NATIONAL IDENTITY
AND THE VARIETIES OF CAPITALISM

STUDIES IN NATIONALISM AND ETHNIC CONFLICT

General Editors: Sid Noel, Richard Vernon

Studies in Nationalism and Ethnic Conflict examines the political dimensions of nationality in the contemporary world. The series includes both scholarly monographs and edited volumes that consider the varied sources and political expressions of national identities, the politics of multiple loyalty, the domestic and international effects of competing identities within a single state, and the causes of – and political responses to – conflict between ethnic and religious groups. The books are designed for use by university students, scholars, and interested general readers.

The editors welcome inquiries from authors. If you are in the process of completing a manuscript that you think might fit into the series, you are invited to contact them.

National Identity and the Varieties of Capitalism

The Danish Experience

Edited by

JOHN L. CAMPBELL, JOHN A. HALL,
AND OVE K. PEDERSEN

McGill-Queen's University Press
Montreal & Kingston · London · Ithaca

© McGill-Queen's University Press 2006
ISBN 0-7735-2996-9 (cloth)
ISBN 0-7735-2997-7 (paper)

Legal deposit first quarter 2006
Bibliothèque nationale du Québec

Printed in Canada on acid-free paper that is 100% ancient forest free
(100% post-consumer recycled), processed chlorine free.

Published simultaneously in Scandinavia in paperback by
DJØF Publishing, Copenhagen
– a company of the Association of Danish Lawyers and Economists
ISBN 87-574-1302-9

This book has been published with the help of grants from the
Copenhagen Business School, Dartmouth College, and McGill University.

McGill-Queen's University Press acknowledges the support of the Canada
Council for the Arts for our publishing program. We also acknowledge the
financial support of the Government of Canada through the Book
Publishing Industry Development Program (BPIDP) for our publishing
activities.

Library and Archives Canada Cataloguing in Publication

National identity and the varieties of capitalism : the Danish experience
/ edited by John L. Campbell, John A. Hall, and Ove K. Pedersen.

(Studies in nationalism and ethnic conflict ; 4)
Includes bibliographical references and index.
ISBN 0-7735-2996-9 (bnd)
ISBN 0-7735-2997-7 (pbk)

1. Denmark – Economic conditions.   2. Denmark – Politics and
government.   I. Campbell, John L., 1952–   II. Hall, John A., 1949–
III. Pedersen, Ove Kaj, 1948–   IV. Series.

HC355.N38 2005   330.948   C2005-905603-7

Typeset in 10/12 Baskerville by True to Type

Contents

Contributors

PETER ABRAHAMSON is associate professor, Department of Sociology, University of Copenhagen. He has written extensively on welfare states and welfare state retrenchment, particularly in the Nordic countries. His recent publications include "Liquid Modernity: Bauman on Contemporary Welfare Society," *Acta Sociologica* 47(2) 171–9, 2004; "Social Exclusion: Concepts and Debates" in *Poverty and Social Exclusion in the New Russia*, edited by Nick Manning and Nataliya Tikhonova, Aldershot, 2004; and "The End of the Scandinavian Model? Welfare Reform in the Nordic Countries," *Journal of Societal & Social Policy* 2(2) 19–36, 2003.

JOHN L. CAMPBELL is the Class of 1925 Professor in the Department of Sociology at Dartmouth College. He is also Professor of Political Economy at the International Center for Business and Politics, Copenhagen Business School, and Adjunct Professor of Political Science at the University of Copenhagen. His research interests include comparative political economy, globalization, and institutional theory. His previous work includes *Collapse of an Industry: Nuclear Power and the Contradictions of U.S. Policy* (Cornell University Press, 1988), *Governance of the American Economy* (Cambridge University Press, 1991, with Leon Lindberg and Rogers Hollingsworth), *Legacies of Change: Transformations of East European Political Economies* (Aldine Press, 1997, with Ove K. Pedersen), *The Rise of Neoliberalism and Institutional Analysis* (Princeton University Press, 2001, with Ove K. Pedersen), and *Institutional Change and Globalization* (Princeton University Press, 2004).

JOHN A. HALL is the James McGill Professor in the Department of Sociology at McGill University and Professor of Sociology at Dartmouth College. He is also Adjunct Professor of Sociology and Political Science at the University of Copenhagen. His research interests include nationalism, comparative state structures, the rise and fall of empires, and social theory. Among his most well-known books are *Powers and Liberties* (Basil Blackwell, 1985), *The State* (University of Minnesota Press, 1989, with G. John Ikenberry), *Coercion and Consent* (Polity Press, 1994), *Is America Breaking Apart?* (Princeton University Press, 1999, with Charles Lindholm), and *The Nation-State in Question* (Princeton University Press, 2003, with T.V. Paul and G. John Ikenberry). He is currently working on an intellectual biography of Ernest Gellner.

PETER A. HALL is Krupp Foundation Professor of European Studies and Director of the Minda de Gunzburg Center for European Studies at Harvard University. He has published widely in the fields of comparative political economy and public policy making in Europe. Volumes he has written or edited include *Governing the Economy* (Oxford University Press, 1986), *The Political Power of Economic Ideas* (Princeton University Press, 1989), and (with David Soskice) *Varieties of Capitalism* (Oxford University Press, 2001).

ULF HEDETOFT is Professor of International Studies in the Institute for History, International and Social Studies at Aalborg University. He is also Director of the Academy for Migration Studies in Denmark (AMID). His interests include cultural and political issues in international relations, specifically in Europe; nationalism, migration and globalization; transatlantic relations; British, German and Danish history, politics and identity. His publications include *Signs of Nations: Studies in the Political Semiotics of Self and Other in Contemporary European Nationalism* (Dartmouth, 1995); *The Postnational Self: Belonging and Identity* (University of Minnesota Press, 2002); *The Global Turn: Nationalist Encounters with the World* (Aalborg University Press, 2003); and *The Politics of Multiple Belonging: Ethnicity and Nationalism in Europe and East Asia* (Ashgate, 2004).

LARS BO KASPERSEN is Associate Professor of Sociology at the International Center for Business and Politics, Copenhagen Business School. He specializes in comparative historical sociology, political sociology, and social theory, including state formation, globalization, associative democracy, warfare, and the origins of the welfare state. Among his recent publications are *Anthony Giddens: An Introduction to a Social Theorist* (Blackwell, 2000), *Classical and Modern Social Theory* (Blackwell, 2000), and "How Denmark Became Democratic – The Impact of Warfare and Military Reforms." *Acta Sociologica* 47(1), 2004.

PETER J. KATZENSTEIN is the Walter S. Carpenter, Jr Professor of International Studies at Cornell University. His research is at the intersection of the fields of international relations and comparative politics. His work addresses issues of political economy, security and culture in both Europe and Asia, with specific focus on Germany and Japan. His current research focuses on the role of regionalism in world politics. He has written over eighty papers and book chapters and is the author, co-author, editor, and co-editor of eighteen books, including *Small States in World Markets* (Cornell University Press, 1985), which received the American Political Science Association's Woodrow Wilson prize, and *The Culture of National Security* (Columbia University Press, 1996). He is a member of the American Academy of Arts and Science and has served as the editor for *International Organization* and the Cornell Studies in Political Economy series at Cornell University Press.

MORTEN KELSTRUP is Professor in International Relations and Jean Monnet Professor at the Department of Political Science, University of Copenhagen. His main research interests are political theory, theory of international relations, European integration, and Danish foreign policy and relations to the European Union. He has authored, edited, and co-edited several books and articles, including (with Michael Williams) *International Relations Theory and the Politics of European Integration,* 2000; (with Hans Branner) *Denmark's Policy Towards Europe after 1945: History, Theories and Options,* 2000; and (with Ove K. Pedersen and Ib Damgaard Petersen), 2004, *Politiske processeer og strukturer i det 21. århundrede* (Political Processes and Structures in the 21st Century).

OVE KORSGAARD is Associate Professor in the Department of Philosophy of Education at the Danish University of Education, where he directs the research unit on Ethical and Political Education. His main research interests are the history of education and philosophy of education. His books include *The Struggle About the Body: The Danish History of Body Culture through 200 Years* (Gyldendal, 1982), *The Struggle About the Light: The Danish History of Adult Education through 500 Years* (Gyldendal, 1997), *The Race for Knowledge: Education in a Knowledge-Based Society* (Gyldendal, 1999), and *The Struggle for the People* (Gyldendal, 2004).

PEER HULL KRISTENSEN is Professor of the Sociology of the Firm and Work Organization at the Center for Business and Politics, Copenhagen Business School. His research interests focus on the comparative study of national business systems, labour markets, and the organization of multinational corporations. He has published numerous books and articles within these areas, including (with Richard Whitley) *The Changing European Firm: Limits to Convergence* (Routledge, 1995) and *Governance at Work: The Social Regulation of Economic Relations In Europe* (Oxford University

Press, 1997); *The Multinational Corporation: Organizing Across National and Institutional Divides* (Oxford University Press, 2001, with Glenn Morgan and Richard Whitley); and, most recently, *Local Players in Global Games: The Strategic Constitution of a Multinational* (Oxford University Press, 2005, with Jonathan Zeitlin).

PER KONGSHØJ MADSEN is Professor of Labour Market Research at the Centre for Labour Market Research, Department of Economics, Politics and Public Administration, University of Aalborg. His main research interests are comparative labour market policy and European employment policy. He is a member of the European Commission's Employment Observatory. His recent publications include "Flexicurity Through Labour Market Policies and Institutions in Denmark" in Peter Auer and Sandrine Cazes (eds.), *Employment Stability in an Age of Flexibility: Evidence From Industrialized Countries* (International Labour Office, 2003); "Wage Formation, Institutions and Unemployment" in Thomas P. Boje & Bengt Furåker (eds.), *Post-Industrial Labour Markets: Profiles of North America and Scandinavia* (Routledge, 2003); and "Employment Policies and Social Exclusion: An Analysis of the Performance of European Employment Regimes" in R. Muffels, P. Tsakloglou, and D. Mayes (eds.), *Social Exclusion in European Welfare States* (Edward Elgar, 2002).

CATHIE JO MARTIN is Professor of Political Science at Boston University. She is the author of *Stuck in Neutral: Business and the Politics of Human Capital Investment Policy* (Princeton University Press, 2000), *Shifting the Burden: the Struggle over Growth and Corporate Taxation* (University of Chicago Press, 1991), and articles appearing in journals such as the *American Political Science Review, World Politics,* the *British Journal of Political Science, Comparative Political Studies, Governance,* and *Politics and Society.* Her research interests in employers and social policy have been funded by the Robert Wood Johnson Foundation, the Russell Sage Foundation, the National Science Foundation, the Magtudredningsproject, the German Marshall Fund, and the Danish Social Science Research Council.

KEVIN HJORTSHØJ O'ROURKE is Professor of Economics at Trinity College Dublin. He is also a Research Associate of the National Bureau of Economic Research and a Visiting Professor at the International Center for Business and Politics, Copenhagen Business School. He has written about the long-term economic effects of the Irish Famine; late nineteenth-century trade, capital and migration flows, and their economic and political implications; and post-war Irish economic growth. His current projects include: the longer-term history of globalization; the interactions between culture, politics, and economics in late nineteenth-century Denmark and Ireland; and the determinants of individual attitudes towards globalization. He has published widely, including *Globalization and History: The Evolution of a Nineteenth-Century Atlantic Economy* (MIT Press, 1999, with Jeffrey G. Williamson), which won the American Association of Publishers Award for best scholarly book in economics, and "The European Grain Invasion, 1870–1913," which won the Cole Prize for best article published in the Journal of Economic History, 1999.

UFFE ØSTERGÅRD is Head of Department for Holocaust and Genocide Studies at the Danish Institute for International Studies and the Jean Monnet Professor of European Civilization at the University of Aarhus (on leave). He has published numerous articles and several books in Danish on national identity, national political cultures, and nation-states in Europe. His research interests also include conscription and nationalism, historical methodology and theory, comparative studies of Nazism and fascism, geopolitics, and the role of the holocaust in European history. He has been a Visiting Professor at the European University Institute, Harvard University, and Rutgers University and has lectured at many universities all over the world.

OVE K. PEDERSEN is Professor of Comparative Political Economy and Director of the International Center for Business and Politics at the Copenhagen Business School. He has been a Visiting Professor at Harvard University and a Fellow at SCANCOR, Stanford University. He is interested in comparative political economy, institutional theory, and the development of comparative methodology. His latest publications are *Europeanization and the Transnational State* (Routledge, 2004, with Per Lægreid and Bengt Jacobsson) and *The Rise of Neoliberalism and Institutional Analysis* (Princeton University Press, 2001, with John L. Campbell).

HJALTE RASMUSSEN holds the chair of European Union Law at the Faculty of Law of the University of Copenhagen. He is also an Honourary Jean Monnet Professor of European Union law, serves as a distinguished Corresponding Member of Det Norske Videnskaps Selskab (the Norwegian Scientific Society) and since 2004 has been counselling and teaching at l'Université Aix-Marseille III. Formerly, he was a full professor of European Union law at the Copenhagen Business School, and Visiting Professor at the European College of Bruges and the European Institute of Public Administration at Maastricht. His research interests have concentrated for several years on the frontier of the law, such as the clash of EU and national law. His publications include *The European Court of Justice:*

A Comparative Study in Judicial Policymaking (Nijhoff, 1986), *European Community Case Law: Summaries of Leading EC-Court Cases* (Copenhagen Business School Press, 1993), *European Court of Justice* (Thomson, 1998) and *EU-ret i Kontekst* (5th Edition, Thomson, 2003).

Preface

"Where is the beauteous majesty of Denmark?"
Hamlet, Act 4, Scene 5

This book is about Denmark's remarkable political economic success since the mid-1980s, and about the political, economic, and cultural institutions that facilitated it. But it is also a book about how a particular variety of capitalism – one based on small states and corporatist institutions – manages late twentieth- and early twenty-first-century globalization. Indeed, from our point of view, much of the "beauteous majesty of Denmark" is to be found in its institutions and the historical processes that gave rise to them.

The genesis of this project was a conversation between two of the editors, John Hall and John Campbell one summer afternoon, during which they wondered if it might not be interesting to write a short paper about Denmark's capacity successfully to weather the forces of globalization. Their curiosity had been sparked over the years by several trips to Denmark, in the course of which they had gained a certain familiarity and admiration for this little country. After consulting with Ove Pedersen, the third editor, we all decided that it would be fruitful to organize a series of small workshops on Danish history and political economy where this issue would be addressed by some of Denmark's best social scientists, historians, and legal scholars, as well as a few very knowledgeable outsiders. We held four workshops in Copenhagen, and a larger conference at Dartmouth College during 2003 and 2004. Financial support for these meetings and subsequent manuscript preparation was provided by the Danish Social Research Council; the Institutes of Political Science and Sociology at the University of Copenhagen; Finn Junge-Jensen, president of the Copenhagen Business School; the Dickey Center for International Understanding, the Office of the Dean, and the Department of Sociology at Dartmouth College; and the Office of the Dean at McGill University. The Institute of Political Science at Copenhagen University and its chair, Lars Bille, played an especially important role in organizing the Copenhagen workshops. We are grateful to all of them for their generosity. John Campbell also thanks the Danish

National Bank, which provided accommodations for him during a sabbatical in Copenhagen, and Dartmouth College for a Senior Faculty Research Grant.

As this project was coming to fruition, the editors were helping to launch the new International Center for Business and Politics at the Copenhagen Business School. An important part of the centre's mission is to help organize collaborative research projects involving scholars from different countries studying how societies respond to international pressures such as globalization and Europeanization. This project represents this sort of effort, in that it has provided researchers from Europe and North America with an opportunity to investigate and discuss how Denmark has been affected by these pressures. As such, the project benefited from the thoughtful insights of several people. These include Steve Brooks, Francesco Duina, Peter Katzenstein, Michael Smith, and Chris Wohlforth, all of whom attended the Dartmouth conference, and two anonymous reviewers for McGill-Queen's University Press. We owe special thanks to Peter Katzenstein and Peter Hall, both of whom read an earlier version of the manuscript and agreed to contribute concluding chapters to the volume. Last, but certainly not least, we thank all the contributors to this volume whose hard work resulted in much more than the short paper on Denmark that Hall and Campbell initially envisioned. We have learned a great deal from them. Indeed, their generosity is another example of the beauteous majesty of Denmark.

The Editors

NATIONAL IDENTITY
AND THE VARIETIES OF CAPITALISM

The State of Denmark

JOHN L. CAMPBELL AND JOHN A. HALL

"And let thine eye look like a friend on Denmark."
Hamlet, Act 1, Scene 2

Denmark played a particularly important role in *The Competitive Advantage of Nations*, the 1990 bestseller by influential business analyst and international political economist Michael Porter. For Porter, as for Marcellus in Shakespeare's *Hamlet*, many things were held to be "rotten in the state of Denmark," and so he predicted Denmark's certain decline on account of its outdated political economy. However, to continue citing *Hamlet*, for those of us who "look like a friend on Denmark," this prediction, if not some of Porter's particular complaints, seemed almost surely to be wrong. Indeed, subsequent events have shown that Denmark has actually performed much better than he predicted, even as this small country has had to cope since he wrote his book with a more politically and economically integrated international environment. This volume explains why Denmark has turned out to be so successful.

However, this book is about much more than just Denmark. By examining the Danish case in considerable detail, it raises serious questions and offers several insights into important literatures in comparative political economy. First, it addresses the literature on small states and the corporatist arrangements that enable these states to survive and flourish economically in an increasingly open and internationally competitive economic environment (e.g., Cameron 1979; Garrett 1998; Katzenstein 1984, 1985). It argues that our understanding of the institutional capacities by which small corporatist states compete successfully in international markets needs to be revised and updated in light of the resurgence of economic globalization during the late twentieth century.[1] It also shows that the historical forces that give rise to these capacities are more complicated than previously understood. In brief, the Danish case illustrates how the perception of national vulnerability, particularly geopolitical vulnerability, can have an enormous long-term effect in shaping national identity, the assessment of national interest, and the institutional capacities for negotiation and learning that facilitate international economic competitiveness. Finally, whereas some scholars have argued that small-state corporatism is dying as a result of the increased pressures of recent economic globalization and the international diffusion of neo-liberal ideology (Schwartz 1994), the Danish case reveals something quite different. Danish corporatism has evolved in ways that actually improve its capacities for coping successfully with the pressures of economic globalization today by enabling decision makers to respond more flexibly to these pressures. In contributing to an understanding of these adaptive measures, this book supports those who argue that reports of the death of corporatism are greatly exaggerated (Molina and Rhodes 2002).

Second, this book sheds new light on the literature of the so-called varieties of capitalism (Albert 1993; Hall and Soskice 2001a; Hollingsworth and Boyer 1997). On the one hand, the Danish case reveals that one cannot fully understand the development and competitive success of a nation's institutional capacities without paying close attention to the formation and persistence of deep-seated national identities – that is, culture – as well as the more formal institutional arrangements that tend to receive the bulk of attention in the varieties-of-capitalism literature. However, this should not be received as an indication that we have taken a cultural turn in political economy so extreme as to reject as irrelevant the political and economic factors that others have argued are important ingredients of national success. On the other hand, whereas the varieties of capitalism literature tends to focus on two diametrically opposed ideal types of capitalism – liberal and coordinated market economies – the Danish case illustrates how competitive success nowadays may actually be enhanced by *blending* important elements of each type. In other words, in the Danish case it is the *hybrid* nature of its institutions – political, economic, and cultural – that has given it its distinct competitive advantage. In this regard, we call for a more nuanced look at the organization of national political economies than that provided by the liberal/coordinated dichotomy. But we also argue for the rejuvenation of the sorts of insights into political economy that were once offered by such luminaries as Max Weber, Emile Durkheim, Alexander Gerschenkron, Karl Polanyi, and others, who argued that in order to really explain a nation's political economic performance one must understand its history as well as its political, economic, and cultural institutions.

We should note at the outset that the title of this Introduction, "The State of Denmark," and in particular the word "state" within it, carries two meanings. On the one hand, by state we mean the recent *condition* of the Danish political economy since about 1985, which, as we shall argue, has been particularly impressive. On the other hand, in assessing this condition we focus in part on the Danish *nation-state*, its particular form, and how it contributed to the country's recent success. This is one reason why our arguments bear directly on important issues in comparative political economy and state theory more generally.

That said, however, we do not mean to suggest that the Danish state was solely responsible for Denmark's success. Nor do we mean to endorse any sort of statist view favouring political commands from above, indicative planning, or the like. Very much to the contrary, we accept what seems to be the dominant contemporary view in state theory and political sociology, which stresses that state strength results from the politics of reciprocal consent; that is, from a political centre serving as a coordinator for a civil society that trusts it to act in the general interest. Following Richard Samuels (1987, 2), we maintain that negotiation and compact are at the heart of state-economy relations in situations marked by the politics of reciprocal consent. But we also believe that cultural factors such as a strong sense of national identity developed over centuries contribute to the capacity for such negotiation. In fact, what is important, as we shall see, is that the state enjoyed a prolonged symbiotic relationship with other social actors in civil society and that the bargaining and negotiation that transpired over the years between the state and civil society played a crucial role in facilitating Denmark's recent success.

One might wonder how a volume that focuses on a single case – Denmark, that is – could be used to generate insights about two literatures in comparative political economy. What is the justification for such an analytical move? Certainly, studies based on a small number of cases, let alone a single case, are hobbled insofar as they seek to generalize to other cases (Lieberson 1992). But this does not mean they are useless. First, cases may be inherently *interesting* on their own terms. We find Denmark to be such a case, not least because it has performed so well during the 1990s and the early twenty-first century. It is also a much neglected case in the comparative political economy literature where an understanding of Scandinavia is largely based on the Swedish case.[2] Second, our approach to this case is in large part *historical*. Indeed, by including contributions in this volume that take the long historical view of the development of Danish political, economic, and cultural institutions, we hope to shed light on how the more proximate factors that affected this particular small state's success came into being in the first place. Third, the fact that we have also included contributions on decision making in several different areas of the Danish political economy affords us a set of *comparisons within the Danish case* that can help us address the issues raised above. Following these last two points, we propose that by studying this case in detail we may in effect offer a rough

empirical examination of theories that seek to explain political economic success, notably Peter Katzenstein's (1985, 2003) theory of small states and
Peter Hall and David Soskice's (2001b) theory of varieties of capitalism.
Finally, although studying a single national case may not provide the
basis for analytic prediction, it has proven to be an important tool for
understanding the *processes and mechanisms* that affect various outcomes –
something that quantitative studies based on larger numbers of cases
often fail to do satisfactorily.[3] Scholars of corporatism have recently
lamented the fact that too much attention has been paid to the structure
and outcomes of corporatism, and not enough to conceptualizing the
process of corporatism (Molina and Rhodes 2002; see also Katzenstein
2003; Smith 1992, 10). For all of these reasons, we believe that focusing
on the single case of Denmark is useful and important.

This Introduction proceeds as follows. We begin by showing how successful Denmark has been since the mid-1980s on a number of socioeconomic indicators compared to other advanced capitalist societies. We continue by reviewing the two overarching theoretical literatures that inform
this volume: the literature on small states and corporatism and the literature on the varieties of capitalism. Our intention here is to raise a set of
important theoretical issues in comparative political economy for which
the Danish case is particularly instructive. Third, we offer an explanation
for how Denmark managed to achieve such success. This section previews
many of the arguments developed in subsequent chapters of the book. We
pay particular attention to distant historical legacies of success, including
the development of a strong national identity; the more proximate conditions of success, such as the institutionalization of corporatist bargaining;
and the capacity for policy learning and flexibility that contributed most
directly to Denmark's success. We also discuss briefly some of the challenges that lie ahead for the Danish political economy. We finish by drawing lessons from our analysis which shed light on some of the most important claims made in the literatures on small states, corporatism, and the
varieties of capitalism.

DENMARK'S SUCCESS

Before turning to the evidence in support of our claim that Denmark has
been considerably more successful than Porter anticipated, a little background on the extent to which the world has become more integrated
since the mid-1980s will be helpful. To begin with, the Communist regimes
in Eastern and Central Europe and the Soviet Union collapsed. This led
eventually to the unification of Germany and movement toward membership in the European Union (EU) for a number of postcommunist countries, not to mention membership in NATO, the OECD, and other interna-

tional organizations. The end of the Cold War also led to the increasing economic integration of these countries with the capitalist world. Moreover, the European Union project gathered momentum as its member states embraced harmonization, adopted an increasing number of EU directives, approved the Maastricht Treaty, and eventually introduced a single European currency. North and South America lowered trade barriers by adopting the North American Free Trade Agreement and Mercosur, respectively. Reflecting these and other changes, world trade, foreign direct investment, international portfolio investment, and international currency transactions all increased sharply in the late twentieth and early twenty-first centuries, with much of the increase occurring in the so-called triad region of Western Europe, North America, and Japan (Campbell 2003).

As for Denmark itself, although this country has long been integrated into the international political economy, its level of integration has increased significantly since the mid-1980s. Table 1 shows that between 1989 and 1999 Danish trade in goods rose from about 58 percent to 68 percent of GDP (a growth rate of about 1.7% annually) and was substantially larger than average for 22 advanced capitalist countries, members of the European Monetary Union (EMU), and the high-income countries in the world. Furthermore, Danish gross foreign direct investment increased from about 3 percent to 13 percent of GDP, levels that were again generally larger than the average for this group of countries, the EMU, and the high income countries of the world.[4] Finally, the flow of Danish gross private capital into and out of the country jumped from about 17 percent to 25 percent of GDP.[5] Thus, in many respects Denmark has either kept pace with or exceeded the average levels of international economic integration experienced by the other advanced capitalist countries. And even though Denmark voted "no" by referendum on the Maastricht Treaty and, more recently, on the adoption of the European common currency, it has become increasingly involved in politics, policy making, and institution building at the level of the European Union (Jacobsson et al. 2003). But how successful has Denmark been in navigating through these increasingly integrated international political economic waters?

Defining success is not always straightforward. First, what we take to be important indicators of success may not be those that other people would emphasize. But many of our indicators are those that have been central to debates about political economic success as defined in the literatures on small states, corporatism, and the varieties of capitalism with which this book is concerned. We will return to this point later.

Success also ebbs and flows. Denmark has not always been as successful as it has been during the last decade or so. For instance, its ranking among the advanced industrial countries in terms of growth rates (measured by

Table 1   Trade and Capital Flows

	Trade in Goods (% of PPP GDP)[a]		Growth in Real Trade Less Growth in Real GDP (%)	Gross Private Capital Flows (% of PPP GDP)[a]		Gross Foreign Direct Investment (% of PPP GDP)[a]	
	1989	1999	1989–99	1989	1999	1989	1999
Australia	28.2	26.9	4.0	13.9	13.2	4.5	2.9
Austria	50.8	65.1	3.4	9.3	42.5	1.0	3.0
Belgium	—	129.6	2.7	—	—	—	—
Canada	43.5	57.3	5.7	7.8	15.1	2.4	6.0
Denmark	**58.3**	**67.8**	**1.7**	**16.6**	**25.4**	**3.2**	**13.3**
Finland	54.2	61.3	5.2	16.7	49.4	4.2	14.3
France	37.6	44.0	3.8	19.1	29.2	3.0	10.9
Germany	51.9	52.0	3.0	10.4	36.0	1.8	7.8
Greece	20.7	25.5	3.4	1.9	7.7	0.7	0.7
Ireland	92.1	120.0	7.0	24.3	179.3	0.2	25.2
Italy	30.5	35.0	4.0	9.0	27.0	0.4	1.2
Japan	20.8	23.2	—	11.1	30.9	2.0	1.2
Luxembourg	—	—	—	—	—	—	—
Netherlands	85.4	101.4	2.4	33.6	81.3	9.4	20.3
New Zealand	35.8	36.7	3.2	13.3	19.8	7.1	12.0
Norway	62.7	62.2	1.7	15.0	32.8	3.6	7.3
Portugal	29.9	38.9	4.1	5.7	27.0	1.7	3.2
Spain	24.2	35.8	7.2	5.1	28.2	2.1	6.4
Sweden	66.1	76.5	4.9	34.3	86.2	8.0	39.4
Switzerland	70.9	82.7	2.2	34.4	139.2	8.7	22.9
United Kingdom	36.8	44.8	3.6	37.6	66.1	7.4	23.0
United States	14.9	19.8	5.2	7.4	13.6	2.5	5.2
Average	**45.8**	**57.5**	**3.9**	**16.3**	**47.5**	**3.7**	**11.3**
EMU average	**38.7**	**52.7**	—	**14.0**	**37.1**	**2.4**	**7.8**
High income country average	**28.5**	**37.4**	—	**12.7**	**29.2**	**2.9**	**7.2**

[a]GDP is measured in purchasing power parity in order to adjust for differences in domestic prices.

Source: World Bank. 2001. World Bank Development Indicators. Washington, D.C.: World Bank, Table 6.1.

GDP per capita) rose after World War II, declined between 1973 and 1990, and then rose again after that (Smith 2004). Nevertheless, as we will show, during the 1990s and the early years of the twenty-first century, Denmark has outperformed most of the advanced capitalist economies in this and many other ways.

Third, success comprises a number of dimensions that need to be taken into consideration. These include indicators of socioeconomic – not just economic – well-being. In other words, success is best measured by means of a bundle of indicators each representing an important dimension of success. This is especially important because what scholars in the comparative political economy tradition deem to be the most important dimensions may shift over time. During the late 1970s and early 1980s, success for national political economies was typically defined as the ability to manage the twin evils of economic stagnation and inflation, phenomena whose control was said by many to require wage and price restraint as well as elaborate welfare state policies (e.g., Goldthorpe 1984; Lindberg and Maier 1985). More recently, as globalization has emerged as an important concern among policy makers and business leaders, success has been defined more broadly in terms of the ability of countries to maintain international competitiveness in the face of increasingly volatile markets and a more open international economy; to effectively manage their budgets and minimize deficits; to sustain high standards of living for the citizenry; and to reduce poverty (Albert 1993; Hall and Soskice 2001a; Hollingsworth and Boyer 1997). So, in order to determine how successful Denmark has been since the mid-1980s, we need to examine a variety of relevant indicators. But, the evidence we will present is clear. Denmark has done rather well during this period in terms of the indicators held dear within the comparative political economy literature.

Finally, while the preceding discussion and much of what follows emphasizes Denmark's relatively short-term success, as measured over a few decades, it is important not to lose sight of some much more basic long-term indicators of success. Not the least of these is the fact that Denmark has managed to survive as a nation-state for several hundred years, during which time it has managed to accumulate great wealth. This is not for lack of internal political turmoil or external economic and geopolitical threats. Indeed, Denmark lost a succession of wars – and with them territory – over the last few centuries, experienced civil war (1848–50), had to contend with a rising labour movement during the late nineteenth and early twentieth centuries, faced the trials and tribulations of the Great Depression during the 1930s, withstood Nazi occupation during World War II, and successfully confronted the challenges of stagflation during the 1970s and globalization since then. Of course, Denmark's ability to survive depended at critical moments upon assistance from more powerful allies; Britain, for example, who, at the end of World War II, insisted that Denmark not be incorporated into Stalin's Soviet Union. But the same cannot be said for several other European states, which have come and gone as a result of war and the subsequent redefinition of national borders. For example, Catalonia was absorbed by Spain. Ireland, Poland, and the Baltic states were also absorbed by more powerful neighbours at one time or another, but subsequently regained their independence. In other words, Denmark, unlike some other countries, has managed to adapt quite successfully to a variety of challenges throughout its long history. Understanding how

Table 2 Central Government Fiscal Performance

	Government Revenues (% GDP)		Government Expenditures (% GDP)		Budget Deficit (% GDP)		Debt (% GDP)	Interest (% current revenue)
	1990	1998	1990	1998	1990	1998	1998	1998
Australia	24.9	23.6	23.3	23.7	2.0	2.8	16.8	6.1
Austria	33.9	37.5	37.5	40.5	-4.4	—	60.2	9.3
Belgium	42.6	43.7	47.7	45.7	-5.5	-1.8	114.6	16.7
Canada	21.6	21.8	26.2	21.5	-4.8	0.4	75.1	16.7
Denmark	**37.8**	**38.5**	**39.0**	**37.3**	**-0.7**	**1.7**	**64.0**	**12.2**
Finland	30.6	31.9	30.3	33.4	0.2	-0.3	61.0	14.3
France	39.7	41.4	41.8	46.2	-2.1	-3.5	—	7.4
Germany	27.5	31.3	29.3	32.6	-2.1	-0.9	38.6	7.3
Greece	27.5	23.5	51.7	30.8	-22.7	-4.4	113.1	38.4
Ireland	33.6	31.9	37.7	33.0	-2.4	0.7	—	13.3
Italy	38.2	40.6	47.4	43.8	-10.2	-3.1	—	18.1
Japan	14.4	—	15.7	—	-1.6	—	—	—
Luxembourg	—	—	—	—	—	—	—	—
Netherlands	45.0	44.1	49.5	45.9	-4.3	-1.6	55.6	9.5
New Zealand	42.6	34.1	44.0	33.4	4.0	0.5	38.7	7.1
Norway	42.4	41.8	41.3	37.2	0.5	-1.6	19.9	4.1
Portugal	31.6	34.7	37.9	39.0	-4.4	-1.2	0.8	8.4
Spain	29.1	28.8	32.4	32.9	-3.1	-2.9	55.6	14.1
Sweden	42.6	38.2	39.4	41.6	1.0	-0.5	—	15.7
Switzerland	20.8	24.8	23.3	28.3	-0.9	0.5	28.8	3.7
United Kingdom	36.1	37.2	37.5	36.9	0.6	0.6	49.8	8.8
United States	18.9	20.7	22.7	19.9	-3.8	0.8	42.8	14.1
Average	**32.4**	**33.5**	**36.0**	**35.2**	**-3.1**	**-0.7**	**52.2**	**12.3**
EMU average	**34.7**	**37.1**	**38.6**	**40.0**	**-3.7**	**-2.3**	**57.9**	**11.8**
High income country average	**23.9**	**28.7**	**27.0**	**30.2**	**-3.0**	**-1.1**	**49.2**	**8.6**

Source: World Bank. 2001. *World Development Indicators.* Washington, D.C.: World Bank, Table 4.11.

Denmark has managed to remain so adaptable for such a long time is another lesson this volume offers and, we shall argue, is an important key to its more recent success.

Let us turn now to the more immediate indicators of Danish success to see how well this nation has done in recent years. Insofar as central government finances are concerned, table 2 indicates that while the Danish government collected and spent more revenue than the average advanced capitalist country, it was much better at avoiding serious budget deficits. Indeed, in 1998 Denmark was running a budget *surplus* of 1.7 percent of

Table 3   Unemployment Rates (% labour force)

	Average Unemployment Rate		
	1986–90	1991–95	1996–2000
Australia	7.1	9.6	7.5
Austria	4.1	5.0	5.4
Belgium	8.5	8.3	8.7
Canada	8.4	10.5	8.3
Denmark	**5.9**	**8.1**	**5.1**
Finland	4.3	13.4	11.8
France	9.8	11.0	11.1
Germany	5.5	6.9	8.3
Greece	7.4	9.1	10.8
Ireland	15.5	14.4	7.9
Italy	10.0	10.1	11.5
Japan	2.5	2.6	4.1
Luxembourg	1.5	2.2	3.1
Netherlands	7.4	6.4	4.4
New Zealand	5.7	8.9	6.6
Norway	3.5	5.5	3.7
Portugal	6.4	5.6	5.5
Spain	14.1	15.6	14.6
Sweden	1.9	6.4	6.6
Switzerland	0.7	3.4	3.7
United Kingdom	8.3	9.3	6.4
United States	5.9	6.6	4.6
Average	**6.6**	**8.1**	**7.3**
OECD **average**	**6.3**	**7.1**	**6.7**

Source: OECD. 2002. *OECD Economic Outlook, No 72*. Statistical Annex, Table 14.

GDP while on average these other countries were running *deficits*. The fiscal downside was that it endured higher than average levels of debt and interest payments, which had been incurred during previous periods marked by less budgetary restraint. Nevertheless, this has not apparently hurt Denmark's economic performance, which has recently been impressive. Table 3 reveals that during the early 1990s the Danish unemployment rate averaged 8.1 percent of the labour force, the same as the average for twenty-two advanced capitalist countries and a point higher than the OECD average. However, the Danish unemployment rate dropped to 5.1 percent during the second half of the decade – a substantial improvement over both groups of countries. Moreover, the average duration of unemployment in Denmark was the shortest of all the EU countries except for Norway (Danish Council of Social Welfare 2002, 46, 53). Additionally,

Table 4   Labour Productivity in the Business Sector

	Average Annual Change in Percent			
	1975–85	1986–90	1991–95	1996–2000
Australia	1.9	0.2	2.1	2.5
Austria	2.7	2.9	2.2	2.6
Belgium	2.9	2.3	1.6	1.7
Canada	1.0	0.5	1.5	1.8
Denmark	**2.3**	**0.6**	**3.0**	**2.3**
Finland	2.9	3.7	4.2	3.0
France	2.7	2.7	1.5	1.4
Germany	2.0	1.3	2.2	1.1
Greece	1.1	0.6	0.8	3.2
Ireland	3.8	4.5	3.0	4.3
Italy	2.4	2.4	2.4	1.0
Japan	2.8	3.6	0.7	1.4
Luxembourg	—	—	1.3	2.8
Netherlands	2.2	1.1	1.4	1.1
New Zealand	0.7	1.6	0.3	1.4
Norway	2.1	0.3	3.0	1.1
Portugal	2.2	4.3	1.3	2.5
Spain	3.3	1.0	2.2	0.8
Sweden	1.5	1.6	3.6	2.2
Switzerland	0.9	-0.2	0.0	1.3
United Kingdom	2.5	1.1	2.1	1.1
United States	1.2	1.1	1.3	2.2
Average	**2.1**	**1.8**	**1.9**	**1.9**
OECD **average**	**2.0**	**1.8**	**1.6**	**1.9**

Source: OECD. 2002. OECD Economic Outlook, No 72. Statistical Annex, Table 13.

table 4 shows that labour productivity grew faster on average during the 1990s in Denmark than in either the group of twenty-two countries or the OECD.[6] Table 5 demonstrates that inflation in Denmark remained rather stable at about 2 percent during the 1990s. However, as table 6 suggests, one area where Denmark has not performed as well as either the twenty-two-country average or the OECD average is economic growth, although the shortfall in the Danish growth rate compared to these other countries was not more than about 1 percent during the 1990s. On balance, then, Denmark's recent economic performance has been quite admirable. Indeed, on the basis of a comprehensive survey of thousands of leading business executives and entrepreneurs from around the world, as well as a wide range of political and economic indicators for 102 countries, the World Economic Forum recently ranked Denmark the fourth most com-

Table 5   Inflation Rates

	Average Percentage Change in Consumer Price Index			
	1975–85	*1986–90*	*1991–95*	*1996–2000*
Australia	9.4	7.9	2.5	1.9
Austria	5.0	2.2	2.8	1.2
Belgium	6.7	2.1	2.5	1.6
Canada	8.1	4.5	2.3	1.7
Denmark	**9.2**	**3.9**	**2.0**	**2.3**
Finland	9.4	5.0	2.6	1.6
France	10.1	3.1	2.3	1.3
Germany	3.9	1.4	3.6	1.2
Greece	18.4	17.4	13.9	4.6
Ireland	13.2	3.3	2.5	2.7
Italy	15.0	5.7	5.1	2.4
Japan	4.7	1.4	1.4	0.3
Luxembourg	6.7	1.7	2.8	1.7
Netherlands	5.1	0.7	2.3	1.9
New Zealand	13.4	9.4	2.1	1.4
Norway	8.7	6.3	2.4	2.3
Portugal	23.3	11.4	7.0	2.4
Spain	15.4	6.5	5.2	2.6
Sweden	9.7	6.2	4.2	0.5
Switzerland	3.3	2.5	3.2	0.7
United Kingdom	10.6	5.2	3.9	2.5
United States	7.2	4.0	3.1	2.5
Average	**9.8**	**5.1**	**3.6**	**1.9**
OECD average	**12.5**	**10.2**	**7.8**	**6.2**

Source: OECD. 2002. *OECD Economic Outlook, No 72.* Statistical Annex, Table 19.

petitive economy in the world, surpassed only by Finland, the United States, and Sweden (World Economic Forum 2003).

It is also important to note that Denmark's economic achievement has translated into an exceptionally high standard of living for the Danish population. Table 7 shows that during the 1990s GDP per capita increased from $18,463 to $22,123 in Denmark, third best in 1998 among the 22 advanced capitalist countries. And despite rising incomes during the late 1980s and early 1990s, inflation was low and Denmark remained one of the world's most egalitarian societies. Although income inequality increased slightly during the 1990s, table 8 shows that in 1997 Denmark had a Gini coefficient of 0.21 – the lowest in the European Union.[7] Given the relatively egalitarian distribution of income as well as a very high level of government transfer payments, it should not be surprising that the Danish poverty rate was also

Table 6   Economic Growth

	Average Percentage Change in Real GDP			
	1975–85	1986–90	1991–95	1996–2000
Australia	3.0	3.4	2.8	4.1
Austria	2.4	3.2	2.1	2.6
Belgium	2.1	3.1	1.6	2.7
Canada	3.2	2.9	1.7	4.0
Denmark	**2.6**	**1.2**	**2.0**	**2.7**
Finland	2.9	3.3	-0.6	5.2
France	2.3	3.2	1.0	2.8
Germany	2.2	3.5	2.1	1.8
Greece	2.1	1.3	1.3	3.4
Ireland	3.5	4.7	4.7	9.9
Italy	3.0	2.9	1.3	1.9
Japan	3.8	4.9	1.4	1.5
Luxembourg	2.4	7.5	4.0	6.8
Netherlands	1.9	3.1	2.1	3.7
New Zealand	1.7	1.0	2.7	3.0
Norway	4.0	1.7	3.7	3.1
Portugal	3.0	5.7	1.7	3.9
Spain	1.6	4.5	1.5	3.8
Sweden	1.6	2.5	0.6	3.0
Switzerland	1.6	2.7	-0.1	1.8
United Kingdom	1.9	3.3	1.8	2.9
United States	3.4	3.3	2.4	4.0
Average	**2.6**	**3.3**	**1.9**	**3.6**
OECD **average**	**3.2**	**3.6**	**2.1**	**3.2**

Source: OECD. 2002. *OECD Economic Outlook, No 72.* Statistical Annex, Table 1.

very low by West European standards. During the mid- to late 1990s, only
about 4 percent of the Danish population lived at or below the poverty line,
measured in traditional fashion as 50 percent or less of the median national
household income. This was among the lowest levels of poverty in the
European Union and well below the EU average of about 12 percent. Finally,
the level of social trust toward fellow citizens and public confidence in representative democratic institutions in Denmark, as in the other
Scandinavian countries, was among the highest and most stable in the world
(Katzenstein 2000; Zak and Knack 2001, 306). In fact, the World Economic
Forum's (2003) study ranked Denmark first over all in the quality of its public institutions – an index that included, among other things, measures of
political corruption, favoritism in political decision making, judicial independence, enforceability of contracts, and quality of property rights.

Table 7 GDP Per Capita (1990 dollars)

	1973	1990	1998
Australia	12,759	17,043	20,390
Austria	11,235	16,881	18,905
Belgium	13,945	17,194	19,442
Canada	13,838	18,933	20,559
Denmark	**13,945**	**18,463**	**22,123**
Finland	11,085	16,868	18,324
France	13,123	18,093	19,558
Germany	11,966	15,932	17,799
Greece	7,655	9,984	11,268
Ireland	6,867	11,825	18,183
Italy	10,643	16,320	17,759
Japan	—	—	—
Luxembourg	—	—	—
Netherlands	13,082	17,267	20,224
New Zealand	12,513	13,825	14,779
Norway	11,246	18,470	23,660
Portugal	7,343	10,852	12,929
Spain	8,739	12,210	14,227
Sweden	13,493	17,680	18,685
Switzerland	18,204	21,616	21,367
United Kingdom	12,022	16,411	18,714
United States	16,689	23,214	27,331
Average	**12,020**	**16,454**	**18,811**

Source: Angus Maddison. 2001. *The World Economy: A Millennial Perspective.* Paris: OECD, Table A1-c.

Now, we do not mean to be naïve. We recognize that Denmark has not surpassed its competitors in all areas. It is not a perfect society. We have already acknowledged that in comparison to other advanced capitalist countries it has incurred higher levels of debt and interest payments, somewhat lower although still respectable rates of economic growth, and higher levels of unemployment, at least during the early 1990s. Moreover, Denmark has registered what to some of us may be surprisingly high levels of social unrest, at least judging by the number of working days lost per 1,000 employees each year as a result of labour disputes. Although the average number of days lost in Denmark was well below the EU average during the first half of the 1990s, it soared during the second half of the decade, easily surpassing all of the other EU countries. Indeed, between 1996 and 2000, the average number of work days lost in Denmark was slightly more than six times greater than the EU average (Monger 2003, 20).[8] And Denmark's average life expectancy rate and, by some measures, its average level of education lag those of other European countries. Thus,

Table 8   Income Inequality and Poverty

	Gini Coefficient		Poverty Rate[a] (% all households)	
	1995	1997	1995	1997
Austria	0.28	0.25	7	8
Belgium	0.37	0.34	10	10
Denmark	**0.22**	**0.21**	**4**	**4**
Finland	—	0.23	—	3
France	0.30	0.30	9	11
Germany	0.31	0.29	11	8
Greece	0.35	0.35	16	16
Ireland	0.34	0.33	8	10
Italy	0.33	0.32	13	13
Luxembourg	0.29	—	—	—
Netherlands	0.29	0.28	7	9
Portugal	0.38	0.38	17	15
Spain	0.34	0.35	12	13
Sweden	—	0.23	—	7
United Kingdom	0.34	0.34	13	16
EU **mean**	**0.32**	**0.31**	**11**	**12**

[a]The poverty rate is expressed as the percentage of households with disposable income 50 percent under the median disposable income for that country.

Source: Danish Council of Social Welfare and Center for Alternative Social Analysis. 2002. *Social Trends: Social Policy in Denmark in a European Perspective.* Copenhagen: Socialpolitisk Forlag, 30, 35.

to reiterate a point made earlier about indicators of success, we recognize that the way success is defined and measured and what sorts of data are appropriate for determining how successful Denmark is remain important issues that may be subject to debate. Nonetheless, we still believe that Denmark's performance during the 1990s is impressive compared to that of most other advanced industrial countries – at least in terms of the criteria deemed important in the comparative political economy literature. So for us there is much to be admired in and learned from the Danish experience.

While it is hard to underestimate the pleasure of having been proven right, the purpose of this volume goes well beyond correcting Porter's error with obvious empirical findings about the state of Denmark – understood first as the socioeconomic condition of this particular Nordic country. Most immediately, we seek to explain why Denmark was able to surmount the problems it faced in the 1980s and ask why that period of difficulty did not lead to something even worse. This will lead us to analyse the Danish case as a political and cultural as well as economic system whose strengths and comparative advantages can only be fully understood in an historical light.

THE OVERARCHING THEORETICAL ISSUES

This volume has its being within two sets of literature. The first is that offered by scholars studying small states and corporatism. This work is represented most famously by Peter Katzenstein's classic book, *Small States in World Markets*, which was published in 1985. The second is the more recent literature on the varieties of capitalism, which modifies and extends some of the work on small states and corporatism. It is represented perhaps most succinctly by Peter Hall and David Soskice's edited volume, *Varieties of Capitalism*, which appeared in 2001. It is worth reviewing briefly the central arguments in both of these works insofar as they bear on the Danish experience. Indeed, as we shall see, the Danish experience has important lessons for both sets of arguments. Suffice to say, however, that since both sets of arguments are complex and sophisticated, our review will cover only the most relevant points for Denmark's recent success.

Small States and Corporatism

Katzenstein held that the size of states mattered a great deal in terms of political and economic behaviour. Roughly speaking, large states could hope to bend the rules of the game so as to suit themselves. In contrast, smaller states had no option but to swim within larger seas, whose rules they could hardly influence. Hence, state size was defined in terms of the amount of territory a state controlled as well as by the state's ability to control the international political economic system and especially international trade (Katzenstein 1985, 21–2). However, there was more to it than this. Katzenstein's (2003) latest reflections on the book spell out what was involved in a slightly different way: "Small size was a code for something more important. I learned from my interviews, readings and reflection that it was concealing an underlying and politically consequential causal connection. What really mattered politically was the *perception of vulnerability*, economic and otherwise" [our emphasis]. Minds were concentrated and conflicts diminished by this brute, Darwinian condition. Cooperate or else!

Furthermore, Katzenstein argued, the ability of leaders to meet and draw upon these perceptions of vulnerability facilitated *flexible adjustment* to various challenges that, in turn, paved the way for successful economic performance. Why? The reason was that small size generated a unique capacity for leaders in small states to engage in *policy learning*. According to

Katzenstein (2003): "Small size favors debate and learning, and economic openness and international vulnerability mean control over fewer resources and the probability of greater loss. Hence, the environmental conditions in which small states operate are particularly conducive for high learning."

But what are the capacities for high learning and flexible adjustment that small states possess? For Katzenstein (1985, chapter 1), they consist of a set of institutions known as *democratic corporatism*. In brief, this involves three things: an ideology of social partnership expressed at the national level; a centralized and concentrated system of interest groups; and voluntary and informal coordination of conflicting objectives through continuous political bargaining among interest groups, state bureaucracies, and political parties.[9] The classic example is national-level collective wage bargaining between labour and business peak associations – that is, trade union confederations and national employers' associations – as organized and moderated by the state. Through the institutions of corporatism, he argued, small states pursue a twin strategy. First, they accept international liberalism (e.g., economic openness and low tariffs) in the belief that to do otherwise would trigger retaliation from larger states in the form of trade barriers to small state exports and higher prices for small state imports, both of which would undermine the international competitiveness of small states. Second, they adopt policies of domestic compensation, which means the development of generous welfare programs (e.g., transfer payments, manpower policies, incomes policies, reserve investment funds, etc.) to buffer their populations from the potentially harmful effects of international liberalization.[10]

The Varieties of Capitalism

The literature on the varieties of capitalism, as described by Hall and Soskice (2001b), seeks in several ways to move beyond the corporatist literature that Katzenstein's work typifies. First, it emphasizes the importance of the role of trade unions, business associations, and the bargaining that transpires between them, as Katzenstein did; but it also underscores the role of *firms* per se and the relationships among firms in the coordination of the economy. In this sense, the approach is explicitly firm-centred and regards firms as the crucial actors in capitalist economies.

In addition, this literature focuses largely on the *strategic interactions* that are central to the behaviour of economic actors, and the way these interactions are conditioned by a variety of proximate institutional factors. In doing so, it relies on rational choice, game theory, and other analytic approaches that emphasize strategic decision making. And it attempts to understand how strategic interactions in different institutional contexts deal with a variety of coordination problems (e.g., industrial relations, vocational training, corporate governance, inter-firm relations, and employer-employee relationships).

Third, it distinguishes between two basic *types of capitalism* – liberal and coordinated market economies. Liberal market economies (LMEs) coordinate their activities primarily through markets and corporate hierarchies, where actors respond to price signals and make strategic decisions accordingly. Coordinated market economies (CMEs) coordinate their activities more through non-market relationships, such as informal networks and other collaborative arrangements. According to Hall and Soskice: "In contrast to liberal market economies, where the equilibrium outcomes of firm behavior are usually given by demand and supply conditions in competitive markets, the equilibria on which firms coordinate in coordinated market economies are more often the result of strategic interaction among firms and other actors" (8). In other words, different institutional arrangements lead to different *equilibrium outcomes* – that is, different yet stable patterns of investment, production, innovation, and the like.

Further, much like Katzenstein, Hall and Soskice stress the importance of institutions in CMEs that provide capacities for deliberation and discussion to help actors reach collective agreements with each other. *Deliberative institutions* are important, they suggest, because they facilitate the sharing of information about interests and beliefs that then boosts everyone's confidence in the actions of the others. That is, information sharing facilitates trust, in part by helping actors strategically to determine the risks and gains involved in cooperation and resolve the related distributional issues. Deliberation also enhances the capacity of actors to cope with new or unfamiliar challenges by enabling them to develop common diagnoses of situations and agree to a collective response.

A fifth factor that Hall and Soskice attend to, in addition to acknowledging the formal institutions typically emphasized in much of the literature in comparative political economy, is the role of informal *cultural institutions*. By cultural institutions they mean informal rules and understandings that help actors coordinate their behaviour. These are important, they maintain, because "in many instances, what leads the actors to a specific equilibrium is a set of shared understandings about what other actors are likely to do, often rooted in a sense of what it is appropriate to do in such circumstances" (13). In this sense, history matters. On the one hand, such shared understandings provide the foundation for the establishment of formal institutions. On the other hand, repeated historical experience forges a set of common expectations that enable actors to coordinate their activities with each other. Although it is not entirely clear, given that Hall and Soskice's approach is influenced by rational choice and game theory, what they seem to mean by historical experience is the expectation about another actor's behaviour that can be assumed, given that actor's performance in prior strategic interactions.

Finally, the varieties-of-capitalism literature argues that different types of political economies each possess different institutional capacities for coping with market challenges and for competing effectively in an increasingly global economy. In other words, both LMEs and CMEs have what Hall and Soskice (36–44) refer to as *comparative institutional advantages*. In both cases, firms enjoy certain institutional advantages that enable them to engage successfully in specific types of activities. For instance, LMEs are more adept at radical innovation that involves substantial shifts in product lines, the development of entirely new goods, and major changes in production processes, in part because firms in LMEs can quickly shed or acquire labour, close down production facilities at will, and rapidly transfer capital from one sector to another. CMEs are better at incremental innovation involving continuous small-scale adjustments to existing product lines and processes, in part because they entail extensive institutional support for lifetime vocational training and close labour-management collaboration not only for wage bargaining, as is often the case in LMEs, but also for the organization of shop floor activity, the adoption of new production technologies, and the like. Furthermore, in terms of policy making, LMEs are better at promulgating policies that sharpen market competition, whereas CMEs are better at promulgating policies that reinforce the capacities of actors for non-market coordination (45–51).

In sum, by situating this volume within the literatures on small states, corporatism, and the varieties of capitalism, we intend our focus on Denmark to be fully social-scientific in nature. We seek to deepen understanding of the Danish case by means of contemporary analytic tools – and equally to sharpen these tools by detailed consideration of an often neglected social formation. It is as well to underscore the analytic nature of this project by saying that nothing is taken for granted. On the one hand, much of the discussion that follows centres on institutionalized bargaining and cooperation among political and economic actors, as often captured by the term "corporatism." Every attempt will be made to unpack this protean term and to raise questions about the precise extent to which corporatist countries in general, and Denmark in particular, should be considered as successful political economies. On the other hand, we will also pay close attention to how well Denmark fits the arguments made in the varieties-of-capitalism literatures – or doesn't. And we will examine what Denmark's comparative institutional advantages are. Let us turn now to an account of Denmark's success.

THE DANISH ROAD TO SUCCESS

Before turning to the important insights for literatures on small states and corporatism and on the varieties of capitalism that the Danish case offers, we must explain why, in our view and taking into account the contributions to this volume, Denmark has been so successful. We argue that distant historical legacies as well as more proximate factors were at work and that these helped determine how Denmark responded successfully to the problems it faced at the end of the twentieth century and the beginning of the twenty-first. We also briefly discuss some of the problems that will challenge Denmark in the future. With this in mind, we then explain how this all sheds light on arguments made in the literatures on small states, corporatism, and the varieties of capitalism.

Historical Legacies

It is important to understand that several historical factors conspired over the long run to give Denmark a comparative edge relative to many other countries. To begin with, as Uffe Østergaard's paper shows, Denmark was once a composite state that held territory in the Caribbean, Norway, southern Sweden, northern Germany, and elsewhere, in addition to that which it possesses today. It was, in fact, a small empire. And, as a result of its military and other international exploits as well as its absolutist rule at home, which spanned the period 1660 to 1814, Denmark built a state apparatus that was very well developed compared to many other European states both in terms of its administrative and its revenue-collecting capacities. A well-developed state apparatus was necessary, in particular, to administer and finance what, during the early eighteenth century, was the second largest army and navy in Europe (Sørensen 1998, 41). But the period of absolutism also involved the creation of a highly centralized bureaucracy, the modernization of government, and the unification of systems of legislation, finance, local administration, main roads, and weights and measures (Royal Danish Ministry of Foreign Affairs 1974, 81–4; 1996, 436–8). More important, however, Denmark realized early on that it was vulnerable, particularly to surrounding geopolitical forces. This was a lesson learned through the repeated loss of wars and in turn of territory, most notably in 1864, when Denmark lost a portion of southern Jutland to Prussia and the German-speaking duchies of Holstein and Schleswig.[11] Territorial loss and perceived vulnerability had three immediate effects that would reverberate throughout modern Danish history.

The first effect was cultural. Loss of territory – and with it the loss of a heterogeneous mix of peoples – meant that the Danish population became not only smaller, but increasingly homogeneous linguistically and ethnically. In Brendan O'Leary's (2001) terminology, the Danish state became "right-sized" and "right-peopled" in the sense that its homogeneity facilitated the development of a strong, politically stable, and unified nation with a strong national identity.[12] In other countries, right-sizing and right-peopling were not achieved; so for them a strong national identity, and with it political stability, did not obtain as early or as easily (e.g., Mazower 1998). Contributing considerably to this nation building were two things. First was a process of democratization, as described in the respective chapters of Østergaard and Ove Korsgaard, through which a peaceful progression from absolutism to democracy helped generate a sense of solidarity among the monarchy, state officials, and other social actors that was absent in countries where the transition to democracy was less peaceful and orderly.

Another contribution to nation building was a grassroots movement, described by Korsgaard, which was based on the teachings of Nikolaj Frederik Grundtvig. During the mid-nineteenth century, Grundtvig and a dedicated group of supporters took it upon themselves to define for the Danish population its national identity. The Grundtvigian movement cut across social classes and stressed the importance of individual freedom, classical liberalism, voluntarism, free association, popular education, and the development of civil society and social solidarity. Grundtvigianism went a long way toward cultivating the normative foundation for Danish nationalism and state building from below. Among other things, the Grundtvigians established a private educational system for the masses alongside the system that the state had already established during the period of absolutist rule. Grundtvigian schools (alternative folk schools) emphasized the teaching of Danish history, poetry, literature, and the like much more than the traditional educational system, and thus served as a key mechanism for the dissemination of the Grundtvigian cultural perspective and the development of a Danish national identity (see also Østergaard, chapter 1). Education such as this is often among the most important mechanisms for the development of national identities (O'Leary 2001, 32; Smith 1991, 118–19).[13]

The second major effect was political. Lars Bo Kaspersen shows (chapter 2) that the monarchy, landed elites, and representatives from other social classes recognized that further territorial loss could completely wipe out Denmark as a sovereign nation-state. This realization provided another early impetus to the development of nationalism but also helped to assuage social conflict and facilitate cross-class consensus. In particular, moderates from the left and right began working more closely together and eventually agreed to a series of social acts in 1891. Notable among them was a budgetary reform that for the first time explicitly accounted for state expenditures on a variety of social programs. According to Kaspersen, the social legislation accomplished two things: on the one hand, the acts reinforced political stability from that point forward; on the other, they led to the establishment of a strong set of national institutions designed to reduce inequality and class differences and to further unite the people of the nation. These institutions provided in embryonic form a basis for the development of the extensive Danish welfare state. Of course, the roots of the welfare state stretched back even farther to the period of late eighteenth-century absolutism. In that period the monarchy and its agents, strongly influenced by a Germanic tradition of Lutheran Pietism – that is, the idea that a paternalistic ruler should care for the well-being of his devoted subjects – established, at least for a time, a comprehensive set of welfare benefits for the Danish people, first in Copenhagen and then in the countryside, which was quite uncommon in Europe at the time (Sørensen 1998). But the broader point is that in response to perceived geopolitical vulnerability Danish elites devised a set of policies now often referred to by scholars as the *internal front strategy*. This was a strategy designed to bolster the defence of the nation by providing for the welfare of the population in ways that would unite it as a people – encouraging a unity that would help the nation resist future geopolitical threats should they arise.[14]

The third effect of territorial loss was economic. Kaspersen also shows that concern with geopolitical vulnerability led Danish elites to foster strong economic ties with Britain. Germany had previously been a major trading partner. And while trade with Germany eventually resumed after the 1864 defeat, a deliberate effort was made to cultivate exports to Britain. The reasoning here was that by providing exports to Britain, she would become a powerful ally in the event that Denmark's sovereignty was threatened again. So, while Danish agriculture had long sought international markets, further impetus was given to that endeavour by concerns over geopolitical vulnerability. The result was that Denmark integrated itself more fully into the international economy; and it has remained a comparatively open economy ever since.

Another important historical legacy was a tradition of consensus and cooperation within and among social classes. Of course there have been conflicts, but, as Østergaard illustrates, Denmark has a long tradition of negotiation and compromise that extends back at least to the late 1700s when, during the period of absolutist reign, the king consulted frequently with the social elites. These consultations eventually led to state reforms that included civil service and tax reform and the expansion of civil rights and education. They also led to land reforms and the dismantling of feudalism, which transformed many of the large Danish agricultural estates into a class of relatively well-to-do small and medium-size farmers. Today, the political system is still characterized by a culture of compromise and consensus among political players, and there are many opportunities for broad popular participation in the political process through membership in political parties, interest groups, and a variety of organizations and associations (Bille 2002).

The tradition of consensus building and compromise has in fact been enhanced by the fact that Denmark has long held voluntary associations in high regard. Notable among them were the agricultural cooperatives, discussed in Kevin O'Rourke's paper, for which Denmark became quite famous and which enabled its producers to adopt the necessary technologies (such as expensive cream separators) to compete very successfully in international markets for processed goods such as butter and cheese, during the late nineteenth and early twentieth centuries. Indeed, the success of Danish cooperatives made them the envy of many other countries and a model that was emulated on both sides of the Atlantic. The cooperatives came into their own in response to a national crisis during the 1870s; having lost its southern provinces to Prussia and with its grain production devastated by foreign commerce, Denmark worked its way back to prosperity by shifting from grain to the production of high-quality dairy and meat products, and by pooling the strengths of her farmers in a variety of production cooperatives (Rodgers 1998, chapter 8). However, O'Rourke shows that the absence of nationalist conflict, derivative of the cultural homogenization noted earlier, contributed to the ability of Danish farmers to organize cooperatives more successfully than farmers elsewhere. The Grundtvigian doctrine favouring voluntary associations contributed as well. But the broader point is that since the last quarter of the nineteenth century commerce and working life have become increasingly organized. Today, virtually all interests in Denmark are organized regardless of whether they are in the worlds of work, business, culture, or leisure. In 2000, every Dane between the ages of 18 and 70 belonged on average to three such organizations (Bille 2002). Moreover, as we shall see, cooperative response to national economic crisis would become a recurrent theme in Denmark after World War II. O'Rourke's paper, then, provides wonderful examples of two agricultural precursors (cultural homogeneity and cooperative organizations) to the industrial flexibilities, learning capacities, and comparative institutional advantages that were crucial to Denmark's more recent success.

One clarification is in order concerning the reciprocal and symbiotic relationship between state and civil society. By civil society we mean simply the organization of social groups outside the state (for example, cooperative associations, guilds, labour unions, business associations, sports clubs, women's organizations, and so forth) and their activities.[15] At least since the time when the absolutist monarchy began to consult groups in civil society about matters of state and economy, Denmark has exhibited a tradition of cooperation between state and civil society in which the strength of one depends on the strength of the other. For instance, the Grundtvigian movement in civil society was enabled by the state insofar as the Grundtvigians enjoyed constitutional protection of free association. And the state passed legislation permitting them to establish the folk schools. Conversely, the Grundtvigian movement's success in forging a national identity provided a crucial source of political support upon which the state could draw as it later promulgated a variety of policies, such as those associated with the internal front strategy. In short, the Danish case suggests that a strong state requires a strong civil society and vice versa.

Finally, it is worth elaborating briefly on the importance of the land reforms that stemmed from the consultation between the king and elites. Of prime significance is that land reform came initially in 1788 – rather early relative to other European countries. It minimized the sort of landlord-tenant conflicts that O'Rourke shows fettered agricultural development in other small countries. Harmony in the countryside was another important reason why Denmark competed so successfully in international markets for agricultural products during the nineteenth century. Land reform in turn created a class of farmers and smallholders who owned their own land and therefore were able to finance their cooperative associations through joint liability agreements among the members. That is, land reform was another factor behind the strength of the Danish cooperative movement (Royal Danish Ministry of Foreign Affairs 1996, 119). What's more, land reform resulted in social inequality being relatively moderate compared to other countries. As Dieter Senghass (1985, 95–122) has demonstrated so convincingly, this provided a relatively egalitarian resource base in the countryside that, when coupled with the development of agricultural cooperatives, gave an enormous boost to agricultural modernization and further stimulated agricultural exports. In turn, this paved the way for the development of domestic markets for a variety of goods required in the countryside; this market expansion then led to industrialization (although rather late relative to most other advanced capitalist countries) and further economic success later.

In sum, Danish history provided several important legacies that, as we argue in the next two sections, helped twentieth-century decision makers respond effectively to the challenges of the modern era. These legacies included: a sense of national vulnerability; a culturally homogeneous population; a strong national identity that blended values of classical liberalism and social democracy; a concern with promoting solidarity between elites and masses and thus a modicum of egalitarianism; a relatively well-developed state apparatus; an inclusive and consensus-oriented approach to decision making; a respect for cooperative organizations and well-organized civil society; and an open economy that depended heavily on exports and imports.

Proximate Conditions

It could be argued that all of this history contributed to the development of several more recent and proximate conditions that underpinned the modern Danish success. It is, of course, difficult to delineate exactly how distant historical legacies influenced the more proximate conditions associated with Denmark's recent success. To do so would require a much lengthier and more detailed historical analysis than we can provide here. Nonetheless, there are clear indications that such legacies have survived and informed the development of these proximate conditions as well as the policies that stemmed from them.

To begin with, Denmark is characterized by an extensive set of *collectively organized economic groups* in civil society. When coupled with a growing labour movement during the late nineteenth and early twentieth centuries, the eminently popular agricultural cooperative movement provided legitimacy for the development of modern labour unions and employers' associations that were organized nationally and covered a large percentage of employees and employers.[16] Respect for free association, an important component of Grundtvigianism and Danish national identity, surely contributed to these developments as well. Similarly, during the first half of the twentieth century Denmark devised a type of cooperative capitalism based almost entirely on small and medium-size firms that were often organized in legal cartels, monitored by the state, and accepted culturally as a proper way of doing business (Schröter 1997). Certainly, the development of unions, employers' associations, cartels, and other collectively organized forms of economic activity was not a smooth and automatic extension of either the cooperative movement or Grundtvigianism; political and economic struggle were involved. But in other countries, such as the United States, there were far more serious obstacles to the formation of such collective organizations. For instance, in the United States cartels were outlawed in the late nineteenth century after much political conflict, and agricultural cooperatives remained illegal under antitrust law until they received a special exemption from Congress in 1922 (Young 1991). Furthermore, prohibitions against labour unions, absent for the most part in Denmark after the 1890s but present in the United States until at least 1935, generated much class conflict in the United States and militated against the formation of a labour movement as broadly encompassing and inclusive as occurred elsewhere (Hattam 1993; Katznelson 1985). Surely Denmark's success in organizing social classes and other groups at high levels was facilitated further by religious, ethnic, and racial homogeneity –

the absence of which undermined such organizational efforts in other countries.

Denmark also developed what Ove Pedersen (chapter 6) refers to as a *negotiated economy*. This consists of a complex set of institutions built up during the 1960s and 1970s whereby matters of economic and social policy were negotiated among all the major political and economic actors. As he explains, these negotiations initially included representatives from government and the major associations representing business and labour. Institutionalized negotiations enabled participants to learn from each other's experience, raise problems, search for mutually acceptable solutions, and continuously define the national interest in economic, political, and social terms. Eventually, this became a more generalized system of negotiation and learning that included an even wider array of social actors. But it always blended principles of social democracy (i.e., large welfare state) with those of classical liberalism (i.e., respect for markets, private ownership, and private investment) – principles that had also been central to Danish national culture at least since the days of Grundtvig, particularly as Grundtvigianism instilled in the people the notion that they were all participating voluntarily in a shared community of fate.

Central to this process and the modern Danish political economy more generally has been the ability to reach decisions through *compromise and consensus*. Indeed, the institutions of the negotiated economy very much reflect and embody Denmark's long-standing traditions of consultation, compromise, and collective organization – especially those existing between business and labour since their first collective agreement was established in 1899, which were predicated on an approximate symmetry of power in business-labour relationships (Pedersen 1993). Compromise and consensus have often been possible in part because the Danish state has had the institutional capacities, developed over a long period of time, to help social groups get organized (even in some cases by providing material resources to that end), to coordinate negotiations among these groups, and to implement and sustain decisions made through these negotiations.

Compromise and consensus building have been important to modern Danish politics for other reasons too. Denmark's strong agricultural sector and late industrialization produced a large and well-organized rural petite bourgeoisie and peasantry as well as a working class that was largely craft-based and an urban population that was also predominantly petit bourgeois in character. The Danish system of proportional representation frequently required the social democrats, representing labour, to form coalition governments with the liberals (large farmers) and radical liberals (leftist peasants) during the twentieth century, and especially during the 1930s, when the country struggled with economic depression. Notably, in

1933 the Social Democratic Party's prime minister, Thorvald Staunning, struck an historical settlement with the four major political parties for a series of social reforms. These reforms built upon past welfare legacies, whose origins stretched back to the absolutist paternalism of the late eighteenth century. They also launched the modern Danish *welfare state*, which was expanded after World War II to become one of the most extensive and generous welfare states in the world (Esping-Andersen 1985). We shall see that the welfare state was another important proximate condition for Danish success during the late twentieth century.

Let us be clear. Although we have argued that Denmark has long been characterized by compromise and consensus, we do not mean to suggest that this is a country without political conflict and struggle. On the contrary, Danish political history is full of conflicts and struggles between state and civil society, between workers and employers, between political parties, and so on. However, all of this has occurred for the most part against a background where the important actors in both state and civil society have tended to agree on certain very fundamental issues, such as Denmark's vulnerability vis-à-vis geopolitical forces. For instance, the defeat to Prussia in 1864 helped generate consensus for the internal front strategy. World War I caused Denmark to establish a number of centralized tripartite war planning boards that included representatives from business, labour, and the state, and which provided an institutionalized means for bargaining and compromise on a wide range of economic issues. And the historic compromise of 1933 that Staunning engineered was reached shortly after Hitler took power in Berlin – an event that Danish leaders feared would threaten the future of Denmark as well as Europe more generally. As a result, the 1933 compromise was in part a return to the old internal front strategy. Major economic challenges have had similar effects. In particular, as Pedersen describes, deterioration in Denmark's economic competitiveness during the 1970s and early 1980s focused the nation on the need for the cooperative development of structural adjustment policies. The point is that major challenges like these have helped to keep everyone focused and in agreement on the big picture – that is, on basic national objectives – so that the conflicts and struggles that transpire have revolved primarily around how best to achieve these common objectives.

But all of this is institutionally reinforced. That is, the conflicts that occur are civilized by a set of institutions that facilitate negotiation and bargaining, and tend to help actors keep in mind the fundamental issues and broad national objectives that are most important for the country. One example of this, referred to by Pedersen, is the institutionalized wage bargaining between employers' associations and labour unions that helped control wages and prices during the 1980s and 1990s. Another example is the formalized negotiations among government ministries that help set

macroeconomic policy (Jensen 2003, 172). A third example is the system
of proportional representation in government, which tends to force governments into power-sharing arrangements. Indeed, since 1903 the government has been run exclusively by coalition, minority governments. This
has ensured that negotiation, compromise, and consensus building were
central to the political decision-making process and that all the important
social actors were included in these deliberations (Bille and Pedersen
2004). In such cases, conflicts are managed, kept under control, and ultimately resolved through institutions that facilitate negotiation and bargaining, and tend to produce mutually acceptable compromises.

A final proximate condition involves the Danish legal system. Hjalte
Rasmussen's contribution to this volume (chapter 5) shows that the
Danish judiciary provided a context of *constitutional laxity* that was especially favourable for negotiated policy making. Much like the dog that did
not bark in the classic Sherlock Holmes tale, the courts refrained from
reviewing, overturning, or otherwise undercutting decisions that were
made through the process of negotiation and compromise. Constitutional
laxity subsumed the rights of the individual under the national interest.
And in so doing, the courts gave policy makers an impressively free hand
to pass laws and promulgate policies as they saw fit, on the basis, of course,
of negotiation, bargaining, and compromise. In other words, unlike many
countries in which the courts have accepted challenges to public policy,
there has been virtually no constitutional review of government policy and
statutes in Denmark. As Rasmussen argues, although this may pose a threat
to liberal democracy, it helps prevent the machinery of the negotiated
economy from grinding to a halt.

Over all, then, by the time Denmark confronted the problems of stagflation and rising international economic competition after the mid-1970s, a
number of proximate conditions had been established that facilitated the
sort of inclusive, consensus-oriented policy learning and flexibility that
small states often require in order to maintain their competitive edge.
These included: collectively organized economic groups, institutionalized
negotiations governing political economic affairs, the capacity for compromise and consensus; a generous welfare state, and a judicial system
whose approach to political and economic decision making can best be
described as one of constitutional laxity. It is hard to imagine that these
conditions would have been possible without a strong national identity
that had unified people across political parties and social classes at least
since 1864; without a long history of inclusiveness and cooperation that
stretched back to the days of absolutism, when the monarch first consulted
regularly with the social elites on matters of state and economy; without
Grundtvigian beliefs in the virtues of voluntary association; and without a
tradition of collective organization in civil society dating back at least to

the agricultural cooperatives of the late nineteenth century. It is also hard to imagine that these conditions would have been possible without the sense of national vulnerability that developed over many years in response to repeated geopolitical threats, or the long tradition of welfare reforms upon which the modern welfare state was based.

Policy Learning and Flexibility

How has all of this affected the policies that enabled Denmark to achieve such remarkable success in the 1990s? In the most general terms, the institutions of the negotiated economy enabled policy makers and representatives from business, labour, and other groups from many policy sectors to respond to stagflation and a decline in Denmark's international competitiveness during the 1970s and early 1980s. According to Pedersen, through the processes of collective problem solving that were institutionalized in the negotiated economy, decision makers learned that several structural barriers were to blame for Denmark's economic plight. As a result, they agreed to remove these obstacles by reforming public sector operations, economic regulation, labour market policy, research and development policy, the welfare state, and more. None of these issue areas was treated in isolation. Rather, discussions of reform were integrated across areas, and attention was paid to pursuing reforms that not only would improve economic performance and competitiveness but would also preserve the relatively egalitarian distribution of resources in society. That is, a genuinely multidimensional socioeconomic frame of reference guided negotiation and reform with much success as decision makers, once again, acted in the belief that the groups they represented all shared a common national fate.

Although the range of policy areas that came under consideration during this period was extensive, a few were particularly important. One was the reform of the so-called system of labour market flexicurity, described in this volume by Per Kongshøj Madsen (chapter 9), which had three components: flexible labour markets, generous unemployment benefits, and active labour market policies – all coordinated to reduce unemployment and improve the quality and supply of workers to the labour market. Denmark has long had one of the *lowest* levels of employment protection in the OECD, so firms can discharge workers more or less at will and labour market turnover is high. This has been a liberal part of the Danish system for a long time, and it has resulted in a very flexible labour market that can respond quickly to shifting economic conditions. However, workers are buffered from the shock of lay offs by a welfare state whose unemployment benefits have been among the most generous in Europe since the late 1960s, often at levels nearly replacing one's lost wages. Thus, labour market flexibility is combined with a strong system of income protection. In addition, Denmark now spends considerably more than many other advanced capitalist countries on active labour market policies, which provide for the retraining and job placement of the unemployed. As Madsen explains, during the early 1990s active labour market policy was both fortified and reformed to cope with rising levels of unemployment that had emerged in the late 1980s. Spending was increased, the program was decentralized in order to better tailor it to the needs of local employers – particularly insofar as vocational training was customized to local labour markets – and job placement incentives were increased. According to Madsen, this was done by agreement among the government, unions, and employers' associations. The result was a dramatic reduction of barriers to the supply of qualified labour. When this supply was combined with an upturn in economic growth and, thus, a demand for jobs, unemployment was reduced during the 1990s; what is more, the supply of labour better matched the needs of employers, thereby enhancing Denmark's international competitiveness. Furthermore, the elimination of supply bottlenecks in the labour market coupled with an agreement between unions and employers to restrain wage increases – another benefit of the negotiated economy – kept inflation in check (see also Nielsen and Kesting 2003).

It is important to understand that underpinning the success of Danish active labour market policy reform was a willingness among employers to support the system. As Cathie Jo Martin shows (chapter 7), although active labour market policies were attempted in other countries during the same period, they were often not as successful, in part because they lacked the backing of employers. Why? Interviews with employers reveal that in countries like Britain, the government tried to foist these policies on employers without much consultation or input from them. But in Denmark, the government consulted with national employers' associations (and unions) to determine what their needs were and how best to satisfy them. Through these negotiations, it was learned that employers often needed workers with more education and skills in order to deploy the sort of flexible and technologically sophisticated production methods demanded of them by a post-Fordist economy in which the capacity to respond rapidly to shifting market demands was critical. Once this had been settled, the government mandated local corporatist committees to implement at a decentralized level the sorts of active labour market policies that were favoured in these discussions. Throughout the process, the employers' associations played a key role in educating member firms to the fact that it was in their collective interest to participate in these programs. As a result, nearly 70 percent of Danish firms interviewed participated, as opposed to only 40 percent in Britain. Moreover, as noted earlier, both labour and employers benefited.

The development of capacities for negotiation and learning has enhanced Denmark's international competitiveness in other ways too. For instance, as Peer Hull Kristensen describes (chapter 8), when the oil crisis hit in the 1970s, causing firms to close and workers to lose their jobs, managers and workers began to negotiate changes at the level of the firm through a kind of micro-level corporatist bargaining process. Hence, since the early 1980s, the organization of Danish firms has increasingly involved teamwork, flatter hierarchies, cooperative labour-management relations, flexible job definitions, in-house vocational training, continuous skill upgrading, learning, and experimentation with production and project management techniques. Indeed, according to Kristensen, all of these strategies help to account for the recent competitive success of Danish firms. At first, many of these organizational changes occurred at the firm level and in very informal and quiet ways, so as not to violate national agreements between unions and employers associations. But as the benefits became apparent in the ability of Danish firms to compete successfully in an increasingly global economy, some of these principles gradually worked their way into national agreements. Even so, Kristensen argues that centralized corporatist institutions could do more to facilitate the adoption and diffusion of these innovations. This may be true. Nevertheless, organized collaboration among producers, users, state regulators, and others at a more macro level has still enabled Danish firms to generate important technological innovations, adapt flexibly to changing circumstances, and compete more effectively in international markets than countries without such collaborative arrangements (e.g., Garud and Karnøe 2001; Karnøe 1995). In sum, close social interaction and trust across organizations and across departments and management levels within organizations have enabled Danish firms to achieve high levels of joint learning and flexibility in the use of resources, including the rapid diffusion of new technologies even among low- and medium-tech sectors of the economy (Kristensen and Zeitlin 2002; Nielsen and Kesting 2003).

It is worth mentioning briefly that Kristensen has found elsewhere that this sort of adaptive flexibility at the level of the firm is based in part on a shared cognitive framework whereby workers and managers conceive of the firm as a collective actor. This mindset enables them to set aside their individual differences and work for the collective good of the firm. As a result, it is an important cultural support for learning and organizational flexibility (Kristensen and Zeitlin 2002). It is also the sort of mindset that has permeated Danish culture for a long time – that is, concern for cooperation in pursuit of the collective good.

Welfare policy is another area where changes and adjustments were made through negotiation. This was in part due to concerns with bringing government spending under control in order to reduce budget deficits and the national debt, both of which had worsened during the 1970s and early 1980s as various Danish governments grappled with stagflation with typical Keynesian bridging policies (Schwartz 1994). In this volume, Peter Abrahamson (chapter 10) argues that since 1993 both social democratic and conservative governments pursued a series of welfare reforms. These included the bolstering of the active labour market policies described earlier, partial privatization of pension and health care insurance programs, more restrictive eligibility rules for various welfare programs, and reductions in benefits for some recipients. Reform also involved increased obligations for welfare recipients, such as workfare programs, and greater citizen involvement in local educational and childcare programs. Over all, then, although welfare coverage and rights remained largely universal and quite generous compared to those of other OECD countries, greater emphasis was placed on individual responsibility, private means, and labour-market–based contributory insurance schemes. These reforms were framed by proponents in very traditional terms – often with references to the Danish Constitution, which requires citizens to have the opportunity to work in order to promote the common welfare (Cox 2001, 478). As was true of flexicurity, these reforms represented a blending of liberal and social democratic principles. Moreover, the revenue base for these programs shifted somewhat from central government to county and municipal governments – another indication of a drift toward decentralization. While this has helped to shore up the public finances and, according to Madsen, to reduce unemployment, the results of reform have not been all sweetness and light. Abrahamson reports that benefit reductions have contributed to an increase in poverty since 1995.

The basic point is that in both the public and private spheres the institutional capacities – political, economic, and cultural – of Danes to engage in well-organized, cooperative, and consensus-oriented deliberation and negotiation have helped them to adjust to the challenges and opportunities of an increasingly global economy. They have been able to engage in policy learning and to respond flexibly at both the micro and macro levels. The papers by Pedersen, Kristensen, Madsen, and Martin provide windows into some of the processes and mechanisms by which this deliberation, negotiation, learning, and flexible adjustment occur.

Challenges Ahead

Many challenges lie ahead that will confront Denmark's socioeconomic fortunes in the twenty-first century. Two are especially important, insofar as they cut to the very core of some of the most deeply ingrained traditions of the Danish political economy.

The first is Denmark's role in the European Union. Since at least the

1970s, Danish elites have favoured European integration. And until the 1990s they had enough political support from the citizenry to pursue that objective. Recently, however, things have changed. Two national referenda, one on the Maastricht Treaty in 1992 and another on the single European currency in 2002, were defeated at the polls despite the fact that members of most political parties, unions, and employers' associations supported them. In other words, a split has developed between elites and masses over issues of continued European integration.

As Morten Kelstrup explains (chapter 11), this change of direction is having serious consequences. The presence of policy making by referenda challenges the very basis of the corporatist, negotiated economy, insofar as decisions regarding EU monetary policy are now being taken outside of traditional policy-making channels. In a sense, a dual political system is developing around EU economic issues which could spread to other areas of EU policy (e.g., national security, common citizenship) – areas that have already witnessed conflicts among the major political parties. This could undercut the institutionalized bargaining and negotiation processes that have served Denmark so well for so long. Moreover, the EU question has contributed to a growing nationalist concern over the potential loss of state sovereignty that could further widen the split between elites and masses and could add an increasingly important new dimension to politics. Whereas Danish political debate has traditionally occurred along an axis ranging from conservative/right to social democratic/left positions, now a second axis cuts through the traditional one – an axis that ranges from pro- to anti-European integration.

Of course, there is a certain irony to all of this. Political elites failed to obtain "yes" votes on the two referenda concerning Denmark's further participation in the European Union in part because Danish voters were concerned with preserving their national identity (Friis 2002). Hence, if a willingness to adapt flexibly to international challenges is a key to success these days (Ikenberry 2003) – a point to which we return later – then Denmark's strong national identity may be inhibiting the sort of flexibility required of it today. In other words, while a strong national identity may once have contributed to Denmark's success, as we argued earlier, it may now be working against it – at least from the perspective of political and economic leaders, most of whom wanted to adopt these EU treaties. All of this, incidentally, also supports the arguments of other scholars who have suggested that the EU project, and with it the attempt to create some sort of large-scale transnational or continental identity, may actually reinvigorate and intensify nationalist sentiments among European countries (Smith 1991, 176). In any case, it remains unclear how the Danish political system will handle all of these challenges and whether their response will further undermine the capacities of parties to compromise.

A second, but related, challenge to the Danish system involves immigration. Ulf Hedetoft argues (chapter 12) that as European integration increases the likelihood that foreigners will migrate to Denmark, and as Denmark continues to accept immigrants and refugees – presumably attracted by its generous welfare state, standard of living, and job opportunities – the homogeneous foundation of the Danish nation is drawn into question. A kind of xenophobic nationalism is emerging, at least in political rhetoric, which may jeopardize the strong feelings of national identity that have underpinned the welfare state, economy, and society in general for well over a century. Despite the fact that there is little evidence to support the view that an influx of immigrants has put undue stress on the welfare state, the issue is very much in the public eye (see also Sørensen 1998, 41–2). Indeed, this issue alone enabled a small, populist, anti-immigrant political party, the Danish People's Party, to win enough votes to help form a bourgeois coalition government in 2001 and push immigration onto the legislative agenda. Whether the immigration issue destabilizes the institutions of the Danish negotiated economy, consensus-oriented parliamentary politics, national solidarity, or societal trust more broadly remains to be seen. The outcome will likely depend on how well new immigrants can be integrated and assimilated into society.

But there may be cause for concern here. Recent studies suggest that the more heterogeneous a population is, the less generous its welfare support is likely to be (Alesina and Glaeser 2004). Indeed, Abrahamson's paper reports that the current bourgeois government recently passed legislation whereby full social assistance benefits will only be made available for people who have been living in Denmark for eight years. Modified benefits – a so-called "start allowance" set at roughly 45–65 percent of the standard benefit – will be available to everyone else. In effect, this is a program designed largely for ethnic immigrants and refugees. Hence, we may be witnessing the development of a dual system of entitlements and rights. Insofar as Denmark's generous welfare system has been an important part of the country's recent economic success, as Madsen argues in discussing labour market policy, political struggles over the immigrant issue may change the welfare state in ways that have significant consequences for Denmark's economic performance in the future.

There are, of course, additional challenges confronting Denmark. One is the problem of an aging population and the pressures it puts on one of the world's largest and most expensive welfare states. These pressures will continue to grow as the baby boom generation moves into retirement. This demographic challenge is one that most other advanced capitalist countries will no doubt face too. Another is the increasing concern for enhancing productivity in the face of competition from low-wage countries, especially the new East European members of the European Union.

This could lead Danish employers to lay off more workers and outsource production and information processing. This is one example of a whole set of challenges associated with continued economic globalization. The challenges – as well as the opportunities – of globalization will surely test the adaptive capacities of the Danish political economy, as they have done for well over a century.

We are reasonably confident that Denmark will successfully meet these challenges. Why? Because Denmark has developed a strong set of political, economic, and cultural capacities for managing conflict through bargaining, negotiation, compromise, policy learning, and flexibility. These capacities have enabled its decision makers to adjust effectively time and time again to a variety of political and economic challenges. Chief among these capacities are those institutions associated with a strong, socially liberal, democratic state that enjoys much popular support from a strong, well-organized, and nationally unified civil society – capacities that facilitate the politics of reciprocal consent that we mentioned at the outset. We suspect that Denmark will continue to do well as long these capacities remain intact.

LESSONS FROM THE DANISH CASE

Given our arguments about Denmark's success, what lessons can we draw for the literatures in comparative political economy that we summarized earlier? Several assert themselves quite clearly.

Small States and Corporatism

Let us begin with Katzenstein's work on small states. The first lesson concerns the important *differences among small states*. Katzenstein (1984, 1985) concentrated his attention on the differences between Austria and Switzerland. To summarize briefly: Austria, he argued, involved a "social corporatist" ideology and politics that favoured, among other things, active industrial policy, selective intervention in market processes, greater political control over the allocation of investment capital, extensive public expenditures, a large welfare state, and a greater emphasis on maintaining social equity while adjusting to international economic trends; Switzerland, on the other hand, exemplified a "liberal corporatist" ideology and politics that favoured passive industrial policy, heavier reliance on the market for industrial adjustment, less political control over investment capital, smaller public expenditures, a smaller welfare state, and a greater emphasis on promoting economic efficiency while adjusting to international economic trends.

While these distinctions may be beneficial, others may be beneficial as well, especially insofar as explaining Danish success is concerned. As noted earlier, and in contrast to many other small states, Denmark had been an imperial state, ruling not just over Norway, southern Sweden, and much of the southern Baltic coastland but over territorial possessions overseas as well. Many of those territories were lost, thereby lending Danish history a particular character. Specifically, its early prominence and power were followed first by the diminution of power and wealth and then by the riches achieved by the smaller unit over the course of the last century and a half. But underneath this rhythm was a continuity – the political capital of early state capacity – which was eventually used to help a peripheral society move to the core. That is, as a result of its imperial past, modern Denmark inherited a state apparatus that was well developed compared to that of many of its competitors and which was relatively well equipped to organize bargaining and negotiations among groups in civil society and to implement the policy decisions that resulted from this process. Moreover, the Danish state was able to draw constructively upon a certain type of nationalist sentiment – forged through the experience of repeated territorial loss – which helped it mobilize consensus among the important social groups regarding what was in the general national interest. The point is that among the small European states, Denmark had certain advantages with respect to state capacities and national identity which stemmed from its having at one time had an empire, thereafter becoming as a result a "big small state" (Hroch, 1985). We have explained that these advantages contributed indirectly to its later successes. Hence, the static distinction between social and liberal corporatism that Katzenstein employed may mask important *dynamic and historical* distinctions among small states which account for their different capacities for socioeconomic success.

That said, it is important to reiterate that Denmark's ability to remain flexible and adaptable in the face of adversity and challenge is not just due to the capacities of its state. It stems also from the particular and very well-organized nature of its civil society, which took well over a century to develop, led to the formation of a strong national identity and, in turn, produced a high degree of social solidarity upon which the state has often relied in coping with various challenges. In other words, what has been crucial is the symbiotic relationship between state and civil society by which each enabled and reinforced the other. In this sense, the Danish case represents a blending of statist influences emanating from above and civil society influences arising from below – a blending that has resulted in the politics of reciprocal consent.

The second lesson we offer concerns the *preconditions of effective smallness*. Bluntly, the theoretical claim here – variously made by others in connection with democracy, economic advance, and welfare (e.g., Dahl 1971; Gellner 1983; Mill 1975; Miller 1975) – is that national homogeneity enables high levels of social solidarity. Indeed, Denmark is an extremely homogeneous society. Foreigners made up only about 3 percent of the Danish population in 1990, up from a half percent in 1960, but still a lower proportion than in virtually any other West European country throughout this thirty-year period, including Sweden, often noted for its homogeneity and whose population in 1990 included 5.6 percent foreigners (Soysal 1994, 23).[17] As suggested earlier, the loss of territory that Denmark experienced as it suffered defeats in a series of wars contributed directly to both this homogeneity and to an enhanced sense of social solidarity among the populace. Of course, the removal of minorities as a result of territorial loss does not ensure national cohesion. Nation building must still take place. Here the role of Grundtvigianism was important in facilitating the nation-building process. But the social solidarity that stems from such homogeneity, geopolitical loss, nationalism, and nation building suggests that these are all important factors underlying Denmark's ability to forge consensus around important policy initiatives and implement them effectively. In turn, these policy initiatives contributed directly to Denmark's impressive recent performance. The literature on small states and corporatism largely neglects the importance of the roles that cultural homogeneity and nationalism play in providing a foundation upon which modern consensus building and economic success often rest. Indeed, cultural homogeneity helps to generate the sort of social trust that other scholars have found to be associated with national economic success (Zak and Knack 2001). Cultural as well as political and economic institutions matter.

We are not arguing that cultural homogeneity is either a necessary or sufficient condition for political-economic success, although there are additional examples of small states that have performed well in the 1990s which were culturally homogeneous, such as Austria and Ireland. But there are also examples of successful small states that were much more heterogeneous, notably Belgium and Switzerland. These states have found various institutional ways, such as consociational democracy, to channel, regulate, and otherwise temper the conflicts that might arise from their more heterogeneous populations and undermine the learning, cooperation, and flexibility that are required for success (e.g., O'Leary 2001). Moreover, homogeneity is no guarantee of success, as the recent case of Albania demonstrates. Our claim is only that Denmark enjoyed a significant advantage because it was homogeneous. Interesting questions can be drawn from our investigation of the Danish case as to whether homogeneity is generally more important in a broader array of cases and in comparison to other political and economic factors. But such questions cannot be resolved with reference to this single case alone; further cross-national research would be needed.

The third lesson we draw from Katzenstein's analysis concerns the *timing of important events*. Katzenstein (1985, 30) maintained that the institutional foundations for small state success had their origins in the catastrophic changes of the 1930s and 1940s. While this may be true for some of the formal institutional conditions affecting the success of small states, at least in Denmark's case the story has a much longer historical trajectory. For example, in Denmark the origins of one of the most important of these institutions, the modern welfare state, stretch back at least to the mid-nineteenth century when political and social elites agreed on the need to reduce inequality and facilitate the development of national identity and social solidarity. This was part of their plan to establish the internal front, mentioned earlier, to protect Denmark as a state from obliteration at the hands of external geopolitical forces. So perceptions of national vulnerability, not just in the 1930s and 1940s but much farther back in history, were important in the Danish case. And, of course, these perceptions concerned geopolitical rather than economic vulnerabilities of the sort that Katzenstein emphasized. In any case, at least for Denmark, the seeds were sewn for the development of the welfare state long before the deals were struck between liberals and labour during the twentieth century which a number of scholars, including Katzenstein, mark as the beginning of Scandinavian welfare states (e.g., Esping-Andersen 1985; Hicks 1999).

The fourth lesson to be drawn from Katzenstein's work concerns the *organization of corporatism*. Katzenstein (1985, 32) defined corporatism as "an ideology of social partnership expressed at the national level; a relatively centralized and concentrated system of interest groups; and voluntary and informal coordination of conflicting objectives through continuous political bargaining between interest groups, state bureaucracies, and political parties." These traits, he insisted, made for "low-voltage politics." However, the Danish case suggests that corporatism may have changed significantly in at least two ways since Katzenstein published his work twenty years ago. First, although Denmark is still characterized by institutions that support negotiation, compact building, and cooperation among social partners, this is no longer a phenomenon restricted to the national level. Since the mid-1980s Danish corporatism has become increasingly *decentralized*. Policy implementation, and to a lesser extent policy formation, has devolved to the regional and communal levels (see also Kjær and Pedersen 2001; Martin forthcoming). For instance, tripartite wage setting has devolved from the national level to the sectoral level (Nielsen and Kesting 2003). Hence, one wonders in light of recent Danish experience whether the key to success for corporatist countries is centralized bargaining at the national level, as Katzenstein and many others argued, or rather just consensus-oriented bargaining and negotiation per se – regardless of the level at which it occurs (e.g., Molina and Rhodes

2002). Indeed, following arguments made by others, including Kristensen, Madsen, and Martin in this volume, it may be that in an increasingly globalized economy where markets are much more volatile and the need to respond to them rapidly and flexibly is at an all-time high, the decentralized nature of Danish bargaining may be especially important insofar as it enables increasingly rapid learning and adjustments to these markets.[18]

Second, rather than just including organized business and labour interests in corporatist bargaining, Denmark now also frequently incorporates other organized interests, such as environmentalists, municipalities, citizens' groups, and the like, into the negotiation process. And it does so in part because it has created a more extensive set of linkages among policy areas besides just the macroeconomic and incomes policies with which corporatist bargaining was traditionally associated. In short, Danish corporatism has become more *inclusive* and more *extensive* than Katzenstein's analysis suggested in the mid-1980s (Nielsen and Pedersen 1991; Pedersen 1993). This broadening may pose certain hurdles to consensus building, such as the problem of large numbers bargaining (Olsen 1965), but it may also present certain advantages. The consensus that emerges may better represent the broad national interest because it is defined by a more representative set of interests than was typically the case in other corporatist countries during the 1970s and early 1980s. Furthermore, higher levels of inclusiveness may be one explanation for public confidence in government institutions being so high and so stable in Denmark relative to the rest of the OECD countries (Katzenstein 2000). Finally, once such a diverse group agrees on a particular policy, implementation of that policy may be smoother and more sustained than elsewhere because a wider array of social actors has agreed to support it.[19]

The last lesson to be gleaned from Katzenstein concerns recent arguments about the *fate of corporatism*. Many scholars in the early 1990s believed that corporatism was in decline as a result of pressures from economic globalization and an apparent drift toward neoliberalism. Moreover, some implied that because Denmark was one of the slowest countries to adopt neoliberal reforms, its economic performance was likely to lag behind those of other small states who adopted these reforms more quickly (Schwartz 1994, for example). As we have shown, none of this seems to be true now. In Denmark corporatism has not been replaced. Rather, it has become more decentralized, more inclusive of a wider array of well-organized social actors, and more extensive in terms of the number of policy areas that are linked together and subject to corporatist bargaining. As a result, it has become a more flexible system of negotiation and consensual decision making. In all of these respects, Demark is a paragon of a new and revitalized style of corporatism that is beginning to receive much attention from scholars of comparative political economy who seek to better understand how corporatism evolves and continues to facilitate successful socioeconomic performance (e.g., Molina and Rhodes 2002).[20]

The Varieties of Capitalism

Our arguments about Danish success also contain lessons for the literature on the varieties of capitalism. The first one concerns the *organization of coordinated market economies* and resonates very much with a point we made earlier about Katzenstein's characterization of corporatism. Recall that this literature, as portrayed by Hall and Soskice (2001b), seeks to bring firms back into the spotlight. Hall and Soskice's intention is in part to correct for what they believe to have been excessive attention in the earlier corporatist literature to the peak associations that represent the interests of business and workers in CMEs like Denmark. Certainly this makes some sense insofar as firms per se were neglected in the corporatist literature. However, as noted earlier, two things impress us about the organization of interests in Denmark since the mid-1980s. One is how much wider an array of interests is represented in decision-making negotiations. Not only firms, business associations, and labour unions but also representatives from environmental groups, local municipalities, and many other groups are involved in the bargaining process. The other thing that impresses us is that, insofar as public policy is concerned, bargaining occurs to a significant degree now at the regional and local level. In short, decision making in Denmark involves a broader range of social groups and more decentralized negotiation and bargaining than the varieties of capitalism literature tends to acknowledge for CMEs.

The second lesson concerns the *time frame* of importance to social actors. Hall and Soskice argue that the bargaining that transpires in all capitalist economies focuses largely on short-term strategic games – even where cooperative outcomes result, as in CMEs like Denmark. While we do not doubt that this is true, in Denmark there has also been a rather persistent and widespread concern among groups involved in the bargaining process to ensure the long-term collective good of Danish society. This is most apparent in the idea that Denmark needs to maintain the internal front as a bulwark against external challenges to Danish political sovereignty. For over a century this has provided a long-term strategic backdrop against which short-term bargaining and negotiations have taken place around issues of more immediate concern. Concern for the long term was also evident, according to Pedersen (chapter 6), in the development of structural policy during the 1980s and 1990s, which was a deliberate attempt not only to improve learning and performance in a wide range of policy areas but also to connect and coordinate changes in one policy area with those

in others for improvement of Danish society over the long run. At a more
micro level, Kristensen's paper demonstrates that concern for the long-
term collective good was also of concern with employers and workers when
they negotiated new production practices, particularly insofar as they had
the firm's long-term survival in mind as well as its short-term profitability.
Thus, to fully understand how the Danish variety of capitalism has
responded to an increasingly global economy, we need to consider the
long-term view of social actors as well as their short-term strategies.

The Danish case also offers a lesson about how the varieties of capitalism literature treats the issue of *culture*. Remember that the idea of the
internal front as well as a variety of principles associated with
Grundtvigianism and national identity have provided important and long-
standing ideological and cultural influences on policy making in
Denmark. Of course, Hall and Soskice (12–14) grant the importance of
informal as well as formal rule-based constraints, acknowledging in particular the importance of norms that define what is appropriate to do or not
in a given strategic situation. But what we have in mind here is something
deeper and much more taken for granted than simply norms of appropriate behaviour or expectations about the behaviour of others derived from
previous strategic interactions, which seems to be what they have in mind
when they refer to culture (see also Culpepper 2001, 303). While this is
surely important, particularly to the extent that it provides a strategic context within which bargaining takes place, we are concerned more with the
sort of deeply held beliefs associated with national identity that are so
taken for granted that decision-making elites and citizens are unaware of
them most of the time (Smith 1991, 77). While the influence of such
beliefs and identities is usually difficult to observe precisely because they
are so taken for granted, conflicts may arise occasionally that dredge them
to the surface and reveal their importance. For instance, the recent debate
over restricting welfare benefits for immigrants that Hedetoft's paper
describes reveals that one important institutional support for the Danish
welfare state has long been the belief that those who would benefit from it
are culturally very much like those who pay taxes to support it. The immigrants in question are principally from Northern Africa, the Balkans, and
Asia and do not fit the homogeneous Danish cultural profile. That is, they
are not white, Lutheran, and of Scandinavian or at least West European
descent. Another deeply held part of the Danish national identity which
influences policy making is the belief in the virtue of social equality.
Despite recent restrictions of welfare benefits for immigrants, even new
arrivals to Denmark remain eligible for benefits that are far more generous than in many other OECD countries. And the Danish state ranks first in
the world in terms of the government's effectiveness in reducing income
inequality (World Economic Forum 2003, see Danish country profile, 42).

The point is that the literature on varieties of capitalism often neglects these very basic cultural influences on decision making (but see Locke and Thelen 1995).[21]

The importance of this lesson is worth some elaboration. National identity is important not just because it influences the range of policy-making options available to decision makers. It is also important because a strong national identity can actually enhance state power and, by extension, the capacity of political economies to perform well in the long run. This point is often neglected by students of comparative political economy but has recently begun to receive more attention (e.g., Baldwin 2003; Hall 2003). The Danish case illustrates this point. After all, a sense of geopolitical vulnerability has long pervaded this particular country's national identity. As a result, decision makers have managed to cultivate a certain degree of social solidarity among various status and class groups in order to cope with geopolitical and, more recently, international economic challenges. This has also involved the development and modification of institutions that are inclusive of a wide range of interests. All of these factors have, we suspect, contributed to the high levels of social trust and public confidence in governmental institutions that others have noted (e.g., Katzenstein 2000; Zak and Knack 2001). Trust and social capital are now more generally recognized by some scholars as being an important determinant of successful economic performance (for example, Zak and Knack 2001; Putnam and Goss 2002, 5–7). Public confidence, trust, and social solidarity have certainly bolstered Denmark's capacity to learn, react flexibly to changing circumstances, and succeed economically in recent years.

Another lesson involves the *assumption of societal equilibrium*. The studies in this volume indicate that Danish society (and we suspect other advanced capitalist societies) is no longer in equilibrium as it once was. That is, whereas Hall and Soskice argue that in both LMEs and CMEs equilibrium outcomes emerge in response either to supply and demand conditions or to strategic interactions, respectively, the recent Danish experience challenges the basic assumption of equilibrium in the first place. For example, Danish active labour market policy and shop floor bargaining and negotiation seem to have institutionalized the capacity of Danish firms and workers constantly to adjust to new circumstances. In other words, Danes seem to have learned that at least in the recent period of globalization there is no economic equilibrium – everything is more or less in a constant state of flux. Indeed, this may be one of the most important reasons why Denmark has achieved such success since the mid-1980s. A sizeable literature argues that market signals change so quickly now in response to recent revolutions in transportation and telecommunications that the situation is never really in equilibrium at all (e.g., Piore and Sabel 1984; Powell 1987). Hence, firms and others need to remain ever-vigilant for new opportunities and must maintain the institutional capacities for learning and socioeconomic adjustment that are necessary to keep pace. Danish managers seem to understand this, given the fact that their firms have been successful internationally in recent years, as Kristensen shows (chapter 8), by developing the capacity to quickly modify process technologies and put them to different uses as the market requires. The same seems true for public policy makers, given the fact that they have developed a set of policy-making institutions based on negotiation, consensus, and trust which facilitate constant policy learning and adjustment. To return to a point made briefly above, some scholars have argued that the strength of states in the twenty-first century no longer lies so much in their traditional administrative or coercive capacities as in their ability to be flexible, and that this new form of flexible strength often stems from an underlying normative consensus within which these states operate and that empowers states to work effectively with society (Ikenberry 2003, 368–9; see also Weiss 1998). Denmark proves the point. As mentioned earlier, it also proves that a new, more flexible form of corporatism may be evolving that will better enable small states to cope with the pressures of economic globalization (Molina and Rhodes 2002).

There is also an important lesson here for the basic *distinction between LMEs and CMEs* that sits at the heart of the varieties of capitalism literature. Certainly Hall and Soskice intend that these are ideal types to which no empirical case will conform perfectly. Nevertheless, there is an emerging literature that criticizes this scheme as an oversimplification and suggests that real-world capitalist political economies are more often hybrids containing important elements of each type, and that it is the hybrid nature of political economies that is important to grasp if we want to understand how they operate and why they are successful – or not (e.g., Zeitlin 2003). Some of the most successful countries during the 1990s, Ireland, the Netherlands, and Portugal, for example, were arguably hybrids of this sort. The importance of hybrid arrangements is particularly clear in the Danish case. On the one hand, we find that at least since the days of Grundtvig, Danes have held dear the principles of individual liberty, freedom, and responsibility. And Denmark has always had great respect for the market – particularly the international market – as a focal point toward which public and private policy ought to be oriented. On the other hand, Danes have also held in high regard the principles of social democracy, including the importance of the welfare state. Indeed, as several chapters in this volume indicate, Danish policy making has generally involved a blending of the two sets of principles. In other words, key elements of the ideal typical LME (orientation to the market) and CME (social democracy) have long been a part of the Danish political economy. This is perhaps most evident in Madsen's paper on the flexicurity system, which involves quite low levels of employment protection, as well as quite generous unemployment and active labour market policies, thus affording employers the right to hire and fire workers as they please in response to market signals. In other words, the flexicurity system deliberately combines liberal/LME and social democratic/CME principles in such a way as to resolve the problem of labour market rigidity. The LME/CME dichotomy is certainly useful in identifying important institutional factors that vary across countries and affect political-economic performance. But it fails to capture the fact that the hybrids may be much better equipped to compete in today's "new economy" – that is, in an economy that is marked by a greater reliance on learning and information processing, flexibility, shortened product-life cycles, interorganizational cooperation, and more intense international competition (e.g., Powell 2001).

In sum, if there is any truth to Hall and Soskice's notion that comparative institutional advantage matters for national economic success, and we believe that there is, then what constitutes institutional advantage needs further elaboration along the lines that we have suggested here. Among other things, a complete understanding of comparative institutional advantage requires that we pay much more attention to its cultural aspects (e.g., national identity), its historical aspects (e.g., perceived external threats), and its hybrid nature (e.g., blending of liberal and social democratic principles). The chapters of this volume do this for an important, interesting, and recently very successful case. So, contrary to those who, like Michael Porter, believed that there was something "rotten in the state of Denmark," we believe that the evidence suggests just the opposite.

NOTES

Thanks for comments go to Lars Bo Kaspersen, Peter Katzenstein, Ove Korsgaard, Kevin O'Rourke, Ove Pedersen, and the two anonymous reviewers.

1 As is now generally acknowledged, economic globalization – that is, the movement of capital, goods, services, and labour across national borders – has ebbed and flowed for more than a century. It increased during the late nineteenth and early twentieth centuries, declined with the onset of World War I, remained low until the 1950s when it began to increase again, and then escalated more sharply beginning in the mid-1970s (e.g., Campbell 2004, chap. 5).

2 The inordinate attention that Sweden receives reflects Swedish success in the academic tourist market as well as the fact that Swedish social scientists generally have been better connected to the international academic community (Sørensen 1998, 365).

3 There has been much attention lately to the need for studying processes and
   mechanisms in social science, rather than letting analysis based on statistical
   correlations suffice for theory construction. See, for example, Campbell
   (2004, chap. 3), Hedström and Swedberg (1998), Lieberson and Lynn
   (2002), Reskin (2003), and McAdam et al. (2001, 24–8). Our focus on
   Denmark as a case is very much in this spirit.

4 Gross foreign direct investment refers to inflows and outflows of investment
   seeking to acquire significant control of an enterprise operating in an economy other than that of the investor.

5 Gross private capital flow refers to the sum of all inflows and outflows of
   direct, portfolio, and other investment recorded in the balance of payments
   financial account.

6 The fact that labour productivity was growing while unemployment remained
   low is impressive. After all, with productivity rates rising, employers can get by
   with relatively fewer workers than they can at lower rates. Indeed, some
   experts argue that this is one reason why the United States is currently experiencing a so-called "jobless" economic recovery – U.S. productivity rates are
   rising and so employers are laying off workers (Gilpin 2003).

7 A Gini coefficient equals 0 when income is perfectly equally distributed; it
   equals 1 when all income is concentrated at the top of the income distribution.

8 The comparatively high number of working days lost in Denmark through
   labour disputes in the second half of the 1990s should be interpreted with
   caution. It stems almost entirely from a large general strike in the private sector in 1998 (Monger 2003, 21). Perhaps ironically, the 1998 strike was associated with Denmark's very successful economic performance during the preceding few years. The late 1990s was a period of considerable prosperity so,
   unlike previous years, the government and employers could not argue convincingly that the unions should refrain from striking lest they further hurt
   an economy already in crisis – an argument that was heard frequently during
   the 1970s and 1980s. Instead, when their contract expired unions entered
   into wage negotiations with employers in 1998 and used the strike as a means
   of applying pressure during the negotiations.

9 It is worth clarifying briefly the commonly held distinctions among statist,
   corporatist, and liberal political economic institutional arrangements.
   Typically, statism refers to arrangements whereby the central government
   plays a powerful role in creating incentives that influence the decisions of
   market actors, principally business and labour, often through indicative planning and the use of a wide variety of powerful policy instruments whose
   effects can be targeted at particular economic sectors or firms. Corporatism
   refers to arrangements whereby market actors are organized through peak
   associations, such as centralized business and employers' associations and
   labour unions, and engage in national-level bargaining, often with the gov-

ernment, over wages and macroeconomic and other relevant policies that shape the incentives for market actors. Liberalism refers to arrangements where the state plays a more distant, arms-length role in regulating, rather than coordinating, economic activity and lets markets establish the incentives to which private actors respond. France is often cited as an example of statism; Germany is often cited as an example of corporatism; and the United States is often cited as an example of liberalism. For further discussion, see, for instance, Crouch and Streeck (1997), Katzenstein (1978), Shonfield (1965), and Zysman (1983).

10 For a review of the vast literature on corporatism, its fall from academic grace during the 1990s, and its subsequent revitalization, see Molina and Rhodes (2002).

11 Ove Korsgaard's paper explains that this lesson of vulnerability was reinforced by the Nazi occupation as well as the threat of internal communist agitation in the wake of the Russian revolution.

12 The concepts of nation and national identity should be distinguished from that of the state. In the West, the *nation* constitutes a cultural and political bond – that is, an identity – based on an historic territory or homeland, common myths and historical memories, a common mass public culture, common legal rights and duties for all members, and a common economy that includes territorial mobility for its members. The *state* refers to a set of public institutions, such as parliaments, administrative bureaucracies, and the military, that are set apart from other social institutions and that exercise a monopoly of coercion and extraction within a given territory (Smith 1991, 14–15).

13 Korsgaard explains that education was also used to reinforce Danish national identity during the Nazi occupation in the 1940s as policy makers strove to bolster the idea that the Danish people were one, regardless of religious, class, and other distinctions, and did so by referring directly to long-standing shared beliefs in social democratic values.

14 Korsgaard argues that the internal front strategy was deployed again in response to the threat of Communist agitation during the 1930s, which policy makers perceived as a possible precursor to full-blown revolution. During this period, steps were taken to establish the modern Danish welfare state. This was viewed in part as a way to defend the nation-state from revolutionary forces by bridging the gap between elites and masses and creating social solidarity among all segments of society.

15 We recognize that there are debates over the term "civil society." Some, for instance, would equate civil society with the market and with actors motivated primarily with the pursuit of profit. We prefer a broader definition that includes both market actors like unions and business associations as well as non-market actors like the Grundtvigian movement. Both played important roles in Danish political and economic history.

16 Trade union density in Denmark has always been high by international stan-
    dards. It was 78.3 percent in 1995 (Rubery and Grimshaw 2003, 161).
    Similarly, there is a comparatively high degree of cooperation and association
    among firms, although not as high as in the other Scandinavian countries,
    Germany, Austria, or Japan (Kenworthy 1995, 171). Not surprisingly, there-
    fore, labour market institutions in Denmark are among the most centralized
    in the OECD, in that there is mutual recognition of the rights of peak associa-
    tions to bargain for unions and employer affiliates (Western 1997, 33–4). In
    1996 nearly 70 percent of Danish workers were covered by collective bargain-
    ing agreements (Rubery and Grimshaw 2003, 161).

17 According to another study, during the mid-1980s if you selected two people
    at random from the Danish population, the odds that they would be from dif-
    ferent ethnic groups were about 6 out of 100. Among the advanced capitalist
    countries, only Ireland, Japan, and Portugal had lower odds. On average, the
    odds for the entire set of advanced capitalist countries were 28 out of 100
    (Roeder 2001).

18 We do not mean to quibble over the best or most appropriate definition of
    corporatism. In addition to Katzenstein's definition, there are many defini-
    tions as to what corporatism is and how it works. These range from elite types
    and types that tend to exclude labour from negotiation to more tripartite,
    consensual, and democratic types of the sort that Katzenstein described
    (Schmitter 1979; Schmitter and Lehmbruch 1979). Our point is simply that
    there may be particular elements of corporatism that are more fundamental
    than others, as least nowadays, to ensuring economic success for small states
    with open economies.

19 The high degree of inclusiveness exhibited in Denmark – especially insofar as
    policy learning is concerned – is well illustrated by Danish think tanks. These
    organizations play a particularly important role in the policy-learning process.
    Here we have in mind organizations, such as the Business Development
    Council, which focuses on industrial policy, and the National Labour Market
    Council, which focuses on labour market policy. These organizations bring
    together business leaders, union officials, politicians, civil servants, experts,
    and others to learn from the past experiences of both Denmark and other
    countries. They do so by evaluating past performance, setting benchmarks
    against which to gauge future performance, and predicting through model-
    ling and other analytic techniques how policies will affect both macroeco-
    nomic and microeconomic outcomes. They also discuss how to translate ideas
    and practices observed outside Denmark into local Danish practice. These
    organizations are explicitly designed for policy learning. They are both very
    inclusive and *consensus-oriented* in their approach to policy learning and in
    making policy recommendations. In this regard, they are very different from
    think tanks in other countries (e.g., Ricci 1993).

20 This is not to say that reinvigorated corporatist institutions are the sole cause of Denmark's recent success. National identity, constitutional laxity, and other things discussed earlier have also been important. Indeed, there is debate about how much of an effect corporatism has had on socioeconomic success in the OECD (e.g., Garrett 1998; Hicks and Kenworthy 1998; Smith 1992; Western 2001).

21 The absence of attention to these issues is apparent from an examination of the index of Hall and Soskice's volume, *The Varieties of Capitalism*, which contains 473 pages of text. The term "culture" is mentioned in just two locations, while the terms "national identity," "norms," and "values" are not mentioned at all.

PART ONE

Inventing Denmark

1

Denmark: A Big Small State

The Peasant Roots of Danish Modernity

UFFE ØSTERGÅRD

How is one to characterize Denmark? One could begin by saying it is a small-to-mid-sized European nation-state with approximately 5.4 million inhabitants; it is affluent, always a high scorer on indexes of happiness, welfare, and national product; and a huge majority of her population belongs to the Protestant Lutheran national church, the so-called Peoples' church (*Folkekirken*). In many ways Denmark is the very archetype of a Northern European "small state" or a "small power," concepts that have often been used in analyses of her foreign policy, as discussed in a comprehensive volume on Denmark's policy toward Europe since 1945 (Branner and Kelstrup 2003). A classic description of the behaviour and self-imposed limitations of a small power was put forward by Robert L. Rothstein in 1968. According to Rothstein, "a Small Power is a state which recognizes that it cannot obtain security primarily by use of its own capabilities, and that it must rely fundamentally on the aid of other states, institutions, processes, or developments to do so" (quoted from Hans Branner 1972, 24). Branner's book is the fundamental work on Denmark as a small state and it introduces the lamentably unimpressive literature on "small states." The situation, as I will demonstrate, is more complicated.

Other observers have preferred to label the country a "small nation," and Danish a "small language." The latter designation is obviously false, confusing the absolute size of a language with its relative importance. In the European Union the established terminology for "small languages" is now "lesser used languages" (Wilken 2001), a term meant to describe minority languages within the individual member states. In Denmark, Danish is obviously not a minority language but a "big" language, though at the European level it is spoken by fewer people than, for example, Catalan, which has not yet received full recognition as a national language, despite its being spoken by about 9 million people and rising.

The same criticism applies to the concept of a "small nation" as used by the Czech historian of nationalism, Miroslav Hroch. According to Hroch, "small nation" describes the position of an ethnic group within a multinational state (Hroch 1985, building on two works published in Prague in 1969 and 1971). Today Hroch avoids the somewhat derogatory term "small nation" and prefers the term "non-dominant ethnic group" for ethnic groups living in multiethnic empires without statehood, or with their medieval statehood interrupted or seriously weakened, with no ruling elites to identify with ethnically and no literary tradition in their own language (Hroch 2000, 11, 39–40). This has obviously never been the case for Denmark and the Danes, who have an unbroken state and linguistic continuity dating back more than 1000 years. Danes and the Danish language have been in unrivalled command of Denmark ever since their crushing defeat of the German states in 1864, which often is taken as the beginning of small state Denmark.

At other times Denmark has been referred to as a "small people" on a par with the Catalans, the Scots, the Bretons, the Corsicans, or the many other so-called "stateless" peoples of Europe. But that is obviously incorrect. Yes, Denmark is a small state, but it is hardly a small people. Denmark is a nation-state with uncontested sovereignty, as demonstrated by her being a founding member of the United Nations and by her very long historical legitimacy. Countries like Denmark belong to a restricted, privileged group of small states ranging from Luxembourg to the Netherlands, who by historical accident[1] exercised national independence in the crucial years in the mid-twentieth century when European cooperation was launched on the basis of sovereign nation states. It is hard to determine any precise logic behind the difference in status of regions such as Catalunya, Scotland, and Bavaria, on the one hand, and sovereign states such as Luxembourg, Denmark, Ireland, the Baltic States – and even Malta – on the other. "Historical accident," as I use the term, seems to be the only common denominator in these cases. The sovereignty of the latter states is now a fact that has allowed these particular entities an over-proportional say in European – and therefore global – political and economic matters.

Independent statehood plays a major role in the era of nation states, regardless of its formality. Therefore it is not completely ridiculous when electorates such as the Danes cling to the sovereignty of their country, however imprecise that concept may seem, while Germans and Italians, at least until recently, have seemed fairly keen on handing over their national sovereignty to European institutions. The problem for Denmark as a player in international politics is that many Danes mistake formal sovereignty for real power in deciding the outcome of European politics. Thus, they feel frustrated or cheated upon realizing the limits of the influence of a small state, regardless of the strengths and cohesiveness of its society. In this sense, Danes tend to act as if their state should be seen on a par with (still) great powers like the United Kingdom and France and as much greater than, for example, Italy or Spain.

On the other hand, if one investigates the Danish political debate over European integration and related elements in the political culture, one finds in it a number of features normally taken to be characteristic of the recently independent Central European states, Slovakia and Slovenia. The latter offers a particularly interesting case for comparison with Denmark, as there are a number of similarities between the national mentalities of Danes and Slovenes as expressed in political discourse, world view, and drinking habits. However, the geographical and geopolitical differences between the states are equally striking. The Slovenian lands have as long a history as Denmark, but only as separate provinces in what eventually became the multinational Habsburg Empire, without the legitimate basis of a recognized unbroken "national" monarchy of their own (Gow and Carmichael 2000). The Slovenes are thus a small people or nation who kept together as a cultural nation because of their language. Only in 1991, with its break from Yugoslavia, did Slovenia make it into the rank of nation-states, as a truly ethnonational small state (see Connor 1994).

Denmark, on the other hand, has been around as a state for more than a thousand years. An entity carrying the name Denmark can be identified back to the formative years of Europe in the early Middle Ages. From the sixteenth century, Denmark was a rather typical state-nation[2] consisting of several entities. Unlike other old state-nations such as France, Spain, and the United Kingdom, Denmark was defeated in its wars with Sweden and Prussia, and consequently lost most of her territories. In contrast to the case of the union of Poland and Lithuania (*Rzeszpospolita*), however, Denmark was not swallowed by its stronger neighbours, thanks to the interests of the great powers of the day in preserving a sovereign state at the entrance to the Baltic Sea (Østergaard 1997a). In the nineteenth century, after the dissolution of the multicultural and multilingual composite state[3] (*Helstaten*), the core provinces were gradually transformed into a homogeneous nation-state with a political culture based on language, people (*folk*), nation, state, and religion.

I intend to analyse the confluence of the long legitimacy of the composite state on the one hand and the small nation-state on the other. At first sight, the combination of a strong civic, or civil, nationally homogeneous society, a state with a long and relatively uncontested sovereignty and legitimacy, with a bragging – though at times insecure – national identity discourse, with traces of the integral nationalism of recently independent nation states, may seem paradoxical. A small state with only 5.3 million inhabitants and a limited military may, at times, behave as if she were a big state. But at other times she may stress her smallness, particularly when confronted with handing over well-defined national sovereignty to the European Union. Thus the title of the chapter, which I owe to stimulating discussions with Miroslav Hroch, although my use of the concept "small" differs somewhat from his, as I will demonstrate.

A COMPOSITE STATE IN NORTHERN EUROPE

Until the loss of the Norwegian part of the realm in 1814, the name "Denmark" referred to a composite state, typical of the European era of territorial states. The official name of this mid-sized sovereign power in Northern Europe was the "Danish Monarchy," or the "Oldenburg Monarchy." Today, to the extent that this entity is remembered at all, it is known by such politically correct terms as the "Dual Monarchy," "Denmark-Norway," or "the Twin Kingdom." However, these polite terms are so imprecise as to be misleading. Following the loss of Skåne, Halland, Blekinge, Bohuslen, Herjedalen, and Gotland in 1658, the Danish king in 1660 became the absolute ruler of the kingdoms of Denmark and Norway as well as the duchies of Schleswig and Holstein. Holstein was part of the Holy Roman Empire (*Sacrum Imperium*), an allegiance that complicated the constitutional situation considerably: as duke of Holstein, the Danish king formally was subordinate to the German-Roman emperor. Thus, the situation in Denmark can be compared to the situation in the larger states, Austria and Prussia, in the eighteenth and nineteenth centuries. They were also composed of large territories outside the Holy Roman Empire and territories within the Empire, with the difference that the centres of the latter two lay within, whereas Denmark never was part of the Holy Roman Empire except for a brief spell in the twelfth century (Østergaard 2005b).The situation was further complicated by the fact that in 1460, in the Treaty of Ribe, the knights of the two duchies had compelled Christian I to recognize that the two regions should "always" be ruled together – in Low German, "dat se bliuen ewich tosamende ungedeelt."

In addition to the four main realms, the three North Atlantic territories of Iceland, the Faroe Islands, and Greenland comprised the composite state. Originally affiliated with Norway, these three countries in the course of the seventeenth and eighteenth centuries gradually came under direct rule from Copenhagen. Finally, the Danish monarchy in this period acquired a number of colonies in the West Indies (St Croix, St John, and St Thomas), West Africa (the Christiansborg fortress in today's Ghana), and India (Frederiksnagore, today Serampore outside Calcutta, and Tranquebar). By virtue of this colonial empire, Danes and Norwegians played an ignominious role in the Atlantic slave trade[4] and profited from the "triangular trade" between a European centre, slave-producing West Africa, and the sugar-growing West Indies (Degn, 1974). This trade, furthermore, was complemented by a stake in the East Asian trade (Feldbæk and Justesen, 1980). The multinational character of the realm is evidenced by the fact that by the end of the eighteenth century the biggest cities of the composite state were Copenhagen and Elsinore in Denmark proper, Altona and Kiel in Holstein, Flensburg in Schleswig, and Bergen in Norway, while the seaports of Charlotte Amalie in St Thomas and Frederiksnagore ranked second and sixth, respectively, as measured by trade volume.

Customs duties on traffic to and from the Baltic through the Øresund contributed significantly to the relatively large revenue of the Danish state. The monarchy owed no small part of its strong position to its location at the entrance to the Baltic. In 1420–25, Erik of Pomerania built a castle at Elsinore. Frederik II rebuilt it as a spectacular Renaissance castle, which was sufficiently well known in Europe for Shakespeare to use it as the setting for his *Hamlet*. For more than 400 years, until the mid-1600s, the Danish monarchy, thanks to its geopolitical position, ruled a dominion in Northern Europe that was formalized in the Kalmar Union from 1397 to 1523, a loose union of the three Nordic crowns. From the fifteenth to the mid-seventeenth century, the Danish state dominated the Baltic region by virtue of its strong fleet and its possession of the islands of Gotland, Dagö, Ösel, Bornholm, and Rügen ((Østergård 1998, 231 ff., Ahnlund 1956; Sørensen 1992).

The multinational history of the Danish state is further illustrated by the establishment of its universities (for a full analysis, see Østergaard 2003b). Conventionally, the university in Aarhus, from 1928, is considered Denmark's second-oldest and second-largest university. Copenhagen University, established in 1479, is agreed to be the oldest. But the second was actually Kiel University, established in 1665 in Schleswig-Holstein – although its language of instruction was German and it was founded by Count Christian Albrecht of the House of Gottorp, a vassal of the Danish king, who was simultaneously his competitor in alliance with the Swedish enemy (Lange 1996, 224). Following the incorporation of the Gottorp parts of Schleswig and Holstein into the Danish monarchy after 1720, the university served to educate officials of the composite state, even after the 1776 adoption of a citizenship requirement restricting administrative positions to citizens born within the borders of the kingdom (*Lov om Indfødsret*). The third university was inaugurated in Christiania (today's Oslo) in 1811, just before the loss of Norway in 1814. The fourth was the Seramporan College, established in Frederiksnagore (Serampore) in northeastern India in 1821–27. Although the college was run in English by British Baptist missionaries, its charter (*oktroyen*) was issued by Frederik VI and is filed at the National Archives. Its mission, apparent from its official title, "College for the Instruction of Asiatic and Other Youth in Eastern

Literature and European Science," was to educate Christian Indian youth in Sanskrit, other Asian languages, and European science (Rasch 1966, 238; Østergaard 2005a). Even after the dissolution of the composite state in 1864, universities were founded in different parts of the surviving federation: the university in Reykjavik (Háskoli Íslands) in 1911; Frodskapasetur Føroya in Tórshavn in the Faroe Islands in 1952; and the University of Greenland, Ilisimatusarfik, which was founded in Nuuk in 1983 after the establishment of home rule in 1979.

When the Danish king was forced to cede territories to Sweden in 1658, the Swedish state immediately established a new university in Lund (1668) as an alternative to the University of Copenhagen, which previously had been the natural centre. (Øresund, the narrow strait between Denmark and the newly acquired territories Scania, Halland, and Blekinge, became a divide to such an extent that only in the 1820s could Swedes and Danes legally cross the Sund.) The political logic behind Lund University was to influence the loyalty of the population by educating Swedish-oriented ministers to succeed the Danish, and to Swedenize Denmark's rural population, or at least to direct its loyalty away from the Danish crown. This policy was far more successful than in comparable European countries such as Bohemia-Moravia or Alsace (cf. Fabricius, 1906–58; Åberg, 1994), even if today several modern historians think the policy ought to be understood as "Scania-nization" – that is, neither Danish nor Swedish – than an actual "Swedenization" (Gustafsson, 2000, 19–20).

The weakening of the state that followed the Oldenburg monarchy's relinquishment of Skåne, Halland, Blekinge, Bohuslen, Herjedalen, and Gotland between 1645 and 1658 led to the introduction of the absolute monarchy in 1660, which implied an administrative reorganization or "modernization" of the state. At the same time Denmark began a geopolitical reorientation toward Schleswig and Holstein, which were now gradually incorporated into the core of the kingdom as the competing state-nation project in Northern Europe of the Gottorp family in parts of Schleswig–Holstein 1490–1720/73, gradually lost out to the Oldenburg family. This realignment was of a similar magnitude to the simultaneous transformation of Sweden from an East-West to a North-South axis. The Danish Monarchy was to prove unsuccessful in its attempts to regain the provinces lost to Sweden in the two wars of revenge of 1675–79 and 1709–20. It was compensated to a degree through the annexation of the Gottorp regions of the duchies Schleswig and Holstein in 1720.

During the war of 1675–79, the Duchy of Schleswig was occupied by Danish troops, though no lasting result was achieved, and in 1689 the king was forced to accept the reinstatement of the Duke of Gottorp. In 1700 Denmark again fought Sweden, each allied with different powers in the great clash of European power politics. As a result of the Swedish defeat by the Russians at Poltava in 1709 in present-day Ukraine, Denmark achieved its revenge but gained no lands. As compensation, Sweden, France, and Britain in 1720 finally accepted the incorporation of Gottorp by the Danish king, enshrined in the *Act of Incorporation* of 1721. The *Law of Succession* of 1665 (*Lex Regia*) was now extended to the whole of Schleswig. Administratively, however, Schleswig was to remain together with the royal portions of Holstein, both of which were to be administered by the German Chancellery (since 1523 situated in Copenhagen), which functioned as the "Ministry of Foreign Affairs" for the whole state in the absolutist period.

All in all, as a multinational monarchy, Denmark in the eighteenth century still ranked as a medium-sized European power at the level of Prussia and Sweden (with present-day Finland). Thanks to Norway, Denmark possessed the third-largest navy in Europe at the end of the eighteenth century. In 1767, after a major military crisis with the Russian Empire (Østergaard 1999), an agreement was reached with the Gottorp heirs, who had married into the Russian ruling dynasty. According to this agreement, the Danish king gained unchallenged possession of all Holstein. The act of incorporation was put into effect in 1773, thus laying the foundations for the great reform process in the various parts of the multinational state from 1784 to 1814. These reforms were initiated primarily by representatives of the German-speaking aristocratic elite within the composite state. This elite, however, saw no reason to make any adjustments to the administrative division of the realm, with the result that the Danish-speaking regions in Schleswig were to continue to be administered together with Holstein, as was stipulated in the earlier-mentioned Treaty of Ribe of 1460.

Even after the loss of the eastern third of the realm in 1658, the composite state was geographically large. The Danish king ruled over lands stretching from the North Cape to Hamburg, a distance equal to that between Hamburg and Sicily (and one must add to that the far-flung North Atlantic parts of the realm). The military, technological, and political backbone of the empire was its fleet, which was manned to a large extent by fishermen from Norway and the North Atlantic islands. This fleet was big enough to fight a growing Swedish rival in the Baltic and to protect the extensive possessions for more than 150 years. However, after exhausting its resources, the realm suffered a series of humiliating defeats against the fast-rising Swedish competitor, which established a vast Baltic Empire in Northern Europe that lasted until 1720 (Roberts, 1979). Nevertheless, the Danish fleet proved capable of inflicting massive losses on Sweden in the Scanian War of 1675–79. Only the superiority of the Swedish land forces and the Swedish success in the battle at Lund on 3 December 1676 enabled Sweden to safeguard the newly conquered territories of what today is South Sweden. These losses notwithstanding, even in the late eighteenth century Denmark-Norway-Schleswig-Holstein ranked as a medium-sized European power, surpassed only by such great powers as France, Great Britain, Austria (the Habsburg empire), Russia, and the budding Prussia.

The foundations of this tightly organized state were laid in the 1670s and 1680s, when the absolutist monarchy reformed itself on the pattern of the France of Louis XIV.[5] The all-encompassing bodies of laws, the *Danske Lov* of 1683 and the *Norske Lov* of 1687, modernized, systematized, and standardized the many varying medieval provincial laws, introducing a chancellery in the European mould (Horstbøll and Østergaard 1990). A completely new survey of the productivity of the arable land and other natural resources enabled the state to collect taxes on a fairer basis than previously. The central administration was rebuilt on the Swedish-European model of specialized "colleges" somewhat similar to today's ministries. The administration of the army and navy was the first to be modernized. This was followed by the administration of the finances in a Collegium made up of four nobles and four burghers. That a path to a government career was now open to persons of non-noble birth was something quite new. The old regional administration of state territories in the Danish and German chancelleries, respectively, was incorporated into the college system as "domestic" and "external" administration, and by the end of the seventeenth century the territorial state had gradually been replaced by a tax-based "Machtstaat" ("power-state," cf. Ladewig Petersen 1984).

MODERNIZATION OR REVOLUTION:
THE DANISH EXPERIENCE OF ABSOLUTIST REFORMS

The price the Scandinavian countries paid for their position as middle-ranking powers was a higher degree of militarization of the relatively poor and sparsely populated Danish and Swedish lands than was the case in the more affluent and densely populated European states (Ladewig Petersen, 1984). Considered alongside this comparatively high level of exploitation of the population, it is rather remarkable that the geographically far-flung and economically overburdened Danish state succeeded nonetheless in modernizing itself much earlier than most Central and Northern European states. This happened in a kind of revolution from above at the end of the seventeenth century, and once again in the late eighteenth century (Horstbøll and Østergård 1990). The Danish kingdom underwent a revolution akin to France's, through a timely self-reformation between the years 1784–1814. In many respects this Northern European monarchy personified the ideals of the Enlightenment thinkers. From Venice to London state political systems were eagerly debated among political observers – not always in flattering terms, as we know from Montesquieu's excoriation in *De l'esprit des lois* (1748), which in 1753 provoked the Norwegian-Danish writer Ludvig Holberg (1684–1754) to publish a fierce refutation in French. The fact remains that the state was an object of discussion in intellectual circles all over Europe (Østergård 1995a).

Theoretically, Denmark's political system was the most autocratic in Europe, formalized, even, in a kind of absolute "constitution" (*Kongeloven* or *Lex Regia* from 1665). But the political reality was far from despotic, a condition that the Norwegian historian Jens Arup Seip somewhat paradoxically has termed "opinion-governed absolutism" (Seip 1958). This tradition of consulting public opinion is the main reason that the Danish monarchy succeeded in revolutionizing itself from above through a series of relatively continuous reforms of the agrarian system, civil rights, customs, trade, and education, and through the emancipation of the Jews from 1784 to 1814 (Horstbøll et al. 1989). In contrast, the French king lost legitimacy with the tax-granting assembly of the States General, a loss that triggered an uncontrollable democratic revolution, subsequently hailed as giving the only meaning to history, despite the enormous costs and the brutal terror it involved. Thus, the Scandinavian experience casts a new light on the relationship between modernization and revolution.

The Italian historian Franco Venturi, unrivalled master of the history of Enlightenment Europe, in 1989 introduced the English translation of his third volume of *The End of the Old Regime* (1979) with a telling comparison:

The first links in the long chain of reforms and revolutions, projects and delusions, rebellions and repressions that led in the eighteenth century to the collapse of the old regime, are to be sought not in the great capitals of the West, in Paris and London, or in the heartland of Europe, in Vienna and Berlin, but on the margins of the continent, in the unexpected and peripheral places, on the islands and peninsulas of the Mediterranean, among lords and peasants in Poland and Bohemia, and in Denmark and Sweden to the North. There emerged the passions and hopes, and the revolts and protests of the sixties and seventies, which proved in the end to be incompatible with the political and social realities inherited from traditions of the past. The end of the old regime presented itself at first as a peripheral event in the Europe of the Enlightenment. (Venturi 1979, ix).

According to Venturi, the seminal process of democratic revolutions began in the peripheries of eighteenth-century Europe and only gradually made it to the core lands. But was the "ancien régime" of pre-revolutionary France doomed to disappear in a revolution which for good or bad overthrew the existing order? Not necessarily. Other outcomes might have been possible. It was not the old regime as such but the experiences of the months of May, June, and July 1789 that turned some liberal reformers

into democratic revolutionaries and other liberal reformers into reac-
tionaries. Until then, a large variety of different outcomes had been
equally possible. The overwhelming majority of informed observers of the
day regarded most likely outcome by far to be a political modification of
the absolutist rule from within, leading to some constitutional arrangement or other. This route was indeed taken by a number of other absolute
regimes of the day.

The prime example of such successful reform in an absolutist regime
was the double monarchy of Denmark and Norway. There, a set of liberal
reforms were carried through without the king compromising his God-
given absolute power. I am not referring to the aborted attempt of the
Enlightenment reformer Johann Friedrich Struensee, physician to the
absolutist (and insane) King Christian VII, who in a brief episode from
1770 to 1772, tried to revolutionize the whole state of Denmark and
Norway by introducing radical reforms from above of the types recommended by Enlightenment philosophers. Though raised in Altona—that is
within the borders of the multi-national Monarchy—most of his career had
taken place outside Denmark and he was thus perceived a foreigner by the
majority of population. His reforms quickly ran into disrepute when he was
exposed as an adulterer and the queen's secret lover, and subsequently
executed (Feldbæk 1991, vol. I).

In 1776, in an attempt to forestall further criticism, the government
passed the "Indfødsret," a law reserving government jobs for those born
inside the realm. This law was backed by a whole series of well-meant – but,
as it turned out, futile – attempts to build a common patriotic feeling in
the whole of the realm in general and for the king in particular (Feldbæk
1991, I–II and Rasmussen 1995, 28–9). Examples of this ideological enterprise were the publication in 1776 of a history of the monarchy (Suhm
1776), and Ove Malling's *Lives of Eminent Danes, Norwegians and
Holsteinians* in the tradition of Plutarch (Malling 1777). This attempt to
roll back the enlightened reforms and replace them with a "patriotic," anti-
German ideology for the whole composite state in its turn provoked a virtual revolution from above led by the young heir to throne, Crown Prince
Frederik, son of the insane Christian VII. (In 1808, upon the death of his
father, he became King Frederik VI.) On 14 April 1784 he carried out a
peaceful *coup d'état*. At the very first meeting of the royal council that he
attended after having reached the age of sixteen, he persuaded his father,
Christian, to dismiss the prior cabinet and grant the reins of government
to Frederik himself. The former ministers were caught off guard and put
up no resistance. The young prince was not well prepared for this task, but
had the good fortune of an extremely gifted group of advisers. They were
headed by the minister of foreign affairs, Count Andreas Peter Bernstorff

(1735–97) and the minister of finances, Count Ernst Schimmelmann (1747–1831). Both men followed illustrious German-born predecessors bearing the same family names, an uncle and a father respectively. They were joined by the influential Danish-born aristocrat count, Christian Ditlev Reventlow (1748–1827) and the Norwegian lawyer Christian Colbiørnsen (1749–1814).

With the exception of Colbiørnsen, these were all noble landowners, among the biggest in the country. Yet they immediately followed up earlier endeavours to reform the agriculture, which had been discussed in learned journals from 1757 onward. Andreas Peter Bernstorff, together with Christian Ditlev Reventlow, chaired from 1786 the Great Land Commission, with Colbiørnsen as secretary. It worked with unprecedented speed and immediately influenced a series of measures that in time granted the Danish peasant as much personal freedom as his English counterpart, but with better protection against economic exploitation. Of course, that applies solely to the middle and larger peasants. First, in 1786 and 1787 landlords were deprived of their right to impose such degrading punishments as flogging on the "wooden horse" on their tenants, and tenants were granted the right to economic compensation for improvements they had made if they were evicted from their plots. In 1788 the Danish equivalent of serfdom, the Stavnsbånd ("adscription") was abolished. (This had been a peculiar form of servitude binding peasants to estates where they were born, enforced as of 1733 by the state on tenant peasants; oppressive serfdom, in the East-Elbian sense, had never made it further north than Holstein.) The Stavnsbånd was to be terminated in stages that would leave all peasants completely free by 1800; but the year 1788 was from the beginning seen as the point of no return for the agrarian reforms in particular, and the whole complex of reforms as well. Lately, the real degree of freedom under the Stavnsbånd has been questioned by Danish historians, and the intent of the legislation appears to have been primarily to secure peasant recruits for the army. Yet, the abolition of the Stavnsbånd and the many other reforms at the time and later on gained a symbolic importance that was to have an enormous political impact on all of the subsequent development of Danish society, regardless of its initial background.

Labour services remained, but landlords were encouraged to define these in a contract with their tenants –with the help of state arbitrators if necessary – and preferably to convert the terms into cash payments. Landlords were not compelled by law to sell off their lands; nor were peasants bound to buy the land they cultivated. However, both parties were heavily encouraged to do so. Many landlords found it more profitable to sell their estates and rely exclusively on the *demesnes*, which they worked with hired labour. The plight of these landless labourers, or very minor smallholders called "husmænd," was the other side of the coin of Danish agrarian reforms (Kjærgaard 1979). Labourers' numbers had been rising all through the eighteenth century, but the end-of-century reforms were to deprive this rapidly growing class of all hope of entering the middle strata of society for more than a century. As in most other cases of successful modernization, the poor paid the price by becoming even poorer. Likewise, the reforms never threatened the central economic interests of the manorial class; the reforms were meant to create a middle class of entrepreneurial peasant farmers – and that they did. Over the next thirty years more than half of the tenant peasants purchased their own middle-sized farmsteads. This process, together with other reforms, did away with the old system of communal village farming. In less than a generation the Danish state, though still thoroughly absolutist, had for all practical purposes done away with the feudal agricultural structure and laid the foundations of a new agrarian capitalism dominated by a self-conscious class of capitalist peasant farmers. When the feudal system was formally abolished in 1919, it had long since ceased to exist as a social reality.

The agrarian reforms of 1784–88 and 1793–96 were followed by a series of other reforms. The legal system was thoroughly overhauled of in the spirit of the Italian legal theorist Cesare di Beccaria, and with the unmistakable imprint of Christian Colbiørnsen.[6] Legal processes were rationalized and prison conditions improved. A regular system of poor relief was instituted, financed by compulsory contributions from the peasants, under the supervision of the priests in their capacity as local representatives of the state (the king had been head of the church in this Lutheran country since the Reformation in 1536). The system worked relatively well until the mid-nineteenth century, when, as a result of the democratization, the peasant farmers took over local government themselves. A more liberal tariff abolishing many import prohibitions was introduced in 1797, and the corn trade was liberalized. In 1792 Ernst Schimmelmann took steps to end the slave trade in the Danish West Indies. When this was effected in 1803 it was the first time in history. However, he failed to abolish slavery itself on these islands because of intransigent resistance among the planters and fear of loss of revenue (Degn 1974). He also presided over a commission which in 1789 proposed the introduction of universal free elementary schooling for all children between seven and fourteen, a measure that was enacted in the *Great School Law* of 1814 in the midst of military defeat and economic catastrophe. Likewise, Jews were emancipated in 1798, with full rights to marry Christians and enter secondary schools. This unprecedented period of reforms lasted twenty years, from 1784 to 1814.

The whole reform program was accomplished in an atmosphere of almost unlimited free debate, as censorship was banned from 1770 until 1799. In the wake of the coup of 1784, freedom of the press had become even more extended, and the abolishment of censorship was put into law in 1790. The agents of these reforms were some of the most influential nobles in the double monarchy. They did not act on an impulse of pure idealism, although the noble landowner Reventlow, like the American republican Thomas Jefferson, left office poorer than he had entered. They were sufficiently far-sighted to give up the untenable political prerogatives of their class and gamble on future economic gains. The majority of the owners of large estates did indeed profit from this policy in the nineteenth century, while the initiators were sufficiently well off to be able to risk the gamble. This was not the case for many of the smaller estate holders, especially in the Jutland peninsula, where, in the summer of 1790, 103 of the greatest proprietors rebelled. This somewhat confusing rebellion took the form of an "Address of Confidence" to the Crown Prince at the occasion of his betrothal to a German princess. The landowners protested against the newly proposed civil reforms and drew attention to the rising "insubordinance of the peasants encouraged by the French example." The latter was the real meat. Anxiety among the nobles over the rising expectations of the liberated peasants triggered off a reaction that has gone down in history as the "Revolt of the Proprietors of Jutland" ("Den jyske Proprietærfejde," Bjørn 1979). The outcome, however, was to contrast completely with that of the protest against the nobility in France two years earlier.

The reform ministry reacted swiftly and with determination to the challenge. Colbiørnsen, besides serving as secretary of the Great Agrarian Commission, in 1788 had also been appointed Procurator General and legal porte-parole of the regime. In this capacity, in October 1790 he published the address and a detailed refutation of the uprising (Colbiørnsen 1790). He stressed the privileges of the grand holders of estates and denounced the signatories and their motives publicly. This perceived offence forced the main instigator of the protest, a German noble by the name of Lüttichau to sue Colbiørnsen privately in order to protect his honour. Thus, the ministry cleverly succeeded in manoeuvring the revolt into the courtroom, while mobilizing the predominantly non-noble "public opinion" of the capital to support its cause. Lüttichau was completely isolated, as the signatories in the following months one by one withdrew their signatures or even denied that they ever signed. When the verdict was pronounced in Colbiørnsen's favour on 7 April 1791, Lüttichau was finished, as was the Danish revolt of the nobles. He sold his manors and moved to Brunswick in Germany, while the reform of the Danish absolutist state continued as planned.

THE DANISH IDEOLOGY OF ABSOLUTISM:
RULE BY CONSENT

The revolt of the nobles was the epitome of the very peculiar and apparently paradoxical Danish ideology, "absolutism guided by public opinion" (Seip 1958). A less clumsy rendering into English could be "absolute monarchy by consent," if consent is understood as openly expressed opinion. A key thinker in this tradition was Jens Schelderup Sneedorf (1724–64). In a book called *Om den borgerlige Regiering* (*On Civil Government*) he combined the notions of "justice" and "common good" from the tradition of the German-Swedish author Samuel von Pufendorf (1632–94) with Montesquieu's concepts of "honour" and "civic virtue" (Horstbøll 1988, 17). Sneedorf followed Montesquieu in claiming these two sets of "mentalities" to be typical of monarchical and republican regimes respectively, but added that civic virtue was all too easily corrupted under the unstable republican form of government, but it could also blossom under monarchy if the "exercise of government aimed at the common weal." According to Horstbøll's analysis, civic virtue was expressed in the patriotism and public spirit of the citizens, while concerns about the common weal originated in the public debate over the proper advice to give to those in power (Horstbøll 1988, 17).

Apart from the title, which is copied from John Locke (1690), this patriotism is a highly original ideological construction developed in the second half of the eighteenth century by Danish and Norwegian historians and lawyers. As Sneedorf said in his speech in 1760 at the commemoration of the centenary of Danish absolutism: "We are the only people who have given ourselves unrestricted monarchs" (Sneedorf 1760, 504). As these writers were of non-noble descent, they feared more than anything else the selfishness and egoism of the aristocracy. The only instrument capable of policing this class and its excessive and inappropriate privileges was a king with absolute powers. Only he could rule in the interests of the whole people and not just of one class.

Thinking of this nature had a long and honourable tradition in Denmark. The proponents of the theory referred to the circumstances in 1660 when King Frederik III had assumed absolute power, dismissing the aristocratic Council of the Realm (*Rigsrådet*) with the support of the Estates General. They called this a contract between the ruler and the ruled. This was definitely not the opinion of Frederik III. He ordered his prime minister, Peder Schumacher (1635–99) (later ennobled as Griffenfeld and even later condemned to prison for life for high treason) to render the new absolutist system in writing. This he did 1665 in the *Lex Regia*, (*King's Law*), a document heavily inspired by the writings of Hugo

Grotius (1583–1645) (Fabricius 1920, 1–21 and 270 ff.). It confirmed the king's divine right to rule relying on the kind of advice he found best. However, even if this absolutist "constitution" was not published until 1709, the very existence of it lent some credibility and legitimacy to the theory of the king's "absolute rule by law," even if the absolute monarchs never openly accepted any restrictions on their power (Horstbøll 1988, 6ff.).

In absolutist France, between the December 1788 decision to convene the Estates General and the proclamation of "*la Constituante*" in June 1789 the king's absolute power turned out to be absolute only as long as it was exercised according to "the law" or a constitution. The problem was only that nobody agreed upon what was "the law." Here we find the fundamental difference between the apparently similar Danish and French absolutisms. The Danish absolute monarchy had from its very beginning taken on the task of formulating a comprehensive system of coherent laws. Under the names *Danske Lov* and *Norske Lov* respectively, they were published in 1683 and 1687 (Horstbøll et al. 1989). Obviously these laws did not amount to a bourgeois *Code Napoléon* but they were much more than a simple codification of feudalism. The relationship between these laws and the *Lex Regia* was ambiguous, but the Danish absolutist state had a modern, reasonably coherent and comprehensive set of laws to refer to when it reformed the society from the top down. Louis XIV, in striking contrast, had never bothered to modernize and rationalize the structure of his state apparatus and thus left his successors without references outside their own persons when their governments ran into troubles.

This is not to suggest that the alliance between the tenant farmers and their "liberators" could necessarily have endured such stresses as those put on the French agrarian society during the revolution; the fundamental precondition for the success of the reforms was the economic boom of the "flourishing epoch of commerce." Under less fortunate circumstances the alliance of peasants and landlords of the Vendée against revolutionary Paris might easily have been repeated in Denmark (Kjærgaard 1989, 229). The agrarian reforms of Denmark had the good luck never to be seriously challenged. They thus had the time to ripen and stabilize, and to lay a solid basis for civil society under the state before Denmark underwent the turmoils of civil war and military defeat that marked the transition from the composite state-nation to the homogeneous and small national state of the nineteenth century. Nevertheless, it seems fair to claim that the foundations of the present negotiated economy were laid in the period of enlightened absolutism ruled by "patriotic" consent between 1750 and 1850.

CIVIL WAR:
BREAK-UP OF THE COMPOSITE STATE
AND NATIONALIZATION OF THE PEASANT MASSES

In 1800 the Danish king still ruled over a vast, though thinly populated realm that stretched from Greenland, Iceland, and Norway to the suburbs of Hamburg, a distance that amounts to almost half the length of Europe's Atlantic coastline. According to the reliable census of 1801, the total population of the kingdom was then 2.5 million: Denmark-Norway counted for 1.8 million, of which 51 percent resided in Denmark proper; Schleswig-Holstein had 600,000 inhabitants, of which 54 percent were in Holstein; other German possessions counted for some 90,000 people, and the North Atlantic islands some 50,000. No reliable census for the colonies exists, as their status was different (Rasmussen 1995, 25). As we have seen, the enlightened reforms of the late eighteenth century had pivoted upon these most important changes: reform of the civil laws, which ended the personal dependency of peasants upon landowners; a reform of the system of cultivation comprising the abolition of the common field system and the fencing-in of the individual holdings; establishment of a comprehensive school system; and liberalization of the customs. In 1805 serfdom in Holstein was abolished, a move that alienated the German landed aristocracy of this province and made it an embittered opponent of the monarchy they had until then supported, or at least accepted as legitimate (Hvidtfeldt 1963). From 1720 to 1807 the Danish Monarchy enjoyed a hitherto unparalelled prosperity, based on the higher prices it received for its agrarian products and its huge profits in neutral trading during the repeated European and colonial wars. In the early nineteenth century, however, Denmark-Norway overplayed its hand and ended up an adversary of Britain in the Napoleonic wars. The Battle of Copenhagen in 1801, the British bombardment of the capital in 1807,[7] the subsequent loss of the navy, and final defeat at the hands of the anti-Napoleon coalition led to bankruptcy of the state in 1813 and the loss of Norway to Sweden in 1814.

These events completely altered the balance between the German and Nordic elements in the composite state. The number of German speakers rose from less than 20 percent to 35 percent, and nationalist sentiments began to tear the state apart (Rasmussen 1995, 26). In 1806 the Duchy of Holstein was annexed to Denmark as a consequence of the disintegration of the Holy Roman Empire. However, with the establishment of the German Confederation in 1815, Holstein was re-established as an independent duchy, a status that implied that the Danish king participated in the German Federal Assembly in his capacity as Duke of Holstein. As punishment for the alliance with France, the Danish king was compelled to cede the kingdom of Norway to Sweden. As "compensation" he received the tiny German duchy of Lauenburg (Nørregaard 1954). Though reduced, this state was still a composite state in legal terms and multinational in character. The *Helstat*,[8] the centralized, unified state, consisted of the kingdom of Denmark proper (Jutland to the river Kongeåen plus the islands) and the duchies of Schleswig, Holstein, and Lauenburg. The latter, no larger in size than the minor Danish island of Lolland, retained its independent status and its particular institutions. Furthermore, the realm comprised the dependencies of Iceland and the Faroe Islands, and the colonies of Greenland, the Danish West Indies, Tranquebar, and Guinea. In short, it was still a multi-nation polity in the mould of the Austro-Hungarian monarchy, only smaller. As was the case with the Habsburg Empire, however, the multinational state was soon to be torn apart by two antagonistic, national programs: one a Danish-Swedish and the other a German-Schleswig-Holsteinian.

The demand for the creation of a national state with a written constitution was first formulated in minority circles of liberal academics in the first half of the nineteenth century, primarily among students and officials. In Denmark and Holstein, the move away from international or supranational liberalism to national liberalism occurred with a vengeance between 1836 and 1842. Up to that point the liberal movements in Copenhagen and Kiel had been allied in their resistance to the almost unlimited power of the absolute monarchy, which continued to prevail even after the introduction of the consultative assemblies in 1830–34. Being small in number, the official bourgeoisie was in no position to shake the despotic regime alone. Had this not been apparent before, it certainly became so after the accession to the throne of Christian VIII in 1839. The liberals had placed their faith in the new monarch on the basis of a naïve idea that he would transfer the free Norwegian constitution over which he had presided in 1814 to Denmark. Astute as he was, Christian VIII nourished no desire whatsoever to curtail his own power and deliver himself into the hands of the increasingly nationalistic liberals. Under these circumstances the two liberal reform groups in the capitals of Copenhagen and Kiel each entered into their own strategic alliances. In Denmark this was to take the form of an alliance with the peasant farmers, an alliance that was crowned in 1846 by the establishment of a political party, "Bondevennerne" (Friends of the Peasant). In Holstein a more informal alliance was established with the landed aristocracy; it later developed into the Schleswig-Holsteinian movement. The confrontation in 1848 was the result, not primarily of the situation in Schleswig, but of the fact that neither of the two national liberal groups was able to gain power without such polarization over an abstract ideology (Waahlin and Østergaard 1975).

The nationalist radicalization of the language eventually led to war in 1848–50. The conflict escalated with the political upheaval of March 1848 in Copenhagen – the Danish version of a bourgeois revolution. The dividing lines on both sides ran parallel to social or class-based affiliations. Liberal academics, officials, and other pillars of the liberal community sought to conceal this division by shrewdly elaborating appeals in the name of "the people." The means to the creation of this alliance that was to cut across class divisions was the "national revival" (or more aptly, the "nationalistic incitement") in regard to the status of the duchy of Schleswig (Sønderjylland) within the national framework. In the first years of the conflict, Prussia and other German states helped the Schleswig-Holsteinian rebels. Eventually, however, other European powers led by Russia took the side of the Danish king, whom they considered the legitimate ruler,. After obtaining neutrality from outside powers, the Danish army fought a hard battle against the Schleswig-Holsteinian army at Isted in Schleswig on 25 July 1850 and won a narrow victory.

After the defeat of the rebels and the survival of the unstable bilingual *Helstat*, the Danish administration took revenge and tried to roll back German language and culture in the disputed territories. Neither side would give in, and an intransigent Danish government in 1863 proclaimed the annexation of Schleswig. The international political climate and international agreements notwithstanding, the ruling National Liberals demanded a Danish nation-state within the "historical" framework, that is, all of Schleswig to the river Eider, regardless of the opinion of the inhabitants. This move would have resulted in a large German-speaking minority within Denmark. As things turned out, the move led Prussia and Austria to take all of Schleswig and Holstein with a large Danish minority in Northern Schleswig (Østergaard 1996a). As it happened, the unilateral act provided Bismarck's Prussia with an opportunity to settle the scores after a crushing defeat of the Danish army at Dybbøl on 18 April 1864 and the subsequent conquest of the remaining parts of Schleswig.

Stubborn and intransigent quibbling on the part of the irresponsible Danish National Liberal politicians and their misjudging of the international situation made it possible for Bismarck to establish a united Germany without Austria, under Prussian dominance (Nielsen 1988). Denmark had gambled and lost it all. The state survived as a sovereign nation-state only by the skin of its teeth, primarily because its monarchy was still regarded as a legitimate part of European politics, and because of the interest of the great powers – first and foremost Russia and Britain – in maintaining a neutral power at the entrance to the Baltic. Had this not been the case, the country would have become either German or Swedish (the latter eventuality being termed Scandinavianism). Today we have grown used to considering the rise of small state Denmark as both inevitable and positive. The reason for this was the swift exploitation of the exceptional situation by the popular movements: a whole sovereign state had been rendered so weak that it allowed first the peasant movement and later the worker's movement to gain control over the state. Popular movements attempting to take full power at the national level are not altogether uncommon in an international context, but it was quite unprecedented that they were able to gain a cultural, economic – and eventually political – hegemony within a sovereign state. This is what the slogan "Outward losses must be made up for by inward gains" came to mean for the Danes in the period following on from 1864.

THE PEASANT-FARMER ROOTS OF DANISH NATIONAL IDENTITY

The program for a romantically, ethnically, and historically motivated definition of the nation was formulated by the National Liberal "party" – party here being placed in quotation marks because the liberals in principle did not recognize political parties at all, but only representatives of the whole nation, the nation's finest or "best," motivated solely by their own convictions (Lehmann 1861). This conception, however, was out of tune with political and social realities. The years 1830–48 had witnessed the rise of modern political ideologies in Denmark. As a result, the lower classes, primarily peasant farmers, began to organize according to their own interests. According to the liberals, members of society ought to organize themselves on the basis of ideas and compete for political power through free elections (although the liberals meant that only those who understood how to govern should vote). But this was all theory.

The victory of German forces under the leadership of Prussia in 1864, 1866, and 1870 led to the proclamation of a new German Empire in 1871. The presence in the middle of Europe of this new, unstable and domineering major power provoked trends toward national unification in Denmark, as well as in neighbouring countries. In Denmark this was achieved in an exceptional manner through a combination of outside pressures and initiatives from below (that is, from the class of peasant farmers). It was on the basis of this conscious self-demarcation as distinct from Germany and all things German that the modern, popular, and democratic Denmark – everything Danes today celebrate as being particularly Danish – was to emerge (Østergaard 1984). During the 1870s the opposition successfully engaged in a virtual "Kulturkampf" with the conservatives and the urban liberals over the control over schools and congregations.

The struggle over control of the schools was to have far greater importance for the establishment of a cultural hegemony than the more-often-described conflict of literary cultures during the 1880s (Østergaard 1984). The latter has always been the subject of attention from social-liberal intellectuals, owing to the quality of the contributions from the critic and politician Edvard Brandes (1847–1931), the literature historian Georg Brandes (1842–1927), the journalist and politician Viggo Hørup (1841–1901), and other so-called "Europeans." Despite the brilliance of these names and their apparent victory with the founding of the newspaper *Politiken* in 1884, the cultural hegemony they sought did not materialize. The religious and social movements, the Grundtvigians and their opponents in the "Inner Mission," however, were more successful. From their efforts a hegemony formed that would later be taken relatively painlessly over by the Social Democratic workers movement in alliance with the successors to the European left.

The price for social unification, however, was a high degree of national mobilization among the rural masses and in the rest of the nation. This nationalism, in its turn, made it extremely difficult for the responsible government to strike the necessary compromises with the rising German power next door. Only with the defeat of the German Reich in World War I did Denmark have an opportunity to retrieve the Danish speakers in North Schleswig. Because of unwise attempts at Germanization these expatriates had become ardent Danish nationals and organized a sort of parallel society. Yet it took almost superhuman efforts on the part of courageous and far-sighted representatives of the Danish minority in Schleswig (such as H.P. Hansen Nørremølle [1862–1936]), to bring about the necessary change in the Danish political line and arrive at a vital national compromise with the great neighbouring state south of the border (Østergaard 1996a).

One of the prerequisites was the building of new self-confidence within Denmark's populace. An important element in this process was a reorientation away from Europe and toward Scandinavia (Østergaard 1996b). Whether the shift from European to Scandinavian or Nordic culture has been worth the cultural and political price is hard to determine. However, it is incontestable that in the short term the reorientation involved major political advantages in terms of empowering a homogeneous and self-confident nation-state to stick together, even after having surrendered to German forces almost without firing a shot on 9 April 1940. The cohesion of the nation was demonstrated by the fact that Denmark and Bulgaria were alone in Europe in rescuing virtually all of their Jewish citizens. This laudable fact is testament to the strength of the small nation-state democracy and the social cohesion that resulted from the debacle of the dissolution of the composite state.

Contrary to the situation in most other nineteenth-century nation-states, the very size of the small, truncated Danish state had allowed a numerous class of relatively well-to-do peasants-turned-independent-farmers (through the reforms of the late eighteenth century) to take over economically as well as politically. Gradually, and not without opposition, the middle peasant farmers took over from the despairing ruling elites throughout the latter part of the nineteenth century. The latter were recruited both from the tiny urban bourgeoisie – the officials of the state trained at German-style universities inside the Monarchy as well as outside – and the manorial class. They had lost faith in the survival of the state after the debacle of 1864 and the subsequent establishment of a strong united Germany next door. Some even considered joining this neighbouring state, which already dominated the culture of the upper classes.

In this situation, however, an outburst of so-called "popular" energy proclaimed the strategy of "winning inwards what had been lost to the outside." This *bon mot* was turned into a literal strategy of retrieving the lost agrarian lands of Western Jutland, which had become deserted after the cutting of the forests in the sixteenth and seventeenth centuries. It also stimulated an opening up of the so-called Dark Jutland in an attempt to turn the economy of the Jutland Peninsula away from Hamburg and redirect it toward Copenhagen. This movement has provocatively been called the "Discovery of Jutland" (Frandsen 1995 and 1996), meaning the exploitation of Jutland by its capital, Copenhagen, which is situated on the far eastern brim of the country as a leftover from the former empire, much like Vienna in present-day Austria. This battle is not yet over, as demonstrated in the heated controversies surrounding the decision whether to build a bridge between the islands Fyn and Sjælland or between Sweden and Copenhagen. The attempt to keep the Danish nation-state together and Jutland away from Hamburg won out, as the former bridge was built first. However, it was decided on a very narrow margin.

What is more important, though, is the cultural, economic, and political awakening of the middle peasants who became farmers during this period of time. The reason for their success lies in the relative weakness of the Danish bourgeoisie and the country's late industrialization. This awakening happened only in the 1890s, with the final breakthrough coming as late as the 1950s (Hansen 1970). The middle peasants developed their own class-consciousness and understood themselves to be the real backbone of society. That their ideology supported free trade is of no surprise, as they were beginning to rely heavily on the export of food to the rapidly developing British market. This was so much the case that Denmark became, in economic terms, a *de facto* part of the British empire from the mid-nineteenth to the mid-twentieth century. What is more surprising is the fact that their ideology also contained strong libertarian elements because of their struggle with the existing urban and academic elites. The peasant movement won out basically because it succeeded in establishing an independent culture with educational institutions of its own. This, again, was possible because of the unique organizational device applied in the agrarian industries – the cooperative.

Basic agrarian production was still largely a typical individualistic production on independent farms, albeit of a larger average size than was usual for Europe. However, the processing of these products into exportable products took place in local farm industries run on a cooperative basis. The cooperatives were managed democratically on the basis of equality, regardless of the initial investment. The cooperative movement formulated this principle in a slogan of votes being cast "by heads instead of heads of cattle" (that is, one man, one vote – in Danish, *hoveder* and *høveder*). This pun is less true when one starts investigating the realities of the cooperatives. Yet the myth stuck and produced a sense of community which through means of various political traditions has been transformed into a hegemony that has lasted so long that it has laid the ground for a national consensus. This consensus is hard to define, as it is precisely what makes it possible for members of a community to communicate through means of words, symbols, and actions. Humour and understatements thrive on a common understanding that anticipates the spoken word.

Libertarian values were not originally applied to the other segments of the population, however. The agrarian system was based on a crass exploitation of the agricultural labourers by the farmers, who, together with the urban elites, were often not even considered part of "the people" by the peasant-farmers. However, in an interesting and surprisingly original ideological maneuvre, the rising Social Democracy adapted its ideology to the unique agrarian-industrial conditions in Denmark and developed a strategy very different from the Marxist orthodoxy of the German mother party. The Danish Social Democracy even agreed to the establishment of a class of very small farmers called "husmænd" (cottagers). Thus, although they fulfilled the expectations of their landless members among the agricultural workers, they at the same time undermined the possibility of ever obtaining an absolute majority in the parliament, as did their sister parties in Sweden and Norway.

This apparently suicidal strategy, as well as later compromises in the housing policy, ruled out any possibility of a Social Democratic monopoly of power, much as in Norway and Sweden (Esping-Andersen 1985). Yet as far as we can judge today, they did it knowingly and intentionally. In the course of World War I it became clear to the Social Democratic leadership that the party would never be able to achieve absolute political majority. Under Thorvald Stauning's thirty-two years of charismatic leadership (1910–1942), the party restructured its line from class-based to more populist. The popular line was first openly formulated in 1923, and later on adopted in slogans such as "the people's cooperating rule" and, somewhat less clumsily, "Denmark for the people" (1934). The platform resulted in a stable governing coalition, from 1929 to 1943, of the Radical Liberals (*Det Radikale Venstre*) and the Social Democratic Party. The Social Democratic leaders apparently accepted the ultimate check on the influence of their own movement in the interests of the society at large. Or perhaps they did not distinguish between the two. Many things might have turned out differently in Germany had the Social Democracy in that country in the 1920s adapted a policy directed toward the people as a whole and not just toward the working class in the Marxist sense.

As eminent a German socialist theoretician as Karl Kautsky (1854–1938) never really came to an understanding of the role of agriculture in modern societies. He saw it as something of the pre-capitalist past which would be better run according to the principles of mass-industrialization. The Danish Social Democrats had a better understanding of agriculture in their practical policies. They failed, however, to turn this understanding into coherent theory. At the level of doctrine, the party stuck to the formulations of the 1913 program, which reflected the international debates in the Second International rather than the Danish reality and the practical policy of the party. The very fact that the 1913 program remained unchanged until 1961 testifies to the lack of importance that this most pragmatic of all reformist Socialist parties attributed to theory. Danish Social Democracy never was strong on theory, but the labour movement, on the other hand, has produced an impressive number of capable administrators and politicians – until recently, at least.

This lack of explicit strategy enabled remnants of the libertarian peasant ideology to take root early on, in the party and in the labour movement itself. As early as 1914 the Social Democrats embarked upon a policy for the people as such, and not just for the working class. This testifies to the importance of the liberal-popular ideological hegemony, which dated back to the last third of the nineteenth century. It is also evidence that the leaders realized they would never gain power on their own. The farmers proper constituted only a fragment of the whole population, but small-scale production permeated the whole society then as it still does today. Ironically, the Marxist who understood Denmark the best was Lenin. In a discussion of the Agrarian Program of the Social Democracy (Lenin 1907), he had a long section on the Danish cooperatives, which he had studied on the spot (or, more properly, in the Royal Library in Copenhagen). Lenin viewed their self-reliant strategy rather positively, but refused to endorse it for Russia for any number of reasons. Maybe he should have done so. That a strategy directed toward the majority of the people would turn out to be more rewarding seems pretty obvious from today's perspective. Yet even as sophisticated a socialist party as the German Social Democrats only embarked on the strategy as late as 1959 in Bad Godesberg; the British Labour and the French Socialist Party took even longer to make up their minds; and what will happen in Eastern Europe still remains to be seen.

The main reason that a libertarian ideology of solidarity could dominate an entire nation-state was the small size of this particular state. Danish historians and sociologists have eagerly discussed whether the peasant ideological hegemony resulted from a particular class structure that dated back to the 1780s or even further back to the early sixteenth century, when the number of farms was frozen by law, or whether it was this ideology that created the particular class structure of Danish nineteenth-century society. Put in such terms, the discussion is almost impossible to solve as both of the protagonist's positions reveal some part of the truth. I explain the outcome in terms of the existence of the particular ideology of populism or "popular" (*folkelighed*), stressing the importance of consensus among people. This status was first and most coherently formulated by the important but virtually untranslated and untranslatable philosopher, historian, priest, and poet Nikolaj Frederik Grundtvig (1783–1872). That is by historical "chance" or "accidence" (see note 2).

THE GRUNDTVIGIAN SYNTHESIS: NATIONAL AND SOCIAL CONSENSUS

Depressed by the defeat of Denmark by Great Britain in the war of 1807–14, the young priest N.F.S. Grundtvig took it upon himself to re-establish what he took to be the original "Nordic" or "Danish" mind. He translated the Icelandic Sagas, the twelfth century historian Saxo Grammaticus, the Anglo-Saxon poem *Beowulf,* and many other sources of what he considered the true but lost core of "Danishness." His sermons attracted large crowds of enthusiastic students. His address on *The Light of the Holy Trinity,* delivered in 1814 to a band of student volunteers willing to fight the English, inspired a whole generation of young followers, including the priest Jacob Christian Lindberg (1791–1857), who later organized the first Grundtvigian movement. When Grundtvig embarked upon a sharp polemic with his superiors in the church on matters of theology, he was banned from all public appearances and from publishing. This drove him into what he called his "inner exile" in the 1830s. This inner exile, however, gave him time for reflection, and so he formulated a program for a revival of the stagnant official religion. When the ban was lifted in 1839 he burst out in a massive production of sermons, psalms, and songs, a literary legacy which at least until few years ago was the core of the socialization of most Danes. Grundtvig then formulated an all-embracing view of nature, language, and history. In 1848, after the outbreak of the civil war over Schleswig, he produced a refined definition of national identity which helped set the tone for a nationalism less chauvinistic than most in the nineteenth century. As is sometimes the case with prolific writers, his most precise theoretical expressions were to be found in the disciplined form of the verse:

People! what is a people? what does popular mean?
Is it the nose or the mouth that gives it away?
Is there a people hidden from the average eye
in burial hills and behind bushes,
in every body, big and boney?
They belong to a people who think they do,
those who can hear the Mother tongue,
those who love the Fatherland.
The rest are separated from the people,
expel themselves, do not belong.[9]

This definition, produced in the heat of the battle with the German-speaking rebels in the duchies of Schleswig and Holstein, resembles most of all the definition of national identity engendered by the French thinker Ernest Renan in what has since become one of the standard texts on nationalism, *Qu'est-ce qu'une nation?* (1882). Originally Renan's intention was "scientifically" to demonstrate the right of the French population in Alsace-Lorraine to its French nationality, even after the provinces had been signed over to Germany by the peace treaty in 1871. After their defeat in the Franco-German war, the French changed their minds as to whether "nation" should be defined in cultural or political terms. The same happened in Denmark after the defeat in 1864 which in 1867 was followed by the incorporation into Prussia of all of Schleswig. But Grundtvig anticipated this change of thinking – at least in some of his writings.

Renan's statement has since become the standard formulation of an anti-essentialist definition of national identity. This could be labelled a vol-untaristic-subjective definition, as it stresses the importance of the expressed will of people. The rival definition in modern European think-ing could be called the objective-culturalist definition. It dates back to the German thinker J.G.H. Herder and has permeated all thinking in the nineteenth and twentieth centuries, until the rise of Fascism and Nazism (Østergaard 1991a). It is surprising that the Danish thinker Grundtvig should present a democratic definition of nationality as early as 1848. No military defeat had preceded it as had been the case in France. Until 1870 French thinkers had defined nationality in terms no less essentialist than any German would after that date. On top of that, it must be remembered that Grundtvig wrote these lines in a highly explosive political situation when a majority in the two predominantly German-speaking provinces of

Schleswig and Holstein had just seceded. Admittedly, Grundtvig allowed those who opted for the German language their own choice as non-Danes, which in his opinion was a most deplorable fate. But he left them the choice and never dreamed of interfering with it.

Through a long and complicated history this understanding of national identity later became official Danish policy and has been successfully applied in the border region between Denmark and Germany after 1920 and in particular after 1955. There is much more to say about the thinking of Grundtvig and his influence on Danish political culture. The core of his thinking was the assumption that culture and identity are embedded in the unity of life and language. Although this kind of thinking invites the labelling of chauvinism, Grundtvig himself, like his counterpart, Herder, did not assume a hierarchy of nationalities. Cultural diversity, yes – cultural dominance, no. Whether these assumptions are really viable need not concern us here. What does concern us, though, is the fact that his thinking caught on among a class of people in the small state left over from the wars of the middle of the century. Grundtvig and his followers accomplished what amounts to a real cultural revolution.

It began with students immediately after 1814. The breakthrough happened only around 1839, when different religious and political movements decided to transform Grundtvig's thinking into practice. First, it influenced the revivalist religious movements; later, the more explicitly political movements. Eventually, it came to serve as the foundation for independent economic and educational institutions. Grundtvig himself did not seek such popular support. He delivered his message either in writing or orally, and then stood aloof when others decided how to apply it. This is why some of today's guardians of the thoughts of Grundtvig speak of him as having been "taken prisoner by the Grundtvigian movement" when his message was transformed into an ideology by the name of "Grundtvigism."

The revivalists came to Grundtvig of their own accord, attracted by his independent interpretation of the Lutheran heritage. This religious movement of the first half of the nineteenth century resembled many other Pietist movements throughout Europe. Because of the negative attitude of the official Lutheran state church, they chose to meet outside the churches and were called *Forsamlingsbevægelsen* ("the meeting movement"). Grundtvig, however, succeeded in giving an optimistic tone to the normally somewhat gloomy Pietism of German origins. In their struggles with the officials of the absolutist state, these revivalists learned an organizational lesson that they would soon put to political use. The leaders of the peasant movement of the 1840s were recruited from their ranks. Initially working under the tutelage of the liberal intellectuals – the National Liberals, as they called themselves – the peasant party gradually broke away.

Soon, though, the various political factions of the peasant party began to establish independent institutions. They began with the church. With the transformation of the monarchy from an absolutist to a constitutional regime in 1849, the organization of the church had to be changed accordingly. The result of these endeavours differed in important ways from the otherwise comparable situation in the Lutheran monarchies of Sweden and Norway. A state church with a proper constitution never came into existence, though it had been envisaged in the constitution of 1849. This was a result of the influence of Grundtvig and the revivalist movement. They wanted guarantees of religious freedom, so that the church would be the creature of the state, or its agent of socialization, as it had been under absolutism. These guarantees they found best preserved in an anarchic form (Lindhardt 1951). In this way Denmark has acquired a most peculiar mixture of freedom and state control in religious matters. There is a minister of religious affairs called Minister of the "People's Church" – a contradiction in terms that does not seem to bother Danes. He or she presides over church administration and the upkeep of church buildings, most of which is financed by a separate tax. However, it is left to individual priests and their congregations to interpret the actual teachings of the church within a broad understanding of Christianity. Local councils, elected every four years, run these congregations. Still today the most influential groups in these councils are the vaguely fundamentalist Inner Mission and the Social Democrats. In spite of their differences, they often collaborate in order to control the freedom of the academically educated priests. The latter are normally academically trained at universities and represent an intellectually refined Lutheran theology that does not appeal to ordinary believers.

Yet most of the apparently non-religious Danish population belongs to this church in the sense that they pay the taxes even if relatively few attend services other than for Christmas, baptisms, burials, and weddings. Still, I think, the Lutheranism of the People's Church plays an enormous and insufficiently recognized role in defining the political culture of Denmark. In fact, we should probably talk of Lutheran or Protestant Democracy rather than Social Democracy when analysing the social and political model advocated by Denmark in particular and the Nordic countries in general. In the 1870s the ideological battle was carried into the educational field. The National Liberals, who now sided whole-heartedly with the conservative owners of the manors in a party called *Højre* (the Right), wanted a comprehensive school system under the supervision of the state. This, the majority of the farmers' party *Venstre* (the Left) vehemently resisted. They believed in the absolute freedom of education and attacked the "black" schools of learning where Latin was still taught. This they could do because the peasant movement from 1844 had established a network of "Folk High Schools" throughout the country. Over the years Grundtvig had produced a series of programs for a new and more democratic educational system. Like most of his other thoughts, his ideas on education did not comprise a coherent system; rather, they can be seen as an appeal for a practical schooling in democracy. However, what these schools lack in coherent programs they make up for in flexibility. Today most of them are institutions of adult education, supplementing the formal educational system.

Grundtvig hated the formal teachings of the official school system and favoured free learning with an emphasis on story telling – "the living word" – and discussion among peers. Grundtvig's anti-institutional thinking in the end permeated the Danish educational system to such a degree that even today there is no compulsory schooling, only compulsory learning. This thinking gave rise to a system of free schools for children, plus folk high schools and agrarian schools for farmers'sons and daughters in their late teens and early twenties. Whether one is educated in a state school or a so-called free school is a personal choice. Although this might not sound very surprising to a North American audience, taken in the context of the highly centralized European states with a Lutheran heritage, it is most unusual. What is more, these free schools helped produce an alternative elite. Until very recently there were three different ways of recruiting the political, cultural, and business elites. The university system was one, the workers' movement another at (least until the democratization of the official educational system in the 1960s). Both are well-known in other countries. The third, recruitment through the folk high schools, however, is (or rather was) a peculiarly Danish phenomenon.

It is difficult to estimate the importance of the Grundtvigian schools in precise quantitative terms, as their influence has been almost as great outside the schools as within them. There is no doubt, however, that the very fact of the existence of two competing elites has helped agrarian and libertarian values to make inroads into the mainstream of Danish political culture and thus has contributed heavily to defining "Danishness." The informal and anti-systematic character of the teachings of Grundtvig was what made them so well suited to the peasant movement. They could provide inspiration without restricting innovation. It also helps explain why Grundtvig has never been a favourite of academics; his thinking does not amount to a coherent theoretical system. His enmity toward all systems led him even to deny that he himself was a "Grundtvigian" (much as Marx denied that he was a "Marxist"). "Grundtvigians" never used this term themselves; they talked of "Friends" and organized "meetings of Friends." This organizational informality also turned out to be a major advantage, at least in the early stages of the movement. Furthermore, it is the reason why the influence of this farmers' ideology was able to cross the boundaries of the class it originally served.

The teachings of Grundtvig were permeated by a fundamental optimism with regard to people's capacities. He demanded economic and ideological freedom and the universal right to education. This program corresponded precisely with the needs of the large class of highly self-conscious and class-conscious farmers, men and women alike. In Danish literature and history it has become a commonplace to interpret Grundtvigism narrowly as the religion of the well-to-do farmers, an identification of class and ideology that dates back to the communist author Hans Kirk (1888–1962). He contrasted the farmer religion of Grundtvigism with the more traditionally revivalist Inner Mission (*Indre Mission*) founded in 1853. According to him, this competing religious movement was better suited the poorer farm hands and fishermen. Lowly farm workers and fishermen would have to wait until the next life, while Grundtvigian farmers could reap their rewards in this life.

Kirk's convincing description defines three different social environments, each with a specific religion. A most satisfying materialist explanation, it has dominated Danish social history ever since, as the overview by Lindhardt (1953) exemplifies. The only problem with the explanation is that it is wrong. Comprehensive research has called into question the simplistic association between class position and religious belief (Thyssen 1960–75; Waahlin 1987). Examinations of membership lists of Grundtvigian parishes show, for example, that they included more than just well-off farmers. The general pattern was rather that entire parishes were either Grundtvigian, or Inner Mission, or nothing at all. The determining factor seems to have been the choice made by the elites of the parishes. In most parts of Denmark, in spite of openings toward other social classes, the well-off farmers constituted the core of both Inner Mission and Free Grundtvigian churches. But they also dominated the great number of parishes that did not undergo any sort of revival, whether Grundtvigian or Inner Mission. These so-called "dead" parishes – that is parishes not religiously committed to either of the two dominating movements – actually accounted for 50 percent of all votes at the first parish church council elections in 1909.

These results do not completely refute class-based explanations of religious beliefs, but they do force us to refine them. We now know that Grundtvigism was not the only relevant ideological medium for the rising class of petty bourgeois entrepreneurs. What is more important, however, is the function of both ideologies as a means of achieving self-reliance. Both revivalist movements had their roots in, and helped to express, the needs of this class vis-à-vis government officials and influential businessmen. The difference lies in the content of the religious doctrines, yet their function was similar. Apparently it was not important what was said; what mattered more was that it was independent of the authorities. Most countries witnessed the spread of revivalist movements such as Inner Mission during the transition to industrialized modernity. The United States is full of them. In Sweden the revivalists stayed outside the state church, as is the case in England and Wales. Only in Denmark these movements were integrated into the loose comprehensive institution of the "People's Church." Hence the popularity of this institution, which to many seems to have risen in the 1990s to a degree where it is perceived as the last barrier against European integration and foreign immigration and threatening "foreign" religions such as Islam.

GRUNDTVIG AND BRANDES: TWO VERSIONS OF SMALL STATE NATIONALISM

What is particular for the Danish Grundtvigism is its emphasis on the unity of land, country, God, and people (*folk*). It has proved virtually impossible to export this particular synthesis. This is why Grundtvigism has played a negligible role among Danish immigrants to the American Mid-West and today has almost vanished in those communities (mainly in Iowa and South Dakota where it was transported in the nineteenth century), whereas in Denmark the Inner Mission is still thriving (Simonsen 1990). Grundtvigism must thus be understood as a shorthand for all the revivalist ideologies of self-reliance thriving in Denmark in the mid-nineteenth century, regardless of their precise teachings. The common theme in these ideologies is the notion of the "middle road" in all facets of life. In a now classic account of Danishness, Robert Molesworth (1656–1725), British ambassador to the king of Denmark from 1689 to 1692, denounced what he called Danish "mediocrity and pittiness." Molesworth hated everything Danish – their petty peasant slyness and shortsighted scheming. He apparently loathed every minute he spent in the country. The conclusion of the account runs as follows:

I never knew any Country where the Minds of the People were more of one calibre and pitch than here; you shall meet with none of extraordinary Parts or Qualifications, or excellent in particular Studies and Trades; you see no Enthusiasts, Mad-men, Natural Fools, or fanciful Folks; but a certain equality of Understanding reigns among them: every one keeps the ordinary beaten road of Sence, which in this Country is neither the fairest nor the foulest, without deviating to the right or left: yet I will add this one Remark to their praise. That the Common People do generally write and read.[10]

Molesworth's book was presented to the British audience as a travel account, but the actual intention was to warn the aristocracy, who in 1688 had expelled James II, of the dangers of absolutism. (Denmark had been proclaimed an absolutist regime in 1660.) It was Molesworth's intention to warn against this ominous fate, and his descriptions are probably no more realistisc than those of his friend and contemporary Jonathan Swift when describing the country of the Lilliputians or Brobdingnagians. Yet his characterizations are reminiscent of any number of subsequent descriptions by Danes as well as foreigners. What varies is the valuation of "mediocrity" and "mundaneness" in a society, which some see as the peak of boredom, others as the egalitarian haven on earth.

Another way to look at this ideology of mediocrity is to accept it as the prerequisite of popular consensus. If laws and reforms are to work they must be based on general acceptance among the people. And acceptance has more often than not been the case in Denmark. At a time when the overwhelming majority of intellectuals in a Europe of rising nation-states talked of the necessary "nationalization of the masses" or the necessity of transforming peasants into citizens through top-down policies, Grundtvig developed an ideology centred on the concept of *folkelighed* ("popular"), denominating a common feeling in the population. According to Grundtvig, the feeling is manifested in actions of solidarity and can only take root in a historically developed national community. By means of easily remembered lyrics and *bon mots* such as "Freedom for Loke as well as for Thor," Grundtvig influenced the mentality of a whole nation.[11] At the level of ideological discourse at least, he transformed the traditional amorphous peasant feelings of community and solidarity into symbols and words with relevance for an envisioned modern industrialized community. It remains to be seen whether the resulting mentality can survive being transplanted to entities larger than the Danish nation-state. Maybe it cannot. However, for a time at least, it was capable of influencing the majority of an industrial working class and establishing a welfare state.

The original Herderian concept of the nation in Germany, which also served as inspiration for Grundtvig and Denmark, was independent of state unity. However, the Danish and German handled the theoretical inspirations from Herder and Romantic nationalism in different ways. National identity in the "Germanic" tradition rested with a notion of a people (*Volk, Folk*) that does not necessarily coincide with the inhabitants of the territory. After 1870 Germans came to identify power of the state and national unity. In Denmark, on the other hand, although unity of the state was also of utmost importance for the national identity, and a prerequisite for national survival, national identity took the form of the reactive defensive nationalism of a small state, not the aggressiveness of a large and strong state.

Ideologically, Danish identity belongs unequivocally to the family of Germanic, Celtic, and Slavic identities, where national identity, in the tradition of Herder, is conceived primarily in terms of language and culture.

(This differs from French thinking, in which the state-nation is a core concept, and state and nation mutually help in defining the other.) The ethnocultural notions of *Volksgemeinschaft* (Danish *Folkefællesskab*) as an organic, linguistic, or racial community were first formulated in the early nineteenth century by German intellectuals who sought to distance themselves from what they saw as the shallow rationalism and cosmopolitanism of the Enlightenment and the French Revolution. This rejection led them to celebrate cultural particularism. In the social and political thought of Romanticism, nations were conceived as historically rooted, organically developed individualities, united by a distinctive *Volksgeist*, and extended infinitely in language, custom, culture, and law .

Through an interesting turn of events, this interpretation came to dominate the German understanding of nationhood. That is surprising; the unified Germany of Bismarck was originally not inspired by nationalism, let alone by ethnocultural nationalism (Østergaard 1995b). And the original Herderian concept of nation did not envisage the political unification of Germans; on the contrary, one could claim that its *culturalis* compensated for the lack of a unified German state. Thus, in the "Germanic" tradition, national identity came to rely on the existence of a people (*Volk, Folk*) that did not necessarily coincide with territorial definitions. The Danes, on the other hand, after having lost the wars with Prussia and Austria, had to depend on being a sovereign state if they were to preserve their identity. This nation-state, however, was difficult to define theoretically, as the Danes and their German adversaries shared ideological positions . Hence the intellectual paradoxes of Danish attitudes toward sovereignty and integration, paradoxes still to be identified in surveys of Danish values (see Gundelach 1993, 2002).

In the German *Reich* of 1871 there was no unified citizenship; the Germans were citizens of individual principalities such as Bavaria, Hanover, Württemberg, and Prussia. Prussia, of course, dominated the others as it made up two thirds and its king was simultaneously emperor. In principle, both the German Empire and the Weimar Republic were organized as federal states. The federal system was only cancelled after 1934 as a result of Nazi *Gleichschaltung*. German citizenship only came to be defined in linguistic, cultural (and therefore eventually biological) terms in 1913 in *Bürgerliches Gesetzbuch* the law code of Prussia; this definition has survived into the present German constitution of 1949 (Brubaker 1992). Nonetheless, Germany was understood as a nation-state and gradually came to understand itself as such. This change was due to the paradoxical combination of inclusion and exclusion. As *kleindeutsch* it excluded millions of German speakers in the Austrian-Hungarian Empire. At the same time the state included millions of French-thinking, though German speakers in Alsace-Lorraine, Poles in eastern Prussia and Danes in North

Schleswig. The intensifying conflict between Germans and Poles in eastern Prussia reinforced the ethnocultural and differentialist strand that had always existed in the intellectual German understanding of nationhood and helped translate it into practical politics.

How this notion was carried into the twentieth century by defeat in World War I, perverted by Nazi *völkisch* propaganda, and translated into official doctrine in the Federal Republic because of the massive migrations of Germans from Eastern and Central Europe after 1944 need not occupy us here. Simply consider the striking similarity between the Danish and the German understandings of nationhood at the level of ideology. On the other hand, the Danish version of this common ideology of national identity took root precisely because of the fatal clash with Germanness in and over Schleswig. The clash was inevitable because both sides demanded a sovereign state based on parallel ethnonational principles. This parallelism, however, has left a profound duality in Danish political thinking which helps explain some of the country's ambiguities concerning sovereignty, European cooperation, and national identity.

On the one hand, Danish identity is firmly rooted in ancestry, language, and an entire way of being. In reality it is based on blood, not soil (*ius sanguinis* not *ius soli*), although it is still easier for a culturally alien immigrant to acquire citizenship in Denmark than in Germany. In other words, Denmark belongs firmly in the group of ethnonational European nations for which culture has priority over state in defining the political nation (see Brubaker 1992). On the other hand, as we have seen, Danishness has always has always been intimately linked with its existence as a sovereign state. For long periods this state was multinational in character; however, because of the continuity of the name Denmark, the Danish version of the ethnopolitical program monopolized the multinational prehistory and reserved the name of "Denmark" for its own collective memory.[12] This continuity is demonstrated at the symbolical level in a number of ways: the use of the flag, which supposedly fell from heaven in present-day Estonia in 1219, pride in the impressive cultural heritage of the absolutist capital of Copenhagen, and the contradictory nature of today's uneasy co-existence of three nations within the so-called *Rigsfællesskab* (Commonwealth) of Denmark, Greenland, and the Faroe Islands, which in reality is a subtle mixture of commonwealth and empire (see Østergaard 1996a).

After the defeat of 1864, the national identity depended even more heavily on a nominally sovereign state than was the case with the French and even the British. This dependence explains the apparent contradictions in Danish collective mentality and political behaviour as the country is confronted with the prospect of European integration. In an ever more closely collaborating Europe, with state characteristics dispersed at more levels, the ethnocultural concept of nation seems to contain a number of relative advantages over the exclusively state-based concept we find in the traditional British identification of national sovereignty, with the sovereignty of Parliament and unlimited parliamentarism (Clark 1991). The French notion of republican state-based national identity, on the other hand, eventually might come to grips with the new Europe-wide dispersal of sovereignty, provided the definitions are clear-cut. The great loser, eventually, will be Denmark, with its peculiar conflagration of the two. It therefore makes some kind of sense that a majority of the Danish populace, for different reasons, have ended up rejecting the transfer of national sovereignty, although this sovereignty is hard for hardheaded outside observers to detect in real terms.

Traditionally, the other side of the coin of Danish national identity, the open and international spirit, has been embodied by the Jewish intellectual and author Georg Brandes (1842–1927). Georg Brandes was "a Jew, a Dane and a European," writes Jørgen Knudsen in his masterly and authoritative biography of Brandes ("I am myself alone. Jøden, danskeren og europæeren," Knudsen 1998, IV, 16). The order is deliberate, though the mentionof a person's Jewish background today seems slightly politically incorrect. After the Holocaust on European Jewry, analysis of the place and the role of Jews in European civilization and in individual nation states has become virtually impossible. Yet, Knudsen demonstrates convincingly how Brandes's Jewishness played an important though attenuated role for him all his life.

Brandes himself, apparently, did not see any problem in distinguishing between the identification as a Dane and a European, either in theory or in practice. Through the influence and widespread reception of his writings in all the dominant – and many of the smaller – European languages, Brandes acquired status as the most read single intellectual in Europe since Voltaire. In his later years he alone constituted a European public sphere – in German *Öffentlichkeit* – the very type of European public sphere many observers of today deplore that we do not have and probably never will get, regardless of the common European market, the common political institutions, and the reluctant common European policy vis à vis the rest of the world. But around 1900, before the two World Wars (which in reality were European civil wars that spilled over into the rest of the world and wars that cost Europe its dominant place in the world), such a common public sphere did exist ... that is, for a limited number of literate men and – in particular – women.

With well-earned self-confidence Brandes wrote in *Thoughts at the Turn of the Century (Tanker ved Aarhundredskiftet)* in 1900, as Knudsen reports, that he personally:

had known and communicated with some of the foremost spirits of European culture of his day, among others Ernest Renan, Hippolyte Taine, Clemenceau, John

Stuart Mill, Kropotkin, Sienkewicz, Gottfried Keller, Arthur Schnitzler, Hugo von Hoffmannsthal, Giuseppe Saredo, Pasquale Villari, Auerbach, Heyse, Eduard von Hartmann, Gerhard Hauptmann, Friedrich Nietzsche, Verhaeren, Maeterlinck, Henrik Ibsen, Bjørnstjerne Bjørnson, Lie, August Strindberg. He could as well have mentioned Amalie Skram and Selma Lagerlöf, Rainer Maria Rilke, Henry James and Benedetto Croce and a few years later as well Anatole France, Romain Rolland, André Gide, Hjalmar Söderberg og Per Hallström, Maxim Gorki, Gabriele D'Annunzio, Giuseppe Marinetti and Bernard Shaw. (Knudsen 1998, 41)

It is an extremely impressive list at a time when writers really counted, politically as well as culturally. In 1912 he had spoken in 42 European cities and securing his interest was considered enormously important by struggling or suppressed minorities as well young writers and people who just wanted to attract the outside world's attention.

Yet, this all-European intellectual, well versed in most European languages, was a Dane, and at times even a nationalist Dane. Most of his life, of course, he strongly opposed the extremely conservative regime under the county squire Estrup, who dominated Danish politics in the second half of the nineteenth century. Although he was often heavily criticized as antinationalist by conservative, he often took a strong stance in favour of the suppressed Danish minority in Prussian-ruled Schleswig, at times when it was most inconvenient for his personal career. In his farewell address upon taking leave of Berlin in 1883, he openly criticized the German suppression of his countrymen in this northernmost part of the newly united German empire. This intervention, however, was not just an expression of narrow-minded Danish nationalism. In principle it was no different from his interventions on behalf of other suppressed nationalities such as the Poles in Russia, the Armenians in the Ottoman empire, or the Alsacians in Germany.

That Georg Brandes was a European with a specific national background does not single him out as anything particular. At least, that is, as seen from today, when the existence of nation-states seems so natural that it is supra- and transnational identifications that have to be explained – and that Europeans have had to invent a whole new set of cumbersome organizations and the complicated political framework of the European Union in order to take some of the most lethal dents out of the aggressive and potentially suicidal nationalism of these nation-states. But I suggest taking a further step in understanding the very "Danish" nature of this epitome of a European intellectual who, despite all the languages he mastered, still only felt fully comfortable in Danish. As he put it in 1871, when his friend Giuseppe Saredo tried to lure him to Italy with all the possibilities this step would open for a man of his abilities: "I am deaf to that. I love the Danish language much too much to ever leave it" (Knudsen 1998, 34);

or "The Danish language happens to be my fatherland," as he wrote to the editor Henri Nathansen in 1903 (Knudsen 1998, 34).

Brandes was born in 1842, when the last remnants of the Danish-Schleswigian-Holsteinian-Icelandic multinational state (with the dependencies of Greenland, the Faroe Islands, and the Virgin Islands in the West Indies) was approaching its final demise in the civil war of 1848–50 and defeat by the Prussian and Austrian armies in 1864. The latter event left an enormous impression on the young Brandes, as it did on all his contemporaries. We should, however, not lump all the figures living at the same time under one hat. Precision in chronology is in this case, as it so often is, of utmost importance. The small, rather provincial capital of Copenhagen was between 1800 and 1850 home for a surprisingly large group of artists, writers, and philosophers, some of whom even acquired world fame at that time or later. They included writers as Søren Kierkegaard and H.C. Andersen, the sculptor Berthel Thorvaldsen, the scientist H.C. Ørsted and his brother, the legal scholar and civil servant Anders Sandøe Ørsted, the linguist Rasmus Rask and the architect C.F. Hansen, all of whom left a lasting imprint on Danish and European culture in the first half of the nineteenth century. Furthermore a large group of painters such as C.W. Eckersberg, Christian Købke, J. Th. Lundbye ,and Jørgen Sonne sprang from the fertile soil of the small capital, painters who led to the period called the "Golden Age" of Danish culture (Scavenius 1994).

What all the analysts – critics as well as admirers – have overlooked is that the background for this surprising outburst of creative energy was the larger composite state of Denmark-Norway-Schleswig-Holstein, with dependencies all over the world. These figures lived in an extremely restricted and narrow urban world inside the walls of Copenhagen, a city that in a European context must be considered a small town. But small size does not necessarily imply narrow horizons when it comes to creative energy. On the contrary, the very experience of concentrating resources from a larger world in a limited space can turn out to be very productive – for a time at least. The same happened in Vienna between 1867 and 1918, when it was a large capital in a truly multinational empire and, together with Budapest, Prague, Trieste, and Kraków in the same empire, and in fruitful exchange with Paris and Brussels, was the prime instigator of the modernist movement in arts and sciences (Schorske 1980, Østergaard 1985, and Østergaard 1992, 213–69). This energy lived on in the much reduced and poor capital of Austria until the *Anschluss* with Nazi Germany in 1938 and the annihilation of the Jewish intelligentsia, as described in Stefan Zweig's *Die Welt von Gestern* in 1942.

The same analysis that applies to Vienna ought to be applied to Copenhagen after the loss of the Norwegian half of the multinational state in 1814. The outburst of creative energy can best be explained, in my opinion, as a sort of sublimation of hitherto dissipated energies. Those responsible for the "Golden Age" of Danish culture were not the reduced and narrow-minded nationalists of the later epitome of a small state. The philosopher Kierkegaard may serve as an example. Although he deliberately shied away from involvement in politics, his recently unpublished diaries and correspondence reveal him as an ardent critic of what he saw as the unhealthy nationalization of politics in the composite Danish state of the 1840s. He cannot be reduced to the existentialist, apolitical figure he has normally been portrayed as. The same goes for H.C. Andersen. Grundtvig, of course, is another case, as he was partly responsible for the nationalization of politics and the subsequent disastrous civil war. Yet even he, as previously mentioned, was at times able to formulate a civilized and non-tribal understanding of national identity, even at the height of the conflict with the German-speaking side in Schleswig and Holstein in 1848.

The call for the creation of national states with written constitutions made its impact on minority liberal groups in the first half of the nineteenth century particularly among students and officials, and led to a shift in liberalism from international to national orientation. In Denmark, as we have seen, this was to occur around 1842. Up until that point liberals in Copenhagen and Kiel had been allied in their opposition to the almost unlimited power of the absolute monarchy that continued to prevail even after the introduction of the consultative assemblies (*Rådgivende Stænderforsamlinger*) in 1830–34. Alone, the official bourgeoisie, as numerically small as it was, was in no position to shake the absolutist regime. The most obvious means to this end was polarization over an abstract nationalism. This occurred in a Danish, a Schleswig-Holsteinian, and a Pan-German version. As I mentioned earlier, after the victory in 1850 the Danish regime experimented with the introduction of the Danish language into the administration in mid-Schleswig (*Regensburg reskripterne*, named after a Danish official in the government for Schleswig and Holstein). The first Prussian administration in the duchies after 1864–66 was, on the contrary, largely uninterested in the national issue. Carl von Scheel Plessen, who in his capacity as prefect led the administration until 1879, was content as long as the Danish peasants behaved like loyal German citizens. Provided they accepted living under Prussian law and had sufficient command of the German language to be able to acquit themselves in daily life, they were free to live as they were accustomed, without interference from the Prussian state. He thus advised against the introduction of compulsory German lessons in the schools.

Subsequent Prussian governments, however, were to show little reluctance to jettisoning this old-fashioned outlook. To them, the Danes, like the Poles, were a foreign element in the new German state, one that had to be combatted by means of an intensive policy of Germanization. The population of Schleswig was neither Danish nor German in the national-political sense until after the civil wars. The overall majority first exhibited national consciousness as a result of the national struggles toward the end of the century, and not vice versa, as one otherwise reads in practically all historical expositions, Danish as well as German (and Schleswig-Holsteinian). It was not until the attempts to Germanize the Danish as well as the French- and Polish-speaking populations within the newly established German empire that these peoples were prompted to openly declare themselves as Poles, Frenchmen or Danes in the political sense. Earlier in the nineteenth century, many people had changed their language without too much consideration, among them many solid, South Jutland– (*sønderjysk-*) speaking farmers in North Schleswig, the same group that later was to constitute the stock element of the German minority. Concurrent with the triumph of the new national-political principle, however, it became increasingly difficult for individuals to change language without at the same time changing their personal identity.

Thus the National Liberal proponents of the Eider policy, for example, had much in common with the Schleswig-Holsteinian movement. Conversely, other national movements in the other Nordic countries in many ways resembled the Danish movement in North Schleswig, examples being the *riksmål* (national language) movement of south-west Norway and the Icelandic and Faroese national movements, in which the fishing communities played a similar role to that of the peasant-farmers in the Danish movement (Østergaard 1995c). Brandes, though strongly influenced by all these events in the first half of the nineteenth century, was primarily a child of the period after 1878, when Denmark became the very epitome of a small state. He himself rose beyond his national background and became a European. But he became a European with a distinct, local, regional, and national background. He was European through his national identification. This affiliation was demonstrated by his involvement in the politics of "national self-determination." If anything, his ideals were the ideals that lay behind the redrawing of the map of Europe in the post–World War I peace treaties signed at the chateaux of Versailles, Trianon, and St Germain outside Paris in 1919 and 1920 (Østergaard 2003d). Today these principles have become so obvious that we tend to neglect any alternatives – alternatives that were debated in Brandes's times. In actual fact he must be considered partly responsible for the outcome of these political struggles.

Brandes and Grundtvig symbolize the two faces of Danish national identity since 1864. Instead of contrasting the two, as is usually done in analyses of Denmark, one should, however, see them as supplementing each other. They were both nationalists in the sense that they valued the cultural and political independence of their country. They only disagreed as to the best ways in which to keep this independence. Grundtvig rooted independence in cultural identity, often understood almost as nature, whereas Brandes operated at a European level and regarded all European national manifestations as results of the same basic civilization. Yet, this common European civilization he saw best furthered through the principle of national self-determination for Poles, Alsatians, Armenians – and Danes, whether in Denmark proper or in North Schleswig under German rule. Understood this way, these two national paradigms still seem to characterize Danish political debates over how best to adapt to the challenges of globalization.

THE RESCUE OF THE DANISH JEWS: NATIONAL COHESION AND PEASANT VALUES

The Danish state after 1864 became so small that all her citizens, regardless of political ideology and cultural affiliation, came to formulate their identity within the same conceptual hegemony of national values of peasant farmer extraction. "Denmark is a little land." Danes say this all the time when they want to impress foreigners with how amazingly well we have done. The saying dates back to that philosopher of Danishness, Grundtvig, who in a 1820 poem struck a chord with the Danish attitudes of social levelling and search for the middle ground:

Far whiter mountains shine splendidly forth
Than the hills of our native islands.
But we Danish rejoice in the quiet North
For our lowlands and rolling highlands.
No towering peaks thundered over our birth.
It suits us best to remain on earth.

The song ends on a note of flat-hill self-satisfaction: "Even more of the ore, so white and so red (the colours of the flag). Others may have got mountains in exchange. For the Dane, however, the daily bread is found no less in the hut of the poor man; when few have too much and fewer too little then truly we have become wealthy."[13] This is not a program of social or economic equality; Grundtvig at this time was a conservative. But it is clearly a proclamation of the political anti-elitism and egalitarianism that later permeated the ideology of Danishness.

There is a certain unpretentious, self-ironic note in this version of the Danish national discourse. It is hard for foreigners to detect because it is considered bad form to be a nationalist in Denmark as it has been in most other European countries since 1945. Nevertheless, an intrinsic nationalism surfaces immediately when foreigners start criticizing anything

Danish. Danes love to criticize everything "themselves," but put up their defenses as soon as somebody else points out a fault with Danish behaviour or something Danish. Luckily, Danes are not very often confronted with such criticism, as Denmark has had surprisingly good press in the international community – that is when she is not mistaken for Sweden. This attitude is of course mainly a reflection of the relative lack of importance attributed to this small country in world affairs, but it has nevertheless engendered a feeling of what we could call "humble assertiveness." We know we are the best, therefore we don't have to brag about it. So never mistake the apparent Danish or Scandinavian humbleness for real humility. It often conceals a feeling of superiority.

Over the last ten to fifteen years this security has been challenged by the arrival of immigrants, some 370,000 foreigners out of a net total population of 5.3 million; that is, little more than 7 percent. Many of these newcomers have been uncomfortable with the unspoken Danish way of life and have challenged it in ways never experienced before. These challenges have produced a certain uneasiness among the public. May the reason that there was no racism earlier on be that there was nobody to discriminate against? An American colleague, the cultural sociologist Jonathan Schwartz, who has been living in Denmark for more than thirty years, has characterized Danish culture as follows:

Danish Academic culture, like agriculture, tends to be enclosed, fenced in and hedged. The *gård* (farm) likewise, is self-contained, and even the house is surrounded by protective trees and bushes. What is Danish in Denmark is so obvious to the foreigner here. *Hygge* (cosiness), *Tryghed* (security) and *Trivsel* (well-being) are the three Graces of Danish culture and socialization. Faces look toward a common gård (yard), or a table with candles and bottles on it. Hygge always has its backs turned on the others. *Hygge* is for the members, not the strangers. If you want to know what is Danish about Denmark, ask first a Greenlander and then a guest-worker ... An American asked me the difference between Denmark and America. I ventured an answer. In America there's one politics and fifteen ways to celebrate Christmas. In Denmark there are fifteen political parties and one way to celebrate Christmas ... "Denmark is a little country." That's canon number one. A close second is: "Danish is a difficult language." How many times have I been chastised for my foreign accent?" (Schwartz 1985, 123–24)

Ultimately this is a rather different way to say the same thing most Danes do when they brag about their friendly, small, and democratic culture. Of course, Danes tend to read as positives what irritates an American like Schwartz. That only demonstrates how difficult it is to be accepted in such a closely knit national culture. Yet both positions agree on the importance of the size of the country as an explanation for the specifics of the political culture. For some, small is beautiful, for others small means petty, mediocre, and tedious. From a cultural and historical sociological perspective, the Danish nation-state of today represents a rare situation of virtual identity between state, nation, and society. But, as has been shown, that is a much more recent phenomenon than normally assumed, in Denmark as well as beyond.

To sum up, Denmark represents a series of apparent and some real paradoxes. On one hand, Danish policy since World War II has been supremely active in advocating international norms in areas where power politics predominate (that is, security). Though the United Nations has been the primary arena where Danish active internationalism has, in recent years, undertaken its own independent initiatives, Denmark has not relied solely upon UN actions and even joined the U.S.–led intervention in Iraq in 2003. On the other hand, Denmark's policy of reluctance in regard to the European Union has severely undercut her possibilities for effectively using these international norms because of the difficulties in building strong alliances with other members of the EU and the EU itself.

Altogether Denmark is held in high esteem. This holds true particularly as regards the saving of the Jewish Danes during World War II. The rescue of the Danish Jews in October 1943 is a major and unrivalled event in Danish history and the basis of the country's uncommonly good reputation in this domain. The rescue is internationally recognized to a remarkable degree, given visual prominence both in the Yad Vashem Institute's exhibition in Jerusalem and in the Holocaust Memorial Museum in Washington. Both exhibitions contain original examples of the fishing boats in which the Danish Jews were sailed over the Sound, along with inscriptions thanking the people of Denmark for their heroic deeds. This collective expression of thanks has a particularly strong effect, in that only individuals recorded by name are given prominence in Yad Vashem's park. The Jewish-American scholar Hannah Arendt emphasized in her well-known book on the trial of Adolf Eichmann in Jerusalem (1963) that Denmark was a little, "stubborn" country where it proved impossible for the Nazis to make the Danes accept their perverted thoughts on their Jewish fellow citizens.

Such spontaneous popular efforts in Denmark can also be regarded as an expression of those virtues and values that Danes wish to have associated with what it means to be Danish. Especially seen in the light of what Denmark otherwise contributed during World War II, it may be said that this popular contribution redressed the balance a little when we take into account the cowardice and direct collaboration which otherwise was characteristic of official Denmark during the occupation. For a long period the Allies were, with very good reason, in doubt as to whether Denmark should be classified as an ally of Germany or as an opponent. By the skin of its teeth Denmark was included in the group of allied victors when the United Nations was founded in 1945. These doubts have again been raised in recent years in the public debate after a new generation of historians and journalists have emphasized how considerable and willing an effort Danish business circles made for the German side, an effort which among other things extended to participating in the German exploitation of the conquered territories in Eastern Europe, including the use of forced labour in some Danish-run factories and the participation of Danish volunteers in the Waffen-SS.

The saving of the Jews does not wipe the blots off the Danish national conscience but it serves to redress the balance of condemnation for the lack of a moral stand on the part of the small state in the most crucial test of strength in the twentieth century. This experience is useful when one is confronted in today's political debate by a forcefully expressed resentment toward having to integrate the so-called aliens. Is this ill-will an expression of animosity toward those of foreign origin, a pronounced racism, a welfare nationalism, or simply an economic reluctance accentuated by the cost of giving public welfare to unproductive immigrants, who on top of everything else do not appear to accept basic Danish values? The saving of the Jews shows what a people is capable of when it shares the same values and the same political culture; it also illustrates the importance of the individual committing himself and making a choice – "courage to care," as it is called in the widespread international debate and extensive research on the subject. Doing something has a beneficial effect, and existential commitment is as important as it proved to be in the resistance. At the same time, while this self-praise may be justified, it is important to remember two circumstances in particular.

First and foremost, it was possible to save the Danish Jews because the shores of Sweden were so close at hand and that country was neutral. The existence of Sweden and the geography of Sealand offer the best explanation for why things turned out so differently for Dutch and Danish Jews. The extermination of the Dutch Jews has left an open wound in the collective memory of that country, something not amenable to excuses. However, as Danes we should remember that it was infinitely more difficult to sail Jewish fellow citizens from the Netherlands to Great Britain than from Denmark to Sweden. Moreover the Dutch suffered under a much harsher Nazi regime, led by the fanatical Austrian, Arthur Seyss-Inquart. This difference in war experiences, one may mention *en passant*, has certainly gone far toward explaining the great difference in attitude to binding European cooperation that one finds when comparing public attitudes in Denmark and the Netherlands. Yet these countries have in many areas views and values that resemble one another's, and their structural placing and interests as smaller states in Europe are therefore parallel.

Second, the Danish rescue of the Jews was possible because of conflicting attitudes within the German occupying power. The Wehrmarcht had no interest in provoking any resistance in Denmark that might have led to a change in the situation that allowed the Germans to use Denmark as a base for exhausted soldiers to take their ease, an arrangement that in fact continued unaltered until the final battle in April 1945. The Danish population did not see the situation in this light, but for Germany, Denmark was throughout the war a comfortable billet where German soldiers could regain their strength after the horrors of the Eastern Front. Moreover, not all German officers shared the Nazi regime's anti-semitic ideology and saw no reason to carry out orders to the letter in hunting down those whom both they and the Danish population regarded as Danish citizens (that is, citizens of a nation that was not at war with Germany). This was not known to the organizers of the escape route, nor did those who fled know it – and it does not in any way detract from the heroism shown. However, the fact is that the Germans were not tremendously interested in capturing the fleeing Jews.

Something else we can learn from the attitude of the Danish population during World War II, which has a more extensive relevance than the actual saving of the Jews but is presumably closely connected to it, is the Danish population's surprising immunity when faced with the temptation of totalitarian ideologies (Lindström 1985). This can be said first and foremost of Nazism, the party receiving fewer than 2 per cent of the votes registered in the free election of 1943. The communists were unable to vote after the Germans had instigated a law excluding them from the right to vote, which was passed in 1941. They would presumably not have received many votes at that time even if they had been allowed to stand for election. The strong support that the communists received in the election of the autumn of 1945 was primarily an expression of protest against the politics of collaboration and an expression of admiration for their "patriotic" efforts during the war – an admiration that did not last many months beyond the summer of liberation.

This is what I mean by the phrase, the "peasant roots of Danish modernity" or the "peculiarity of the Danes." The concept helps explain many of the apparently paradoxical features of Danish political and social life, right down to the anarchistic party political system. Real national values are at stake in the present process of European integration, and many Danes fear they will disappear when society, nation, and state are no longer identical, as has been the case for the last hundred years or so. This is why they have been reluctant to wholeheartedly participate in "the construction of Europe." What they have failed to realize is how recent this experience is and how dangerous the geopolitically exposed situation in the centre of Europe at the entrance to the Baltic Sea. When the Baltic region opened up to the rest of Europe with the fall of the Iron Curtain, old continuities from before the rise of the nation-states re-emerged and put back on the table the necessity to choose between different international options. Denmark cannot have it both ways, as she did during the Cold War.

There is a massive satisfaction in being Danish among Denmark's citizens which at times produces a negative feeling toward European citizenship. "Danish" values thus help to explain Danish behaviour in foreign politics (see Gundelach 1993). The major problem, however, is that the "Denmark" referred to is far from unequivocal. On the one hand, the name denotes a typical multinational state-nation with a long-standing role in European politics; yet the very same name simultaneously refers to an atypical homogeneous small nation-state. This duality is nicely reflected in the use of two national anthems (see Knudsen 1992). The first is "Kong Christian," written by Johannes Ewald in 1779; this martial song praises the warrior king who defeats the enemies of the country – and politely forgets how he lost everything in the end. The other song is "Der er et yndigt land," written in 1819 by the Romantic poet Adam Oehlenschläger, praising the beauty of the friendly and peaceful country and its national inhabitants. Denmark, the Danes, and the "Danish" national consensus are caught between such competing and at times even antagonistic notions of Danishness.

NOTES

The present article is a rewritten and much shortened version of a former work, Østergaard 2000d. Parts of the argument also have been published in a special issue of *thesis eleven* on "Nordic Paths to Modernity" (Østergaard 2004b).

1 Social science–biased readers should note that for historians "accidence" and "coincidence" are not to be confused with pure chance. On the contrary, these *termini technici* refer to outcomes that can be explained afterward, once they have happened, but hardly could have been predicted before, as the combination of the necessary structural factors only happened because of a particular historical *conjuncture.* The sudden demise of the Soviet Union between 1989 and 1991 is a major example of a development that historians would label accidental in this sense. I have written on the use of counterfactual analyses and historical accident in historical explanations in Østergaard 1997d.

2 State-nations are the territorial states that originated in early modern Europe between 1500 and 1800, mainly in the West. Some of these states later developed into nation-states with a national identity created in more or less top-

down process. The distinction between state-nation and nation-state dates back to Hans Kohn's classic account, *The Idea of Nationalism* from 1944. It is developed in E.J. Hobsbawm, *Nations and Nationalism* 1990. Confusingly a nation-state is called *état-nation* in French. Regardless of these terminological difficulties it is important to uphold the distinction between the two types. Many state-nations were organized as monarchical unions or composite states (see note 4).

3 "Composite state," "conglomerate state," etc. have become accepted technical terms for the territorial states of early modern Europe. A definition with particular relevance for the United Kingdom is proposed by the British historian Jonathan Clark in Østergård 1991b. An examination of the phenomenon in a European context is found in Elliot 1992. Early attempts to apply these terms to Danish and Nordic history include Ole Feldbæk in Johansen et al. 1992, Jens Rahbek Rasmussen in Sørensen 1995, and Harald Gustafsson 1994 and 1997. For the concept *Helstat* see note 8.

4 See the works by Green-Pedersen 1973 and 1975. He unfortunately died before finishing the ultimate treatise on the Danish slave trade. His preliminary publications are still the fundamental works on this ignominious episode in Danish history, which does not fit into the national self-understanding of Denmark as a victim.

5 According to the highly original research of Gunner Lind and others, the structural foundations for these legal innovations actually date back to the wars between 1614 and 1660, the Danish version of the Europe-wide military-political revolution of the seventeenth century (see Lind 1994).

6 Cesare di Beccaria lived from 1738 to 1794. His influential work *Dei delitti e delle pene* (*On Criminal Offenses and Punishment*) was published in Italian in 1764. In 1796 it was translated into Danish, but the influence of the work can be detected as early as the 1767 law abolishing capital punishment (Østergaard 2003e, 53).

7 Which gave rise to the expression "to Copenhagen a city"; that is, to expose a civilian population to a terror bombardment.

8 *Helstat,* in German *Gesamtstaat,* was originally a term employed in the nineteenth century for the entire Danish monarchy, made up of the kingdom of Denmark and the duchies of Schleswig, Hostein, and Lauenburg. The policy of the unitary state was to unite the entire realm against two competing national programs, the national-liberal Danish and the Schleswig-Hosteinian-German, respectively, both of claimed all of Schleswig/South Jutland. In recent years, the term *Helstat* is used in Danish historiograhy for the multinational Danish state of the eighteenth century too (i.e., including Norway), in particular by the influential eighteenth century historian Ole Feldbæk in a large number of works.

9 Quoted from the poem *Folkelighed* from 1848 by N.F.S. Grundtvig (author's translation).

10 Robert Molesworth, *An Account of Denmark as It was in the Year 1692*, London 1694, 257.

11 Grundtvig, *Preface to "Nordens Mythologi,"* 1832, *Udvalgte Værker* I.

12 This interpretation has formed the ideological backbone of Danish historiography, professional as well as otherwise. See the critiques in Østergaard 1992b, Engman 1991, Kjærgaard 1989, Rasmussen 1995,32

13 N.F.S. Grundtvig, *Langt højere Bjerge* 1820 (author's translation).

The Formation and Development
of the Welfare State

LARS BO KASPERSEN

How and why did the Danish welfare state arise and develop? Analysts have looked at this question from many points of view. Did it develop as a consequence of conflicts and negotiations between political parties, economic classes, organized interests, and key persons? Is it an outcome of policies based upon a master plan embedded in a clear and single-minded political ideology? Or is its normative foundation embedded in a moral-religious discourse? If so, which norms and from where do they stem?

This chapter takes an alternative path and attempts to answer the question about the origin and development of the Danish welfare state from a slightly different approach. I shall argue that the welfare state does not originate in a clear-cut political ideology or norms but in "exceptions" – situations in which norms are abandoned (Schmitt 1988[1934]; 1996 [1932]). The normative and legal foundation is set in a "state of exception," in which norms are either disappearing or undergoing radical change. These are most often situations in which the survival of the state is at stake. During the last two centuries Denmark has experienced such states of exception several times, often in relation to wars. Thus the conflicts with the British Empire in 1801 and 1807, the wars against Prussia in 1848 and 1864, World War I in 1914, World War II, and the German Occupation 1940–45, and the 1945–49 period with a new world order emerging are all examples of different "states of exception." Also the external shock to the foundation of the agricultural structure when cheap grain was sailed in from the United States, Russia, and Australia can be seen as a "state of exception" that demanded action.

This chapter will illustrate, with several examples, how the development of the Danish welfare state must be seen in the light of specific "moments" or periods in which the survival of the Danish state has been at stake and in which the state has been forced to demonstrate a strong political will. I shall point out certain periods and "breakpoints" or "states of exception" in which Denmark has been vulnerable, and in which decisions have become crucial in the short and long run to secure autonomy and sovereignty, with deep implications for the development of the welfare state. The rationality of survival at crucial moments has overruled any other political ideology, whether social democratic, social liberal, or conservative. In other words, beyond the internal political struggles, and social mobilizations driven by certain political ideologies, the Danish welfare state must also be conceived as a response to external pressure in a struggle for survival as a sovereign state. Consequently, the distinctive character of the Danish welfare state is also a distinctive form of defence. To put it in its most acute form: the welfare state in Denmark can be seen as a defence mode in the widest sense of the word. More precisely, as we shall see, the welfare society became the means of defending the state.[1] Moreover, the development of the welfare state and a welfare society went hand in hand with the consolidation of Denmark as a nation-state. A specific welfare ideology was merged with a form of popular nationalism (see Korsgaard, chapter 3).

The welfare state did not develop overnight, The creation of a specific state form always has a longer history, and consequently, we have to encompass aspects of the state-formation process that extend even further back, in this case to the seventeenth century, in addition to the period from the mid- and late nineteenth century and onward.

A caveat is in order. This is not a traditional exposition of the development of the Danish welfare state stressing the various social reforms and social policies. The concept of the welfare state itself is contested, as well as terms such as "welfare society" or "welfare regime" also found in the welfare literature. No clear-cut definition is available, but a good part of the literature on welfare focuses on matters such as redistribution of wealth, social policy, and social rights. This chapter operates with a different and broader understanding of the concept of the welfare state. One of its aims is also to reconceptualize the concept of the welfare state. Social policy issues play only a minor role in this context. Consequently, the reader should not expect a detailed and careful description of the development of social reforms, social policies, and their content or implications (see Abrahamson, chapter 10); Andersen 1983; Esping-Andersen 1985, 1990; Baldwin 1990; Flora 1988; Hornemann-Møller 1992).

My point of departure is a conceptual effort to clarify my use of the concepts of state and welfare state. It is crucial for the reader to understand that the definitions of "state" and "welfare state" applied here differ from conventional uses of the concepts. An analysis of the first segment of the history of the Danish welfare state from the mid-nineteenth century onwards follows. Most important in this regard is Denmark's friend-enemy

relationship with Germany and its impact on the political and social structure of the Danish state and society. After this, the third and fourth sections take us into the twentieth century, in which the shift from Germany
to the USSR as the principal enemy is of importance. The last segment of
this chapter focuses on the most recent ten years and asks whether
Denmark is currently undergoing a process of change from a welfare state
to a security state.

THE POLITICAL, ECONOMIC, AND NORMATIVE FOUNDA-
TION OF THE DANISH WELFARE STATE

When we address the foundation of the Danish welfare state, we often look
to the area of political ideologies. We tend to approach the problem by
asking which political ideologies were crucial to the principal political
actors in shaping the welfare state and its institutions during the foundational years. Over the years historians and social scientists have discussed
which political parties, interest groups, and social movements can be singled out as the major driving forces in the development of the welfare state
in Denmark. Several scholars argue that the Danish welfare state can be
seen as an outcome of a struggle between the political powers of social
democracy and the economic powers of capital (Esping-Andersen 1990).
Others argue that the Danish welfare state has strong bourgeois roots
(Nørgaard 2000) or that class alliances and ideologies have changed over
time (Baldwin 1990). These various accounts differ as to which political
ideologies have been most influential at any given time: Is Denmark a
social democratic or a social liberal welfare state? How influential have liberalism and conservatism as political ideologies been on the Danish
"model"? The role of religion and the church is another aspect of the normative foundation of the welfare state that has also been discussed
recently. Sørensen (1998) and Knudsen et al. (2000) claim that the
Danish protestant church and its ethics have played a major role; in other
words, that the normative foundation must be found in a religious-moral
rather than in a political-ideological discourse.

An alternative explanation of the development of the Danish (welfare)
state comes from "development theory," as expounded in Senghaas's *The
European Experience* (1985). Senghaas is interested mainly in the relationship between the world economy and the development prospects of individual national economies. In focusing on the way the logic of the (world)
market is interrelated with the national political system, he offers an
important insight on the material and economic foundation of the Danish
state and society. The material foundation of Danish development lay an
export-led path, in which agriculture first played the key role. Later the
close intermeshing of agriculture and industry became the foundation of

Danish success. The Danish development was entirely dependent on a process of displacement of competition (Senghaas 1985, 15–16). Inexpensive grain brought in from overseas by the new methods of transport in the 1870s and 1880s caused a change in world markets and generated an agricultural crisis in Denmark. By rapidly transforming the agricultural sector toward butter, eggs, and meat production, and introducing a selective protectionist policy to guard the emerging industry, the Danish state and society responded to these new conditions. Senghaas continues his analysis into the twentieth century, stressing the importance of the economic crisis in the 1930s and its implications for Denmark in the diversification of its industrial structure. Senghaas's perspective emphasizes the way structural changes in the world economy stimulated economic and political responses from the Danish society; he is not primarily concerned with political ideologies or which economic and political actors were most influential.

This chapter attempts to step along still another path. I shall argue that any political ideology that becomes a ruling ideology (that is, an ideology that is a part of the normative basis of the ruling political parties and political actors) is constrained and framed by another rationality embedded in any state, notwithstanding state form or regime type. Political parties or movements embedded in a ruling political ideology often come to realize that ruling a state is something different than seeking power and influence as an opposition party. A state is more than a reflection of the interests of powerful actors in society; it is a political entity with its own agenda and a life of its own. In theory a state must always possess a rationality that directs its activities toward reproduction and survival. Without some form of willingness to survive, a state will wither away. In order to survive as an independent entity, a state must possess some form of locus or centre with the ability to formulate a political will and make decisions. The political will emanating from such a centre – whether it be a monarchy, a state council, a government or a dictatorship – must successfully orchestrate as many "elements" of a state and its society (citizens, political parties, state institutions, companies, local political institutions, trade unions, and many other interested organizations) as possible toward a common will to survive. In order to survive, a state must always seek to remain a sovereign entity in a system of states, and at certain moments, the will to survive must totally override any political ideology or any other rationality.[2] This seems to be difficult to prove because when a prime minister, dictator, king, government, state council, or any part of the state elite makes a decision, that decision will often be interpreted as being in the interests of the involved actors themselves in a more narrow sense. Of course, a government is interested in saving the country by any means because the country is the government's own power base; I shall argue, however, that (crucial) decisions are sometimes taken for the sake of the state, with more than narrow-minded interests at heart. The decision by the Danish prime minister in 2003 to go to war against Iraq, for instance, was hardly a decision taken to please his own electors or to secure his own mandate. When the Danish prime minister Jens Otto Kragh in 1971 decided that Denmark should have a referendum to join the European Community, it was not a decision made to please the social democratic voters. He knew that only a minority in the party and among its supporters would vote for EC membership. It was a decision to secure the survival of the Danish welfare state.

State survival is more than an issue of military security. Remaining sovereign, continuing to be recognized by other states, surviving as a state entity – all these imply a continuous orientation of several areas and activities of state and society toward this goal. Apart from military strength, a strong defence involves several matters: education level, health, population size, economic strength, access to raw materials, legitimate political institutions, a degree of consensus and social cohesion, and the avoidance of extremist ideologies that otherwise could cause tensions and divisions in society. All these elements can be seen as important from the point of view of defending the state. In other words, the normative foundation of any state – welfare state or any other state form – is not only based upon norms stemming from a political ideology but also is embedded in decisions about survival and recognition. These decisions can at times overrule and undermine official political party ideology. Moreover, these moments tend to have a more lasting impact in structuring the state, society, and state-society relations, and have important implications for citizenship, rights, and obligations.

My key argument about the development of the Danish state and society includes an element of political existentialism. States are political entities that struggle for survival, and only alertness and a political will to defend the state and its sovereignty can secure independence and maintain sovereignty.

The intermeshing of geopolitical and international changes, on the one hand, and domestic changes, on the other, is an important aspect of this perspective. Here my argument is somewhat similar to the position of Senghaas, through his Listian influence. Inspired by Frederick List, Senghaas also looks at the interplay between external changes and national economic decisions driven by the state. There are, however, more differences than similarities between a Senghaas/List type of argument and the position adopted in this chapter. First of all Senghaas is rather "economistic"; he concentrates mainly on changes in the world economy, whereas this chapter also stresses military and political changes at a global and European level, as well as providing a theory of the state which is absent in Senghaas's work. By acknowledging that some form of political existentialism and a "will to survive" as a state are necessary components in a theory of the state, we can begin to understand why these Listian national economic policies are advanced by governments and powerful agents. From his more world system–inspired perspective, Senghaas tends to neglect key agents – not least the state, its leading politicians, and the state elite in general.

CONCEPTS AND FRAMEWORK

Research in the welfare state, its origin, development, character, effects, and apparent crisis has proliferated over the last two or three decades (Schwartz 2000; Esping-Andersen 1985, 1990; Korpi 1979; Flora 1988; Flora and Heidenheimer 1995; Baldwin 1990; Skocpol 1992; Briggs 1961 – just to mention a few!). Within welfare state studies the term "welfare state" is rarely clearly defined. The term consists of two elements: *welfare* and *state*. In common definitions of the term it is almost always the *welfare* part of the term that is defined.[3] *State* is not defined, but *welfare* becomes the key to conceptualizing the welfare state. Much welfare state research has a strong emphasis on social policy, and welfare is often simply equated with social policy.

The focus on social policy leads to development toward three types of welfare state regimes or models. Esping-Andersen's three regime-types of welfare states, as outlined in his 1990 book *The Three Worlds of Welfare Capitalism*, loom large in the debate.[4]

Although "welfare modelling" can be quite useful in some cases, especially when we need to specify distinctive characteristics of different ways of designing and implementing social policies in different welfare states, it does not provide us with a definitive characterization of a welfare state in contrast to other state forms. If we take a closer look at political organizations that can be called states, those that can be characterized as welfare states for the most part provide some form of welfare, either by the state itself or by market or family. So how can we specify the state form that we call a welfare state? A first and necessary step is a conceptualization of the state. My conceptualization of the modern state can be condensed into the following propositions:

- The state is constituted in its relationship with other states – in a mutual struggle of recognition; the state is essentially and existentially defined by its relationship to other states.
- The modern state emerged slowly in early modern Europe as a consequence of the interplay between external warfare and an internal cen-

tralization, territorialization and hierachialization, and often with war as an important driving force.

- A central government and administration is a characteristic feature of the modern state.
- The modern state is demarcated and territorialized; the domain of its sovereignty is demarcated.
- The modern state tends to have monopoly on the means of violence and taxation.
- The modern state emerged in most West European countries during the eighteenth century, during which most states created a (civil-) society (a market). The French Revolution marked the fulfilment of this endeavour. Civil and political rights, the right of property, and the market were in place. Here we have a *Rechtsstaat* with a state-society separation. This was the first time in history that a state developed a market society, and it was the first time these two entities were separated.
- In the following centuries the welfare state, or more precisely the Sozialstaat/ welfare state, developed. It is characterized by state intervention in society. In other words, a welfare state is a state form characterized by the state's intervention to mitigate the social question and increase its strength by optimizing its resource base and strengthening social cohesion.
- The modern state is confronted with the "social question."

These propositions are very general, but I submit that they are common denominators for all states in Western Europe.[5] How, then, are states different? States are very different in that, among other things, they are situated in very different geopolitical spaces, they have different social structures and different resource bases (for example, natural resources, raw materials, ethnic composition, geographical size, and population size). Thus, in order to specify the distinct character of the Danish welfare state, we need to undertake a detailed study of Denmark, its history, its geopolitical location, its social structure, and other factors. Such a study can only be sketchy in this chapter, but we must keep in mind that the differences among welfare states are determined by these factors.

The modern state emerged slowly from the late fifteenth century (Machiavelli's *stato*) to the seventeenth century (Hobbes's *Leviathan*), but it was not until the late eighteenth century that there appeared the demarcated territorial sovereign state with its dual monopoly and with a state-society separation – the state as often described by Weber. In many places in Europe the territorial sovereign state form developed into a nation-state during the nineteenth and twentieth centuries. It is beyond the scope of this chapter to deal in any length with a more theoretical discussion of the nation-state. As a state form , however, it is characterized by a correspondence with the following:

- The defence of the state with a monopoly on the means of violence
- A domain of sovereignty (a territory)
- A government, administration, and legal system covering this domain
- A national economy
- A national identity
- National citizenship and some loyalty between state and citizen.

The transformation of the citizen into a national citizen contributed to the development of a nation-state as a strong state form. For the first time in history, the whole population became involved in the struggle of the state for survival. Each citizen now became a participant in the nation-state project and each citizen was in the last instance willing to sacrifice health and life in order to protect the state and secure the survival of the nation. Almost everybody realized that it was now a matter of defending one's own conditions of life – a defence of one's own rights, identity, and right to property. The nation-state became further consolidated during the nineteenth century and right up to the period after World War II. As already indicated, the Danish nation-building project later merged with the welfare state/society project.

The French Revolution and the Bourgeois Revolution can be seen as the establishment of the *Rechtsstaat* with civil and political rights. The key element of the *Rechtsstaat* was "provision and safeguarding of legal equality, universal freedom of acquisition and contract, freedom of movement and settlement, and the guarantee of acquired property" (Böckenförde 1991, 152). During the nineteenth and twentieth centuries a transition took place away from the *Rechtsstaat*, with its separation of state and society, to a *Sozialstaat*, or in a post-1945 term, a *welfare state*, in which the state increasingly intervenes in society. The *Rechtsstaat* contains a contradiction. Although the state underwrites the basic principles of equality before the law, freedom of employment, and the guarantee of acquired property, the realization of these principles generates social problems. Social inequality based upon property emerges, and, as a consequence of the legal consolidation and perpetuation of that inequality through the property guarantee, class antagonism increases. The social question becomes a reality.

If this development, which is inherent in society as a result of the way in which it is constituted, is given free rein, unrestrained by the state, then the state's guarantee and protection of legal liberty and equality becomes a meaningless formality for an ever-increasing number of people. What ought in principles to be the freest society, founded on the equality of law, exudes material unfreedom. So the state, in line with its original relationship to society and in accordance with its function as guarantor of the free society and its basic constitution, is bound to intervene by making selective use of its sovereign regulatory power in order to keep society from destroying itself ... The state must counter the social inequality continuously spawned within society out of the dialectic of liberty and equality; it must modify it through the medium of social conciliation and social services in order effectively to maintain the reality of individual and social liberty and equality before the law. (Böckenförde 1991, 166–7)

Böckenförde argues that state intervention takes place in order to prevent society from destroying itself. The argument must, however, be extended: the state intervenes to prevent society from destroying itself – and, consequently, also to prevent the state from undermining itself. State-society is mutually conditioned in the modern state, and the existence of society is crucial to the state in order for it to survive in a struggle of recognition with other states in the state system. The state needs a society from which resources can be extracted.

In other words, the welfare state – or in Böckenförde's terms, the *Sozialstaat* – can be defined as a state form developing in Western Europe and America whereby the state intervenes in society to protect society from itself, and to strengthen the state and its resources in order to remain recognized as an independent sovereign state. According to this definition, welfare state means more than social policy, even in its broadest sense. Therefore, the intervention that characterizes the welfare state must be seen in the light of two interrelated processes: the state intervenes partly in order to strengthen its own position toward other states and partly in order to mitigate and reduce the "social question." Poverty, malnutrition, poor living conditions, a poor health standards, and low level of education are all matters that can weaken a country's defence capability.

Different actors of course have different motives for intervening in regard to the social question, but from a statist perspective the social question is not important for ethical reasons alone. It can be crucial to remove incentives for rebellion and civil disorder that can weaken the state's position toward other states and weaken the power position of the state elite.

In other words, a welfare state is a state form that developed during the nineteenth century as a response to an incipient crisis of the liberal state. The liberal state that emerged in different variants in the eighteenth and nineteenth centuries was a state that was separate from the market (society) but which preconditioned it. When market forces expanded, with the ensuing poverty and other problems, a social question arose. In some states such as Denmark the attempt to resolve the social question led to a specific variant of a welfare state. Thanks to the character of its geopolitical situation, Denmark developed a distinctive national welfare society in which national welfare institutions constituted the defence of the Danish people.

THE INCEPTION OF THE DANISH WELFARE STATE

The origins of development of the Danish welfare state must be traced back to the 1660 revolution. In 1660 absolute monarchy was introduced in Denmark, and the period from 1660 to the mid-nineteenth century can be characterized as a long reform process that unintentionally, with the loss of the German-speaking territories, led to a territorialized demarcated nation-state in 1864. Many of the changes that gradually brought about the rise of the modern state and civil society in Denmark go back to the sixteenth century, but the advent of absolutism in 1660 was a pivotal event. Absolutism in Denmark occurred as an unintended consequence of the war against Sweden (Kaspersen 2004, 79–80); the king had outmanoeuvred the nobility and forced absolutism through as a response to the defeat and as a way of reconstructing the defence and cohesion of Denmark. With the introduction of absolutism, external and internal sovereignty fused into one subject – the king's person. The various estates – even the old nobility – were stripped of most of their privileges. The monarch was now the sovereign active subject and the people had become a passive object. In practice, the mediating link between king and subject was the government official and the civil servants. This was codified in the *Lex Regia*, the Royal Law.[6] This strict separation of monarch (state) and people (society), which was mediated by the civil servants and the bureaucracy, created a more transparent society and transformed the existing structure of closed feudal spheres into one public social sphere. Here we find the germ of civil society, which became full-grown only when the modern nation-state developed during the nineteenth century.

The state expanded and centralized, and a civil society (the market) gradually emerged, generated by the state. The fulfilment of a society (market), and as a corollary the state-society separation, was achieved with the liberal-democratic Constitution of June 1849 and the *Freedom of Trade Act* (1857). The emergence of the liberal-democratic constitution can be seen in the following responses to outside forces: i) being part of a context of Europeanization processes with changes in the relations between states; ii) a war against Prussia in 1848 and iii) a social mobilization in Denmark with inspiration from the processes of nationalism, and political and economic liberalism elsewhere in Europe. The year 1848/49 was crucial to the development of the Danish state. The problem of the duchies (Holstein and Schleswig) and Prussia led to radical reforms and a reorganization of the Danish state, by now based upon a liberal-democratic constitution that limited the king's capacity to form the political will (Skovgaard-Petersen 1985, 74–94, 218–49; Bjørn 1990, 338–46). Under a liberal democracy, the individual takes primacy, and with the *Freedom of Trade Act* in 1857 the individual had finally become liberated from the old medieval guild structures. The liberal-democratic constitution heralded the atomized society celebrating the individual and individualism. It did not last in its pure form, however, since a new organization of the various political interests was already taking place in the late 1860s (Hvidt 1990, 145–60; Rerup 1989, 163–77), Denmark was on its way to become a national organizational society.

From the mid-1860s forward, a new situation emerged which had a deep impact on the Danish state and society. Bismarck's strategy to unify Germany involved wars against Denmark (1864), Austria (1866), and France (1871). Denmark's defeat to Prussia in 1864 came as a deep shock to the country. With the loss of the southern part of Jutland and the two duchies Schleswig and Holstein (Hvidt 1990, 127–40), Denmark had to reorganize herself again, and a revision of the constitution took place in 1866 (Rerup 1989, 149–55). The most important consequence of the defeat was that Denmark realized that Germany was now a great power and a threat to Danish sovereignty and independence. Germany had become the principal enemy.

Between 1864 and World War I, Germany/Prussia was the enemy, a reality that led to various internal measures and alliances in Denmark. First it resulted in a major conflict between left and right concerning the constitution and the defence of the country. I shall return to this conflict and its "solution" later. Second, it reinforced nationalism, which already had taken off in the early nineteenth century but which now became extremely strong. Third, the defeat also led to a shift toward Britain, which was now regarded as the coming key trading partner. Thus, a major development of the Danish infrastructure taking place after 1864 was oriented toward a new international political situation. The railway to Esbjerg (West Denmark), railway ferries over the Belt (Little Belt) and the construction and extension of the harbour in Esbjerg were all measures taken to enable Denmark to redirect its export from Germany to Britain (Hvidt 1990, 253–6).

The construction and expansion of the railway lines is an important and illuminating example of how problems were solved in a "state of exception" by the leading politicians and centrally placed civil servants. When railways first appeared in England and Germany, it became clear that new railway lines could be useful. From the beginning, the Danish state took a strong interest in railway building. It established a "Railway Commission" in 1835 in order to be on the leading edge in development. A planned line between Hamburg and Lübeck, which would connect the North Sea and the Baltic Sea, could threaten Copenhagen as a port of transit. Consequently, it became vital to the Danish state to respond to these plans. The involvement of the Danish state in these matters also underlines List's observation of how normal it was during the nineteenth century for the state to intervene to secure development and prosperity (List 1999 [1837]). During the 1840s, 1850s, and 1860s, many agents demonstrated very diversified interests in terms of the railways lines. The Jutlandic farmers preferred a line form the northern part of Jutland right down the middle of the peninsula to Germany in order to facilitate their export opportunities. The market towns at the east coast of Jutland argued for a line along the east coast to link them, a suggestion that was supported by the Ministry of War. Others wanted a line across the country connecting Copenhagen and the islands to the western part of Denmark in order to facilitate increasing exports to England. After the repeal of the Corn Laws in England in 1845, this country was seen as the new export market for grain (Hvidt 1990, 50). Despite a huge expansion of railway lines in the early part of the 1860s, the crucial question was never really solved: what to prioritize – a strengthening of the east-west connection or a further elaboration of the north-south link? The solution came with the war in 1864. After her defeat to Prussia, Denmark lost the two most important harbours of disembarkation to the west (England), in particular Tønning and Husum (Hvidt 1990, 159). Moreover, with the defeat, and with Prussia becoming a great power, it became clear to Danish politicians that the connection to England was vital. Thus, under the nickname "The Railway minister," the Minister of Interior Affairs, J.S. Estrup (who later became prime minister) forcefully persuaded the parliament to vote for his bill. The Bill, passed in 1865, contained a plan for building the railway in the east-west direction and a plan for building a harbour in Esbjerg to enable a stronger link to England (Tamm 1996, 159–61).

The solution of the conflict between different agents came in the wake of the 1864 war. This was a truly "state of exception" that forced Estrup and others to make a clear decision in the interests of the survival of the Danish state. It is a clear demonstration of the link between changing external conditions, a new geopolitical situation, and decisions taken by politicians within the country. The most powerful social groups – the farmers and the national liberals – were ignored despite their economic and political arguments. Estrup and the state apparatus acted in the clear interests of the state; consequently, the link to England had to be developed.

These developments became crucial to the evolution of the Danish state and society when the rapid internationalization of the economy changed the conditions of the Danish economy in the 1870s and 1880s. Cheap grain from the "new" states – the United States, Australia, and Russia – was sailed into Europe with the new steamships, and this new commerce undermined Danish agricultural exports. The Danish agricultural structure transformed itself almost within a decade as farmers established cooperatives and went from vegetable production to animal production. The new products (bacon, eggs, and butter) were sold in England. This structural change of the agricultural sector and the reorientation of the export market from Germany to Britain could only take place because Denmark had invested enormously in infrastructure after the 1864 defeat and, moreover, had directed railways, ferries, and harbours toward the west. In other words, it was crucial to the success of the cooperative movement and the agricultural "revolution" that a political, military, and ideologically new orientation took place after 1864. This was a precondition of the Danish "cooperative miracle." It is important to stress, however, that other decisions could have been made, with a better or worse result. At least in retrospect we can see that this amalgam of decisions taken at a specific moment in the history of the Danish state had a character and strength enabling Denmark to survive.

The importance to Danish development of the transformation of the agricultural sector in the last decades of the nineteenth century cannot be underestimated (Senghaas 1985, 82–92). The new products were exported and the income financed the import of much needed raw materials for emerging industry in Denmark. Early industrial development in Denmark was intimately connected with agricultural modernization, and was characterized by a fairly wide spread of industrial plants (Senghaas 1985, 83). The link between agricultural modernization and agriculture-based industrialization provided the impetus for the economic development of Danish society.

The second half of the nineteenth century offers a clear example of how new external circumstances forced the state elite to make decisions. The German problem after 1864 and the internationalization of the economy beginning in the 1870s and 1880s confronted Denmark with new and difficult circumstances that compelled Denmark to respond in order to survive politically, militarily, and economically. Among the responses were: a revision of the constitution, an agricultural structural change, infrastructural changes, and a shift from Germany to Britain as major trading partner.

The problem of Germany and the revision of the constitution had a number of implications. First and foremost, the problem of defence was heavily discussed throughout the last four decades of the nineteenth century, and it was a key point in disputes between right (the conservatives, landowners, civil servants, and bourgeoisie) and left (the farmers). This conflict became even more tense after the revision of the Constitution in

1866. The farmers and others saw this revision as a major deterioration of the democratic basis of the constitution. The 1866 constitution strengthened the right and the landowners and increased the problem of reconciliation between the two houses of the parliament.[7] The wide gap between right and left was a huge problem. It was due partly to the fact that the country faced an unsolved problem of defence and partly to the intensifying social problem caused by the fact that more and more young people were leaving the countryside for the towns and cities, leaving old people behind without any income. A constitution without a solution to the problem of reconciling the two houses of the parliament made it difficult to find sustainable solutions to the problem of defence as well as the social problems.

The Conservative government outplayed the opposition between 1875 and 1894 under the prime ministership of J.B.S. Estrup. Despite the opposition majority in the Folketing (House of Commons), Estrup managed to keep the opposition out of influence by governing through provisional finance acts. The first act was passed in 1877, and during the Period of the Provisional Laws between 1877 and 1894, Estrup and the Conservatives forced through a measure for the building of the fortifications around Copenhagen. However, the conflict between government and opposition never took a character that paralysed the country. Underlying this conflict there existed a common project that generated some level of consensus – the national project (Hornemann-Møller 1992, 62). The defeat to Germany in 1864, the loss of the Danish-speaking North Schleswig, and a general fear of the new Germany created nationalism. This, again, generated an ideological and to some extent a military mobilization and contributed to reproducing the consensus.

Daily politics was, however, characterized by a policy of obstruction from the left, but the left was internally too weak to bring about a change of the system. Consequently, the moderate part of the opposition began to cooperate and negotiate with the conservative government, and in 1891 a majority in the *Rigsdag* passed a number of social acts. In 1894 the two parties came to an agreement, which brought about a political stabilization. The series of social acts introduced as of 1891 inaugurated a new period in Danish history. For the first time the state budget contained an account of social expenses next to the expenses to the King, the Church, the army and the navy. In other words, the state intervened for the first time in society at a larger scale. It can seem odd that it was Estrup and the right who started an intervention in societal matters to solve a social question. It would hardly have had happened if Bismarck had not set the example in Germany some years prior to Estrup's intervention. The inspiration from Bismarck is very conspicuous, but, in contrast to Bismarck the social acts passed in Denmark did not target the working class but the old and poor who had been left alone in the countryside as a result of migration to the towns and cities. The Danish system was optional and not restricted to the working class; it was open to all persons, including agricultural labourers and craftsmen. "The basis of the system was not a state intervention in the labour contract but financial subsidies and legal support for voluntary associations in civil society. This principle was called a 'help-to-self-help' and applied to associations with members with an income equal to or less than a skilled worker. Thus the associations for sickness insurance – the 'sick-clubs' – would be recognized by the state and subsidized only if their rules and number of qualified members met the standard. The same held true for associations for unemployment insurance, the 'unemployment clubs,' even if they were organized and run by the trade unions" (Bernild 2003, 2).

Crucial to the inception of these welfare elements were a number of decisions taken by Estrup and the state apparatus which, again, were driven by an underlying rationality: to sustain sovereignty and to remain in power. Decisions related to the survival of the state overrode ideologies of the left and the right at that time. State intervention on this scale was not the norm but an outcome of decisions to survive as a state and, of course, the imperative to remain in power as a party.

THE IDEA OF A "WELFARE SOCIETY": THE SOCIAL LIBERAL AND SOCIAL DEMOCRATIC ALLIANCE, 1905–1947

During the last years of the nineteenth and early twentieth century, the behaviour of Denmark's German neighbour led to increasing tensions between the two countries, especially when Germany annexed the whole of Schleswig. The threat became clearer to Denmark, but most politicians realized that an armed conflict with Germany would only cause pain and defeat. Peter Munch, leader of the small Social Liberal Party founded in 1905 (*Det Radikale Venstre*) and later Minister of Foreign Affairs, took the stance that Denmark should avoid military conflicts with Germany. A defeat would be inevitable. Munch argued that the Danish state as a sovereign entity would disappear in a military confrontation with Germany. Denmark should therefore remain neutral and stay out of any great power conflict. The politics of neutrality was not new but it was strongly emphasized during the years of governments that included the Social Liberals and later Social Democratic–Social Liberal coalition governments. The strong emphasis on disarmament policy was new, as until the 1870s Denmark had been one of the most militarized countries in Europe.

These circumstances led Munch to rethink the relationship between state and people. He argued that the state and the people are not a unity. The state might come under severe threat – it might even disappear for some time – but the people can continue its existence as a people. By strengthening society or, more precisely, the people's community, Denmark might survive. Therefore, the only strategy for Denmark was to develop a strong national community or society that could resist the external enemy. Referring to the fate of Poland, Munch argued that even though the state might wither away, the people would remain a national people and survive as a unity. It required, however, that a responsible government provide the conditions for the growth of a strong national community. Here, according to Munch, it was important to remove class inequality and huge class differences in general: "The state and the people are not a unity. If the unlikely accident were to overtake the Danish people – to be subsumed by a foreign state – then the People shall exist anyway ... And the people will have a stronger and more secure life with a more developed spiritual and material culture when there are no class boundaries that split and divide a people in contending parties with different worldviews" (Munch 1905, 55) (author's translation).[8]

He went even further in 1908: "We can no more defend the Danish state with culture than with fortifications. Culture can, however, forge the Danish People into a spiritual protection ... If the sad situation occurred that the Danish state was conquered – it is fitting to realize the truth that it could happen – then a unique and highly developed Danish culture as far removed from the militaristic culture of the conqueror state as possible, would guarantee that the Danish People could preserve its own national life until external independence was returned." (Munch 1908, quoted in Lidegaard, 1998a) (author's translation).[9]

These quotations demonstrate that Munch's vision and political ideology were embedded in a worldview in which the lines between international and domestic issues were blurred. Domestic politics are the crucial element in the survival of the Danish state. In the short run the state may wither away, but in the long run it will survive if the Danish society and community prove to be strong and coherent enough. The aim was to protect Danish sovereignty, but the means was to develop national institutions – welfare institutions or welfare society, to put it in modern terms. It required, among other things, a strong national health system, a system of social protection schemes, and an education system. Building such institutions could unite the people in a strong national project.

Thus we find a close connection between Denmark's international situation, its geopolitical location, and its domestic political circumstances. Munch's social vision, stressing a strengthening of the nation, fitted well into an alliance with the Social Democrats. The ideas about the welfare state of the leader of the Social Democrats (and later prime minister) Thorvald Stauning corresponded in a number of ways with Munch's vision about the need for an internal armament process as a response to external threats. To Munch it was crucial not only that the Danish people were well educated and morally rearmed but also that they existed in an environment free of serious class conflicts and tensions. Consequently, the people would not become susceptible to totalitarian ideologies and, moreover, would feel more responsible toward their own society and nation.[10] Munch juxtaposes the external defence strategy of the state and the internal construction of society: "The defence consists of an internal organization of society – developing education and culture levelling out social differences" (Lidegaard 1998a).

This compatibility of vision enabled the Social Liberal party to build a bridge to the Social Democrats. This alliance has been a key element in the construction of the Danish welfare state throughout the twentieth century. Whereas the welfare society was a goal for the social democrats, who strove to create a society for the working class from cradle to grave, the welfare society and its institutions were merely a means for the Social Liberals. Perhaps the whole party did not see it that way, but at least Munch, its leader, was more concerned about the state and society as a whole and not so much about particular class interests. The primary goal for Munch was to secure an autonomous and sovereign Danish People!

The transition toward a welfare society was not a clearly defined project with clear goals and intentions. It was, rather, the outcome of new external conditions, an underlying rationality to stay sovereign combined with various ideologies taking part in the development. The response from Munch and Stauning to the new external situation and the internal social problems was a welfare society.

The Crucial Years: 1914–1919

A modern total war has certain predictable effects on the social problems of the warring nations. It absorbs the unemployed, it stimulates health services in both their technical and their organizational aspects, and it creates a housing shortage, either by destroying houses or preventing them from being built, or both. In a more general sense total war obliges governments to assume new and heavier responsibilities for the welfare of their peoples, especially by controlling the production and the distribution of scarce necessities, like food and fuel, and by looking after those who have been made homeless by invasion, evacuation, or aerial bombardment. The experience of total war is therefore bound to have an effect on both the principles of social policy and the methods of social administration. But the nature of this effect will depend to a considerable extent on the fortunes of war – on whether a country is invaded or not, on whether it is victorious or defeated, and on the amount of physical destruction and social disorganization it suffers. (Marshall 1975, 82)

As Marshall clearly observed, "total war" has a strong impact on state intervention and social policies, as most European countries found after the two world wars. World War I became the crucial event, with long-term consequences for the development of the welfare state in Denmark in the second part of the twentieth century.

As important as Munch's political vision was the coalition between the Social Liberal party (*Det Radikale Venstre*) and the Social Democratic party. Munch was far from the only politician or intellectual with this perception of the political and geopolitical realities; these ideas were widely shared among members of the political elite. A certain perception of the world does not in itself lead to a country with stronger social cohesion, or stronger cooperation between the political parties and the many organizations and interest groups. Willingness to compromise, the ability to listen to one's opponent, and a consensual culture are elements of a political culture which, in the Danish case, were more an outcome of necessity than the natural product of a good-hearted people. Tough choices and hard compromises require a sense of urgency. This urgency was felt in the years after the defeat to Prussia in 1864, and during the agricultural crisis in the 1870s and 1880s; and it was felt again during World War I.

Despite the fact that Denmark stayed neutral during this war, it became clear that Denmark was constrained by the war as much as any other country. The impact of the war was intense. Blockades and mines in the seas threatened exports as well as imports of raw materials. The outcome was a shortage of supplies and goods and resulting price increases. The suffering of low-income social groups, in particular, threatened to lead to greater inequality and social tensions. Consequently, the state adopted a new strategy to solve the problems. Massive state intervention and regulation was the answer. This intervention was, however, based upon a corporative structure in which the key societal organizations representing the major social groups and economic interests took part (Vigen 1950, 440–69).

On 7 August 1914, immediately after the war broke out, the Danish government, with full support from the Parliament, established a commission (*den Overordentlige Kommission*) with the Minister of Interior Affairs, Ove Rode, in charge. The strong support for the commission indicated a truce between the otherwise conflicting parties in the Parliament. The minister appointed representatives from all major organizations, interest groups, and social classes in Denmark. Farmers, small landholders, industry, trade unions, ship owners, consumers, social democrats, liberals, and scientists were all represented (Vigen 1950, 444; Rasmussen 1965, 72). The *Act of August 7* gave the minister and the commission extended powers to intervene, regulate, and control society. The commission constructed an elaborate system of regulations that affected every economic and social area, including price policy, supply policy, rationing systems, and, to a certain extent, income distribution policy. As mentioned above, the state had already began to intervene with the first social reform in 1891, and since then a number of acts had gradually been passed in Parliament which demonstrated that the state was no longer the good old liberal state abstaining from any form of intervention (Rasmussen 1965, 87). However, it was not until World War I that state intervention on a massive scale took place. The commission's efforts met with considerable success: Denmark succeeded in coming through the war without major wounds, tensions, or social conflicts.

Rode found the commission so successful that in 1916 he emphasized in a speech (the Gimle-Speech, 26 October) that state intervention and state regulation were the key to solving societal problems and therefore should form a policy for the future (Rasmussen 1965, 88; Vigen 1950, 454–5).

Although World War I is crucial to understanding state formation and societal development in Denmark, the widespread state intervention and regulation of that period are only one aspect. Also important is the welfare dimension. The state's attempts to regulate society were intended to benefit all social classes. For the first time, redistribution of income and welfare took place on a massive scale. Crucial to this development is the means by which the state succeeded both in getting support for these policies and in implementing them. Other states also intervened in their societies but in Denmark the intervention took place through an extensive corporatist strategy. The state increased its power, but so did all the major organizations representing the economic interests in the country. In 1899 the state had already recognized and accepted that the labour market was run by employers and employees. The state also had some years before acknowledged the presence and importance of the other organizations, not least the farmers and the industry. Only with World War I, however, were these organizations invited to take part in all sorts of commissions and committees set up by the government or a governmental institution. This process gave the organizations considerable influence and transformed them into more stable and strongly institutionalized entities. They became indispensable organizations, co-responsible for societal development in Denmark.

It would be no exaggeration to say that World War I became the point of crystallization of the Danish welfare state, the Danish model of "effective corporatism," and the organizational society in Denmark. Despite a setback for state intervention and state regulation after the war, it was only a bit more than a decade before it was back on the agenda. In the first years after the war, "back to normalcy" was the policy. The political truce broke down immediately after the end of the war, and the Opposition, which then consisted of the Liberals and the Conservative People's Party (until 1915 *Højre*, "Right"), demanded that the regulations be abolished.

The government hesitated, however, because of the delicate social balance and the fear of a post-war crisis. Despite this division, a number of land laws were passed in 1919, which changed the system of ownership for the large estates and took over land that was used to set up approximately 6,000 small-holdings. This was a serious piece of welfare state policy, once again on a very large scale. By passing this Act, the Government basically created new conditions of existence for a class in society – the small-holders.

The April 1920 election brought in a Liberal government that was supported by the Conservative People's Party. The new government faced difficulties as a result of the post-war crisis. The policy was, however, a move back to the liberal state and a retreat of from state intervention. This policy lasted only until the early 1930s, when the new government – a coalition between the Social Democrats and the Social Liberals led by Stauning and Munch as prime minister and foreign minister respectively – were forced to bring state intervention and the corporatist system back in.

The agricultural sector faced problems with sales and prices. Many farmers were affected by the debt crisis. In 1931 towns also began to feel the crisis as businesses went under and jobs were lost; in 1932 unemployment rose to over 40 percent. The government attempted to ease the situation through trade agreements with Great Britain and Germany, and at home, it made a number of emergency agreements with one or both opposition parties. In 1932 the Exchange Control Office was set up to control the external sector of the economy, and all parties gradually acknowledged the need for state intervention in the country's economy.

The most important of these agreements was the Kanslergade Agreement, which was entered into by the government and the Liberal party (*Venstre*). It provided for a number of measures, including the first of many extensions by law to the collective labour agreement between employers and employees, a devaluation of the currency, and state subsidies to the farmers and small-holders. The Kanslergade Agreement also contained a set of social acts. K.K. Steincke, the Minister of Social Affairs, designed a new social reform in order to alleviate the repercussions of the crisis for the poor. More or less a continuation of the social reform of 1891–92, the Social Reform of 1933 simplified legislation and laid down the principle of law; it also introduced fixed charges for social services.

Steincke's social reform in 1933 changed the structure of Danish social insurance by making it compulsory for every adult to be a member of a "sick-club" (Bernild 2003, 4). The sick-clubs became responsible for many administrative tasks as well, old-age pensions in particular, but not unemployment benefits. The change had the effect of making it possible to abolish the old and humiliating Poor Law that took care of the non-members of sick-clubs. However, on the other hand it necessitated a new distinction between active members, who could receive benefits, and passive members, who could not, because of their increased income. And though the contribution of the poor was merely symbolic, an obvious contradiction had emerged (Bernild 2003, 4).

The emergency agreements blurred the ideological divisions between the parties and social groups in the country. On the one hand, purely liberalistic objectives were in decline and on the other, the Social Democratic Party had abandoned its original socialist goals and was becoming a party for the workers and the people with greater appeal for a wider sector of the population. Their new position was underlined in 1934 by the introduction of Stauning's program entitled "Denmark for the People." The international and national crisis brought about a "state of exception" that forced politicians to act, and so they did. Again, it also led to closer cooperation between the state, the administration, the trade organizations, and the two sides of industry. State intervention, regulations, and effective corporatism were back on the agenda. World War I had demonstrated the efficiency of state-initiated welfare policies and a corporatist system; consequently, it was easy to recall the important experience and bring it back again.

When World War II came, the "model" had already been "invented." State regulation and state intervention, supported and legitimized by all major social classes and economic interests, and implemented by civil servants and the major organizations in a corporatist system, were repeated during this war. By 1943 the model was so strongly institutionalized that the civil servants and the major economic organizations could run the country and the remaining years of the war even though the government stepped down in August 1943. After World War II the system and the corporative model was here to stay and it became institutionalized.

Munch' s political vision and political strategy, developed in the first decade of the twentieth century, proved its worth. However this political vision, emphasizing the need for a set of strong national welfare-state institutions in order to reduce inequality and strengthen social cohesion only materialized because two major wars and a world economic crisis generated "states of exception" that forced politicians into a truce in order to act together to save the country. The size of the country, the already-constructed popular nationalism, the associational and organizational features developed during the nineteenth century, and other factors facilitated that the vision could be carried out during these crises. Without these "states of exception," which generated a state of necessity, the Danish welfare state would likely not have developed, at least not in this extended form.

World War I, the crisis of the 1930s, and World War II are all events that clearly demonstrate the relationship between, on the one hand, geopolitical changes and "states of exception" and, on the other, domestic changes and policies; only external changes created a space for structural changes within the state and society. The Danish case illustrates how politicians, mainly ministers, and highly positioned civil servants acted rather determinedly in relation to these new, threatening external changes. The imminent threat to Denmark when World War I broke out was quickly perceived not least by Munch, but also the Minister of Justice, C. Th. Zahle and, of course, the Minister of Domestic Affairs, Ove Rode (Vigen 1950, 440–58). They acted together with their civil servants and then later with other politicians (from the opposition parties) and representatives from the major organizations as a state elite determined to struggle for survival of the Danish state and society. Initially, it was the politicians who demonstrated a strong political will to act, but they needed help from the state bureaucracy and they got it. In other words, it was politicians as well as state civil servants who demonstrated the political will and who pushed national economic development in the Listian manner by intervention, regulation, and protection.

One could argue that Munch's policy came to a test on 9 April 1940. He hoped that Denmark would avoid German occupation but, as we know, that did not happen. But Munch's policy passed the test in another respect. The internal defence of the nation proved to be very efficient. The policy of cooperation with Germany became, "despite the humiliations, tragedies, and compromises which necessarily follow from a foreign occupation, a spectacular success" (Lidegaard 1998b). The Danish nation was never threatened during the occupation. But the increasing struggle of resistance against Germany led to a hard critique of the politics of neutrality. This break with the policy of neutrality inaugurated a new phase in Danish history and in the development of the welfare state.

THE WELFARE SOCIETY AS A TOOL AGAINST COMMUNISM

After the victory of the Allied forces in World War II, a new international situation emerged. Denmark became a part of the American sphere of interest. Denmark's geopolitical position at the entrance to the Baltic Sea made Denmark strategically important, and Greenland, its possession in the North Atlantic, was vital to American strategy (Villaume 1999, 22). It became crucial to the United States – and to the Danish government/ Social Democrats – to keep the Russians and Communism at bay. In Denmark the Communist party gained enormous support after the war, winning many parliamentary seats in the post-war election. The Social Democrats feared that a continuation of this development would in the long run undermine the position of the Social Democrats and the whole country (Gravesen et al. 1999, 3). Despite conflicting views on many issues between the Social Democrats and the Americans, the problem of Communism made it more acceptable for the Danish Social Democracy to become an American ally. This situation, combined with the general short-age of resources after the war, led to the acceptance of the American offer of Marshall Aid in 1947 and, as a corollary, membership of NATO in 1949 (Sørensen 2001; Villaume 1999; Lidegaard 1996, 1999). It was a difficult and contested decision (Lidegaard 1996, 549–60).

This was a fundamental break with Danish foreign policy – the most decisive break since the end of the Napoleonic Wars. The first part of the twentieth century had reflected a policy that kept Denmark out of all conflicts and alliances. This position now changed radically. If the Danish welfare state was to survive under these new conditions of exis-tence, it required: i) security – not least from the external and internal Communist threat, and ii) the best possible opportunities for trade and economic stability.

In order to solve the security issues it became vital to find a strategy that could deal with the external as well as the internal threat from Communism. One of the "solutions" to this problem was to develop a "strategic alliance" between the Social Democratic Party as the leading party and the United States (Lidegaard 1996, 578–88). In order to dimin-ish the Communist threat in the east, the Americans saw clearly that they had to prevent Communist fifth-column activities in Denmark (and other Scandinavian countries) which could facilitate a Russian invasion. Consequently, the best strategy from an American point of view was to sup-port a welfare state project that would minimize the number of social prob-lems and thereby prevent the spread of Communism. The most important American ally in Denmark therefore became the Social Democrats and not the bourgeois parties. The Social Democrats were ready with their welfare project and the Social Democrats themselves regarded the Communists as the principal enemy. The United States had another strategic interest in Denmark, which was Greenland. During World War II, Greenland had become crucial to the United States, and the control of North Atlantic. After the war this interest increased, and air bases became vital to American defence. Since Denmark used to be a neutral country, Greenland became a problem for Denmark. It was a very sensitive and difficult issue for the Danish government to handle, but eventually the Social Democratic prime minister, Hans Hedtoft, realized that although Greenland was a problem it was also an asset for Denmark. Thus it became important in solving the Danish defence problem and it led to participation in the U.S.-led NATO alliance (Lidegaard 1996, 551).

A strengthening of the social democratic–social liberal welfare state with extended social rights to protect the poorest was the best means of undermining the strong Communist position in Denmark. Thus the welfare state was a fusion of a social project and a defence project. Joining NATO implied that Denmark was subject to American dominance in a military sense but at the same time it led to a situation where the United States paid Denmark's defence bill, leaving the country free to develop a stable welfare society.

The post-war welfare state was a defence project intertwined with an attempt to solve "the social problem." It was important to remove the problem of unemployment because it reduced the incentive of the working class to support the communists. Welfare policies and unemployment became a means of immunizing the working class against Communism.

Despite the strong impact of social-democratic policies, the structure of the Danish welfare state in the post-war years was still based upon an alliance between the Social Democrats and the Social Liberal Party, but often with support from the bourgeois parties in vital issues. The Cold War and its frozen friend/foe picture was an obstacle for the social democratic vision of the welfare state as a society based upon universalism and individual social rights. For some decades it was still a welfare state that supported a class-based welfare-state structure. The state protected the four major classes and tried to keep a balance among them. A strong Anglo-American influence was evident, but the Marshall-type of individual rights-based welfare did not become the basic structural principle of organizing welfare services until the 1970s (with some clear exceptions such as the pension reform of 1956) (Bernild 2001).

A further precondition of the evolution and consolidation of the Danish welfare state, in addition to the previously mentioned security problem, was a continued development of trade and industry. Denmark needed access to the world market and it was in Denmark's interest to have an open market (especially for agricultural products) and a stable monetary regime. The two key trading partners, Germany and Britain, were both in very difficult situations, but for different reasons. Thus neither of the two countries was ready to import Danish products to the extent needed for Denmark to create a better economy and provide better living conditions for the working class.

The Marshall Plan was one step toward improving the European and the Danish situation. Most European states feared American dominance in Europe but eventually most countries accepted the plan along with the Americans' conditions (Lidegaard 1999, 40; Dalgas Jensen 1989, 62). In 1947 Denmark had no reserves of foreign currency and no prospect of obtaining credit in the near future. Moreover, the country had developed a large deficit in its balance of payment in just two years. Consequently, the $278 million that Denmark received from 1948 to 1953 constituted an important injection into the economy and its future prosperity. The country needed a process of industrialization, and the only opportunity to develop more jobs lay in a new and modern industry. It required coal, iron, chemicals, metals, and other resources but, in order to finance these resources, Denmark needed an increase in export. A higher income from export – foreign currency (dollars) – could only come from agricultural products, and an opening of the market was desirable in the big countries, especially Britain and Germany, who protected their own agricultural sector (Schmidt 1993, 267–8). After difficult negotiations in the OEEC, Denmark found some willingness on the part of other countries.

The cost of receiving the financial injection was basically an acceptance of American economic and political architecture. The Americans had several demands, such as an organization with the purpose of organizing the Marshall Aid (OEEC), and new policies within areas of customs, trade, currency, and technology. The period from 1948 to 1953 was crucial in the development of new structures within these areas. Thus, again, we see that new external conditions virtually determined certain aspects of new economic and social structure in Denmark. A former key civil servant, Erik Ib Schmidt, reminds us that Denmark was even forced to raise taxes as a consequence of its new membership in OEEC and NATO – a step which had not even been taken by the European Union (Schmidt 1993, 272–89).

The acceptance of the Marshall Aid and membership in NATO took Denmark into the Alliance and represented a definitive abandonment of neutrality and non-bloc policy. It was a very difficult step for the Social Democrats, who throughout the first half of the twentieth century, had argued for neutrality and staying out of any blocs or alliances. The approval of Marshall aid was seen as a necessary economic decision that continued the previously initiated welfare policy (Lidegaard 2002, 286). The NATO decision was, on the contrary, a clearly political decision to join the Alliance and leave the non-bloc ideal.

Two other important aspects of post-war development with relevance for Denmark deserve mention. First of all the American policies that were structuring the Western world also included the evolution of a monetary and exchange rate regime that could be characterized as a "semi-fixed rate dollar standard" – the Bretton Woods system (Hirst and Thompson 1999,

33). This monetary system was a key element in Denmark's quite remarkable growth and increasing wealth during the late 1950s and throughout the 1960s. It provided the necessary stability and, when combined with the new markets, allowed Denmark to flourish as a trading nation.

The other element of major importance was access to markets. The changing Danish governments knew very well that free trade and the opening of markets were keys to the further development of the welfare state. Again, export of agricultural products was crucial to Danish welfare but it was also important to the expansion of small- and medium-scale industries with potential for export. First of all, membership in the European Coal and Steel Union and the EEC raised an important question to be faced. Denmark was here in a dilemma. A strong majority of the grass roots in the Social Democracy and the Trade Unions opposed the idea of joining the EEC. Moreover, Britain, the largest market for Danish agricultural products, was not member. Consequently, Denmark stayed outside until Britain joined in 1972. Among leading Social Democrats, most notably Prime Minister Jens Otto Krag, membership of the EEC was considered a necessary political and economic decision. Already from the early 1960s, industry export had overtaken agricultural export and Denmark was no longer a "farm nation" but depended on industrial growth. Krag saw it as his mission to take Denmark into the EEC to provide the foundation for future development and expansion of the welfare state (Lidegaard 2002, 568–85). When Britain decided in October 1971 to apply, Krag wanted to follow. More than 25 percent of Danish export went to the EEC countries and more than 20 percent to Britain. According to Krag and his welfare state strategy, staying outside the EEC would have had disastrous consequences for Denmark; a Denmark outside Europe would mean no future prospect for the welfare state. In 1972, with the support of voters from the bourgeois parties and a minority of his own party voters, Krag succeeded in taking Denmark into the EEC.

The period from the early 1950s to the early 1970s provided a fairly stable and advantageous set of conditions of existence of the Danish welfare state. A rapid increase in social expenditure, and expansion of the public sector facilitated by economic growth contributed to further development and consolidation of the welfare state. In the late 1960s and early 1970s successive governments and leading civil servants elaborated more policies and institutional changes in order to strengthen the welfare dimension. Among politicians and civil servants it was emphasized that Denmark was a "society of change," no longer a stable society with predictable "social events" such as old age and unemployment. The old social insurance system had been developed to respond to such foreseeable events. According to leading politicians, social reform was needed. The Commission for Social Reform was established in 1964 with the main objective of reforming the administrative machinery of the old social insurance system. Its strategy was to centralize all the casework into a single social security office, but to decentralize the administration of this system by locating it at the local level. "The guiding line for social casework was to make less use of cash-benefits and instead to mobilize the individual to adapt to the possibilities in the labour market by re-education and help to geographical change. The overall aim was, in short, to enhance social and geographical mobility in order to adapt to the changing demands from the labour market in a dynamic economy" (Bernild 2003, 5). The reform was introduced by several acts decided by the Parliament between 1971 and 1978. These reforms together were seen as the creation of the "world's best welfare state."

The social reform went hand in hand with the administrative reform that was introduced in the 1970s at the municipal level (Knudsen 1993, 187). This new municipal structure provided better conditions for the set of social reforms. The administrative reform changed the institutional and administrative structure of the Danish public sector. Denmark went from more than 1300 small local parishes to 275 municipalities governed with the same administrative structure (Knudsen 1993, 187). These new municipalities all had to provide welfare services according to the new set of acts from 1971 onward. Each citizen in Denmark now had the right to claim certain services, and these services required a social security office equipped with a professional staff. Around 1950, in more than 800 of the parishes, no personnel had been employed to offer social services in Denmark; even if a person had rights there was no place to claim them. All this changed with the homogenization of the administrative structure and the professionalization of the system under the reforms of 1970.

This quite remarkable expansion of the welfare state was based upon a policy of continuous growth and full employment. Consequently, several events in the early 1970s had severe implications for the Danish welfare state, as well as for others. A conjunction of events from the late 1960s, but mainly from 1971 onward, caused a completely new situation. A radical change in American foreign and economic policy combined with the oil crisis gave rise to a political, ideological, and fiscal crisis for the welfare state. The 1969 Nixon doctrine was the first significant shift in American foreign policy. The United States terminated its policy of global containment of Communism (Reifer and Sudler 1996, 28) and directed its efforts to the pursuit of a *détente* with the USSR and a dramatic change in the relationship to China. When Kissenger in July 1971 (and later Nixon in 1972) shook hands with Chairman Mao, the world – not least Japan – was taken by surprise (Calvocoressi 1991, 78).

This policy shift gave a simultaneous signal to the Western allies that they had to fend for themselves to a greater extent. The restructuring of the alliance implied a new prioritization of its aims: internal communist revolts were no longer seen as a real threat. This signal was repeated in the United States' decision to close the gold window. On 15 August 1971, Nixon declared the end of dollar-gold convertibility, bringing about the collapse of Bretton Woods system.[11] This event also signalled a new economic policy with new priorities. The key priority was now to reduce inflation by all means, including the acceptance of a higher level of unemployment. Keynesian economic policy was replaced by Friedman monetarism; that is, the employment policy that to some extent was the key to welfare collapsed. These political and economic changes had severe consequences for welfare states and coincided with the 1973 and 1979 OPEC oil crisis (Hirst and Thompson 1999, 5). The oil shock was more consequential for the United States' main competitors, especially the European countries, because oil was paid for in U.S. dollars. The dollar surplus that had accumulated in Europe and Japan during the 1960s disappeared, and trade balances went into deficit. Also the rise of oil prices involved higher production costs (Reifer and Sudler 1996, 28).

A change in American policies, the collapse of the Bretton Woods system, the two oil shocks, some domestic failures, and the generally more unstable international economy put Denmark in a difficult situation. In the 1960s and early 1970s Danish politicians and civil servants thought that the peak of the welfare state was close to being reached and it remained only for the true welfare society based upon genuine universalistic principles to be implemented. Major social and administrative reforms were introduced and everything was ready, when, as a result of these mainly external events, the model ran into major problems: higher production costs, deterioration of the trade balance, currency problems, higher inflation, and rapidly increasing unemployment, which again became a major financial burden. These developments sucked the treasury dry and stunted the further development of social policies in years to come.

The 1970s ushered in a new situation that placed Denmark in a set of new conditions. It is beyond our scope here to examine how Denmark responded to these new circumstances. It is, however, a well-known story that it took several Danish governments and more than twenty years to bring Denmark back to a situation with low unemployment, a trade balance surplus, and controlled inflation. The Danish state has survived as a welfare state, but changes and modifications have had to take place.

The welfare state and the welfare society as a defence mode are now, however, under pressure. The importance of the anti-communist struggle diminished after the 1970s, and as of 1989 it disappeared. The Americans had no longer any strong geo-political interest in Denmark except for Greenland and its important position for the Strategic Defense Initiative.

Without an external enemy, the state – the welfare state as well as the nation-state – loses a part of its basis of legitimization. With the end of the Cold War, Denmark is out of the shadow that first Germany and later the USSR cast over it. These countries functioned as external enemies and motivated a mobilization of Denmark.

The welfare project as an inner fortification against the external threat has also changed character. Even today we find a division in Danish political life over the purpose of the national welfare project. One group argues for its strengthening so that it can serve as an internal fortification and as a countermeasure against increased European integration. Moreover, a part of this strategy is a total mobilization of Danish values as an attempt to protect against the "increasing Europeanization devoid of identity." In contrast to these opinions, another wing argues that the survival of the welfare state depends upon a development of increased active participation in the European project. This group sees the strengthening of Denmark through the development of the common European market as a primary tool for the survival of the Danish welfare state.

The picture has been even more complex since 11 September 2001, when Denmark again strengthened its international involvement in fighting terrorism, and the country has demonstrated a surprisingly high will to send troops to support America's war. A new external enemy is looming large – an enemy that has to be fought both externally (terrorism and Islamic fundamentalism) and internally (the Islamic population living in Denmark who potentially could become fundamentalists). Can the welfare state become a means of preventing the disillusioned Islamic people living in Denmark from turning into supporters of terrorism? Or must the welfare state change itself into a security state to protect its own population? These questions need to be addressed further in the coming years.

CONCLUSION

The normative foundation of the welfare state can be explored from different angles. Here I have paid attention to the importance of the decisions taken by the state (or more precisely by the centre or locus of the state in which the political will to survive has been formulated) in order for the country to survive My claim is that we tend to neglect the fact that the state has its own agenda – to remain independent and sovereign – an agenda that is always there, notwithstanding the political ideologies that dominate the ongoing debate in the country among parties and interest groups. At crucial moments, mostly when new external conditions of existence emerge, this rationality tends to override any other agendas brought forward by individual political parties. Any state must struggle for survival as a state, and many welfare aspects must also be viewed in this light.

The claim that the state is an actor with its own autonomy and rationality has often been criticized by scholars who find it methodologically or theoretically unacceptable. I argue, however, that certain developments can best be understood from a statist perspective as long as we keep in mind that it is only a limited – albeit neglected – view of the processes leading to a welfare state we see from this angle. Here I emphasize that the development of the Danish state during the last 150 years can be conceived as a process in which the nation-building project merges with the welfare project as a response to developments in the international environment. The welfare state developed a welfare society as a strategy to survive in the international environment – the welfare society became a defence mode.

In order to contextualize this chapter in the debates raised by Katzenstein in *Small States in the World Market* (Katzenstein 1985), and in his epilogue to this book, it is important to emphasize that a part of my research supports Katzenstein's argument about the ability of leaders to perceive vulnerabilities and act upon their perceptions. In this chapter I have demonstrated how certain moments such as 1864, the 1880s, 1914, and 1945–49 were perceived by the elite as crucial moments and how responses to these moments facilitated flexible adjustment. The actions taken by the Danish government at the outbreak of World War I give a good example. Before the war, strong state intervention in society was not even thinkable and was not perceived as a possible solution to any crisis. The war, however, was a crucial moment: action was needed and the system demonstrated "flexible adjustment" to a new situation. The same process illustrates how politicians, civil servants, and institutions went through a learning process during World War I. State intervention and democratic corporatism developed and became institutionalized during this period and, when compelling external events – the crisis of the 1930s – were again perceived as a crisis, experiences from 1914–18 were revitalized and further developed.

Another discussion that has been important and inspirational to this book is contained in the literature on varieties of capitalism. This literature has not directly been addressed here, but some common elements can be found. First of all, this chapter argues that Denmark can be seen as an example of a coordinated market economy. Although I have emphasized the state level more than the market, I argue that the interaction between state and societal actors in the Danish case leads to a strong and close coordination of market activities. Subsequently, as mentioned above, the idea of the presence of deliberative institutions in the Danish context has also been illustrated. The chapter also points, however, to the importance of decisions taken by the state elite in "states of exception" – decisions that can lead either to the establishment of new, or the transformation of old, institutions. The importance of the "decisionist" aspect at the political level is underrated in the varieties-of-capitalism literature. This is hardly any surprise, since the market and the corporations are key elements in this approach. Finally, Peter Hall and David Soskice, as representatives of this approach, stress the importance of cultural institutions (defined as informal rules and understandings) coordinating the actions of the actors. In this chapter it has been demonstrated how a common perception of specific situations among important actors is needed in order for a shared understanding of a common strategy to arise. The defeat to Prussia in 1864 raised a strong national consciousness among the population in Denmark and, as Korsgaard also shows (chapter 3), this strong version of popular nationalism facilitated a strong social cohesion and a willingness to negotiate to solve problems. The same story can be told about World War I and other events that prompted major social partners to meet and negotiate solutions to respond to a new crisis. In that respect, this chapter provides evidence for the argument in the Hall-Soskice version of the varieties-of-capitalism literature.

Another question that needs to be addressed before closing this chapter concerns the problem of the uniqueness of the Danish case. How different is the Danish case really, compared to other small states such as the Netherlands, Sweden, Austria, Switzerland, or Finland? This is a difficult issue, and a proper response needs to be theoretical and methodological as well as sociological. It is beyond our scope to give a full account, but a brief answer can be the following. Yes, the Danish case is exceptional. Yes, the Danish path to a modern wealthy and prosperous society with a high degree of differentiation, flexible institutions, and an ability to adapt to new external conditions of existence is unique. But how unique and how exceptional? And compared to what?

Since this chapter and this book constitute a single case study, we cannot answer questions of comparative matters in the most appropriate way. However, this study and my theoretical framework suggest that all state formation processes are different and exceptional in many respects. Despite the fact that I endorse the endeavour to make comparisons and generalizations, this ambition is highly problematic. I have argued that, among other things, geographical size and position, geopolitical context, state structures, state-society relations, population size, character, and composition, education levels, resources, and societal institutional structures differ from one state history to another. The fact that every single state has a different geographical position, with different neighbours and different access to sea and rivers, constrains and empowers each state in a particular way. Consequently, some structural frameworks are always fundamentally different from state to state, and each state will always develop along a particular path.

In this respect every state-formation process is exceptional and unique. Only Denmark and Sweden are located at the entrance to the Baltic Sea and only Denmark has ruled Greenland and the Faroe Islands for centuries. This position provides Denmark with special opportunities and problems. In recalling Montesquieu's emphasis on the climate as an important dimension for differences in state-building processes, Kevin O'Rourke (chapter 4) illustrates how a climate difference between Denmark and Ireland had an impact on the way cows were treated during the winter and the consequences for milk production and technological innovation in the two countries. In other words, by stressing geography and geopolitics in particular, this chapter has argued that the Danish state-formation process is unique – but not more exceptional than that of the Dutch or the Swedish. They are, however, all three different.

Similarities can be found as well; consequently, some generalizations can be made in the history of state building and state-formation processes. Thus, I claim that a logic of survival is present in all states, and for some centuries European states were located in a fairly coherent system in which they all interacted intensively. This survival logic intensified over the centuries and, particularly the period from the late fifteenth century and onward, was crucial. States imitated each other's best practices in order to survive. They copied military systems and institutions, tax and legal institutions, and education systems from each other, and therefore, many similarities between states can be found as history has unfolded. This volume and this chapter illustrate, however, that in our endeavour to develop general categories, types, models, and regimes we tend to overlook strong differences between the states – differences which only can be brought to light through serious single-case studies. The next step for me will, of course, be to take the Danish case into a comparative study, but once again taking my point of departure in geopolitics and geography in order to pinpoint the clear differences and similarities that such an approach can demonstrate.

NOTES

1 This chapter and the thesis of the welfare state as a defence mode is an outcome of a research project, "Life-modes and welfare state at a crossroad" (*Livsformer og velfærdsstat ved en korsvej?*) sponsored by the Danish Research Council (humanities). For further reading see T. Højrup, 2003, *Livsformer og velfærdsstat ved en korsvej?*, Copenhagen: Museum Tusculanums Forlag.

2 We cannot necessarily assume that a state or state elite makes the best decisions or develops the best strategies. Many states in history have been punished as wrong decisions and poor strategies led to a weakening of state and
   society. In the worst cases states have withered away, as Poland did four times.

3 More recent examples are C. Pierson (Pierson, 1998, 6–7) and Esping-
   Andersen (Esping-Andersen 1990, 21–3).

4 Esping-Andersen distinguishes between the "liberal" welfare state regime
   (U.S.A., Canada, and the UK), based upon the principle of means-tested
   assistance, modest universal transfer or modest social insurance plans; the
   conservative, corporatist welfare state regimes (Germany, Italy, France), based
   upon social insurance schemes and traditional familyhood; and, finally, the
   social democratic regime-type (Scandinavia), based upon extended universalism and decommodification of social rights (Esping-Andersen, 1990, 26–9).

5 There are some similarities between these propositions and the theoretical
   bulk of work on the state developed by the historical "state" sociologists such
   as Michael Mann (1986;1993), Theda Skocpol (1979), Anthony Giddens
   (1985), and Charles Tilly (1992). There are also some crucial differences. In
   brief, the approach taken in this chapter comes from a more radical statist
   perspective because it is argued that the state is a political entity constituted
   in its relationship to other states and that this mutual struggle of recognition
   has some form of primacy over the struggle of internal sovereignty. Moreover,
   warfare is even more strongly emphasized in this perspective (for a clarification and elaboration of my position in contrast to that of historical sociologists see Kaspersen [2002]).

6 See the *Royal Law* of 1665, for example §4 and §5. See Danske
   Forfatningslove, 1958, 17.

7 The House of Lords (*Landstinget*) was controlled by the right – the conservatives. The House of Commons (*Folketinget*) was controlled by the farmers and
   others.

8 "Staten og Folket er ikke eet. Skulle den usandsynlige Ulykke ramme det
   danske Folk, at blive lagt ind under en fremmed stat, saa lever Folket alligevel
   … Og Folket lever stærkere og sikrere jo mere udviklet dets aandelige og
   materielle Kultur er, jo mindre der er tilbage af de Klassegrænser, som splitter
   og deler et Folk i stridende lejre med forskelligartet Tænkevis." (Det ny
   Aarhundrede, 2. Aarg., 2. Bd., 1905, s. 55.)

9 "Vi kan lige så lidt forsvare den danske Stat med Kultur som med
   Festningsværker. Derimod kan Kulturen skabe det danske Folk et aandeligt
   Værn … Hvis Forholdene skulde stille sig saa ulykkeligt at den danske Stat
   blev erobret – det sømmer sig at se i Øjnene den Sandhed at dette kan ske –
   da vil en ejendommelig, højt udviklet dansk Kultur saa fjern fra
   Erobrerstatens militaristiske Kultur som muligt betyde Sikkerhed for, at det
   danske Folk kan bevare sit eget nationale Liv, indtil det faar ogsaa sin ydre

Selvstændighed tilbage." (Munich 1908; the quotation is from Lidegaard, *Radikal Politik*, nr. 9/1998a, 17/6).

10 The attempt by the Social Liberals to reduce tensions and inequalities in Danish society and at the same time strengthen the common cultural and spiritual dimension of the population appears clearly in the first party program in 1905 (Odense-programmet, 21 May 1905).

11 The closing of the gold window was an unintended consequence of the Vietnam War. The enormous trade surplus changed in 1971 to a huge deficit. As a consequence the U.S.A. printed more dollars to pay for the war. This led to inflation and to other countries preferring gold rather than dollars (Reifer and Sudler 1996, 26).

3

The Danish Way to Establish the Nation in the Hearts of the People

OVE KORSGAARD

"A decade before the constructivist turn in security studies and international relations, scholars of comparative and international political economy simply did not know what to do with ideology as an explanatory construct. With a few notable exceptions, the impermeability of the field of political economy to considerations of identity persists to date. In the rationalist world of political economy actor identities are assumed to be fixed and unproblematic, an intellectually untenable position in the case of the small European states." Peter Katzenstein makes this statement in the article "Small States and Small States Revisited" (Katzenstein 2003), in which he reviews his own book *Small States in World Markets* from 1985.

This chapter is about the modern history of the state of Denmark. Upon rereading Katzenstein's statement about identities, it became clear to me that it is really impossible to understand modern Danish history without considering the question of identities. It was to some extent the outbreak of a new feeling of identity that changed Danish society and made it modern.

When the democratization of the Danish state occurred, nationalism was gradually replacing religion as the kernel of European collective identity. The process of democratization did not, however, bring about a gradual progression toward modernity. Rather, this process led to a radical destabilization – in fact, a complete breakdown of the existing multinational and multilingual state. Only after this breakdown could the nation-state become the exemplary model for the modern Danish state.

The process of democratization in Denmark is an exceptional illustration of the tension between collective identities, political systems, and state-form. In 1789, when democracy began to be implemented as a new political system in Europe, there was as yet no fully realized nation-state. As a consequence of the Napoleonic wars, the Danish-Norwegian union was dissolved in 1814 as Norway came under Swedish sovereignty. But the state, the so-called United Monarchy, was still a multinational and multilingual composite monarchy consisting of the Kingdom of Denmark and the duchies of Schleswig, Holstein, and Lauenburg; the north Atlantic isles – Iceland, Greenland, and the Faroe Islands – and a few small colonies throughout the world. The majority of the population in the kingdom spoke Danish, though in Holstein they spoke German, and in Schleswig half the population spoke Danish and the other half German. The 1815 Congress of Vienna determined the borders of the United Monarchy, making the big question from 1830 on: Could one, in a single process, implement democracy and still keep the United Monarchy together? The problematic consisted in whether democracy could be implemented in a United Monarchy or whether the implementation of the new political system required an alteration of state-form. If the latter were to be the case, what should the guiding principles of this alteration be?

Democracy's problem is, of course, that it requires a *demos*, that is to say a people. But who were the people of the United Monarchy? Did the people correspond to population? Or, were there several peoples within the state? The answer to this question depended upon the understanding of the notions of *people* and *nation*. Should they be understood as a political, cultural, or social category?

In the pre-democratic social order, the notion *people* was simply a category for the subjects. The people were subjects – to the master of the house, the lord of a manor, the father of the country, or God. However, with democracy the people became sovereign and thus could no longer be categorized as mere subjects. The origin of this change and transformation in the history of ideas can be traced back to Rousseau and Herder, who in the 1760s and 1770s wrote key texts on pedagogic and political philosophy. Rousseau was the first to formulate the groundbreaking idea that the people hold the political power. Thus from Rousseau came the impulse to regard the people as the ultimate sovereign within a new kind of political and governmental structure. Herder also formulated a groundbreaking principle, the principle that people hold cultural power. With Herder the notion *people* also came to denote specific peoples, independent of political systems. At the core of Herder's "cultural" conception of the notion *people*, is an understanding of collective identity as a deep-seated reality shaped by language and culture, the understanding of people as ethnic groups. Rousseau and Herder both broke with the old notion of the people as subjects; however, they put forth two distinct senses of people as the sovereign. While Rousseau tied his conceptions of sovereignty to establishing a social contract, Herder linked his to the recognition of a language pact.

The relationship between state-form and political system was, as I mentioned, not clear when democracy knocked on the United Monarchy's door in the spring of 1848. As democracy would threaten the existing state-form, a series of royalists opposed its implementation as a political system. Further, there was a great difference of opinion among advocates of democracy as to the future of the state-form: the fundamental issue was whether democracy actually required a new state-form or whether the new political system could be incorporated into the old state-form. In other words: Does the *demos* require a state with only one dominating *ethnos*, or could there be one *demos* in a state consisting of competing *ethnos*? The advocates of democracy proposed three different state-forms.

A Federation: Cosmopolitan democrats proposed a free constitution within a federative configuration of the state and suggested Switzerland and North America as models. According to journalist and author Meir Goldschmidt, Denmark should – as Switzerland did in 1847 – create a "federation of states wherein the different nationalities are thriving and are ensured by the means of freedom" (Goldschmidt 1849, 344). This vision was a "rainbow-state" within which the different nations – Holstein, Schleswig, and the Kingdom – could live in the same state under a common constitution.

The Eider-state: The national liberals in Copenhagen fought for a free constitution within an Eider-state, which meant that Schleswig should be included in the Kingdom and Holstein should be excluded. The large German-speaking minority within the Danish state was regarded as a threat to the future existence of the Danish nation. It was feared that a fiercely expanding Germany would use this minority as an excuse to turn against Denmark. Later, history proved that this fear was well founded.

Two States: Schleswigholstein and the Kingdom: The national liberals in Kiel fought for a free constitution within an autonomous state, which was to include Schleswig-Holstein. Essentially, they demanded that Schleswig-Holstein secede from Denmark in order to be included as an autonomous state in the German confederation.

When the demand for democracy resulted in the fall of absolute monarchy on 21 March 1848, disputes over the state-forms surfaced. The proponents of democracy in the United Monarchy could not come together in one *demos*, and a civil war broke out. It was not a war played out between the proponents of the old and the new political systems, but a war among the various proponents of democracy. The first battle in this civil war took place near Bov on 9 April 1848. The war ended in 1851 without a solution to the fundamental problems, in part because the major powers in Europe would not allow changes to the borders that had been agreed upon in the *Congress of Vienna*.

The constitution that was instated on 5 June 1849 was regarded as radical, and the Eider-state was therefore connected with the democratic constitution in a dangerous way for Prussia, Austria, and Russia. Even though democratic voices were suppressed in Germany and Austria and never had a foothold in Russia, the rulers of these countries did not find it desirable to have the constitution extended to Schleswig as well. This meant that the democracy instated in 1849 ended up applying only in the Kingdom (that is, to Kongeåen). The fact of the matter was that the United Monarchy got two constitutions: one for the Kingdom and one for the duchies.

From 1851 to 1864 the main question was still whether it was possible and desirable to implement democracy as a political system in a federation, in the Eider-state or in two states – the Kingdom and Schleswigholstein. In 1850 the lawyer and civil servant A.S. Ørsted tried to reason with his fellow countrymen by warning them against new nationalistic movements in the Kingdom as well as in the duchies. He published a historical and state-judicial writing, *For the sake of the Danish state's preservation in its entirety*, in which he defended ethnic pluralism against the national liberals. In the introduction, he wrote: "The considerations, in regards to the relations between Denmark and the duchies Schleswig and Holstein, which I hereby put forth to my fellow countrymen are so divergent from the conceptions, which, in stark internal conflict, by now have developed and finally achieved an almost absolute control, in one or the other part of the state's population, that there seems to be no prospect of them getting through"(Ørsted 1850, iii).

Ørsted knew that the odds of reasoning with the two parties, the Danes and the Schleswigholsteinians, had not improved with the events that had "caused dissension and finally civil war in our previously happy fatherland" (Ørsted 1850, iv). Indeed, they had done quite the opposite. Nonetheless, he made a final heroic attempt to avoid the dissolution of the United Monarchy by working out a plan for its preservation. He proposed a renewal of the monarchy, "wherein all peoples, united by the Danish sceptre, ought to seek out their salvation" (Ørsted 1850, 338). Ørsted considered the king to be the symbol of unity that was to bring the people together in one common state. This way of thinking, however, was in opposition to the demand for a free constitution with the people – rather than the king – in the symbolic centre. This turned out to be decisive.

Not until the defeat in 1864 to Prussia and the loss of Holstein, Schleswig, and Lauenburg did the solution appear. With the loss of the duchies, Denmark was close to fulfilling the ideal requirements of a nation-state (that is, the co-extension of state, language, culture, and territory). There were, however, two elements that disturbed the idyllic image.

One of these elements was that the North Atlantic isles could not, without further ado, be regarded as a part of the Danish nation-state. The other – and far more crucial – problem was that 200,000 Danes fell under German rule. The last matter did not get straightened out until the reorganization of Europe after World War I, which led to a plebiscite in Schleswig and the subsequent division of the old duchy. The northern half was incorporated into Denmark; the southern part remained German.

THE ETHNOS-STRATEGY

Why was it possible to establish a democratic federation in Switzerland and Belgium but not in Denmark? Why was a federal model not chosen in Denmark? What went wrong? As Brendan O'Leary points out, there are few good examples of the establishment of democratic federations that have been able to concurrently and successfully regulate the conflict between different ethnic communities. In successful cases, the communities have lived in relative segregation. "In Belgium, Canada and Switzerland the success of federalism in conflict-regulation, such as it is, had been based upon the historic accident that the relevant ethnic communities are quite sharply geographically segregated" (O'Leary 2001, 50). In the United Monarchy of Denmark, there was actually a relatively clear-cut division between the German and the Danish-language communities that went right through the middle of Schleswig – approximately where the current border was drawn in 1920. This indicates that it was possible for the United Monarchy to become a democratic federation like Switzerland and Belgium.

The ethnically based nationalism played a major role in the creation of the Danish nation and was in part the reason that no federation was founded. The predominant view turned out to be that the borders of the *demos* and the *ethnos* should coincide.

This emphasis on language as the "natural" foundation of socio-political unions had enormous political consequences for Europe. The politicization of language, which Herder founded but did not unfold, shaped the political basis of the growing national groups in Europe by conferring major importance on all language communities. Poets, philologists, literati, and historians became the main champions in those "language-battles" that broke out in Europe during the nineteenth century. Even though other weapons were in use, it was language itself that turned out to have the sharpest edge.

It is ironic – or perhaps tragic – that the tropes through which the linguistic or cultural nationalism took part in the construction of a Danish national sentiment were developed by the "enemy" – the Germans. And the more one depended on the German conceptualization of "nation" and "national sentiment," the weaker the multinational United Monarchy became. The multilingual United Monarchy was weakened as a political entity with the politicization of the language and the nationalization of the culture. There were in Denmark – as in the multinational states of Austria and Switzerland – people who warned strongly against instating an ethnic principle of nationality as a state ideology. There was a successful balancing of the ethnic tensions in Switzerland and the Swiss maintained a multinational state by clearly distinguishing "ethnos" and "demos." There was not, on the other hand, a successful creation of a multinational state in Denmark or Austria. Though the Danish multinational state ultimately collapsed in 1864, the Republic of Austria did not break down until after World War I.

Seen in a power-political perspective, neither of the two major languages, Danish or German, was strong enough to produce a linguistically homogeneous state such as France (Weber 1976). With only marginal domination, neither a policy of "German-ization" nor one of "Danish-ization" could fulfill the goal: one people, one language, and one state. Neither of them could obtain a hegemonic status within the existing multiethnic and multinational state. And when no accord on a federal state could be attained, the aforementioned civil war ensued in 1848–51 and then the war against Prussia and Austria in 1864.

There is a remarkable difference in the ways in which Denmark and Norway came to their democratic constitutions and were transformed into modern nation-states. In Norway the 1814 revolution was a double-revolution: an implementation of the constitution as well as national independence. While Norway turned "modern" in one go, Denmark did it in three. First, the assembly of the Estates of the Realm in 1831–34; then the implementation of the democratic constitution in 1848–49, and finally, Denmark was transformed into an (almost) ethnically homogeneous nation-state from 1864 to 1920.

The modern Danish nation-state was not formed by liberating itself from a larger political unit, as was the case with Norway, Belgium, Ireland, and Hungary. Neither did it unite hitherto separated territories the way state formation occurred in Germany and Italy. Rather, "foreign" territories such as Norway, Holstein, and Schleswig were detached until the remaining part more or less corresponded to the ideals of the new nation-state – accordance of state, people, and language.

There were, however, crucial differences in the processes of linguistic homogenization in Norway and Denmark. In Norway the process was complicated by "the era of the Danes," which by 1814 had lasted for 434 years. The question there was whether the new Norwegian nation-state should maintain the old written language, which it had held in common with Denmark for hundreds of years, or, whether it should develop its own written language. Disagreement over the question resulted in an intense language feud that led to the formation of a new Norwegian written language alongside the old Danish written language (*bogmål*). It was the poet and linguist Ivar Aasen who, through the study of Norwegian dialects, created the basis of a new-Norwegian written language. In Ivar Aasen's mind *bogmål* was an improper language – it was un-Norwegian. He left Kristiania, today's Oslo, where the "elite" spoke and wrote in *bogmål,* and ventured out amongst the "people" to find the roots for a recreated Norwegian language. Arne Garborg was a distinctive spokesperson for those forces in the country that, in the last decades of the eighteenth century, advocated for the establishment of the new-Norwegian language as the sole standard language in the country. The language-feud was to Garborg a struggle for national liberation, in which the class of civil servants and officials represented the old colonists. The Danish colonists did indeed lose political power in 1814, but if the "language of power" had not been replaced with the "language of the people," the Norwegian state would still be subject to an "alien" yoke.

An essential difference between the ways the debate about nationalism played out in Denmark and in Norway is that the Norwegian language-feud between *bogmål* and new-Norwegian was not interpreted as a conflict between two different *ethnic* groups, but rather as a feud between *social* groups – the "upper class," who tried to maintain the old language of power, Danish, and the "people," who wanted to speak their own "original" language. In Denmark, however, the language-feud was made an ethnic issue. Even if the social question played an important role in the process toward democracy the feud was interpreted not only as a social struggle between the "upper-class" and the "people" but also as an ethnic-cultural struggle between Germans and Danes – between the "people" and the "foreigners" (Korsgaard 2004, 304). This element was fatal to the United Monarchy's attempt to stay united.

What was it that led to the defeat of 1864? This is one of the questions that has most occupied Danish historians. Among historians there has previously been a strong tendency to focus on the military aspects of the matter, principal among them the withdrawal from Dannevirke and the defeat at Dybbøl. But by focusing on the military aspects in the sequence of events, attention is drawn away from other aspects of identity-politics and cultural circumstances that also played a part in these events. The future of the state-form was actually not settled on the battlefield. It was settled by the particular sort of ethnonationalism that developed in Germany as well as in Denmark. While the army's withdrawal from Dannevirke must be considered an inconsequential detail in the reshaping of the Danish state, the development of national tales and edification of a symbolic order must be ascribed vital significance. It was not the fight for Dybbøl that sealed the destiny of the United Monarchy; it was rather the figure of thought and the structures of sentiments that nationalism brought out (Korsgaard 2004, 296–301).

Today, it is easy enough to scorn the nationalists of those days. The crucial question is, however, whether the Danish state could have survived as an independent state in Europe had it not been for the Danish nationalists' demand for the state to be transformed into a modern nation-state. For not only was nationalism in fashion during the nineteenth century, but the nation-states' creation of an international state-system was underway as well. And if we grant that Ernest Gellner is right, nationalism and the establishment of nation-states must be regarded as a necessary and integral part in the development of the modern industrialized state (Gellner 1994).

What we obviously cannot know is what would have happened in Denmark if Rousseau's social contract – political nationalism – had been ascribed more importance and Herder's language contract – cultural nationalism – less. We can never know if this would have led to the conservation of the multinational and multilingual state-form, or to the obliteration of the entire state: Jutland swallowed up by Germany and the isles united with Sweden. But however that may be, Denmark was, by the defeat in 1864, reduced to being a small state in Europe.

Because the ethnically homogeneous nation-state had been regarded as the obvious framework of democracy since 1864, the question of whether a functional democracy within the framework of the United Monarchy could have been established has hardly been raised. The reason why this question has not been posed is related to the fact that nationalism, as a homogenizing factor, relies not only on the ability to remember but also on the ability to forget. After the war and in the wake of nationalism's advance, new stories and tales of what it had been like to be Danish in times past were developed and Denmark's past as a multinational state was soon forgotten.

Nationalism stages certain historical myths and allows others to slip out of our field of vision. Such a manoeuvre requires an active and conscious effort in a politics of remembrance. Danish national histories began to tell the tale of the Danish state as a historical power that had existed since the dawn of time. But in order to establish and maintain such a way of recollecting history, it was necessary that historians partook in "forgetting" and "suppressing" certain events and processes related to the creation of the nation-state. To the Danes it was about "forgetting" how bloody the transition to democracy as political system and to the nation-state as state-form had been in Denmark (Korsgaard 2004, 304–6).

THE DECLINE OF THE DANISH MANDARINS

It is common in political theory to distinguish between political nationalism and cultural nationalism. But in order to describe how the nation was built in Denmark, we need to make a further distinction between state-nationalism and popular-nationalism – a distinction between top-down and bottom-up nationalism. The state and the civil society constitute the symbolic centers of the two kinds of nationalism, and these two centers are a part of all national and democratic movements. However in certain national movements the state is regarded as the most important factor, while in others it is civil society.

As mentioned, German language- and cultural-nationalism aided the collapse of the United Monarchy. It is, however, extraordinary that Danish nationalism after 1864 came to differ radically from German nationalism. There are multiple explanations as to why the same kind of nationalism developed differently in the two countries. One is that state-nationalism in Denmark was seriously weakened by the defeat in 1864, whereas the nationalism of the populace was strengthened. This is connected with the different roles played by the academic elite in Denmark and in Germany. While the academic elite in Denmark lost its political and cultural legitimacy after 1864, in Germany, it was the academic elite who helped establish the legitimacy of the new German nation-state.

As the American historian Fritz K. Ringer documents in his classic book *The Decline of the German Mandarins* (1969), the "mandarins" in Germany constituted a significant ideological factor in the development of the German nation-state. By "mandarins" Ringer is referring to the bourgeoisie of higher civil servants (priests, lawyers, professors, and doctors) that appeared in the nineteenth century. These academic elite based its authority on cultural knowledge rather than on aristocratic traditions or economic and political power. For the mandarins, *Bildung* became a key notion; it was related to "culture" and internal cultivation rather than to "civilization," with its origins in rationalism's focus on utility. As the holder and administrator of a German *Geist*, the academic elite came to be very important to the legitimacy of the German state.

In the attempt to implement democracy and create an Eider-state, the Danish national liberals came to have great cultural importance as well. When the sovereign king abdicated his throne on 21 March 1848, a new partly national-liberal government was formed. D.G. Monrad, the government's "strong man," became the first Minister of Cultural Affairs. Already by the 22 March 1848 he had taken charge of the newly established Ministry of Affairs under the official name of the Ministry of Education and Ecclesiastical Affairs (Ministeriet for Kirke-og Undervisningsvæsnet). Monrad regarded the new ministry as a ministry of nation building. His idea was to create a ministry that administered everything related to "the creation of the nation and the spiritual interests of the state in general" (Petersen 1984, 16). From the initial steps of democracy, he emphasized that the Ministry of Cultural Affairs should be involved in everything that could further the creation of the state, and this applied in particular to the field of education. He wanted to separate school and church and unify the institution of education. It is often overlooked that when Denmark became democratic there were two separate schools, the school of the common people and the school of the learned. The two institutions had each their own language of education. While Latin was the basis of the school of the learned, Danish was the language in the school of the common people. To Monrad it was crucial to the construction of the nation-state, that the difference between the two educational institutions be bridged. "For the department of education might well contain different sorts of schools but these do, however, collectively constitute a unity wherein they in junction create a chain of institutions whose individual joints interconnect and support each other" (Petersen 1984, 16).

In this passage, Monrad actually formulates the ideological foundation of the national union school (*enhedsskole*). However, more than fifty years had to pass before this ideology acquired structural and institutional consequences, and more than 100 years before the union school was fully realized.

Because Monrad was head of the government during the war with Prussia, and therefore particularly associated with the catastrophe, his power was broken in 1864. After the defeat, broken down by sorrow and an apocalyptic anxiety, he immigrated to New Zealand. But it was not only Monrad who was struck; the entire political elite of national liberals and thus the related cultural elite were crushed as well. When the Prussian soldiers stormed Dybbøl on 18 April, the political power of the national liberals was shot down, so to speak. In the parliament (*Rigsdagen*), they did not play a role in working out the revision of the constitution that was necessitated by the breakdown of the United Monarchy. Even though the national liberals rightly considered the 1849 constitution as of their making, they were left with no influence when some representatives from the peasant class joined the landowners in making the so-called revised constitution of 1866.

The defeat of the national liberals came to be a determining factor in the development of the Danish nation-state. The defeat caused a new social group, namely the peasants and their cultural shock troops – the so-called Grundtvigians – to influence this development to a degree unparalleled in the rest of Europe. In the power-vacuum that appeared in the wake of the fall of the national liberals, the Grundtvigianism of the populace was the only movement with a fairly broad appeal. The workers' movement only appeared in 1871. It was thus not the national liberals but the Grundtvigians who came to influence the establishment of the state up until the workers' movement began to take hold after World War I.

Grundtvigianism got its name from the poet, priest, and politician N.F.S. Grundtvig who lived from 1783 to 1872. As no other did, he created myths, images, and tales that added to the evolvement of a kind of nationalism among the populace in Denmark. After 1864 greater attention was paid to Grundtvig's constant call to the people for active involvement, and far greater sympathy felt for his powerful critique of the Danish mandarins' educational program, characterized by state-paternalistic ideas. In the parliament Grundtvig fought to promote a liberal society; he would by that same token phase out a series of state institutions. He proposed abolishing the military draft, and making participation in defence voluntary. He was also an advocate for the highest possible economic independence and a spokesman for the abolishment of all coercive guild systems. Freedom of choice in regard to churches and schools was of particular importance to him, and he opposed all kinds of coercion when it came to schools and education.

The Danish mandarins kept on trying to assert themselves after 1864. On the initiative of the heads of the national liberals, the Committee for Advancement of the Enlightenment of the People was founded in 1866. Liberals saw a dire need for such a committee: "Our common people, the countryside people in particular, have yet appropriated so little of the middle-class' culture and spiritual interests." The common people in particular had not really acquired an awareness of their nationality. Thus, the main task was to enlighten the people so "that the social life and the state life can be saturated by the national spirit and consciousness" (Steenstrup 1865).

In 1870 the national liberal professor H.N. Clausen all but implored from the podium at Copenhagen University for the Danish people to conform to the enlightenment that emanated from the university. "I cannot descend from this podium, whose engraving says 'in spirit and in truth' without pleading – to our people: that it must become more and more worthy of help from above, more and more able to use the help, when the time of help is at hand" (Clausen 1870, 14). In short, with the guidance of the Danish mandarins, the rest of the population should partake in academic enlightenment.

But the Danish mandarins' plea to be heard was violently swept aside by Grundtvig. In his last speech at Marielyst Højskole on 2 November 1871, less than a year before his death at 89, the always ready-for-revolt Grundtvig rejected, with an edge-of-hand blow, the thought that his own notions of cultivation were meant to bridge the gap between the learned and the people. Such a prospect, according to Grundtvig, was a great misunderstanding. In order for the people's college (højskole) to lead to human enlightenment and cultivation it must: "emanate from the people itself, [because] the so-called academic enlightenment and cultivation that emanates from the foreign ... never reaches the people as living words, nor does any good for the fatherland, but leaves the people dumb and spiritually defenceless to be ridiculed by foreigners" (Grundtvig 1965, 108).

After 1864 the Grundtvigians projected an impressive self-awareness. As the movement advanced, the "popular" became more than ever understood as a counterpoint to the state. Grundtvigians lunged at the state educational system (the common school, the Latin school, and the university), hoping to create an alternative, more "popular," system with private schools (for children) and people's colleges (for young adults). By the time of the 1864 defeat, Grundtvig's "popular" elite had begun to found a vast number of Grundtvigian private schools and people's colleges, desiring a people's enlightenment, but this time, an enlightenment by the people, with the people, and for the people. The mandarins' enlightenment, coming from "above," was to a large extent bested by this enlightenment coming from "below." For instance, the Grundtvigians succeeded in establishing a private school system alongside the public system. If we turn to the 85-year-old parish official Hans Christensen, we find a concise example of the opposition to the Danish mandarins. In 1865 he made the following proclamation in regard to the private school in Vejstrup, Fyn: "I expect these schools to provide a great deal of good for the Danish people." He was hoping that a private school would be founded in every town, "so that the other little hells [i.e., the public schools] will be left empty." Adding to that he said: "And if we look at it politically, it is then in actuality the greatest of stupidities to think that state officials can educate a people to be free" (Markussen 1988, 330).

The Danish mandarins and the Grundtvigians differed on the role of the state in the new ordering of society. Although they were in agreement in wanting to break with the strong state of the absolute monarch, they were in stark disagreement as to how radical that break should be. To the founding father, D.G. Monrad, the state had the authority to speak on behalf of the people and by that authority could intervene and regulate social behaviour. The invisible hand of liberalism cannot alone realize a society as "a good community"; it takes the control of politics' visible hand and the "morality" of society's institutions. To Monrad, the institutions of society were the corporal aspect of the community's ethical norms. To Grundtvig and the Grundtvigians, it was not the state institutions but the "free" institutions that, ethically speaking, were the corporal aspects of the national community's norms.

It was, as we know, the Danish mandarins who began to reshape the state institutions of the absolute monarchy into democratic institutions. It was Monrad, for example, who, during the making of the constitution, formulated the notion of the people's church – *Folkekirken*. Later, the "common school" was renamed the "people's school," the "common library" the "people's library," and so on. But to many of the Grundtvigians it was not enough to change old state institutions into people's institutions; rather, new people's institutions had to be founded, as for instance "open" or "free" schools, "open" congregations, and "open" associations. According to Grundtvigianism, the public school could not, due to its ties to the state, be regarded as truly "popular." Only the "open" school could be popular. By virtue of their liberal vein, the notion of the "popular" had become almost synonymous with what was outside the state. And in this manner, the notion of "popular" in Denmark came to be equivalent with the liberal notion of voluntariness.

To be "free" or "open" – as an individual, an association, a school, or a church – was to Grundtvigianism, as well as to liberalism, to be free from the power of the state. In order to maintain such freedom it was vital that the people be willing to make an effort voluntarily. Freedom and the volunteer-spirit are, in both traditions, two sides of the same matter. Freedom cannot ultimately be guaranteed by the state; only the people can secure freedom. And that can happen only with a foundation in "popular" and "civil" society. Open associations were seen as a sign of a voluntary social solidarity, which in turn was seen as the ideal for a grander popular and national society. Willingness to render voluntary and unpaid assistance was thus regarded as the ultimate test of one's civil virtues. Neither the state nor the free market could guarantee national solidarity; that depended on whether or not "popular" and "civil" society made up the moral groundwork of society in general. Grundtvigianism's ideology and its norms of behaviour were coloured by the thought that one should manage without help from the state.

The educational politics of the Danish mandarins and the Grundtvigians were alike in having an obviously national point of departure, but they differed as to their views on the state and the people. While the bourgeoisie continuously bestowed essential significance on the state institutions, in the building of the nation, the Grundtvigians relied more on institutions outside the state. The national liberals and the Grundtvigians wanted to build the nation by means of, respectively, a state-nationalism and a popular-nationalism.

Even though the Danish mandarins retained considerable influence throughout the century, it does not compare to the influence of the German mandarins in the building of the German nation-state. In Denmark, as opposed to Germany, the connection between political power and the academic elite was broken by the events leading up to the national catastrophe in 1864. While German academics intensified the effort to legitimize the state as the heart of the German nation, their Danish colleagues lost their legitimacy to act as the pillars of the state. In this way, it was of great significance to further development in Denmark that power shifted from the state-oriented academics to the non–state-oriented

Grundtvigians. This meant that the Danish version of culture-nationalism diverged from the German, which had been the common background of both the Danish mandarins and the Grundtvigians. In Denmark, popular-nationalism contributed to the democratization from "below" and popular-education contributed to the formation of the nation in the hearts of the Danish people (Korsgaard 2004, 342–7).

Not only did the Grundtvigian cultural revolution have a tremendous impact on the civil society's growth but it affected the Danish capitalist market economy as well. The internationalization of the 1870s – the first step toward globalization – meant radically increased agricultural competition. Cheap grain, predominately from the United States, gained a footing in European markets. New railroads and steamboats were the technological precondition that gradually made it possible to transport American grain to Europe while still keeping prices competitive. The crisis in Danish farming brought a demand for customs regulations; however, the call for protectionist policies never really caught on, and the agricultural industry instead responded to the crisis by shifting from grain to livestock production. This shift called for educational research and reforms of existing farming education, the establishment of a new agribusiness (i.e., the processing industry: dairies and slaughterhouses), as well as the setting up of a new distribution network. A key concern was whether agribusinesses should be governed by the laws of capitalism – as the urban industries had been – or whether they should be based on ideas of cooperation. The Danish farmers' prevailing choice was to organize agribusiness and its distribution network as cooperative companies. In the eighteen-year period from the founding of the first cooperative dairy in 1882 to 1900, no fewer that 1066 cooperative dairies were founded, as well as a considerable number of cooperative slaughterhouses. Danish agricultural products were soon thereafter considered the finest in the steadily growing British market. The developing agriculture powered general Danish industrialization up until the 1960s, and it was not until 1963 that industrial exports exceeded agricultural exports.

The way out of the agricultural crisis in the last decades of the nineteenth century has been a "grand narrative" in Danish written history. This has often been a story about a close connection between cultural and material revolution – the Grundtvigian cultural revolution and its obvious material consequences. The people's college, regarded as an institution of formation as well as an educational body – not only educating, but also creating the citizen – produced mental and cultural conditions that greatly contributed to the Danish peasantry's choice of the cooperative model (Korsgaard 1997, 191–208). The story of the Danish people's college and the cooperative movement earned international renown in the twentieth century and inspired a series of reform movements in Eastern Europe in the interwar period and in the Third World in the decades succeeding World War II.

The war of 1864 is another grand narrative in modern Danish history. The defeat meant a groundbreaking change in political thinking, as it had been expressed in Danish culture through literature and art, in historiography, and the overall Enlightenment. The Danish perception of themselves and the rest of the world were entirely altered.

The war was a turning point in German history too. With the war against Denmark in 1864, Germany, under the leadership of Bismarck, started on a road of expansionist politics, attacking Austria in 1866 and France in 1870–71. These three wars altered the geopolitical situation in Europe and confronted Denmark with the following dilemma: Was the country to be defended to the last man standing, or, was Denmark to surrender the moment it was attacked by a major power? It was an extremely intense problem. The majority of the population regarded Germany as the enemy. But it was nevertheless a hard geopolitical fact that Denmark, with its two million inhabitants, at this point was a neighbour of Europe's – and therefore the world's – strongest power. In the days following 1864, Danish military policy was based on the possible scenario of retrieving Schleswig by joining a major European power in a war on Germany. This scenario had already broken down in France's defeat in the war against Germany (1870–71). From then on, it was no longer a matter of whether Denmark should join a war in order to retrieve Schleswig, but rather whether Denmark could protect its sovereignty by military means at all. If this was not possible, could sovereignty be defended by other means? The ensuing debate came to have a considerable focus on defence priorities: Was it the nation or the state that should be defended? Should state security be based on military might? Or, should the future of the nation be grounded in the hearts of the people?

Rousseau's *Considerations on the Government of Poland* (1772) can shed light on the Danish situation. With Russia, Austria and Prussia as neighbours, Poland was surrounded by states with superior military capacity: "She has no strongholds to stop their incursions. Her depopulation makes her almost entirely defenceless" (Rousseau 1991, 167). What is Rousseau's advice to the Poles? Mainly, it is to ground the Polish republic in the hearts of the Polish people. "I can see only one way to give her the stability she lacks … it is to establish the Republic so firmly in the hearts of the Poles that she will maintain her existence there in spite of all the efforts of her oppressors" (Rousseau 1991, 167–8).

In addition, Rousseau directed the Poles on how to ground the republic in the hearts of the Polish people. It could only happen through a national system of education that fortifies the country by engendering patriotism: "It is education that must give souls a national formation, and direct their opinions and tastes in such a way that they will be patriotic by inclination, by passion, by necessity" (Rousseau 1991, 172). Poland needed a new type of defence as well: "Poland is surrounded by warlike powers which constantly maintain large standing armies which she herself could never match without soon exhausting herself" (Rousseau 1991, 182). It was impossible, in the foreseeable future, for Poland to defend herself by means of an expensive, ready army, said Rousseau. However, he added: "You will soon, or more accurately speaking, you already have the power of self-preservation, which will guarantee you, even though subjected, against destruction, and will preserve your government and your liberty in its one true sanctuary, the heart of the Polish people" (Rousseau 1991, 183). Rousseau suggested arming the people in the Swiss model: "Why not, then, instead of regular troops, a hundred times more burdensome than useful to any people uninterested in conquests, establish a genuine militia in Poland exactly as in Switzerland, where every inhabitant is a soldier, but only when necessary?" (Rousseau 1991, 185).

A hundreds years later, in a debate over Danish defence, a part of the left wing put forth a number of viewpoints similar to those found in Rousseau's *Considerations on the Government of Poland*. While the right wing proposed a ready army as the key element in the country's defence, the left wing advocated a defence based on arming the people. Grundtvig had already vehemently opposed the idea of a ready army in 1848, because he saw it suppressing the peasant class. Therefore, as Rousseau had advised the Poles, so Grundtvig recommended to the Danes: "*Men of Denmark, as truly as we all constitute a freeborn royal people; no ordinary military service of bondage, but an arming of the people in freedom*" (Grundtvig 1909, 174). And in the defence commission of 1866, hardly any of Balthazar Christensen's many contributions did not defend the idea of a "people's army," a "national guard," or an "arming of the people." As leader of the left wing group in the parliament, he wanted, as Rousseau had wanted, to make "the people an armed people" (Nielsen 1979, 77). To the left wing it was a matter of securing the people's autonomy even in matters of national defence.

The two predominant positions in the Danish defence debate were: a ready army in combination with a strong fortification of Copenhagen, or an arming of the people. There was, however, a third stand whose foremost spokesman – as pointed out by the Danish ethnologist Thomas Højrup – was the historian and politician Peter Munch. As a young historian Munch had begun to develop a new defence strategy in the 1890s. The fundamental question was: How can a minor country maintain its sovereignty in a world dominated by major powers? Munch's analysis of the international system told him that the disproportion between Denmark's and Germany's military power had, since the 1864 defeat, become impossible to overcome: "Denmark, in any battle it could possibly end up in, will be pitched against such an overwhelming superiority that no matter how great the enthusiasm, it cannot lead to anything but more peril, more bloodshed and more destruction before the already given defeat" (Højrup 2002, 333).This perspective implies that military defence was hopeless: "If the Danish people built their future on military defence it would not build on the foundation of reality but on the most fragile of illusions." To Munch neutrality was the only possible way for Denmark to preserve itself, and furthermore, neutrality alone would not be enough. The sovereignty of the country must still be defended but with means other than military. The sovereignty must be defended by establishing a society and a culture that make it possible to survive as a people even if the territory is occupied for a while. Here Munch drew on Poland as an example. Even though the Polish state had been conquered a hundred years earlier (Poland was split between Russia, Prussia, and Austria in 1795), the Polish nationality was, according to Munch, "stronger today than it had been a hundred years ago." And went on to predict: "*It is not impossible that Poland, yet again, can partake in world history*" (Højrup 2002, 333). In Denmark it was fundamental to avoid creating the illusion that the country could be defended by the military: "And truly, it is of no misfortune to the people that they cannot sustain the creation of such a belief in defence. It is a quite unfounded and unsound claim that believing one can defend oneself is a vital-necessity for a people, a precondition for it to maintain its vitality and liveliness" (Højrup 2002, 334).

The lack of capacity to defend the country militarily must, according to Munch, be met with a will to form a society that the population appreciates; that is to say, with a national project that the people can be proud of and identify with.

The means for this end is to enlarge our culture and to create solidarity in the Danish people by developing such states in the society that all layers of the people have reason to embrace our country and its people with warm affection. Often is this sentence mocked: It is by culture and not by weapons that we shall defend ourselves. This mockery comes from people who are not capable of understanding the meaning of the sentence. The intention is of course not that the weapons shall fall from the hands of enemies in respect for our culture. It follows that no culture ever so distinguished can guarantee the subsistence of a state as state. But a free and self-reliant culture that permeates all layers of the people can, however, create safeguarding for the subsistence of the people's national life, even if the misfortune should come upon us, and the state, by the brutal laws of war and conquest, succumbed to the will of foreign violators. (Højrup 2002, 334)

This perspective on the future of Denmark became the basis of the party platform of the Social Liberal Party *(Det Radikale Venstre)*, in the so-called *Odenseprogram* of 1905. The *Odenseprogram* was prefaced with the statement: "Denmark declares itself continuously neutral." Then five platform planks laid the foundation of the society and culture that were to replace the military defence of the state. Munch's policies were: to defend the country by arranging the foreign and military politics according to the will of the major neighbour and, as an alternative to conventional defence, to build a strong internal defence primarily through social, educational, and cultural politics. What could not be known in 1905 was that the *Odenseprogram* formulated what later came to be the basic principle of the welfare state, which was established in the twentieth century. The main founders of this state-form were the Social Democrats *(Socialdemokratiet)*, but it took place in close correlation with the Social Liberal Party.

THE *DEMOS* STRATEGY

For the Social Democrats, the relations between socialism, democracy, and nation-state were an unresolved ideological issue up until World War I. First of all, was it possible to implement socialism within the framework of liberal democracy? Second, was it possible to implement socialism in only one nation-state without a concurrent world-revolution? In different ways, two events helped reveal the solution: the outbreak of World War I and the Russian Revolution. The breakout of World War I was to many social democrats a painful realization of how national comradeship proved primary to international relationships. At the same time, the Russian Revolution in 1917 finally split socialism into social democratic and communistic factions. The essential difference between the two factions was their relation to democracy. While the Leninist version of communism sought to implement socialism through a dictatorship of the proletariat, the social democrats wanted to implement socialism through democracy.

In Denmark, it was the leading social democrat F. Borgbjerg who first formulated the ideological consequences of the experiences leading up to the commencement of World War I. In a speech on the First International and the war in August 1914, he emphasized that the national was a prerequisite for the international and that the aim must be to establish national social democratic parties. After World War I the social democratic strategy in Denmark and the rest of Scandinavia was laid out in order to create socialism on a national and democratic foundation; the democratic nation-state was now the main framework for building the social state.

It was the Swedish social democrat Per Albin Hansson who in 1928 made "the People's Home" *(Folkhemmet)* a key notion in the party's ideology. Rather than *Folkhemmet*, the political platform "Denmark for the people" *(Danmark for folket)* became the ideological motto among social democrats in Denmark. This platform was passed under the leadership of the social democratic prime minister, Thorvald Stauning, in 1934. The same year Oscar Hansen wrote the song *"Danmark for folket."* No longer should there be a people's table and a master's table but "room for us all by the table of society" (*Højskolesangbogen* 1994). Stauning's greatest political achievement was *Kanslergadeforliget* in 1933, whereby the four leading parties entered a historic settlement on a series of social reforms intended to counter the social consequences of the Great Depression. This was the foundation of the welfare state, though the establishment did not really catch on until after World War II.

It was not only the Nordic social democrats that had a social armament, however. Soviet Communism and German National Socialism had in their platforms distinct ideas of the welfare state (Mazower 1999, 76–103). The coupling of socialism and nationalism was a common element in Stalin's communism, Hitler's national socialism, and Stauning's socialism. But only in Stauning's version were these elements coupled with democracy.

The coupling of the democratic and the social is key to the understanding of the nation and the people that was gradually developed by the social democrats in the interwar period. The strategy was to create as strong a tie as possible among the "social," the "national," and the "democratic." The national and democratic foundation of Denmark's society should be strengthened by means of a social, rather than a military armament. In order to protect the country from external threats, neutrality should be the basis of the foreign policy. Likewise, social policy should secure the country internally by offering society solidarity; this would be effected by bringing those in the worst positions to acknowledge the state and the society as theirs.

What everybody had feared came true on the 9 April 1940 when the country was occupied by Germany. Denmark surrendered with virtually no military resistance. (Munch was foreign minister at this point.) The belief that the Danish nation could be maintained even though the Danish state was occupied was now to be tested. The leading national strategist of this battle came to be the theologian Hal Koch. He did not pay too much attention to the contrast between Denmark and Germany. According to his interpretation, it was not as much a war between nations as it was a war between political systems – a war between democracy and totalitarianism. In the struggle against the occupiers it was crucial to strengthen and maintain a democratic mindset in Denmark, particularly in the youth (Korsgaard 1997, 348–57; Korsgaard 2004, 452–6).

In the fall of 1940 Koch was asked to be the president of the newly established Danish Youth Association (*Dansk Ungdomssamvirke*), whose aim was to counter the impact of Nazism on young Danes. He stipulated that the aim of the association should be to politicize Danish youth. In dissociating itself from the common view of the "cultural" as unifying and the "political" as dividing, Koch's understanding of the political came as a surprise to a lot of people.

"Usually I would be one to caution people who talk too much about the 'cultural.' As it is a very dangerous word it leads to abstract talk of 'our thousand year legacy,' 'what it means to be Danish' and the 'deep cultural values.' It is things like these that make Nazism flourish. If you dig down into the cultural it shows, that 'the cultural does not unify, it divides.' And that is the way it should be. There is a vast difference between cultures in the life of a peasant woman from western Jutland as opposed to a lady of the bourgeoisie in Copenhagen. What is common is to be found elsewhere: 'When it comes down to it, it is the political that ties us together'" (Koch 1942, 16). That is to say, the democratic.

Nazism and fascism confronted Koch with a question: what was supposed to keep the Danish society together? When the anti-democratic ideologies began advocating national-cultural values it was necessary, according to Koch, to change strategy and emphasize *demos* at the expense of *ethnos* as the binding or unifying factor. Political-democratic values should be strengthened instead of national-cultural values. The key term in Koch's theory of democracy was for that reason not a national-cultural mindset, but rather the notion of democratic fellow-citizenship.

Koch is an exponent of the general tendency that shows up after the war, giving low priority to the *ethnos* and high priority to the *demos*. At that same time an extension of the notion of democracy was coalescing. It is perhaps illuminating to refer to David Held, who distinguishes between two types of democracy, a *protective* and a *developmental* democracy (Held 1996, 99–116). In protective democracy the most important task of society is to protect fundamental human rights, such as the right of property. That means that there are certain limits to the kind of decisions that can be made within a democracy. A majority cannot, for instance, make an act to considerably reduce the right of property, or of freedom of speech or the press. In a developing democracy, democracy is regarded as being more than a fixed set of rules. Democracy is something that needs to evolve in order to include economic, social, and cultural dimensions as well.

In Denmark, the preparations for the shift from *protective* democracy to *developmental* democracy was made during World War II, and then realized by the Social Democrats after the war. While liberal democracy was emphasizing the protection of the individual's freedom *from* the acts of state, social democracy was emphasizing a realization of the economic and social rights *via* the state (Slagstad 1987, 257). There is a marked difference in state size in these two models of democracy: on the one hand we have an idea of a highly restricted authority, and on the other, an expansive state-regulation wherein the accomplishment of political aims determines the extension of the state.

In Denmark, Koch became the leading advocate of the *demos*-strategy. In an important article, "The Hour of Reckoning" (*Opgørets time*) from December 1943, he stressed vehemently that the *demos*-strategy would be the template for the politics of the post-war period. These politics must be based on strong ties between "the social," "the national," and "the democratic," he wrote. "The postwar period's real – not to say only – problem is whether national solidarity can be exchanged with an actual economic community where the burdens dealt match the abilities to carry – not the ability to shove ... We have to demand that future economic and social regards turn out so that we in D.U. (*Dansk Ungdomssamvirke*) can retain the same praise of solidarity and community – retain it even when we are faced with the pressure from within" (Fonsmark 1990, 54–5).

With this article, Koch clearly drew out his position on the priority of "the social" and "the economic" in the post-war period. He reckoned on the acknowledgment that everybody was in the same boat by virtue of a national and cultural community. His position was that a national 'boat-community' required a prior social and economic community; and a national community could only be established if there was a just distribution of goods. He therefore proposed a decisive displacement in the understanding of "the national." The national had to be made of social and economic content rather than spiritual and cultural. The welfare state can be seen as an incarnation of the view that democracy is not only a form of politics, but a form of society and a form of life as well.

Hence Koch referred several times to Russia as an ideal when talking about social and economic rights, even though he simultaneously maintained a critical distance from the political system. In "What is democracy?" (*Hvad er demokrati?*) from 1945 he wrote: "Soviet-Russia does not yet seem to have reached democracy politically. On the other hand, one must not forget that they have made an effort in another respect: They have first and foremost been preoccupied with creating an economic democracy. In that respect Western Europe still has a lot to learn" (Koch 1970, 25–6).

In Koch's view, the financial crisis of the 1930s had been a vital factor in the advance of totalitarian systems and the crisis of democracy. He therefore did not believe that a political democracy could last without a concomitant social and economic democracy. Koch became one of the great ideologues in the building of the welfare state after World War II.

With the war coming to an end, it was time to breathe life into some of the thoughts on the organization of society and democracy which had been developing during the war. Many of the political controversies that had characterized the period from 1920 to 1940 were minimized considerably thanks to the war's politics of cooperation. There was for that reason a strong political agreement to solidify democracy, and it was intended to come about through a democratization of new areas of society. This point of view came out most clearly in the Social Democrats' party platform "The Future Denmark" *(Fremtidens Danmark)*, which was passed in 1945. The platform emphasized that "democracies have to show, not only that can they win the war but that they can also provide safety" *(Fremtidens Danmark* 1945, 6). Democracy should include not only the political field but the economic field as well: "Democratization must be followed through. Concurrent with the completion of the political democracy, economic democracy must be realized" *(Fremtidens Danmark* 1945, 14). Economic democracy was a catchword with broad appeal just after the war. Even five of the Parliament's seven political parties used the term in their political platforms. This bears witness to a broad appeal of the *demos*-strategy after the war.

The Social Democrats regarded education as a boon that should be more justly distributed; it was also a weapon against the class structure of society. The strategy of the parties' educational politics was based on two principles. On one level, the access to education had to be democratized; on another, the educational institutions were to bring people up to be democratic citizens. After the war, when Koch was head of the Youth Commission, the commission put out it "Report on Youth's Access to Higher Education" *(Ungdomskommissionens betænkning om ungdommens adgang til den højere uddannelse)*. It argued that the liberal principle of formal equality in education needed to be realized and that longer education should be made accessible to more children and young adults. "The desire for education to be democratized is therefore first and foremost a demand for society to uphold the inherent justice in the concept of democracy to the individual citizen regardless of standing and social position" (Korsgaard 1999, 91).

The ideology of the school system during the first decade after the war was based on a social notion of equality more than a liberal notion of freedom. But it was a part of the consensus in education policies that equality presupposed schools' autonomy in contributing to the realization of political aims. Schools should be allowed to develop the field independent of market forces. Even though education policies in general were put in an economic growth perspective, this did not mean that schools had to be organized accordingly. Their primary task was not to produce economic growth but social equality. An ideological demarcation was drawn between schools on the one hand and capital, market, and production on the other. This demarcation was supposed to ensure schools' undivided attention to democratic upbringing. Union-schools were regarded as the main resource for furthering democracy. Schools should train students in tolerance and cooperation in spite of differences in social situation and skills.

In order to reach this goal many hoped to uproot schools' competitive mentality by, for instance, reducing the pressure from examinations.

WELFARE AS DEFENCE

When Denmark joined NATO in 1949, the country made a radical break with more than a hundred years of a politics of neutrality. This shift in defence policy and matters of national security was linked to a demand for a higher defence budget, which was a particular sore spot for the Social Democrats. Confronted with NATO and the American government's demand for increased defence budgets, the Social Democratic leaders were nevertheless successful in getting sympathy for their views; that welfare should not be regarded as a luxury, but as an essential element in the defence strategy against Communism. Jens Otto Krag was the strategist accountable for conjuring up the image that displayed the communists inside Europe as the greatest threat. Countering that threat primarily required a struggle against communism inside the country, and this struggle could not be won by military means; it required social means. "Moderation must be displayed in the demands on defence in the European countries. What good does it do us to arm Europe with a strong defence if we at the same time lower the standard of living, which will allow the internal communism to flourish." And in addition he said: "What good does it do us to have a defence that keeps ... communism away from the main gate, if it comes sneaking in the back?" (Lidegaard 2001, 425).

The Social Democrats argued from this perspective on national security, claiming that increased welfare would rob communism of its strongest weapon: social impoverishment, ignorance, and misery. When this strategy was developed, the Soviet Union still had social and material results to show for itself that were alluring to many in Western Europe. The Social Democrats' argument against the American demand for an increase in defence budgets was that if the population's living conditions were not improved quickly, no armaments or ideological war, no matter how strong, would be enough to remove the attraction of communism. It was for that reason vital that capitalism got a social face. And in reverse, if capitalism could show a bigger production and a distribution of goods broad enough to supply everyone, it would provide a greater security than any military armaments could ever do. The Social Democrats managed to get some sympathy for their point of view in the American government and were therefore able to continue their old social and educational policies alongside the new defence politics and matters of national security.

With the acceptance of welfare as a form of defence, it was possible for Denmark, with the Social Democrats as the primary advocates, to establish a welfare state. An important prerequisite for the party's welfare policy was an economic policy based on two pillars: plan and market. The Social Democrats' congressional manifesto of 1953 stated that *regulating* methods as well as open competition should be used. With this manifesto, the structure was laid out for the production sector that would finance the construction of the welfare state. It was thus prime-minister-to-be Jens Otto Krag's abiding idea that it was possible through a proper control of the national economy to create unprecedented wealth and economic drive. Crisis and massive unemployment were not given, but were merely social phenomena that could be countered through state planning and political control. Their reason for the confidence in the state as a regulating factor was without doubt the financial crisis and the massive unemployment of the interwar period. After 1945 there was sympathy for the point of view that public intervention in the market economy should protect society from problems like those of the interwar period. The economy should be placed under political restrictions.

The Social Democrats were the main driving force giving the state a social form. The kernel of this state-form was that the state should intervene and create symmetry within the population by compensating for the asymmetry the market created. Social rights should be strengthened in order to correct the inequalities that came with the market economy. Inspired by J.M. Keynes, young economists with social democratic affiliations drew up the blueprint of the welfare state. The welfare state should: secure the basic social and economic safety of every citizen; provide everybody with a decent residence, and access to hospitals as well as education; and replace poverty-aid with the right to receive aid. Further, democratic citizenship was to be based on certain rights that would be valid for everyone without regard to social or economic status. It was important to experience "the feeling of being a citizen with rights," wrote Krag in reference to the law on public pensions of 1956, which guaranteed everybody a basic amount of money. And he added, "Democratic freedom now has a social content" (Krag 1956). The underlying political idea was that social rights ensure an equality of status in relation to the state and an independence from the market.

A key element in the social democratic model was the concept of the "friendly state." The strategic aspect of the model was a strong and expansive public sector, a strategy at odds with a series of liberal ideas and Grundtvigian concepts, which, as mentioned, had a fundamental state-scepticism at their core. But during and following World War II, a number of Grundtvigians – like Koch – began to approach the social democratic perspective on the state. The establishment of the welfare state did not lead to a complete abandonment of liberal ideas, however. The welfare state – as opposed to a totalitarian system – was ultimately based on a liberal view of the state. Of course, the state did to a large extent take over the roles of the family and private institutions as up-bringers and norm-setters, but this upbringing and disciplining was combined with individual participation and influence. Furthermore, it seems that the welfare state's individualization of rights has furthered the individualization of the last decade's progression of society. According to Ove Kaj Pedersen, the welfare state has managed to allow the individual to take responsibility for the community without intruding upon the individual's rights to freedom. On the contrary, these rights have been furthered. Making the individual responsible for the community is a needed new form of regulation which is founded on individualization (Pedersen 1994, 125).

A CLOSING REMARK AND A QUESTION MARK

Looking back on the procession of events since the mid-1800s, the development of Danish identity and society has been propelled by political programs of three different "classes." The National Liberals caused the shift that replaced the monarch with the people as the centre of the symbolic order. In spite of their economic liberalism, the National Liberals emphasized the importance of state institutions in matters of national integration. A national fellowship had to be created, not by the "invisible hand" of the market, but by the "visible" hand of politics and the moral conduct of state institutions. The National Liberals' loss of political and cultural legitimacy after 1864 was significant for the future face and shape of Danish nationalism.

In the power vacuum that appeared in the wake of the National Liberals' demise, and before the workers' movement had emerged, popular Grundtvigianism was the only movement with any general appeal. In contrast to the National Liberals, the Grundtvigians regarded civil society, not the state, as the complement of the people; "popular," in the Danish context, became almost synonymous with what is understood as external to the state in the liberal tradition. This move from state to civil society was more than just an ideological shift; it was also a shift dictated by the fact that, up until 1901, landowners and the king had the power to block access to the government.

The Social Democrats clarified the notions *people* and *nation* during World War I. The nation was not just a stage in historical development that belonged to the past; rather, the nation was the basis for the realization of democracy and socialism. This link between democracy and sociality, developed by the Social Democrats during the interwar period, came to be at the heart of the future conception of the nation. Stauning's greatest political feat was to make the Social Democrats accept the notion of the people as politically correct, a feat that was completed by the party platform of 1934 "Denmark for the People" *(Danmark for folket).* The developed conception of people was fundamentally different from the Nazi notion of people. It was a conception based not on a race-ideology but on a combination of social and political ideology. During the war, it was Hal Koch who made the greatest contribution to formulating a national compromise uniting the liberal and the social democratic conceptions of state, nation, people, and democracy. This compromise became the foundation for the creation in the postwar period of the welfare state, governed by socialistic as well as liberal ideals. The welfare state, however, was based not only in a social political, but also in an identity political program. Welfare and Danishness were one and the same. To be Danish was to identify with the Danish welfare project.

During the last fifty years the welfare state, more than anything else, is what has grounded the nation in the heart of the Danish people. Today, however, we are confronted with the alarming question: Is this way of grounding the nation losing its power as a result of expanding globalization and migration?

NOTES

Translation by Kelly and Christopher Kyst

4

Late Nineteenth-Century Denmark in an Irish Mirror

Land Tenure, Homogeneity, and the Roots of Danish Success

KEVIN H. O'ROURKE

Denmark is not only a smaller country than Eire but her climate is less equable, her soils are, in general, lighter and poorer, she has no coal and no water power to compensate for its absence, nor has she any iron ore or other metallic ores to serve as a basis for industrial activities. Yet, in comparison with Eire, she has a bigger population, a greater agricultural output, a more extensive industrial system, a larger foreign trade, a lower national debt, a higher national income and a better standard of living. It is the purpose of this paper to throw some light on this unusual economic paradox. (Beddy 1943, 189)

It might seem odd for a book about Denmark to have a chapter focused on Ireland. However, much can be learned about late nineteenth-century Denmark by comparing the two countries. The strategy of placing the countries in a comparative context can help us not only to evaluate the scale of Denmark's economic achievements but also to think more deeply about the roots of Danish success. Indeed, any convincing explanation for that success is ultimately going to have to be comparative in nature, whether the comparisons are explicit or implicit. The method typically used by economists seeking to explain why some countries grow more rapidly than others is the cross-country growth regression; yet the average correlations that such exercises yield can often conceal as much as they reveal. An important motive behind this chapter is precisely the desire to move beyond such regressions; as the editors emphasize in their introduction to this volume, country studies (and, I would add, comparative country studies) can yield important additional information about the mechanisms at work in particular places and at particular times. Serious comparative studies of the economic growth experiences of different economies have been rare in recent years, although they were a staple of an earlier generation of economic historians: Joel Mokyr's (1976) dissertation on industrialization in Belgium and Holland remains one of the few examples of the genre within an explicitly cliometric framework. Such studies are of particular use when they focus on pairs of countries which a priori seemed to have equivalent growth potentials, but which ex post performed very differently; in this case, Mokyr's method may help us isolate the factor or factors that were particularly important in shaping the different outcomes.

Ireland is a good country with which to compare Denmark, since the two countries were in so many respects similar during the late nineteenth century. Not only did both have access to large markets, but their major market was the same: Britain. Since Britain was an open economy at the time, any differences between the two countries' performances must be due to supply side, rather than demand side, factors. Geographically, Denmark and Ireland are Britain's two next-door neighbours, and both have northern European climates and abundant coastlines, factors generally associated with successful economic performance (Mellinger et al. 2000). They are of similar size, with Ireland being larger: 20.3 m. acres (13.3 m. ha) as opposed to Denmark's 9.6 m acres (6.3 m. ha).[1] Their natural resources are also similar: lacking the large coal and ore deposits so often associated with growth in the late nineteenth century, they both specialized in similar agricultural products. Finally, they both pursued liberal economic policies, adhering in particular to agricultural free trade throughout the late nineteenth century.

There were, however, some important differences between the two countries, largely if not exclusively in the political and social domains. First, and most obvious, Denmark was an independent country, with its own government, whereas Ireland was a part of the United Kingdom. Denmark's generally liberal policies were thus the result of Danish decisions, while Irish liberalism arose from British decisions. Second, Denmark was an extremely homogeneous society, as a result of the territorial losses emphasized by Uffe Østergård (chapter 1). By contrast, there were important religious and political cleavages within Ireland, and so Irish political debate involved competing nationalisms, as had Danish debate prior to 1864. Third, Irish emigration by far exceeded Danish emigration, although the exodus from Denmark was by no means insignificant in the late nineteenth century. While this difference was presumably related to Ireland's less successful economic development, the very fact that Irish labour markets were so tightly integrated with their American counterparts had potentially important knock-on implications for the way in which its economy and society operated. And finally, as mentioned in the intro-duction to this volume, land reform came early in Denmark – as early as the late eighteenth century – while in Ireland the "Land Question" was still inflaming passions a hundred years later.

This chapter can only be a first step in a thorough comparison of eco-nomic growth in these two countries in the late nineteenth and early twen-tieth centuries. As such, it aims more to set out a research agenda than to provide comprehensive answers to what are, after all, difficult questions. In the first section I present some comparative data on the two countries' economies between the middle of the nineteenth century and World War I, identifying some of the stylized facts that any comparative history of the two countries should address. After placing both countries' economic per-formances within the context of the highly globalized economy of the late nineteenth century, I ask to what extent the recent literature on the first great wave of globalization can explain those relative performances. The bottom line is that the international economic literature is helpful in this regard, but in many ways leaves us with even more questions to answer.

I next survey the existing economic history literature, asking why Ireland did not do as well as Denmark (not surprisingly, there has been much less interest among Danes in comparing the two countries). After identifying hypotheses that might help resolve the question, I shall evaluate them on the basis of recent research by Ingrid Henriksen and myself. The dairy industry is a major focus, since it was a key sector in both countries, and since the dairy cooperatives that emerged in Denmark at the time repre-sented a rapid technological and institutional innovation in response to an external shock that threatened traditional Danish agriculture (the inva-sion of overseas grain, combined with German agricultural protection). The episode thus illustrates both an early Danish capacity for learning and flexibility and the Danish ability to devise mechanisms that built up trust in society – all features of late twentieth-century Denmark stressed else-where in this volume.

COMPARING DENMARK AND IRELAND: FROM THE GREAT FAMINE TO THE GREAT WAR

Unfortunately, no official Irish GDP statistics are available from before the late 1930s, so what little we know about late nineteenth-century trends in Irish living standards comes from two benchmark estimates (Mokyr 1985 and Ó Gráda 1994). Joel Mokyr's revised estimate of about £80 m. in 1845 puts Ireland's GDP per capita at roughly 40 percent of Britain's; Cormac Ó Gráda's 1913 estimate of £135 m. places Ireland's relative income per capita at about 57 % of Britain's on the eve of the Great War. We can com-pare these numbers with the ratio of Danish to UK (not British) income

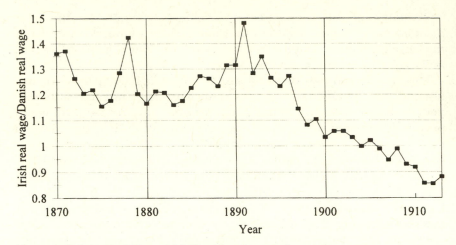

Figure 1   Relative Real Wages, Irish/Danish real wage, 1870–1913
Source: Williamson (1995), amended in O'Rourke and Williamson (1997).

per capita in 1840 and 1913; but unfortunately, the latter figures depend on the methods used to compare prices in the two countries. The two best estimates available are those of Angus Maddison (1995) and Leandro Prados (2000), which imply that Irish national income per head rose from 56 to 68 percent of Danish GDP per capita between the two dates (according to the Maddison data, revised in Prados 2000, Table 9) or from 63 to 71 percent (according to the Prados data, ibid.).

However, this rise in per capita income does not imply that Ireland's late nineteenth-century performance was superior to Denmark's, for one simple reason: 1840–45 was the eve of the Irish Famine, which reduced the Irish population from some 8.5 million to roughly 6.5 million in just six years. Moreover, since those who died were the poorest members of society, the famine thus raised the country's average income by an unknown but presumably significant amount.[2] Until we know to what extent Irish incomes per capita were raised as a result of the famine, it will be impossible to assess the relative GDP performances of these two economies from the mid-nineteenth century onward.

We do have wage data for unskilled, urban male workers in the building trades from 1870 onward, however (the Irish data going back to 1830), and these have been purchasing-power-parity adjusted to make them comparable across countries (Williamson 1995). Figure 1 shows the ratio of Irish to Danish real wages; what may be surprising to some readers is that Irish wages were substantially higher than Danish wages between 1870 and the mid-1890s, with the margin in Ireland's favour ranging between 20

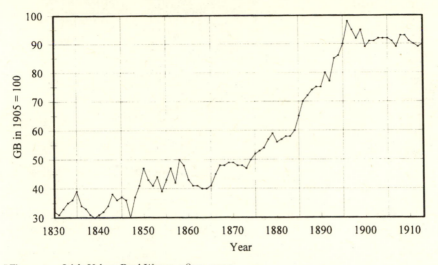

Figure 2   Irish Urban Real Wages, 1870–1913

Source: Williamson (1995), amended in O'Rourke and Williamson (1997).

and 40 percent. As Figure 2 shows, however, these high Irish wages were achieved largely as a result of the famine and the ensuing emigration: Irish real wages were stagnant from 1830 to the late 1840s, rose discretely in the aftermath of the famine, and then continued to rise from the mid-1860s onward.[3]

From the mid-1890s, however, Danish wages caught up strongly on Irish wages, and overtook them in the early twentieth century; Irish wages were between 10 and 15 percent lower than their Danish counterparts on the eve of World War I. Living standards therefore became substantially lower in Ireland than in Denmark from the 1890s onward. Even more telling are data that show how many people could be supported at these wage rates. In 1841 the Irish population stood at 8.2 million, while Denmark's population was a mere 1.3 million (Figure 3). Even after the famine of the late 1840s, there were still 4.5 times as many people in Ireland as in Denmark. Uniquely, however (since populations typically recover after famines: see Watkins and Menken 1985 and Ó Gráda and O'Rourke 1997), Ireland's population continued to decline, and stood at only 4.4 million in 1911; on the eve of World War I, Ireland's population was only 53 percent higher than Denmark's, which had grown steadily throughout the period. An economy that maintained its wages largely as a result of population decline (of which more later) was evidently not as healthy as one in which living standards could grow alongside population. It was above all the declining population (which, in the twenty-six counties that later formed the Irish

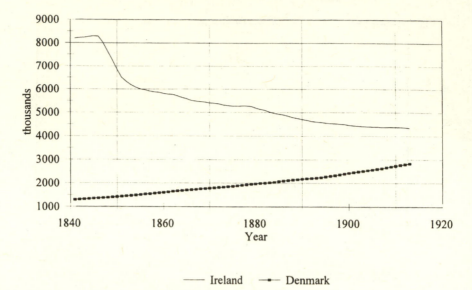

Figure 3   Population, 1841–1913

Source: Johansen (1985), Mitchell (1988).

Republic, persisted until the 1960s) that perturbed Irish commentators and symbolized for them Irish "failure."

Both Ireland and Denmark were largely agricultural economies in the late nineteenth century. Ó Gráda (1994, 383) estimates that agriculture accounted for about 38% of Irish national income in 1914; the corresponding figure for Denmark was 31.8% (Johansen 1985, 392). Agriculture's share of the male labour force (including forestry and fishing) declined from 58% to 48% in Denmark between 1860 and 1911; the corresponding Irish figures were 56% (1861) and 54% (Mitchell 1992, 143, 148). Figure 4 shows that while Ireland's real agricultural output was flat between the Great Famine and the Great War, Denmark's output more than quadrupled over the same period. In nominal terms, while Ireland's agricultural output had been more than four times that of Denmark in 1850, it was lower than Denmark's by 1914 (Figure 5).

Table 1 shows that this relative performance was not due just to aggregate population movements; between 1871 and 1911, real output per male agricultural worker almost quadrupled in Denmark, but rose less than 80% in Ireland. Nominal output per worker was roughly similar in the two countries in the 1870s, but Ireland was overtaken in the crucial 1880s, and by 1911 Danish output per worker was more than 50% higher than Ireland's. These contrasting productivity performances are reflected in milk yields, which in Ireland on the eve of the Great War were at most

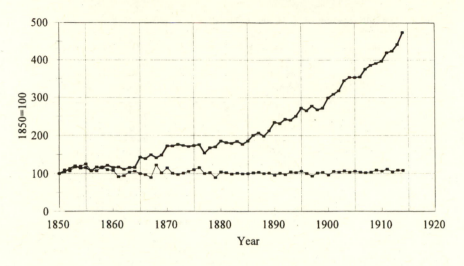

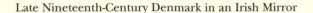

Figure 4   Real Agricultural Output, Ireland and Denmark, 1850–1914

Source: Turner (1996), Hansen (1984).

Figure 5   Nominal Agricultural Output, Ireland and Denmark, 1850–1914

Source: Turner (1996), Hansen (1984).

Table 1   Agricultural Output per capita, 1871–1911

	Real output/male agricultural worker		Nominal output/male agricultural worker	
Year	Denmark 1871=100	Ireland 1871=100	Denmark pounds	Ireland pounds
1871	100	100	41.9	42.6
1881	94	105	40.6	45.0
1891	110	110	49.1	45.4
1901	239	138	73.6	51.4
1911	388	178	106.0	68.2

Sources: Index numbers taken from Turner (1996, 159). Nominal output per capita figures calculated from Turner (1996), 108, Johansen (1985, 153–5), Mitchell (1976, 154, 157) and Mitchell (1988, 108). Danish figures converted to pounds at the gold standard exchange rate of 18.16 kroner per pound.

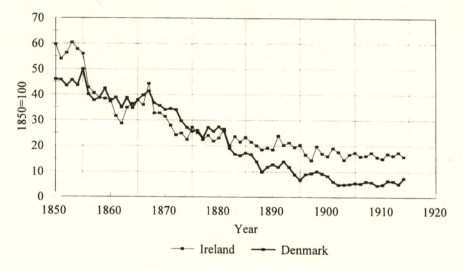

Figure 6   Crops' Share of Agricultural Output, Ireland and Denmark, 1850–1914
Source: Turner (1996), Hansen (1984).

400 gallons per cow, up from maybe 350 gallons in the mid-1850s (Solar 1989–90, 153) – an increase of 14% over some sixty years. It was reckoned by contemporaries that they were maybe 100 gallons lower in Connaught (IAOS 1914, 11). By contrast, Danish milk yields rose by 22% in the 15 years before 1914, by which time they stood at some 700 gallons per cow (Statistiske Meddelelser 1915, 42; Smith-Gordon and Staples 1917, 111).

What was happening to the structure of agricultural production in the two economies? Figure 6 shows that the share of crops in agricultural out-

Table 2   Distribution of Agricultural Land (Percent)

Denmark

Year	Cereal	Potato	Other root	Grass
1861	45.5	1.4	0.1	53.0
1866	46.0	1.6	0.1	52.3
1871	45.9	1.8	0.3	52.1
1876	46.0	1.7	0.4	51.9
1881	45.2	1.7	0.7	52.4
1888	45.5	2.0	2.0	50.5
1896	45.1	2.0	3.3	49.7
1907	42.0	2.0	9.3	46.8
1912	43.8	2.3	11.0	43.0

Ireland

Year	Cereal	Potato	Other root	Grass
1861	18.0	7.3	2.8	71.8
1866	15.7	6.8	2.8	74.8
1871	14.5	6.7	2.9	75.8
1876	12.6	5.6	3.1	78.7
1881	12.6	5.6	2.7	79.1
1888	11.2	5.3	2.9	80.6
1896	9.8	4.6	2.9	82.6
1907	9.3	4.0	2.8	83.8
1912	9.1	4.1	2.9	83.9

Source. Jensen (1937, 389); Johansen (1985, 129–33); Mitchell (1988, 190–1); Turner (1996, Appendix 1).

put was falling sharply in both countries between 1850 and 1914, plummeting from 60% to 16% in Ireland, and from 46% to 7% in Denmark. These declines can be explained by the grain invasion of the late nineteenth century, which depressed cereal prices throughout Europe; in countries such as Ireland and Denmark, which maintained free trade, a fall in cereal production was inevitable (O'Rourke 1997). This overall similarity disguises a profound divergence in land use, however. Ireland had always devoted more land to grass than had Denmark (Table 2), but this difference intensified, with the percentage of land devoted to grass rising in Ireland, and falling in Denmark. Denmark accommodated its additional animal production by increasing the production of fodder crops from the 1880s onward and by stall-feeding cattle with grain, a development often encouraged by reformers, but not realized, in Ireland. One implication of these differing strategies (since Irish agriculture was becoming less and less labour-intensive) was that while total male agricultural employment

Table 3   Cattle Numbers, 1861–1914

Year	Ireland			Denmark		
	Cattle	Cows	% cows	Cattle	Cows	% cows
1861	3472	1545	44.5	1121	758	67.6
1866	3746	1483	39.6	1194	812	68.0
1871	3976	1546	38.9	1239	808	65.2
1876	4117	1533	37.2	1348	898	66.6
1881	3957	1392	35.2	1470	899	61.2
1888	4099	1385	33.8	1460	954	65.3
1893	4464	1441	32.3	1696	1011	59.6
1898	4487	1431	31.9	1745	1067	61.1
1903	4664	1495	32.1	1840	1089	59.2
1909	4700	1549	33.0	2254	1282	56.9
1914	5052	1639	32.4	2463	1310	53.2

Source: Turner (1996, Appendix 1); Jensen (1937, 393).

Table 4   Butter and Milk Production, 1850–1914

Year	Ireland		Denmark	
	Million pounds	Share of output (percent)	Million pounds	Share of output (percent)
1850–54	5.1	15.3	1.4	16.1
1855–59	8.6	21.6	2.0	17.8
1860–64	7.6	21.3	1.9	18.2
1865–69	8.9	22.6	2.7	18.0
1870–74	10.0	23.0	3.5	19.4
1875–79	9.3	21.3	4.3	23.9
1880–84	7.4	18.7	5.3	27.7
1885–89	6.2	18.0	5.9	33.4
1890–94	7.0	19.1	8.2	37.2
1895–99	6.6	18.6	9.1	39.9
1900–04	7.3	18.3	12.2	42.1
1905–09	8.1	18.8	14.9	41.6
1910–14	8.8	18.1	16.9	37.1

Source: Turner (1996, 108, 116); Johansen (1985, 153–5).

Note: Irish figures are for butter production, Danish figures are for milk and milk products.

fell in Ireland, from 1.1 million in 1861 to 0.7 million in 1911, in Denmark it rose over the same period from 0.37 million to 0.4 million (Mitchell 1992, ibid.).

In the crucial dairying sector, the story is again one of a relatively strong

Table 5   Shares of British butter market, 1860–1914 (percentages)

	1860	1870	1881	1885	1890	1895	1900	1905	1910	1914
Ireland	46.6	38.3	24.5	20.7	22.0	19.3	16.8	12.1	11.9	15.2
Denmark	0.6	6.8	10.3	12.5	31.7	33.2	36.6	34.5	35.2	37.2
France	6.3	15.4	18.3	14.9	20.2	13.0	7.9	7.4	7.4	5.8
Russia	0.0	0.0	0.2	0.5	0.3	3.7	5.2	9.8	11.9	13.1
Netherlands	20.8	21.7	27.5	35.7	6.0	5.5	7.0	4.4	3.1	3.9
Belgium	5.1	4.5	1.8	2.0	1.4	0.7	1.9	1.1	0.0	0.0
Sweden	0.0	0.5	2.4	4.2	8.6	8.9	4.8	4.0	7.0	5.8
Germany	8.9	8.6	4.0	4.8	4.0	3.2	0.9	0.1	0.1	0.0
USA	5.2	0.9	6.4	2.6	3.3	1.9	1.4	1.8	0.0	0.2
Australia	0.0	0.2	0.5	0.0	1.6	7.4	8.7	9.7	13.6	9.3
New Zealand	0.0	0.0	0.0	0.0	0.0	1.5	4.0	6.4	7.4	7.6
Other	6.4	3.1	3.9	2.0	0.9	1.7	4.8	8.6	2.4	1.8
Sum (cwt. '000s)	1572	1878	2712	3026	2599	3503	4062	4719	4908	4697

Source: Solar (1989–90, 159–60); Nüchel Thomsen and Thomas (1966, 152); Ó Gráda (1977, 206); *Agricultural Statistics, 1914.* Note: before 1887 the figures include margarine imports.

Danish performance. Table 3 gives the evolution of cattle numbers in the two countries from 1861 onward. In 1861 there were more than three times as many cattle in Ireland as in Denmark, but in 1914 there were only slightly more than twice as many. Ireland had a comparative advantage in "dry" cattle, with the share of milch cows falling from 45% to 32% (note that the share in Denmark also fell, from 68% to 53%).

Table 4 gives the contribution of the dairy industry to agricultural output in the two countries from 1851. The share of the industry in total Irish agricultural output was slightly over 20% from the mid-1850s to the late 1870s, and slightly more than 18% thereafter. In Denmark, dairying was of roughly comparable importance in the third quarter of the century, but from the late 1870s, resources were shifted into the sector, and by the early twentieth century it accounted for more than 40% of Danish agricultural output: evidence of substantial flexibility on the part of the Danish agricultural sector. As late as the 1870s, the Irish industry dwarfed the Danish one, but again the 1880s proved a crucial turning point: by the early 1890s Irish dairying had been overtaken, and on the eve of World War I it was only half the size of the Danish industry. The Danish industry was producing 83,800 tons of butter annually in 1900–04; 104,400 tons in 1905–09; and 112,600 tons in 1910–14, of which 90,000 were exported (Johansen 1985, 150, 201). In 1914 Ireland produced about 66,399 metric tons of butter (O'Donovan 1940, 326), of which 36,222 tons were exported

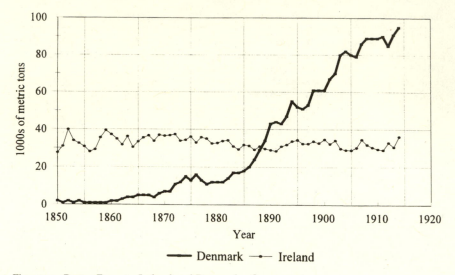

Figure 7   Butter Exports, Ireland and Denmark, 1850–1914
Source: Johansen (1985), Solar (1989–90).

(Solar 1989–90, 160). Figure 7 shows that Irish butter exports were static throughout the late nineteenth century, whereas Danish exports grew explosively, with a sharp acceleration during the 1880s, during which decade Danish exports pulled ahead of Irish exports. Both Ireland and Denmark exported almost all their butter to Britain; Table 5 compares the countries' shares of the British import market (assuming that all Irish exports went to Britain, and that all UK imports were consumed in Britain). Before 1887 the statistics include margarine imports, mostly from Holland, which were quite substantial; this implies that Ireland probably held somewhat over half the British butter market in 1860. Yet again, it had been overtaken by Denmark by 1890, and also faced strong competition from French, Russian, and eventually Australasian butter.

Not only was Ireland losing market share; it was also getting relatively less for its butter over time. Figure 8 gives official average butter prices in the two countries from 1846; in principle these should capture overall movements in butter prices and changing average qualities as well. According to the data, Irish prices were well above Danish prices in mid-century, the gap was rapidly eliminated after the mid-1870s, and average Danish prices exceeded Irish ones from the early 1880s. The gap averaged almost 15% between 1905 and 1914: 15% of the value of butter production on the eve of the Great War was equivalent to one percent of national income.

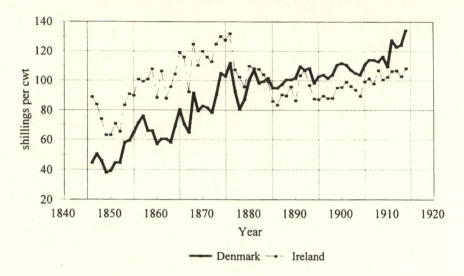

Figure 8   Official Butter Prices, Ireland and Denmark, 1846–1914
Source: O'Rourke (1999).

Tables 6 and 7 give some intuition as to what was the underlying source of these average price differences. The gap between average export prices realized by the two economies was 13.2%, somewhat lower than the average domestic price gap; when like is compared with like, the price gaps are even smaller. Thus, Danish creamery butter fetched between 6.4% and 7.3% more than Irish creamery butter in Britain; this presumably reflects quality differences. The gap between creamery butter prices in the two domestic markets was 8.1%. Table 6 suggests that about half of the average price gap [(6.4+7.3)/(2*14.8)=46%] was due to Irish butter being inferior to Danish butter, within given product classes; the remaining half was due to an inferior Irish quality mix.[4]

Table 7 shows that there were substantial price gaps between different types of butter in Ireland, and between the Irish provinces.[5] Creamery butter was produced using the new cream separator technology invented in Scandinavia in the late 1870s. Separators extracted more cream from the milk, and did so more quickly and hygienically. They diffused quickly in Denmark, and by 1914 the vast majority of butter there was being produced with the new methods. However, as late as 1907, only 37.2% of Irish butter was produced in creameries. According to a witness to the 1911 Irish Milk Commission, 50% of total output was farmers' butter, produced on farms using traditional methods; the remaining 12.7% was "factory butter," that is farmers' butter which was bought up by factory owners and

Table 6   Butter prices, 1905–14 (s. per cwt.)

Price	Official		Creamery		UK 1st quality		UK 2nd quality		Average export	
Year	IRL	DK	IRL	DK	IRL	DK	IRL	DK	IRL	DK
1905	99.5	110.8	102.1	110.1	109.5	115.0	106.0	112.5	99.5	109.0
1906	101.5	114.1	103.8	114.1	111.5	119.0	108.5	116.0	101.5	114.0
1907	98.0	114.1	101.8	110.8	108.5	114.5	106.0	112.0	98.0	110.4
1908	107.1	113.0	109.2	117.0	116.5	122.0	113.5	119.0	107.1	115.2
1909	100.8	116.4	104.8	114.0	112.0	118.5	108.0	116.5	100.8	113.1
1910	102.6	109.7	106.8	113.2	112.0	120.0	109.0	117.5	102.6	115.4
1911	106.7	127.6	112.9	119.3	119.0	125.0	115.5	123.0	106.7	120.4
1912	106.8	123.1	113.5	123.8	119.0	130.0	116.0	127.5	106.8	125.5
1913	103.0	124.2	110.3	122.4	117.0	127.0	113.5	124.5	103.0	123.1
1914	108.5	134.3	114.8	122.9	122.5	130.5	118.5	127.0	108.5	125.1
Average	103.4	118.7	108.0	116.8	114.8	122.2	111.5	119.6	102.9	117.1
DK-IRL (%)	14.8		8.1		6.4		7.3		13.2	

Sources: Irish and UK Agricultural Statistics (various years); Report on the Trade in Imports and Exports in Irish Ports (various years); Statistisk Aarbog (various years); Jensen (1937, 373–4).

Table 7   Butter prices in Ireland, 1905–14 (s. per cwt.)

Year	Ireland	Leinster	Munster	Ulster	Connaught	Creamery	Factory	Farmers
1905	99.5	100.4	99.5	94.9	95.9	102.1	94.8	89.9
1906	101.5	98.4	101.8	95.5	91.9	103.8	88.7	89.8
1907	98.0	94.1	98.3	91.3	88.5	101.8	85.0	86.1
1908	107.1	103.4	107.3	101.3	100.3	109.2	97.8	98.4
1909	100.8	98.3	100.9	97.6	94.3	104.8	90.1	89.6
1910	102.6	100.8	102.9	97.8	93.8	106.8	94.5	94.0
1911	106.7	103.4	107.1	96.4	104.1	112.9	95.4	95.0
1912	106.8	109.0	107.0	104.9	96.1	113.5	98.8	98.0
1913	103.0	108.5	102.8	100.3	94.5	110.3	95.4	92.9
1914	108.5	114.0	108.3	100.8	107.3	114.8	99.3	99.8
Average	103.4	103.0	103.6	98.1	96.7	108.0	94.0	93.3

Source: Irish Agricultural Statistics (various years).

blended to produce a more uniform consistency. Table 7 shows that cream-ery butter fetched 15% more than factory butter, and 16% more than farmers' butter; the market clearly regarded traditional butter as being inferior to the modern creamery product. The big difference between the

Irish and Danish dairy industries was that the Irish product mix was more old-fashioned and of lower average quality.

In addition to producing smaller amounts of creamery butter than the Danes, the Irish were slower in adapting another, organizational innovation: the cooperative creamery. The use of cream separators was only financially viable when they were processing the milk from a large number of cows – 300 to 400, say – and so it clearly made sense for centralized creameries to process the milk output of several farms.[6] In principle, this could be done by privately owned creameries as well as by cooperatives. Ingrid Henriksen (1999) has, however, emphasized the efficiency advantages of the cooperative: by tying a group of farmers into supplying only one creamery, which they jointly owned, a higher average milk quality was ensured. Farmers had an incentive to provide high quality milk, and if necessary, to monitor each other; social sanctions could be applied to farmers who underperformed; and of course their property rights in the creamery might be forfeit. A privately owned creamery, on the other hand, would always be on the lookout for enough milk suppliers to ensure an efficient scale of production (not having suppliers who were locked in); this would give suppliers more leverage, and might enable them to sell poorer quality milk.

The first Danish cooperative was established in 1882, although proprietary creameries had been in existence for some 10 years. Figure 9 shows that the number of Danish cooperatives increased dramatically over the next decade; by 1914 there were almost 1200 in the country, of which over half had been established by 1890. Diffusion was almost complete by the turn of the century. Irish cooperatives started later (in 1889); their numbers jumped between 1896 (70) and 1903 (356) and continued to increase up to the Great War, at which stage there were 445 in existence. Thus diffusion in Ireland was slower, and the innovation was never as widespread, as a glance at maps of Ireland and Denmark early this century will confirm (Ó Gráda 1977, 290; Bjørn 1988, 373). Ireland's cooperative performance looks even weaker when set against the two countries' milch cow herds; by 1888 there was roughly one cooperative per 2000 milch cows in Denmark, and there was almost one cooperative per thousand milch cows by the turn of the century; in Ireland, there was only slightly more than one cooperative per 4000 milch cows by 1914 (Table 8).

Things look better if proprietary creameries are added to the total. In 1896 there were 207 private creameries in Ireland, or 279 in all; in 1906 there were 800 creameries in all, of which just 339 were cooperative. In Denmark, by contrast, cooperatives displaced private creameries during the 1890s; cooperatives accounted for 54% of all creameries in 1888, but 81% in 1894, a proportion that was to remain roughly constant until the war.[7] Thus, there were 0.19 creameries per 1000 cows in Ireland in 1896,

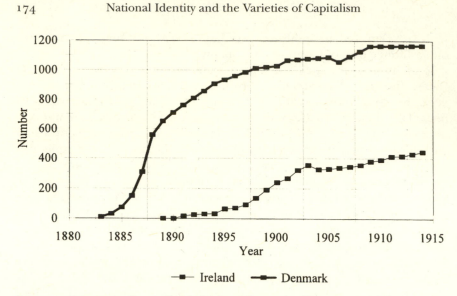

Figure 9   Cooperative Creameries, Ireland and Denmark, 1882–1914
Source: IAOS Annual Reports; Danish data kindly provided by Ingrid Henriksen.

as opposed to roughly 1.1 per thousand in Denmark in 1894; and there were 0.53 creameries in Ireland per 100 cows in 1906, as opposed to roughly 1.18 in Denmark in 1903. Nevertheless, Ireland's total creamery density was less than half that of Denmark throughout the period, as further evidenced by the large proportion of non-creamery butter in total output. If the arguments concerning the efficiency advantages of cooperatives are to be believed, Ireland chose the wrong type of creamery.

Does this failure to adopt new creamery techniques, and the cooperative organizational form, constitute economic failure, or was it a rational response to the circumstances in which Irish farmers found themselves? The decade of the 1880s was crucial for creamery diffusion in Denmark. The fact that Denmark's agricultural productivity and butter exports overtook Ireland's in the 1880s, the fact that on average Ireland was producing butter of a lower quality (as reflected in her average butter prices), and the fact that even her premium creamery butter sold at a discount against her Danish rival all suggest that some failure may have been involved. This is certainly how contemporaries perceived things, although in fairness our perceptions of what contemporaries thought are largely coloured by the energetic and vociferous attempts of Ireland's cooperative movement to displace traditional technologies and privately owned creameries. The timing of the decline in Ireland's relative butter prices is consistent with the argument that Danish innovation and a sluggish Irish response were responsible for Ireland's displacement in international markets. Thus, the

Table 8   Cooperative Creameries per 1000 Milch Cows, 1888–1914

Year	Ireland	Denmark
1888	0.000	0.585
1893	0.021	0.849
1898	0.095	0.949
1903	0.238	0.989
1909	0.245	0.907
1914	0.272	0.892

Source: Creamery totals from IAOS Annual Reports, Bjørn (1988, 371), Statistiske Meddelelser (1915, 9), Henriksen (1999, Table 1). Cow totals: see Table 3.

official figures in Figure 8, which embody information about changing quality mixes, show the early 1880s as being the crucial period during which Denmark overtook Ireland.

Clearly, Denmark's economic performance was much stronger than Ireland's in the late nineteenth century. In the next section, however, I put this relative success into a comparative context.

IRELAND AND DENMARK IN COMPARATIVE CONTEXT:
GLOBALIZATION, EDUCATION, AND GROWTH

In recent years, several economic historians have emphasized the highly globalized nature of the late nineteenth-century international economy, and have explored the implications of this for the performance of peripheral European economies (e.g., O'Rourke and Williamson 1997, 1999; Taylor and Williamson 1997). Both Denmark and Ireland participated fully in this globalization experience. As already mentioned, Ireland was a completely free-trade economy by virtue of its membership in the United Kingdom, while Denmark distinguished itself by its refusal to impose agricultural tariffs in the wake of the European grain invasion of the late nineteenth century (Kindleberger 1951, O'Rourke 1997).[8] Just as important, Ireland and Denmark both had capital and labour markets that were tightly integrated into global factor markets. Both sent emigrants abroad, mostly to the New World; while capital flowed freely into and out of both economies.

In principle, free trade, migration and capital mobility should have helped poor countries, such as Ireland and Denmark around 1870, catch up with richer countries, such as Britain or the United States. And in fact, it is the case that the late nineteenth-century Atlantic economy was distinguished by a general convergence of poor countries on the core (Williamson 1995, O'Rourke and Williamson 1999, chapter 2). Figure 10

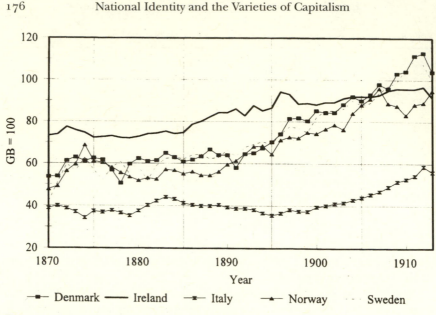

Figure 10   Wages Relative to Britain, 1870–1913

Source: Williamson (1995), amended in O'Rourke and Williamson (1997).

shows real wages in five peripheral European economies (the three Scandinavian economies, plus Ireland and Italy), expressed as percentages of the real wage in the leading European economy of the day, Britain. In all five cases, the wages caught up on British wages, and in two (Denmark and Sweden) they actually overshot them. Figure 11 replicates the exercise, this time expressing real wages in the five countries as percentages of U.S. real wages; once again the picture that emerges is one of convergence.

This is important in evaluating Denmark's success vis à vis Ireland: Ireland was by no means a basket case economy by the 1870s. Its living standards were high by the standards of the time, and even more important, they were growing rapidly; more rapidly even than living standards in the two leading economies of the day. This was on the face of it no mean achievement; and makes Denmark's performance seem all the more impressive.

All five countries in Figures 10 and 11 were heavily involved with the international economy. Norway, Italy, and above all Ireland, sent vast numbers of emigrants to the Americas, with Irish and Norwegian emigration rates of 142 per thousand and 95 per thousand per decade during the 1880s; Italian migration started later, but exceeded 100 per thousand during the 1900s, which is exactly when Italian real wages started to converge

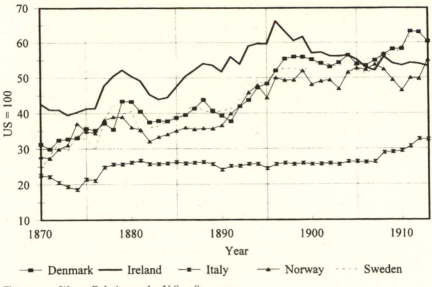

Figure 11   Wages Relative to the U.S., 1870–1913

Source: Williamson (1995), amended in O'Rourke and Williamson (1997).

on Britain. Swedish and Danish emigration rates were more modest, but still significant, with respective emigration rates of 70 and 39 per thousand during the 1880s (Hatton and Williamson 1998, Table 2.1). Furthermore, Sweden and Norway received important capital inflows, while Norway pursued a relatively liberal trade policy.

It turns out (O'Rourke and Williamson 1997) that globalization can explain a large fraction of the convergence of these countries on Britain and the United States. This pattern is exactly what simple trade theory predicts, although in this case there are a few surprises along the way. Table 9 gives a decomposition of each country's convergence on either Britain (Panel A) or the United States (Panel B) into those portions that can be explained by three dimensions of globalization (mass migration, capital flows, and trade), as well as by cross-country differences in schooling.[9] In all cases, the entries in the table give the percentage of the relevant country's observed convergence, on either Britain or the United States, that can be explained by the relevant variable. Thus, for example, the first entry of Panel A says that between 5 and 8 percent of Denmark's convergence on Britain can be explained by its superior levels of schooling.

This table contains several main messages. *First,* schooling accounted for only a small share of these countries' convergence on Britain and the United States, simply because even though the Scandinavians in particular

Table 9   The Sources of Catch-Up and Fall Back around the European Periphery, 1870–1910 (in percent)

	Schooling	Mass Migration	Capital Flows	Trade	Residual
A How Much of Real Wage Convergence (or Divergence) on Britain Explained?					
Denmark	5–8	3.9–5.7	30.0	> 3.9	< 52.4–57.2
Norway	5–6	8.9–20.0	35.1	> 4.4	< 34.5–46.6
Sweden	4–5	2.9–8.4	43.0	3.1	40.5–47.0
Italy	0	64.8–67.8	positive	positive?	< 32.2–35.2
Ireland	0	83.6-86.9	small positive	0?	< 13.1–16.4
B How Much of Real Wage Convergence (or Divergence) on America Explained?					
Denmark	0–9	31.9–49.2	16.3	>12.1	< 13.4–39.7
Norway	0–9	40.6–67.7	20.0	>13.9	< 0–25.5
Sweden	0–8	24.6–41.4	34.0	9.4	7.2–32.0
Italy	0	all	0?	0?	0
Ireland	0–5	all	0	0	0

Source: O'Rourke and Williamson (1999, Table 14.4).

were well educated, so were the British and the Americans. *Second,* trade-induced price shocks accounted for very little of the convergence either. *Third,* Irish and Italian convergence on the core was almost entirely due to emigration, which reduced their labour forces by 45 and 39 percent respectively between 1870 and 1910, and which raised their real wages by 32 and 28 percent during that period (O'Rourke and Williamson 1999, Table 14.2). Migration accounted for a smaller but still significant share of Scandinavian convergence, particularly on the United States (where immigration lowered real wages) and particularly for Norway. *Fourth,* capital flows also facilitated Scandinavian real wage convergence on the core, particularly on Britain (where capital exports lowered real wages), and particularly in the case of Sweden. The surprising fact is that capital probably flowed out of Ireland and Italy, thus lowering real wages there, whereas simple theory suggests that it should have flowed into those economies in search of cheap labour. Sadly for peripheral economies then and now, this prediction did not and does not hold; in the late nineteenth century capital flowed toward resource-abundant countries in the New World (which was already rich) or in the Old (i.e., Scandinavia and Russia). Finally, note the large residuals for the Scandinavians, in particular for Denmark: more than half of Danish convergence on Britain cannot be explained either by globalization or by schooling, and was thus due to superior technological progress; while between 13 and 40 percent of Denmark's convergence on the United States is similarly unexplained by these exercises. The fact that such a large share of Denmark's convergence cannot be explained by factors that do a good job of explaining convergence elsewhere further highlights the unique nature of Danish success.

Denmark and Ireland are thus alike to the extent that a large share of their convergence on the core economies of the late nineteenth century can be explained by globalization. However, there are very important differences. In the Irish case, convergence was almost entirely due to emigration: Irish wages caught up with British and U.S. wages because there were fewer people at home (a shift up the labour demand curve) not because of rapid capital accumulation or technological progress (an outward shift in the labour demand curve). Emigration also played a role in Danish convergence, but Denmark was able to attract capital from overseas,[10] and enjoyed relatively rapid technological progress, factors which helped her not only to converge on British real wages, but actually to overtake them.

To make matters more precise, Danish real wages (and thus the living standards of ordinary workers) grew at some 2.6 percent per annum between 1870 and 1913, while Irish real wages grew at only 1.8 percent per annum: the growth gap that we would like to explain thus amounted to some 0.8 percent per annum. But adding emigration into the equation does not help in explaining this difference, since nearly 0.7 percentage points of the Irish growth rate can be explained by emigration, but only 0.2 percentage points of Danish growth: without emigration, the growth gap would have been 1.3 percent (= 0.8 + 0.7 − 0.2) per annum, not 0.8 percent. On the other hand, the growth regressions suggest that superior education could indeed help in explaining Denmark's superior performance; but this is simply based on average correlations across a group of countries.

Thus, several new questions must be asked. Why did Ireland, like Italy, rely so heavily on emigration to advance its living standards? Why was Denmark able to attract capital from overseas when Ireland was not, despite the fact that Denmark did not enjoy the natural resources that helped attract capital to Sweden (iron ore) and Norway (timber)? Why is the residual for Denmark so impressively large in Table 9? If education helps explain the difference between Danish and Irish performance, then precisely through what mechanisms did education matter? In many respects, it seems as if a broader comparative perspective has made the Irish-Danish comparison more puzzling, rather than less so; and has made the Danish achievement of very rapid growth in living standards without the advantages of either mass emigration or large natural resource endowments seem even more impressive.

EXPLANATIONS

Why was Denmark's late nineteenth-century performance so successful? Perhaps a review of the literature on why Ireland failed to keep pace with her can yield some insight into the question.

Rational Actor/Comparative Advantage Arguments

Cow density: One difference between Ireland and Denmark, which was emphasized by Ó Gráda (1977), is that Ireland had almost twice as many acres per cow as did Denmark. "Creamery viability demanded a minimum milk supply: in areas where that milk supply implied a catchment area too large for many individual farmers to consider switching techniques, it seems reasonable to expect few if any creameries. For small herds, or for herds located some miles from a creamery, the overhead cost incurred by the farmer in bringing milk to the creamery might be prohibitive, and there might then have been no demand for the new technique" (Ó Gráda 1977, 292). Ó Gráda found that the number of cooperative creameries in each county (or poor law union) in 1913 was well explained by cow density, milch cow numbers (a scale variable), and population (representing the demand for non-butter uses of milk, i.e., liquid milk). In areas such as Limerick, which most resembled Denmark, creameries (both private and cooperative) were widely diffused; they had "spread as far as was viable in the Irish context by the 1910's" (299).

In O'Rourke (2004), I test Ó Gráda's assertion by exploring whether the diffusion of cooperative and private creameries across counties in 1906 could be explained solely by the economic variables he suggests, or if other, non-economic, factors were also important. The bottom line is that while his economic variables had the expected impact on creamery numbers, so did a number of other factors, a matter to which I return below.

Climate: It has also been argued that Ireland's relatively favourable climate retarded Irish agricultural development. Ireland's mild winters and the yearlong availability of grazing made it possible for farmers to leave their cattle outside all year round; in Denmark this was impossible. Thus Danish farmers had to invest in stalls for their animals; this in turn favoured stall-feeding and tillage (especially root crop) production, the collection of dung, and dairying rather than beef production. Irish cattle were bred for beef far more than for milk, and were indeed often exported "on the hoof," as is still the case today. Thus Irish animal husbandry was as labour-extensive as possible.

Stall-feeding also implied a year-long supply of milk, and therefore, for Denmark, a yearlong supply butter. By contrast, in 1909 Ireland, creameries produced just 22% of their annual output in the six months from November to April; fully 45% of annual output came in the three summer months – June, July, and August (BPP 1913, 174). Annual reports of the IAOS (Irish Agricultural Organisation Society, the official body representing and promoting cooperation in Ireland) are full of complaints about the impact that this limitation had on the movement's ability to market its butter in Britain; the concern was that not only did Irish butter only sell during the summer, when prices were substantially lower, but that creameries, having lost their position on the British market during the winter months, were forced to "bribe" their way back into the market in May or June by offering their product at a discount.

James Beddy (1943) made this climatic argument most forcefully, and since his is the only Irish work with the express purpose of comparing Irish and Danish economic development, it is worth quoting him at some length. He claimed that Denmark's "rainfall and general climatic conditions did not point the way to grazing," and went on to describe Denmark's agricultural policy:

[It] involves the growing of large quantities of cereals and forage crops for animal fodder which is supplemented by imported feeding-stuffs of high protein content ... Climatic conditions are such that animals must be housed for a comparatively large part of the year and hence extensive farm buildings are required not only for this purpose but for the storage of fodder. This constant care of livestock is associated with that regular, as opposed to seasonal, production of livestock products which is so important a feature of marketing ...

Eire, on the other hand, with her heavier soils, her milder winters and her ample rainfall, adopted a system of animal husbandry based upon grass ... Unlike Denmark, our selection had not the same element of compulsion. While our choice was not open to Denmark, hers was not closed to us. Our system ... involved pure grazing for livestock export and seasonal – and hence restricted – production of livestock products partially for export at the most highly competitive period of the year to markets with which our dealings had not the advantage of regularity. There resulted less employment, less activity on the land, fewer farm buildings and less farming capital. From the strict economic standpoint it no doubt represented our natural contribution to the international division of labour in a world of Free Trade; from the social standpoint, however, its effects have been in many respects deplorable. (Beddy 1943, 196–7)

While Beddy elsewhere mentions cooperation and education as being important determinants of Danish economic progress, he concludes that emphasis on these factors may "distract attention from what has been stressed in this paper as the fundamental explanation of the differences between Eire and Denmark in economic prosperity and social welfare.

Primarily, and indeed, paradoxically, it is our climatic advantages which are the cause of our relative economic and social disadvantages" (Beddy 1943, 208).[11]

How is one to evaluate these claims? In a world without imperfections, the addition of an extra constraint (e.g., an unfavourable climate making certain agricultural systems impossible) cannot lead to greater economic welfare. The Beddy argument therefore must rely on some imperfection(s). For example, maybe the path which Denmark embarked on turned out ex post to be more technologically progressive than the extensive grazing path that Ireland followed. Thus what might have appeared the better option in the short run turned out, unexpectedly, to be the worse option in the long run. The logic here would be similar to that demonstrated by Alwyn Young (1991), in which a country switching to free trade may gain in the short run for the usual static reasons, but lose in the long run. That would occur if the good in which the country specialized (and into whose production the country was subsequently locked) was less technologically progressive than the country's import good. Alternatively, if technological innovation responds positively to bottlenecks and the severity of binding constraints (Landes 1969; Porter 1990) then an extra constraint can indeed benefit a country. Specific technological innovations, whose primary purpose was to cope with Danish climatic conditions, may have raised the productivity of Danish agriculture.

However, these arguments would rely on the new technologies not being easily transferable to Ireland. In fact, there was no technical obstacle to specific innovations such as separators and cooperatives being transferred to Ireland, as is shown by the fact that both innovations were introduced there; if the argument reduces to one stating that new technologies were not diffused rapidly enough within Ireland, it merely restates the basic question underlying this chapter: Why did Ireland did not grow as rapidly as Denmark?

Seasonal price gaps:[12]   It should be noted that Einar Jensen's standard English-language history of Danish agriculture primarily attributes the Danish system of winter dairying, not to the Danish climate, but to historical chance: "During the formative period of specialized dairy farming, butter prices during the winter months were so much higher than summer prices that it paid well to develop winter dairying. This fitted in so well with the system of farming that it paid to retain high winter production even after increased supplies from the southern hemisphere changed considerably the seasonal variation in butter prices" (Jensen 1937, 328). Of course, if winter butter prices were higher in Ireland too, then Irish farmers should also have had an incentive to develop winter dairying.

Is it the case that prices fluctuated more in Denmark than in Ireland, at the stage when crucial decisions were being made about long run dairying strategies? Henriksen and O'Rourke (2005) explore this question in some detail, using prices collected from newspapers and other primary sources, and their answer is a definite "no": winter price premia were no higher in Denmark than elsewhere during this period, and indeed this is what you would expect in a well-integrated international market. It is not the case that Danish farmers faced a price incentive to develop winter dairying that did not exist elsewhere. The Jensen hypothesis on it own will not suffice, therefore, to explain the different path taken by Danish farmers. Second, however, Henriksen and O'Rourke find that there was an increase in the winter premium precisely at the time that the Danes began to develop an intensive dairying sector, based on winter production and cooperative creameries. The incentive to develop winter dairying was indeed at its height when Danish agriculture moved in that direction. While the incentive on its own was not sufficient (since it also existed in Ireland and presumably elsewhere in Europe), Jensen may be right in his assertion that price incentives were important in the Danish case, and that they presented Danish farmers with a moment of opportunity that was seized with both hands.

Third, it is not the case that the incentive to develop winter dairying had vanished by the time that Irish cooperative creameries started to emerge around 1890, since Henriksen and O'Rourke find that the winter premium only began to fall significantly in the mid-1890s. Again, the difference between Denmark and elsewhere seems, at least initially, to have involved different responses to the same price incentives, not different incentives. However, it is true that by the early twentieth century the incentive to develop winter dairying was indeed lower than it had been in the early 1880s.

Land Tenure Arguments

The most common arguments traditionally advanced to explain Irish economic backwardness in the nineteenth century have to do with land tenure arrangements. The traditional claim was that the landlord-tenant system that prevailed in the decades after the Famine discouraged investment in agriculture: absentee landlords did not invest, while tenants feared that if they invested, the benefit would be appropriated by landlords raising their rent. A series of reforms, starting with the (half-hearted) *Land Act* of 1870, ensued, culminating in the transfer of ownership to the Irish peasant. By the early twentieth century, the major impediment to the development of Irish agriculture was gone.[13]

The problem with this traditional view is that Irish landlords did not rackrent or capriciously evict in the years prior to 1870, as would have had to have been the case for tenant investment to have been discouraged. Barbara Solow (1971) showed this convincingly, and went on the counter-offensive: not only were the land reforms of the late nineteenth century based on a mistaken analysis of landlord tenant relations but they actually hurt Irish agriculture. The 1870 *Land Act* made landlords compensate tenants for (i) eviction (unless the eviction was for non-payment of rent), and (ii) the value of any improvements the tenants had made to their holding. Solow claims that one effect of the latter was to cut off landlord investment, as landlords were afraid that tenants might claim compensation for investments the landlords had funded. Thus the Act reduced investment in Irish agriculture at precisely the time when globalization, and developments in Denmark and elsewhere, made such investment essential (Solow 1971, 86, 198). However, Ó Gráda's (1975) figures on landlord investment between 1850 and 1875 cast doubt on this assertion.

Raymond Crotty (1966) also argues that 1870 marked a downturn in the fortunes of Irish agriculture, but for reasons other than Solow's. Contemporaries agued that making peasants owners of their land would increase the efficiency of Irish agriculture; Crotty argues the opposite. According to him, peasant proprietorship is a fundamentally inefficient institution for the simple reason that it does not embody the equivalent of an effective market for corporate control. A landlord might have ejected a lazy or inefficient tenant, but a peasant proprietor will not eject himself (nor will he sell the land for a good price to a better farmer: there must be a strong non-economic motive for staying on the land for this argument to work). The gradual move toward tenant right during the three decades from 1870 progressively eroded the competitive market for land; farmers became increasingly old, conservative, and inefficient.

In Denmark, as mentioned in the Introduction to this volume, peasant proprietorship was given a boost by the government during the "period of reform" from 1784–1807, and the transition to that institution proceeded throughout the nineteenth century. Already by 1835 there were 41,695 peasant proprietors in Denmark, as opposed to 24,795 tenant farmers (Jensen 1937, 125–6). If Crotty is right, therefore, then Danish agriculture should have been less efficient than Irish agriculture, *ceteris paribus*. Crotty salvages the "land market hypothesis" by appealing to the climatic differences between the two countries: an inefficient Irish farmer could adopt an extensive farming system that involved little pecuniary loss compared with an intensive farming system; the lazy Danish farmer had no such option, and would be forced out of business (Crotty 1966, 94–6).

So much for speculation; is there evidence that can be brought to bear on the issue? In research reported elsewhere (O'Rourke 2004), I find that the counties with higher levels of owner-occupancy in 1906 had greater numbers of creameries, *ceteris paribus*, than counties in which more farmers were still tenants. While this is hardly a direct measure of farmer efficiency, on the face of it this finding is consistent with the traditional view that tenancy was bad for progress, and inconsistent with both Solow and Crotty. It also provides indirect empirical evidence for the argument advanced elsewhere in this volume, that its history of early land reform was one of the advantages enjoyed by late nineteenth-century Denmark.

However, the fact that owner-occupancy was beneficial does not necessarily imply that the *process* of land reform was without cost. For example, Solow emphasizes that one effect of the turmoil over property rights in land was that enormous effort and resources went, literally, into rent-seeking activities. The effect of the 1870 Act, she writes, was "a signal to both sides to 'look to their rights' and gird for further battle. But the real problem in Ireland was not the division of a given pie, but the provision of a larger one" (Solow 1971, 88). She is even harsher about the effects of the rent-fixing 1881 *Act*:

Incentives to adjust the economy in the face of new international conditions were to some extent paralysed. There is no need to take too seriously landlord contentions that everybody rushed to court and neglected his farming, but if tenants could increase income more by litigation than by changing agricultural techniques, they would certainly do so. If valuers were swayed by appearances, a premium was even put on worse farming, and consequent dilapidation. "They calculate on getting the reduction, and put an exaggerated value on what it is going to do for them," a land agent told the Cairns Commission ... "They look to some political machinery or result to give them that which should come from their own industry?" asked Lord Tyrone. "Yes" was the reply.

Not alone from their industry, but from intelligent economic policy, too. But with the tenants of Ireland crowding into court, no one was thinking about agricultural education, credit and marketing programs, improved cropping, selective breeding, and, in general, ways of assisting tenants to adjust to changed economic conditions. (Solow 1971, 165–6)

This analysis makes sense in the context of the work of William Baumol (1990), who argues that talent will be allocated to where it earns the highest return, and that consequently it is important to ensure that the returns to entrepreneurial behaviour are higher than the reward to rent-seeking, criminality, or other potentially remunerative activities. Horace Plunkett took the argument one step further, by asserting that this emphasis on government policy, itself a byproduct of earlier harmful policies, led to a weakening of the national moral fibre: "We in Ireland have yet to free ourselves from one of the worst legacies of past misgovernment, the belief that any legislation or any legislature can provide an escape from the physical and mental toil imposed through our first parents upon all nations for all time" (Plunkett 1982, 61).

While the above arguments seem difficult to test, an additional factor was the widespread violence associated with the "Land War," as well as boycotts and similar tactics; the bitterness of the dispute was exacerbated by the fact that, outside of Ulster, tenant farmers were typically Catholic, while their landlords were typically Protestant, implying that the land conflict became intertwined with broader ethno-religious cleavages within society.[14] This must surely have retarded economic development in parts of rural Ireland, at least to some extent. In O'Rourke (2004) I test for a relationship between a history of land war violence (as measured by agrarian outrages per 10,000 population during 1880–82) and the number of creameries per county in 1906. As might have been expected, land war violence was associated with fewer creameries; but the effect was statistically insignificant at conventional levels. However, there was a very strong negative relationship between a history of land war violence and the propensity to cooperate (as measured by the share of cooperatives in total creamery numbers). While it might seem that trust between the farmers themselves should have been the crucial factor in determining the success of agricultural cooperation, it seems that traditionally poor landlord-tenant relations hampered progress in this area. One reason for this may have been that the cooperative movement was interdenominational; in which case it may have been viewed with greater suspicion by the majority Catholic population in regions where intercommunal tensions were higher.

Politics and Nationalism

Following on from the last point, the argument has been made that the unsettled political condition of Ireland during much of the period 1870–1930 profoundly retarded economic development there. The land war and nationalist politics were inseparably intertwined, as the landlord class whom the tenants were seeking to dispossess were viewed by many as the representatives of British rule in Ireland. The second and third decades of the twentieth century also saw widespread violence, connected with the Irish War of Independence and the ensuing Civil War. "If the Irish sacrificed economic progress on the altar of Irish nationalism, who can say it was the wrong choice?" asks Solow in the concluding sentence of her book (Solow 1971, 204). Why might the struggle for independence have involved such a sacrifice?

One can think of at least five reasons. The first has already been mentioned: violence cannot have helped the economy. The empirical question then becomes: to what extent did violence hurt the economy? To this end one might attempt estimates of the material damage done to infrastructure as a result of violence, or look for evidence of risk premiums being demanded by investors in Ireland.[15] However, the period from roughly

1900 to 1914 was an unusually tranquil one; once the Land Wars had been settled, the country was at peace, and thus this factor cannot have been important, at least in the years leading up to the Great War.

A second, extremely Danish, argument was put forward by a Danish observer of Ireland during the 1920s, Jørgen Pedersen (1926). His argument was that the Irish had little respect for the law under British rule, as the law involved was British law. This phenomenon, if it existed, may be referred to as the "Playboy effect," after Christy Mahon of Synge's play, who achieved fame and fortune in a remote Irish village by claiming to have killed his father. Pedersen went on to speculate that with independence, the Irish might become more law-abiding, which would benefit the economy. This sort of argument might make sense in the context of a world where imperfections (for example, the existence of collective action problems) make government legislation necessary. Note, however, that many of the agricultural reforms that made Denmark prosperous arose spontaneously out of the private sector, without the need for government action. The first cooperative contract, for example, was drawn up by a farmer rather than by a civil servant or intellectual, and cooperative creameries were diffused from the bottom up; and the "Lur" butter brand, which started out as a certificate of national origin and became a guarantee of quality as well, was voluntarily adopted by 98 percent of Danish farmers before the Government stepped in to legislate for the remaining 2 percent (Jensen 1937, 326–7). If government involvement was more important in Ireland (and indeed cooperative reform was more "top down" there than in Denmark), this would raise a series of questions about the different social contexts in the two countries, and once again push key questions back one stage further, rather than answering them.

Third, in line with the argument of the previous section, and with Baumol (1990), the "national struggle" may have diverted talent from economically productive activities, hence lowering Ireland's growth rate. An instructive case is that of Horace Plunkett, the leader of the Irish cooperative movement, who was committed to the ideal of interdenominational cooperation to solve Ireland's economic problems.

Although Plunkett himself felt that politics played far too important a role in Irish life, he took a seat in Parliament in 1892 as a unionist candidate for south Dublin. His willingness to ally himself with nationalists to pursue his economic agenda lost him unionist support, and cost him his seat in 1900; while his 1904 book, *Ireland in the New Century*, with its attacks on the influence of the Roman Catholic Church and the tactics of the Nationalist party, its advocacy of the union and its comments on the defects of the Irish personality, alienated many nationalists. The failure of unionists to advance a positive Irish program led to Plunkett's conversion to Home Rule in 1911, but he was not sufficiently radical for many nationalists. In 1919 he proposed that Ireland be a self-governing dominion (not a republic) within the Empire: for this he was attacked by all sides (West 1986, 184).

Thus it was that Plunkett, who felt that "politics are by no means the most useful, or indeed the most edifying, of a nation's activities,"[16] became diverted from what he saw as the greatest Irish issue of the day (the economy) into a personally damaging involvement in constitutional politics. Not only did this distract his attentions from the economy; it earned him many enemies, which did not help his cooperative movement. Plunkett was appointed to the Irish Senate in 1922, the first year of Irish independence. The following year his house was burnt down by Republicans, Plunkett resigned his Senate seat, and the founder of the Irish cooperative movement emigrated to England, where he spent the rest of his life (West 1968).

Fourth, as indicated above, politics introduced a divisiveness into public life which could make it difficult for collective action to be effectively embarked upon. On one famous occasion, R.A. Anderson, an associate of Plunkett, was prevented from addressing a local meeting on the subject of cooperation, when a local solicitor discovered that the cooperative movement was apolitical and non-denominational. The solicitor informed Anderson that cooperation "would not suit Rathkeale. 'Rathkeale,' said he pompously, 'is a Nationalist town – Nationalist to the backbone – and every pound of butter made in this Creamery must be made on nationalist principles, or it shan't be made at all.' This sentiment was applauded loudly and the proceedings terminated."[17]

Finally, reformers claimed that the cooperative movement and other attempts to improve Irish living standards were viewed with suspicion by some Nationalists, not just because many leaders of these movements were of the wrong religion or political persuasion, but because, if the attempts were successful, their success might undermine the demand for Independence. "It had been enough to see the powerful lever of the land agitations weakened by agrarian legislation. To improve the position of the people further was to destroy Home Rule utterly" (Smith-Gordon and Staples 1917, 47). The IAOS frequently complained that they had to contend, not just with the vested interests of traders, but with a hostile Nationalist press, and the opposition of local politicians.

Once again, many of these arguments seem difficult to test empirically. However, as mentioned earlier I did find (O'Rourke 2004) that land war violence was negatively associated with cooperation. This is consistent with the notion that trust was important for the sort of horizontal cooperation that made creamery cooperatives work; and that religious and/or political divisions could undermine this trust. More generally, Denmark was a country without ethnic or religious cleavages, at peace with itself. The Irish comparison makes it clear that these were probably important ingredients in the Danish success story, and thus provides powerful indirect evidence in favour of one of this volume's key arguments: that homogeneity has been one of the factors underlying Denmark's historical success.

Education

As noted earlier, there is a significant cross-country correlation between education and the growth in urban real wages during the late nineteenth century, and it is well known that such a correlation can also be found for other measures of economic performance, such as GDP per capita growth, both then and now. In turn, several authors have speculated that the mechanism by which education makes a difference in growth is that it increases the ability of countries to adopt best practice technology (Abramovitz 1986; Barro 1991; Easterlin 1981). Might relative Danish success during the late nineteenth century simply be a reflection of her relatively high levels of education?

Certainly, several commentators have claimed that Irish peasant farmers were too conservative, suspicious, poorly educated, or ignorant to adopt cooperation and the milk separator. Smith-Gordon and Staples (1917, 47–8), the former an employee of the IAOS, wrote in 1917 that "the most serious obstacle to the co-operative movement was and remains the conservatism of the Irish farmer. Many projects that would have brought great benefit to the country have been abandoned because the lords of the soil were suspicious, or did not understand," an opinion with which Liam Kennedy (1976, 177) concurs. Even when these landlords did establish creameries, they were often reluctant to invest adequately in them:

It seems absurd to some farmers to sanction the payment of a salary to a skilled Manager (of the creamery) in excess of their own incomes. This is one of the chief short-comings in productive co-operation, and it is this that gives the proprietor his chance. His business instinct shows him plainly that a good man is worth a good wage, and hence it is that some of the very best men the movement has produced have been tempted to leave it for situations outside, where their brains and skill will be adequately rewarded. The Co-operative Creamery Manager is too often driven by circumstances to become a "rolling stone" ... He seldom is provided with an adequate residence and his wages are frequently cut down during the winter months, though he has been obliged to compress more than a year's work, done at high pressure, into the summer months. (IAOS 1904, 16)

Similarly, the Irish farmer's refusal to engage in winter dairying was often decried as an example of self-defeating conservatism, although the counterargument was just as often heard, that it would not be worth the farmer's while. The IAOS continually brought up this issue in its annual reports, variously suggesting that more root crops, or higher milk yields, or greater use of agricultural machinery would provide the solution to the problem. Whatever the cause of this failure, it was important for the creamery sector's ability to market its output in Britain, as noted above.

How did education in Denmark and Ireland compare at this time? Denmark was clearly a more educated society than Ireland in the nineteenth century. Compulsory education, for 3 days a week between the ages of 7 and 14, had been introduced in Denmark as early as 1814; in 1849 compulsory education was extended to cover a six-day week. Although there are comparatively few data to support the claim, it seems clear that near universal literacy had been achieved in Denmark, certainly by the middle of the century, and probably a lot earlier. In 1859–60, only 3% of military recruits in Denmark were completely illiterate, while 9% could read but not write (Cipolla 1969, 14).

By contrast, in Ireland only 74% of bridegrooms could write their names as late as 1880 (Flora 1983, Vol. 1, 82).[18] In 1841, 53% of the Irish population over the age of five could neither read nor write; with succeeding censuses, the figure fell to 46.8%, 38.7%, 33.4%, 25.2%, 18.4%, and 13.7%; by 1911 it was 11.9% (Flora et al. 1983, 72; 1911 Census, *General Report*, lii). While a successful national elementary school system had been established in Ireland in 1831, education was made compulsory only in 1892 (1898 for rural areas). Ireland was clearly less literate than Denmark; it is, however, important to note that Ireland was not a backward society educationally for the time. Mokyr and Ó Gráda show that this was true even for the pre-Famine period, and conclude that pre-Famine Ireland "was something of an 'impoverished sophisticate,' in the sense that its literacy level was probably higher than its income level would indicate" (Mokyr and Ó Gráda 1988, 226). In 1900, literacy was higher in Ireland than in Italy and Austria, insignificantly higher than literacy in Belgium, and insignificantly lower than literacy in France (Flora, 72).[19]

However, there were large regional variations in literacy within Ireland; the proportion of the population aged 9 years and over which could neither read nor write in 1911 ranged from 3.4% in County Dublin to 20.6% in County Donegal. One might think that this would help explain the diffusion of creameries across counties; but I have found (O'Rourke 2004) no evidence that literacy mattered for creamery numbers. It may well be that educational levels were a key difference between the two countries at this time, but more research would be needed in order to sustain such a hypothesis.

CONCLUSIONS:
DENMARK IN THE IRISH MIRROR

Why did Ireland see its living standards, output, and productivity grow less rapidly than those of Denmark, and why did it rely so heavily on depopulation in order to achieve what income increases it enjoyed? How did Denmark manage to enjoy such rapid real wage growth in the absence of mass emigration, and how did it manage to attract significant capital inflows without the lure of abundant natural resources? Why was Danish performance in key sectors such as dairying so much more impressive than Ireland's, when the two countries were so similar in so many respects? A broader comparative perspective only serves to further highlight the extraordinarily successful nature of late nineteenth-century Danish economic development; what can explain it?

These are big questions, which no one paper can hope to answer. This chapter has reviewed evidence that suggests that rational actor arguments based on different comparative advantages can indeed help to explain why Ireland adopted a less intensive, less high-value-added approach to dairying, and indeed to farming in general, than did Denmark. The fact that cow density was lower in Ireland than in Denmark probably did influence the spread of cooperative creameries in Ireland; although an obvious counterargument in principle is that the number of cows per acre was not necessarily fixed, and that it could have been increased, had the demand from the creameries been there. Other differences in the economic circumstances facing Danish and Irish farmers, which have not been sufficiently explored by the literature, concern factor prices. Figure 1 showed that Irish wages were actually higher than their Danish counterparts until the mid-1890s or so; might this have prompted Irish farmers to chose a less intensive route than the Danes? If so, then Ireland's high emigration rates, which did so much to raise Irish living standards, might have indirectly led to a less technologically progressive agricultural environment.

Another argument is that capital may have been relatively abundant in Denmark, as a Danish expert visiting Ireland argued in 1909:

For the Irish butter exports to be tolerably distributed over the year the present system will have to be revolutionized. The calving is timed in the spring for the sake of raising the young calves. Should this be changed byres will have to be built and feed stuffs imported ... Purchase of feeds and building of byres requires big outlays and, in addition to that, the whole working of the farm must be changed from permanent grass to arable land. The Irish farmer lacks the funds for making this transformation and unlike the Danish farmer he does not reckon the manure to be of value. Since he owes the whole purchase sum of his farm no money can be raised unless the government will lend it to him. And the crux of the matter is, I suppose, whether butter is more profitable than beef. A change towards whole year butter production necessitates the growing of roots [beets] and these plants take, besides some experience, more labour. (Schou 1910, 266)

It is unlikely that capital was scarcer during this period in the United Kingdom, of which Ireland was a member, than it was in Denmark; after all, Britain was the world's foremost capital exporter of the time, and the available evidence suggests that Ireland was exporting capital as well (O'Rourke and Williamson 1999, chapter 11). It is possible, though, that capital markets may not have worked sufficiently well to channel investment funds to Irish farmers. Credit cooperatives never really took off in Ireland as they had done in Germany (Guinnane 1994); while in Denmark small local savings banks to a large extent fulfilled the same task as credit cooperatives did elsewhere, supplying credit to people with little or no security for loans (Guinnane and Henriksen 1998, 52–4). Besides, cooperative creameries in Denmark in some instances granted credit for the purchase of feed stuffs (Henriksen and O'Rourke 2005). Furthermore, the transfer of land from landlords to farmers was taking place in Ireland at this time, whereas in Denmark land reform had taken place much earlier: in addition to occupying peoples' energies and fuelling agrarian unrest, this may have locked up farmers' capital in the purchase of their own land, as the above quotation suggests, when it might have been more usefully employed in various productive investments, including facilities for stall-feeding.[20]

However, it is a key conclusion here that not all of Denmark's relative success during this period was due to different comparative advantages. For example, the price incentives which, Jensen argued, prompted Danish farmers to adopt winter dairying existed elsewhere; what differed was the ability of societies to respond positively to these incentives. Future research could profitably focus on three spheres in which conditions may have favoured Denmark: politics, culture, and the legal system.

As mentioned earlier, land war violence was negatively associated with the diffusion of cooperative creameries within Ireland, suggesting that political factors were important in hindering the spread of new agricultural technologies there. Denmark was a politically stable, homogeneous society, whereas Ireland was divided both culturally and politically. Conflict over property rights, and the national question, may well have been important obstacles to progress there, even though the end results (that is, owner-occupancy) may have been desirable in themselves. Denmark was not only religiously and ethnically homogeneous; it was relatively economically homogeneous, with a large, well-educated class of peasant proprietors. Indeed, this egalitarianism persists today within the workplace, with important implications for the way Danish industry functions (see Kristensen, chapter 8). Homogeneity in Denmark not only meant the absence of conflict; it also facilitated the rapid transmission of organizational and technological innovation. It is notable that the one region of Denmark (eastern Hjørring) where cooperatives were less widespread was also characterized by a slightly different cultural and/or political environment than the rest of the country, with more support for evangelical Lutheranism and the conservative party (Henriksen 1999). Whether this indicates that mainstream Danish society was particularly receptive to cooperation, or whether it was rather the homogeneity of society that was crucial in diffusing cooperatives, remains to be seen.

More speculatively, cultural factors may have made cooperation easier to achieve in Denmark. Timothy Guinnane (1994) argues that an unwillingness to sanction neighbours who were making a poor use of the cooperative's funds was one reason why credit cooperatives spread less rapidly in Ireland than in Germany, where such an unwillingness was apparently absent. Creamery cooperatives also relied on sanctions to maintain a high quality milk supply, and it has been shown (Henriksen and Hviid 2002) that Danish creameries did indeed impose heavy sanctions on members whose milk threatened the quality of the creamery's butter. Might Irish culture have made this kind of strategy more difficult? Remarkably, 82 percent of creameries in largely Protestant Ulster were cooperative in 1906 (roughly the same proportion as in Protestant Denmark); whereas in the rest of the island – overwhelmingly Catholic – just 28 percent of creameries were cooperative (O'Rourke 2004). Is there some feature of Catholic culture that makes economic cooperation more difficult than in Protestant societies?[21] Several authors (e.g., Putnam 1993; La Porta et al. 1997) have recently argued that hierarchical religions such as Catholicism or Islam inhibit the development of trust and social capital; on the face of it, the discrepancy between Ulster and the other three Irish provinces, and between Denmark and Ireland as a whole, is consistent with such arguments. On the other hand, the difference between Catholics and Protestants in nineteenth-century Ireland had as much to do with political and national identity as with religion; and the correlations in the data between Catholicism, agrarian violence, and landlord-tenant agreement are very strong. Moreover, Ulster was much more industrialized than the rest of the island. More detailed historical work is therefore necessary if we want to fully understand the difference in the propensity to cooperate between Protestant Ulster and the Catholic portion of the country: it could have to do with Weberian cultural factors, or it could have to do with other (political or economic) differences between the two communities. The tentative conclusion (O'Rourke 2004) concerning the different propensities to cooperate in Ulster and the rest of

Ireland is that politics was more important than religion *per se*; while Catholicism is negatively correlated with the cooperative share of creameries across Irish counties, this effect disappears once land-war violence has been controlled for. A homogeneous population, rather than a Protestant one, emerges as the key Danish advantage in this period (a conclusion with which Henriksen 1999 concurs).

A final set of speculations concerns the role of law and the state. Being resident in a common law country, Irish cooperatives may have been hampered by a legal tradition that took a dim view of restraints of trade. Thus, attempts to introduce a "binding rule" that would have tied cooperative members into supplying only the creamery of which they were members ran into repeated legal difficulties in Ireland, while such rules posed no problem within the Danish legal system (Henriksen and Hviid 2002). Further, a key difference between Ireland and Denmark was, as stated at the outset, that Denmark was an independent state. While Danish agricultural reforms were largely initiated by the private sector, the state may have played an important supporting role, for example by funding such institutions as the Agricultural University, which carried out important research into the links between winter stall-feeding and productivity (Henriksen and O'Rourke 2005). The obvious strategy for evaluating such an argument would be to look at the development of Irish agriculture between Independence in 1922 and the shift to protectionism in 1932; but such an investigation belongs in another study.

The comparison between Denmark and Ireland brings to the surface several of the main themes of this volume. As small economies, Denmark and Ireland were both vulnerable to external shocks, and certainly the Danish example illustrates the flexible adjustment and rapid learning emphasized by Katzenstein. Even though the labour market institutions of the post-1945 economic miracle did not exist at the time, late nineteenth-century Denmark did see the rapid development of a nationwide cooperative system that not only ran creameries at the local level, but represented the sector's interests in its interactions with a supportive, but not intrusive, government. Furthermore, the reality of large-scale emigration, which had served as a safety valve for Irish society for decades, and led to large and receptive overseas communities that always offered an exit for Irish farmers, may have meant that the Irish felt themselves less vulnerable than did the Danes: they were able to pursue a labour-extensive strategy, and did so, whereas the Danes felt far more obliged to generate prosperity through employment at home. It was not until the late 1980s that the Irish, now inhabiting a smaller and therefore more homogeneous state, and – crucially – faced with a potential fiscal meltdown and spiralling unemployment, embarked on the peculiar blend of low-tax and corporatist policies that would lead to the explosive growth of the 1990s.

Overall, though, this chapter speaks more to the varieties of capitalism literature, in its stress on cooperatives as prime agents of economic change, on the importance of mechanisms for coordinating the behaviour of individual suppliers, and on the importance of trust and those cultural and political factors that either promote or inhibit its development. More generally, the chapter confirms the editors' assertion that "history matters": late eighteenth-century land reforms played an important role in Danish agriculture one hundred years later, while the homogeneity and group cohesion generated by earlier territorial losses proved to be crucial in developing the cooperative structures that would in turn go on to influence the political and economic development of Denmark in the twentieth century.

NOTES

This paper was written while the author was an IRCHSS Government of Ireland Senior Fellow. I am grateful to the Irish Research Council for the Humanities and Social Sciences for their generous funding, and to Ingrid Henriksen and Jeff Williamson for allowing me to draw on my joint work with them. The usual disclaimer applies.

1 Before 1921, Irish Agricultural Statistics, 1913, 2–3; Bjørn (1988, 252).
2 In addition to killing the poorest members of society, the Famine also raised land-labour ratios, thus raising the income of survivors: see Ó Gráda and O'Rourke (1997).
3 Boyer et al. (1994) confirm this interpretation, using a small-scale CGE model of the Irish economy calibrated to 1907–08 data. They estimate that if there had been no emigration between 1851 and 1911, the real urban wage would only have been 66–81 percent of its actual 1908 level.
4 In principle higher transport costs between Britain and Ireland could also have been to blame, but in fact Anglo-Danish price gaps were higher than Anglo-Irish ones for most of the period.
5 For an extensive discussion of the different types of butter, see BPP (1910).
6 The average mid-sized Danish farm owned 6 to 14 cows (Henriksen 1999). The next three paragraphs draw heavily on O'Rourke (2003).
7 Based on Henriksen (1999, Table 1), except for the 1888 figure for cooperatives, which is taken from Bjørn (1988, 371).
8 On the other hand, it should be noted that Denmark did impose tariffs on manufactured products, something which is not always appreciated: see Bairoch (1989).
9 The numbers for the globalization variables come by (i) estimating the impact of migration or capital flows on local labour or capital supplies, and

then estimating the impact of these factor shocks on real wages; or (ii) estimating the impact of commodity market integration on domestic goods prices, and then simulating the impact of these price shocks on real wages. The estimates for the schooling variable are derived by estimating growth regressions for real wages, and then using the estimated schooling coefficients to calculate the growth differentials which arose from differences in educational levels.

10 Which boosted her capital stock by some 16 percent between 1870 and 1910: O'Rourke and Williamson (1999, Table 12.3).

11 Crotty (1966, 69–70), makes a very similar argument to account for the differences in the Danish and Irish agricultural systems; moreover, he appeals to this climatic argument to bolster the argument for which he is best known, which has to do with the effects of peasant proprietorship on the market for land: see Section 4.2.

12 This section draws on Henriksen and O'Rourke (2005).

13 See Armstrong (1989) for a readable account of the traditional view.

14 For an entertaining account of the land war in Kerry in the 1880s, see Grousset (1986).

15 Ó Gráda (1994) has done this and has not found them.

16 Cited in West (1986), 21.

17 Cited in Plunkett (1982), 190–1.

18 Army recruit data and bridegroom data are fairly comparable for other countries at the time: see Flora (1983).

19 Irish literacy was less than Belgian literacy in 1870/71 (64.1% of the population 10 and over could read and write in Ireland, compared with 69.4% in Belgium); Ireland had caught up by 1880/81.

20 More useful, that it, for total agricultural output, but not necessarily for individual farmers' incomes. On the Irish Land Wars, see also Solow (1971) and Guinnane and Miller (1997).

21 For recent contributions on the possible effects of culture on economic performance, see Greif (1994), Putnam (1993), and Temin (1997).

PART TWO

Mechanisms of Success

5

Constitutional Laxity and High International Economic Performance: Is There a Nexus?

HJALTE RASMUSSEN

For the better part of the twentieth century, Danish lawyers were, as a rule, the only readers of works on Danish law written by Danish legal scholars. It was primarily the same circle of readers who, in turn, asked new questions to which legal scholarship would begin designing pertinent answers. Topically and methodologically, this chapter cannot draw much intellectual comfort from the Danish law tradition; it must seek its own way. Softening links to tradition becomes compelling in view of its context – research about Denmark as "One Small State in World Markets" (Katzenstein 1985). It must answer questions of interest for scholars from other social science disciplines than law, who are often without an insider's knowledge about Denmark's legal system.

A PAPER NOT ON LAW BUT ABOUT LAW

The pertinent questions are not *on* but *about* Danish law. They target the law's role in Denmark's noticeable international economic and political success. More specifically, they deal with a narrow segment of Denmark's constitutional laws and practices as well as with some problems regarding the interface between higher European Union (EU) laws and Danish legal politics (Rasmussen 1998, 2003). I refer summarily to these rules of a small state as "the relevant constitutional laws."

My working hypothesis is that to analyse Denmark in the context of the present study without accounting for law's place and role would be arbitrary. A truly notorious constitutional lack of rigidity – laxity may be a better word – characterizes the Danish legal system. Arguably, the capacity of the country's 150-year-old constitution (*Grundloven*) to curtail political

initiative has been eroded to such an astonishing extent that it may be analytically helpful to conceptualize the Small State of Denmark as if it were
in reality governed by an unwritten set of unenforceable constitutional customs and conventions. This was a metamorphosis that mattered. In the
course of the first quarter of the twentieth century it remade Denmark's
free constitution of 1849: from posing a binding challenge to societal
change, it moved to making such change constitutionally virtually unbinding. The constitutional reshuffle did more than make it possible for
Denmark's companies to accomplish the high international economic performance they are renowned for (Campbell, Hall, and Pedersen 2006). It
handsomely oiled processes of the Danish political quest for the enhancement of Danish companies' technical and structural international com-
petiveness (Dahl et al. 2002) in circumstances where a genuine or liberal
version of constitutionalism (U.S.A., Norway, Germany) would have played
it out like a bull in a china shop.

At this point, a short illustration in five parts may clarify what I mean.
(i) Section 75 of the constitution emphatically declares that government
must make it possible for every fit citizen to work in conditions that will
secure his or her livelihood. (ii) Although Section 75 is placed among
undoubtedly legally binding provisions, Parliament (*Folketinget*) never
treated this constitutional provision as if it were binding. It may well not
have been intended to be binding, but activist courts might have made it
become precisely that. (iii) During the latter half of the last century, consecutive Danish governments socialized the citizens of Denmark while
sharpening the international competitive edge of Danish companies
within a domestic framework of capitalism with a human and social face.
(iv) In this process, companies were given a remarkably free hand to hire
and fire workers, while citizens out of work received handsomely distributed public funds offering them economic conditions that secured their
livelihood. (v) The courts of the Realm were not asked their opinion:
workers representing the unemployed minorities did not judge it worth-
while to bring in-court actions to argue that the nation's company-friendly
laws were unconstitutional.

My plan for this chapter is as follows: With bold strokes I begin by pleading the case for the significance and relevance of the law, mapping out
where law has assisted politics in becoming more efficient. Introduced
here is the key notion of a national political management characterized
by a truly pervasive reliance on politicians' agreement (agreement politics). The meaning of this notion is detailed in the following section, in
which I offer illustrations of various types of agreement as they occur in
political and legislative practice in Denmark's negotiational democracy.
After giving examples to corroborate my contentions, I deal with the formal constitutional amendment procedure – which, in practical terms, is

unavailable. Here, I seek to establish a link between the virtual absence of access to formal amendment and the beginning of the demise of constitutional review. In the next section I show that the oft-heard postulate about the Danish courts' empowerment to exercise constitutional review is but an empty shell. With this in mind, I present and discuss a series of case laws and try to identify the societal forces that funnelled negotiational democracy or agreement politics – we have many names for the things we love.

PLEADING THE CASE OF THE LAW

An absolutely indisputable line of causation connecting the relevant constitutional laws and international high performance and economic success does not, of course, exist. To contend otherwise would be arbitrary. However, as I said, to analyse Denmark in the context of the present study without accounting for law's place and role would be equally arbitrary.

The Demise of Constitutionalism

Several indicators testify to the relevance of the constitutional laws. One is the almost complete demise since the 1920s of two crucial features of the previous period's emerging liberal democracy. These were: its formal constitutionalism and a nascent institutionalization of judicial review of legislation for its constitutional compatibility with the *Grundloven*. Another was evidence that, along with the exit of constitutionalism, a new form of democratic governance was taking root, which I call negotiational democracy to mark its main characteristic: a political and legal majoritarian rule, remarkably unrestrained.

These are noteworthy innovations in view of the fact that the *Grundloven* provides for a system of separation of powers, lays the foundations of judicially protected individual rights, and restricts transfers of national sovereignty to non-Danish organizations like the European Union. Instead, the Danes preferred to be governed not by law but by man. As it is, the institutions of parliamentarism and negotiational democracy, its two-egged twin, draw almost complete consensual political support in Denmark. Why? The nation's political allegience to parliamentarism from 1901 gives a simple answer to the declining importance of a supreme law. The reference to parliamentarism does not tell the whole story, if only because other countries have parliamentarism without virtually eclipsing the role of higher laws and constitutional review. The explanatory value of parliamentarism is in want of supplementary rationales.

It is not a valid rationale that the supreme law's own insufficiency or fatigue led to its demise. Instead, a combination of political constellations dictated its fate. Across the Danish political spectrum it was deemed to be in the national interest to subordinate rule by law to rule by politicians' agreement. In this view, the place of law shrank in accordance with a significant shift in the Danish society's list of value priorities during the period under study. In this process, the interest in protecting the individual against encroachments of fundamental and human rights by public authorities gave way to what was seen as the State's overriding modern responsibility: to provide for social peace, cohesion, and prosperity – in short welfare. To illustrate: the state, with the voters' consent, diluted most of the citizens' constitutionally guaranteed rights and gave them a statutorily entrenched right to a state-paid generous old age pension instead.

To accomplish the state's overriding high economic goals, consecutive centre-right and centre-left governments installed regulatory regimes and mechanisms that freed companies' hands – with the view of maximizing Danish companies' international competitiveness. The ensuing, hopefully ever-increasing national economic wealth and welfare was to be distributed to a massively socialized voter force (Fonsmark 1990; Pedersen 2006). *Folketinget* also involved companies, not only as money machines, but as proactive agents in shaping tomorrow's body politic. In fact, *Folketinget* made private corporations and companies socially co-responsible for implementing the politically designed welfare programs; and did so increasingly throughout the latter part of the twentieth century.

Deregulation encompassed the *Grundloven*, including its chapter on basic classical, fundamental, and human rights. "Classical" came to connote belonging to a previous age and an outdated perception of democracy. To be sure, this did not lead to any formal abrogation of the constitution nor of its legally binding nature, although it became increasingly difficult to say what "legally binding" precisely meant. It implied instead that less formal and essentially unenforceable constitutional conventions took its place; the achievement of a constant growth in national economic wealth should have its day, untrammelled by legal niceties.

These are surely remarkable innovations in their own right. They are no less striking in that Denmark's constitutional decline coincided with the growth of constitutionalism and of constitutional review in the European Union and almost everywhere else in Europe; except perhaps (but not without caveats) for Finland and Sweden.

Was this, then, a Small State particularity? *Prima facie*, constitutional amorphousness is not a small state attribute. Among bigger Western states, the United Kingdom likewise features an amorphous constitution. The obvious difference, however, is that the United Kingdom never had a written constitution that could disintegrate. It is therefore still possible that the radical shift of emphasis in Danish constitutional and democratic discourses from citizens' legal rights to their political, social, and welfare rights could well be unparalleled among its equals – a Small State privilege or prerogative.

Some of the inherent peculiarities of Danish political organization may have contributed to this paradigm shift. I refer to the prevalence of radically proportional elections, of a very low, two-percent threshold to representation in *Folketinget,* and of a monocameral legislative system. From this it almost inevitably followed that if there were (rarely) majority governments they were always composed of two, three, or four political parties. The rule has been governance by minority governments, as it were. A majority of only one parliamentary seat has often been all that separated a coalition of parties from being in government or in opposition. Needless to say, government by weak parliamentary majorities or minorities is regularly associated with a lack of determined, farsighted, and strong economic leadership. Alliances and coalition building obviously offer themselves as viable and indispensable alternatives. A more innovative perspective on the cumbersomeness of the said political inadequacies is that their negative societal effects would, *ceteris paribus,* be magnified if paired with an efficient judicial review of legislation's compatibility with the *Grundloven.* This circumstance bears its share of responsibility for the deligitimization of constitutional review, a phenomenon that is key to this chapter.

The decline of constitutional review began when parliamentarism was introduced in constitutional guise in 1901. Decline accelerated when a formal amendment of the constitution's Section 88 in 1915 made constitutional change by way of formal amendment virtually impossible. In fact, Section 88 prescribes an utterly cumbersome – and risky – formal constitutional amendment procedure; to launch it is any prime minister's nightmare. I later argue that formal constitutional unamendability contributed to and perhaps even justifies Danish judges' remarkable self-restraint in litigation concerning the constitutionality of legislation. This judicial hands-off policy is the essence of the notorious constitutional laxity to which I referred in my opening observations: in short the noted deregulation of constitutionality.

A main ingredient of these company-fixated policies was the desire to compensate their victims economically (Fonsmark 1990). For example, the State guaranteed to all workers being laid off that the loss of a job would not bring with it severe losses in income. Similarly, government spends huge amounts of money in order to find new employment for the jobless, including providing for small meshed frameworks for upgrading of qualifications and retraining workers for new job-functions. More about this below.

Alliance and consensus building did in fact become the name of the game of Danish political life. Since the early twentieth century, but most systematically since the 1970s, political leaders have cultivated in common a style of national political management that is characterized by a truly pervasive reliance on politicians' agreements, independently of whether centre-left or centre-right parties were forming government. Borrowing the term *forhandingsdemokrati* from Morten Kelstrup (Kelstrup 1998), I shall speak of it as "negotiational democracy." This is a style of governance that can be likened to the particularities of corporate governance – if one does not forget that Denmark is not a private corporation but a sovereign state (Kaspersen 2006). The comparison is rife with clues to a better understanding of several aspects of the following presentations.

Danish law-and policy making by politicians' agreement is a fairly unique phenomenon. It does not compare to the way politicians and parties negotiate in democracies everywhere. In post–World War II Denmark, the entire constitutional and political structure was upheld by negotiation – entailing agreement in order to continue the dance around the Golden Calf of sharp company-driven increases in the wealth of the nation – as results of successes on export markets. Politicians' agreement politics is not only the absolutely dominant mode of policy formation; it is unstoppable, almost like an addiction. Take it away and the Danish Model's often spectacularly ideology-free, inter-party, welfare-generating democratic policy-making structure is likely to implode. The lifeblood that keeps it alive, well, and flourishing is Denmark's unique ethnic, religious, educational, and linguistic homogeneity. The fact that the country's small, fertile land is flat and densely populated is another important key to understanding the premises to the essentials of the functioning of Denmark's specific brand of "democracy plus international economic success."

The large stakeholders in negotiational democracy are both the members of the government of the day and the leaders of the opposition in Parliament. While I have already noted this, the point will be developed further here. In fact, the doers in this policy-making machinery have mostly come from the Liberal, the Conservative, the Social Democratic, and the Radical Liberal parties. They and their leaders have together formed an exclusive and politically distinguished *Privy League*. Politicians belonging to a number of more decidedly leftist and rightist political parties existed during the post-war period but they rarely took part in privy agreement politics (Kaspersen 2006). In fact, over long periods of time it would be the same small group of men and women who made up the core of agreement politics – wearing one or the other hat.

The glue that held them together was not a desire or necessity to hammer out class compromises; far more mundane concerns were at stake. In light of the constantly fluctuating world economy, the top political priority was to enhance Danish companies' competitive edge abroad. An important means deployed for this purpose has been to adapt society to the needs of its companies. What companies and their organizations said would be good for them was, by implication, deemed to be good for Denmark. What they asked for would often be granted to them at the expense, if it could not be otherwise, of groups of individuals and their interests and rights – thus reinforcing a democratic-corporatist ethos that has old and deep roots in Danish society (Martin 2006).

From it all emerged a political system characterized by huge concentrations, in the hands of relatively few leading political characters, of discretionary powers of appalling size – powers to mould virtually all aspects of life and death in Denmark.

Human Rights Lacunae

So much for generalizations. Two randomly chosen cases will illustrate the practical importance of this constitutional unconstrainedness and show how it worked. The first case deals with constitutional protection of human and fundamental rights. The second looks at conflicts between European Union law and Danish domestic law.

To begin with the case about human rights. The fact that the EU-treaties from 1952 and forty years onward gave fundamental and human rights absolutely no legal protection caused headaches in some EU Member States – but never in Denmark. It was not a Danish problem, simply because the national legal room was itself virtually empty of such protection (more to follow below). In contrast, the absence of such protection caused major constitutional and political difficulties in, for example, Germany – one of the European Union's founding members. At home, German citizens enjoy a privileged, high, constitutionally entrenched protection of a great many human and fundamental rights (under the *Grundgesetz*). Against this backdrop, it was of serious public concern that every transfer of a regulatory power from some German authority to an EU counterpart implied a corresponding loss of protection. On several occasions the German Constitutional Court (*Bundeverfassungsgericht*) protested sharply, threatening not to apply EU law that did not comply with the German constitution. The problem of lack of protection occasionally restrained (but on such occasions, severely) the German government's freedom of –action within the European Union.[1] If Norway had joined the Union, its judicial traditions of high level protection of human and fundamental rights would likewise have been irreconcilable with the existence of a basically protection-free EU room. Like Germany, the Irish Republic has gone through a series of hard-fought court battles and constitutional amendments in order to bring Irish constitutional law into line with Ireland's obligations as a member of the Union. Far from this, the Danes and their courts did not raise an eyebrow over the European Union's human rights lacunae.

Sovereignty and the Courts

Even more important is the fact that the Danish courts have backed away from explaining whether Section 20 imposes legally enforceable limits to the degree of sovereignty that it authorizes Denmark to transfer to the European Union. Complainants have twice, in 1971 and in 1993, but without avail, turned to the Danish courts for help against what they perceived as *ultra vires* sovereignty transfers.

The Supreme Court refused to dispose of the 1971 case on its merits, declaring that the plaintiff lacked standing.[2] The plaintiffs of the second case could not individually muster more *locus standi* than their 1971 predecessor. The case was rather a sort of class action, which the Danish procedural code does not provide for. The Supreme Court admitted the case for a hearing on its merits nonetheless, thereby jumping up as a lion.[3] Eventually, it dropped down as a mouse, acquitting the government of the charges levelled against it. It reasoned that judicial help was in short supply because it was primarily a political question to identify the constitutional limitations to Section 20's legal basis for transfers of sovereignty.[4] The Court, in other words, returned the sovereignty-transfer ball to the smoke-filled backrooms of politicians' deal-making. If the Privy League hereafter considers more transfers of sovereignty to be in Denmark's and its companies' best interests, the judicial branch of government will not help those who feel disentitled (about whom more details below).

The preceding account makes it plain that the judiciary could not or would not stand up against statutory enactments on behalf of citizens, claiming that the application of such an act had wrought injustice. The following narrative illustrates that the courts of the Realm surely disposed of resources to help distressed governments.

The situation in which this example is played out is the era after Denmark's entry into the European Union, which brought with it the full and, in principle, unfettered direct applicability and primacy of EU law in Denmark. More specifically, this meant that the following three fundamental EU legal principles would set up insurmountable boundaries to Danish governmental action. The first strictly limits the freedoms of legislative action of Member States' parliaments. Danish laws are henceforth not to be enforceable if promulgated in areas of competencies delegated to the European Union. Second, after membership, EU law is to be honoured as the supreme law of the land, prevailing over all withstanding national laws. Finally, the founding treaties vest in the high EU Court an empowerment to enforce these principles and limitations strictly (Rasmussen 1998).

All these legal principles are the vestiges of a rigorous constitutionalism quite unlike its domestic Danish counterpart. Thus, Danish lawyers, judges and politicians would have to learn to deal with a membership-created dilemma of considerable proportions, namely that of respecting a law higher than political expediency. On the one hand, EU membership was seen as instrumental to a continuation of sharp increases in wealth in Denmark. On the other, if Small State Denmark were to grant EU law all it asked for, ruin would be threaten the much-hailed principles of agreement politics and the Danish State's unilateral and unlimited promotion of its companies' international competitiveness. Was the sacrifice of the unfettered national lawmaker's Garden of Eden too high a price to pay for this? Was there, possibly, a third way that could be explored – a middle way to be carved out between non-membership and full EU -law compliance in consequence of membership? What to do?

In answer to this question we may begin by restating that no chain is stronger than its weakest link. In the context of the interface problems between EU law and Denmark's negotional democracy, this link is Article 234 of the EU treaty. This article provides for a cooperation mechanism between the EU court and the courts of the Member States, the "preliminary questions procedure." The aim of this procedure is not only to enable the EU court to exercise its monopoly of interpretation of EU law; it is no less than to ensure that the monopoly goes unchallenged by national courts and authorities. The problem is that an enabling act of a national judge is required in order to trigger the EU court's interpretetive competence. However, anticipating abuses by negligence, the drafters of Article 234 made it a solemn duty for national courts beyond which there lies no higher national appeal to refer any relevant preliminary questions to the EU court. Now, where is then the sought-after weak link? It lies hidden in the fact that non-compliance with Article 234's obligation is not sanctionable – not as a matter of law but as a matter of the Union's political and constitutional practices. It follows that if the enabling national act is not issued, the EU court's prerogative will be emptied of much of its content and purpose. Against a national unwillingness to cooperate, the European Court's interpretation monopoly will be turned into an hollow postulate – in many hard cases at least.

This weakness opened a window of vulnerability and opportunity which lawyers acting on behalf of the Danish government were not unwilling to exploit. In fact, in a number of instances where the sovereignty of Denmark's agreement politics came under threat of the EU law's supremacy, these distinguished lawyers sought to activate the loophole in Article 234. Intermittently, they used the same technique and argumentation, which on the face of it is entirely appropriate and legal. It consists in arguing before the domestic courts that a litigated provision of EU law, typically one that gives a citizen or a company a right against the Danish state, does not actually pose a genuine and real problem of interpretation – at least not one serious enough for the courts to trigger the preliminary references procedure. In the language of EU law, the lawyers argue that the case is about an *acte clair* which, according to the EU court's own case law, falls outside the ambit of Article 234. Notorious among such tactics have been court cases dealing with core fields of EU law such as the fundamental economic freedoms. These give economic actors entitlements to unhindered border-crossing activities such as intra-union trade in goods and services and the free movement of persons and capitals.

The circle is squared if the competent Danish courts accept the government's *acte clair* argumentation, and there is solid evidence to suggest that they often will in hard cases. Before continuing I should answer the question of how the courts can get away with finding *acte clair* where there is interpretive obscurity? This facility is a simple consequence of the Danish judicial tradition of offering utterly taciturn motivations for judicial decisions.

Transparency or not, it is the result that counts. The result is that the European Court can, if necessary, be kept at bay and that the disputed statute translating a high priority political agreement into Danish law can be enforced without EU judicial interference. It follows that the discretion of the Privy League's politicians will often not be strait-jacked by the necessity to calculate the risks associated with EU constitutional litigation. To sum up, it is no wonder that Danish governments involve themselves deeply in sovereignty-protective courtroom battles involving EU law. It is a greater surprise that our courts seem to embrace the government's *acte clair* argumentation, also in instances where it is not wholly convincing. However, when they do, the result is to shield politically important Danish statutes from a potentially destructive Union-judicial scrutiny. Astonishment or not, the Danishness of it all is truly remarkable.

Danish voters' trust in and patience with the Privy League has been notorious, at least on this side of World War II (Volz 2006; Pedersen 2006).The big question, of course, is why? That voters representing the political mainstream are satisfied poses a lesser problem than to understand what makes the country's minorities go along as well. Their impressive allegiance to the rights-denying, company-well-being–focused, and politico-constitutional system reflects, it seems, the sustainability of agreement politics and, especially, of its systematic recourse pay offs. Allegiance has been obtained by lavish public economic subsidizing, respective financing of the big and small necessities of life of both not-so-well-off and well-to-do Danes. This generosity is such that the livelihood of one in every three Danes' is fully dependent on solicited and unsolicited money hand-outs by the welfare authorities. Another result is that recipients of payments and subsidies by the end of the twentieth century encompass children and elderly people alike, students in schools and at universities, home owners, unemployed and employed, middle class consumers of the state's multifarious cultural offers, and private and public companies being at the receiving end of state subsidies – just to illustrate (Fonsmark 1990:167). On the receiver's side of economic and non-economic favours (on an unbelievable scale), and of government hand-outs has been, *inter alia,* the AP Moeller and Maersk companies, which have recently been listed as one of the world's biggest enterprises (Benson 2004). It is a truly egalitarian redistribution of the fortunes made by Danish companies operating in world markets. It has been succinctly pointed out that 90 percent of the citizens pay via their taxes for a slightly differently composed other 90 percent.

This unique intertwinement of law, legal culture, and history (see Part Six for more) on the one hand, and of politics, political culture, and definition of democracy on the other, is intrinsically linked to and preconditioned by the smallness of the Danish state and nation.

After having thus in general terms pleaded law's case, let us now focus on the gist of politicians' agreements. We go on to present a more detailed account of how and why law matters. This will be done by dissecting each of the relevant constitutional laws, showing its role in the processes of oiling agreement politics – and thereby, indirectly, Denmark's taking of a more than proportional part of international growth in wealth.

THE GIST OF "POLITICIANS' AGREEMENTS"

The preceding passages have expressed my contention that the Small State Denmark is characterized by its body politic's conviction that it is in the country's best interests to be governed by agreement politics with an obsession for economic growth.

In its own odd ways the Small State Denmark managed to free its legislative processes from most existing constitutional ties while constricting acceptable national policy making to the furtherance of fairly well-defined substantive policy objectives. Above and in what follows, the notions of "politicians' agreements" and "agreement politics" are ubiquitous. At this point, two or three things should said about them and illustrations given of how they operate.

First, the durability that their politically but not legally binding nature makes possible, is an important characteristic. "Politically binding" means that any party privy to an agreement is, as a rule, entitled to veto the other parties' law-making activities which may be at variance with the policies agreed upon. Second, one's imagination alone places a limit on the contents of these agreements. A third and final point is that it is possible to loosely identify different types or classes of agreements.

As it is, one class of agreements pertains to the way the political departments handle certain provisions of the *Grundloven*. At issue here is a politicians' agreement that in practice substitutes for Parliament's constitutionally entrenched prerogative of the nationalization of aliens. In practice, it is for the most part not *Folketinget* but the government which affords Danish nationality to foreigners. Once every year, a draft bill with the names of those administratively offered citizenship is laid before Parliament for automatic legislative approval and entrenchment, independent of the presence of a parliamentary majority. Another illustration is that a politicians' agreement has effectively turned the important provision of Section 20 on transfers of sovereignty into a *lettre morte*. Although the Section warrants ratification by qualified parliamentary majority of treaties that transfer sovereignty, it seems to result from a politicians' agreement that this legal basis is disapplied in practice, a matter I shall return to below.

Other agreements are organizational in nature. This goes, for example, for the agreement setting up a hierarchy of governmental committees entrusted with identifying the national interest vis-à-vis European Union policy making. Close to thirty expert committees form the structure at the lowest level of this hierarchy. While the core membership of these committees is made up of civil servants, private interests are also often solidly implanted. Eventually, layers of committees later, a committee on which sit a few centrally placed government ministers will hammer out Denmark's best interests and negotiating position in a forthcoming meeting in the competent EU body – often the European Council or the Council of Ministers.

Enter, next, a new stage of agreement politics. This intervenes when, according to another politicians' agreement (this time one as old as Danish EU membership), the minister who will represent Denmark's interests in Brussels appears before *Folketinget*'s Europa Committee (*Europaudvalget*). The latter is a permanent, seventeen-member committee, the membership of which is representative of the current relative strength of the political parties in *Folketinget*. At this meeting the Europa Committee will give or deny the minister a requested mandate for his negotiations, which will take place the following week in the pertinent

EU body. Whether identical to the minister's proposal or not, a mandate – in real terms a new political agreement – of some kind will in most situations be given. As such, it is binding in the ordinary ways just mentioned.

Still other types of politicians' agreements pertain to high and low political matters alike. One distinct type of agreement regulates Denmark's non-EU, international behaviour. This could, for example, be related to the country's participation in the coalition forces in Iraq; to international trade negotiations; to refugee and asylum politics; to aid to developing nations. Other agreements pertain to questions about, for example, granting licenses to private companies' oil-exploration in the North Sea; or to public and private pensions and/or taxation and other conditions; or to privatization of publicly owned media or companies. One might also mention the agreements which parties conclude on the occasion of the adoption of the budget each year in November – and many more. Thus, the term "politicians' agreements" is most of all about the involved politicians' decisional and legislative technique.

"Technique" is not to be taken in any precise or technical meaning. The ways and means of agreement making are not subject to rules of procedure or the like, exception made perhaps for untimely rescindments of agreements. Most politicians' agreements serve the purpose of avoiding – if at all possible – any show of confrontation in public and of conveying the message to the voters that the Privy League is in control and the country healthy, safe, and well-governed in its leaders' trustworthy hands. It follows that many agreements were never meant to lead to or prepare for the adoption of legislation. Others serve as preparatory steps for later legislation and will frequently orchestrate in impressive detail – as we shall see in three examples that follow (i–iii). A hallmark of virtually all politicians' agreements is, thus, the remarkable informality that characterize all their aspects. These pertain to time of beginning and ending, to their venue; and to who will take the initiative to new negotiations. Their existence is often not even known to the public (again, examples i–iii are illustrative). As for their objectives, these range from the spheres of economics (often), organizational (i) or political (iii) concerns; or they may pertain informally to overcoming some existing legal barrier (ii).

So much for the presentation in the abstract of negotiational democracy's politicians' agreements. Now follow three more detailed descriptions of agreement politics "at work." The presentations are drawn from a series of factual and legal circumstances which ended up in court. Discussions of these court cases will, from a different angle, be continued in the penultimate section of the chapter.

The Tvind Judgment

(i) There is, first, Parliament's Tvind statute and the factual and legal circumstances leading up to the so-called Tvind judgment of 1999. Under judicial scrutiny in this case was the Tvind statute, which succeeded in depriving a number of private schools of their entitlement under existing legislation to apply for and receive grants of certain public funds (the Fund Law). The funds had been designed so as to make more efficient the administration of a variety of precisely defined educational purposes in pursuance of which the legislation had been enacted (which we need not discuss here). A number of the relevant schools were assembled in one common organization, Tvind – which the media often nicknamed "Tvind's Empire."

When the Tvind statute eliminated the entitlements of Tvind under the Fund Law, *Folketinget* was quite aware of what it did. Its action was based on a well-established assumption that the Tvind schools had grossly abused the entitlement. It was assumed that they had bilked the State's finances of hundreds of millions of DKK. Of these monies, Tvind had likely used a good deal for certain vaguely understood but presumably unauthorized (including private) purposes.

Tvind's behaviour could undoubtedly be reproached for lack of social solidarity. The schools' administration had likely also violated a number of principles of Danish law. In the words of one MP, the Public Auditor had given "full insight into the School's illegal practices and reproachable conditions" (Koch 2002). In the past, many administrative initiatives aiming at regularizing Tvind had been undertaken, but all had petered out. While MPS across *Folketinget*'s political spectrum were aware of much, they had little solid proof of misconduct in their *dossier* and would therefore not under normal circumstances have begun legislating. Yet, in this case the Chamber was full of resentment caused by most MPs' complete and definitive loss of confidence in the Tvind organization's ways of doing business. In the end it ignited the legislative powder so that the media burst forth with well-intentioned indignation, requesting loudly and repeatedly that something had to be done about Tvind.

One course of parliamentary action, and an efficient and constitutional one at that, would have been to abrogate the Fund Law. Although attractive in theory, this route was repugnant in practice – for one reason. This reason was that *Folketinget* considered it to be of paramount importance that the Fund Law be able to continue financing all other eligible schools, not just those assembled in Tvind. Some of them had, more or less like Tvind, been peacefully milking the Fund and joyfully spending the proceeds, often for their own pleasures. But unlike Tvind, they had not aroused much public fuss, in part because they had powerful allies inside

Folketinget. All of these schools fit into the wider context of this study in view of their undisputed contributions to raising the general educational level of the Danish workforce, among other things.

Profiting from some sort of protection were, in particular, two school conglomerates which included *folkehøjskolerne* (folk high schools). Historically and actually, these schools have been affiliated with the Radical Liberal and Liberal Parties. These schools, as well as *Arbejderhøjskolerne* (workers' high schools) which are run by the trade unions whose companions in arms in Parliament are the Social Democrats, were thus both indirectly linked to agreement politics. All this placed several of the key players of the Privy League in a squeeze. In this situation, the parliamentary majority, controlled by the Privy League parties, fell victim to the temptation to single Tvind out for separate legislative treatment.

This in itself well illustrates the functioning of agreement politics. Moreover, answering the following two questions will shed additional light – especially on the extent of *Folketinget's* sense of the freedom of uncensurable action. Why did the majority chose not to set in motion the specific administrative procedures that the Fund Law had designed to apply in the event of cases of alleged abuses of grants? The majority simply stated that it would be too time-consuming to go by the law's own administrative sanction rules!

The second question is hypothetical. Had the administrative sanction rules been applied and, in the end, a negative administrative decision had gone out against Tvind, what would have transpired. Tvind would in that case undoubtedly have had standing to challenge the decision judicially. Aware of this, the majority simply perceived the possibility as another good reason for not applying the specific administrative procedures of the Fund Law. It reasoned that legal proceedings would add another unknown and unacceptable number of years to a time sheet already incommensurable. In sum, the majority succumbed to the public demand for "justice" now.

Folketinget thus chose to wrap itself in the clothes of legislator, administrator, and judge. Needless to say, it thereby disregarded the command of any thinkable principle of separation of powers, including that in the *Grundloven's* Section 3. Specific to the Danish situation was, however, that Section 3 had never before in Denmark's constitutional history been applied by the courts against the legislature. Therefore, when Tvind sued and the Supreme Court struck down the Tvind statute, the Danish legal community was greatly surprised, many of its members in shock.

The Tvind statute was obviously not the result of a momentary parliamentary absentmindedness. Instead, the majority was fairly well informed, had a plan, and followed it through – unfortunately to some absurd consequences. On this assumption, the relevant political Tvind agreement and subsequent legislation offer another vivid illustration of negotiational politics at play. Namely, the lesson seems to be that friends are protected while fiends are given short shrift – the *Grundloven*'s Section 3 notwithstanding.

The acuity of this conclusion is mind-boggling in all circumstances. It stands out the more sharply only if the Privy League's parties assumed that their combined interests represented a higher value than the relevant constitutional provisions, including Section 3. A discussion of what the majority's yes-voters were actually thinking will be taken up below.

The AMBI Legislation: Ends and Means

(ii) The embroilment surrounding the AMBI -legislation also offers a good illumination of the lengths of illegality to which Danish politicians are willing to march in pursuance of a given national interest. This legislation (*ArbejdsMarkedsBidrag*) introduced a 2.5 percent sales or cascade tax to be charged on sales of all goods in Denmark. It applied irrespectively, but not indiscriminately, of whether the goods were locally produced or imported from other EC Member States. It did so in spite of the acknowledged fact that the good Danish intentions with this legislation were flatly incompatible with two of EU law's most fundamental principles: its clear prohibition against Member States' enactment of cascade taxes; and the equally important legal ban of national discrimination on grounds of nationality against goods originating in other Member States. As usual, the proposed legislation was not objectionable – or more precisely, not judicially attackable – on any domestic constitutional grounds.

As a large parliamentary majority in *Folketinget* perceived the situation, they must have hated it. However, the necessity of solving no fewer than three major political problems forced them to act, and act quickly. First, an overheated national economy necessitated that a very substantial amount of buying power be mopped up – one way or another, forthwith, and by new taxes. Second, imports of cheaper foreign goods were weakening Danish companies' competitiveness on the home market. Massive layoffs, which would increase the current, already double-digit rate of unemployment were a real threatening. Third, the centre-right parties in power had won the last general election promising their voters not to increase the VAT – which at a general rate of (then) 22.5 percentage points was already high enough. Raising the VAT level would, had it not been for this promise, have been the most effective, as well as the most legal, simple and, therefore, politically attractive solution. Now it was felt that the road to an increase of the VAT was absolutely barred.

In these circumstances the Privy League Parties agreed that the adoption of a sales tax was the best way to get their backs off the wall, EU law withstanding or not. This would immediately cool the economy but not do away with the unemployment challenge. To counter the latter, the new tax was in a very ingenious and complex manner construed so as to place a lighter tax burden on imports of raw materials and semi-manufactured goods than on most goods manufactured domestically. This measure would usefully stimulate the competitiveness of homemade goods on the domestic market – but, of course, contravene EU's fundamental prohibition against discrimination on the ground of nationality.

EU law was an annoyance but one, as the Privy League saw it, to be overcome by simple disregard. Going ahead with its plans, the Danish Parliament tried to conceal the EU infringements, especially by taking shelter behind statutory texts of great regulatory complexity. It was moreover – and as usual – assumed that the inaccessibility of the Danish language would enhance chances of getting away with the law's irregularities unpunished. This mask would not of course help if the legal game's real losers, the Danish importers, were to bring in-court actions. Yet, it could not realistically be counted on that importers would shy away from initiating the traditional tough and costly uphill battle that it is to win a court case against the government in Denmark. If the importers were to sue, it was foreseeable that they would urge the national court to cooperate with the EU court under Article 234 (above). Were the case in this manner to reach the EU court, the Danish government's control of the situation would de-escalate fast.

Two importers did bring court actions, claiming their tax monies back. Facing the challenge of the case reaching the EU court, the government followed its usual *acte clair* strategy (explained above). The Danish courts did not trigger the preliminary questions procedure in time to prevent the European Commission from suing the Danish government before the EU court, urging it to knock down the AMBI statute (an Article 226 procedure). Then, the Danish courts sent their AMBI case to the EU court as well. At home, no-one really seriously doubted that the EU court would make it clear that the cascade tax was in violation of the said two fundamental EU prohibitions. The EU court's reputation of being an unabatedly strict enforcer of both the spirit and the letter of Community law is of long standing. When it actually did, the AMBI statute's life looked doomed – even in Danish court, to which the EU court would address its ruling under Article 234. The deposition of massive claims to reimbursement of illegally levied AMBI tax money would be the case's next stop. In short, national economic disaster was an eventuality to be reckoned with.

Enough of the theory – now on to how Danish agreement politics, combined with judicial loyalty, plays the game when damage control is needed. This story, which includes a tale about how the Danish courts in the end came to the rescue of the government (against all odds), will be retold in the penultimate section below. At this juncture, the important point was merely to illustrate the frequent high risk-taking functioning of agreement politics, a point that is also borne out by the fact that Denmark loses almost a hefty two-thirds of all the other EU-tax-legislation infringement cases that reach the EU court.[5] Add to this toll the cases decided by the Danish courts without asking a preliminary question under Article 234. The end often seems to justify the means.

Referendum by Politicians' Agreement

(iii) The Privy League's contribution to finding a solution to what began as the Social Democratic Party's difficulties vis-à-vis their rank and file membership on the issue of Denmark's accession to the EC/ EU offers a good third illustration of the functioning of politicians' agreement-making. The Social Democratic Party, it is recalled, has for nearly a century been one of the country's major government-bearing political parties. Especially after World War II, it has been at the helm of several, mostly minority governments.

In his capacity as prime minister, the social democrat Jens Otto Krag in 1971 concluded, on behalf of Denmark, a Draft Treaty with the European Union (or the European Economic Community, as it was then). If the treaty was ratified following the procedures prescribed by Section 20 of the constitution, Denmark would become an EC Member State from 1 January 1973. Section 20, which has already been discussed above, stipulates the conditions to be met in case of transfers of Danish sovereignty to organizations like the EU. Its first paragraph provides that: "The powers vested in the authorities of the Realm under this Constitution Act may, by statute and to a specified extent, be delegated to international authorities set up by mutual agreement with other states for the promotion of international rules of law and co-operation." The Draft Treaty on Denmark's EC membership was clearly about a transfer of sovereignty in this sense of the first paragraph.

For cases in which a sovereignty transfer is foreseen by an international treaty, Section 20's second paragraph prescribes two alternative modes of procedure for its ratification. One mode is by a decision taken by a five-sixths majority of all MPs, necessitating at least 150 yes-votes. Alternatively, the sovereignty transfer can be ratified if a lesser parliamentary majority votes in favour and a majority of voters representing 30 percent of all registered voters participating in the ensuing referendum do not vote no. If there is a negative vote it means a full stop to the process of ratification, which was the case when a majority of Danish voters in 1992 refused to go along with the proposed ratification of the Maastricht treaty.

However, while Krag and most of the other social democratic and trade union leaders were very much in favour of membership, well over 50 percent of the party's rank and file squarely opposed it. This was in itself a serious divide that could only get worse if the intra-party split was to become widely publicized. And it would be if 150 MPs or more, including all the social democratic MPs, voted for ratification. For Krag it was crucial to prevent this hypothetically calamitous situation from becoming real – but not at the price of not getting Denmark into the EU (Kapsersen 2006). Two solutions offered themselves to his problem. The first consisted in organizing a referendum on EU entry which would dilute political responsibility – even in the case of a five-sixths yes-vote in Parliament (the confirming referendum). The second possible exit consisted in preventing a qualified majority from being seen to exist. While hindsight informs us that the second solution prevailed in the end, Krag could not have known this. To play it safe, he had to gather political support for holding a confirming referendum.

In the face of a qualified parliamentary yes-vote, safe play was not assured, however. Although Danish legal scholars are not of one mind on this issue, the problem arguably is (or was) that under the circumstances a confirming referendum might be unconstitutional. Violation or not, the simple fact that the Privy League's pursuance of a high priority policy might contravene some constitutional provision would normally not suffice to prevent its transformation into law.

Krag's real problem, therefore, was of a different nature. It was that no other political parties privy to agreement politics were grappling with a comparable elite/non elite divide. While he was dependent on others' political support, what course of action should he follow in order to obtain it? Although there was no self-evident answer to this question, he managed to square the circle. En route, a first provisional victory was pocketed when the leader of the Radical Liberal Party – at the end of an "under-four-eyes" conversation – declared that he was willing to go along with planning for a confirming referendum. Next, these two politicians persuaded the rest of the League's members that a politically legitimizing, confirming referendum had to be organized. The group's third step consisted in letting the competent, permanent parliamentary committee, *Markedsudvalget* (now *Europaudvalget* or the Europa Committee) vote in favour of the arguably unconstitutional project. The final step consisted in that the same parties induced *Folketinget* to adopt a so-called *beslutning*, to the effect of organizing a confirming referendum.

In this series of events, two things are important for our purposes here. The first is the episode's demonstration of the forcefulness and resourcefulness of agreement politics in the absence, for all practical purposes, of constitutional review. If the confirming-referendum trick was *ultra vires* the constitution, no-one would ever know because of the courts' hands-off policy. That it all was to no avail in the actual circumstances of the case, because fewer than 150 MPs voted for ratification, is not the point of the present analysis. It is, instead, that the 1972 course of events did not deprive the confirming referendums of a bright future. Indeed, throughout the following thirty years prime ministers facing successive situations of ratification of sovereignty deftly prepared drafts enabling legislation for holding confirming referendums. Negotiational democracy's rooms for manoeuvre are certainly impressive.

Two final observations should be added. The first remark is that Krag's 1971 strategy paid off in one more respect than initially envisaged. His plan not only made the five-sixths rule's legal exclusion of an affirming referendum redundant; it has also been successful in turning voters' attention at general elections away from the Privy League Parties' EU platforms ever since. In fact, according to recent opinion polls, a mere 7–8 percent of voters let a party's EU platform influence their decision about where to cast the ballot! Nor do these parties compete for voters' favours when referendum campaigns are fought – by explaining, for example, on which policy issues they stand divided. Instead, the Privy League Parties are bent on agreeing, prior to the launching of each new campaign, about the conditions and arguments – a sort of musketeer's oath – on which they will conduct the referendum campaign. Competition is deemed to be a luxury in the face of the overriding interest of all involved in not ruining the continued national enjoyment of the economic and political benefits of European Union membership. Ideological differences have therefore been reduced to a barely audible background noise (Kaspersen 2006).

My second remark emphasizes that it will require an unusually fertile imagination to prophesy that the courts, in case an action were brought, would invalidate a supplementary draft referendum bill. The Privy League's public interest in such a bill, and in a referendum, will weigh heavily against a judicial finding of a sufficiently clear violation of the *Grundloven*. It argues strongly against judicial censure that agreement politics favours referendum practice, including the shape of affirming referendums. These are seen by the League as propitiously oiling the conduct of the country's necessary EU public policies. A normal Danish judge will in such circumstances be inclined to reason that these practices therefore *must* serve a major national interest and therefore be constitutional – constitutional, if necessary, in the forms required for a constitution-derogating new customary or conventional law to have emerged. The pervasiveness and perseverance of Danish politics by agreement is daunting.

It should be remembered that I did not set out to prove the existence of a direct line of causation between the relevant constitutional laws and the country's international high performance. My objective was less ambitious. It was to demonstrate that the absence, in any meaningful sense of the word, of binding constitutional laws and of the courts' exercise of constitutional review (more to follow) has really set free the hands of Danish policymakers and policy enforcers – almost beyond imagination.

When the ends justify the means, goal accomplishment flows more smoothly.

In summing up, three points may now be made. First, light has been shed on the art and nature of politicians' agreements. Second, we know something more about the interests that agreements regularly pursue. Third, it has been established that – within certain substantively defined limits – the Privy League is virtually unconstrained to mould at its will both the headlines and the details of Denmark's policies.

My intent in the three following sections will be to dissect each of the relevant constitutional laws, showing its role in the processes of oiling agreement politics – and thereby, indirectly, Denmark's taking more than a proportional share of international growth in wealth.

FROM "CONSTITUTIONAL AMENDMENT UNAVAILABLE"
TO THE DESTITUTION OF CONSTITUTIONAL REVIEW

In the present and succeeding sections I shall try to corroborate my contention about the international-economic relevance of Denmark's peculiar constitutional configuration. The role of this section in this is twofold: first, to place the entire discussion about relevance in the context of the constitutional history of the unitary state of Denmark; second, to shed light on the significance of the unavailability of both constitutional amendment and legislation review for the purposes of adapting Danish society to altering international conditions of competition.

The first point recalls that the nation's omnipotent monarch in 1849 gave the citizens a free, written constitution, replete with a catalogue of fine fundamental and human rights. It is remarkable that, as of the writing of this chapter in 2004, its text has been virtually unamended from its wording in the mid-nineteenth century. In comparative terms this is a truly unique feature.

It was the 1915 amendment of the *Grundloven* that enshrined this textual durability. Since then, four cumulative conditions have had to be met in order to carry through any formal constitutional amendment. These conditions are among the world's toughest. The road to a successful constitutional amendment is so barrier-laden that politicians tend to shy away from trying.

These amendment conditions are the following. First, the sitting Parliament must adopt a draft proposal of the amendment. Past experience informs us that this draft will not be submitted to Parliament unless a politicians' agreement makes it certain that the draft will draw a strong affirmative vote. Second, a general parliamentary election must be organized, the main issue of which must be the politics pertinent to the proposed constitutional amendment. The third step is the incoming Parliament's adoption of the draft without adding or detracting anything from it. Up to and including this point, the success of the procedure can by and large be controlled by intelligent campaigning and party discipline.

A referendum constitutes the fourth and final barrier, which cannot, of course, be won by effective political management or agreement making alone. At this referendum, a majority of the voters must vote to uphold the twice-adopted draft amendment bill. When the Social Democratic and Radical Liberal parties initiated the 1915 amendment, Section 88 did not prescribe that a referendum be called. Since the 1915 amendment, a majority constituting 45 percent of the registered voters must cast an affirmative vote. If the 45 percent yes-threshold is not passed, it means a full stop and failure. This was, in fact, what happened in 1939, the first time the 1915 conditions were applied – the very atypical amendment situation in 1920, right after World War I, needs no mention here. The orchestration of an amendment project that fails is not what prime ministers want to be remembered for.

After World War II, another attempt to amend the *Grundloven* had become overwhelmingly compelling, although still politically unattractive. Several existing political institutions were greatly in need of an overhaul. One was the constitutional entrenchment of parliamentarism. This entrenchment, which has been in political practice since 1901, had politically made *Folketinget* the country's supreme institution and, by implication, made the courts wary of undoing parliamentary enactments. Yet, the legal basis had not been established. Another high priority was to pass from a bicameral to a unicameral organization of the legislature. Third, it was proposed that the 45-percent nightmare threshold be reduced – to 40 percent. When, then, the required yes vote was obtained and the amendment passed, it was a moment of relief. Yet, in spite of the successful 1953 amendment, the aborted 1939 call for constitutional change still haunts putative Danish constitution-amenders. It petrifies prime ministers into inaction. Fifty-one years have passed since the 1953 updating and modernization of the *Grundloven* – a remarkable lapse of time in view of the fact that these have been years of unprecedented social change, both at home and globally, change including a constitutionalization of the EU treaties, the destitution of the Cold War, the rule of communism, and the advent of globalization.

It is important to understand that the absence of constitutional amendments thus is not due to a lack of political and/or legal need or desirability. The main cause of torpor is the rigidity and complexity of the amendment procedure. It is a safe guess that another one or two decades will pass with the present constitutional texts intact. Formal constitutional amendment has not, thus, really been available as an instrument of constitutional modernization and updating for the better part of the twentieth century and, most notoriously, since 1953.

In view of all this, the following two questions call for an answer: first, might some sort of a causal link exist between the unavailability of formal amendment and the demise of constitutional review (more about this demise to follow below)? Second, might the 1915 addition of the referendum requirement have been inspired not only by a longing for direct democracy but by political anti-review sentiments and convictions as well – legitimated by the introduction of parliamentarism a good dozen years earlier? Since historical sources do not give any clear answers to these questions, analysis based on circumstantial evidence must suffice for the purposes of concluding this chapter.

A first point is that nobody can have doubted that the 1915 referendum requirement would make future amendments far more cumbersome to enact. Second, it can be assumed that an enhanced legitimacy would attach to amendments adopted with the consent of the voters. An indirect weakening of the institution of constitutional review would be a side effect of both points. The reason is that the referendum roadblock to politician-led constitutional amendments was more than likely to inspire the visionary to keep judge-made constitutional interpretations at bay. This was a likely tendency if only because the political processes would in reality be unable to correct or reverse a "wrong" judicial constitutional decision. Add to this, that constitutional review had never enjoyed a strong status in Danish society. At the 1848 Constitutional Convention, political support and opposition to the principle had been equally strong – and equally uncompromising. For this reason it had been agreed neither to constitutionally entrench a prohibition against nor to authorize judicial review of legislation (Andersen 1954, chapter x). Add to this that once the metaphor of the *Grundloven* as a living instrument, as the updated and inspired umpire of society's great issues and conflicts, bolstering the exercise of constitutional review was gone, the legitimacy of judge-conducted constitutional change had to be going through a rough patch. However, a very large proportion of Danes still revere the national constitution as a sea captain his compass – probably as a symbol of national unity.

However, if neither the country's revered *Grundloven* nor its highest judges could be seen to set the body politic's agenda, someone else must. Who could this be but the politicians who, in Denmark, are united in the Privy League, the hands and action of which are, as I have repeatedly submitted, immune to judicial interference on behalf of the *Grundloven*. Is this immunization against constitutional review to be seen as a side effect of popular confirmation of formal constitutional amendments – when they have been, rarely as it is, carried through? The Supreme Court's ruling in the Maastricht Ratification Case (on the limits to sovereignty transfers) affords circumstantial evidence of the existence of such a link. Most remarkable was the Court's constitutional tiptoeing and eventual negation of any real judicial responsibility for defining the scope of the legal basis of Section 20. This was the first, and so far the only, litigation turning on a constitutional provision inserted in the *Grundloven* under the tough post-1915 version of Section 88. I shall analyse this ruling in more detail in one of the sections below (UfR 1998 800 H).

At this juncture, the very important practical effect of the 1915 amendment of Section 88, namely that the exercise of constitutional review petered out, raises a new series of questions. Was the demise of constitutional review not only the practical result but possibly also the effect intended by those who initiated the amendment? Some evidence actually suggests that a hesitant yes can be given on this question (the intentional version). There is, first, the fact that it seems unlikely that one would propose such an amendment without forecasting its consequences, including the indirect ones. Moreover, among the latter looms the possibility that constitutional review would become the notorious fall guy. With it weakened, the principle of separation of powers was prone to become the next probable victim. We know that this sort of forecasting did not hold the amendment's authors back. To postulate from this that it was also what actually (co-)inspired them is another step. The step does not appear to be a big one to take, though, in view of the fact that the acting political parties were among the nation's stiffest ideological antagonists to constitutional review. The Social Democratic Party, the national stature of which grew steeply throughout the first quarter of the twentieth century (Korsgaard 2006), was especially lean on constitutional review. After World War I, the Party often espoused a clear anti-review stance in public debates. Party spokesmen developed the argument that review of legislation was an instrument by which appointed, presumably politically conservative, judges could – and would – block socially progressive (social-democratic) legislation. In this, they may rightly have been inspired by what actually happened in the United States during the same years. It emboldens this sort of argumentation that one of the mid-century's most prestigious constitutional law scholars, also a social democrat, endorsed the opposite view in his scholarly writings (Ross 1959, chapter 14).

Second, we know for a fact that the institution of constitutional review sank into disrepute. It must have seemed an attractive solution for someone wishing effectively to marginalize the institution of constitutional review, without saying this in so many words, to add the referendum requirement to Section 88's procedures. Moreover, there is not really another credible explanation as to the reason the referendum model was preferred as a new, last limb of the formal amendment procedure. This model is a classic instrument of governance in direct democracies and therefore fits oddly with Denmark's otherwise wholly representative democracy. All these instances of notorious anti-review advocacy and manifestation must have impressed Danish judges. Even the convictions of the most uncompromising pro-review member of the Supreme Court must have been mollified in response to the massive societal forces he was up against. In sum, these are considerations testifying to the validity of the intentional version, although they cannot claim to offer bullet-proof evidence.

With constitutional review abridged, the *Grundloven* was the next victim. Its devaluation from once being the country's highest law was almost inevitable. What remains of it to day is not a living instrument or a regulatory reality of any significance but rather a symbol of national unity. It may be for this reason that Danes hold their constitution in uniquely high esteem.

This sequence of events functioned to clear the ground for politics by uninhibited politicians' agreement. On a broad scale, this was perhaps the two parties' ultimate vision: a vision of a policy-making situation freed from having to calculate for unfriendly constitutional amendments and judicial reviews of legislation. Politics and not legal niceties should, from then on, govern how Danish society ought to evolve in the course of the twentieth century. If the intentional version is accepted, why was it desirable to enable agreement politics to fill the vacuum left by the higher law's devaluation? This is the theme of my final discussion.

But first, some case analyses to illustrate my contention that the absence of constitutional review has set politicians' agreements free from higher legal constraints. The purpose of the coming section is thus to flesh out how freely the Privy League was enabled to design and pursue the nation's top policy of an ever-sharper international-competitiveness-edge; in a political room free of constitutional constraints and of constitutional review. This, in other words, is the final corroboration of the point made in the beginning about law mattering in a uniquely Small State manner for the international success of the Danish Model. The relevant constitutional laws oiled success by their virtual absence.

THE VIRTUAL ABSENCE
OF CONSTITUTIONAL REVIEW

Books on Danish constitutional law set forth the implications of Section 3's principle of the separations of powers. On the one hand, they say, each department is supposed to ensure that no single branch of government trespasses onto the powers constitutionally vested in another. On the other, the courts are deemed to be more responsible than the other departments for ensuring that all abide within the principle of separation of powers.

In this, Danish law and text books very much resemble their counterparts in most other nations of the Western European/Anglo-American type. However, within this international pattern one also remarks notable differences. One is, for example, the American-style essentially rigid insistence on the observance and enforcement of the constitution's principle of separation of powers (checks and balances). Another is the less rigorous separation maxim prevalent in countries like the United Kingdom and Denmark, where varying degrees of interdepartmental functional interdependency entail overlapping circles of competence.

The Dormant Principle of Separation of Powers

In this context, Danish constitutional practice is at variance with even the scantiest version of a soft separation-of-powers regime. As I said earlier, the Tvind statute was the first in 140 years of constitutional history to ever suffer the thankless fate of being vilified for its violation of Section 3. What is more, even in the grotesque circumstances of *Tvind*, the court below the Supreme Court was unable to identify a judicially sanctionable breach of Section 3! Therefore, the Supreme Court's boldness in *Tvind* surprised most of us and shocked some, perhaps even the Court itself. This we shall never know. As it was, some Danish constitutional commentators did interpret *Tvind* as a precursor of a new era now marked by a more vigorous judicial review of Parliament's compliance with the *Grundloven*, or at least with its Section 3. They saw a hint in the circumstance that *Tvind* in time coincided with the Supreme Court's admittance of the litigation on the Maastricht Treaty ratification. *Tvind* was innovative because it invalidated a statute on substantive law grounds (violation of the principle of separation of powers). The *Maastricht*-case made headlines because it looked like the Supreme Court's acceptance of a kind of class action. Yet, these were single swallows: judicial facts since *Tvind* and *Maastricht* exclude the likelihood, as already noted, that more judicial review is in the offing that would patch up existing constitution-free territory.[6] The Supreme Court has, since *Tvind*, realigned itself and now pays obedient tribute to Denmark's non-judicial-interventionist tradition. Hence, a threatening discontinuation of Denmark's high international economic performance will not fall victim to some sneaking, twenty-first-century reconstitutionalization.

A different question asks if a closer look at Parliament's handling of the Tvind situation can tell us anything about the separation-of-power relationships between Denmark's lawmaking and judicial institutions. Some points can be made.

One may begin by asking what caused the Supreme Court to speak out here against the political department's easygoing relationship with Section 3, after so many years of silence and complacency. However, before I address this question, a caveat should be interjected in order to avoid misunderstandings. I therefore stress that my discussion of the "more-review" issue does not imply a quest for a fundamental overhaul of the power relationships between *Folketinget* and the judiciary. On the one hand, *Folketinget* is – under the rule of parliamentarism and beyond any doubt – the institution *primus inter pares* – perhaps even higher ranking than that. Alternatively, it is disturbing that Parliament's Tvind-majority apparently assumed that it could get away uncensured with the outrageous Tvind statute. Against this backdrop, it is arguable that a bit more strict judicial scrutiny might perhaps add a beneficial corrective to Parliament's tendency to occasional self-indulgence. This should not be too appalling in view of the fact that the EU court and the European Human Rights Court have both, for quite a number of years, been in the business of setting aside Danish parliamentary enactments (for their incompatibility with the Union Treaties or the European Convention on Human Rights). Why should the Danish courts not do just a little bit of the same – from time to time at least? It lends some support to the "a-little-more-domestic-review" argument that since the *Grundloven* is professed to be the highest law, it ought to be the highest law for everybody, Parliament included. If elected majorities are not stoppable by judges, the argument runs, the attractiveness of democratic government – perhaps even of parliamentarism – might come to an end, possibly devolving into tyranny. I mention this because the Tvind situation represented a unique situation in which a majority tyrannized its opponents. As it is, the actual and almost complete disallowance of constitutional supremacy is possibly a Small-State specificity. Be this as it may, it has become a Danish national practice that the courts trust that Parliament – or, even better, that they – are to identify the boundaries to its powers flowing from Section 3. Therefore, when asked about a statute's possible violation of the *Grundloven*, they look through the wrong end of the telescope.

The following point has, on the preceding background, become more important than it would seem at first glance. The Tvind situation comes to us as a late warning, as an eye-opener to the possibility that many other, less gross but still serious violations of the *Grundloven* did actually, year after year, pass through Parliament's wide-meshed Section 3 net. From the perspective of this chapter, this possibility is of interest because it informs us about the magnitude of the unrestrainedness of the national policy formation processes under the constitution. For the purposes of this volume and its non-Danish readership, the problem is not so much that the courts have shown trust in *Folketinget*; the real concern should be about how blind this trust was. The blinder it becomes, the more far-reaching will the judiciary's grant of discretionary power to the political departments be. Blind trust implies an empowerment to obfuscate even the simplest "natural" commands flowing from the *Grundloven*'s Section 3 and other provisions. How blind did Parliament's members perceive that trust to be?

First, would it be a sustainable hypothesis that scores of Tvind-MPs were victims of the flawed perception that judicial review of legislation was alive and well? If so, it will be a viable assumption that they must in some non-negligible measure have felt restrained in their law- and policy-making endeavours in pursuance of the most ideal competitiveness policies. I submit with some caution that such a false impression had an impact on the MPs' behaviour. In fact, this hypothesis is not implausible if for no other reason than that few others besides constitutional law scholars know for sure that the courts have long ago buried their constitutional battle-axe. Outside the narrow circle of specialized professors, it is not rare to hear people comment about constitutional review as if it were a living institution and the *Grundloven* more than simply a great and unifying symbol. Many "wannabe" MPs share with ordinary folks the fact that they are not in the habit of regularly consulting constitutional law books. To this might be added that the Supreme Court has frequently stated that the courts enjoy a constitutional entitlement to review legislation for its compatibility with the *Grundloven* – only to add, however, that in the case at hand the plaintiff had not proven, with the clarity required for the courts to set aside a parliamentary statute, that the repugned law was in violation of the Constitution. This proof-test has been repeated in the very large majority of cases where the Court has had to dispose of constitutional cases on their merits. This judicial "we-could-if-we-would" language might in the uninitiated and not so critical listeners' minds have caused the impression to take root, false as it is, that the institution of constitutional review remained viable and vigilant. (The cases are documented in Germer 2001, chapter 10).

Let us, if only for the sake of argument, place ourselves in the situation of a newly elected, and probably unexceptional MP. Because constitutional review for him represents a living reality, he will assume that the judiciary will strike down laws which he votes for in violation of the constitution. Let us further surmise that our MP, in situations a, b, c, and d, votes for a law that he privately suspects is constitutionally *ultra vires Grundloven*. For each time a foreseen or perhaps even predicted invalidating judicial decision fails to tick off, this MP's first idea will not be that constitutional review is suspended. He will rather feel some comfort in thinking that the *Grundloven* must simply have been more accommodating than he first supposed. However, as time goes by, he will slowly but steadily stop worrying about the *Grundloven*, including its separations-of-power doctrine. Why worry, when none of Parliament's acts, the problematic as well as the unproblematic ones, bring out the judges' red card. Note, that I have not said that all or most MPs go down this sort of intellectual slide. The described scenario is hypothesized, and necessarily so, because research work shedding light on what MPs actually know or assume has not been done, to my knowledge. I would suggest that someone do something about this lacuna in our knowledge.

At the present, however, we may be reasonably satisfied with conjecture and speculation. This is because the Tvind-majority was large enough to justify some tentative extrapolations about how participating MPs actually reasoned – in close situations at least. It can be assumed that the yes-voting MPs must have had their minds set on one of the following four constitutional alternatives: (1) either they largely viewed the principle of separation of powers as a legally unbinding politico-constitutional ideal; or (2) they assumed that Section 3 did actually contain a legally binding restriction, limiting Parliament's discretion, but also, and perhaps a bit *naïvely*, that the new enactment might be in compliance with the Section 3's directive and no further; and (3), on the assumption that the majority could well be acting in violation of the separation of power principle, that the courts' self-restraint would keep them from declaring the law inapplicable on the ground that the legislation was *ultra vires* Section 3; or (4) that Parliament adopted the law envisaging with open eyes that the courts would subsequently proceed to invalidate it.

Of these, the fourth alternative seems to me to be too far-fetched to attract the slightest credibility. It is flawed if only because the government, *per* the Justice Ministry, had assured that the Tvind-bill was not tainted with unconstitutionality. This assurance, on the other hand, should not be used by the yes-voting MPs as a sleeping pill, in view of the fact that each branch of government is individually responsible for upholding *Grundloven*. Of the remaining alternatives (i) through (iii), the unhappy fact is that it is difficult on the basis of what we know to judge which is the better one. The good point is that a detailed discussion and insight can be dispensed of for the present paper's purposes because the three alternatives have one important thing in common. This is that the majority of MP s assumed that the courts would not mingle with the affairs of Parliament. Whether their rationales for thinking so vary, is of lesser importance.

This picture of the (i) through (iii) reality review is telling. It is telling about how courts' trust in parliament fared at the receivers' end. Here, all or most of the involved MPs assumed that *Folketinget*'s discretion is virtually limitless. Obviously, on this assumption one's imagination only places a limit to how often parliamentary majorities have legislated *ad libitum.* From a traditional rights' point of view, that is, on the other side of the coin, it is mind-boggling reading that the law makers may have trammelled unnumbered individual and group rights and interests. From our perspective here, the important point is not whether this happened *bona fide* or not. The thrust of the matter is that these would-be violations of the *Grundloven* all (but one) went unchecked.

Where does the special Danish nexus reside in all this? It is not only that the courts are in reality looking over Parliament's shoulder – on behalf of the legal essentials of the country's revered written Constitution. Neither does the secret reside uniquely in the circumstance that the two other branches of government are left with an impressively free hand to define, pursue, and realize the policy objectives that they at any time deem fit. Both are sub-elements of the key to an understanding of the nexus between Danish constitutional laxity and the international successes of agreements politics.

From the Small State perspective, most crucial of all are the pervasive effects of trust and consensus; it is all fine and constitutionally impeccable as long as it works. In this Sleeping Beauty's Palace there is also room for the following frightening paradox: The political institutions and individual actors within them construed their agreements to the enhancement of Danish companies' international competitiveness ever more creatively and irrespective of the constitution's commands, guided by a conception according to which everything they did was not only possible but constitutional because the courts did not rule otherwise.

The Courts and the Rights Chapter

The present subsection investigates the judicial department's enforcement – or lack thereof – of the *Grundloven*'s Chapter VIII on fundamental rights and freedoms (the Rights Chapter). This chapter contains many provisions guaranteeing a rich variety of the finest traditional human or fundamental rights, such as the right to property, to free speech, to freedom of organization and assembly, to work, to children's education at public expense, to the inviolability of personal freedom and of domicile – and more. Yet, in tune with the hands-off policy they apply in respect of the separation-of-powers principle, Danish courts do very little to enforce these rights and guarantees against the legislature. The contrast between the words of the *Grundloven* and judicial laissez-faire is perhaps even sharper in relation to the Rights Chapter. In fact, judicial restraint is more easily justifiable vis-à-vis the enforcement of the arguable ambiguities of the separations of powers principle than, say, the rights provisions which are largely drafted in clear language. Moreover, a thorough judicial protection, at least of the core of traditional human rights, seems to have found favour in many other jurisdictions practising parliamentarism. Some would even see it is a benchmark of a high quality modern parliamentary democracy that its judicial protection of non-economic human rights be beyond criticism.

The few words spent on Section 75 in my opening section testify to the fact that this is not the situation in Denmark. The case of Section 72 guaranteeing against searches of a person's domicile without a judicial warrant brings out the same point. According to this provision, the domicile is inviolable except under at least one of the following conditions. The protection can be lifted (i) if a judge warrants a search and (ii) if exceptions are provided for by statutory law. Yet, no fewer than 200 laws "provide exceptionally" for searches without a judicial warrant. The courts have not measured any of these against the words and spirit of Section 72 and found the legal basis of many of them too thin-legged. The conclusion seems inevitable that if the welfare state has successfully managed to make the individual responsible for the community, that success has taken its toll. The price has been the public authorities' uncensured inobservance of, intrusions into guaranteed rights, not only of that in Sections 72 and 75 but a good many other rights and freedoms (Pedersen 1994, 125). When citizens have turned to the courts for help they have been met either by dismissals due to a lack of standing or by the we-could-if-we-would (exercise constitutional review)-but-not-in-the-case-at-hand language. The result, of course, is the operation of a strong presumption of constitutionality of any legislative act (Zahle 1997).

In sum, depending on one's perspective, the courts' remarkable self-restraint is both a virtue and a vice. It is a virtue in that the interests associated with negotiational democracy and its proliferation, self-restraint, and constitutional laxity are undoubtedly beneficial, although not a *sine qua non* of international economic success. It is a vice from the rights point of view. I ought here, for the record, to add that the Danish courts have, since the integration of the European Convention on Human Rights into Danish domestic law in the early 1990s, in some spectacular instances disapplied parliamentary statutes on the grounds of their incompatibility with the Convention – in situations where the *Grundloven* was to no avail. This is presumably, however, not a judicial activity announcing a nascent revitalization of constitutional review.

Section 20 and National Sovereignty Transfers

As I noted earlier, Section 20 was one of the most interesting innovations of the 1953 constitutional amendment. It stipulates that national sovereignty can be transferred to international organizations like the European Union without following Section 88's impossible procedures (see the preceding section). By inserting Section 20, Denmark joined company with the popular forces propagating the post–World War II view that warfare would break out anew if the European states could not be convinced to join some of their sovereignties together in supranational institutions for the common good of peace and prosperity.

The aspect of Section 20 policy making that is pertinent here was that bills of ratification of sovereignty transfers are never adopted by qualified parliamentary majority. Instead, all important orientations of Denmark's EU policies are placed in the hands of the voters, who discuss them and decide them in referendum's halls of direct democracy.

Other perspectives on the relationship between Section 20 and negotiational democracy deserve mention: (a) looking at the history of the provision; (b) clarifying the courts' role in defining the constitutional limits to sovereignty transfers (c) illuminating the frequent half-heartedness with which the nation's courts enforce Denmark's EU obligations when negotiational democracy's legislative outcomes are accused of violating EU law.

(a) When the Danish 1953 Constitutional Committee worked on the idea of entrenching something like a Section 20, its inspiration was not that European integration or union was in itself a good thing. It was rather one of expedience: If one day it could be taken to serve the nation's economical and political interest to join a supranational organization – founded by or together with other states – it would be silly to find the road barred by the *lourdeur* of Section 88's procedures. Facing this challenge, and realizing that the next occasion to amend the constitution would probably lie many years ahead, the Danish *constitution makers decided to insert a transfer-of-sovereignty clause* into the constitution. However, because few, if any, knew what supranationalism was really about, drafting the new text was not an easy task.

The committee steered its way through this confusion, holding to two basic assumptions. On the one hand, a provision that unduly restrained the nation's future political decision makers' liberty of choice might soon become an impractical dead-letter-law. Alternatively, a too-open formulation would risk alienating many voters, who would become no-voting Eurosceptics for fear that the politicians were planning to sell out Denmark's national silver. The formula eventually chosen – that is, that sovereignty can be transferred "*i nærmere bestemt omfang*" ("to a specified extent") – was a genial trick because the wording conveys the impression – false as it would prove to be – that the potential scope of sovereignty transfers was legally thoroughly circumscribed, and presumably also judicially reviewable. Even to the trained eye and reader, Section 20 conveys an atmosphere of "hereto and no further."

However, if the material scope of the Section's legal basis for operating sovereignty transfers was ambiguous, its procedural prescriptions were sharp and clear: a qualified majority of five-sixths of MPs could adopt a draft bill of ratification. Only if this majority were not obtained, could recourse be had to Section 20's alternative, a two-step adoption: first by a simple majority of MPs and second by a favourable vote in a referendum.

The early drafts of Section 20 did not envisage the direct involvement of the voters in the ratification procedure. It was at the initiative of the parties which in 1915 were responsible for adding the referendum requirement to Section 88 on constitutional amendment that a similar requirement was inserted into Section 20 – and became a stab in the back for Danish representative democracy. Between 1972 and 2003, six out of seven EU ratification bills were submitted to the alternative adoption procedure.

If this cannot be denied, the pros and cons are not self-evident. The con is the loss of representative democracy in respect of most crucial EU policy making. Weighing the pros and the final balancing is more complicated. The weighing is simple enough, though, insofar as Danish EU membership has been of crucial economic and political importance to the Small State Denmark. The big unknown of the equation is this: could Denmark have continued to integrate its economy and politics along with the rest of the Member States if the Privy League had not decided, by way of the introduction of the affirmative referendum (above), to always grant to the voters the final say on sovereignty transfers at domestic referenda? That is, if parliament and government had preferred to ratify using parliamentary qualified majorities? We know that the Euro-sceptic mood of the population was such in 1992/93 that Denmark could ratify parts of the Maastricht Treaty only. Could representative democracy have obtained better results? The point is that a stricter political and/or judicial enforcement of the spirit of Section 20 might have done more harm to the vital national interest in joining the EU and staying in, than the price that Denmark has paid by watering down its representative democracy. One observation seems quite clear though: there is a legal canyon which divides the relatively narrow amounts of sovereignty that most informed people in the early 1970s prophesied that Section 20 warranted and the inclusion, forty odd years later, of Denmark into an emerging federal union, which has resulted from the combined effect of that Section and the voters' decisive say about how much sovereignty they were prepared to give up.

(b) This brings us to a further query. *How did the courts define their role* in the process of making more sense of Section 20? At bottom, their role definition is reminiscent of the constitutional tradition that I have accounted for in earlier sections – with a few innovations.

History repeated itself, however. I refer to the already-mentioned 1971 dismissal on grounds of the plaintiff's lack of standing in the first court case about the limits to Section 20's legal basis. The second time Danish citizens turned to the courts for help against existing political plans to enmesh Denmark further into the European federalist project, the first court to hear the case declined to have competence – again because of the plaintiffs' alleged lack of *locus standi*. This was in the *Maastricht Ratification Case* and the acting court was the Court of Appeals for the Eastern Circuit (1995).

Eventually, in 1996, the Supreme Court reversed the dismissal of the Appeals for the Eastern Circuit. The Supreme Court reasoned that the courts were under an (hitherto unheard of) obligation to hear and decide the plaintiffs' case on its merits. This was so, the Court said, because the actual Section 20 litigation represented a special case – wherefore the ruling did not let class actions in by the back door. Hearing the case anew, now on its merits, the Court of Appeals without much ado or finesse found it to be beyond reasonable doubt that Section 20 was the proper legal basis and that the government's ratification of the Maastricht treaty was not *ultra vires*.

On appeal of this decision, the Supreme Court had to draft its own suitable solution to the problem about limiting what Section 20 warranted. Needless to say, the situation was highly contentious. On the one hand, the Court's admission of the case in the first place suggests that its majority, if not all the judges, had felt that a judicial redress was necessary under Section 20, which had become politically and legally volatile and lacking in transparency. On the other hand, the Court hardly had the option to find against the government. If it ruled the latter's Maastricht ratification to be *ultra vires* Section 20, this EU treaty would become *lettre morte* after having been in force in five years in 12 states. One of the required twelve signatures would retroactively have been withdrawn.

As it was, a unanimous Supreme Court acquitted the government. However, unlike the lower court, the Supreme Court wrote – by Danish standards – an unusually long, subtly argued, and informative judgment. Space permits me to focus only on two crucial passages, the first of which makes it clear that legally identifiable and judicially enforceable limits to Section 20's warrant of sovereignty transfers do exist. Next, the Court qualified this statement by adding that, within wide margins, the other departments' decisions about the location of these limits were non-justiciable political questions. The judges should keep a low profile as long the amounts of sovereignty transferred did not cast in serious and obvious doubt Denmark's continued "survival as an independent state."[7] Welcomed as this judicial intervention should be, the independent-state test is not really easier to apply than Section 20's own "more-specified-extent" test. The merit of the judgment is therefore basically that it signalled to the political institutions that their agreement politics could continue untrammelled by the judiciary. Thus, the day of the Supreme Court's judgment became yet another festive moment for negotiational democracy.

(c) *Denmark's EU policy formulation* is not only a major national political playground; EU law is also important because it guarantees fundamental economic rights to companies and workers and, today, even to non-economic movers. These rights include the freedom of movement of capital, persons, companies, goods, and services. Not only shall the individual economic operator's exercise hereof be unrestricted by national law but in addition, the EU court will not relinquish its insistence that where EU law applies, it must be enforced unconditionally, against big and small subjects alike. This judicial philosophy obviously was a poor match for Denmark's easygoing agreement politics. Thus, clashes between two antagonistic regimes would surely be forthcoming – in fact, they have been numerous. The way the so-called AMBI legislation fared through the Danish political and judicial institutions offers a spectacular illustration of the strength of agreement politics – even in the face of the powerful EU law and its mighty court.

I reported above that the AMBI legislation introduced a cascade tax in clear violation of EU law. The problem was that the EU law's commands were at odds with what best served concrete national interest. However, after the Danish state had levied some 50 billion AMBI-kroner, the EU court ruled that the levying was illegal under EU law.[8] At the time of the events, this amounted to a chilling 6–7 billion Euros, a huge amount of money as far as Denmark's state finances are concerned. This was the point where the above narrative ended.

At this point we take up the thread in order to explain in more detail how concern for safeguarding the national interest was allowed to influence the Danish judiciary's handling of the reimbursement litigation, which thousands of companies initiated. Of course, the windfall cash had long before been spent. Now, repayment to the rightful owners of the money would wreak havoc on national economic stability and growth, a situation completely at odds with all that the Privy League's negotiational democracy yearned for.

According to the EU court's case law, repayment is due of such nationally collected EU-law-violating taxes which their contributors have not been able to pass on to subsequent resellers or to consumers. If passed on and reimbursement was nonetheless granted, the sum would amount to an unjust enrichment, which EU law then considered unacceptable. Crucial for the outcome of all this litigation was the right answer to the question: on whom would the burden of proof of passing on or not passing on impinge? Yet, at the time of the events, EU law was unclear on most points of proof. In particular, it did not rule out clearly whether a debtor state could rely on passing on presumptions that would disadvantage the companies seeking reimbursement. EU law was really clear on two points only. The one was the statement that tax payers' claims were to be processed in accordance with national procedural rules and regulations. The other was a prohibition against a Member state's unilateral imposition of more onerous procedures and/or requirements of proof as compared with similar claims under domestic law in cases where reimbursement of monies levied in violation of EU law was sought.

The Danish government acted as if this EU law did not exist. It moved swiftly and with a firm hand by letting Parliament pass a statute specifically regulating AMBI reimbursements. This statute was rife with provisions about repayment formalities and procedures, which included the setting up of a special public authority for these purposes. Moreover, it placed a tough burden of proof on those who wanted their AMBI taxes back (the Reimbursement Statute).

When claimants argued that the Reimbursement Statute was simply yet another blatant violation of Denmark's EU obligations – which it was – the government put on a poker face. No, it postulated: EU law was ambivalent and the rules of the new statute did not exceed this ambivalence. In the face of two so diametrically opposed interpretations of EU law, the better view often is that the legal situation is not as clear as either party professes it to be. Where there is uncertainty and a reasonable doubt about an interpretation, the EU treaty's remedy is the so-called preliminary references procedure (Article 234; see Part Three, title 2). This remedy provides for a special cooperation mechanism between national courts and the EU court which, at the end of the procedure, in an authoritative ruling, will declare what is the right interpretation. The problem with this procedure is that it does not come into play unless the relevant national courts turn to the EU court for assistance. No need for that, the Danish Supreme Court boldly ruled: all the elements of the Reimbursement Statute arguably observe the limits to an interpretive margin within which national institutions are presumed to operate in compliance with EU law's various commands. At the utmost, some of the statute's marginally important rules perhaps violated EU law, perhaps not. The government pleaded that it was unnecessary to trigger the preliminary references procedure. Wrong, the plaintiffs submitted: and rightly so because the statute discriminated between claims for reimbursement and was totally indefensible in so doing.

It is probable but not provable that the Supreme Court followed the government because the judges understood that it had a very bad case – a case that could become worse only if the EU Court was given an opportunity to develop its case law in still less sovereignty-friendly ways. If this was the Court's anticipation, hindsight informs us that it was a correct prophecy. As the EU court's case law stands today, a decade later, it is clear that all the statute's major procedural provisions, including its operating presumptions of unjust enrichment against the tax payer and laying the burden of proof on him, were in violation of Denmark's EU obligations. However, in the event, the Supreme Court invoked a doctrine of margins of discretion, which does not exist in EU law. Why? Presumably in order to save the life of the reimbursement statute and to avoid abiding by its duty under Article 234 to submit a preliminary question to the EU court.

The Supreme Court having thus ensured the survival of the Reimbursement Statute, it was now the government's turn to save reimbursement monies *en masse*. A conservative estimate has it that at least forty billion kroner ought have been reinstalled in the pockets from where they had been illegally taken. The Danish state has gotten away with repaying only one billion d-kroner.

Three lessons may be drawn from this narrative. The first is the impressive lengths of illegality to which the Danish political and judicial institutions are willing to go to in depreciating the rights and other advantages that EU-law grants some Danish citizens and companies – in cases where the state stands with its back against the wall. From many perspectives, including that of liberal democracy, this is appalling. The second is that the role of the *Grundloven* – and its Rights Chapter – in this was once again that of the passive bystander.

The third is that the biggest winner in all this was neither the Danish Treasury nor the government's shrewd lawyers. It was the national obsession with maximization of the international muscle and success of Danish businesses in general. Economic flexibility was in this case the brand under which the Golden Calf was marketed – *sotto voce*.

WHAT FUELLED THE ADVENT AND VICTORY OF NEGOTIATIONAL DEMOCRACY?

By now we have explored the destitution of constitutionalism and of constitutional review in Denmark and highlighted some of the politico-legal circumstances preconditioning decline. From a variety of angles this chapter has also shed light on Denmark's conflict-laden and ominous cohabitation with the sovereignty-absorbing higher laws of the European Union. Consecutive Danish governments sought beyond reasonable doubt for ways and means to circumvent fully honouring Denmark's EU obligations.

This endeavour typically culminated in situations where EU law threatened to obstruct the Privy League's pursuance of its best-for-Denmark's-economy-and-companies policies. In these developments EU law's most fundamental principles of direct effect, supremacy, and non-discrimination were treated with benign neglect by both the nation's political and judicial departments. A great illustration of one such instance is this chapter's presentations of the AMBI course of events. It was obvious that all of this was really one manoeuvre in a larger political game. The ground rules of this game were dictated by the interaction between the Privy League political parties, the voters' taste for consensus politics and negotiational democracy, and the League's agreement politics.

Two questions remain unanswered. The first is: What fuelled the advent and victory of negotiational democracy in the first place? We know by which legal acts and political advocacy the Radical and Social Democratic political parties militated against constitutionalism and constitutional review. The preceding narrative also includes a note about the latter party's fear that Danish judges would erect a judicial fortress against social-democratic laws.

We registered, moreover, that the Danish population has learned and accepted to keep quiet and act stably and predictably whatever its government does. Was it an unknown variable as to whether this pattern of laissez-faire would survive the day when the welfare state might no longer be able to deliver? We do not know. What we know is that those who have suffered diminished individual rights-positions have in the Danish welfare state experienced that constitutional docility is in practice richly compensated for by all sorts of public money handouts. Here emerges the link between the necessity of Denmark's larger-than-size cut of international growth in wealth and the acceptance of negotiational democracy. A satisfying and pacifying effect is dissociable from the several decades of massive tax-led redistributions of foreign-trade–generated wealth and growth in incomes and public services that were outlined in my second section above. Why not stay put, remain solidified, and let the welfare state soldier on, as long as it is able to justify all its right-denying legislative outputs and actions by the preponderance of just one of them: an ever stronger international competitive edge?

Or, on the other hand, could we face the wider societal question pertaining to the more deeply rooted, politically motivated *whys*, which I have postponed for analysis in the present section. Could we ask whether the causes underlying the emergence and acceptability of a virtually constitution-free, corporate governance – like negotiational democracy – can be identified as genuinely Small-Statish-Danish in nature?

For the purposes of this research, four circumstances need particular attention: (i) Denmark's geopolitical location at the northern frontier of the great German Nation; (ii) the geographic smallness of the country's population and territory; (iii) Denmark's remarkable ethnic, religious, educational, linguistic homogeneity and the fact that its flat and fertile land is densely populated; (iv) the fact that rule by minority or multi-party, and often-weak majority governments has been a Danish benchmark and not the exception throughout the post–World War II period. For far more complete accounts of this period, see Uffe Østergård (chapter 1) and Ove Korsgaard (chapter 3) in this volume.

The power relations between the German-speaking nation(s) and Denmark has changed radically over time. In the eighteenth and much of the nineteenth centuries German land was ruled by a multitude of mostly small and militarily and politically weak sovereign entities. In comparison, Denmark was a large, multinational, multilingual, powerful, and often bellicose kingdom from as far back as the Early Middle Ages. This changed in the course of the nineteenth century. The balances of power shifted, especially in the wake of Germany's mid-century unification, which led to a remarkable growth in military and political might. Germany's subsequent pursuit of territorial expansionist policies was all too often successfully executed at the expense of, among others, its northern neighbour. In the nineteenth century's second half, Denmark lost both wars and land to Germany (Østergård 1996).

For entirely different reasons, Denmark's territory had been curtailed by the loss of Norway in 1814 and Iceland (plus a couple of smaller colonies) in course of the last century. The territory of the former international power player which Germany occupied from 1940 to 1945 had shrunk dramatically – to the size of present-day Denmark.

The Danish population survived all this as a nation. Undeniably, during the twentieth century a new sense of nationhood or national identity has been emerging – because of these foreign policy calamities rather than in spite of them (Østergård 1996). Be this as it may, the overarching problem for the nation's mid-twentieth century political planners was related to the durability of this sense of nationhood. Was it strong enough and sufficiently cemented to survive another foreign onslaught, coming perhaps in the shape of some Iron Curtain occupation? It had to be considered that such an occupation might last for longer. If the answer could not unequivocally be given in the affirmative, what then?

In these calculations, the Danes' sense of national unity and cohesion became a crucial parameter. It was believed that if some critical mass was not at hand, the Danes' survival as one people could be jeopardized. From this type of analysis, an acute awareness grew up by the mid-twentieth century that the bringing about, preservation, and possible expansion and intensification of such a critical mass had become the nation's undisputedly highest priority. After the German wars of the nineteenth century, the nascent acknowledgement of the necessity for nation building had eloquently been coined in a sentence that has since acquired proverbial status: "*Hvad udadtil tabes, må indadtil vindes*" ("What is outwardly lost, must inwardly be won") (Østergård 2006). In 1945, after the German occupation of Denmark, the recognition of the acuteness of this problem had been greatly accentuated. One may say that the diagnosis had been made and finalized; the challenging question was now: what cure to apply?

Around the same time that a response to this question of cure was being formulated, something was in the air calling for a revision of the country's conception of its democracy. A certain weariness with the hitherto formal definition prevailed. Should it and could it be replaced by a democracy whose success would be measured by the extent of its accomplishment of more substantive social good (substantive democracy)? Before World War II, in states such as the Weimar Republic, democracy *à la danoise* was defined in purely formal terms. Parliament's entitlement under the *Grundloven* to enact any legislation was absolutely free of substantive constraints – except for policies expressly commanded or forbidden by the Constitution. Forbidden policies were, for example, laws that violated the provision of the Rights Chapter, exacted taxes without a statutory legal basis, or afforded the franchise to persons without Danish citizenship or permanent residence in Denmark, Section 29. Except for such constitutionally ordained limitations on *Folketingnet*'s entitlement to regulate, all and anything could be legislatively decided.

I cannot say which came first: the quest for another democratic rationale or the requirement of intensified nation-building. The better view is probably that it was the national survival rationale which took its toll on the prevailing entrenchment of formal democracy, causing it to begin buckling (Kaspersen 2006). Welfare and socioeconomic solidarity took pride of place as the top national defence strategy, thereby reversing earlier periods' emphasis on the best possible military defence as Denmark's highest valued policy priority (Korsgaard 2006; Kaspersen 2006).

The hallmark of the new democracy can be said to be this: If new legislation does not demonstrably promote domestic, social, and economic solidarity and quality of life, there is no space for it under the metamorphosed constitution and democracy, which has become negotiational. Almost no policy enhancing the international competitiveness of Denmark's economy and companies will conceivably be met with anything other than judicial acceptance under the Constitution. Thus, in spite of the incoming substantive legislative standards of due process, a renaissance of a legal constitutionalism will not take root, and neither will the courts begin to strike down incompatible legislation. Constitutional review had in course of the preceding quarter of a century suffered some fatal blows from which resurrection is hardly possible.

In sum, a new variant of the Danish tradition of consensus policy making was in the making in the twentieth century. Its top priorities were greater solidarity, economic equality, and more welfare for all. And its main protagonists were the Radical Liberal and Social Democratic parties. These, it will be remembered, had also promoted the 1915 constitutional amendment of Section 88, an event whose importance for the decline of constitutional review was underlined above. This is not to say that the Liberal and the Conservative parties also immediately liked what they saw coming after World War II. However, the new mood was already, by the mid-twentieth century, strong enough for some to acknowledge that a modernization of the constitutional theory of democracy would not take root. Obviously it was influenced by the threats to the nation's survival experienced during the Nazi occupation (Fonsmark 1990, citing Stephan Hurwitz, 61). It is noteworthy that, after the German occupation, the Danes did not yearn for more individual freedoms, or a more robust judicial protection of civil liberties. To be sure, all sorts of freedoms had often been brutally suppressed, especially during the last years of the occupation. But the Danes were asking for fewer real rights and less protection – as long as an ever-increasing national wealth would be provided for. Admittedly, it has long been a claim of Danish national pride that this was a country in which "*få har for meget og færre for lidt*" ("few have too much and fewer too little"). However, after 1945 it was no longer enough to pay lip service to this ideal.

The new brand of solidary democracy is remarkable from another viewpoint as well. This is that one will look in vain for some major footprint of pre-existing ideologies such as religion, Marxism, socialism, or liberalism on the new socioeconomic dimension of policy formulation. It is instead a typically Danish melting pot that submerged the dominant influence or taste of any single ingredient. At the most one can recognize some bits of social democratism, a thoroughly watered-down kin of socialist political philosophy; and, on the other hand (among the notions dear to the Radical Liberals) a political party with its roots in a specific Danish culture of *folkelighed* (in the best – but still inadequate – translation: "populism" or "popularism"). The hallmark is that legislation and other public policies ought to emerge and be given life and blood and societal structure from an essentially unstructured debate among independent and well-meaning people – and never social classes. Its Founding Fathers were N.F. Grundtvig, a nineteenth-century priest, historian, and poet (Østergård, chapter 1, Korsgaard, chapter 3) and *Højeskolebevægelsen*, a non-elitist educational movement founded by Grundtvig and his followers. It was these

elements, plus of course the occupation's threat to the survival of the
Danish people, that gave birth and political substance to the new, but in
the event reinterpreted, and de-ideologized concept of solidarity democracy in Denmark (Fonsmark 1990, 234). The new substantive requirement
of economic due process and economic solidarity should promote a new,
strong feeling of identity and community and enhance social cohesion – a
feeling of "belonging-togetherness" ("*Hvad udad tabes, skal indad vindes.*")
While the major ingredients of the new construct were consensus, agreement politics, and the building of a "mental fortress Denmark," it was
never meant to function to the exclusion of individuals or coteries of a different persuasion. Tolerance and free speech were to become the system's
high priests. Persevering disagreement and its twin companion, litigious-
ness, were conceived as uncivic and shameful conduct (Fonsmark 1990,
267).

A national compromise, which encompassed all the (Privy League) parties, was forged during the early 1970s when the Liberal and Conservative
parties eventually gave up their resistance to the new socioeconomic solidarity or welfare understanding of Danish society. This, in turn, tended to
legitimize the new society in the perceptions of the societal groups, the
interests of which these two parties represented (Martin 2006).

The relative political weakness of the Danish left prevented any more
than a few cases of socialization of means of production from taking
place. Yet, public ownership was not a rare phenomenon because the public sector began during the post-war period to produce numerous goods
and services, paid for by tax money. Indeed, being to a still lesser degree
about confronting ideologies, interparty political competition focused
increasingly on parties' willingness to augment taxes to pay for ever more
costly welfare benefits. These benefits were more and more frequently
handed out to everybody rather than to the needy and the weak. As a consequence, by the 1990s the daily livelihood of one in every three Danes
had been turned into some sort of dependency on money handouts by
the welfare authorities. One may rightly say that the four-party block
introduced legislation designed to socialize not the means of production
but the voters.

Vast numbers of privately owned, mostly small- and medium-sized companies were helped and urged to compete domestically and internationally. Existing regulations and other constraints were lifted, often irrespective of deregulation's potential harmfulness to, say, employees' and
customers' interests and "rights." An enhanced ability of Danish companies to perform well and better on export markets became a sort of
Golden Calf. This productivity was to be insulated from much public interference as long as it produced the wealth that the state could subsequently
tax and redistribute. The voters dependent on the state, incapacitated by

their virtual trusteeship, were well versed in accepting that politicians said one thing before election day and did another right afterward. Voters' quite remarkable trust in both the state and its incorrupt administrators and politicians was contingent on one thing, however; namely, that the latter provided for an unabridged (or even better, increasing) flow of money from the state to them.

In one way of thinking, political brinkmanship *à la danoise* is not different from that of politicians everywhere: They must produce results, making it easy for voters to re-elect them. Two important caveats are necessary, though. One is that an essentially de-ideologized voter force will be willing to perpetuate in passivity if well paid. Another important nuance is that in comparative terms most of the relevant constitutional laws or conventions that I highlighted in this paper's first sections are generously greasing the wheels of the Privy League's Danish policy-making machinery instead of imposing procedural or substantive constitutional barriers or restrictions on it.

CONCLUSION

In summary to this chapter, several points or clusters of points can be made. The first highlights the absolute priority and infallibility attributed to the consensus principle. An undeniable concurrence of public opinion targeted the labour market and the national economy's domestic flexibility (one sometimes bordering on deregulation) and encouraged its international openness and competitiveness. The lifeblood that keeps the consensus-principle alive and flourishing is Denmark's unique ethnic, religious, educational, and linguistic homogeneity. The fact that the country's small and fertile land is flat and densely populated is another important key to understanding the essentials of the functioning of Denmark's specific brand of democracy and international economic success.

This specificity is epitomized by the Privy League's essentially higher-law–free conduct of its agreement politics, dominated by a political culture characterized by the governance of mostly weak minority or multi-party majority governments. The term Privy League is used to epitomize the close interaction and agreement making among the leaders of the four or five main political parties that produce most important Danish policy.

The sum of this is what I have called negotiational democracy and its oligarchical style of government and policy making, with its traits of corporate governance. The latter comparison is rife with clues to a better understanding of Small State Denmark – as long as one does not forget that the country is not a private enterprise but a sovereign state.

Higher-law–free is the crux of the matter. An absolutely indisputable line of causation connecting the relevant Danish constitutional laws and international high performance and economic success does not, of course, exist. I submit that to contend otherwise would be arbitrary. However, to analyse Denmark in Katzensteinian ways without accounting for the place and role of law would be equally arbitrary.

Several indicators testify to the relevance of the constitutional laws. One is the almost complete demise since the 1920s of two crucial features of the previous century's emerging liberal democracy – its formal constitutionalism and a nascent institutionalization of judicial review of legislation under the *Grundloven*. Amid much notorious anti-review advocacy and manifestation, the tone of which increased after the 1915 amendment of Section 88 made formal constitutional amendment unapproachable, the convictions must have been mollified even for the most dedicated pro-review protagonists sitting on the Supreme Court. This early twentieth-century virtual exit of constitutional review meant the non-participation of the legal system's fundamentals, such as the separation-of-powers doctrine in Section 3 and of human rights protection, in the way international economic high performance could be and was accomplished.

With constitutional review abridged, the *Grundloven* was likely to become the next victim. Its degradation from being the country's highest law was almost inevitable – and it happened. What remains of it today is neither a living instrument nor a regulatory reality but a mere symbol of national unity. It may be for this reason that it is held in uniquely high popular esteem. This chapter has also shown that EU law, which claims to be the supreme law of the land, was not always permitted to fulfill that role.

The absence, in any meaningful sense of the term, of binding constitutional laws and of the courts' exercise of constitutional review set off the developments that freed the hands of Danish policy makers and policy enforcers – almost beyond imagination. Out of these developments came a system of state governance based on "politics-supremacy," which is not designed to safeguard traditional individual rights-positions and interests. Instead, "flexicurity"9 takes care of the interests of those whose interests end up at the bottom of the heap. Several decades of massive tax-led hand-outs of foreign-trade–generated wealth to these and many hundreds of thousands other Danes have pacified and socialized the workforce, and made them and the rest of the voters nonchalant about legal rights. The favoured few, those the Privy League's policy-making machinery really cares for, are companies and businesses operating in world markets, and the nation's overarching interest is in sharpening their competitive edge. The underlying political philosophy is that wealth in satisfactory amounts can pay for welfare politics' insatiable need for more and more economic resources to be generated by international trade in goods and services. From all of this and more grew both Denmark's larger-than-average cut of

international growth in wealth and the body politic's acceptance of negotiational democracy.

The pact between the voters and the Privy League supposes that the former stay put as long as politicians design and enforce agreements that
serve this one overriding policy objective. Negotiational democracy, thus
delegalized and dejudicialized, has become both master and servant to
some goddess of growth in wealth and welfare. In a system of governance
where ends tend to justify means, goal accomplishment flows with ease. A
prime characteristic of the pact is a unique intertwinement of, on the one
hand, law, legal culture, and history and, on the other, politics, political
culture, and the definition of democracy – a feature presumably intrinsically linked to and preconditioned by the smallness of the Danish state and
nation. Moreover, an elevation of the body politic's socioeconomic and
welfare values to a status above day-to-day politics seems to have happened.
The thrust of all this was possibly to reshape the country's conceptualization of democracy as it moved from a Weimar-type, formal, and political
democracy. The new form of governance substituted an economic substantive, due-process requirement for the constitutionalism of the past,
which had been characterized by ideals of legal and substantive due
process and constitutional review. In the words of one of the militants of
this reorientation or reshaping of democracy: "Concurrent with the completion of the political democracy, the economic democracy must be realized."[10]

Most of all, this was a consequence of the implosion over a couple of
hundred years of Denmark's big-European-state status, followed by the
nineteenth-century unification of Germany and the German Reich's subsequent political and military aggressiveness. During World War II German
belligerency resulted in the five-year occupation of Denmark that jeopardized the Danes' survival as one nation. If Denmark had not for several
centuries been the neighbour of a big imperialist state, the turn of events
discussed in this paper might quite likely have been strikingly different.

NOTES

The present chapter is a revised version of the paper that was presented at
"The State of Denmark" conference, Dartmouth College, Hanover, New
Hampshire, 30–31 January 2004.

1 The German academic literature on this is enormous. In terms of litigation,
   strained German-EU relationships in the realm of human annd fundamental
   rights peaked in the several-hundred-page–long decision by the *Bundevers-*

affungsgericht in the *Maastricht-Ratification-Case* of 28 May 1993; in *Entscheidungen des Bundeverfassungsgerichts* 39, 1 [44].

2 UfR 1973 694 H.

3 UfR 1996 1300 H.

4 UfR 1998 800 H.

5 "Bag om EU-sagerne," *Den danske Europabevægelse,* July to October, 2004, www.europabevaegelsen.dk

6 Notably the Supreme Court's judgments in *Schengen,* UfR 2001 2065 H; and in *Government Information on EU,* UfR 2002 418 H.

7 UfR 1998 800 H.

8 Case C-52/90, *Commission v. Denmark,* ECR [1992] I-2240.

9 The prime minister's recent formulation, *Berlingske Tidende* of 8 January 2005.

10 Quoted from Ove Korsgaard 2006: his translation.

6

Corporatism and Beyond: The Negotiated Economy

OVE K. PEDERSEN

The political economy of Denmark is of particular interest in the contemporary debate on small advanced industrial states and their capacity to react to changes in the international context – economic and otherwise. As a small nation with a population of 5.2 million people, Denmark sits among the most prosperous nations of the world and has done so for more than thirty-five years. Its economy rests on high wages, narrow income disparities, investment in skills and education, and high levels of taxation to fund an advanced welfare state. Compared with other small countries like Sweden and Norway, Danish political history is characterized by a number of distinct traits. First, a long history of lost wars and territories carving into the public mind a sense of national vulnerability (see Kaspersen, chapter 2), making it possible for elites to implement national identity policies and to establish a homogeneous *demos* based on a common understanding of national identity (see Korsgaard, chapter 3). Second, a long history of state authority being centralized in the hands of a small elite, enabling the elite to build up capacities (resources and legitimacy) to rule the country according to national strategies and interests (see Østergård, chapter 1). Third, a history of being a small and open economy, emphasizing the need for politicians to base their conflicts on a politics of pragmatism rather than on a politics of ideals or ideologies (see Rasmussen, chapter 5). Fourth, a political culture marked by institutionalized class cooperation and a high proportion of organized wage earners (Wallerstein and Western 2000), creating possibilities for governments and peak organizations to institutionalize macro policy concentration in the form of routinized bargaining (Pedersen 1993).

On the basis of these distinct traits derived from the long history of Denmark, a new institutional order emerged in the course of post-war developments (Kjær and Pedersen 2001; Jørgensen 2002). In a number of policy areas the organizing principles shifted from those of either a mixed or market economy to those of a *negotiated economy* (Kjær and Pedersen 2001; Nielsen and Pedersen 1996; Pedersen 1993). Whereas both mixed and market economies are based on a clear division of labour between the sovereign state and an autonomous market, a negotiated economy entails political and economic processes and relations that are neither strictly public nor private but are situated between public authority and private autonomy. Thus, the negotiated economy became a system of governance where economic coordination is achieved through organized negotiations among autonomous actors in both public and private sectors. At one level, Denmark developed governance through the decentralization of decision making and the spread of autonomy and authority across private and public institutions. At another level the country remained committed to policy making through negotiations and trust in collective solidarities (Amin and Thomas 1996).

This chapter describes the negotiated economy as a generalized political system of negotiations (Crouch 1990; Marin 1990, 1996) in which adjustments to international challenges are an everyday feature of the system. I emphasize that a negotiated economy is characterized by a combination of institutionalized learning and organized negotiations and that the learning capacity of the system is influenced by the articulation of a shared and mutual understanding of Denmark's socioeconomic problems. I also show that the flexibility of the economy is influenced by the gradual development of a generalized political system of negotiations as an evolutionary form of governance.

The generalized system can be seen as the institutional precondition for a negotiated economy; and a negotiated economy, then, will be defined as a structuring of society whereby an essential part of the allocation of resources is conducted through organized negotiations between independent decision-making centres in the public sector, private interest organizations, and financial institutions. Unlike decisions made by public authorities, negotiation-based economic decisions are reached on the basis of interaction between independent agents, and the relevant public authority is just one of several participants. Unlike market decisions, which are made by individual agents acting on the basis of given preferences and resources, negotiation-based economic decisions are made through a process characterized by the deliberate shaping of preferences. And unlike mixed economies, in which action is taken by sovereign market agents and precluded or followed by supplementary or corrective measures by the state, in a negotiation-based economy decisions are made in a generalized political system of negotiations in which the deliberate shaping of preferences and the mutual understanding of socioeconomic problems put limits to and set targets for multiple arenas of negotiations between public as well as private, and centralized as well as decentralized collective actors.

In Denmark, negotiations have been – and still are – widely used as instruments for decision making in relation to both allocation and (re)distribution. The classical example is the labour market. Wages, working hours, and other conditions of work are generally determined by individual market agents and by legislation, as well as through organized negotiations – at the macro-, meso-, and micro-level – between collective organizations (Nielsen and Pedersen 1991). In the Danish case, negotiation seems to be an appropriate instrument for solving conflicts of interest, especially because none of the involved social partners are in full control of the implementation, thanks to the spread of autonomy and authority across private and public institutions. This is also because none of the partners is able to chose exit as an option on account of the long history of institutionalized class cooperation in the labour market and cross-party coalition making in Parliament. Thus, negotiation is not only a tool for resolving conflicts; it is also an instrument for achieving mutual understanding. It is not only a technique for decision making; it also involves communication, learning, and the development of a shared mutual understanding of Denmark's socioeconomic problems.

The objective in presenting the Danish case of a negotiated economy is to show how organized negotiations and institutionalized learning (Cox 2001; Hall 1993) are used to handle the changing conditions in European and global markets while recreating national political structures in a flexible way. The key point is that collective learning and policy flexibility are facilitated by the development of a particular socioeconomic discourse and the founding of a generalized system of negotiations. I argue that the Danish case is of special importance for the theory of corporatism because it shows that during the 1980s and 1990s the post-war neo-corporatist wage and incomes policy-bargaining system, so aptly described by Peter Katzenstein (1985) and others (Schmitter 1974, 1982; Therborn 1998), was adapted rather than undermined (Molina and Rhodes 2002). I also propose that the Danish case is important for comparative political economy because it shows how an important and often-neglected case of policy learning and flexibility occurs, and points to some of the conditions that facilitate that learning and flexibility (Hemerijck and Schludi 2000; Teague 2000; Katzenstein 2002). The Danish case is especially well chosen for highlighting the discursive as well as the governance side of institutions (Campbell and Pedersen 1996).

DISCURSIVE PREREQUISITES
FOR INSTITUTIONALIZED LEARNING

The way a socioeconomic discourse is institutionalized in Danish politics is important because this discourse contributes to the blend of high learning capacity and consensus making that has enabled Denmark to adjust so well to shifting international economic currents. The particular Danish economic discourse is built around the ongoing deliberative process of establishing a common understanding of *socioeconomic problems*. While macroeconomic phenomena such as inflation, deficits, productivity, growth, and unemployment are objective in the sense that they can be demonstrated by economic statistics and by social events, socioeconomic problems are subjective, given that they are based on interpretations of statistics and perceptions of events. But even if interpretations are subjective and based on individual interests in the first place, they are not exogenous forces with autonomous causal powers. Rather than being exotic to existing frames of meaning they are formed by a discourse that structures actors' experiences of macroeconomic phenomenon in advance and set frames for what counts as a socioeconomic problem in the first place and an appropriate interest (individual or common) in the second (Kögler 1999). Hence, even if socioeconomic problems are based on objective economic phenomena, they are framed by discourse and formed into perceptions of individual as well as common interests.

This discourse is a particular Danish understanding of the Keynesian paradigm built around an ideal conception of socioeconomic balance through negotiated coordination of policies among various autonomous actors in the national economy. It constitutes a blend of liberal and social democratic principles. It is liberal in the sense that it respects the autonomy of economic actors and organized interests; it downplays direct state intervention in the economy, preferring negotiated settlements instead; and it views the Danish economy as an open economy that, being exposed to international competition, must find ways to become and remain internationally competitive. It is social democratic in the sense that it portrays the national economy as a "community of fate" of a multiplicity of social interests, and attempts to secure the interests of the whole by inducing the parts to act responsibly with respect to the overall socioeconomic balance (Pedersen 1999). To illustrate briefly, the gradual articulation and stabilization of this discourse is reflected in three overlapping phases of policy articulation and institution building in the post-war period (Pedersen 1993; Kjær and Pedersen 2001) by which not only was a particular Danish reading of the Keynesian paradigm created but also a set of complementary institutions was developed.

First, from 1945 through the 1960s there was a period during which wage formation and labour markets were of concern. In this phase, the key problem of the Danish economy was conceptualized not only as a problem of macroeconomic management but also as one of socioeconomic coordination between wage formation and the overall development of the national economy. Wage structures and labour markets, it was believed, needed to be maintained in ways that better facilitated economic growth. In this view, responsibility for economic coordination lay both with the state and with the peak organizations in the Danish labour market. This problem of coordination was articulated in a series of public investigations and official blueprints that defined labour market organizations as being responsible for the resolution of the wage and labour market coordination problem but also emphasized the autonomous status of these organizations, thus pointing to the need for voluntary coordination and mutual restraint in the labour market. From the early 1960s, there was gradual organization building in relation to this coordination problem. A complementary set of negotiation and arbitration organizations was established, and the Economic Advisory Council (EAC) of economic experts was designed to create a common awareness of coordination problems in the economy. The biennial wage negotiations between employer federations and the trade unions were to become *negotiation organizations* and *arbitration organizations*, and the EAC became the first example of a *campaign organization* with the purpose of communicating socioeconomic conceptions to the broader public and engaging in processes of persuasion to create focus on particular socioeconomic problems so that they would be put on the political agenda and the agenda of negotiations between labour and capital. There was also experimentation with active labour market and incomes policies, which became stable parts of Danish economic policy making during the 1970s mainly on the basis of proposals formulated by the EAC and implemented through negotiation and arbitration organizations.

In a second set of responses, from the 1970s through the 1980s, new systems were put in place to meet concerns about the increasing size and growth of the public sector. This problem was first articulated by public commissions in two major reports on long-term planning in 1971 and 1973, and was further articulated in later publications from the Ministry of Finance (*Finansministeriet* 1971, 1972). From the 1950s public commissions were the major arena for political exchange among governments, trade unions, and employers' associations. Since then, tri-partite public commissions have developed as the ideal type of *policy organization* where socioeconomic problems could be identified and related to particular policies (e.g., social security, training, and education) and general guidelines for their resolution could be formulated. From the 1960s to the 1970s, public commissions called for the founding of welfare measures and the creation of a welfare state. From the 1970s, the increasing public sector became the most important problem, and commissions called for a significant degree of public sector decentralization by granting the municipalities responsibility for a constantly growing part of public expenditures. The question was how to ensure fiscally responsible municipalities while maintaining their autonomous status vis-à-vis the national government. This was resolved by defining public expenditures as a problem and gradually institutionalizing this idea through the state's creation of new economic models and budgetary systems, and through the creation of a system of budget negotiations between the Ministry of Finance and the municipalities that was governed by the goal of limiting total public expenditures. This system was implemented during the late 1970s and early 1980s.

Third, beginning in the mid-1970s, Danish economic problems were conceptualized as stemming from the structure of the Danish economy itself. The structural problem entailed a concern with the competitiveness of the national economy, a preoccupation with the supply side (i.e., the conditions of production rather than demand and consumption), and a focus on structural as opposed to conjunctural barriers to competitiveness. Initially, the problem of competitiveness was viewed as having to do with the size of the public sector, which put severe constraints on the cost-competitiveness of exporting firms. However, it gradually came to be associated with a number of problems inherent in the structure and organization of the private sector, such as low levels of technological development and an inability of firms to adequately adapt and innovate. During the 1980s this change in the overall understanding of socioeconomic problems was formulated by analytical units in the Ministry of Finance and the Ministry of Trade and Industry. These units came to function as *discourse organizations* with the purpose of creating the theoretical and empirical discourse of socioeconomic problem solving through the development of socioeconomic models and statistics that could depict and predict causal relations and dependencies in the economy as a systematic basis for the ongoing identification of socioeconomic problems. From the 1980s a more coherent structural policy framework was articulated which first involved industrial policy and later public expenditure policy. The emergent conception of structural policy emphasized the continuous and voluntary restructuring of the Danish economy through the creation of various private and public policy-making and implementing bodies. This approach was gradually institutionalized by linking industrial, labour market, education, and public administration issue-areas through negotiations.

So, whereas policy formation and implementation in both market- and mixed economies are centred on state hierarchy, notably the legislature and the executive branches, in the Danish case a more complex set of complementary institutions was developed. Policy organizations (e.g., public commissions) identified socioeconomic problems, related them to particular policies (e.g., wage or labour market policy problems) and formulated general guidelines for their resolution. Campaign organizations (e.g., the EAC) communicated socioeconomic conceptions to the broader public and engaged in processes of persuasion in order to create a focus on particular socioeconomic problems and get them on the political agenda. Discourse organizations (e.g., analytical units in the Ministry of Finance and universities) created the theoretical and empirical language of socioeconomic problems and negotiation. And arbitration organizations (e.g., the biennial wage negotiations between employer federations and labour organizations) facilitated policy negotiations, adjudicated settlements, and resolved disputes. In this set of complementary organizations, a shared socioeconomic discourse was gradually articulated, enabling governments, trade unions, and employers' associations to interpret macroeconomic phenomena as socioeconomic problems; and to formulate policy frames and enter into negotiations that entailed problem solving via institutionalized learning. Policy formulation and campaigning were to become major elements in a generalized political system in which negotiations mixed power, persuasion, and learning in a hybrid way without automatic recourse to authoritative state intervention (Mansbridge 1992).

STRUCTURAL POLICY: A POLITICAL PROJECT

The development of a structural policy in the last twenty years is one of the most conspicuous aspects of modern Danish economic policy making (Kjær and Pedersen 2001). What began as a complement to existing forms of policy and policy making has gradually come to constitute an overarching political project and a generalized political system of negotiations in the context of which policies and institutional arrangements are positioned, given meaning, and coordinated through negotiations. So far, I have emphasized the structural elements of a negotiated economy, I go on to emphasize the evolutionary aspect of a negotiated economy, describing the process through which a structural policy was developed in terms of policy formation and institutionalization. After illustrating the changing institutional order of structural policy, I identify the emergence of a generalized political system of negotiations linking different issue-areas.

Danish economic policy making was traditionally viewed as involving a trade-off between employment and balanced budgets which could be solved through the management of aggregate demand. In this perspective, economic imbalance first and foremost reflected conjunctural trends in the economy, notably vacillation in the business cycle that could be dealt with effectively through fiscal or incomes policies. However, after the first oil crisis in the later half of the 1970s, this conjunctural interpretation of the economic crisis was challenged by a view stressing that Denmark's economic problems were rooted in the structure of the economy itself. This structural conception was formulated in response to the evident failure of various short-term and demand-oriented policy responses to the international recession. In particular, several actors, including the Danish Confederation of Trade Unions (LO) and the Danish Federation of Industry (DI), saw the problems of crisis management as a manifestation of structural problems on the supply side rather than on the demand side of the Danish economy. Whereas labour saw the problem as having to do with the basic organization and orientation of Danish industry, the Federation of Industry viewed it as stemming from the constraints on export-oriented firms caused by a large public sector that tended to favour industries oriented primarily toward domestic markets. As a result, labour called for stronger industrial policy, but capital called for wage restraint and public expenditure policies designed to improve the international competitiveness of Danish industry. The key implication of the debate, however, was a common focus on structural problems in the national economy and a common linking of macroeconomic problems and problems of industrial competitiveness (Pedersen et al. 1992).

As it turned out, the formulation of a more structural view of the problems of Danish industry led quickly to a revitalization of industrial policy, which was now seen as a tool for socioeconomic reconstruction. This led to attempts to formulate a technology policy aimed at improving the technological competitiveness of Danish firms through programs targeted at particular industries or technologies, or at public-private cooperation in the area of technological development. In the technology policy interpretation of structural problems, the key problem was the low level of technological development in industry, which was due in part to the small size and limited financial strength of Danish firms. The key actors in developing this interpretation were policy organizations within the Ministry of Industry and the network of public and semi-public discourse organizations (research and development [R&D] organizations) under the auspices of the Ministry. Inside the policy organizations but outside the discourse organizations, both the Federation of Industry and organized labour, represented by the Danish Confederation of Trade Unions (LO), were involved in a number of conflicts, together with the major political parties (the Conservative Party, the Liberal Party, and the Social Democratic Party), about how to organize research and interpret research results. Main conflicts occurred on the subject of the overall strategy. Industry, together with the Liberal Party, wanted the strategy to be based on liberal principles not targeting particular industries or branches. The Conservative and Social Democratic Parties, for their part, argued for a more interventionist policy. In the end, the idea of using industrial policy to foster structural adjustment and thus international competitiveness became of foremost importance for all parties. Moreover, the development of sectorally oriented technology policy signalled a move away from a traditional non-selective and non-interventionist industrial policy toward an industrial policy that involved a greater directive role for the government. This shift was also reflected organizationally in the fact that significant changes had been made in the Ministry of Industry and elsewhere which led to the establishment of policy organizations oriented toward the development of industrial policy programs. These in turn led to the formulation of new, more active, and more project-oriented policy programs, in the development of which industry, organized labour, and the most important political parties took part.

In the mid-1980s a broader definition of structural problems developed. Discourse and policy organizations within the ministries of Finance and Industry adopted the concept of "structural competitiveness," in which the competitiveness of Danish industry was seen as being dependent on a much wider variety of structural problems in the Danish economy, problems that resulted not just in low R&D but in an orientation toward producing for low-growth markets and a general lack of adaptive and innovative capacities in Danish industry. It was argued – mainly by the Ministry of Finance – that in order to resolve these problems coordinated efforts were needed in areas other than just industrial policy. There was also a need to reform state administrative and regulatory structures in several policy areas.

Furthermore, in 1986 a process of reorganization started in the Ministry of Industry. Several subsidy programs were terminated much against the will of LO, and the administrative structure of the Ministry was changed to more closely approximate a corporate structure; that is, an administrative form based on the management principles of private corporations and intended in part to improve the efficiency of industrial policy. Initiatives toward these changes were taken by higher-ranked public servants inside the Ministry of Finance and the Ministry of Industry many times in conflict with organized labour and the Social Democratic Party then in opposition. A few years later, and in tandem with these changes in the two ministries, several private and semi-public industrial and structural policy organizations began to emerge in an effort to widen the scope of structural policy. This time, members of the Social Democratic Party were to become active participants in developing a new and more interventionist industrial policy strategy. For instance, the Forum for Industrial Development was founded in 1988 and comprised representatives from firms, institutional investors, trade unions, and other private organizations as well as civil servants known for their social democratic leanings and members of the inner circle of the Social Democratic Party. It sought to put issues of industrial restructuring on the agenda and later also pushed for broader issues, such as welfare state reform. Indeed, during the late 1980s there was an explosive growth in local and regional industrial and structural policy initiatives that were favoured by groups representing a broad selection of actors, including public agencies, industrial associations, R&D institutions, and private firms (Pedersen et al. 1992; Amin and Thomas 1996).

Throughout this period a number of neo-liberal ideas and distinctions were introduced into the debate over structural policy. One was the notion that state subsidies to industry presented "barriers" to adaptability and therefore to competitiveness. Another was the idea advanced by the Federation of Industry that public regulation had adverse effects on private firms. Still, it was not public regulation per se that was seen as the problem, but rather a particular form of regulation that posed barriers to industrial adaptation and competitiveness. As a result, ministries, policy agencies, and other administrative bodies related to industrial performance were not to withdraw from their activities, but to reorganize according to the needs and practices of industry and other relevant economic actors. Thus, on the one hand, implementation of the corporate model in the Ministry of Industry was designed not so much to liberalize or deregulate industrial policy but to improve its efficiency. On the other hand, public bodies were to become more goal- and market-oriented, and open to dialogue with a more inclusive group of private actors as well as other public bodies.

Discourse organizations within the ministries of Industry and Finance, as well as the Economic Advisory Council (a campaign organization), participated in formulating the framework for a structural policy that transcended the area of industrial policy, which had preoccupied policy makers during the previous period and entailed the coordination of industrial policy with other policy areas, such as labour market and R&D policy, administrative reforms in the public sector, and changes in issue-areas like training and employment policies (Madsen 2003). In a series of policy publications, the need for economic growth and structural adjustment was linked to initiatives that emphasized much closer coordination among various issue-areas and between public and private actors with respect to industrial development, research, education, labour mobility, and so on. The key problem of Danish industry in this interpretation was not its low degree of technological development but its inability to adjust to new positions of strength in the international competitive environment. In order to develop policy to facilitate this goal, increased public-private dialogue was called for. The key actors in this regard were several sector ministries and a variety of firms, industries, and other private actors.

Around 1990 the conception of structural problems shifted from being oriented toward barriers to growth and adaptation in Danish industry to being oriented toward the adaptation of Danish society as a whole – both the public and private sectors – to a challenging future in a world of European integration and economic globalization. The new conception of structural policy was one of a much more continuous, simultaneous and, importantly, integrated structural adaptation of the public and private sectors. This was foreshadowed by the development of public sector and structural policies since 1985, and points to how participants in the ongoing deliberation learned from past conflicts and experiences to develop strategies through incremental and pragmatic changes in already formulated common understandings. New socioeconomic problems were seldom formulated; rather, old ones were reformulated. Insofar as the public sector was concerned, specifically public expenditure policy and public sector modernization, the long-term development of the public sector was now seen as the most important socioeconomic problem and was increasingly to be connected with the overall structural development of Danish society. Neither one could develop effectively without the development of the other. For instance, it was no longer enough to limit public expenditures and make the public sector more efficient; one also had to consider the relationship between the public and private sectors and the overall dynamics of development of society. In the context of structural policy, the government became increasingly aware of the role of the public sector in facilitating the restructuring of industry.

The key participants were a multitude of both public and private actors at the national and local level, all of whom shared responsibility for the continuous development and adaptation of the Danish economy. For a short period of time the Ministry of Finance came to play the important role of policy organization as well as campaign and discourse organization (Jensen 2003), with organized labour and organizations representing public employees pushed aside. With public sector modernization in focus, industry as well as labour became marginalized, and fights developed between the government and groups of public servants. Hence, between 1985 and 1993, policy conflicts often emerged between organized public employees and the top managers of the central state. Structural policy now merged with public sector modernization policies and was oriented toward restructuring the boundaries between issue-areas and institutions, on the one hand, and between the public and private sectors, on the other. The objective of creating an efficient and adaptive public sector, which had been articulated in 1984 through the Administrative Modernization Program, was now linked to the goal of creating an adaptive and future-oriented industrial structure in the private sector. The pressing problem and object of attention became the adaptation of Danish society to future developments in the European Union and the international economy. As a result, structural policy gradually became more macro-oriented in the sense that it entailed not only coordination and restructuring in and between policy sectors but also a continuous restructuring of the entire Danish economy.

This was perhaps clearest in the area of policy regarding public sector modernization. Here policies that attempted to consider the role and boundaries of the entire public sector were institutionalized. First, starting in 1990, Fiscal Policy Statements that were published by the Ministry of Finance began to treat questions of structural transformation and structural policy making as the overarching consideration toward which most other policies, including stabilization policies, were oriented. Second, several programs and plans were initiated to promote experimentation with new types of public sector governance and new relations between public and private bodies (Lægreid and Pedersen 1994, 1996; Jacobsson, Lægreid, and Pedersen 1999).

During this third phase of structural policy development, which drew attention to the existing boundaries between state and economy as a socioeconomic problem, the macroeconomic efficiency of the entire public sector became a key ingredient in the formulation of structural problems and, consequently, in policy and institutional reform. Of course, the changing of boundaries was usually seen as part of the new problem of improving structural competitiveness vis-à-vis European political and economic integration. Still, although emphasis on state-economy boundaries was paramount in assessing structural problems, the issue was often more one of how better to coordinate and integrate policies and structures on each side of the boundary rather than sharpen and deepen the divide between public and private. The emphasis on the public sector then did not lead to radical changes in the understanding of socioeconomic problems; instead problems and topics were reformulated to include new groups of participants into conflicts. Organizations representing public servants were to become major players, together with private interest organizations representing local and regional authorities. As a result, while the structural policy gradually became more macro-oriented, the number of participants became more encompassing, in the sense that the reformulated socioeconomic problems entailed not only coordination and restructuring in and between policy sectors but also a continuous restructuring of the public sector. Eventually, these reforms were institutionalized through experiments in contracting out public services to the private sector, various forms of public utility privatization, and contractual arrangements between ministries and government agencies. Again, however, these initiatives were articulated as part of a broad program to resolve structural problems by improving the adaptive capacity of Danish society as it coped with increased European integration and competition. For example, the need to liberalize particular regulated industries was motivated by the problem of competitiveness and the potential for development in related industries as well as by the anticipated trend toward liberalization eventually being required by the European community. Furthermore, experiments with contracting out were seen not as ends in themselves but as part of a broader set of structural policies (Andersen 1997) continuing the line of development in the formulation and reformulation of socioeconomic problems that had been ongoing since the 1970s.

STRUCTURAL POLICY:

A GENERALIZED POLITICAL SYSTEM OF NEGOTIATIONS

To review briefly, during the 1980s and 1990s a structural policy was formulated. It developed as part of the discursive history of the Danish polity after 1945, and particularly after 1975. In more than twenty-five years the structural policy gradually became macro-oriented, in the sense that it entailed not only coordination and restructuring in and between the private and the public sectors but also a continuous restructuring of the entire Danish economy. First, it came to be distinguished from Keynesian demand-side politics by its emphasis on the supply-side as an ideal point of departure for economic policy making. Second, it focused on the boundary between public and private sectors and emphasized liberalization – that is, restoring market relations and removing obstacles to free competition. Third, it entailed attempts to introduce market principles of organization in the public sector either by moving functions from the public to the private sector and lifting restrictions on the operation of private markets or by marketizing the public sector through reforms that created or simulated competition among public institutions or depoliticized or individualized decision making in and around public institutions. Fourth, it was distinguished from traditional industrial policy by its emphasis on the coordination between industrial restructuring and reforming of the public sector. This conception of structural policy is one of a continuous, simultaneous, and integrated structural adaptation of both the public and the private sectors. It looks upon the reorganization of the public sector as a prerequisite for restructuring industry; and it looks upon the restructuring of industry as a prerequisite for making the Danish economy internationally competitive.

During the gradual development of structural policy, a multitude of both public and private actors at the national and local level were integrated into a generalized system of negotiations that made all of them co-responsible for the continuous development and adaptation of the Danish economy. On the basis of the socioeconomic discourse, a generalized system of negotiations was established to enable multiple actors in the private as well as in the public sector to adjust and change structural elements in the economy and to do it in an unremitting way. During these twenty-five years of policy development, new organizations evolved as a result of deliberations and learning. Policy organizations, together with campaign and discourse organizations, played an important role, in the sense that they enabled actors to read changes in the international environment as socioeconomic problems and helped them turn specific and individual questions into collective challenges. The ability of these organizations to establish joint interpretations of statistics and events and to translate them into collective socioeconomic problems was paramount for learning and flexibility. The ongoing deliberation made it possible for collective actors: (i) to develop structural policy as a national political project that would gradually involve more policy sectors and integrate additional public and private actors; (ii) to go through several phases of reformulation of a structural policy without radically changing precedent understandings but reformulating these in the view of past experiences and present readings; (iii) and to do so in an incremental way by reaching consensus among the most important social partners on the basis of common interpretations and understandings of socioeconomic problems. Thus, Denmark learned to change to structural policy and learned that it also needed to change its institutions to do that.

During this period of learning and flexibility, a generalized system of negotiations was established with the following capabilities: (i) in terms of content, settling conflicts of distribution between private and public sector, central and local state, labour and capital by establishing nationwide organized negotiations; (ii) in terms of process, linking an increasing number of issue-areas by sequencing negotiations at the national level with negotiations at the levels of policy sectors, local state agencies, and individual firms; (iii) in terms of procedures, allocating representational privileges among social partners by ongoing organizational and institutional reforms; (iv) in terms of mechanisms, developing new and reform old means of policy formulation, campaign tactics and negotiation strategies in the light of past experiences; and (v) in terms of agency, establishing the prerequisites for strategic games among collective actors (Traxler 1997). Let us look at each of these five areas in turn.

Organizing negotiations: Since the end of the 1980s three organized sets of negotiations were established, involving the parliament, the government, peak organizations, and organizations representing local and regional authorities (*Kommunernes Landsforening* and *Danmarks Amtsrådsforening*). The first of these were negotiations over public budgets. Here, the first step is for every minister to negotiate budgets for his or her issue-area with the Ministry of Finance and also with institutions beneath the ministry (departments and directorates); in a second step the government negotiates the state budget with parties in the parliament (*Finanslovsforhandlinger*), agreeing on long- and short-term goals for the public sector. The second of the organized negotiations are negotiations concerning distribution packages. Here, the state budget sets cost limits for negotiations between the government and the local authorities while deciding productivity goals for public organizations and policy targets for welfare institutions (*Kommunaløkonomiske forhandlinger*). Both sets of negotiations take place every year but also set cost limits for a third set of negotiations – wage negotiations, which take place every second year between peak organizations in the public and the private labour market. Lower-level negotiations are sequenced in accordance with the rhythm of the three organized negotiations; they set limits on and policy targets for issue-oriented negotiations at various levels such as the joint shaping of national policies (e.g., labour training, social policy, employment), sectoral wage bargaining, and negotiations at the plant level regarding working conditions. Hence, through organized negotiations, social partners representing all major collective actors link distribution packages (covering incomes policies, pensions, taxation, and social security) to productivity goals (for the public and also the private sector) and set long- and short-term cost limits for the whole economy. The Ministry of Finance is a powerful participant in all organized negotiations. The Ministry is also in charge of the arbitration and sanctioning organizations that conciliate and sanction breaches of agreements.

Interlocking negotiations: Among the issue-areas being linked and sequenced, wage- and incomes policy measures were probably the most important. For years, until the 1980s, wage- and incomes policy had been a favourite macroeconomic instrument according to the demand-side orientation of the socioeconomic discourse. From the end of the 1980s a peculiar institutional arrangement in the labour market made it possible for the government and the peak-organizations to manage wage formation by consensus mobilization, bi- and tripartite negotiations, and inter- as well as intra-organizational control of members. Indirect guidance and control of wage formation rather than discretionary intervention by the government was increasingly used to adjust nominal wages to changing macroeconomic conditions. Negotiations in the public labour market were organized according to the rules of the private market, and negotiations for both markets were sequenced so that the Ministry of Finance could control and manage both wage and income developments for all employed in the Danish economy, within cost limits decided by state budget negotiations. The institutional flexibility involved was based on the willingness of the organizations (both in the private and the public labour market) to implement wage limits without government interventions.

Negotiations dealing with wage formation became blended with issues such as cost-of-living escalators, introduction of new technology, work time reductions, decentralization- and individualization of pay agreements, and job security.

A second issue-area to become locked in to the generalized system of negotiations was labour market policy. From 1982 to 1989 a new active labour market policy was attempted, and in the 1990s four labour market reforms were implemented; these decentralized policy measures to regional corporatist bodies (involving both local and regional authorities, trade unions, and employer's organizations) and to the plant-level (involving firm management, employers' organizations, and shop stewards) (Jørgensen 2002; Madsen chapter 9; Martin 2003). The intention was to restructure the composition of the labour force and its flexibility through pre-employment and on-the-job training programs. Today education and retraining are considered the primary means for adjusting the labour force to changes in the global economy.

Administrative reforms in the public sector became a third issue to be locked in to the system of negotiations. Uncontrolled public expenditures and heavy tax burdens had for years been a major macroeconomic problem. Expenditures came under control as a result of strict austerity measures put forward by the government in the 1980s. New models for managing and controlling the public sector were introduced, and during the 1990s unions representing public employees were forced to accept austerity and modernization measures. In addition, a new set of bi-partite institutions was created, making it possible for the government (in several instances in collaboration with the organizations) to develop new means for reorganizing the public sector through programs for privatization, deregulation, out-sourcing, and decentralization of wage formation to public organizations and individual pay agreements (Jacobsson, Lægreid, and Pedersen 1999).

Allocating privileges: Organizing and interlocking negotiations involved building new arenas for political exchange and establishing new organizational privileges for collective actors. New arenas, such as the regional corporatist institutions and negotiations at the plant-level, were established for collective bargaining (Martin 2003; Madsen, chapter 9). New actors, such as organizations representing public employees or top managers in the public sector, were included in nationwide negotiations (Lægreid and Pedersen 2001). In other words, new privileges were established, and autonomy and authority were spread across private and public institutions and decentralized to the regional, local, and plant levels. The delegation of power and influence was part of the political exchange in which socio-economic problems were reformulated; and the discursive shifts were then followed by the linking of issue-areas, the building of negotiation organizations covering the national economy, and the integration of a growing number of collective actors able to influence the policy process from policy design (policy, campaign, and discourse organizations) via policy negotions (negotiation organizations) to implementation. According to Tiziano Treu (1992), this structure has led to more developed forms of concertation in the sense that the number of participants involved was increased (quantitative integration) and the number of policy areas linked was amplified (qualitative integration). Compared to the traditional wage- and incomes policy forms of corporatism and collective concertation, the generalized system of negotiations is embedded in the collective understanding of more (rather than less) encompassing types of socioeconomic problems and is based on generalized (rather than isolated) negotiations. In the Danish case the institutional shift from traditional corporatist arrangements toward generalized negotiations was based on the dynamic change of collective understandings. The corporatist arrangements were not reduced or undermined, but were extended and adapted (Molina and Rhodes 2003).

Changing mechanisms: Throughout the establishment of this generalized system, three rather basic mechanisms came to play a particularly important role in all the processes we have described above: problem formation, codification, and consensus building. These three mechanisms facilitated collective learning, and each underwent significant change during the 1980s, which was linked, in part, to the gradual introduction of structural policy into Danish discourse and understanding of socioeconomic problems (Kjær and Pedersen 2001).

First, the collective construction and articulation of socioeconomic problems was to become a central feature of the Danish negotiated economy. This is referred to as the *problem formation mechanism.* During the 1980s and early 1990s there was a fundamental change in the way problems were perceived and formulated. During the early 1980s problems were defined in terms of the past. For example, it had long been assumed that policy ought to be directed toward maintaining an ideal socioeconomic balance as reflected in measures such as balanced budgets. Under these discursive conditions, the factors that were perceived as problematic and requiring explanation, evaluation, and policy management were the factors that moved the economy away from the desired balance. However, during the early 1990s problems were defined much more in terms of the future. Specifically, the concern was how the national economy and its position vis-à-vis other national economies related to the future development of markets and political structures, including the development of the unified European market project as well as the more general globalization of economic activity. What had to be articulated now was an imagined future, and the associated problems that might be anticipated with it. Consequently, the policy process became more preoccupied with definitions, predictions, and anticipatory strategies than with descriptions and explanations of past and present conditions.

Second, in the generalized system actors came to verbalize conflicts and disagreements, articulate interests, coordinate behaviour, modify courses of action, create strategies for actions, and ultimately codify decisions through negotiation. This is referred to as the *codification mechanism*. Two important developments occurred here. On the one hand, whereas codification initially occurred within fairly stable cognitive and institutional frameworks, it now took place within more open-ended bounds partly as a result of the more future-oriented nature of problem formation. On the other hand, codification became professionalized. For example, in order to become a participant in the structural policy debate, actors now had to legitimize themselves by reference to being familiar and comfortable, if not masterful, with particular and somewhat exclusive bodies of scientific knowledge. Among other things, this professionalization has been mirrored since the late 1980s in the sharply increasing number of discourse, policy, and campaign organizations in ministries and interest organizations and financial institutions (pension funds for example). The form of writing in many reports published by these institutions increasingly resembled the style of more scientific publications.

Third, a key element of the system was to become the *consensus mechanism*. Here the formulation of problems and coordination of behaviour is made possible and constrained by the continuous production of a basic and widely shared understanding of the situation – the socioeconomic problem – among all participants engaged in the articulation and negotiation of problems and solutions. In the early 1980s this process was closely linked to a traditional corporatist type of institutional arrangement that included bi-partite or tri-partite consultations in various policy fields. During this time a consensus on substantive policy prescriptions became a precondition for joint action. In other words, only those prescriptive measures to which all parties could agree were enacted as official policy. However, beginning in the early 1990s there was less emphasis on consensus over substantive matters and more on methods and procedures for devising policy prescriptions and delegating power and influence. Hence, there has been a shift from substantive agreement to a kind of procedural consensus marked by the establishment of a generalized political system for negotiations.

Strategic games: The generalized political system of negotiation was constituted in an incremental way through the contribution of many actors with diverse and often short-term motivations. However, the system developed into much more than an instrument for preference formulation and decision making. More than anything, it became a rationality context that enabled actors to validate their specific interests in the light of their mutual interests; to evaluate their short-term interests in the light of long-term consequences; and to negotiate social pacts and policy packages based on the rules of log rolling and the like. During the development of the generalized system of negotiations, political exchange became embedded in strategic games of inclusion and exclusion of both participants and problems. At some point, conflicts became formulated as socioeconomic problems, as did the distribution of organizational and institutional privileges, just as political exchange came to be oriented toward an imagined future more than the reality of the present. Strategic gaming, then, came to be built on three different types of games: language games, negotiation games, and round table negotiations.

In *language games,* preferences and interest are formulated and reformulated, and are moulded into a common understanding of the socioeconomic situation, on the basis of which the negotiation game of inclusion or exclusion can take place. Language games developed during the 1980s on the basis of the fact that ministries, peak organizations, and financial institutions established their own discourse and campaign organizations with the goals of positioning their specific understandings of socioeconomic problems on the public agenda and influencing the moulding of mutual understandings. During these years there was a fundamental change in the way problems were perceived and formulated due to the gradual development of the rationality context for language games; socioeconomic problems came to be constructed, articulated, and codified in reports written in a semi-scientific style by discourse organizations.

While language games are about the reading of social events and the interpretation of economic statistics as well as the inclusion and exclusion of problems, *negotiation games* deal with who is to participate in round table negotiations. Again, fundamental changes took place in the 1980s and 1990s. During the days of traditional neo-corporatism, inclusion and exclusion were decided by the lawmakers, and included actors were delegated influence by law. In the system of generalized negotiations, inclusion and exclusion are part of the gaming, and the game is based on the rules of coalition making and log rolling.

The same goes for *round table negotiations.* Here the government and local authorities, in collaboration with organized interests and financial institutions, engage in concrete negotiations to develop compromises on problems and solutions based on the outcome of language games and negotiation games. In round table negotiations, bargaining is founded on common understandings of the socioeconomic problems. Only those who have shown an interest in signing agreements based on a mutual under-standing are invited. Excluded actors are left with the possibility of influencing negotiations only by lobbying, media campaigns, or other forms of manipulation from the outside.

In sum, although a negotiated economy has always been a unique form of collective learning that contributed directly to policy and institutional change, key elements of this – content, process procedures, mechanisms, and agency – changed as structural policy became a major political project in the Danish context. However, it is important to recognize that these changes were themselves driven, at least in part, by the introduction of the policy. In other words, as a new political project was incorporated into discourse, it began to have significant effects on content, procedures, processes, mechanisms, and agency. A generalized system of negotiations was built and neo-corporatism was transformed. In this way the social partners have proven to be capable of verbalizing experiences and transforming institutions and organizations on the basis of interpretations of changing macroeconomic situations and conditions. Also, they have proven themselves capable of formulating a national strategy for structural change, technological renewal, and modernization of the public sector, and of achieving broad acceptance of this among multiple collective actors and in the population in general.

This transformation of neo-corporatist arrangements involved the selection and displacement of socioeconomic problems as well as the triggering of shifts in policy orientation and shifts in the distribution of organizational and institutional privileges. For example, the three mechanisms (problem formation, codification, and consensus making) contributed to the selection of new political-economic ideas in the sense that they determined what ideas and issues could fit into or become part of the learning process. Notably, the problem-formation mechanism ensured that only issues and ideas that could be defined as socioeconomic problems could become part of the discussions about structural policy. Thus, the issue of supply-side structural barriers to industrial growth became part of the existing economic policy discourse because it was possible to formulate this issue as a socioeconomic problem. Once supply-side orientation had been introduced, it transformed policy orientation by opening up a whole new range of possibilities for rearranging processes, procedures, and agency.

The introduction of structural policy into the Danish policy discourse also displaced certain elements of the learning process. For example, neo-corporatist arrangements were altered by the introduction of a new set of arenas for negotiation and by a new set of collective actors. This led to the expansion of formal procedures of participation in policy negotiation and consensus building. The initial conjunctural perspective on socioeconomic problems, especially that which focused on problems associated with business cycle fluctuations, entailed a stable pattern of bi-partite or tri-partite interest representation in negotiation because these were problems to be dealt with through well-established wage negotiation institutions. However, problems of structural competitiveness were more complex, involved a multiplicity of structural difficulties that could not be handled in one negotiation arena, and required a more integrated approach spanning several arenas as well as multiple levels and departments of government. This precipitated a revision of negotiation organizations, notably the inclusion of a wider and often-shifting set of participants, such as representatives from R&D institutes and new government agencies and municipalities, as noted earlier.

Finally the introduction of structural policy triggered a shift in attention toward new aspects of reality, made possible new ways of conceptualizing problems and solutions, and created possibilities for new types of political action and intervention based on strategic games. For example, the emphasis on structural competitiveness shifted policy makers' attention from current to future structural and organizational constraints in the economy. This led to changes in the agency of actors, which increasingly emphasized the strategic aspect of political exchange and the importance of inclusion and exclusion of problems as well as participants. In terms of macroeconomic policy, attention shifted from conjunctural business cycle fluctuations to the formulation of political projects or national strategies for the structural competitiveness of the whole economy. The formulation and implementation of national strategies became important, and key elements of the traditional neo-corporatist arrangements – content, process procedures, mechanisms, and agency – were changed.

CONCLUSION

To recognize the importance of the negotiated economy is not to suggest that every small country can or will have to develop a similar institutional structure to guarantee economic prosperity. It is not even to suggest that the negotiated approach in the Danish case is the only factor to be credited for positive economic results. Denmark is not only a small country but also a little land with a relatively homogeneous population, a developed democratic culture, and, in particular, a small policy and political community drawn from a network of known educational institutions and families. A small elite makes up the Danish power networks. Collaborators as well as opponents are linked through common educational experiences and institutions, institutional rotation, and personal acquaintances (Amin and Thomas 1996).

Even so, I maintain that a national strategy was formulated during the

1980s and 1990s that led to a reformulation of the socioeconomic discourse and profound changes in the articulation of socioeconomic problems. I also maintain that new policy instruments and organizations were created, and that new possibilities for conflict and consensus have been established by the creation of a rationality context for strategic gaming. These achievements ought not to divert attention from the problems and ambiguities, however. The emergence of a structural policy is a rather new phenomenon, and questions remain as to its implementation. Only a patchwork of policies has been implemented. And even if a generalized system of negotiations has been created, many policy fields are not (yet) interlocked with these negotiations (see Kristensen, chapter 8). Also, strained relations developed between the government and public organizations when distribution packages and productivity goals were to be implemented at the local and regional levels. Even the restructuring of the industrial sector has proven to be more difficult than expected, mostly as a result of fierce resistance from certain branches and single companies reacting to being enrolled in the overall strategy of the structural policy.

The overwhelming complexity of a negotiated economy is another of the many reasons why national strategy is still vague and likely will continue to be. Yet another reason is the particular character of the generalized system of negotiations, built as it is on the autonomy of all participants and on deliberation and persuasion as instruments of regulation rather than on state authority and state planning. A third reason for the vagueness of national strategy is the small and open character of the Danish economy. In times of European and global change, small and open economies are forced to enter a period of ongoing adaptation and reformulation of interpretations, and restructuring of organized privileges. The very limited size of their industries and their lack of political muscle force them to adapt to changes on the basis of technologies mainly researched and developed by others and within a political agenda controlled and formulated by others. Therefore, not only is a time lag between changes and adaptation to be expected, but the question of efficiency in adapting is also raised, while the fluidity of institutions makes it difficult to establish the preconditions for measuring the efficiency of an institutional regime. This helps explain why it is difficult to prove conclusively that it was the negotiated approach to policy making that was primarily responsible for the impressive performance of the Danish economy in the 1990s (Madsen 2003).

My key point in this chapter has been that collective learning and policy flexibility are facilitated in the Danish case by the articulation of socioeconomic problems and the founding of a generalized system of negotiation. Denmark is especially well chosen for highlighting the discursive as well as the governance elements of institutions. The Danish case is of special importance for the theory of corporatism because it shows that the post-war neo-corporatist wage and incomes policy bargaining system described by others (e.g., Schmitter 1974, 1982; Katzenstein 1985; Therborn 1998) was adapted and extended rather than abandoned during the 1980s and 1990s (Molina and Rhodes 2002). Finally, the Danish case is of importance for comparative political economy because it constitutes an important and often neglected case of policy learning and flexibility, and points to some of the conditions that facilitate that learning and flexibility (Hemerijck and Schludi 2000; Teague 2000; Katzenstein 2002).

However, an important question remains: How have the social partners been able to govern national changes through joint policy making in a situation of ongoing change in the economic and political environment? To answer this question, it has been important to understand how policy organizations, discourse organizations, negotiation organizations, and other organizations evolved in the 1950s and 1960s to form a particular institutional framework for the evolution of traditional neo-corporatist arrangements toward a contingent and emergent system of generalized political negotiations. While a system for generalized negotiations is the discursive and institutional precondition for a negotiated economy, the system itself can only be identified by understanding the discursive as well as the governance side of the system. Indeed, institutions consist of both discursive structures (i.e., cognitive and normative frames for interpretations of social events and readings of economic statistics), and governance structures (i.e., formal and informal rules and compliance procedures). In order to understand how they function, attention must be paid to both (Campbell and Pedersen 1996).

In the Danish case, the discursive side of the system is especially important because socioeconomic discourse makes it possible for actors to interpret and understand social events from the point of view of the same discourse and to come to a mutual understanding of what kinds of problems to look for and what kinds of solutions to stretch to. The possibility for social actors to differentiate between systems is important for communication to be possible and for mutual understanding to develop (Luhmann 1981). The evolution of a socioeconomic discourse is an important factor in explaining the way organized negotiations participate in a generalized system. Such discourse enables a special type of social actor (equipped with discourse- and policy organizations) to recognize certain social events and problems as socioeconomic problems. Thus, socioeconomic discourse is not an overarching frame of meaning but one among several discourses framing social events; nor is it a general frame of meaning able to be portrayed in other than the Danish case. Rather, it is a particular discourse that has evolved under certain historical conditions that have enabled social partners to act rationally while moulding specific interests into public interests and to implement national strategies while preserving their own autonomy and authority.

The governance side of the system is important in explaining how organized negotiations take part in a generalized system. In the Danish case, the mix of discourse- and policy organizations with negotiation and arbitration organizations makes it possible to combine the reformulation of socioeconomic problems with changes in policy orientation and in the distribution of organizational positions and privileges. On the one hand, the possibility of social partners entering into strategic games and moulding interests by the mechanisms of problem formation, codification, and consensus making enables them to reach decisions on the basis of interaction among independent agents, where the relevant public authority is just one of several participants. On the other hand, the evolution of organized negotiations enables social partners to coordinate decisions without hierarchy and allows them to link levels of bargaining involving strong commitments through the sequencing of negotiations and the interlocking of issue-areas.

Hence, the generalized system of negotiations encompasses both discursive and governance elements. On the discursive side, it is a system based on a discourse that enables social partners to understand social events from the same cognitive and normative point of view. On the governance side, it is a system that has evolved into a set of arenas for sequenced negotiation, which enable social partners to engage in political exchange through strategic games and make it possible for them to reach decisions based on their mutual autonomy and authority.

In political science, theories of pluralism and neo-corporatism have been offered to explain policy making in advanced capitalist countries. The pluralist tradition has its origin in group theory, according to which political groups are autonomous in relation to political institutions and a formal distinction is supposed to exist between the two. The neo-corporativist tradition, on the other hand, originated in functional theories, according to which it was assumed that political institutions and private organizations are no longer separated by a formal distinction. Rather, stable and institutionalized relations among the two are established in an effort to make public decisions more efficient (Kastendiek 1981). Neo-corporatism and pluralism differ in important ways from the negotiated economy. (i) While pluralist as well as neo-corporatist theories focus on relations among organizations representing objective societal functions or interests, I have stressed that interests in a negotiated economy are created or formed in language and negotiation games and that a generalized political system of negotiation can mould selfish interests into common understandings and, subsequently, into public interests. (ii) While plural-ist theory stresses the authority of public institutions and the autonomy of private organizations, social partners in a negotiated economy are autonomous but enter into collective decision making on the basis of strong commitments by all participants to a shared socioeconomic ideal. Notable also is that fact that the government is only one among several participants in this decision making. (iii) While neo-corporatist theory focuses on special or single arenas for negotiation, I have stressed the sys-temic and generalized character of organized negotiations that cut across and link these arenas. (iv) While neo-corporatist theories emphasize the way state and other organizations are formally integrated, I have high-lighted the often informal character of the strategic games that are involved. (v) I have shown how both governance and discursive organiza-tions are important, whereas the literatures on neo-corporatism and plu-ralism neglect the discursive side. (vi) Finally, while both pluralist and neo-corporatist theories point to the stable aspects of relations among social partners, I have underlined the evolutionary and very dynamic character of a negotiated economy, which results in a high degree of insti-tutional flexibility and learning capacity. Especially in this sense, the Danish case is of special interest for comparative political economy because it is an important and often neglected case of policy learning and flexibility that is based on institutional arrangements that are quite dif-ferent from the neo-corporatist arrangements described by Katzenstein (1985) and others.

In describing the Danish case of a negotiated economy, I have under-lined that social partners have built and transformed their institutional framework following a path-dependent, neo-corporatist trajectory that has changed classic neo-corporatism into a generalized system of negotiations (Molina and Rhodes 2002). Even if this resembles what Anton Hemerijck (1995) has described in the Dutch case as a networked variety of economic governance, or what Franz Traxler et al. (2001) have called a development from "classic" to "lean" corporatism, the Danish negotiated economy is a distinct mode of governance because of its systemic and encompassing character. It must therefore be recognized that complex and important discursive and other institutional differences can exist among the small, advanced capitalist countries that are often described collectively as neo-corporatist or coordinated (Hall and Soskice 2002). Indeed, given the right circumstances, some of these countries may evolve into something significantly different and more complex than the simple but telling dichotomy of liberal market economies and coordinated market economies discussed in the first chapter of this volume. Whether Denmark's negotiated economy will continue to evolve in the face of new challenges such as globalization and European integration, and especially during a period in which international organizations like the EU, the OECD, and the World Bank, among others, strongly advocate neo-liberal reform, remains to be seen.

NOTES

This chapter is based in part on Peter Kjær and Ove K. Pedersen 2001, "Translating Liberalization: Neoliberalism in the Danish Negotiated Economy." 219–48 in *The Rise of Neoliberalism and Institutional Analysis*, edited by John L. Campbell and Ove K. Pedersen. Princeton: Princeton University Press.

7

Corporatism in the Post-Industrial Age: Employers and Social Policy in the Little Land of Denmark

CATHIE JO MARTIN

The future of European small-state capitalism – with its attendant, coordinating, political institutions – has been hotly debated of late. In an earlier era, comparative political economists broadly agreed that countries with coordinated market economies (CMEs) and corporatist organizations were better able to reconcile social and economic goals than their counterparts in a liberal market economy (LME), in which markets organized production with limited government interference (Shonfeld 1965; Katzenstein 1985; Hall and Soskice 2001). Vulnerable to the vagaries of international competition, governments in small CME countries encouraged firms to adopt high-equilibrium production strategies to compete in sectors that relied on highly skilled workers (Katzenstein 1985, Hall and Soskice 2001). These competitive strategies required significant investment in human capital; consequently, the needs of economic production were closely coupled to the benefits of social protection. Thus, the strategies both fostered employers' support for social protection and provided an economic rationale for class compromise.

The past two decades have threatened to unsettle this happy equilibrium, undermining faith both in CME economic strategies and in the political arrangements underpinning these strategies. Analysts have argued that de-industrialization, globalization, a weakening of organized labour, the decline of national collective bargaining, an ascendancy of new policy issues on the public agenda, and a decentralization of political decision making to the local and regional levels were limiting the ability of national organizations to engage in consensual decision making. Neo-liberal ideology seemed to capture the hearts and minds of voters and scholars debated whether globalization would bring about a convergence of policy outcomes and the political processes producing them (Streeck and Schmitter 1991; Campbell and Pedersen 2001; Kitschelt et al. 1999; Berger and Dore 1996).

Yet, in a remarkable episode of *déjà vu*, we are once again in an era where high-equilibrium production strategies, social partnerships, and win-win solutions are back in vogue (Rhodes 1998). For example, the latest vehicle for welfare reform – active social and labour market policy – aims to reconcile economic production and social protection by reintegrating the long-term unemployed into the core economy. These policies attempt simultaneously to address concerns about budgetary crises, human capital deficiencies, and social exclusion. Once again small states seem to have something special to offer their big brothers – the "Danish model" and the "Dutch miracle" have replaced the "Dutch disease" (Campbell and Hall, Introduction).

An essential question is whether small coordinated market economies (and Denmark in particular) continue to foster more positive views of the welfare state, despite significant changes in the political economy. Do processes of coordination still encourage positive business views of social investment, or have pressures on collective bargaining turned firms away from their employers' associations for political interpretation? Have the corporatist forms of business association that are so important to processes of coordination changed in response to the pressures of the past decades? With political decentralization, have national corporatist groups lost influence, or do the dynamics of corporatist interaction extend to the local level? If all politics is local, does politics at the local level differ under corporatist and pluralist systems?

This chapter evaluates the continuing utility of the CME model by comparing recent Danish experiments in welfare reform (in the form of active labour market policy) to those of the United Kingdom. The British uncoordinated market economy, with its liberal welfare state, is a useful comparison that highlights the attributes of the Danish model. As expected, Danish active labour market policy diverges from its British counterpart in emphasizing closer connections between production and protection. Danish programs for the long-term unemployed are coordinated with efforts to enhance the skills of regular workers and are encompassed in general efforts to redress projected shortages in the labour supply. As the CME model predicts, the Danish corporatist employers' associations have been more active in the processes of policy development than British businesses, allowing Danish employers greater influence in tailoring plans to employment needs.

In addition, with an empirical study of 107 randomly selected firms in the two countries, I investigate whether Danish firms participate in active social plans more than British employers. I find that Danish firms do participate in greater numbers than British companies and for reasons offered by varieties-of-capitalism models. Unlike English employers, Danish firms participate to gain a better-skilled workforce, demonstrating close links between economic production and social protection. Also diverging from the British experience, membership in Danish corporatist associations has a significant positive effect on participation.

These findings confirm the continuing advantages offered by coordinated market economies and corporatist associations in shaping policy, in providing information and other benefits to members, and in easing the implementation of the social agenda. Those who proclaim the death of corporatist business organizations on the basis of the decline of collective bargaining neglect other important contributions of these groups. Corporatist organizations continue to shape employers' cognitive perceptions of public policy and their understanding of governmental issues. Worried that the decline of collective bargaining will reduce their salience to their members, Danish peak and major sector associations have sought to expand their networking services for members. Today, networks and groups sponsored by the employers' associations may be more important to the cognitive deliberation of employers than the formal positions taken by the associations. Because social pacts must be renegotiated, corporatist forums influence processes of renegotiation even as these networks and informal groups are in the process of replacing the formal structures of engagement.

This study also reveals the changes in corporatist systems since the 1980s, changes that preserve the spirit of the original model despite diverging from it. While original assertions about the importance of corporatist coordination emphasized national structures (Katzenstein 1986; Streeck and Schmitter 1991), much corporatist negotiation today transpires at the local level, a change mirroring the decentralization of the Danish welfare state. Danish corporatist associations have also sought to move into new policy areas, even when these areas address citizens who are outside of the groups' core memberships. For example, Denmark has a long tradition of local partnerships among business, labour, and the state in the local and regional corporatist boards set up to implement active labour market policy. Policy makers have tried to replicate these lower-level labour market boards in social policy areas, reinforcing important ties at the local level and colonizing new policy areas at the same time.

THE REPUTED BENEFITS OF
AND CHALLENGES TO COORDINATION

Two types of literatures link employer coordination to greater business support for social policies: the corporatist literature produces an *institutional* logic for why employers in a coordinated market economy might need public social provision more than managers in a liberal market economy; and the more recent varieties-of-capitalism literature offer an *economic* rationale for this greater support.

First, scholars of corporatism offer an institutional rationale to explain why employers in countries with high levels of coordination support public social provision. Democratic corporatism, a system of interest intermediation, provides a process by which employers and workers can arrive at mutually beneficial equilibria. Democratic corporatism comprises an ideology of social partnerships, a centralized and coordinated mode of interest group representation, and a system of voluntary bargaining among interest groups to resolve conflicting objectives (Katzenstein 1985, 32). Corporatist groups are numerically restricted, singular, functionally differentiated, and hierarchically ordered, whereas the alternative pluralist groups are not restricted in number, have overlapping jurisdictions, and are not hierarchically ordered (Schmitter 1981). The advantages of corporatist systems reputedly appear in several features of social partners' engagement with governmental processes: in the characteristics of the groups, in the mechanisms for involving groups in policymaking, and in the impact of group structure on outcomes (Molina and Rhodes 2002).

Scholars believe that countries with corporatist associations (usually, small countries) are more likely to produce collectively beneficial outcomes than those without such groups (Wilensky 1976; Kendix and Olson 1990; Streeck and Schmitter 1991; Crouch 1993; Hicks and Kenworthy 1998). Because corporatist groups encompass a wider range of interests than pluralist associations, they focus attention on broader, shared concerns and thereby bring members to support collective goals and develop industrywide and enduring positions on public policy (Visser and Hemerijck 1997; Scharpf and Schmidt 2001).[1] In providing information to members, corporatist groups enhance the quality of political deliberation and likelihood of social learning. Participation in such groups helps to overcome the limits to collective action by binding firms to negotiated decisions and bringing members to trust that they will not be punished for committing to longer-term goals (Streeck 1992, 265–84; Rothstein 2000; Katzenstein 1985; Visser and Hemerijck 1997) Because peak associations adjudicate among conflicting demands, large, technologically advanced, export sectors can often force traditionalists in the small business sectors to accept a program of social reform (Crouch 1993). Because corporatist groups participate in the policy-making process through tripartite boards, employers both shape and make a commitment to outcomes from the outset.

Although much of the conventional writing on the welfare state held that weak or divided business led to greater social provision because strong employers defeat social initiatives (Korpi 1980; Castles 1978), the logic of corporatism suggests that well-organized managers are more likely to favour broader, more universal welfare states because the structure of the groups encourages employers to support collective goods (Streeck 1992; Martin 2000). Just as corporatist institutions are functional to economic interests in that they internalize "externalities," they offer similar benefits to social interests. Duane Swank and I have found empirical evidence of this relationship between corporatist organization and the welfare state across developed democracies (Martin and Swank 2004). Corporatist labour and employer associations with centralized systems of collective bargaining have also reputably been able to deliver better outcomes in economic performance. By focusing members' attention on shared macroeconomic goals, these organizations can achieve wage and price restraints in exchange for stable employment and non-inflationary growth (Henly and Tsakalotos 1992, 566–8).

Second, building on corporatist insights, the varieties of capitalism literature recognizes a fundamental difference in the logic of *economic* competition between firms in coordinated market economies (CMEs) and those in liberal market economies (LMEs). CME firms compete in high value-added sectors with high equilibrium production strategies; these strategies allow them to take advantage of their highly educated workforce, to offer high wages, and to help their countries achieve a high standard of living. CME production strategies rely on high levels of investment in training programs that develop workers' skills and other social programs that augment human capital. Thus CME employers realize that in addition to deriving economic advantage from material factors, they can enhance their competitive positions with institutional arrangements that encourage information exchange and consensus. Many institutions reinforce CME production strategies – social welfare regimes, systems of labour relations, employer associations, and methods of financing and corporate governance – and companies' preferences for public policies are reinforced by the tight coupling of these diverse spheres. Alternatively, in liberal market economies such as the United States, labour-management relations tend to be contentious, neither workers nor employers have much incentive to invest in skills, and competitive strategies entailing a highly skilled, productive workforce are discouraged. Scholars generally assume that it is extremely difficult for nations to alter their model economies once in place, and that the persistence of policy in one sphere reflects the constraints imposed by deep linkages to other spheres (Hall and Soskice 2001; Katzenstein 1985).

Coordinated market economies are often found in small countries with large export sectors. Because trade exposure makes economics more dependent on the vagaries of international markets, governments have asserted some control over their domestic economies by expanding social spending (Katzenstein 1985). These strategies create an economic rationale for class compromise, in linking economic production to social protections.

Denmark confirms this picture of a coordinated market economy with a corporatist business community that is sympathetic to social initiatives. Both social democratic and conservative governments have historically appealed to managers to support social initiatives (Jacobsen 1937). Danish employers were centrally organized in 1896–98 and pushed for a more centralized labour federation, asking unions to refuse to work for free-riding firms who stayed out of the business group (Galenson 1952, 2–8, 58, 69–72, 91). At the dawn of the last century the employer-oriented Conservative party had joined with the Liberals in supporting the first mandatory, tax-financed old-age pensions and state sickness funds (Hornemann-Møller 1992). The Danish welfare state made important advances in the 1930s and 1960s, with employer support for most of the expansion (Hornemann-Møller 1994, 111–60). In fact, the right was to brag: "No decisive step in this expansion [of the welfare state] has been undertaken without support from the conservatives in all these parties" (Friis 1969).

Yet myriad economic, political, and demographic changes in the past two decades have made it difficult, some argue, for countries to sustain the levels of social expenditure that can support a high equilibrium production strategy, and have placed concomitant pressures on corporatist interest organizations. Paradoxically, the same internationalization of production that has driven small states to expand their social expenditures programs (Cameron 1979; Katzenstein 1985; Garrett 1998) may now be forcing retrenchment as newly industrializing countries threaten to flood the markets with lower-cost products (Cable 1991; Skidelsky 1979). Iversen (1998) argues that de-industrialization and the lower productivity growth rates in service sectors are making it impossible for governments to expand employment, maintain wage equality, and balance their budgets at the same time. Financial openness has motivated governments to reduce taxes, spending, and other measures that might drive away owners of assets. Rising unemployment has burdened the welfare state (Swank 2001), although some of this reflects an influx of new workers (especially women) into the economy (Huber and Stephens 2001). Low fertility rates and increased life expectancies have added demographic pressures on mature welfare states (Pierson 2001; OECD). Although spending has generally grown more slowly rather than declined (Iversen 2001; Huber, Stephens and Ragin 1993, 2001; Swank 2001), the forms of social provision have changed with deregulation and privatization (Schwartz 2001b).

Events of the past two decades have also threatened to undermine corporatist interests, including globalization, the growing gap between skilled and unskilled workers, and the expanding political power of the European Union. Labour is becoming more diverse with post-industrial production forms, a growing divergence between skilled and unskilled workers, and the increasing strength of public-sector and white-collar workers within organized labour (Lash and Urry 1987; Longstreth 1988; Lange et al. 1995; Crouch 1993). This diversity complicates the efforts of peak associations to negotiate economy-wide wage agreements, and a decentralization of collective bargaining may be underway (Pontusson and Swenson 1996; Katz 1993). Corporatist forms of interest intermediation may also be losing ground in public policy negotiations, as EU-level groups have less representational power than their national counterparts (Streeck and Schmitter 1991; de Swaan 1992, 33–51; Sandholtz and Zysman 1989, 95–128; Kitschelt et al. 1999; Crepas 1992; Coen 1997; Greenwood, Grote, and Ronit 1992.) Economic and political integration has increased the diffusion of policy paradigms across countries (Rhodes 1998). Europe may be moving to a form of weak corporatism, historically associated with weaker economic performance (Henley and Tsakalotos 1992).

Despite these varied pressures on national systems of business organization, recent literature suggests that corporatist arrangements endure in some areas (Traxler 2000). Decentralization of collective bargaining in Germany and Austria has been limited to non-wage issues and, although the Danish peak association has lost strength, its industrial sector groups have gained in importance (Thelen 1998; Due et al. 1994; Schauer 1992). In many countries union coverage (density) has increased while the concentration of union power (concertation) has declined (Wallerstein, Golden, and Lange 1997: 383; Soskice 1990). Measures of corporatism had as much power to predict economic growth in the mid- to late 1980s as they did in the 1970s and early 1980s (Crepaz 1992). Economic integration is, paradoxically, creating an enhanced demand for wage restraint and, consequently, for centralized wage negotiations (Perez 2001).

The various aspects of corporatism are differentially influenced by these challenges. Thus, globalization may complicate collective bargaining enormously because of difficulties in unifying the interests of exposed and protected sectors; yet, tripartite advisory commissions to training programs may be much less affected. Similarly, the European Union may pose larger challenges to the associations' tripartite and legislative activities than to collective bargaining, because EU integration has shifted the development of many rules and regulations to the supra-national level. The fracturing pressures on corporatist groups may be less pertinent to the associations' role in channelling employers' involvement in social programs than to other functions of these groups. In addition, associations may develop strategies to combat the fragmenting pressures associated with globalization and EU integration – political processes rather than functional structures may ultimately matter most to the survival of corporatism (Molina and Rhodes 2002; Treu 1992).

A POLICY RESPONSE TO THE PRESSURES OF THE POST-INDUSTRIAL AGE

In the 1990s countries across Europe tried to adjust their welfare states to the new economic realities with active labour market and social policies that would reintegrate long-term beneficiaries of unemployment insurance and social assistance into the core economy. The policies entail giving the long-term unemployed (for six months or one year) a "new start" in the form of access to training or to subsidized jobs (Ferrera, Hemerijck, and Rhodes 2000; Gilbert 1992; Rhodes 1997, 71–3). The goals of the active approach are ambitious: to curb the growing underclass of multigenerational welfare recipients, to reduce social exclusion, to halt expansion of the public debt, and to contribute to a renewal of human capital. Many believe that countries can now again reconcile social and economic goal policies with this new "competitive corporatism," by which employers, unions, and the state simultaneously negotiate bargains about both growth strategies and social protection (Rhodes,1998; OECD 1994, 43; Matzner and Streeck 1991; Silver 1998).

Active social policies rely on employers and other voluntary actors far more than traditional interventions.[2] Employers are viewed as key to combatting unemployment and social exclusion because private sector training with a wage subsidy has a much higher likelihood of resulting in permanent employment than public sector training or public sector subsidized jobs (Madsen 1997, 8–9; J. Martin 1994, 92). Thus, the 1994 OECD Jobs Study sought to promote "apprenticeship-style training," "incentives for enterprises and workers to invest in continued learning," and "a sharing of the cost burden of life-long learning between the individual, business and the public purse" (OECD 1994, 48, 37). Robert Geyer and Beverly Springer note that in the new policy areas "interest groups are co-opted ... and called on to assume responsibility for formulating and implementing social policy" (Geyer and Springer 1998, 210). Even countries where governments typically provide all social benefits are today turning toward employers as important actors in new public-private partnerships. For example, the Danish labour market and social reforms created subsidies for employers to hire long-term and youth unemployed (Bach and Kylling 1997, 6). The Danish Ministry of Social Affairs explained its new emphasis on employer participation as follows: "From an economic point of view, the purpose of enhanced social responsibility of enterprises is to make social policy more productive in order to achieve social cohesion at the lowest possible costs to society" (Danish National Institute of Research 1997, 10).

There has been considerable support within the European Union for this "emerging European model," officially endorsed with the November 1997 Employment Summit in Luxembourg. Inspired by a shared conception of welfare provision, the Danish and British plans look remarkably similar in terms of the time limits set on the receipt of passive benefits (six months for youth and one year for adults), the compulsory participation by recipients, and the effort to involve firms ("United Kingdom Employment Action Plan 1999"; "*Danmarks Nationale Handlingsplan for Beskæftigelse* 1999"). Although Denmark spends more on general employment policies than Britain, state subsidies paid to employers for hiring the unemployed are similar – about 50 percent of wages (Westergaard-Nielsen, November 2001).

The question is whether coordinated market economies will continue to have different approaches to social protection than liberal market economies even in areas such as active social policy with considerable conceptual convergence across countries. If so, we might expect to find the following cross-national comparisons about the Danish and British experiments in welfare reform. First, the differences between the strategies of small and large states should be evident in each country's development of an active social program. The Danish programs should conform more closely with the needs of a high skills equilibrium production strategy than the corresponding British plan. Second, the Danish corporatist groups should exhibit deeper involvement in formulating and implementing the policies than the British pluralist groups.

Finally, Danish firms should participate in greater numbers in the active programs than the British groups, both because the programs are more closely tailored to their economic needs and because their corporatist groups help them to perceive the advantages of the policies. In addition, the reasons for participating (and therefore the types of companies that participate) should differ across the two models. Yet working against this final expectation is the fact that the active model asks employers not only to support the welfare state but to help to implement it through jobs and training programs. These expectations of private sector involvement represent a monumental break with past programs administered almost entirely by government. In addition, the new programs may have less relevance for economic production, because they are largely designed to met the needs of outsiders – the long-term unemployed and socially excluded.

STRUCTURAL ECONOMIC PRESSURES IN DENMARK AND THE UNITED KINGDOM

Before investigating the impact of model distinctions on active labour market programs, we should consider whether Denmark has been motivated to fix its welfare system by stronger structural imperatives. Denmark had very high rates of unemployment before most European countries and represented something of a worst-case scenario even while Katzenstein was describing the strengths of the small state model. Unemployment went from 0.9 percent in 1973 to 8.3 percent by 1978; wage moderation was abandoned as unit labour costs increased by 80 percent between 1973 and 1980. In Phillips Curve–defying fashion, inflation hovered around 10 percent and the national bank had to raise interest rates significantly to support the Danish krone's connection to the European "currency snake" (Scharpf and Schmidt 2001, 46–7; Iversen et al. 1999).

Yet the Danish economic situation was no worse than that of Britain, and by the early 1990s Denmark was already emerging from its economic doldrums. Denmark began to resolve its economic problems in the mid-1980s: although unemployment rose to 10 percent in 1993, it dropped to a two-decade low of under 6 percent by 1999. Most of the employment growth occurred in the private sector and was concomitant with increasing public budgetary surpluses. Labour force participation by women grew from 48 percent of male employment in 1958 to 84 percent of male employment by the 1990s (Scheurer 1992, 170).

Some of this economic improvement reflected efforts to restrain the growth of public consumption, although policy makers were less successful at restraining the growth of income transfers to households (Andersen 1997, 7–8; Alestalo and Uusitalo 1992; Christiansen 1999). In addition, much of the "miraculous" recovery of the Danish economy was related to solving the debt problem. Danish budget and balance of payment debts became less onerous as global interest rates declined and it became less expensive to finance debt accrued in the 1960s and 1970s. In addition, increases in housing prices combined with a big mortgage tax deduction was a wealth effect fostering demand (Andersen 1997, 3–5; Madsen 1999). Dominated by small and medium-sized enterprises, Danish firms and the economy fared poorly during the 1960s and 1970s, years when Fordist production was in its heyday, as they lacked the economies of scale to make mass-produced goods cost-competitive. Yet when post-Fordist manufacturing came into vogue and consumers craved the well-designed, high-quality, unique (or at least not mass-produced), tailored-to-individual-tastes, and somewhat more expensive products offered by Danish SMEs, production and employment levels naturally rose (Schwartz 2001a, 134.)

Despite these improvements in the Danish economy, reformers were motivated by three types of concerns. First, when active labour market and social policy was initially proposed, structural unemployment was of greater concern than it is today. Granted, despite the decommodifying potential of high unemployment benefits (Esping-Andersen 1990), Danes have high rates of labour market participation (Andersen 1997, 17). Yet policy makers worried that solidaristic wage bargaining limited job growth because the narrow wage spread keeps low-skilled individuals out of the labour market (Ministry of Labour, Ministry of Finance 1996). A growing population of welfare recipients (often multigenerational) suffered from social exclusion and economic isolation, and positive macro statistics did not fully portray the problems of the growing underclass at the micro level. Although economic equality has improved in Denmark since the early 1980s (giving Denmark more equality than Holland, Sweden, Germany, France, or the U.S.A.), economic equality paradoxically has *not* led to social equality in many quarters. Geographical segregation by income and marital status is growing, and employment status is associated with both health and education. Those who grow up in families with heavy poverty risk becoming themselves socially excluded and unemployed (*Mandag Morgen* 1997; Christoffersen 1996). Second, worries about unemployment were linked to concerns about Danish firms' insufficient investment in capital stock and research and development. Thus, proposals for active labour market policy were part of a larger industrial policy initiative pushed by the Danish government in the 1980s (Finansministeriet 1986; Nielsen and Pedersen 1989; Scherer 1992).

Third, many worry about future labour shortages and believe that the economy cannot prosper with a large proportion of the citizenry relegated to non-productive roles. Although Danish fertility rates have been among the highest in Europe in the 1990s, Danes have the second-lowest life expectancy rates among EU countries (Andersen 1997: 9). Labour shortage projections have been exacerbated by an early retirement scheme introduced in 1979 that allowed insured individuals to retire at the age of 60. (The social democratic government finally revised the early retirement scheme in 1998–99.)

Thus, an irony of the active labour market and social policies is that they were initially proposed to solve structural unemployment and expand employment generally, and yet employers now are motivated to participate by an opposite concern about future labour shortages. Unemployment pushed the solution for policy makers, but projected labour shortages have propelled employer participation.

Globalization, unemployment, and gaps in labour supply have also been issues in Great Britain, although the concerns there are somewhat different than in Denmark. While Danish employment languished under Fordism, British employment dropped when post-Fordist manufacturing eroded the demand for unskilled workers in the 1980s. An under-supply of training and a concurrent skills deficit have been chronic problems in Britain, not surprising, given its liberal market economy and its firm preference for low-skilled competitive strategies (Wood 2001). As in Denmark, British employment surged in the 1990s, a process beginning before (and perhaps independent of) the active social and labour market policies proposed by the New Labour government. Yet, although Britain is second only to Denmark in low unemployment rates among EU countries, much of the improvement in employment has been due to the expansion of low-skilled, low-wage jobs, especially in the entertainment and finance/insurance sectors (DfEE 1999, 7–8). In addition, young people were more frequently found to be out of the labour market in Britain (nearly 20 percent of the males) than in Denmark (7 percent of the males) (OECD 2000, 9–17).

It would appear, then, that both countries were motivated by similar sorts of factors to seek the activation of the long-term unemployed. Concerns about growing public expenditures, social exclusion, and projected labour shortages inspired both Danes and Brits to turn to active social and labour market policies, and the two countries have been leaders in these areas within the European Union. There are of course differences between the two countries. Danes worry that training is inordinately concentrated in the public sector and believe private training to be more efficacious, while Brits worry that there is insufficient training – period (Wood 2001). Denmark has a history of subsidized state employment, but state and social partners worry that this fails to provide lasting jobs. Britain has many short-term jobs in the private sector, but these jobs do not last and individuals tend to cycle in and out of employment.

Yet despite similar structural pressures, there is some evidence that Danish plans have had a more genuine impact on employment growth than the corresponding British plans. Danish rates declined with unemployment rates over the course of the 1990s, suggesting that programs matched skills to employment needs. British vacancy rates remained steady even while unemployment dropped, suggesting that social reform forced people back to work without addressing the skills gap (OECD 2001, 13–14).

DANISH AND BRITISH ACTIVE SOCIAL POLICIES

For the distinctions between coordinated market economies and liberal market economies to hold, Danish and British active social plans (despite their common conceptual origins) should diverge in ways that reflect the differences inherent in the models. This, indeed, seems to be the case. In keeping with social democratic values the Danish plans are available to a more universal clientele, in that they offer protected jobs to the unemployed disabled for whom no rehabilitation is possible. The state pays up to 50 percent of wages for these protected jobs and has effectively developed a new category of subsidized minimum-wage jobs, helpful to firms that for reasons of productivity could not retain disabled workers otherwise headed for early retirement (Teknologisk Institut 2000, 11). In comparison, the target population is more narrowly defined in Britain; it serves the long-term unemployed and unemployed youth but does little for disabled workers (King and Wickham-Jones 1998).

Denmark has also sought to tailor active social policy more closely to the needs of a high skills equilibrium economy. The Danish active social plans for the long-term unemployed are linked much more closely to general state training efforts than in Britain, where labour market policy has always been considered a residual service for the unemployed (OECD 1996, 29–30; King and Wickham-Jones 1998, 445–51; Wood 2001, 394–8). Danish plans were connected to broader programs to train low-skilled workers and to expand the labour pool (European Information Service 1997). Job rotation schemes allowed firms to hire the long-term unemployed with state subsidies, while their own employees receive skills training (Arbejdsmarkedsstyrelsen 2000; Interviews; Bach and Kylling 1997; Torfing 1999). Kongshøj Madsen (2000) views the Danish experiments with active labour market strategy as congruous with the values of a highly productive and highly protective society.

The language of the appeals made to employers reflected differences in the two countries' welfare regimes. In liberal Britain, government actors used the language of markets to sell the programs and used "demand-led" strategies to tailor the programs to private market needs (Interviews; Deloitte & Touche 1999). Danish government leaders used the language of collective goals, urging employers to satisfy their own long-term self-interests by participating to advance the collective economic interest of developing an encompassing labour market (*Det rummelige arbejdsmarked*) and the collective solidaristic goal of ending social exclusion.

ASSOCIATIONS AND THE CREATION OF ACTIVE SOCIAL POLICY

In keeping with the theoretical distinctions between corporatist and pluralist countries, Denmark and the United Kingdom have diverged enormously in the political processes by which the plans were developed, with employers' associations playing a much larger role in Denmark. Dansk Arbejdsgiverforeningen (DA), a central employer confederation, represents most of the employers in Denmark; its twenty-five sectoral member associations cover most of the Danish economy. The manufacturing sector body, Dansk Industriet (DI), is the largest and most powerful. A large share of labour market policy (as high as 90 percent) has evolved in negotiations with the labour organization Landsorganisationen i Danmark (LO) (Ministry of Labour 1996); however, social policy has always been under the jurisdiction of the government (Due et al. 1994; Gill et al. 1998).

The Danish peak employers' association, Dansk Arbejdsgiverforeningen, suffered setbacks in its control over collective bargaining in the past quarter century, as collective bargaining became more decentralized down to the cartel level and consensus about national agreements became more difficult to achieve among member organizations. During several recent collective bargaining rounds, failure to reach agreement by the social partners has necessitated state intervention (Due et al. 1994; Gill et al. 1998; Ugebrevet Mandag Morgen, Sept. 1999). DA has retained its monopoly in tripartite corporatist negotiations, but has also lost influence in the legislative realm, as individual firms have increasingly made direct contact with the Danish parliament (Christiansen and Rommetvedt 1999). Other types of networks, which lie outside of the formal corporatist channels of engagement, have also been growing in importance (Pedersen et al.1992).

Despite diminished authority in collective bargaining, the corporatist groups wielded greater influence than British pluralist groups in the development and evolution of the active labour market and social policies. The labour market reforms of the 1990s began with the work of the Zeuthen Commission, which included representatives from the social partners. Christoffer Green-Pedersen et al. (2001) have correctly emphasized the social democratic party's leadership in creating the reforms; yet business and labour were also brought in from the beginning and participated to some degree in each of the labour market reforms. Indeed, in the 1999 reform, the social partners essentially dominated the process, as most of the details were determined in the climate agreement negotiated by DA and LO.

The social partners were less involved in the initial social policy reforms; for example, the Social Commission (*Socialkommissionen*), which laid the initial groundwork for a similar move toward activation in social policy, was composed largely of experts and political representatives. But DA and LO joined subsequent discussions about the creation of subsidized job trials and training for the long-term unemployed and protected jobs for those with reduced working capacities; for example, playing a role in the committee (Udvalget om Skånejobs) to create jobs with special terms of employment. In March 2000 the LO and DA issued a common position paper on the development of a more encompassing labour market, arguing that individuals should be retained if possible in the regular labour market before moving into early retirement or protected jobs. The social partners also made clear that they considered job creation to be a joint project involving the private sector, the municipalities, and the government, rather than solely a private sector responsibility (LO/DA 2000).

British employers' associations, in comparison, have been fairly marginal to the development of active social policies. The programs were developed by the Labour Party with little employer input (Finn 2000). The Confederation of Business Industry and other employers supported the New Deal programs yet their interests seemed related more to winning concessions on business agenda than to benefits from the programs themselves (Clement 1997; *Management Today*, November 1998).

FIRMS AND ACTIVE SOCIAL POLICY IN DENMARK AND THE UNITED KINGDOM

If the distinctions between coordinated market economies and liberal market economies hold true, we should be able to observe cross-national differences in the patterns of firms' participation in the active social programs. I conducted structured interviews of 107 randomly selected employers in Denmark and the United Kingdom to evaluate their participation in active labour market and social policies. The study's dependent variable estimated the firm's participation in the set of active labour market and social programs that were identified by the respective countries in their National Action Plans as mechanisms for expanding employment. I evaluated eight economic independent variables as possible causal sources of firms' participation: estimates of the firms' average wages, skills composition, profits as a percentage of total sales, size in sales, union membership, exports as a percentage of total sales, and percentage of sales going to public sector purchasers. I also evaluated two institutional independent variables: a firm's membership in an employers' association and the size of a firm's human resources department. I estimated the hypotheses with an ordered probit model. By conducting two separate but parallel firm-level comparisons (comparing firms within a country but not between countries), I was able to isolate significant causal factors driving firm behaviours in each country and compare significant variables across countries. It is beyond the purview of this paper to present the full statistical analysis, but the following pages discuss the findings of the study (see Martin 2005 for a full presentation of the analysis).

At the time of the study, 68 percent of the Danish firms were engaged in subsidized jobs and training programs for the long-term unemployed, while only 40 percent of firms were involved to some extent in parallel British programs (and many British employers signed up without actually creating jobs) (Hasluck 2000, 4). The statistical analyses demonstrate that different causal factors brought Danish and British firms to participate, suggesting that the programs offered different benefits to firms in the two countries and that firms learned about these benefits through different processes.

In Britain two economic characteristics of the firms were significant: companies were much more likely to participate when they had higher levels of sales to the public sector and a higher proportion of unskilled blue-collar workers. Institutional characteristics also seemed to suggest the processes by which companies decided to engage in the active programs. British companies with large professional human resources department were significantly more likely to participate in the programs than those with smaller departments. Membership in a group, the other institutional characteristic measured in the study, not only failed to increase the likelihood of employers participating in a social program, but was, oddly, *negatively* associated with participation, an observation that we will return to in a moment.

In the Danish study, three economic characteristics made companies significantly more likely to participate in active social programs: firms with a greater percentage of blue-collar workers (both skilled and unskilled) participated more than those with white-collar workers, as did companies with lower average wages. Smaller companies participated significantly more than larger ones, and, in stark contrast to the British case, firms with a high level of public sector sales participated significantly less than those selling primarily to private purchasers. A firm's institutional characteristics were also significant in the Danish study: companies that belonged to an employers' association were significantly more likely to participate in the active social programs (Martin 2005).

Five general points must be made in regard to these differential findings about Danish and British employers' participation in active social policy and the role of corporatism in this process. The first point is that, in keeping with the expectations of the varieties of capitalism model, Danish employers were much more likely than British employers to view social protections as providing benefits for economic production. Denmark did a better job of integrating the active social programs into a general training project, and employers felt that the programs offered a new labour supply or a mechanism for coping with the declining competencies of their own workers.

The finding that firms with a high proportion of blue-collar workers (both skilled and unskilled) were statistically more likely to participate in active social programs suggests that companies viewed the programs as a mechanism for improving the quality of their workforce. Danish employers believed that the programs would help them gain access to a more highly skilled workforce, either by enhancing the skills of their own employees or by preparing a more skilled labour pool. Some participated in the programs as part of job rotation schemes that allowed them to hire the long-term unemployed using state subsidies, while their its own employees received skills training (Interviews, 2/21/01; 3/29/01). Many firms wanted all of their upskilled workers qualified as "industrial operators," a classification gained through a course to enhance the basic skills and flexibility of workers without specialized training.[3] Danish firms were more likely to view the programs as a way of satisfying their need for labour: despite similar vacancy rates, 31 percent of the Danish firms cited labour shortages as a reason for participating, while only 22 percent of the British firms gave this argument. Although the value of the subsidies was quite similar in the two countries, 39 percent of the Danish firms considered subsidies at least somewhat important, while only 10 percent of British firms reported that subsidies contributed to their participation and could compensate for the many problems associated with taking in the unemployed.

The Danish companies were also able to use the protected jobs programs to retain their own employees who were at risk for unemployment due to a permanent physical or mental impairment that reduced their "working capacities." A skeptic might suggest that this feature of the plan alone could account for the greater participation in Denmark than in Britain. Yet the rules for the protected jobs are fairly strict, and a strong case has to be made that a worker really has lost a significant amount of his or her capacity to work. Few Danish firms (14%), in fact, restricted their participation to their own workers, although many began social projects with their own employees and then moved on to offer jobs to other unemployed persons. Many companies had strong reservations about moving their own workers into the formal protected jobs programs, because they thought that labelling the individual would make him or her feel badly (3/9/01).

By comparison, one had the sense that British firms participated for one of two broad reasons: public relations or cheap labour. Because some firms seemed to be engaged for philanthropic motivations or to derive political credit, it is not surprising that those with a greater dependence on government (in their higher proportion of sales to the public sector) were more likely to try to please the new administration. Indeed, the most prevalent motivation offered by British firms for signing on to the New Deal programs was a political one: 31 percent of the companies credited their participation to strong pressure from government. Because British employers felt that the New Deal did little to improve the skills of the workforce, it stands to reason that the firms most willing to participate in the program would have had few skills needs. While 36 percent of the Danish firms identified skills needs as a constraint against participation, 53 percent of the British firms offered the need for more highly skilled workers as a reason for not participating.

The second general point related to my findings was that the presence of a corporatist business association seems still to be an important determinant of support for social policy. The statistical findings of my study revealed that membership in national employers' associations in corporatist Denmark was a highly salient determinant of participation in the social programs. Membership in British employers' associations was negatively correlated with participation; rather, the size of the HR department was a significant determinant of participation (Martin 2005).[4] The interview data overwhelmingly confirmed these findings. When asked to state their most important source of information about HR issues and labour market policy, 32 percent of the Danes identified an employers' association, as opposed to 14 percent of the British firms (and many other Danish companies mentioned their associations as their second-most important source of information after local governments). British companies learned from trade press, the Internet, or regular newspapers (34%), government or government inspired groups (24%), private consultants (14%), or formal and informal HR groups (10%). Finally, in part because groups remained strong and in part because average firm size in Denmark is quite small, most Danish firms have less-developed human resource departments than their British counterparts.

Danish respondents repeatedly reported that their associations instructed them in the new policy ideas about solutions to unemployment. A leader from DI explained that one of his groups' important functions was to educate member firms about reducing social exclusion and long-term unemployment. The organization does this through the committees that work with the labour organizations to set up conferences on topics such as taking new ethnic groups into the market. In addition it offers management education seminars on the topic of social exclusion through its HRM (Human Resources Managers) network. Danish Industries also sponsors informal topical groups (*Efa grupper*) on wage and social issues (11/22/00).

Through these various activities, Danish employers engaged in a process of social learning. Confronted with the negative policy legacies of the passive unemployment system, Danish employers joined other parts of society in seeking policy reversals of past failures. When suddenly thrust in the role of benefits provider rather than negotiator, employers felt compelled to rise to the occasion. The high level of organization among employers allowed managers to participate in training and subsidized jobs without fear of being penalized for their altruistic behaviours. In short, because employers were so well organized, they were able to take action.

Danish managers also wanted their employers' associations to assume a leadership role in social policy because they preferred that associations rather than government take the lead in formulating public policy. One respondent feared that if the firms did not engage in this issue area, it would be left up to the government – with dire consequences: "If the politicians create the rules off in some corridor, they will not know how to do it and they will create rules that business and labor cannot live with. If the social partners create the rules, these will work better; so the associations should figure out what they want and present the rules to the politicians."

Third, in comparing Danish and British employers' participation, the findings show that in Denmark corporatist associations seem to be most important to firms' deliberations in *local* corporatist forums and in *informal* networks sponsored by the groups. The Danish corporatist employers' associations have themselves recognized the declining importance of collective bargaining and have taken strategic steps to expand their offerings in other areas such as the development of informal networks and discussion groups for their members. Recognizing the pressures on collective bargaining, they have sought to cultivate comparative advantages in other sorts of activities in order to continue to attract members. One of the major sector organizations observed that decentralizing pressures on collective wage negotiations meant that "fewer firms will need organizations to give them advice about collective bargaining." But because "companies will still need other kinds of advice" this group will expand its functions to attract a more diversified membership. The organization moved into a new role of organizing networks: "The networks provide, along with other things, a platform from which firms can figure out what they think about issues ... Today the associations have to come up with reasons for members to pay for belonging to a group, such as to develop political positions ...

Having political influence is a collective good, but you always have the free rider problem. So you have to have some individual goods as well to keep up the membership" (Interview).

Respondents reported being deeply influenced by these networks, such as the Dansk Industriet Think Tank on HR issues. These task forces, ironically, often formulated policy positions that were more liberal than those formal positions taken by the organization as a whole. Employers were also brought into the welfare reform project when they were asked by DA to serve on the local social coordination committees. These committees included representatives from business, labour, and professional doctors; among their tasks, the committees sought to generate support in the local community for welfare reform. DA urges companies to join the local labour market councils (*de regionale arbejdsformidlingsrad* – RAR) in order to ensure that workers get the right qualifications, to avoid bottleneck problems, and to reduce spending on passive social support (DA 1998, 9). One manager recalls planning a "talk show" to teach firms about the programs, in which a TV star interviewed former welfare recipients who had successfully made the transition to the world of work (12/20/00). DI's regional member organizations (*regionale forningen*) also support participants in the local committees such as the RARs and the Sociale Rådsgiving Udvalg.

A fourth point derived from the comparative findings is that the participation of labour market partners in active social policy seemed to be somewhat lopsided, with labour less active at the firm level. Although the issue was allegedly pushed by the social chapters, none of the firms reported that this mechanism had been an inspiration for participation and many did not even know that the social chapters covered active social policy. In Denmark 65 percent reported no labour involvement in decisions to participate and another 7 percent recalled labour opposition; 88 percent of British firms cited no labour involvement. In neither statistical analysis was the unionization variable significant. In the vast majority of the British firms, unions were described as fairly irrelevant to choices about participating in the programs. In Denmark organized labour has been a key source of historical support for the development of the welfare state and the national labour unions have been deeply involved in the policy debates about unemployment and social exclusion (LO). Some employers reported enormous support from the local unions for active social projects; for example, several firms developed their positions in work councils with a union fully supportive of protected jobs (12/11/00; 12/12/00; 4/17/01; 6/29/01; 12/20/02). Yet the national labour movement commitment to welfare state restructuring often did not translate to the local level, thereby creating a juxtaposition between national and local unions (Interview with LO, June 2001). Active social policy poses a problem for unions – recipients are usually nonmembers and a source of cheap state-subsidized labour – and many local unions had mixed feelings about programs (12/19/00; 11/7/00; 2/20/01). One manager quipped: "The unions are as reactionary as I am" (Interview, 7 March 2001).

The fifth point emerging from my findings was that in Denmark the state played a vital role in extending corporatism to the active social policy area and in inspiring (in both intended and unintended ways) organizational commitment to the programs. The state has recently undertaken steps formally to extend corporatism to the social policy area (to become more like labour market policy); a recent law requires each municipality to have a corporatist committee consisting of representatives from business and labour to oversee social policy in the community. Dansk Arbejdgiversforening (DA) has the responsibility for selecting company participants to sit on these local Social Coordination Committees. Many of the employers with whom I spoke identified these committees as an important source of information about the area of corporate social responsibility and came to participate in social partnerships through their involvement with these committees. Of course DA was unlikely to select as representatives employers who were completely hostile to the social arena, but employers usually had limited experience with social partnerships before being called to duty by DA. In fact, firms that participated in such corporatist committees (and in the association-sponsored networks described below) often ended up with positions to the left of those formally specified by their employer associations (Interviews).

Many firms felt that the creation of a company consultant (*virksomhedskonsulent*) position within the local government greatly assisted their involvement with active social policy (12/12/00). In some municipalities, such as Herlev, the firm consultants began holding regular weekly or monthly sessions at the large companies to evaluate problematic employees' needs and to give advice about state programs to meet those needs (4/19/01). Others reported that employees of labour market institutions (AF) were "very helpful" and helped firms "to figure out the bureaucracy" (2/20/01). Some managers reported Herculean efforts on the part of local government social workers to return the socially excluded to the workplace: "In a lot of cases, the major task is to help people become used to having a job. They don't know what it is like to work – have never even tried being on the job. They do not realize that you have to get up everyday at a certain time and go to work even if it is raining. For example, the local government had one project trying to get seriously overweight women into the workforce. These were women who could not stand for very long because their bodies couldn't handle it. The municipal social worker who was handling this project went around to their houses every day, waking them up and getting them to work" (12/20/02).

Danish state actors have helped to mitigate against the fragmenting pressures on employers' associations by efforts to increase support for the policies with information campaigns, new corporatist forums in the area of social policy, and, ironically, with direct appeals to firms. Initially, the Social Ministry sought to bring employers' associations into discussions about social policy, a deviation from the status-quo state control of this issue (Interviews). Later the Social Ministry shifted to a campaign to mobilize individual firms (Social Ministry 1999; Danish National Institute of Social Research 1997; Holt 1998, 9–10). The major employer associations were upset with this campaign. As one respondent explained: "DA and DI were worried that there would be anarchy." But as the ministry moved into the associations' turf, the groups became more anxious to be included.

In comparison with the Danish strategy, the British government has relied much more on attracting corporate participation through market-based incentives, largely sidestepping the established national employers' associations. While Blair sought support for the New Deal programs from the Confederation of British Industries, the administration primarily relied on an extensive and expensive media campaign to engage individual British firms, and sought to involve employers in New Deal programs with personal appeals to the largest British corporations (Wintour et al. 1998). These market strategies reflected the policy legacies of a liberal welfare regime and the constraints of working with a fragmented, poorly organized business community. As a senior aid put it: "We tried to work with business but they couldn't really deliver."

CONCLUSION

Despite its myriad challenges, coordination in Denmark seems to persist in fostering a higher commitment to social protection than is found in the liberal market economy of Britain. In keeping with spirit of connection between social protection and economic production found in coordinated market economies, the Danish active social reforms of the 1990s enjoyed greater employer support than the corresponding British endeavours. Even though the new active social policies have been largely geared toward the needs of the long-term unemployed, Danish employers felt that the plans could expand the labour pool of skilled and semi-skilled labour. The policies have been linked to other programs to enhance training for firms' own workers; for example, job rotation schemes in which the unemployed are brought into the company while normal employees go through an up-skilling program. Danish employers view the measures as addressing real economic problems such as projected labour shortages.

This investigation of the impact of coordination on firms' attitudes and behaviours toward social reform makes a theoretical contribution to the literature on coordination. First, it illuminates the micro impacts of macro institutions. Scholars writing about the varieties of capitalism seek to link micro incentives to macro policy, by observing how institutional structures shape the strategic choices of employers and workers; however, this approach cannot account for inter-firm variations within national settings (Hall and Soskice 2001). In addition, there has been very little rigorous empirical investigation of the impact of coordination on individual firms. The study presented here attempts to fill this gap by allowing us to test the theories and evaluate whether institutions that influenced individual actors during the golden age are losing their salience in these post-industrial, shifting times.

The empirical findings of the study have important implications for how firms are experiencing their corporatist organizations today: peak associations are still important to their members' self-identification and cognitive perceptions of public policy. As theory predicts, corporatist employers' associations helped Danish companies to recognize the advantages of participation. Corporatist business-government relations involved Danish firms in overseeing labour market policies for some time, even though, historically, firms have not been part of the implementation of such programs. Indeed, the deliberative processes fostered by corporatist organization may ultimately be of greater political consequence than the formal political positions taken by the associations.

Second, this investigation illustrates how agency contributes to the renegotiation of cooperative arrangements. Studies of corporatism and varieties of capitalism (which underscore the functional benefits of institutional structures) have a tendency to explain continuity more easily than change and have problems capturing diversity at the sectoral, regional, and firm levels. Yet, as Kathleen Thelen (2001) points out, social pacts between business and labour need to be renegotiated. To address charges of institutional determinism and functionalism, she shifts conceptually from how institutions determine outcomes to how they shape processes, thereby introducing greater contingency into predictive models (see also Scharpf and Schmidt 2001). Different patterns of business association may have a divergent effect on this process, but the outcomes are by no means assured. Like a good marriage, the processes of negotiation, information-sharing and communication rather than de jure agreements (such as prenuptials) may be most important to long-term success.

Two types of agency were important to the Danish story: the leadership of the Danish government and the efforts of Danish employers' associations to redefine themselves. The Danish state was critical in moving the employers' associations to embrace active social policy. The government sought support from the DA for the active agenda, but also developed a parallel strategy of mobilizing individual firms. The government-inspired coalitions of firms served to heighten the associations' desire to engage in social initiatives. Aware of threats to their monopoly on collective bargaining, the groups sought avenues of revitalization. The Danish peak and major sector associations expanded networking services for members in an effort to remain relevant (and financially solvent). Partially at the behest of the Social Ministry, employers' associations became much more involved in the area of social policy, which traditionally had been left up to the state. Again with government encouragement (and legislative instigation), corporatist forums at the local level developed in the social policy area.

Danish employers' willingness to participate in active social programs gives hope about the future of the small state model and offers some cause for optimism about policies designed to address simultaneously issues of social cohesion and unemployment, without harming productivity. These cases illustrate in a very concrete way why firms in coordinated market economies are better positioned to recognize the high-road logic of social partnership. In Denmark, social exclusion has been identified as a collective problem, and Danish firms have been very much engaged in the dialogue about this collective concern. The issue of long-term unemployment has been linked not only to social exclusion issues, but to projected labour shortages, to the training of firms' own workers, and to future needs for expanded human capital as well. Thus, the Danish coordinated market economy exhibited advantages over the British liberal market economy even where one would least expect these advantages: for outsider groups such as the structurally unemployed, and in private sector training and employment.

One must caution against excessive optimism, however, as the study illustrates some contradictions and goal conflicts associated with this new brand of welfare state restructuring. Human resource managers must convince their firms that social partnerships are consistent with the other goals of the company; yet the social strategies for integrating the unemployed are often at odds with companies' other strategies to improve productivity and the working lives of their own employees. Many British managers reasoned that the active social policies did little to improve the stock of available skilled labour, and preferred more fundamental educational programs. Danish firms experienced problems with reconciling participation in active social policy – bringing people with reduced working capacities into production – with their innovations to make their own workers more highly skilled, flexible, and productive. But to some extent policy makers in both countries moved to deal with this goal conflict by changing the clientele of the programs. In keeping with Denmark's social democratic traditions, the Danes sought to make the programs more universal: with programs to those suffering from a reduction in working capacity, firms can use these for their own employees. As befits a liberal state, the British tailored some New Deal clientele to market needs, and firms have been more likely to hire those who resemble individuals in the regular labour pool. If in both countries the popularity of the programs depends on the extent to which these programs can be applied to individuals who are already in jobs or "job-ready," one wonders about the scope of the strategy and the extent to which it can address the needs of the truly disadvantaged. The socially excluded could become even more marginal.

NOTES

The author wishes to thank John Campbell, John Hall, and Ove Kaj Pedersen for their many comments on this chapter. In addition, many thanks go to the Danish Social Science Research Council, the German Marshall Fund, and the Magtudredningen for their support of this project.

1 Interest group theory suggests that the more one group has of a collective good, the more likely it is to act in the collective interest; therefore, countries with corporatist groups are more likely to approximate the collective good (Wilensky 1976; Kendix and Olson 1990; Streeck and Schmitter 1991, Crouch 1993; Hicks and Kenworthy 1998).

2 Aspects of active labour market policy have been around since its development in Sweden in the 1960s (A. Martin 1979), but the 1990s variant of ALMP differs from the past in placing even more emphasis on private sector training and jobs (and less on relocating labour).

3 At the same time, participation in programs for the socially excluded was not always easy to reconcile with productivity concerns. Companies competing globally on a high wage- or high-skilled basis felt pressured to upgrade technologies, to reorganize production on the shop floor, and to alter managerial relations. Managers in several firms reported that incorporating those with reduced working capacities was more difficult than they had anticipated.

4 The significantly negative impact of belonging to a trade association on participation in the programs in Britain initially seems odd; yet this finding becomes more comprehensible when one remembers that in Britain joining a trade association is something of an alternative to developing a large, professional human resources department. Although at least some of the British associations (such as CBI) have endorsed the New Deal programs, British trade associations are generally less activist, less informative, and less important than their Danish counterparts. Thus the British firms that have developed HR departments tend to have more expertise in the HR area, in part because the alternative – membership in the association – gives employers so little in the way of information or inspiration. Seen from this light, it makes sense that one group (firms with large HR departments) has a significantly higher likelihood of participation while the other group (firms in associations) has a significantly lower likelihood.

8

Business Systems in the Age of the "New Economy": Denmark Facing the Challenge

The success of American economic performance in the 1990s may be explained by the simultaneous emergence of a multitude of local high-tech innovative clusters such as Silicon Valley, and the Japanization of traditional mass-producing industries, jointly moving toward a globally networked knowledge economy. The success of both France and Finland could be seen to resemble this template (Hancke 2002; Taino et al. 2001; Moen and Lilja 2003). In all cases, headquarters (HQs) of large corporations have played decisive roles in transforming their host economies. In the United States they have poured capital into high-tech sectors and established a new managerial regime of benchmarks and balanced score-cards in order to globally transform their subsidiaries in the direction of greater organizational flexibility, lean production and the use of sub-contractors (Mueller 1996; Mueller and Purcell 1992; Hancké 2000). This transformation has gone hand in hand with Human Resource Management (HRM), which some see as a deliberate attack on unions, centralized bargaining, and fairness in industrial relations (Ackers and Wilkinson 2003; Mueller and Purcell 1992). This structuration by HQS can also be explained by the new international financial system, which is organizing a new positional game (Golding 2001; Plender 2003; Kristensen and Zeitlin 2005). To play this game, HQS must provide information about how their subsidiaries perform, according to the growing number of benchmarks that financial institutions demand. This leads to competition and rivalry among subsidiaries and their contractors across countries over investment budgets and head-counts, making subsidiaries and labour markets – according to some observers – more uniform and convergent across countries (Mueller 1996; Mueller and Purcell 1992). In this way

HQS transform regions toward low-lost production or highly skilled for innovation, the latter constituting the backbone for the growth of a knowledge economy.

If this were the only way to transform, Denmark would be found to lack most of the agencies needed for bringing a country into the future. However, like Manuel Castells (2000), we will search for the ability of societies to create self-organizing structures and ordering out of complexity and chaos, expecting transitive processes of societies to lead in diverse directions through self-reinforcing mechanisms and path dependency (Arthur 1998). In this view, innovation arises from and is limited by existing institutions (Casper 2000), meaning that different countries and regions will contribute to different parts of innovation processes (Whitley 2000), as different labour markets and business systems provide different advantages. In the varieties-of-capitalism literature, Denmark is characterized (Whitley 1999; Whitley and Kristensen 1996b) as a society that seems able to cooperate pragmatically and informally, governed by reputational links among firms and workers (Kristensen 1997b) though at the same time having a very liberal labour market with different groups of employees pursuing individual careers. Neither in terms of its capital market nor in terms of formal regulation of collaboration does Denmark possess the institutional characteristics of a "coordinated market economy" that observers have seen in Germany (Hall and Soskice 2001). Denmark's problems, as well as its institutional resources for resolving them under the current transformations, differ from those of Germany, as, therefore do the ways in which Denmark will cope with the new challenges.

It will not be the first time that Denmark has responded to a transformation in a novel and highly surprising way. As O'Rourke demonstrates (chapter 4), Danish farmers, by forming cooperatives through a popular movement in the last third of the nineteenth century, created a highly admirable, export-intensive route to prosperity whereby individual enterprises and farms became related to a whole architecture of economic agencies in a very systemic way. However, viewed from the perspective of the elite of that time, Denmark needed more industry rather than more agriculture, and elite circles were trying to create a very different economy, but with much less success than the social movements of that time. Likewise the crisis of the 1930s became highly confusing when it became clear in retrospect that industrial growth during that period had been higher than in any previous period – to be superseded only by industrial growth in the 1960s. While in the former transformation, the farmers and small holders were the prime movers that changed the situation; in the latter period it was small craftsmen and agricultural service providers in small railway towns who, to make up for reduced demand from farmers, initiated industrial production on their own. Again, after World War II, the elite did not see this achievement in a positive light; only much later did they realize that the process had fostered some of the most recognized and highly reputed enterprises in Denmark (Kristensen and Sabel 1997).

Through these many transformations runs a general pattern that we think might also be relevant for understanding what goes on in the current period. First, the regime in Denmark is highly unusual. While abundant negotiations are taking place among political actors and interest groups (see Pedersen, chapter 6), lower-level actors in these negotiations do not necessarily cease their initiatives. So, while legitimate participants in the corporatist system negotiate a possible future, actors of the civil society shape it – often in ways very different from those stipulated in the negotiated outcome. Negotiations at the corporatist level may become complementary to, or contradict, ongoing transformations in civil society, depending on historical circumstances. What goes on in the game played among actors in civil society of course takes a different route, according to which groups are playing the decisive role at the time. But the architecture of this game seems very repetitive and distinct: Social groupings are competing among themselves to prove and improve performance (e.g., the quantity and quality of butter and bacon after 1865; craftsmanship in furniture from the 1930s) as a way to gain social space. This leads them to form new institutions or use existing ones in ways that frequently differ highly from those imagined by participants in corporatist negotiations. A novel pattern of collective learning gradually becomes institutionalized, leading to the formation of working careers that are underpinned by educational institutions, so that complementarities among a range of sectors and professions emerge. This transformative pattern has served to provide for Denmark a distinct, though quite advanced, position in emerging world economic orders in several transformative epochs.

In this chapter, I present a tentative portrait of the nature of current transformations, the way they reflect pragmatic ways of dealing with current challenges, the kind of learning that becomes institutionalized, and how this affects working careers. I also suggest how the possible contradictions between the regime of a negotiating corporatism and an acting civil society might be solved and novel complementarities formed. I focus on Danish subsidiaries of multinationals as they act on the borderline between the new challenges of the globalization process and take part in the transformation of their host localities. The aim is to study how, by directly confronting the new MNC managerial regime mentioned above, they pursue a strategic and innovative leeway for transforming work organization and local labour markets that may develop Denmark's human resources and re-position subsidiaries and regions within MNCs so as also to influence even the way multinationals operate more generally (Kristensen and Zeitlin 2005).

DENMARK: ENTERING THE NEW ECONOMY
BY EXTENSIVELY REINFORCING THE OLD?

Neither Danish firms nor regions have entered the new global economy as template variants of the knowledge economy. Had Danish firms been big players like Swedish and Dutch corporations, they might have entered this game in distinct ways and created successful novel templates for managing MNCs or fostering clusters of innovation. But not since the banking crisis in the 1920s have Danish firms in general been able to make use of either a credit-based financial system (as in Germany) or a capital market of Anglo-Saxon proportions. No corporate coalitions were built, as in the case of the corporate "families" around Wallenberg in Sweden, to make an endogenous strategy for and route to globalization (as was the case, for instance, with ABB in Sweden). Apart from one huge shipping company, most Danish firms are comparatively small, and the founding family often still holds a controlling interest in the firm. Investments in R&D are generally modest in the business sector and very low, by comparative Nordic standards, in the public sector. Small, and perhaps more significantly in comparative terms, medium-sized enterprises dominate the business sector. Thus it is very difficult to register a shift to a radically different production regime and a special version of the new economy.

And yet, during the 1990s, the Danish "employment miracle" rated the country among the highest-performing European economies in the decade (together with the Netherlands, Ireland, Austria, and Finland) (Madsen 1999, 2003, and chapter 9 in this volume). As also demonstrated in the Introduction, Denmark in many ways provided an entirely new set of performance benchmarks in the 1990s; among EU countries, it ranks close to the top in terms of GDP per capita and employment rates among men as well as women (aged 15–64). Despite this high participation rate, unemployment is comparatively low. Such achievements have not been reached by low-income service workers as in the United States. Rather, Denmark positions itself as the country with the least income inequality of all the EU countries. Nor has this been reached by "sweating," as workers in Denmark are very well positioned in terms of both working hours and health and safety risks. In no other EU country is there a lower proportion of workers dissatisfied at work (data for comparative positioning can be found in European Commission 2004, chapter 6). So, in many ways, Denmark seems to have been very successful in coping with new challenges, and we are in need of causal factors to explain this success, as it does not fit with dominant templates.

This "miracle" can probably only be explained by a patchwork of factors rather than any single factor alone. The Maersk-owned shipping and oil company has no doubt played its part in the economy, but less so in terms of employment. Some firms related to health and medicine have captured high positions in the international market. Certain regions have successfully transformed their positions in the international division of labour. The garment-knitting district of Herning-Ikast, for instance, is still one of the most important of its kind in continental Europe, even though employment for knitting-operatives and sewers has been drastically reduced. On the other hand, design, engineering, logistics, and marketing have grown in importance. In a similar vein, wireless radio-producers in North Jutland have changed from batch production to a focus on development projects, often for large MNCs. Also, while most other countries had problems in the late 1990s, meat production in Denmark prospered, not least because of a superior control and quality system, institutionalized jointly by the cooperative movement and the state in the late nineteenth century. Finally, it is worth noting that in 1994 Denmark introduced new labour market and social schemes to reduce unemployment and increase employability using a training system for groups at risk of becoming marginalized (Madsen and Pedersen eds., 2003).

Some of these factors may be seen to represent a special route for Danish firms wishing to become part of a globalizing economy specializing in some of the issues in the international division of labour that emphasizes knowledge, information, and science. However, as noted above, the majority of factors mentioned are far from being part of the core dynamics of this new economy. Some of the additional phenomena revealed during the 1990s in Denmark even contradict the general picture of a knowledge economy. First of all, the employment rate of workers without *formal training* was in general higher than in most other countries. In addition, this unskilled part of the labour force increased its wages to the degree that it outstripped certain groups of the middle classes, with the result that Danish society became more egalitarian, while fast-changing societies such as the United States witnessed increasing dualism and inequality in their labour markets despite similar or higher levels of employment (Andersen 2003).

However, rather than opposing transformation, these phenomena may be significantly related to the way in which Denmark is changing toward the new economy. Well before initiating this change, the organization of work in Denmark differed highly from that of other countries. Whereas many countries had followed the American road to Taylorization, Danish workers, led by craft workers, had captured a skill-intensive road, secure that industrial knowledge rested with the operatives of plants and that superiors were recruited from their ranks, creating very flat hierarchies by international comparison (Kristensen 1995; Dobbin and Boychuk 1999). Frank Dobbin and Terry Boychuk's comparative analysis revealed that job autonomy for Danish workers, supervisors, and middle managers was higher than anywhere else, whereas upper managers were placed lower than supervisors in terms of autonomy. This probably signifies a close-knit coalition among people in production, where the represented groupings leave social space for each other, and upper managers are left with more marginal roles than in other economies.

This can be explained as an outcome of the formation of a technical school system for crafts and craft workers established up to and around the end of the nineteenth century. Initially the crafts as a self-help movement laid the foundations, but later on it also involved the state, leading to the creation of an entire system of uniform skill-formation with an abundance of local schools tied up to craft-specific schools at the national level. On top of this, a technological institute experimented with novel technologies to make them useful for small and medium-sized firms, and continually reformed curricula for craft education or created entire new crafts and vocational training programs. From the 1930s unskilled male workers realized that to compete with craft workers for jobs, they had to upgrade their skills. They accomplished this at first through evening courses at Work Technical Schools. By establishing Schools for Specialized Workers in the early 1960s and by vastly expanding this system in AMU centres (labour market vocational training centres) after the 1970s, they were able gradually but continuously to challenge craft workers over skills. Rival unions with competing vocational training systems effected continuous upgrading of skills and competition among blue-collar groupings, as skills gave them access to jobs with new technologies or within new functions. Skills were thus often developed before jobs, and it became virtually impossible for managerial professions to capture such skills and de-skill workers according to the general formula of Taylorism. Nor could they position these groupings as upper levels of business hierarchies, as workers continually integrated a large proportion of the new skills into their own groupings (Kristensen and Sabel 1997). Skilled workers could study up to the level of engineer and from there embark on careers aimed at top positions in firms. Unskilled workers could gradually combine a number of courses that, aggregated with their work experience, would lead to a formal recognition as skilled workers and thus make them eligible for the training offered to the latter. This vocational training system, combined with the peculiar organization of the Danish welfare system, created a highly fluid labour market in which employees would prefer to look for new jobs than accept degrading authority relations, and in which employers had a freer hand in laying off people than in most other countries. Although this has been the case for almost 75 years, it is only recently that the Danish labour market has captured the term *flexicurity*, which has been seen as especially favourable to the emerging new economy (Madsen 1999; Zeitlin and Trubek 2003).

Just as important for understanding how the Danish economy functions are the unintended effects of this labour market on relations among firms and their mutual rivalry. First, a large number of workers develop their working careers by holding jobs in many different firms and simultaneously attending further training courses or vocational educations. Therefore, when moving up the career ladder, they create a network of collegial ties to many people holding different positions in a variety of firms. In this way the Danish labour market cultivates and reproduces informal, personal networks across firms, networks that are also used to establish novel professional and formal ties. In effect a large number of workers in a given firm have a broad range of contacts to people in other firms, and this network is easy to mobilize for collaborative purposes, should such collaboration be needed.

A second effect is that, despite this dense network of relations among firms, which in other economies could lead to performance deterioration, firms in the Danish labour market can only be taken seriously by the best workers if they are able to accumulate teams of highly skilled workers with high reputations among knowledgeable colleagues. They are forced to compete with each other over their attractiveness to employees and therefore tend to specialize in being best at certain processes rather than at a specific product. The reason is that by specializing in a specific product and up-scaling production volume they risk creating repetitive jobs. Workers habituated to seeking challenging jobs and attending training courses will then start to leave such firms. And a firm's loss of its most skilled workers means loss of reputation and the chance to compete both in the recruitment of excellent workers and for technically demanding customers. The typical firm in Denmark is therefore a configuration that we have called a *Skill Container* (Kristensen 1996b; Andersen and Kristensen 1999), which aspires to become extremely proficient at the processes in which it has specialized by constantly upgrading its labour force and trying to capture increasingly difficult tasks.

Skill containers have their origin in the craft shop. Their organizing principle is that a *Meister* recruits a number of skilled workers and equips them with the necessary machines and tools and a place to work from. This operating core is what makes up the identity of the firm, and other social groups are considered "helping hands" to this core. Two different types of "helping hands" are typical ... Unskilled/specialized workers assist skilled ... an administrative staff ... keep the books, pick up the phone, contact customers, pay wages, etc. The "entrepreneur" is often an active member of the operating core, and sees the evolution of this core as the major aim of his "firm" rather than growth of the firm as such ...

While the typical mass producer is highly dependent on the general level of activity, the skill container is contingent on the functioning of a narrow number of linkages. Customers ask the firm for its services, and as past services are the basis of the firm's reputation, this reputation may lead to new demands as its reputation spreads. Being dependent on this mechanism for growth and survival, the critical growth variable is the firm's capacity to recruit new skilled workers who can meet or improve the reputational standards. (Kristensen 1996a, 119–20)

As this type of firm normally acts as a sub-contractor in the industrial market, it has been easy to set up the other typical type of firm in Denmark, the *Project Coordinator*. Such firms are able to conceptualize a product, and sometimes to do assembly work, but they generally focus on marketing and selling the product. Project coordinating firms do their jobs at very low fixed costs, while the ecology of skill containers takes care of developing and producing the parts that their specialization allows. Only rarely do the dynamics among Skill Containers and Project Coordinators lead to the normal "hierarchically dominated" supplier system (as, for instance, in Japan). Skill Containers will normally only follow the growth of successful Project Coordinators to a certain level, applying the golden rule: never put more than one third of the turnover in one basket. In effect Project Coordinators will be forced to look for foreign suppliers as their needs become more standardized and mass-produced. By following this strategy, Skill Containers have often earned their own international reputation within the narrow boundaries of small sub-branches of industry, because their teams of skilled workers are recognized for being able to meet virtually any challenge within their specialty. In some regions, clusters of Skill Containers have been able informally to institutionalize the rules of mutual conduct so that they have avoided hard-nosed competition. In such regions they have been able to shift mutual roles. Toward certain customers, some firms will act as privileged contractors and then make use of their colleagues as sub-contractors, for instance. In other situations they may become sub-contractors to their sub-contractors when these, in other customer relationships, take on the role of privileged suppliers. In this way even very small firms may mobilize their business networks to help solve very complicated and heterogeneous problems for customers – Danish or foreign (Nygaard 1999).[1]

As a result, Danish firms are engaged in multiple value chains rather than being firmly embedded in a few– in contrast to producers in the traditional Italian Industrial districts. In this way Denmark was, from the 1960s, tied into the global economy by many overlapping, conflicting, or complementary networks of trade and industrial collaboration – long before the global economy started to reorganize toward a networked, global economy. When Alfred Chandler (1962; 1977) was in the United States studying the change from the unified, vertically integrated to the multi-divisional firm, Danish industrialists were discussing how they could deliberately search for niches too small to be of interest for large corporations and yet with the potential to give Danish firms a significant position within – and shares of – the international market (*Industrirådet* 1977). By holding such positions, Danish firms were and are communicating many new technological impulses, and other impulses as well, from many quarters of the international economy without investing in intelligence-services such as R&D and strategic search. Customers address them for solutions to unusual problems. With the dynamics of the labour market and the vocational training institution, firms were and are serviced with skills that are continually upgraded in their capacity to solve such problems with new technologies and craft professions. Continuous learning, so to speak, is an institutionalized part of the game, and, despite low investments in *formal* R&D, a surprisingly high proportion of Danish products are recent innovations.

It should be added that the smooth running of this system has highly benefited from being framed by labour market parties that have cultivated a tradition for cooperation. They have tried to find compromises between employers and employees, and have formalized them in general agreements that communicated effectively the rights and duties of workers and employers. At the same time, they have jointly negotiated with state bodies to secure institutions that gave them access to programs such as training and welfare schemes, in such a way as to facilitate the conditions for cooperation at the level of the firm as well. The welfare state simply removed a number of potential conflicts from the factory floor (Crouch 1993; Regini 1991). With an almost unitary union movement and exclusive agreements among unions and individual employers, the election of shop stewards and convenors representing the workers actually became a tool for establishing the further institutionalization of dialogues and schemes for procedural justice in Danish firms rather than a tool for recurrent conflicts. In this way Danish firms were often better able to play the role of partners with their customers than their counterparts in most other nations. They were able to act in individual situations without first having to conduct internal negotiations. Furthermore, as new entrepreneurs, foremen, engineers, and production managers typically came from the rank and file of skilled workers and shared with them an apprenticeship background, class divisions on the shop floor never made it difficult to "take on the role of others" (Mead 1967). This in turn probably made both employment relations and employee relations, as well as worker aspirations, highly particular in Denmark. It also explains why workers and employers might not wait until the two "parties" had reconciled conflicts and found general solutions through corporatist, central negotiations before they acted and formed new local partnerships.

By being constituted this way, the Danish production system has been able to take advantage of the emerging new economy since the 1980s. If the new economy has had effects on the Danish economy, they have been rather to reinforce the pattern of interaction among and the typicality of the two firm types, cleansing them from the hybridization with Americanization that took place in the 1960s and 1970s (Kristensen 1996a).

STRATEGIZING ACTORS IN THE NEW POLITICAL ECONOMY: DANISH PLAYERS IN GLOBAL GAMES

The gradual adaptation to the emergent new economy could be seen to have reinforced rather than changed the depicted pattern of interaction among the types of firms in Denmark, whereas *actors and agencies* have had to learn to act and strategize in novel ways to adapt this pattern of interaction to new circumstances.

This shift started in many Danish firms in the early 1980s (Kristensen 1996a; 1986), when they were pressed by interest rates as high as 25 percent. This forced them to focus on stores and buffers, and they gradually realized that they had managed non-Fordist firms (producing a lot of different products in many variants) after Fordist principles. A Danish factory had typically been divided by the specialty of processes (drilling, welding, polishing, assembly, etc.), and each operator was provided with batches of blanks to process, allowing for time-measurement techniques. In effect, the put-through time was very high, and blanks had to be zigzagged through factories (depending on the product or the variant) along different routes resulting in huge buffer-stocks and large final stocks that were often irrelevant in relation to customer demand. Managers had focused on increasing the efficiency of individual jobs and machines, while basically ignoring the total functioning of the factory.

It could be argued that these Fordist/Taylorist principles of management within the Danish production system also had highly counterproductive effects in relation to individual jobs, workstations, or workers (Kristensen 1997b, 30 ff.). Because workers "owned" industrial skills, the ability to improve on performance and reduce processing time did not rest primarily within "methods-departments" but rather with the workers. In effect, workers could use their skills to manipulate machinery in ways that increased the ease of their job without letting the firm benefit economically. Therefore Taylorist techniques in the Danish context could be seen as tools for changing this balance; that is, for managers to make the firm benefit from the improvements that workers in fact initiated. However, as workers were competing over their reputation among other workers rather than in the managerial hierarchy, these measurement techniques instituted a game in which workers competed to use their skills to outwit the techniques, their superiors, and their firms. And their opponents had to be very inventive to undermine the ways in which workers undermined them. In effect both managers and workers were using skills in very unproductive ways.

Behind this game of fooling managers, workers performed under very different situations, some being extremely busy (very often the young and newly recruited) and with low piece-rates, while others (with high seniority) had very favourable jobs with plenty of time and pay. This formally fair, but in reality very unfair, system was frequently under the joint protection of shop stewards (under the banner of solidarity) and middle managers (who used it to buy loyalty or to "divide and rule"), but always at the risk of the system blowing up and turning into an all-out war. It was probably the strong regulation of agreements and negotiation procedures at the local level, determined by the central unions and employers' associations, that prevented this system from evolving into manifest and continuous conflicts. This factory regime was not very attractive, even though unions appeared to be strong, decisive, and able to help nominal wages increase fast.

As in most other countries, the factory regime in Denmark underwent serious challenges after the first oil crisis. Firms fell victim to insolvency, or near insolvency, unemployment grew dramatically, and takeovers and mergers became widespread phenomena. By the early 1980s, when I was making my first factory visits (Kristensen 1986), experiments with new organizational forms and computer-based technologies seemed widespread, even before the Japanization debate had reached Danish shores. Some engineers, inspired by the "continuous flow fraction" within the Taylor society, thought that much buffer and final stock could be reduced if different types of machines and workstations were brought together in manufacturing cells that produced by order rather than according to statistics. It would, on the other hand, imply much more resetting and programming time to shift between small batches, but because skills were available on the factory floor it was rather a matter of giving up the piece-rate wage system than implementing more dramatic restructuring. Though it is my impression that dramatic changes happened in this way in Danish factories from the early 1980s, these changes hardly became hot or widely reported news, unlike, for instance, when GM's Saturn-project was launched in the United States in January 1985 (Cornette 1999). Maybe for good reason: while actors in Denmark were making experiments that would fit the administrative system to the country's industrial practice, the United States was trying to alter industrial practice as such.

In Denmark few envisioned what the changes were all about – even among the actors participating in the experimental process. We found shop stewards and convenors busy collaborating with production managers. But they kept secret their experiments with new factory design, new principles for manning new CNC-machines, changes in the hierarchy, reduction of middle-managers, and new time- or bonus-based wage systems so that neither unions nor employers' associations would discover that they were breaking the rules of the "book" (i.e., the General Agreements). Rather than thereby undermining the centralized corporatist system, it could be said that it was being duplicated informally at the level of the firm. Thus, a much more active social partnership may have emerged at local factory levels from the beginning of the 1980s, but at central levels it seemed – at first – as if Danish corporatism was being weakened by the conservative-liberal government, inspired by neo-liberalism and less inclined toward tripartite negotiations than former Social Democratic governments. This change among central-level peak interest organizations and the government can also be seen as a transformation from a mixed/market economy to a negotiated economy in which the parties became less focused on given issues such as wages; that is, to a system in which what is constantly negotiated is actually Denmark's economic challenges and how the state, institutions, and interest organizations can participate in experimenting with novel ways to meet these (Pedersen, chapter 6; Kjær and Pedersen 2001). Industrial competitiveness has become a concern of all, and for each institution it has become an open, continuously discussed, and negotiated issue, whether and exactly how they may contribute to meeting this aim. This change can also be formally seen in a drift toward laws that set a framework for institutions rather than directing institutional behaviour. Pedersen and Kjær's interpretation of the changes of macrocorporatism in Denmark explains why it became structurally possible to engage in a much more experimental approach to how groupings and firms could make novel social use of welfare state institutions. The coming into existence of local partnerships at firm and local levels may explain why, and how this opportunity has been successfully exploited.

One example of this novel vitality of local partnerships is illustrated by the way Pasilac in Horsens in 1987 created one of the first "further training agreements" (Kristensen 1994; Kristensen and Zeitlin 2005). After some very active years, during which the convenor had collaborated with the production manager to change the factory toward just-in-time production, cells, and CNC technologies in a very successful, though secret (as they broke several rules of General Agreements) way, the business group to which Pasilac belonged got into trouble and was sold to a British MNC. The British MNC declared investment stop, and wanted to see employment reductions, and so on. However, to prevent the loss of a highly skilled workforce, the manager and the convenor struck an agreement that offered the employees further training of their own choice for up to four weeks a year. During the time they spent on vocational training, state budgets would pay a considerable part of their wages and all the costs of training.

Consequently, the firm, as a subsidiary of a MNC, could simultaneously report a reduced wage bill to the HQ, upgrade its skills, and rotate people more in production (to compensate for those taking training courses), thereby effecting a very radical up-skilling of the workforce within a short period. This training agreement, which could have been seen as a way of abusing the welfare system, was engineered in collaboration with a local union office, who saw it rather as an experimental way of resolving the employment problem in a proactive way, and therefore developed an infra-structure to search for courses and vacant seats in schools all over Denmark, hoping to diffuse the agreement to other firms of the locality. Within a few years the subsidiary in Horsens had more than regained its former activity level and was undergoing rapid growth. Because it was still under severe limits as to how many workers it could employ, it started to produce on three shifts, a schedule that was only possible because of the training revolution it had undergone. Working on three shifts, however, meant radical increases in demand for its local suppliers and created a pull through the whole local system that reduced unemployment. But it also made it very difficult to stick to the training agreement, because workers were in great demand and difficult to replace because of their skill level. To resolve this problem, local union offices, technical schools, and AMU centres invented a new education for "flyers." The idea was to take the unemployed and give them all the training necessary to enable them to replace the most highly skilled in factories such as the Horsens plant, so that their workers could leave for additional training courses. Obviously, the plant not only had effected a way to preserve its skilled workers in times of crisis, but also had greatly reformed institutions for further training, which previously served only private career aspirations. Now, however, if effected the systematic collective upgrading of skills among employees and generalized this to the unemployed. Later on, this example was one of many that served both to put further training on the agenda in general agreements between unions and employers' association and to inspire the creation of an active employment policy in the 1990s. But it was local actions that provoked a set of other actions that led to the social use of existing institutions in highly novel ways. From the 1980s, the Danish wel-fare state might have come under fire at central and political levels, whereas it was being made social use of in novel ways at micro levels. With unemployment skyrocketing after 1987, numerous factories made local agreements about continuous training, and the use of vocational training institutions pivoted to the extent that Denmark took the lead in further training within the European Union.

Gradually, as the central unions and employers' associations realized what was happening and included issues such as vocational training in the general agreement as rights, they also suggested general principles for new wage systems. They even agreed, on an experimental basis, to make new curricula for apprentices (so that they would work in a number of work-groups, departments, and even several firms during their education). With these general principles in hand, a new "industrial" regime could diffuse throughout Denmark during the 1990s. Even where workers were formally unskilled, an enormous upgrading took place, making Danish workers highly competent in using new technologies, shifting between different types of production, and taking over responsibilities that had up to then rested with middle-managers. Though Danish firms had been allocating much more responsibility to their employees than in any other country by the mid-1980s, the degree to which employees were implementing their own ideas and planning their own work increased dramatically toward the turn of the century (up from 34% to 69 % of respondents between 1985 and 2000), while 76 percent felt by 2000 that they had good or very good possibilities for influencing their factory (Andersen 2003, 176–7). In a comparative investigation inquiring to what extent people felt that they had or had actively tried to gain influence on their jobs, no country reached the level of Denmark (Andersen 2005).

Though unguided by visionary templates, the new factory regime emerging from these experiments revealed a clear logic. Methods departments would now calculate the costs of keeping parts of production inside or, alternatively, outsource them. In this way, workers could see that using their skills would improve productivity and secure jobs for themselves and their colleagues. It became attractive for workers to reveal improvements in working methods, and finding novel improvements would now be seen as an act of solidarity within the workers' collective. In exchange, managers had to reveal the economic data that proved or disproved the contributions of persons, groups, and departments, so as to improve the economic performance of the entire firm – to enable both the administration of bonus systems and the ability to argue fairly when an increase in the use of subcontractors was up for decision. What had formerly been concealed in the deep structures of the informal organization now became transparent, and what used to belong to the formal organization in terms of hierarchical positions and offices became part of the informal game. The formal organization chart gave few clues as to how things were really functioning.

In this dynamic it was important that factories were being bought and sold frequently among business groups and multinationals; in order to follow some form of coherent strategy, "subsidiary-managers," convenors, and shop stewards had to collaborate to gradually develop a factory that they believed served their interest – if not in the long term then at least for some time.

Through the continuation of this process across borders, actors who used to be adversaries in individual factories have been forced to learn new ways of acting independently and mutually by becoming more directly involved with global firms. Either by their own initiatives, seeking the shelter of a MNC HQ to run financial markets (Kristensen and Zeitlin 2001), or by hostile takeovers, many Danish firms have become directly involved with foreign multinationals as subsidiaries. A few have developed from their Danish origins to become MNCs themselves and find that they now need to learn to play new roles in new games. Finally, a large number of firms serving as subcontractors now experience being involved in a larger game, where MNC HQS play them off against subcontractors in much the same way as they organize investment bargaining among the subsidiaries that they fully own. So, despite the seemingly structural continuity of the Danish economy, its actors are busy trying to learn to play new games, transforming their former identities and the larger societal systems of which they are part. In doing so, actors of various positions may, in a highly indigenous way, transform the Danish production system into a knowledge economy with a specific global role.

We first came across this phenomenon in a bottom-up study of a British multinational (Kristensen and Zeitlin 2005). Of the subsidiaries we investigated, the Danish one seemed to be especially capable of developing internal flexibility, creating new cost-effective generations of products, meet shifting benchmarks from the HQ, and preparing itself for the next move. As we noted earlier, it did so by mobilizing resources of its locality in the form of vocational training programs for its employees, by holding a shifting and flexible interaction with its Danish subcontractors, and by playing skillfully with the changing schemes and instruments of the labour market. Formally, the subsidiary was managed by a Danish diploma-engineer with a typical career pattern. In reality the management team was jointly constructed as a partnership between the convenor and this manager. Together, they succeeded – often in strong opposition to what the English HQ had formally decided – in pursuing a strategy that transformed the Danish subsidiary from being a minor plant overlooked by a Danish Holding Company, a German SBU manager, and the British HQ, to itself becoming a SBU HQ in charge of twenty-two companies throughout the world, sending its workers – blue-collar included – abroad as consultants to engineer organizational changes – and simultaneously changing their own plant into a highly elaborate version of the flexible team-based firm, operating skillfully on the principles of just-in-time production and continuous improvement. This case study reveals that it is possible to a very high degree for a subsidiary, and even for workers in formally very low positions, to become engaged in, contribute to, and participate in the construction of globalization. It is even possible for them to learn from it.

A subsequent, broader study of the lives, careers, practices, and strategies of convenors in Danish subsidiaries of MNCs reinforced the described pattern of how Danish subsidiaries, through management-convenor partnerships, were able to move their subsidiaries toward highly elaborate versions of flexible production, and high-performance work systems, that could meet shifting benchmarks, thereby winning a growing role and influence within the larger MNC (Kristensen 2003).

As partners, convenors and shop stewards have contributed to a shift in work organization based on a radical up-skilling of operatives (formally unskilled or craft workers), the introduction of group or firm bonuses, and a consequent transparency as to how improvements on the part of employees effect the benchmarks by which a subsidiary measures its overall improvements. Helping teams to improve performance has become the best strategy for enabling convenors to argue for improvements in wages and working conditions, while it simultaneously serves to gain influence toward HQ managers, as these are increasingly realizing that they can allocate difficult and demanding problems to such Danish subsidiaries. Through emerging channels of influence and by building trust relations with HQs, subsidiary managers and convenors have been able to influence high political decisions such as transfer pricing principles, the appointment and recruitment of persons for managerial positions, budgetary allocation at different levels, negotiations over the choice of fair benchmarks, procedures and responsibility allocation for the choice of plant closings, the formation of European Work Councils, and the establishment of procedures and institutions for joint consultation. Thus, it seems as if Danish employee representatives are engaged in the far-reaching institutionalization on a global level of a negotiation system that they take for granted at home. And our impression is that they do so much more efficiently than is normally reported by studies of European Work Councils.

DENMARK: AN EXPERIMENTALIST INDUSTRIAL LABORATORY

Far from being an economy in which the definition of its new form becomes increasingly fixed, what takes place in Denmark is rather a search for new forms. This search turns nearly all of its dimensions into an unsettled, tentative and experimental activity, in which it is impossible to foresee what the targets and possible outcomes of experimentation will be. This makes learning at the societal level a huge challenge.

One prime example is the *internal work organization* of factories of MNC subsidiaries. In contrast to Germany, it seems as if degrees of freedom in Denmark have been legion, while the absence of institutional restrictions and barriers has provided factory reformers with neither defining building blocks nor guidance. What a team is meant to be, and the organizational framing of its interaction with the larger organizational setting of which it is part, remains very open, and is hardly the focus of direct attention or reflection. In some factories, teams seem to have emerged from quite arbitrary and invisible dividing lines being suddenly rendered visible by the drawing of lines on the factory floor to encircle a team. The concept of teams thus leads to their habituation. In other instances, teams emerged when the technical department made alternative calculations as to whether a factory should produce a component in-house or outsource its production; what needed to be included within was included as a grouping of machines, operators, and administrative functions that could be brought together only incoherently. As in other situations, the components made by the group would belong to a variety of different groupings. In still other cases, continuous attempts to create and parcel out unity among tasks, machinery, equipment, administrative routines, development, and people gradually pointed toward a unit team, although it would seldom be defined and separated from the rest in a tightly consistent way. Finally, in some cases Japanese-inspired consultancy firms have cast the net of theoretical model factories and defined, very consistently, a team structure that has gradually squeezed practice into its pattern (partly by farming out inconsistencies to suppliers or to internal buffer zones). This heterogeneity in task definition has its parallel in the practice of appointing team leaders. In some factories, management simply appoints the team leaders autocratically; in others, the job rotates for a shorter period among the team members on an equal basis. In a third group of enterprises, the members elect the team leaders after democratic vote, while in still others shop stewards and convenors appoint the possible candidates among whom the team members may choose. Consequently, in some factories it is difficult to distinguish between the current team leaders and past foremen, while in others, team leaders must be seen, rather, as a new layer in the hierarchy of shop stewards and convenors.

The variety of patterns in the selection of team leaders is also reflected in their training. In some factories training basically means employer-controlled courses for middle managers, while in others union training schemes for shop stewards constitute their basic training. Some firms, in collaboration with local vocational training institutions, have developed highly advanced courses that elevate team leaders to a unique and highly interesting personnel configuration incommensurate with that of any role-holder cultivated for the former factory regimes. The resulting organizations show a wide variety in both form and substance. In some enterprises team leaders work side by side as equals, and in others they are subordinated to a system of foremen and supervisors. Some have stripped the whole place of middle managers, leaving a collegial system of teams and team leaders linked together within a vastly expanded system, a number of shop stewards, and a convenor who almost autonomously run, for example, the bonus-wage-system, personnel-administration, and vocational training schemes. None of the firms have abandoned their managerial hierarchy/apex entirely, but it is very uncertain, as the teams show, which role different "offices" actually do play, and what remains of managerial staff as seen by the shop stewards is often rather cause for disruption of the productivity of teams than a source of help in their attempts to improve performance. In a few of the factories we visited, top managers and convenors had discussed whether to integrate what remains of the hierarchy into the shop floor teams or, alternatively, to let the hierarchy reconfigure into teams itself, the survival, growth or contraction of which would be dependent on their ability to continuously increase and create demand for their services, internally or externally. Some factories have progressed strongly toward such a situation by handing over to teams and team leaders the responsibility for an entire project (e.g., the delivery of ten trains to Italy). The team then itself decides whether to buy services outside the team, either from internal sources of the subsidiary or from the outside world. In this way a team is run de facto as a distinct firm, not subordinated to the larger hierarchy of the firm. Though this experimentalist variety can be observed by anyone who visits a Danish factory, nobody seems yet to have initiated a more systematic study of what can be learned from all these experiments. Benchmarking happens within the corporations that own these firms, and comparisons are made across countries of MNC HQs, but nobody seems to compare across Danish factories. Nobody seems to have addressed the question of which current organizational forms or experiments are especially favourable for cultivating a Danish version of factories for the new economy. This makes the outcome of Danish experimentation very unpredictable and exciting, but probably also makes it less robust as crucial decisions may be processed by less than informed actors.

This information gap can also be seen in *how Danish subsidiary-partnerships exploit opportunities when a privileged position to MNC HQS emerges.* In a number of the cases studied, partnerships between local subsidiary managers and convenors were able to seize opportunities in a very effective way. Though initially rebelling against the rules of the MNC or strategizing subversively, Danish subsidiaries have often been able to make use of the new work organization much more efficiently than their rivalling colleagues in other countries, so that they have been able to position themselves in the role of "benchmark factory." Thanks to the Danish tradition for decentralized responsibility in production, it has been possible to use normal blue-collar workers for development work as well, meaning that both products and processes could be improved faster (and under current accounts) than in most other countries. Danish subsidiaries have in effect, frequently been better at meeting benchmarks quickly and have therefore been winners in negotiations with HQS. Through this voice in negotiations, convenors and local managers have been able to modify parts of the MNC such as organizational structure and procedures that would have limited a subsidiary's future ability to perform. But it is also through such channels that Danish subsidiaries seem to have been able to take home big stakes in the game played. Partly because they have been able to demonstrate a high record in continuous improvement, and partly because Danish costs show up in a very competitive way (overhead cost for administration, R&D, and management being very low), Danish subsidiaries have been favoured in the best way an HQ knows to favour collaborating subsidiaries, the negotiated premium being the allocation to Denmark of a world mandate for a core product of the MNC. Both subsidiary managers and convenors have readily celebrated such victories as a confirmation and recognition of past performance. New mandates have seemed great for the future, as the promise of large orders enabled them to foresee a logic of automation that would ease the pressure from the high wages of blue collar workers in Denmark and make it easier to protect Danish jobs. Yet, for obvious reasons, this way of celebrating victories is indeed very shortsighted. If the product soon reaches its maturity in terms of further development and in terms of improvements in production, it starts to reduce the challenges to the most skilled workers, who now foresee no improvement in their own skills associated with the production process as such. Either they start to leave or the subsidiary must invent costly compensating measures to hold onto them. In either case, the Danish subsidiary gradually loses its comparative advantage vis-à-vis subsidiaries in other countries. Had the Danish subsidiary instead always concentrated on the most uncertain and most demanding parts of products and production processes, in which there seemed no limit to potential improvements, it would have been able to maintain its comparative advantage and would have served to continuously reproduce the bargaining power of both subsidiary managers and convenors. But to achieve such situations, these local partners would have had to try to allocate production, against their own immediate interests, to countries where subsidiaries were geared more toward mass-production principles. To do so, subsidiary managers and convenors would have had to develop a more long-term view of how to build up and gradually improve the capabilities of the entire MNC – a perspective that is often more advanced than that currently held by executive officers of MNC HQs. On the other hand, they would have to imagine which of the several forms of team-based production was more promising from the point of view of becoming increasingly able to tackle the most innovative, the least mature, and the most uncertain part of the production processes, when the major capability is rooted among highly skilled, and blue-collar workers, who are continuously engaged in upgrading their own skills and thereby enhancing the subsidiary's capabilities (Kristensen and Zeitlin 2005).

A third aspect of the unsettled experimentalist state of the emerging new economy in Denmark can be studied in *the intensive but unreflective way that the country makes use of its vocational training system*. In retrospect, it is clear that this system, which was neither intended nor designed as a system, has grown into a forceful institutional matrix through actions taken on different occasions, in which various social groups managed to create political support for institution building that could enhance their competitiveness among many groups over a variety of job positions. Thus, from the mid-nineteenth century technical schools gradually evolved into a complex system of local and national training facilities that secured the transformation of craft apprenticeships to a regime of industrialization and science, with its own supporting institutes to make new technologies transferable to the crafts. Industrialization based on SMEs rather than on large corporations became possible and acted as a complementary force to decentralized production along the lines of the cooperative movement, where the two would interact in small railway towns. Then in the twentieth century unskilled workers built their own institutions from evening classes – from specialized workers' schools to AMU centres – to underpin their efforts to compete with the skilled workers over jobs in industry, while craft-workers took advantage of the new technical courses that were thought to help foster a Fordist production regime. With these institutions in place, competition both at the level of unions and among training institutions resulted in workers' being able to acquire the skills that made it possible to claim the right to occupy distinct jobs in industry. Consequently, being a worker could equally be seen as simply the start of a career or as a class position; and while it may be a "class struggle" for improved educational institutions, it is simultaneously a system that allows individuals to travel through working careers quite unimaginable in other societies. During the 1980s and 1990s the rivalling dynamics of vocational training institutions and unions were in particular directed toward the introduction of computer-based technologies in both manufacturing and administrative processing, to the effect that such skills were highly and evenly diffused among different professions in the Danish labour market. Observers, who feared the coming of a dual labour market, were overwhelmed by the impressive generalization of computer literacy. Thus, in hindsight, it becomes clear that the gradual composition of a complex vocational training system has been – and probably is – the most important tool by which the labouring classes have continuously transformed their identities to adapt to new phases of modernization in the Danish economy. This system has probably played a much more profound role than univer-

sities and research-oriented institutions in supporting the egalitarian character of the Danish welfare state at its social roots rather than compensating for elite power by modifying the economic effects of such power. The
ownership of industrial knowledge in the current transformation toward
the new economy thus rests also with the immediate producers.

It is also quite telling that several groupings claim responsibility for the
active use and the change of the vocational training system. Observe, for
instance, how Pedersen (chapter 6) sees vocational training as playing an
important part in defining actions within structural policy among the corporatist elite; how Madsen (chapter 9) sees it as an instrument deliberately
used by politicians to form a turn toward an "active labour market policy";
how Martin (chapter 7) attributes its active use to managers who try to
implement policies of social responsibility; while I am reporting how shop
stewards are using it to fight for the improvements of their constituencies.
Rather than being contradictory, this phenomenon probably reflects the
reality that each grouping sees the vocational and educational system as
the core institution for supporting transformative action, just as education
and systems for improvements and learning constituted important back-
bones in Denmark's agricultural transformation in the nineteenth century,
as O'Rourke observes. However, it is also significant that, depending on
the circles in which different actors are engaged, each of them attributes
to the system very different types of rationality, while hardly any acknowledges how important the system is in its totality.

For instance a significant – though politically unintended – effect of the
presence of a strong vocational training system has been that it has served
as *an automatic stabilizer* not by stimulating demand, as do Keynesian-type
stabilizers, but rather by changing the quality of the supply of workers during periods of unemployment. This could be observed in 1930–1950,
when skilled workers flocked to engineering educations and transformed
themselves into the new technicians that they expected would be needed
with the transformation to Fordism, while the unskilled, through evening
classes, tried to prepare themselves to take over the jobs normally held by
the skilled. From 1980–2000 this orientation was rather toward IT-tech-
nologies and new principles for organizing production and administration, but the pattern looked very similar. Taking their departure from each
position, the groupings of workers tried to elaborate their skills to the best
of their knowledge so that they could compete better with the skill level
above them over the unsettled demarcation lines associated with the new
technologies. This competition in turn helped the groups of workers
communicate mutually, as all had achieved at least some part of the new
skills, thereby allowing a transformation to a new technological regime to
take place in a fast, very quiet, and seemingly non-dramatic way. When
unemployment was high in the 1980s and the early 1990s, factory workers

in particular upgraded their skills, while during the late 1990s the vocational training system was used to increase the employability of unemployed. In this way Denmark used the recession to upgrade skills that
could be utilized in the coming boom, and then enlarged the employment
base by diffusing these skills to the wider labour market during the boom
years of the late 1990s.

With this perspective on the vocational training system, it seems paradoxical that the political system has not recognized the core role it has
played and can play. Beginning with the late phase of the Social
Democratic/Radical government in 1999/2000 and continued under the
present Liberal/Conservative government, the state has reduced public
financing of vocational training and wage subsidies, and without provoking strong criticism from either employers' associations or unions, though
the latter have raised a soft critique.

This paradox is even more compelling when one considers what role the
vocational training system could play in the continuous transformation
toward and the systematic construction of a Danish version of the new
economy. For a subsidiary to defend jobs by transforming work organization into teams, which then try individually and jointly to fight for keeping
or enlarging their respective space within the MNC that owns it by a process
of deliberate and continuous improvements, soon puts that subsidiary in a
very dependent position vis-à-vis its local labour market. If it needs to
recruit workers to fill existing positions or expand by enlarging the number of teams, then the whole position of the subsidiary toward the MNC HQ
may be at risk, especially if the newly recruited workers reduce the performance of existing teams or show up in low performance of newly established ones. One way to reduce this risk is to upgrade the qualifications of
new recruits before they become employed, through a range of courses
arranged by the complex of local vocational training institutions. Thus, in
some cases, we have seen subsidiary partnerships engage in creating new
institutions for recruiting workers to "job-banks"; in-coming workers
undergo half a year of job training courses to prepare them for entering
the new industrial life of high performance organizations. As a side effect,
such "job-banks" are training workers for new technologies and team-
based production in ways that also offer other local firms the possibilities
of recruiting workers to help them initiate an organizational transformation similar to what foreign subsidiaries have undergone. This solves
another problem for MNC subsidiaries; while the pressure to reform themselves might have been early and more direct because they had to meet
MNS internal benchmarks, such subsidiaries can only move at satisfactory
speed if surrounding subcontractors also move in a similar way. Otherwise
very few shoulders must master the process of continuous improvement
individually. Consequently, the use of a region's vocational training system

to spread the work organization of teams engaged in continuous improvement greatly enlarges the potential for a subsidiary to defend its position within a multinational. But it means that the whole local labour market must be engaged in the processes of transformation, which then only gets its impetus and inspiration from the transformation that has been evoked in the most successful subsidiaries of MNCs. Denmark is possibly one of the few countries in which it is possible for small subcontracting firms to prepare themselves for the type of bargaining- and management regime that MNCs try to install not only among subsidiaries they own, but also among suppliers with whom they trade. Thus, it could turn regional labour markets into collective entities that jointly develop strategies for firms and employees to cope with the new global economy.

It is apparently to the level of the entire local labour market that institutions and agencies must put the question: How do we build institutions and training curricula that sustain the ability of workers and plants to engage continuously in ongoing improvements? What are the proactive skills that we should supply? How do we define the new skills, which, in the longer term, will help our firms in this locality transform, form, and create the foundation for the type of life we want to live? But, rather than engaging in rivalries among localities over such issues, vocational training institutions under the current political configuration have been trying to survive and trying to rescue, in a defensive way, what they think are core activities for a much more simple-minded reproduction of the labour forces of their local labour markets, because the state is cutting back their financial resources.

AN EXPERIMENTALIST LABORATORY WITHOUT LEARNING?

These three brief drill samples from the ecology of experimentalist laboratories of Danish economic organization reveal several core issues. The first is that, whereas each of the aforementioned parts of the traditional agencies of Danish industry is busily engaged in experimental activities that could help the Danish economy transform toward a vibrant and interesting version of the new economy, these experiments have difficulty connecting into circles of mutual reinforcement so that a process of "cumulative-causation" can take place across different spheres of action. Learning takes place at an incredible pace at the level of individual agencies, but lessons learned and experiences gained are not diffused across firms, regions, and institutional divides or between micro- and macro spheres. In short, Denmark seems currently unable to create complementarities. One side of this coin is very positive; the Danish Inquiry into Power (*Magtudredning*) reveals that people living in different spheres do not in general feel their actions are seriously restricted by interference from other spheres. However, the other side of the coin could be less promising; it points to the fact that no agency is sufficiently powerful to be able to act in such a way that actions in one sphere become coordinated with actions in other spheres so that reinforcement mechanisms, complementarities, and processes of cumulative causation can be established.

This separation of spheres probably has many causes. For instance, leading politicians are generally recruited on the basis of their educational career (as economists) rather than being elected to parliament because they have been *pioneers* in local social experiments and movements, as they often were in the past, when the high-school movement prepared common people to raise their voice in parliament. Mass media are rarely, if ever, interested in trying to reveal ongoing experiments for their positive contributions to developing the country; rather, they attract readers, listeners, and viewers by focusing on scandals or failures. But perhaps the most important part is played by the orientation of interest formations joined in corporatist negotiations that, in the past, used to make consensus and joint action possible in Denmark and other small states.

Institutions for centralized bargaining and tripartite negations in the post-war corporatism of Denmark mutually legitimized the country's participant interest organizations because these were believed to represent underlying constituencies, the interests of which they were each seen to aggregate. During the process of evolution, these interest organizations likely changed shape by mirroring each other rather than by cultivating their respective abilities to speak the current voice of their constituency. The universalized language of economics and political science became used for constructing compelling arguments in discourses and negotiations, and the ability to listen to the numerous and polyvalent voices of constituencies engaged in identity-transforming processes at micro levels became less and less prevalent within unions, employers' associations, and the state. "Enlightened" technocrats from interest organizations preferred to share information rather than speak with their respective constituencies, which they saw as being, if not ignorant, at least ill-informed. It became more and more self-evident during the reign of Keynesianism that interest organizations and the state had to come to agreement and then use their organizations to impose their mutual agreement on their constituencies. Given Keynesian demand management, Fordist modernization of enterprises, and competitive incomes policies, such a regime of coordination may have been very helpful and may partly explain Denmark's economic performance after World War II, which was believed to have taken place by central design. It is possibly this form of learning across interest groups that enabled small states to develop better than the larger ones, as Peter Katzenstein (Campbell et al. 2003) argues. It is also impressive how this regime was able to spread and deepen its interaction, and encourage mutual communication among established interest groups and institutions in such a way that coordinated learning took place among its constituent entities (see Pedersen, chapter 6).

However, for learning within corporate, regional, institutional, and organizational bodies in an age of unlimited experimentation with an economy, the shape and character of which can only be very dimly defined in advance, such a coordination regime is at best very inept. It may seem capable of aligning itself toward a general discourse, often inspired by global debates, and of establishing local versions of universally applied schemes for modernization; but it seems incapable of making sense of the experiments that are actually going on in factories, firms, and local labour markets among entrepreneurs, managers, and employee representatives. What seems to be needed is interest organizations that are so firmly rooted in their constituencies that they actually know about ongoing experiments to the extent that they can assess comparative outcomes, draw conclusions about sameness and difference, and gradually draw out patterns by reinforcing what works and deselecting what does not, so that experiments can acquire a sense of direction and character. In this process, centralized bargaining and tripartite negotiations could potentially agree on priorities and allocate ways and means to benchmark ongoing experiments so as to allow for coordinated change in institutions and organization, rather than attempting reform on the basis of universal discourses. Such a deliberate shaping of the Danish version of the new economy is far from being a reality. As long as the corporatist industry is passive, even though Denmark's potential and raw material are amassing with incredible speed, making the country very prosperous, it can not know why, how, or with which prospects this incredible potential must be managed in the future.

However, despite the inherent dilemma of the modern version of corporatism, whereby institutions and aggregated interest groups engage jointly with the state in a mutual learning process that tends to ignore the learning processes going on at the level of employees, firms, and their relations to local institutions, the two precondition each other. We have seen how local initiatives and experiments have served to create models that could reform the use made of vocational training. But the very fact that subsidiary managers and convenors have been able to form partnerships and establish a highly capable system of negotiation at the plant level and between plants and local labour market institutions shows how the corporatist model equips actors with a technology for reforming the system while at the same time constantly making mutual understanding possible. If employee representatives and managers are able to establish similar systems of ongoing negotiations with their respective central unions and employers' associations, a generalized learning society could be established and make the outcome of the cooperative agricultural system of the nineteenth century look minor in comparison. As we previously mentioned, subsidiary managers and convenors have established similar experimental systems of negotiation with headquarters of multinationals. If this could be systematized and cultivated into an institutionalized practice, it could change the way in which global firms operate and make globalization function in a very different way than it does today. Thus, what a small country does far away from the commanding heights of the new global economy could have significant consequences – in a way reminiscent of the inspiration Danish farmers provided for some of the reforms under Roosevelt's New Deal policy in the United States in the 1930s (Rodgers 1998).

NOTES

1 In other regions (e.g., Copenhagen) such systems never evolved, probably because the industrial milieu was too footloose to find informal solutions in the absence of formal systems as, for example, Germany or the Third Italy (Kristensen and Nygaard 2000).

PART THREE

Challenges

9

How Can It Possibly Fly?

The Paradox of a Dynamic Labour Market in a Scandinavian Welfare State

PER KONGSHØJ MADSEN

Over the past decade, Denmark has experienced what is generally acknowledged as a remarkable shift in its labour market statistics. After several years of rising unemployment, the economy reached a turning point in 1993. A substantial rise in employment was followed by a fairly dramatic decline in unemployment. From a maximum of 12.4 percent in 1993, the rate of unemployment (by national definition) gradually declined to 5.2 percent in 2001, the lowest level since 1976. Figure 1 portrays this development against the background of the Danish post-war experience.

THE DANISH JOB MIRACLE

As figure 1 suggests, development from 1993 onward is characterized not only by a reduction in unemployment but also by a considerable increase in employment to its highest level ever. As a result, the employment rate increased to 76.2 percent, which, as shown in figure 2, represents the top level among EU Member States. In the OECD area as a whole, the employment rate of Denmark is surpassed only by that of Norway and Switzerland.

Table 1 takes a closer look at the main statistical indicators of labour market development in the recent period and also compares it with the economic downturn from 1987 to 1993. During the whole period since 1987, the workforce has been almost constant. Thus the changes in open unemployment mainly reflect changes in total employment. The reduction in unemployment from 1993 to 2002 of just above 200,000 persons mirrors an increase in private employment of about 141,000 persons and in public employment of 68,000 persons. As shown in the last row, the employment rate increased during the 1990s and almost returned to the level of the mid-1980s. In this light, Danish employment success in recent

Figure 1　Total Employment (left scale) and Unemployment (right scale) in Denmark, 1948–2002.

Source: Statistics Denmark. *Databanks of the Macro-Econometric Model ADAM.*

Table 1　Main Statistical Indicators for the Danish Labour Market, 1983–2002

Year	1987	1993	2002	Change 87–93 (1,000 p.)	Change 93–02 (1,000 p.)
Population, aged 15–64 years, 1000 p.	3421	3495	3569	74	74
Workforce, 1000 persons	2888	2880	2885	-8	5
Employment, 1000 persons	2666	2531	2740	-135	209
Private sector employment, 1000 p.	1901	1759	1900	-141	141
Public sector employment, 1000 p.	765	771	840	6	68
Open unemployment, 1000 p.	222	349	145	127	-204
Employment rate (employment as a share of adult population)	77.9	72.4	76.8	*	*

Source: Author's calculations based on the databanks of the macro-econometric model ADAM (Statistics Denmark).

years is not just a reflection of surplus labour being transformed into participants in different labour market programs or being moved outside the workforce.

Turning to the question of the level of unemployment, as opposed to the shifts in recent years, it is important to notice that the number of registered unemployed (labelled "open unemployed" in table 1) to some degree underestimates the size of the labour reserve, because it does not include unemployed taking part in active labour market programs, various

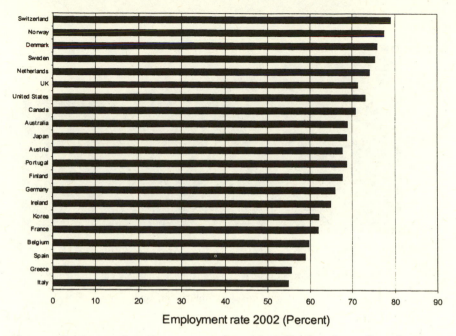

Figure 2   Employment Rates (age group 15–64 years) of a Number of OECD Countries, 2002.
Source: OECD. 2003. Table B.

leave schemes and the Voluntary Early Retirement Pay Scheme. This scheme, under certain conditions, allows both unemployed and employed to retire at the age of 60, receiving a benefit that is similar to unemployment benefits, until they qualify for old-age pension at the age of 65. The recipients of voluntary early retirement pay and participants in active labour market programs are not included in the workforce, as it is normally defined.

Figure 3 presents information on both open unemployment and "gross unemployment," which includes not only the registered unemployed but also the unemployed who participate in various active labour market programs, leave schemes, and the Voluntary Early Retirement Pay Scheme. As can be seen from figure 3, total "gross unemployment" fell from 600,000 persons in 1994 to about 434,000 persons in 2002. This is primarily the result of a strong decline in open unemployment. Also, the number of participants in active programs fell during the upturn. As a result of a steep increase in the number of recipients of voluntary early retirement pay, the total number of persons at the margin of the labour market did not fall as fast as the number of open unemployed. However, the main conclusion from figure 3 is that the reduction in open unemployment reflects not

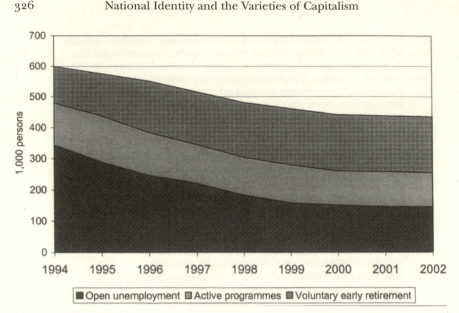

Figure 3   Open Unemployment and Gross Unemployment, 1994–2002.
Source: Databanks of Statistics Denmark.

merely a shift in the composition of persons at the margin of the labour market, but a genuine reduction in the labour reserve.

Finally, one could hypothesize that the positive employment performance could to some extent have been the outcome of a widening of the wage dispersion, which then allowed for the creation of new jobs at the lower end of the wage scale. The statistical evidence available shows that the relative yearly wage of low-wage workers fell slightly from 39 percent of the income of high-income earners in 1994, to 37 percent in 2002 (Dansk Arbejdsgiverforening 2003). However, the decline is only seen after 1999 and is thus more likely the result of the upturn in employment than its cause. Also, from 1994 to 2001, the Gini-coefficient, calculated on the basis of taxable incomes, increased a little from 0.36 to 0.37 (Danmarks Statistik 2003). Again, the increase is observed only at the very end of the period.

In summary, the overall impression of the accomplishments of the Danish employment system in recent years is that of a genuine upturn that reflects a strong increase in private and public employment. Furthermore, these results were obtained without deficits on the external balance of payments (except for 1998) and with rising surpluses for public budgets. Also, this remarkable improvement in the overall employment situation has been accomplished without any significant increase in wage inflation.

Finally, no sharp shifts are observed with respect to the wage or income distribution.

International Interest in the Danish Experience

Not surprisingly, these favourable developments have caused international interest and made Denmark a member of the group of small, successful European economies (Auer 2000; Auer and Casez 2003). To many international observers, Denmark seems to have created a unique combination of stable economic growth and social welfare since the mid-1990s, at a time when liberals were arguing that the classical Scandinavian model was becoming obsolete and was no longer able to face the demands of flexibility and structural change arising out of technological progress and the growing forces of international competition.

The term *flexicurity* is often used to characterize this successful combination of adaptability to a changing international environment and a solidaristic welfare system, which protects the citizens from the more brutal consequences of structural change. In recent years there has been a growing interest in the scientific study of various models of flexicurity, characterized by different combinations of flexibility and security. In this broader perspective the Danish model can be seen as a specific variant, where a high level of mobility between firms (external numerical flexibility) is combined with income security. For an introduction to this new line of research, reference can be made to Wilthagen and Tros (2004). The success of the Danish model of *flexicurity* thus points to a "third way," which combines the flexibility of the labour market often ascribed to a liberal market economy with the social safety nets of the traditional Scandinavian welfare state.

However, reality is, as usual, more complex than the portraits of *model societies* found in international discussions of welfare state systems. The purpose of this chapter is therefore to present a brief, as well as critical analysis of the factors behind the Danish version of a "flexicurity model." I attempt to disentangle the various elements behind the apparent success of the Danish employment system by highlighting the following three aspects:

- The role of the macroeconomic expansion of the 1990s.
- The long-term nexus between a high level of labour market flexibility and a generous system of economic support to the unemployed.
- The contributions of the reforms of Danish labour market policy since 1994.

Finally, the chapter ends with a critical look at the future trends and challenges of the Danish version of flexicurity.

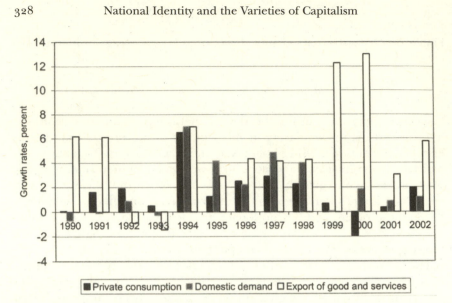

Figure 4   Real Growth Rates of Components of Aggregate Demand in Denmark, 1990–2002.

Source: Statistics Denmark. *Databanks of the Macro-Econometric Model ADAM.*

A Good Old-fashioned Upturn!

A first factor to be noted is that the Danish upturn, and the decline in unemployment since 1993, is not in itself an economic miracle but a standard example of demand-driven growth. Figure 4 portrays the development in different components of aggregate demand since the early 1990s.

The most notable observation from figure 4 is of course the steep rise in total domestic demand (especially private consumption) and in exports in 1994, both showing growth rates above 6 percent. This "kick-start" of the economy was followed by four years of solid growth in both domestic demand and exports. Only in 1999 did the boom in domestic demand level out, with export taking over as the main driving force.

Several causal factors lay behind this remarkable development. First, an expansion of fiscal policy was implemented by the Social Democratic government, which took office in January 1993. Then came falling international interest rates, rising real estate prices, and a credit reform allowing home-owners to convert the fall in long-term interest rates into lowered housing costs. Private demand was therefore strongly stimulated. In 1994 alone, private consumption grew in real terms by almost 7 percent, and investment in housing accelerated. The same happened, after a while, with private investment in general, all according to the standard economic

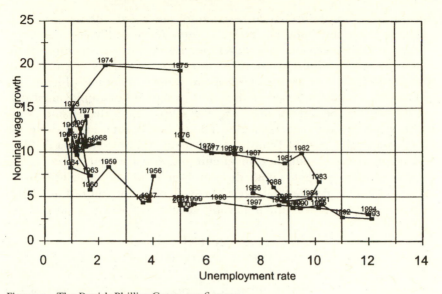

Figure 5   The Danish Phillips Curve, 1956–2002.
Source: Statistics Denmark. *Databanks of the Macro-Econometric Model ADAM.*

textbook. Also, export developed positively thanks to strong international competitiveness, which was, among other factors, the result of slow wage increases during the previous years and the fact that nominal wages during the upturn after 1994 were still remarkably stable.

The Main Research Questions

The success of the Danish economy and labour market in recent years has stimulated ideas about the existence of a particular Danish model of the employment system. Given the correspondence of the start of the upturn in 1994 and the implementation of a number of reforms of labour market policy, it is sometimes argued that the decline in unemployment can be directly attributed to the changes in labour market policy. However, as I have mentioned, the decline in unemployment itself can be explained perfectly well within the framework of standard macro economic analysis. The remarkable feature is therefore not the fall in unemployment as such, but the fact that this reduction took place without any outburst of wage inflation (see figure 5, which shows the Danish Phillips curve since 1956). As shown by the table, the Danish Phillips curve can be subdivided into three distinct sub-periods. Both the first period from 1956 to the late 1960s and the second period from the early 1970s to the early 1990s are characterized by downward-sloping curves, while the third sub-period, after 1993–94, shows an almost perfectly flat curve (Boje and Madsen 2003).

Against this background, the developments of the Danish employment system lead to two different, but related, research questions. The first deals with the long-term relative success of the Danish economy, which – as I indicated – was able to sustain a high and rising level of employment during the post-war period, leading to a level employment that is among the highest found in the OECD countries. The second question focuses on the more spectacular part of Danish employment history: the remarkable – and inflation-free – reduction in unemployment in recent years. In the remainder of this chapter both those questions will be dealt with in an effort to disentangle the longer-term positive development of the Danish employment system from the noticeable success of the last decade.

THE "GOLDEN TRIANGLE" OF THE DANISH EMPLOYMENT SYSTEM

The analysis will be carried forward by applying a simple model of the Danish employment system, which has gained popularity in recent years. It takes the form of the so-called "golden triangle," shown in figure 6 (adapted from Arbejdsministeriet 1999, figure 1.6). The model focuses on three elements of the Danish labour market and labour market policy:

- A flexible labour market with a high level of external numerical flexibility indicated by high levels of worker flow in and out of employment and unemployment.
- A generous system of economic support for the unemployed.
- Active labour market policies aimed a upgrading the skills of the unemployed who are unable to return directly from unemployment to a new job.

The arrows in the model symbolize flows of personnel between different positions within work, welfare, and active labour market programs. The two arrows linking the flexible labour market and the generous welfare system indicate that large numbers of workers are affected by unemployment every year, but that most of them return to employment after a short spell of unemployment. Active labour market programs assist those who do not quickly go back into employment, during the time before they re-enter a job.

The argument underlying the concept of the golden triangle is that the success of the Danish employment system is due to its unique combination of *flexibility* (measured by a high level of external numerical flexibility), *social security* (a generous system of social welfare and unemployment benefits),

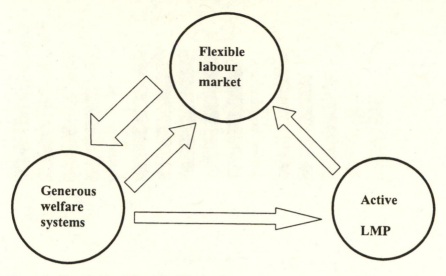

Figure 6   The "Golden Triangle" of Flexicurity

and *active labour market programs*, all of which support the ongoing transformation of the economy. The golden triangle therefore depicts Denmark as a kind of *hybrid* employment system. Thanks to a non-restrictive employment protection legislation, which allows employers to dismiss workers with short notice, the Danish system has a level of flexibility that is comparable to liberal labour markets like those of Canada, Ireland, the United Kingdom, and the United States. At the same time, through its social security system and active labour market programs, Denmark resembles the other Nordic welfare states in providing a tightly knit safety net for its citizens.

The historical background for the model should be seen not as the result of a well-defined grand scheme but as the outcome of a long historical development. The high level of worker mobility supported by a low level of employment protection is a long-term feature of the Danish labour market. Actually, the employers' right to freely hire and dismiss their workers was accepted by the trade unions as a part of the so-called September Compromise between the social partners in 1899. Also, the present version of the system for economic support for the unemployed dates back to the last large reform of the unemployment benefit system in 1969. Finally, the present system of active labour market policy dates back to programs introduced in 1979, which were given a large-scale overhaul in 1993–94.

In the following five sections, I look at each of the aspects of the golden triangle, before returning to the issue of the historical origin and development of what has been considered a unique "Small State Phenomenon."

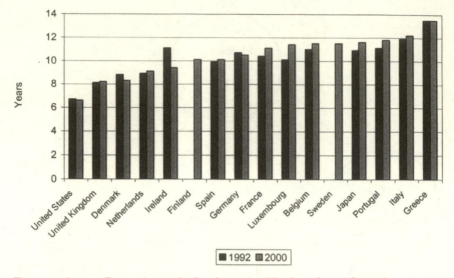

Figure 7   Average Tenure (years) for Employees in a Number of OECD Countries.
Source: Auer and Cazes. 2003. Table 2.1.

Worker Mobility

Compared to the net changes in employment, the underlying mobility of workers between jobs and the level of both job turnover are surprisingly high. A recent study concerning hires, separations, job creation, and job destruction has found that, on average, the level of worker turnover during the period 1980–1995 was about 30 percent, and in no year less than 25 percent (Bingley et al. 2000). The level of job turnover (job creation and job destruction) is also much higher than the level of yearly net changes in employment levels. The overall average of job turnovers is around 12 percent. Furthermore, the level of worker turnover is high for most categories of employees and not concentrated in a minor share of extremely mobile unskilled workers.

Another indicator of the high rate of mobility on the Danish labour market is provided by data on the average tenure of employees. Figure 7 shows the distribution of employees by average tenure in 1992 and 2000 in a number of OECD countries. Denmark is at the low end of the international scale in terms of average tenure, along with countries such as the United Kingdom and the United States. In contrast, other Nordic countries, such as Finland and Sweden, have significantly higher levels of average tenure. Sweden is actually at the top end of the chart, with Japan, Portugal, Italy, and Greece. Moreover, it may be noted that average levels of tenure, in

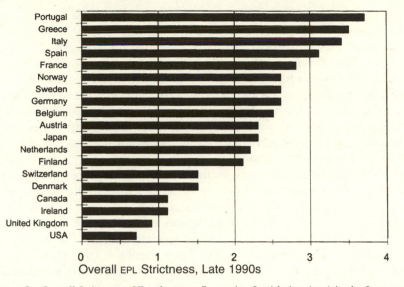

Figure 8   Overall Strictness of Employment Protection Legislation (EPL) in the Late 1990s.
Average Indicator for Regular Contracts, Temporary Contracts, and Collective Dismissals.

Source: OECD. 1999. Table 2.5.

both Denmark and in other countries, are fairly stable over time. The level
of average tenure therefore appears to be an inherent structural characteristic of the employment system of each country. Finally, during the time
span covered by the data, there are no signs of a general decline in the stability of the employment relationship in the countries covered by Figure 7.
For the countries in the sample as a whole, average tenure actually
increased a bit from 10.2 years to 10.4 years during the period covered by
figure 7.

The composite index of labour mobility calculated by Eurostat (based
on its labour force survey) gives a similar impression of a flexible Danish
labour market. The index takes account of job rotation: inflows into
employment following a period of unemployment, after leaving the education system, and after having looked after a family. With the EU-average
at 100, the Danish score of 138 is the highest among the EU Member States
(European Commission 2002, 10).

An important explanation for the high level of Danish worker mobility
is the Denmark's liberal regime of employment protection. A number of
studies have compared the level of employment protection in Denmark to
that of other countries. Figure 8 summarizes the results of an OECD study
on employment protection legislation (OECD 1999, chapter 2). As shown
by the indicator of employment protection legislation, Denmark is ranked

as having a low level of employment protection in comparison to most other industrialized countries, and a much lower level than the other Nordic countries with whom Denmark is commonly grouped. Although there may be differences between the formal level of employment protection and the actual enforcement of the legislation, the data still show a surprising divergence between Denmark and the other Nordic welfare states.

It might be thought that this high level of job mobility and low level of employment protection would lead to a widespread feeling of insecurity among Danish employees. Paradoxically, this is not the case. In a survey conducted in 1996, the proportion of Danish workers *not* strongly agreeing with the statement "my job is secure" was about 45 percent, and therefore considerably lower than for all the other countries in the sample. This feeling of job security was found among all subgroups of workers (OECD 1997, table 5.2). Although this finding may also reflect the positive situation on the Danish labour market at the time of the survey, there are no clear indications that Danish workers are reacting to the high level of numerical flexibility with a strong feeling of insecurity. Similar results have also been found in a more recent survey (Auer and Casez 2003, figure 1.1).

There are at least three explanations for this apparent paradox. One is the predominance of small and medium-sized enterprises (SMEs) in the Danish industrial structure. This implies that strong internal labour markets are less important in Denmark than in other countries. With lower entry barriers at the enterprise level, it is easier to shift from one firm to another. Furthermore, the general improvement in the Danish labour market situation since 1994 may also have influenced the responses, although Danish registered unemployment in 1996 was still at the level of 8.9 percent of the labour force. But a final explanation is the relatively generous level of unemployment benefits paid to unemployed workers from the first day of unemployment and for a considerable period. This is the subject of the following section.

The Danish Unemployment Benefit System

The vast majority of unemployed persons who are members of an unemployment insurance fund receive unemployment benefits calculated at the rate of 90 percent of their previous earned income, with a ceiling of 162,000 DKK (21,800 Euro) per year (2003). Unemployment benefits may be claimed from the first day of unemployment and for a maximum of four years, including periods of activation.

For low-income groups, these and other income-related benefits, combined with the effects of the rather high level of income tax, result in high

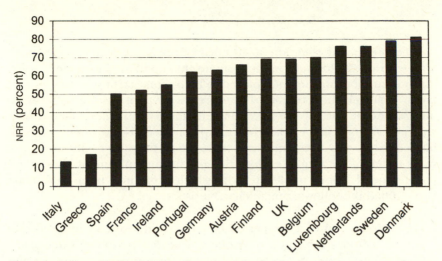

Figure 9   Average Net Replacement Rates (NRR) for 60 Months of Unemployment for an Average of Different Family Types and Income Levels. Percent.

Source: OECD. 2002. Table 3.10.

net income replacement rates (OECD 2002). For an average production worker, for example, the replacement rate is around 70 percent. For low-income groups, the net replacement rate is around 90 percent (highest for single parents). This system puts Denmark at the top end of the EU Member States, when one compares the net replacement rates. Figure 9 shows the results from the comparison provided by OECD.

The minority of the unemployed, who are not members of an unemployment insurance fund (often labelled the "non-insured" unemployed), will receive means-tested social security cash benefits, which for adult family supporters are at a level of around 80 percent of normal unemployment benefits. The most important difference between unemployment benefits and social security cash benefits is thus the means testing. Furthermore, social security cash benefits will depend on the recipient's family situation. In addition, a special low level of cash benefits was introduced in 2002 for newly arrived immigrants.

In the Danish labour market system, the potential disincentives caused by such high income replacement rates are addressed by requiring the unemployed to be actively seeking jobs and by offering mandatory activation after 12 months of unemployment for adults and 6 months of unemployment for young unemployed persons under the age of 25. Activation is therefore seen as fulfilling a purpose in regard to both qualification and motivation.

Danish Active Labour Market Policy

Between 1979 and 1993, the main pillar of the active policies addressing long-term unemployment was a program that combined job offers, training, and support for the unemployed to help them start up in self-employment. However, this program showed relatively poor results, with only a minority of the participants becoming employed on the open labour market. This factor, combined with a sharp renewed rise in unemployment between 1990 and 1993, increased the political pressure to find new measures to break the vicious cycle of long-term unemployment. The result was a general labour market reform, which came into force in January 1994; it had the following main characteristics:

- The introduction of a two-period benefit system, with an initial *passive* period of four years and a subsequent *activation* period of three years; during the passive period, an unemployed person receives benefits and is also eligible for twelve months of activation;
- A change in the assistance provided to individual long-term unemployed persons from a rule-based system to a system based on an assessment of the needs of the individual (with the introduction of *individual action plans* as an important instrument);
- The *decentralization of policy implementation* to regional tripartite labour market councils, which are empowered to adjust program design to fit local needs;
- The *abolition of the connection between participation in labour market measures and the unemployment benefit system,* with the effect that employment with a wage subsidy would no longer prolong the period for which the unemployed are eligible for unemployment benefits;
- The introduction of *three paid leave arrangements* for childcare, education, and sabbatical leave to encourage job rotation by allowing employed (and unemployed) persons to take leave while receiving a benefit paid by the state and calculated as a fraction of unemployment benefit.[1]

Under the governments headed by the Social Democrats from 1994 to 2001, Danish labour market policy underwent a number of further reforms, whose main effect was to shorten the maximum period for which the unemployed would receive benefits (the passive period). As noted above, this passive period was four years in 1994 (with an option of twelve months of activation during this period). In 1996, the passive period was reduced to two years. For young unskilled unemployed persons, the period was reduced to six months in 1996. It was subsequently decided in 1999 to further reduce the passive period to one year for adult unemployed persons. By the end of 2000, Denmark had therefore implemented the element of the European Union's employment guidelines that calls for early activation for both young and adult unemployed persons.

With broad political support, the Conservative-Liberal government in 2003 introduced a new major reform of labour market policy: "More people at work." With respect to active measures, it had the following main elements:

- The number of individual programs of the active labour market policy was reduced from thirty-two different schemes to only three main types of instruments covering: a) guidance, training, and education, b) practical introduction to the enterprises, and c) wage subsidies.
- Higher priority was given to early guidance and other forms of personal contact with the individual unemployed at least every three months. The demands on the unemployed for active job search and mobility were increased.
- The whole administrative system for active labour market policy and benefits was modernized applying an extensive use of digital technologies.
- Other actors (private firms and organizations, including unemployment insurance funds) were to become more involved in implementing active employment policies at all stages.
- All adult unemployed should still take part in an active program after one year of unemployment. However, the exact extent of activation was now specified more vaguely than under the previous system, which had a rule stating that activation should be on a full-time basis (defined as 75 percent of the time in the "active period").
- A long-term target of the reform goal was to fully integrate the two tiers of the present Danish system, which now handles insured and non-insured unemployed separately. Here, an important step is to be taken in 2006, where joint job-centres located in the municipalities will take over the responsibility for both the insured and the non-insured unemployed.

Also as part of the reform, social security cash benefits for some groups (married couples and newly arrived immigrants) were reduced. However the vast majority of recipients of social benefits and of normal unemployment insurance benefits have not been affected by this element of the reform. Therefore the major effect of the reforms of labour market policy since the change in government in 2001 is that the main policy profile has been kept intact as a reflection of a broad political consensus about the merits of the style of labour market policy that was developed during the second half of the 1990s.

The change in the profile of Danish labour market policy since the mid-1990s has placed Denmark in the upper range of OECD countries, in terms

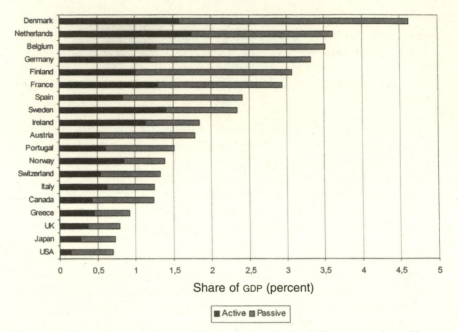

Figure 10   Expenditure on Active and Passive Labour Market Policy, 2002 or Latest Year. Share of GDP.

Source: OECD. 2003.

of expenditure on both active and passive labour market policy measures. The data in figure 10 illustrate the high level in Denmark of total expenditure on active measures and passive benefits (unemployment benefits including early retirement for labour market reasons).[2] Also when it comes to expenditure on active measures alone, Denmark is ranked high among the OECD countries, surpassed only by the Netherlands.

Evaluations of Active Programs

As in many other countries, the net effects of active labour market policy are disputed. One reason is that active programs have both positive and negative effects on the future employments prospects of the individual participants:

• The *motivation effect* implies that an unemployed person seeks work more actively in the period immediately *before* she or he has to participate in a mandatory activation program. The strength of the motivation effect is indicated by the change in the probability of leaving unemployment in the period immediately before the person is obliged to take part in an activation program.

- The *"locking-in" effect* means that job-search activities are reduced during the period in which an individual takes part in a program.
- The *training (or qualification) effect* stems from the rise in the level of qualifications during activation, which should improve the possibilities of finding a job for those who have participated in one of the active programs.

In a study published in 2000, the Ministry of Labour presented some of the first results based on a new database, which it had developed (Ministry of Labour 2000). The database contains information on the labour market situation of all individuals, including their participation in labour market programs and their contacts with the social security system.

First of all, the study revealed significant motivation effects, as measured by an increased probability of taking up employment in the period immediately before having to take part in mandatory activation programs. Such effects have been confirmed by later studies (e.g., Geerdsen 2003; Rosholm and Svarer 2004) and play an increasing role for the proponents of active programs. However, the specific dilemma posed by such observations should be borne in mind. If the wish is to increase the motivation effect, there may be a temptation to change the content of activation programs in order to make them less attractive to participants. But this would also likely imply that the *quality* of the programs themselves would be lowered in terms of their training content and other activities the offer to improve the skills of the participants. As a result, the overall outcome might be less positive for unemployed persons who are unable to find a job before entering activation.

Another potential effect for the individuals taking part in activation programs is that they may increase their chance of gaining employment through the improvement in their qualifications and therefore their employability. In the study by the Ministry of Labour, improvement in employability is measured by the reduction in the proportion of the year for which the persons concerned receive any form of transfer income (such as unemployment benefits, social assistance, or sickness benefits). A reduction in this proportion is a reliable indicator of a genuine improvement in the employment situation of an individual, either because she or he has found ordinary employment or has taken up some form of ordinary education.

Such qualification effects of the various types of labour market programs are of considerable interest (see figure 11).[3] In this respect, the largest improvement in the employment situation (as measured by an increase in the economic self-dependency of the participant) is found for participants

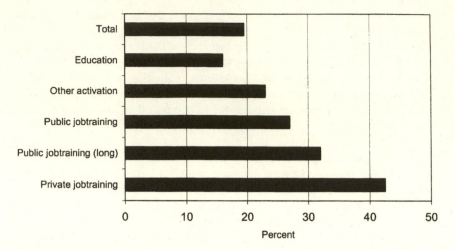

Figure 11   Increase in Economic Self-Dependency after Taking Part in Different Programs. Averages for 1996–98.

Source: Beskæftigelsesministeriet. 2002. Figure 9.

in private job training. For public job training and labour market education the effects are positive, but less significant. These findings are in line with international experience (Martin 2000).

Other studies have been more skeptical about the positive net effects of active programs, often pointing to the existence of significant locking-in effects. For example, the Chairmen of the Economic Council, in their report from December 2002, ascribe about a third of the reduction in unemployment since 1993 to the improved structural performance of the Danish labour market and attributes part thereof to improved labour market policy (*Det økonomiske Råds formandskab* 2002). However, the report gives a rather critical account of the majority of the instruments applied within active labour market policy and points especially to the significant locking-in effects of several measures. Only job training in private firms seems to have large positive net effects and seems to be cost-effective. Job-training in the public sector and many other forms of education have dubious or negative net outcomes for the participants. Against this background the Chairmen propose improvements in the use of active measures (including giving higher priority to job search and private job-training).

Concerning international comparisons, it is difficult to assess the efficiency of active Danish labour market policy in a comparative perspective. Figure 12 gives some data on overall unemployment, long-term unemployment, and youth unemployment for a number of European countries. As indicated by figure 12, Denmark is among the best performers among

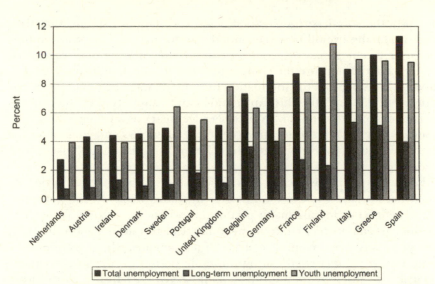

Figure 12   Total Unemployment (unemployed as % of workforce), Long-term Unemployment (long-term unemployed as % of workforce), and Youth Unemployment (unemployed as % of age group) in a number of EU Member States.

Source: European Commission. 2003. *Statistical Annex.* The countries are ranked according to the sum of the three indicators..

the European countries, when assessed by various aspects of unemployment. Also, when measured by other indicators of labour market performance such as lifelong learning, gender pay gaps, and employment rates of older workers, Denmark is among the top performers of the EU Member States.

Labour Market Reforms and the Functioning of the Labour Market

The evaluation findings discussed above have focused on the micro-level. However, the coincidence of the implementation of labour market reforms and the dramatic fall in unemployment has of course stimulated discussions about the extent to which the inflation-free macro-economic upturn can be attributed to the shift in labour market policy in the 1990s. A lowering of the level of wage inflation for a given size of unemployment is taken as an indicator of greater flexibility in the functioning of the labour market. As noted above, the Danish Phillips curve has since 1994 become almost horizontal, indicating a steep fall in structural unemployment.

Of course, there could be a number of factors behind these developments. The changing attitudes of the social partners could be important.

In 1987 the social partners issued a joint declaration stating that they would take the overall macro-economic performance into consideration and therefore negotiate wage increases below the international wage inflation in order to improve the competitiveness of Danish industry. This declaration has since laid the foundation for general wage negotiations. From a theoretical perspective this explanation can be supported by the concept of the "negotiated economy," which sees Denmark as a prime example of a society where a joint conception of the overall targets and constraints for macro-economic development has been established (Nielsen and Pedersen 1991).

Furthermore, Danish wage negotiations have to an increasing degree been decentralized to the level of the individual firms. In the collective agreements covering the major part of the private sector, only 15 percent of the agreements had centrally negotiated wage rates in 2000. In 1989 the share was 34 percent. The share of agreements, which mentions no wage rate at all, increased during the same period from 4 to 20 percent (Dansk Arbejdsgiverforening 2003, table 8.10). According to the well-known Calmfors-Driffill hypothesis, this development could also explain slower wage growth (Calmfors and Driffill 1988).

Combining the conditions for wage negotiations at the central and "decentral" level, one could therefore point to a shift in the norms for wage negotiations. This would imply both a recommendation of wage restraint from actors at the central level and a higher acceptance of the need to keep wages in line with (foreign) competitors at the firm level. Thus, shifts in norms and in the organization of wage formation overruled the potential inflationary effects of a large reduction in unemployment. Following the argument of Smith (1992) this seeming paradox points to the complexity of the forces that determine inflation and to the fragility of the traditional Phillips curve.

In this context one must furthermore emphasize the lowering of the international level of inflation (including wage inflation) as an important factor behind the lower internal pressure for nominal wage increases. In their report from December 2002, the Chairmen of the Economic Council presented a new model of Danish wage formation, which includes wage increases abroad as an important explanatory variable. The estimate for the influence of foreign wage growth implies that Danish nominal wages increase by almost 0.6 percent, when foreign wages increase by 1 percent (Det Økonomiske Råds Formandsskab 2002, 155–6).

A final point worth bringing into the argument concerning the lowering of nominal wage inflation is the difference between the development of nominal and real wages during the last decades (figure 13). The main message is that stable growth in real wages of about 2 percent per year can be reached also at a moderate level of nominal wage growth, as indicated by

Figure 13   Growth in Nominal and Real Hourly Wages for Workers in Manufacturing Industry, 1980–2002.

Source: Statistics Denmark. *Databanks of the Macro-Econometric Model ADAM.*

the experience of the 1990s. The opposite lesson was learned during the years from 1977 to 1986, when increases in nominal wages of 5 to 12 percent resulted in increases in real wages of around zero. An added factor during the period from 1994 onward was the further increase in private consumption made possible by the growth in prices of private homes and the easy access to cheap mortgages. Therefore, the perception of the need to moderate nominal wage growth was strongly supported by the daily experience of the wage earners themselves – slow wage increases and rising living standards could easily go hand in hand.

While one can therefore offer a number of explanations for the shift in the unemployment-inflation nexus on the Danish labour market since the early 1990s, one can also point to evidence that supports the view that *reforms of labour market policy* during the 1990s made a significant contribution to the improved functioning of the labour market. Thus the Chairmen of the Economic Council, who, as indicated above are rather skeptical about the merits of active labour market programs, nevertheless ascribe a little less than half of the reduction in unemployment since 1993 to the improved structural performance of the Danish labour market, and attribute a significant part thereof to the reforms of labour market policy, although they find it difficult to provide a more exact estimate. The Chairmen furthermore point to an increase in the share of unemployed who are actively looking for work, and relate this to the shortening of the period of passive benefits payments and the stricter demands to take part in activation (Det Økonomiske Råds Formandskab 2002, 163–5 and 153).

A study from the Danish National Institute of Social Research in 1998 summed up the evidence from a large-scale evaluation program studying the initial labour market reform of 1994 (Larsen and Langager 1998, 34–6). Concerning the importance of the activation strategy, the analysis showed that:

- The employment goals specified in the individual action plans indicated that there was *considerable planned mobility* among the unemployed;
- Labour market policy seemed to function effectively, in that planned mobility among the unemployed was *greater* in regions where the need for mobility was the highest (because of threats of bottlenecks);
- There were *significant positive employment effects* of both job training and education for unemployed;
- The *effective supply of labour among the insured unemployed seemed to have increased* from 1994 to 1997 probably as a result of the stricter demands made on the unemployed during the second phase of the reform (for instance in relation to the increased demands on the young unemployed).

Concerning the activities directed at the firms, there were indications that the reform has contributed to the absence of bottlenecks since 1994:

- There was a (weak) indication that *the quality of the services of the Public Employment Service to the firms has improved* since the reform, judging by the ability to fill the needs for qualified labour (though there were also examples of labour shortages in the short run).
- The introduction of new forms of placement services (in the form of "open" self-service placements) had – together with surveillance activities and regular contacts with employers – led to *an increase in the transparency of the labour market* and thus improved its function as a system to match demand for and supply of labour; the market share of the Public Employment Service, however, was still rather low.

Thus, on the basis of positive evaluation findings for both the process and the effect of the labour market reforms, there is a well-founded case for arguing that the change in Danish labour market policy in 1993–94 has made a separate contribution to the improved functionality of the Danish labour market in recent years. The absence of labour shortages and wage pressure since 1994, in spite of the fall in unemployment and the strong growth in employment, indicates that the functioning of the labour market has improved.

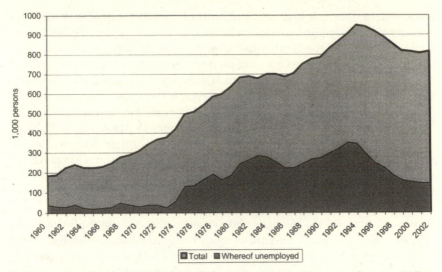

Figure 14   Number of Adults Aged 15–65 Receiving Transfer Income, 1960–2002. Full time equivalents.

Source: Statistics Denmark. *Databanks of the Macro-Econometric Model ADAM.*

Also, as indicated in figure 14, both the number of unemployed and the total number of adult persons receiving transfer income has been falling since 1993. Besides the unemployed, the number of adult persons aged 15–65 years and receiving transfer income includes persons on sickness benefits, invalidity pension, and voluntary early retirement schemes. The number of recipients of transfer income had been steadily rising since the early 1960s, but started falling in 1993. To what extent this is due to the labour market reforms, the economic upswing, or to another of the above-mentioned factors cannot be definitively determined on the basis of the available evidence. However, on the basis of the data in figure 14, it is hard to judge Danish labour market policy during the 1990s as having created social exclusion or having in other ways been destructive to the function-ing of the labour market or the welfare state.

A SMALL STATE PHENOMENON?

Given the interest in the Danish experience in recent years, it is appropri-ate to address the question of the background and uniqueness of the inter-play between labour market flexibility, social security, and active labour market policies that has been spelled out in detail in the previous sections.

As already indicated, the Danish model of flexicurity is not the result of a well-defined grand scheme, but is the outcome of a long historical development. Thus, a high level of worker mobility supported by a low level of employment protection is a long-term feature of the Danish labour market. Already in the September Compromise between the social partners in 1899, the trade unions accepted the employers' right to freely hire and dismiss their workers. Since then, a number of agreements and norms have developed, which put some restrictions on the practices of the employers with respect to dismissals. For example, a revision of the General Agreement between the social partners in 1960 stated that dismissals should not be arbitrary and that suspected unfair dismissals could be assessed by a special tribunal (Kristensen 1997, chapter 10). However, as suggested by the indicators provided by the OECD, the Danish regime concerning dismissals still places relatively few restrictions on employers (OECD 2004, chapter 2).

Similarly, the system for economic support for the unemployed is not new, but has its origin in unemployment insurance funds founded by the trade unions and regulated by law since 1907. The last large reform of the unemployment benefit system took place in 1969, when the state undertook the responsibility for financing the extra costs of unemployment benefits that were caused by increases in unemployment (the principle of financing "at the margin"). Members of unemployment insurance funds would therefore be obliged to pay only a fixed membership contribution, independent of the actual level of unemployment. Furthermore, as shown by Niels Kærgaard and Henrik Hansen (1994), the average compensation rate of unemployment benefits almost doubled during the late 1960s and 1970s. Data from the databank of the macro-econometric model ADAM indicates that the amount of compensations then levelled out at about 60 percent. During the 1990s the average rate of compensation slowly fell to around 50 percent. Finally, as described in detail above, the present system of active labour market policy dates back to programs introduced in 1979, which were given a large-scale overhaul in 1993–94 and subsequent years.

A further observation can be made concerning the foundation for the present model. The relationship between the liberal regime of employment protection and the well-developed state-financed system of unemployment compensation is strongly supported by both trade unions and employers' organizations. This support becomes manifest every time political proposals for restrictions in access to unemployment benefits are put forward. In such cases a strong alliance between trade unions and employers' organizations is formed, whereby the employers' organizations point to the risk of claims for better employment protection in case of deteriorations in the benefit system. An illustration of the strength of this alliance was given in August 2003, when the Minister of Employment, as part of the negotiations for the budget for 2004, put forward a proposal to reduce unemployment benefits by a number of reforms, including the introduction of a longer waiting period for high-income earners. Originally the aim for this and related proposals was to reduce public expenditures by around 100 million Euros. The proposals immediately met with strong resistance from the trade unions, especially in the construction sector. Longer terms of notice were called for, if the rules were to be changed. Then the employers' organizations moved in and supported the views of the trade unions, referring to the lower flexibility that would be the outcome of cutbacks in the benefit-system. At first the protests lead to a reduction in the intended savings to around 20 million Euros, and in the end the Minister had to drop the proposal altogether.

Active labour market policy, the third element in the triangle, is also the outcome of a long tradition of intervention in the functioning of the labour market. When it comes to settling wage negotiations, the September Compromise in 1899 is often taken as the starting point, because this agreement between the social partners also laid the foundation for the state's role as mediator in collective agreements. In 1907 the first law on Unemployment Insurance Funds was passed, and in 1913 a public employment service was established. In 1942 the Ministry of Labour was established as a separate ministry. Thus, labour market policy in Denmark has a long political legacy, although it developed into a distinct policy area only in the mid-1950s (Jørgensen and Larsen 2002, 171–5). Being partly based on a system of private unemployment insurance funds affiliated with the trade unions, and having traditionally a large number of tripartite bodies responsible for labour market training and other institutions, Danish labour market policy is a prime example of the negotiated economy: "The September Compromise provided the foundation for labour market regulation that emphasized negotiation early on, and organizational representation in government committees, boards and commissions has remained strong ever since. The state has learned to delegate authority to the labour market organizations, and they almost always assist in the design of initiatives. The organizations also have a strong sense of "ownership" of the post-war labour market policy" (Jørgensen and Larsen, 2002, 171).

Also the reforms of labour market policy in the 1990s were the outcome of a compromise between the government and the social partners, which was struck in the early 1990s in a special tripartite committee (the Zeuthen Committee). The committee hammered out the foundation for the active and decentralized profile of Danish labour market policy in the following years. The background for the Zeuthen Committee was an increasing dissatisfaction with the general design of labour market policy, which had been the outcome of the previous reform in 1979. Also, the dramatic rise in open unemployment in the early 1990s pushed the need for reform higher on the political agenda. Recent studies of the political processes behind the reform of labour market policy in 1993 and its successors have pointed out a number of factors behind this development (see the various contributions in Madsen and Pedersen 2003b):

- The changes in the discourse whereby active labour market programs were increasingly described as an important instrument for lowering structural employment, and received support from proponents of both workfare-oriented and human-capital-oriented strategies (see also Torfing 2004);
- The need of the newly elected government lead by the Social Democrats to demonstrate its ability to "break the curve" of unemployment;
- Broad public support for reforms, including the various leave schemes;
- While the social partners had a dominant role during the work of the Zeuthen Committee, their function in the subsequent adjustments has been somewhat ambiguous. In some years, especially in 1998, they played an important part, while the government took the lead in other situations, thus shifting between different political channels for decision making (see Winter 2003).

Most observers will agree, however, that corporatist structures play an important role in explaining the development and robustness of the particular Danish version of flexicurity (Mailand and Due 2003; Jørgensen and Larsen 2003). Furthermore, the above observations also fit well with Peter Katzenstein's view on small-state democratic corporatism, in the sense that the Danish version of flexicurity allows for flexible adaptation of the level and composition of employment to a changing international environment with ongoing shifts in the demand for goods and services (Katzenstein 1985). In a slightly different context, Peter Auer (2000) has also pointed to the importance of strong corporatist governance as a factor in explaining the success of a number of small European countries, including Denmark.

With reference to the literature on the varieties of capitalism, Denmark, on the other hand, provides an interesting case of a variety that does not fit well with the idea of regimes clustering around either the liberal market economy (LME) or the coordinated market economy (CME) (Hall and Soskice 2001). From the varieties-of-capitalism perspective, Denmark would be seen as having an unstable configuration of institutions and being on the move in the direction of one of the two clusters. However, when looking at the historical background for the Danish model of flexicurity, the main notion is that of a model developed through a long time period and underpinned by stable institutions and class compromises.

Concerning the question of the relation between the longer-term traits of the Danish labour market and the specific developments of the 1990s,

Table 2   An Overview of the Danish System of "Flexicurity"

	Basic traits of the Danish system of "flexicurity"	Specific developments in the 1990s
Political environment	• Strong corporatist structures • Implicit social contract concerning balance between security and flexibility	• Broad political support for reforms of labour market policies • Acceptance by social partners of need for wage restraint • New government headed by the Social Democrats
Macroeconomic environment	• Changing international economic conditions • Active fiscal policy, but constrained by external balance	• Strong internal demand • Favourable external balance • Lower level of international inflation
Employment situation	• High employment rate (around 75 percent) • Shifting levels of open unemployment • Rising share of persons receiving transfer income	• Significant reduction in both open and gross unemployment • Reduction in structural unemployment
Worker mobility (external numerical flexibility)	• High by international standards	• High by international standards
Employment protection	• Weak	• Weak
Unemployment benefits	• Significant increase in compensation rate with reform in the late 1960s • Cash benefits for non-insured unemployed	• Slow decline in compensation rate, but still high by international standards • Reduction in duration, especially for passive benefits
Active labour market policy (LMP)	• High expenditures on LMP in general • Incremental policy adjustments since 1979	• Decentralized • Individualized • Right and duty to early activation

it is important to note that neither the flexibility-security nexus nor a well-performing employment system (indicated by a high employment rate) is anything new. In spite of the difficult years of the first and the second oil crisis, the post-war economic and social history of Denmark must in most respects be seen as a successful transformation from an agrarian to a modern society, which has kept its place in the top strata of nations on the basis of most indicators of economic and social performance.

Table 2 aims at summing up the basic traits and the more recent developments of the Danish model of flexicurity. The main points from table 2 are that the combination of high employment rates, weak employment protection, and generous economic support for the unemployed has been a characteristic of the Danish employment system since the late 1960s. The features added during the 1990s were, first, a more favourable macroeconomic environment, and second, a more ambitious labour market policy.

The interesting aspect of the most recent Danish development in the 1990s is therefore that Denmark has been able to keep its position as a successful economy at times when the Nordic welfare states were criticized for being ill-adapted to face the pressures from increased internationalization. However, the present situation of the Danish employment system is not without strains and tensions, as we discuss in the upcoming section.

TENSIONS IN THE DANISH EMPLOYMENT SYSTEM

As noted in the introduction, the dramatic fall in open unemployment in Denmark since the mid-1990s has attracted the attention of international observers. In many respects, there are real grounds for this admiration. But on the other hand it may be useful to take a closer look at some of the drawbacks and tensions in the Danish model of flexicurity. Returning to the concept of the golden triangle, a number of problems can be identified in the Danish employment system.

Large Groups Expelled from the Labour Market

The highly dynamic nature of the labour market, while involving frequent shifts between jobs, also implies a continual testing of the productivity of employees. One outcome of these ongoing selection processes is that some workers are gradually expelled from the labour market if they fail to meet the productivity criteria set by employers. The few restrictions placed on employers with regard to lay-offs may of course add to the risk of workers' exclusion from the labour market. There may also be many other (often inter-related), causes of marginalization, such as health problems, lack of formal or informal skills, age, or ethnic background.

Over the forty-year period from 1960 to 1999, the number of full-time persons receiving some form of transfer income increased from about 200,000 to over 800,000, equivalent to about one quarter of the adults aged 15–66 years. This number does not include persons covered by active labour market measures for the unemployed, who accounted for another 87,000 persons in 1999, or for persons above the age of 67 receiving old-

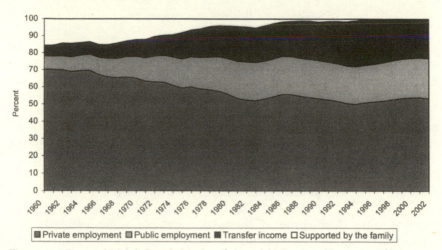

Figure 15   Denmark: Adult Population (15–65 years) by Source of Income, 1960–2002. Full-time equivalents.

Source: Statistics Denmark. *Databanks of the Macro-Econometric Model ADAM.*

age pensions. One price paid for the high level of efficiency of the Danish labour market therefore appears to be that a large number of persons are being gradually squeezed out of the labour market and placed on transfer income.

However, the growth in the number of persons supported by transfer income has not been at the expense of the share of employed adults. Figure 15 shows the distribution of the adult population (aged 15–65 years) from 1960 to 2002 into the number of persons receiving some form of transfer income, the number of adults supported in the family, and the employed (divided into public and private employment). During the last forty years, the proportioon of adult Danes in employment has been around 75 percent. The rise in the share of adults receiving transfer income has therefore been reflected solely in a corresponding decline in the share of adults being supported in the family (mainly as married women).

The second factor of note is that a high level of the population receiving transfer income is not purely a Danish phenomenon. All four Scandinavian countries experienced growth in the share of inactive adults receiving transfer income up to the level of about 25 percent in the late 1990s, indicating that the mechanisms involved cannot be attributed solely to special features of the dynamics of the Danish labour market, but are due also to more general aspects of the interplay between welfare states of the Scandinavian type, modern labour markets, and the business cycle.

Unemployment Benefits and Poverty Traps

Another debate related to the golden triangle has already been foreshadowed. The high replacement rates in the Danish unemployment benefit system increase the risk of financial disincentives, especially for low-income groups (Finansministeriet 2001). While such effects are theoretically plausible, they have been hard to verify empirically as being important in their magnitude. Indeed, the general remedy has been to rely on early and intensive activation measures to counter potential problems related to the disincentives of the unemployment benefit system.

Problems of Active Labour Market Policy

Turning to the third corner of the golden triangle, some further critical points may be made to supplement the discussion of the micro-effects already touched upon. Danish labour market policy has been given a more active profile during a period of economic expansion. In the event of a change in the business cycle, the cost of maintaining the necessary level of ambition to activate the unemployed at an early stage would lead to a sharp increase in public expenditure at a time when revenues would be falling due to the economic downturn. The political pressure to cut active programs could therefore become overwhelming, and would be compounded by Denmark's *de facto* need to comply with EMU budget criteria.

And on the Horizon...

Taking a longer-term perspective, a number of further problems may be identified which could increase the forces that are already causing a rise in the number of persons excluded from the Danish labour market. These include:

- Demographic changes over the coming decades, which imply a growth in the number of older workers, with higher risks of marginalization;
- The rising share of immigrants in the Danish population, with the proportion of persons from non-European countries rising from about 4 percent today to about 10 percent in 2020;
- The increasing wage competition from low-wage countries, also within Europe, which will be strengthened in the event of the accession of a number of Eastern European countries to the European Union

These challenges to the Danish model will place the need to reduce the upward trend in the numbers of persons left outside the golden triangle high on the Danish political agenda in coming years (Nordic Council of Ministers 2000).

CONCLUSION: THE FEASIBILITY OF "FLEXICURITY"
AND THE ROLE OF ALMP

This analysis of the Danish version of flexicurity can be summarized in three steps. First, one can identify a high level of worker mobility (external numerical flexibility) as a structural characteristic of the Danish labour market. An important factor explaining this situation is the liberal regime of employment protection found in the Danish labour market. Second, this high level of numerical flexibility is made acceptable for the trade unions and more broadly within the framework of the traditional value system of a Scandinavian-type welfare state by the development of a state-supported unemployment insurance system supplemented by cash benefits for the uninsured unemployed. These two elements constitute the basic flexibility-security nexus. Third, during the 1990s a more ambitious active labour market policy added both stronger motivation and stronger qualification effects to stimulate the flow of workers between employment and unemployment.

Figure 16 sums up the argument, applying a modified version of figure 6. The dotted ellipse indicates the basic flexibility-security nexus, which combines a high level of numerical external flexibility and a generous system of economic support for the unemployed. In this context the main role of active labour market policy is to support flows from unemployment back to employment by creating motivation effects for all the unemployed in the target groups and by upgrading the skills of the unemployed actually taking part in the programs.

Finally, the positive Danish experience during the 1990s illustrates the importance of the macro-economic environment. Labour market policies alone cannot generate ordinary jobs. Sufficient pressure from the demand side is a prerequisite. On the other hand, once the upturn is underway, active labour market policies play an important role in securing the supply of skilled labour and avoiding bottlenecks.

Thus, the Danish experience points to the economic feasibility of a "hybrid employment system" combining, on the one hand, the traditional virtues of a liberal labour market with few restrictions on employment contracts and, on the other hand, a reasonable level of economic protection for individual wage earners. The Danish model therefore fits the picture of a possible "trade-off" between a very flexible employment relation and a social protection system combined with active labour market programs, which defends individuals from the potential costs of a low-level of employment security. In this respect the model represents a genuine alternative to the common idea of making firms more responsible for employment by developing a high level of individual employment protection at the company level.

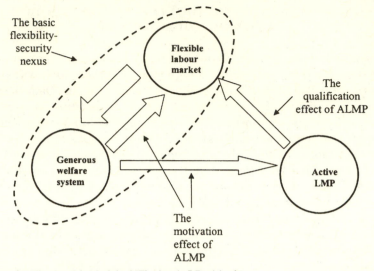

Figure 16   The Danish Model of "Flexicurity" Revisited

However, one should remember that the Danish model of flexicurity is itself the outcome of a long historical process involving a series of negotiations and compromises among the social partners, the evolution of the welfare state, and – in recent years – a gradual development of a more active profile of labour market policy. The model is thus a prime example of the specific Danish version of the negotiated economy. It should therefore be taken as a source of inspiration for new ideas about alternative configurations of flexible labour markets and economic security for the individual. The Danish model of flexicurity is not a simple scheme that is ready for immediate export.

NOTES

The author is Professor of Labour Market Research, Department of Economics, Politics and Public Administration, Aalborg University. The chapter draws on the author's contributions to studies initiated by ILO and by ISSA (see Madsen 2002, 2003). Inspiration is also taken from his work within the EXSPRO-project financed by the European Commission (see Madsen et al. 2001). Thanks for comments go to the editors and the two anonymous reviewers.

1   For a detailed account of the introduction of the three leave schemes, see Compston and Madsen (2001). The schemes were later integrated into

other pieces of legislation (concerning maternity leave and adult education).

2 One should mention that expenses for the Danish Voluntary Early Retirement Pay is included in the figures for Danish passive expenditure and constitutes about 1.7 percent of GDP. However similar schemes, or substitutes for them, are found in other countries. I have therefore chosen to present the aggregate figures for public expenditure on labour market programs

3 The estimated effects in figure 11 are based on a version of the so-called "fixed-effect" method, which applies information about the labour market history of each participant to estimate the effects of participation on subsequent employment and unemployment. Each individual is therefore used as his or her own control-group. Space does not allow for a more elaborate presentation of the Danish debate on the relative sizes of the different effects of active programs and of further effects (like dead-weight and substitution effects) to be included in a full-fledged evaluation of active labour market programs.

Welfare Reform

Renewal or Deviation?

PETER ABRAHAMSON

Welfare states are currently being changed around the globe. Denmark is no exception. Depending on one's method of approach and the specific case, such changes may be conceptualized as welfare states being either reformed, recalibrated, recast, or retrenched – or simply renewed (Clasen 2000; Ferrera and Rhodes 2000; Ferrera, Hemerijck, and Rhodes 2000; Kuhnle and Alestalo 2000; Leibfried and Obinger 2000; Pierson 1994, 1996). It has also been common to characterize current changes as a crisis for the welfare state, as seen in Joakim Palme (1999, 13); yet others, such as Duane Swank (2000, 114) and Miko Kautto et al. (1999, 2001), find no cause for alarm. But which labels are most appropriate in the case of Denmark? Given its changes, does Denmark still belong to the Scandinavian family of nations? The overall conclusion of the very impressive conference, *L'État-providence nordique,* held in December 2003 was that the Scandinavian countries have all gone through the crisis of the 1990s pretty much intact (see Strobel 2003). However, a somewhat more skeptical view is presented elsewhere (Abrahamson 2003) on Scandinavia in general. This chapter concentrates on developments in Denmark.

Within the framework of Peter Hall (1986, 1993), one can distinguish between first-, second-, and third-order changes. First-order changes refer to incremental and quantitative changes (e.g., a slight reduction or increase in benefit level or benefit period). Second-order changes refer to institutional changes, qualitative changes (e.g., changes in financing a scheme from public purse to social partner contributions or vice versa). A change of the third-order indicates a change of policy goals or policy objectives (e.g., when the intent of measures toward the unemployed changes from providing for them while unemployed to making them employable through forced participation in activation schemes). This tripartite scheme is applied here to the Danish case as it has developed during the 1990s and the early 2000s.

This chapter seeks to answer what might be called the question of the direction of change. Has change moved Denmark away from what has become the Scandinavian model of welfare? Or is it a necessary adjustment of the same model, allowing it to stay true to its principles, as suggested in general terms by Kees van Kersbergen (2000, 31): "The paradox is that in order for the welfare state to survive, it must be transformed"?

THE SCANDINAVIAN WELFARE MODEL:
AN IDEAL-TYPICAL ASSESSMENT

Within the social sciences it is now common practice to divide the world of welfare states into various models or regimes. These models reflect the fact that the commonality of a welfare state, the state's obligation toward the well-being of its citizens – the institutionalization of social citizenship – has come about in different ways. The first distinction, chronologically, was that between residual and institutional welfare states; the former were seen as immature or developing, expected to develop into institutional ones. The independent variable was the total amount of social expenditure: the more developed, the more institutional, the more expensive – or so the argument ran (Wilensky and Lebaux 1958). This view was challenged, however, by Richard Titmuss (1972), who claimed that the residual and the institutional models appeared simultaneously with a third model, which he named the "achievement-performance" model of social welfare. He also qualified the definition of the institutional model by adding the concept "redistributive" to its merits. This three-dimensional understanding of the post–World War II welfare state went on rather unnoticed by welfare researchers until the publication of Esping-Andersen's *The Three Worlds of Welfare Capitalism* (1990). In this influential book Titmuss's models were renamed according to the political ideologies promoting them: the residual model was named the liberal regime; the achievement-performance model was named the conservative-corporatist regime; and the institutional-redistributive model was named the social democratic regime. Esping-Andersen's claim is that this differentiation of welfare state experience covers all cases, or can meaningfully be applied to any welfare society, be it Asian, South-American, or other (1996, 1997). Others have challenged this view and have developed additional models or regimes, such as a rudimentary model to cover the Latin-Rim in Southern Europe (Leibfried 1992); a Confucian to cover South-east Asia (Jones 1993); a post-communist to cover Eastern Europe (Deacon 1993), and a labourist to cover the antipodes (Castles and Mitchell 1990; for a general overview, see Abrahamson 1999).

Table 1   Four Ideal Typical Welfare State Models

	Southern	*Continental*	*Atlantic*	*Scandinavian*
Criteria for entitlement	Need (contribution)	Contribution	Need	Right
Political ideology	Christian democratic	Conservative	Liberal	Social democratic
Central institution	Family	Voluntary organizations	Market	State
Extent	Limited	Encompassing	Limited	Encompassing
Financing	Voluntary organizations	Social partners	State	State
Demarcation of entitled population	Member of family and local community	Affiliated with the labour market	Citizen	Citizen

Despite these differences of view, the welfare state literature is in agreement about clustering the Scandinavian states within the same regime or model, despite naming them differently (Scandinavian, Nordic, Social Democratic, institutional, encompassing, etc.) To summarize the characteristics of the Scandinavian welfare model, table 1 above indicates differences among four models according to their central dimensions:

In Scandinavia the criteria for welfare entitlements are based on (Constitutional) rights; not on a selective assessment of needs as in the Atlantic model, or on the basis of contribution as in the Continental model. Entitlement is then based on membership of different communities from model to model. In both the Scandinavian and the Atlantic models, legal residence is the primary criterion – being a member of society, a citizen – while affiliation with the labour market is the criterion in the Continental model, and belonging to a family or local community is the criterion in the South. The political ideology promoting a particular Scandinavian way is social-democratic, whereas the Southern model, for example, reflects a Christian Democratic ideology. The dominant societal institution responsible for welfare provision in Scandinavia is the state; not the market as in the Atlantic model, nor voluntary organizations as in the Continental one, nor the family as in the South. Both the Scandinavian and the Continental welfare model are expected to be extensive, appropriating many resources, whereas both the Atlantic and the Southern models are expected to be cheaper. Small or large, welfare financing comes from different sources: ideally both the Scandinavian and the Atlantic model are financed out of general taxation; the Continental one is financed out of contributions from the social partners of the labour market; and the Southern model is financed by collections and donations from the religious organizations.

In other words, and with a few qualifications, the Scandinavian welfare model :has the following characteristics: it is universal and (therefore) expensive; it is tax-financed; it is based on public provision of both transfers and services; it emphasizes personal social services vis-à-vis transfers; it provides high quality provision; it has high compensation rates and is therefore egalitarian; and it is based on a high degree of labour market participation for both sexes. Palme (1999, 15) summed it up thus: "The Nordic model is about ... universalism, generous benefits, social citizenship rights, dual-earner model, active labour market policies, and extensive social services." Duane Swank also included tax policies and full employment: "The Nordic countries are generally characterized by publicly funded and administered programmes that have comprehensive and universal coverage and relatively egalitarian benefit structures. Traditionally, they have been supported by redistributive general taxes and strong work orientations, in terms of both programmatic emphasis on work and economic policies that stress full employment" (Swank 2000, 85). The question, of course, is: do these characteristics still hold?

CHANGES IN DENMARK DURING THE 1990S

Social citizenship is often equated with social rights; but in the Danish case we are reminded that citizenship entails both rights and *obligations*. The general trend is to emphasize and clarify the obligations that citizens have with regard to claiming social rights. This was coined the "something for something" principle by the former Minister of Social Affairs Aase Olesen and is still valid (Ministry of Social Affairs 1990, 1991). The principle has been institutionalized with the so-called *activation* approach to social policies in general. Participation in active labour market policy measures, or workfare schemes, has become mandatory if continued financial support is to be expected. Also, the requirement for proof of active job-seeking behaviour has been strengthened.

Another tendency is one toward greater *choice*: free hospital choice in the public secondary health care system, and the possibility of choosing private/market solutions by opening up commercial segments in hospitals and clinics. Predating this trend, free choice of GPs was introduced; and free choice of primary school *except for immigrants!* In some municipalities, immigrants are subject to quota systems that reallocate their children geographically in order to obtain a more "even" spread across municipal schools. The emphasis on free choice echoes elements of a neo-liberal approach to social citizenship; but it has been implemented in a universal regime.

A third tendency is a stronger emphasis on *citizens' involvement* in decision making and administration of social services such as childcare institutions, primary schools, or elder care. Everything else being equal, this indicates a strengthening of Danish political citizenship. A childcare guarantee was issued by the government; but the responsibility for it lies with the municipalities (and a considerable part of them have not complied – or have not been able to). This is an example of the decentralization process being challenged by the central government, and has led some observers to talk about introducing a process of *re*centralization (Hegland 1994). Various leave schemes have been introduced and then reduced because of their popularity – and by 2002 had disappeared again! Yet, taken together, their introduction indicates a strengthening of social citizenship rights. Pension rights have moved toward the performative model because of a strengthening of occupational pension schemes. Such arrangements are currently, albeit slowly, being extended to blue-collar workers. Denmark has experienced a continuation of the so-called *experimentation* strategy, which means a diversification of social services with greater involvement of civil societal institutions and actors such as volunteers, self-help groups, charities, and businesses. This strategy implies a *complication* of social rights. Finally, the campaign for corporate responsibility (the "social responsibility of companies") and the quest for more social clauses in industrial relations agreements point toward the performative model of social rights.

This development is not unique to Denmark. Reporting on the situation in Sweden during the 1990s, the Welfare Commission found that benefits had been cut, the universal element had been reduced regarding pensions, and services had been somewhat privatized. The middle classes are now buying in services from the market, and the lower income segments have to rely more on informal help from relatives (Palme et al. 2003). A similar situation exists in Finland, as Maija Sakslin (2002) has shown. She maintains that the link between contributions and entitlements has been strengthened, and that solidarity has thereby been weakened.

Welfare Reform Under Social Democratic–Led Government 1993–2001

A new series of Social Democratic–led governments came into power in 1993 and stayed in office until late 2001. The major changes they introduced are indicated below:

• Leave schemes with the labour market reform of 1994 (childcare leave; education leave; sabbatical leave);

- New *Social Assistance Act* of 1997 (split into: the *Active Social Policy Act* and the *Social Service Act* plus the *Social Provision Administration and Legal Guarantee Act*);
- Stronger financial and ideological support to the voluntary sector;
- The campaign: "The social responsibility of companies."

With the labour market reform of 1994, a couple of experimental leave schemes were made permanent. The *education leave* was a scheme enabling insured workers twenty-five years of age and older to take time out – for at the least one week, at the most one year – to participate in some kind of recognized education, receiving benefits equivalent to unemployment benefits (UB). In 1994, 80,000 people and in 1995, 53,000 people took advantage of this opportunity. The *childcare leave* was a scheme allowing parents with children up to eight years of age to take time out to care for their children for up to one year and at least for thirteen weeks. The scheme is open to everyone affiliated with the labour market, whether insured or on social assistance. Because of its popularity, the benefits were reduced from 100 percent of UB to first 70 and then to 60 percent of UB. During childcare leave, children cannot occupy a space in a public child-care institution. In 1994, 47,000 people and in 1995, 80,000 people took this leave. Finally, the *sabbatical leave* was a time-limited experiment running until 1999, which allowed employed insured people twenty-five and older to take up to one year, and at least thirteen weeks, out from the labour market, provided they could find a substitute for themselves, to fill their spot during that period of time. When benefits were reduced to 60 percent of UB in 1994, 13,000 and in 1995 3,000 people went on sabbatical leave (Andersen, Appeldorn, and Weise 1996).

These schemes were meant to increase circulation in the labour market between unemployment and employment; but as the schemes became increasingly popular the government feared that they might create bottlenecks by reducing unemployment too much, and the schemes were therefore made less attractive. The childcare leave must be viewed as a universal right, while the other two leave schemes were reserved for workers belonging to the social insurance system, and thus represent a performative trend.

With the new *Social Assistance Act* of 1997 the active labour market/workfare strategy was strengthened, indicating a stronger emphasis on the *obligation* of the claimants to participate in some activity they arranged or were referred to by the municipality. The majority of the claimants viewed this positively insofar as they claimed to be quite satisfied with the offer received; yet many also described it as a means of social control. This development is a demonstration of the government's focus on marginalized and socially excluded people; this targeting is a clientistic trait.

The government, through the Ministry of Social Affairs, has for some time encouraged the *voluntary sector* to be more engaged in fighting social problems at various levels and in various ways. The encouragement has taken the form of financial support for voluntary organizations. With its emphasis on new partnerships between public and private sectors, this trend is intended to strengthen the welfare-mix approach to social policy. This was expressed very clearly in a government document entitled *Social Trends 1999*: "The discussion of private-public partnerships is hence part of the debate on how our welfare society can be renewed and modernized so that it lives up to the demands and needs of the future" (Ministry of Social Affairs 1999, 95). The same can be said for the campaign for corporate citizenship: "The social responsibility of companies." The government was trying to involve businesses more in fighting the marginalization and social exclusion that companies had, in the first place, produced (Holt 1998). This is clearly a performative trend in the development of social citizenship rights in Denmark.

With respect only to transfers, H. Hansen (1998) has indicated changes concerning the unemployment benefit system (social insurance) and early retirement:

The duration of the benefit period was shortened from seven to five years in 1996 ... Active labour market measures will no longer prolong the benefit period.

Substantial changes were implemented in 1996 for young persons under 25 years of age. Unemployed young persons with no or only little formal education will be offered education after six months of unemployment unless they have a solid work record, in which case they will be offered job training. The benefits for those participating in education are 50 percent of maximum UB; those in job training will receive maximum UB ...

From 1997 the working condition was 52 weeks within the last three years, up from 26 weeks, before benefits could be received.

Unemployed who are over 50 years when their UB rights expire can continue receiving benefits until the age of 60 years if they continue membership of the UB scheme; at that time they will qualify for the early retirement scheme (*efterløn*). For unemployed over 60 years the duration of the benefit period is only two and a half years as a maximum, and there are no active labour market measures for this group...

The temporary schemes for early retirement from the labour market [concerning people between 50 and 60] were closed for new entrants from February 1996. (Hansen 1998, 46, 53).

The tightening of eligibility rules for receiving unemployment benefits witnessed here must be interpreted as a reduction of social rights with a simultaneous strengthening of the obligations that unemployed people have to actively change their situation.

Finally, user rates are quietly becoming a part, albeit still a small part, of Danish welfare policy. From 1993 to 1997 they were increased by 20 percent to 36 billion DKK; within the area of education they increased with 50 percent to 9.3 billion DKK; in health care they doubled to three billion DKK (Information 1998).

Summing up Policy Changes during the 1990s in Health Care, Pensions, and Employment

Two closely related principal issues have developed during the last years of the twentieth century. Since responsibility was transferred from the state to the individual citizens, an ongoing individualization of the systems can be detected. Indicators of increased private responsibility can, to a greater or lesser extent, be found within all the three parts of the welfare system. In relation to the increased degree of private responsibility, a number of the universal public schemes have been supplemented by private insurance-based initiatives that share the common feature of covering only those who obtain labour market participation. Within the field of health care services, the rising number of contracted private health care insurance schemes illustrates these tendencies. Employer-paid Private Hospital Insurance especially has started to grow dramatically and continues to rise. Furthermore, the free choice of hospitals could be seen to reflect individualization tendencies, since the patient has the right, but not the duty, to pick a hospital of his or her own choice.

The above-mentioned characteristics can also be found within the pensions system. Even though the public old-age pension and the anticipatory pension scheme represent and remain universal schemes, labour market pensions, and to some extent civil service retirement payments, contain elements of labour market participation-based insurance. For instance, the fact that the size of civil service retirement payments depends both on the length of employment as a civil servant and on the salary received can be seen in this light. Also, the voluntary early retirement pay scheme clearly contains the insurance element, especially after the introduction of the earmarked voluntary early retirement contribution that has to be paid as a precondition to entering the scheme. In the labour market as a whole, the labour market pensions represent a sort of mandatory insurance, like a supplementary pension for labour market participants to the public old age pension.[1]

Even though the division into the social assistance system (non-insured) and the social insurance system (insured) represents the labour market participation dependency, it is within the area of the dual unemployment system that the first of the two tendencies is most clearly reflected. In the late 1970s – in the shadow of high unemployment rates – the assumption that unemployment was a public and not an individual responsibility started to change, along with the introduction of the active line in labour market policies. The "give and take" perspective that is the essence of the "right and duty to activation" principle can be seen as a consequence of this increased individual responsibility, in that it is up to the individual to improve his or her qualifications by participating in the different activation measures.

What impact, then, could these trends be said to have for basic notions of social security in Denmark? The labour market participation-based insurance initiatives (private health care insurance, for instance) as well as labour market pensions, may lead to a division of the population into those who obtain a job, and thereby participate in the labour market, and those who do not. A consequence of this may be that groups who have an unsteady labour market connection, if any at all, are excluded. The demand for labour market participation in the insurance-based elements in this way makes state-financed, universal schemes such as old age pensions (and to a lesser extent the public health care reimbursement scheme) a sort of last social security safety net for those who have nowhere else to go. This reflects the "unemployment model," in which the social assistance system functions as a kind of subcategory to the social insurance system. In sum, even though the Danish welfare model remains by and large a universal welfare state, a move toward a system based more on insurance and labour market participation can be detected. If this development continues, groups who already experience some kind of marginalization from the labour market will have a more detrimental position in the future (Abrahamson, Kambskard, and Wehner 2002).

The Development in Numbers

A few statistics may illuminate the overall development as it has taken place in Denmark recently.

Table 2 takes stock of the value of transfers paid to the unemployed, the sick, and the aged. Since 1995, the tendency has been clearly in the direction of less coverage. Benefits have been reduced in all risk categories to the magnitude of 3 percentage points, which can be considered modest, yet significant. The table also demonstrates the huge differences in coverage offered through the various programs. For those who are members of an unemployment insurance fund, compensation will keep them out of income poverty since they can expect to receive the equivalent of nearly two-thirds of an average income, which is the same for sickness pay and pension with a record of full contribution. It is equally obvious that single social assistance recipients are by any standard income-poor, their income being about 45 percent of an average income; pensioners who have to rely

Table 2   Compensation Rates* in Denmark 1995–2001, Various Risks

	1995	1996	1997	1998	1999	2000	2001
Unemployment insurance, single, no children	67	66	65	64	65	64	64
Social assistance, single, >30 years, no children	47	46	45	44	44	44	44
Social assistance, single, >30 years, one child	77	77	76	74	71	68	73
Illness, single	67	67	65	64	65	64	63
Old age, single	65	64	64	63	62	62	62

* Calculated as the relative value of the provision in percent of a production worker's average net disposable income December
Source: NOSOSCO. 2003.

Table 3   Activity and Employment Rates in 1995–2003, Men and Women, 15–66 Years of Age, Third Quarter

	1995	1996	1997	1998	1999	2000	2001	2002	2003
Activity rate (%)	78.0	78.1	79.0	78.8	79.6	78.7	78.8	78.1	78.4
Employment rate (%)	72.4	72.6	73.9	74.0	74.9	74.6	75.0	74.3	74.0
Unemployment rate (%)	–	9.2	8.1	6.9	5.8	5.3	5.3	5.1	5.8

Source: Statistics Denmark, Data Bank. 2003.

only on the old age pension receive compensation of around 50 percent of an average income, so they are also to be considered income-poor (NOSOSCO 2003). For *Social Tendencies 2003* the rate of risk of income poverty, as the official European Union now defines the 60 percent of median disposable income, was calculated in 2001 at 9 percent of the Danish population, while the old measure using the 50 percent cut-off line gave 5 percent (*Social Årsrapport 2003*, 29).

These are moderate levels by any comparison, but what is interesting in this respect is that most of the poor are people who rely on welfare state provisions for their livelihood. The welfare state is, hence, producing income poverty.

The previous government, which took office in 1993 when unemployment was at a record high in Denmark (at 13 per cent of the workforce), was very happy and proud to see that in 2000 it was down to 5 percent. Since then it has gone up half a percentage point, but it is still moderate, at around or just under 6 percent. The former government attributed this positive development to its emphasis on activation, which has been taken to be able to bring the unemployed back into the labour market. Elsewhere I have discussed that this is not the case (van Oorschot and Abrahamson 2003). What has occurred, rather, is a reclassification of people. Instead of being labelled "unemployed" they have been labelled "on leave" or "in activation." Further, as can be seen from table 3, despite the decrease in registered unemployment, the activity rate of the population has stayed unchanged since the mid-1990s: 78 percent of the Danish population aged 15–66 are affiliated with the labour market, and the employment rate in the third quarter of 2003 was at the same level as in 1997, namely 74 percent. As a consequence of this, we have calculated the rate of persons of working age *not in ordinary employment*, which we find to be a better indicator of *real* unemployment. In Denmark in 2002, the not-in-ordinary-employment rate was 9.2 percent, which was 50 percent higher than the registered unemployment rate (*Social Årsrapport 2003*, 48).

In relation to the national economy (GDP) the situation was quite stable during the same period: Denmark devotes about 30 percent of its total economy to maintaining social citizenship of some sort. Measured per capita, it tends to spend more and more; but social expenditure has been a relatively declining part of total public spending since 1979 (Statistics Denmark 2003). It is with respect to the financing of social expenditure that Denmark experiences the most substantial changes in regard to social citizenship; a declining share is financed by central government, and more and more is being paid by the employees themselves, as well as the municipalities and counties. In addition to indicating a trend toward further decentralization of financial responsibilities, this shift in burden also indicates a turn toward a performative model of social citizenship.

Changes are not Big Bang, but They All Go in the Same Direction

In summing up the Danish case, one can identify numerous first-order changes all leading in the same direction: toward less security. Second-order changes were noticeable in regard to pensions and health care (individualization, marketization, and pluralization), as well as a third-order change regarding unemployment measures (activation obligation). Both these second- and third-order changes can be said to have moved Denmark further away from the ideal-typical Scandinavian welfare state; hence, perhaps, making it converge more toward what might be labelled a European social model, as is also the case in the other Scandinavian countries (Abrahamson 2003; Abrahamson forthcoming).

THE MOST RECENT DEVELOPMENTS: TWO YEARS WITH A BOURGEOIS GOVERNMENT[2]

In November 2001 Denmark changed government, indicating a move from a centre-left to a right-wing government (the former headed by the Social Democratic party with then prime minister Poul Nyrup Rasmussen,

Table 4 Development of Total Social Expenditure in Denmark 1990–2002, Relative and Absolute

	1990	1991	1992	1993	1994	1995	1996	1997	1998	1999	2000	2001	2002
Social expenditure/GDP in %	28.9	29.9	30.3	31.9	32	31.3	30.6	29.6	29.1	28.9	27.6	28.2	29.1
Social exp. in fixed prices 1997 = 100	80	85	87	92	100	100	100	100	101	102	102	104	106

Source: Statistics Denmark. 2003.

Table 5 Development of Financing of Total Social Expenditure in Denmark 1990–2002, Relative in Percent

	1990	1991	1992	1993	1994	1995	1996	1997	1998	1999	2000	2001	2002
State	49.3	48.7	49.4	49.7	43.1	39.3	37	34.5	32.4	30.4	28.6	27.6	26.4
Counties and municipalities	36.6	38.4	38.1	37.6	34.6	35.1	35.6	36.8	38.4	39.1	39.8	39.7	40
Employers	8.4	7.7	7.4	7.4	10.8	10.9	11	9.4	9.5	9.9	9.8	10	10.3
Employees	5.7	5.3	5	5.1	11.4	14.7	16.4	19.3	19.7	20.5	21.8	22.7	23.3

Source: Statistics Denmark. 2003.

and the latter headed by Anders Fog Rasmussen). The most recent government is a minority government consisting of the Liberal and the Conservative parties, and it obtains its parliamentary majority through the support of the Danish People's Party, a xenophobic, anti-immigrant, right-wing political party. This government has announced that it is committed to enhancing employment, a goal that has had a least a semantic consequence with the renaming of the Ministry of Labour to the Ministry of Employment. Per Kongshøj Madsen judges that the change *is* indeed only semantic (2003, 9); in what follows this is verified.

Labour Market Reform: "More People in Work"

The success of commitment to employment is measured by calculating recipients' degree of self-supportiveness about a year and a half after they have been through an activation offer (i.e., measuring to what extent former unemployed people, after having received "help" in the form of workfare from the welfare state, are able to provide for themselves). Technically, a cohort of recipients that received an activation offer in week

Table 6   Consequences of Receiving Various Active Provisions in Week 9, 2002, Calculated in Week 25, 2003

	Private job training	Public job training	Municipal activation	Special activation	Education
Self-supportive	59	25	24	36	32
Ordinary education	1	1	4	1	4
Activation	9	32	37	16	27
Unemployment	22	31	37	16	27
Outside labour market	1	3	0	2	1
Sickness	8	8	4	10	9
Total	100	100	100	100	100
N		2.53	11.438	39.887	5.081	30.25

Source: Social Årsrapport (Social Tendencies) 2003, 60.

nine in 2002 was checked in week twenty-five in 2003. The same calculations were made for recipients of passive measures (transfer payments only).

The findings, given in table 6, were that job training with a private employer yielded the best results with regard to achieving self support: 59 percent of those who went through private job training in 2002 were self-supportive in 2003. In contrast, only 25 percent of those who received public job training, or municipal activation in 2002 were self-supportive in 2003. Of those in special activation and education in 2002 approximately a third were self-supportive in 2003. Unfortunately, most clients do not receive the offers that tend to produce the best results; relatively few people take private job training, while the large majority receive public job training or municipal activation, neither of which apparently does much to get them to a situation where they are able to support themselves. So, the overall effect of the heavy emphasis on activation proves to be very small. Education does rather well in comparison, and it is interesting, but also sad, to notice that the present government has down-prioritized this provision (Social Årsrapport 2003, 59–60).

For purposes of comparison, the same calculations were made for recipients of passive provisions, as shown in table 7. Not surprisingly, unemployed members of an unemployment insurance fund do better than various categories of social assistance recipients. Of those unemployed in 2002, 45 percent of the insured were self-supporting in 2003, while only, at best 30 percent, or 20 to 22 percent of social assistance claimants, had obtained self-sufficiency in 2003. A relatively large share of the cohort were on sickness benefits – nearly one out of ten – in 2003. It can be con-

Table 7   Consequences of Receiving Various Passive Provisions in Week 9, 2002, Calculated in Week 25, 2003

	Insured unemployed	Social assistance unemployed	Social assistance other	Introduction provision
Self-supportive	45	30	22	20
Ordinary education	1	5	2	2
Activation	10	15	14	10
Unemployment	28	46	54	68
Outside labour market	7	0	0	0
Sickness	9	4	8	0
Total	100	100	100	100
N	144.625	19.879	73.04	11.193

Source: Social Årsrapport (Social Tendencies) 2003, 61.

cluded that, except for the very few who go through private job training, people were doing equally well without activation. It had no or very little effect with respect to bringing unemployed people to a situation of self-support.

Another priority of the present government, as well as one pursued by the former one, is the creation of a "spacious" labour market, which means a labour market spacious enough to hold people that are not considered 100-percent effective and productive. One means of achieving such a spacious labour market has been the creation of so-called flexi-jobs. They are jobs under regular conditions of pay but adjusted to the ability of the individual who has a chronic reduction of work capacity. If one becomes unemployed after having been employed in a flexi-job, one is *not* entitled to unemployment benefits; instead one is eligible for a so-called redundancy benefit (*ledighedsydelse*). It is set at 91 percent of unemployment benefits. The number of people receiving redundancy pay can be seen as an indicator of the degree of spaciousness of the labour market: if there are few people on redundancy pay the labour market must be considered spacious, since it has room for those wanting to work. Unfortunately, the number of people on redundancy pay has increased dramatically: from March 2002 to March 2003 it more than quadrupled. During the same period of time the registered unemployment increased by 9 percent, while unemployment for those waiting for a flexi-job increased 408 percent (*Social Årsrapport 2003*, 65–8.) By these measures the government has failed to create a spacious labour market.

This is very disappointing since the government announced its intention to enhance employment in general through its reform entitled "More people in work!" Here it forecast that employment should have increased by 84,000 people by 2010, (which, of course, remains to be seen). A number of changes were introduced: a liberalization of labour exchanges in the form of contracting out of a number of the services provided; a reduction in the number of "tools" (i.e., activation measures including a reduction in the possibility of receiving an education offer, which, as mentioned above, has had a reasonable success rate), The general idea is that it must pay to work and that everybody should be eligible for work. This is being accomplished by means of tougher rules for taking any job, (e.g., the demand for geographical mobility has been increased: up to four hours a day must be accepted). Social assistance for couples and for people under twenty-five years of age has been reduced after six months of unemployment. New candidates can no longer qualify for maximum unemployment benefits. Sticks and carrots have been distributed very unevenly: all the carrots have gone to employers, who are now able to employ unemployed people with a wage subsidy, while the sticks are banging the unemployed (*Social Årsrapport* 2003, 51–6).

Changes in Social Assistance: Start Allowance

In line with the previous government, the present one has found it imperative to reduce transfer payments to refugees and immigrants as a way of motivating them to seek employment and self-support. Ethnic minorities have a high level of unemployment in Denmark; roughly double the average for the whole population, and the former Social Democratic–led government had already enacted the so-called introductory provision in 1999. It was meant for people who had recently arrived in the country, and payments were about two thirds of regular social assistance. However, the government was compelled to withdraw the act after complaints were filed against Denmark for discrimination and non-compliance with international conventions. Nevertheless, the current government has succeeded in creating legislation that is not formally discriminatory. It is called the *start allowance*, and it can be given to people who are otherwise eligible for social assistance but who have not been residing in Denmark for seven of the last eight years. So, now one has had to have been living in Denmark for at least eight years in order to claim social assistance; if not, one can claim the start allowance. The start allowance provides claimants with somewhere between 45 and 64 percent of social assistance and is equivalent to state student grants (*Statens Uddannelsesstøtte*). Most recipients are refugees, and the ethnic composition of recipients is highly biased toward people from "less-developed countries."

A number of poverty thresholds have been calculated for 2003: 50 percent and 60 percent net disposable income, a standard budget, a discount budget, and a basic living level. In all cases start allowance were lower than any threshold, and that was the case for all family types (*Social Årsrapport* 2003, 112–14). This social policy invention is deliberately producing income poverty at a level not seen before in Denmark.

The Terminology of Freedom

Claus Olsen and Idamarie Svendsen (2003) have analysed the recent changes regarding transfer payments within the Danish welfare state and concluded that all changes "refer to what can be labelled 'the terminology of freedom.'" In comments about acts or government programs, concepts such as self-determination, personal development, resources, or "putting the individual at centre stage" dominate. These terms are evidence of what Lone Moritz (2003) sees as a change from the family principle to the labour market principle within social assistance legislation. Earlier there was a holistic approach, in which the situation of the individual was interpreted with reference to the environment in the form of family, labour market, or housing; when material and psychological dimensions were concerned, on the other hand, the focus was more on the history and past of the client, the new focus is now more on the present and future situation, emphasizing labour market ability and willingness within a contractual environment that ties help to certain benchmarks. Olsen and Svendsen (2003, 99) are very critical toward such contractual thinking, which presupposes an equal relationship between client and social worker, which, of course, never has existed and never will. "This kind of norms carries with it a risk of a downplayed, invisible and in principle unlimited power domination: through a dramatic and obscure number of legal rules, through lack of stipulation of limits for what is relevant the legal judgement, and through omission of relating to the reality (power, financial matters, security, distribution), substituted by a general consensus about the general, ethically loaded starting point." They conclude that "the ethical formulations and procedural rules may perhaps express a liberation of the individual for some, but simultaneously they seem to produce rules of control and sanctions toward others" (2003, 100).

Changes in Family Policy

The chairman of the Danish Social Policy Association, Per Schultz Jørgensen, has summed up the development with regard to family policy since the new government took office. Generally, he sees the government's obligation not to increase taxation and the introduction of the start allowance as leading to a deterioration in the conditions for many families.

Specifically, he considers the change regarding parental leave as reduction in social rights for families. Earlier, a combination of parental leave and childcare leave gave the possibility of caring for children for up to two and a half years, while the introduction of the new *Parental Leave Act* has meant that childcare leave has been abolished. As a consequence, the effective period of leave has been reduced. Furthermore, Jørgensen emphasizes the lack of gender equality due to the lack of a specific period assigned to fathers; there is no "use or lose" element in the parental leave scheme. Within day care, a clearly liberal element has been included with the introduction of the possibility of financial subsidies to parents who decide to care for the children themselves. This is conditional upon the parent leaving the labour market and not, of course, utilizing public day care in any form. Finally, in regard to policies toward "exposed children and youth" Jørgensen (2003, 137) concludes that they are a continuation of earlier approaches but with "a particular twist in a bourgeois, liberal direction."

Continued Liberalization and Privatization

The present government has continued its efforts to involve market and civil societal actors more in social policy. In Frederiksborg county north of Copenhagen, contracting out of services has tripled since 1997 (MetroXpress 2003a) and as a consequence the counties are now employing fewer people; the situation is similar within Roskilde county, west of the capital (MetroXpress 2003b). The counties are responsible for health care and this is where marketization has taken place alongside elder care, which is the responsibility of the municipalities.

Volunteering has also been emphasized by the present government as it had been by the previous one. Bjarne Lenau Henriksen (2003) sees a tendency toward exposing and accepting voluntary work within social work to a degree where it, more and more, is given the responsibility for solving social problems. During the last ten years this has happened through a process of professionalization, but that has changed the identity of volunteering from how it was originally understood. If the voluntary organizations are successful in this transformation, they may lose their potential as a critical counterforce and provocative alternative to the established help system, as well as their ability to be path-breaking and border-crossing. Instead they will develop into publicly driven and controlled private organizations.

FUTURE CHANGES?
THE WELFARE COMMISSION

Of course, no one knows the future, and two years of government is a short time span from which to extrapolate trends. Yet, some qualified guesses can be made from existing knowledge. First, what we have seen above all points in the same direction: changes, small and incremental as they may be, are unanimously toward more performative and liberal elements. Put together, they push Denmark away from the ideal-typical Scandinavian model outlined above, and there is no reason to suppose that the immediate future will bring about a change in that respect.

Second, the government has formed a Welfare Commission, which is expected to conclude its recommendations for the structuring of the future Danish welfare state in late 2005. From its mandate (*Kommisorium*) we learn that the likelihood of greater numbers of elderly people in the future will lead to a pressure for more welfare state expenditure. A similar pressure can also be expected because of the general increase in standard of living in society. However, it is then stated as a premise that "taxes cannot be increased since they already are at a high level." The consequences will therefore be "that the welfare systems to a higher degree must be targeted to those groups most in need of help, and the policies must support the greatest possible labour market participation" (Ministry of State 2003). From these premises the commission will investigate the possibilities of financing welfare provisions into 2020, given unchanged tax levels, and will consider various ways of financing the provisions. Furthermore, the government wants to learn how other countries have solved similar problems.

The mandate lays out a straightforward liberal program: "no more taxes" and the targeting of welfare provisions are taken right off the page of a textbook manual for liberal politics. The government also wants to learn from other countries, which necessarily will bring experiences of retrenchment and liberalization, since that has been the dominating picture. Furthermore, the commission, which is stated to be "broadly composed of knowledgeable experts" (Ministry of State 2003) actually consists of eight economists and a lawyer, which is as narrow a range as it gets. So, if the mandate, premises, and composition of the Welfare Commission are indicative of future changes within the Danish welfare state, going down the liberal road is certainly confirmed.

CONCLUSION

Taking the four Scandinavian countries together, I conclude that the Scandinavian model of welfare is still distinct, but less so than it was (Abrahamson 2003). Developments during and since the 1990s in Denmark lead toward the same conclusion. Legal residency still entitles one to a fan of basic social rights, provided that one is able and willing to fulfil a set of corresponding obligations. Yet, entitlements are increasingly tied to membership in various funds, contributions and contractual commitments;

market solutions are becoming more and more common; and the liberal ideology of placing the individual at centre stage has become more and more widespread. Most changes have been of the first order, but the question remains: how many incremental changes can a system absorb without changing profoundly? In other words, when do quantitative changes turn into qualitative ones, to employ the vocabulary of Marxism? Considering the two most important elements of welfare state provision – health care and pensions – a trend toward dualization is manifesting itself: social citizenship is split between a universal coverage of basic entitlements, and a coverage supplemented by contributory and purely market-based provisions and services. From an institutional perspective, this is a decisive deviation from the ideal-typical Scandinavian welfare model; yet, considering outcomes in the form of employment and poverty rates, Danes still receive the security promised by their welfare regime. But the trend is toward a stronger division in society between middle class people and marginalized segments. The former enjoy integration into society through an increasing reliance on market and corporate solutions, while the latter are exposed to exclusionary processes because of their dependence upon public provisions which, deliberately or not, places them outside the mainstream.

NOTES

Parts of this chapter have been previously published in Abrahamson (2002), Abrahamson (2003), and Abrahamson, Kambskard, and Wehner (2002).

1 For a detailed account of pension reform in Denmark, see Abrahamson and Wehner 2003.
2 This section draws on work produced for the yearly publication *Social Tendencies [Social Årsrapport]* of which I am an editor. I am indebted to the statistical analyses made by Finn Kenneth Hansen, Henning Hansen, and Mette Marie Juul, Centre for Alternative Social Analysis.

11

Denmark in the Process
of European Integration
Dilemmas, Problems, and Perspectives

MORTEN KELSTRUP

Danish policy toward and within the European Union is *analytically* a complex topic and *politically* a complicated problem area. *Analytically* the topic is "slippery" in the sense that it we are rather unclear exactly what we mean when we talk about "Danish policy" in this area. Are we talking about a special aspect of Danish foreign policy? Or are we talking about the actions of the Danish government as a "semi-integrated actor" within the multi-level governance system of the European Union? Here, I shall talk about *Denmark's EU policy* as the policy that is formulated by the Danish government and called Denmark's EU policy; it includes the foreign policy aspect as well as the government's actions within the European Union's multi-level governance system.[1]

Further, Denmark's position in the process of European integration is a broader topic, which also includes the many *direct and indirect effects* that EU participation has on Danish society, administration, and politics. I shall return to the point of view that Denmark might increasingly become a semi-integrated actor in the EU system of multi-level governance.

COMPLEXITY AND PARADOXES
IN DENMARK'S EU POLICY

Politically, Denmark's EU policy is rife with complications and frustrations. Some of the complications stem from the fact that the EU policy that Danish governments pursued together with other major parties has been rejected twice by a majority of the Danish voters. This occurred in the 1992 referendum on the Maastricht Treaty and again in the 2000 referendum on Denmark's adherence to Euro-cooperation.[2] On these occasions the "no"s hit hard because they came after most of the Danish elite groups and most other parties had supported the policy of the government in a very intensive campaign. In some ways the "no"s represented a revolt on the part of a majority of the Danish population.

Other complications and frustrations stem from the fact that the government and the elite groups has had to – and still must – live with the Danish reservations from 1993. The rejection in 1992 of the Maastricht Treaty led in 1993 to what is known as the National Compromise, which stipulated that Denmark could accept the treaty only with four important reservations: that Denmark is *not* taking part in the third part of the EMU (the Euro-cooperation); that Denmark is *not* part of the European Union's defence policy; that Denmark is unwilling to accept the supranational aspect of a common EU policy on justice and home affairs; and that Denmark is against a European citizenship that would substitute for national citizenship.[3] These reservations were accepted by the major political parties in Denmark in the fall of 1992 and included in the so-called Edinburgh Agreement with the other EU Member States in 1993. The majority of the Danish voters accepted this agreement, combined with the Maastricht Treaty, in a new referendum in 1993. Although the major political parties have for a long time openly declared that they consider the reservations to be in contradiction to Danish interests, these reservations are still in force.[4] They played an important role in Denmark's EU policy in the 1990s and are still an unavoidable part of the Danish EU debate.

We can add also that in the Danish population there is widespread dissatisfaction with Denmark's EU policy. Yet, different groups are dissatisfied for very different reasons. The groups that support full Danish participation in the EU, are unhappy that Denmark still acts as a reluctant participant in the integration process of the EU, seemingly unable to direct its policy away from the old reservations. Many euro-skeptics are, on the other hand, frustrated because they feel that the two "no"s have not been respected, and that the reservations have, at least partially, been undermined. The greatest reason for the dissatisfaction of the Danish population is likely that neither the former nor the present political leaders – in spite of many declarations – have been able to formulate Danish policies that create a "new credibility" in the EU area.

Despite these problems, there has long been a high degree of agreement on Denmark's EU policy between the major political parties, an agreement that comprises, in particular, the Liberals, the Social Democrats, the Conservatives, and the Social Liberals. This agreement was renewed as a basis for the Danish presidency in the fall of 2002, and it was manifested again in March 2003 in a common policy paper concerning Danish views toward the Convention on the Future of Europe (Regeringen et al. 2003). It is in some ways a paradox that such a common platform in the EU area has existed in the present period of Danish politics, because since November 2001, when the Liberal-Conservative government came to power, Danish politics has been characterized by a "new divide" between, on the one hand, the government and its parliamentary base (the Danish People's Party) and, on the other hand, the other political parties, including the "middle" (the Social Liberals and the Christian People's Party), the Social Democrats, and the "left" (the Socialist People's Party and the "Unitarian List"). There have been some problems in preserving the EU consensus among the major parties.[5] Yet, in November 2004 a new agreement among the major parties (now including the Socialist People's Party) was reached on Denmark's attitude to the new Constitutional Treaty (Regeringen 2004). Thus, the main picture – that the EU policy is marked by a high degree of consensus among the major Danish political parties – still prevails as of the beginning of 2005.

Behind the paradox in the present Danish EU policy lies a greater paradox. On the one hand, Denmark is participating very actively in basic aspects of European integration. Denmark is fully engaged in the single European market and, more generally, in the European Union's "negative integration" (that is, the opening of markets and the creation of transnational deregulation). Denmark is an active proponent of economic globalization and liberalization, and in its economic policy it has had relatively great success, being one of the wealthiest countries in the European Union with a BNP per capita surpassed only by Luxembourg. Yet, on the other hand, Denmark is a reluctant participant in important aspects of the European political project. The situation is *not*, however, that Denmark takes part only in the European Union's negative integration. Denmark is also actively engaged in the formulation of – and support of – "positive integration" (that is, the formulation of common European policies) in major areas, not least in regard to the CAP and environmental issues.[6] Denmark is only reluctant to participate in *some* dimensions of political integration in the European Union. In regard to environmental policy and consumer protection, for instance, Denmark is very actively engaged in positive integration. The new agreement from November 2004 specifies a number of areas in which Denmark can accept that issues in the future may be decided by qualified majority vote – minimum levels of indirect taxation, and rules concerning the structural funds, for instance (Regeringen 2004). Danish reluctance is evident, in particular, in regard to supranational regulation of social and welfare politics and in the areas affected by the Danish reservations from 1992. Denmark still does *not* take part in Euro-cooperation; it is *not* part of European Union defence policy; and has reservations in regard to the supranational aspect of a common EU policy on justice and home affairs.

On the basis of this complex situation, one might pose the simple question: Why is it that Denmark, which after all is considered to be a rather successful state that has been able to participate in the international economy in a rather open way and has developed its own form of democracy and its welfare state in many positive ways, has such great problems in regard to the process of European integration? In view of the present development of the European Union – a development that seems to encompass not only an enlarged European Union but also a much more integrated union with a new, constitutional basis – we might also ask: What are the perspectives for Denmark in regard to the European Union's new developments? There is no doubt that the present Danish EU policy is challenged by the new developments in the European Union, partly because of the changes in the Union's institutional structure and competences and partly because the Union is undergoing rapid development in the areas most affected by the Danish reservations (defense, euro-cooperation, and justice and home affairs). Yet, it is very uncertain whether the major pro-EU parties will be successful in getting rid of the reservations and allowing Denmark to play a more pro-active role in the European Union in the future, or whether Denmark in the future faces even greater problems in its relationship to the EU.

The purpose of this chapter is to describe the complications inherent in Denmark's EU policy and to address the questions just posed. How are we to view Denmark's difficulties in regard to the European Union in light of the optimistic interpretation of Denmark as a successful, small, democratic state with a mature welfare system and an open economy? The basic view of my analysis is that it is quite understandable that states, and in particular small states, from a certain stage in a process of supranational, political integration, reach a serious dilemma in regard to the integration process, an "integration dilemma." This dilemma, which I shall discuss more later, has to do with the uncomfortable choice between supporting a supranational political "integration" (with the consequence of being bound by new institutional structures) and preserving formal state-based "sovereignty" (which leads to exclusion from the benefits of integration). Basically, all states are in principle exposed to such a dilemma at a certain stage in any integration process. Yet, the interpretation here is that this dilemma is particularly strong for Denmark because of the historically close relationship between people and state in Denmark. Denmark has managed to live with its ambivalence toward European integration for a rather long time, with a high degree of pragmatism and adaptation. But this pragmatism and adaptation has been achieved at the cost of cleavages in the Danish polity and further dilemmas. And we cannot exclude the possibility that there may be limits to such pragmatism and adaptation, an eventuality that is relevant in discussions about the prospects of Denmark's future participation in the European integration process.

This analysis is structured so that the following section briefly presents a broad historical interpretation of Denmark's political and economic development as a successful small, democratic state. The purpose is to go beyond the relatively narrow approaches from foreign policy analysis and integration theory to the broader discussion of political economy that Peter Katzenstein developed in his book *Small States in World Markets* (Katzenstein, 1985), and to pose questions regarding Denmark's EU participation in this light. In the third section I attempt to characterize Denmark's EU policy and its internal tensions as they have manifested historically. The fourth section deals with the areas of Denmark's political and administrative life in which we find indirect effects of Denmark's EU participation; in relation, for instance, to the character of elections and referenda, the position of the political parties, the relationship between elite and mass, and decision-making procedures related to EU policies. Has Denmark's participation in these different areas strengthened the corporative and democratic Danish state or, perhaps, weakened it?

In the final section, I return to the overall interpretation of Denmark's EU policy. How, in particular, might the Danish difficulties be interpreted in view of the integration dilemma? Is there a real dilemma, so that Denmark either has to choose to take part in a wide-reaching integration process in an attempt to preserve some kind of – maybe only formal – national sovereignty? Or is it possible, somehow, to live with the integration dilemma or even use it for institutional change and learning? I conclude with some important perspectives on Denmark's participation in the European integration process and the debate on Danish policies.

DIFFICULTIES IN DENMARK'S POLICIES TOWARD TRANSNATIONAL AND EUROPEAN INTEGRATION

Let us take a broad view of Denmark's historical development as a liberal, democratic state that has also become a mature welfare state, and pose a couple of questions. What has characterized the Danish experience in regard to democratization and the development of the welfare state? And, how are the characteristics of this historical development of importance for Denmark's relationship to the European Union?

One line of interpretation in such a broad perspective is that Denmark, like some other small states, in particular the other Scandinavian states, has developed as a democracy in such a way that cooperation across classes and cleavages has dominated. This is the perspective we find in Peter Katzenstein's analysis from 1985. The basic thesis is that the small

European states have been able to combine open economies with special forms of democratic corporatism and that, in this combination, they have been able to reach political stability as well as economic flexibility. Open economies, which also create high vulnerability, are seen as a basis for special kinds of corporatist arrangements. And the success of such political institutionalization within small states is also seen as a possible model for the way in which larger states could deal with world markets and what we today call globalization (Katzenstein 1985, 9). The Scandinavian states, including Denmark, are seen as examples of such successful small states.

Other authors have also dealt with the ways in which small states have reacted to economic globalization. German sociologist Dieter Senghaas, for instance, has discussed different strategies that individual states and societies might use to address the problem of marginalization in regard to the global economy, and has offered Denmark's historical experience in the late nineteenth century as an example of a successful adaptation strategy. The different developmental policies of states might be characterized as different ways of reacting to the pressure of being marginalized in the capitalist economy (*"Reaktionsweisen auf Peripherisierungsdruck,"* Senghaas 1982, 41ff). Basically, states might choose among different types of dissociative or associative strategies toward new markets, with greater or less success. Obviously, it is interesting to discover how some states (and national economies) succeed in "catching" up with the economic development of more advanced economies even in situations where they have become somewhat marginalized. In Senghaas's analysis, the Scandinavian countries are also taken as examples of states which, in earlier phases of economic globalization through openness, adaptation, and institutional learning, actually managed to develop economically and socially.[7]

Senghaas's analysis of Denmark's industrialization in the latter part of the nineteenth century and Katzenstein's interpretations of the Danish strategy toward the open global economy in later periods can in my view be regarded as supplementary. Of course, this should be said with the necessary reservations and with respect for the need for differentiated analyses. But there seems to be broad agreement that Denmark was able to take part in the global economy in a successful way, and that the special characteristics of Danish politics – consensus-orientation related to a high degree of pragmatism and based also on class-cooperation and democratic corporatism – were factors in this success. Also, the development of the Danish welfare state can be seen as part of this picture.

That Denmark developed in its early adaptation to the world market as a democratic state should, of course, also be seen in the light of other aspects of the country's history. Because of the wars in the nineteenth century and the dissolution of the former multicultural Denmark, the rest of Denmark, in particular after 1864, had a high degree of homogeneity and an unusually strong articulation of national identity in a period of enlightenment. Clearly, the national identity was articulated more strongly in some sub-cultures than others. The "Grundtvigian tradition," particularly dominant in the countryside, was articulated in rather national terms, while the conservatives and workers in Copenhagen and other cities were less explicitly national. In the second wave of adaptation to open economies, after World War II, there was a certain marriage between the projects of national identity, the revival of democratic norms, and, in particular from the 1950s, the project of the welfare state. Thus, in this period, democracy and the welfare state all became part of the Danish national identity.

This sketch links our discussion of Danish EU policy to the interpretation of the Danish experience as a special kind of success story, as expressed by Katzenstein. Basically, the picture of Denmark in the period after the 1950s becomes that of a coherent, small nation state that opened itself successfully to world markets and which – maybe not least because of its internal coherence and its practices related to democratic corporatism and the welfare state – experienced this success economically, socially, and politically. Of course, for some this is a far too rosy a picture. But let us at least for a moment accept this perspective.

If we accept this perspective, how are we then to interpret such a state's relation to the project of European integration? Can we explain that such a state might be open to negative integration in the EU and at the same time be a reluctant participant in the political, supranational aspect of European integration? And can we explain why so many difficulties and contradictions emerge for such a country in its relation to the European project?

My simple answer to these questions is: *yes!* And the answer falls into two parts. The first is that a small state engaged in an open market economy will actively support not only economic liberalization (and negative integration within the EC) but also international organizations and regimes that regulate the international market economy but at the same time respect the individual states. A small state will, if it is competitive, have an interest in fair trade, but will also be interested in a global international system that respects and protects small states as actors in the international society. Such a view fits well with Danish history. After World War II Denmark was able to compete – at least relatively well – in the opening economy and supported the opening of markets. But at the same time it was skeptical about giving up its sovereignty. It emphasized trade liberalization as its preference for EFTA over the EEC indicated.[8] In its relation to international organizations, Denmark engaged actively in what we sometimes have called "pragmatic functionalism": cooperation in specific, functional areas without surrendering its fundamental position as a sovereign state.

The second part of the answer, however, is that problems arise in regard to more advanced and supranational, regulative political integration. If it is true that the success of small states in relation to world markets was caused in part by a high degree of national democratic corporatism, also comprising specific national traditions, it is understandable that a more extensive positive integration in the form of supranational decision-making and regulation through common policies might cause problems. In other words, the importance that national corporatism, in particular, might have for the success of the small state in regard to the open markets might be the very reason that skepticism emerges when a more advanced and supranational, regulative political integration begins to interfere in the mechanisms of this national corporatism. A central question is: how are mechanisms of national corporatism and national democracy affected by the new integration? If the new political integration affects the institutions of national democracy and national corporatism in a negative way, it is not surprising that skepticism would arise in successful small states toward this new development.

Of course, this reasoning also presents a simplified picture – perhaps too simplified. We should also ask: what happens when political integration continues anyway, as it seems to do in the EU, despite the reluctance of the state in question? Many questions follow from this perspective: Is it possible that the relatively coherent and relatively democratic, but also corporatist state in question can settle new imbalances in its own domestic sphere and develop into an active player in the new integration system? If this new system emerges as a system of network governance, under what conditions could the former successful, corporatist state play an active role that allows it to exploit new possibilities of influence? Is there any alternative but a retreat to a defensive position in which it attempts, above all, to preserve its basic features? If the state in question takes a defensive attitude, what would the central feature of its defensive policy be? The national culture, formal sovereignty, or the central mechanisms of established corporatism? I shall in the following sections try to relate some of these questions more specifically to Danish EU policy and to the ways in which Denmark has adapted its participation in the European Union.

TENSIONS IN THE HISTORICAL DEVELOPMENT OF THE DANISH POLICY TOWARD EUROPE

In an analysis entitled "Denmark's Policy towards Europe,"[9] undertaken in 1997–2000, the researchers showed that Denmark's deep historical traditions played an important role in the formation of Danish policies. Danish foreign policy traditions are rooted in fundamental traits in the history of the Danish people and the Danish state. On the one hand Denmark has a "small state tradition" that leads to a passive adaptation policy, possibly supplemented with "compensatory internationalism"; on the other, Denmark has a more independent internationalistic tradition that builds upon the earlier – and in some periods stronger – multicultural Danish state that existed until the mid-nineteenth century. Clearly, characteristics of both these traditions can be found in Denmark's European policy after 1945. While Denmark's EU policy has in some ways been rather reactive, in others, especially since the end of the Cold War, it has revitalized its former "active internationalism" (Branner 2000).

More concretely, Denmark gave a relatively low priority to its European policy in the first decades after 1945. Its European policy was dominated by the option of comprehensive European cooperation, and its preference for a liberal economy and the preservation of intergovernmental cooperation in international organizations. Reminiscences of this preference for broad European, intergovernmental solutions can be found in later Danish policies – in the rapid decision to join Britain in applying for EEC membership in 1961 and 1967, for instance, and in Denmark's participation in EFTA and in the NORDEK experiment at the end of the 1960s. The decision-making elite's emphasis on economic advantages and concrete results, and its disinclination for political integration in the debate on Denmark's entrance in the EC in the early 1970s can be seen in this light. In parallel, Denmark's hesitant and half-hearted approach to later plans for a political union, its reservations to treaty obligations in 1992, and its enthusiastic endorsement of EU expansion plans in the 1990s can be seen as a fundamental Danish preference for broad European and intergovernmental cooperation.[10]

Denmark joined the European Community in 1973 with a highly selective identification with EC goals (Petersen 2000, 73ff). The primary motivation was economic, and the politicians advocating membership focused almost entirely on the economic benefits of joining the referendum campaign prior to membership. Denmark's identification with EC goals was low in the areas of foreign policy and security policy, especially in regard to constitutional-institutional policy. Thus, Denmark's priority was that security and defence should be handled within NATO. In relation to EC /EU's institutional side, Danish policy was mostly reserved, skeptical about supranational and federalist elements and with a clear preference for intergovernmental structures. This was especially true for the first two decades of Danish EU membership.

Denmark's policy toward the EC/EU in the period from the 1960s to the late 1980s has, correctly in my view, been characterized by "limited engagement,," "fragmentation," and "pragmatism" (Branner 2000). One might claim that there was a change toward greater commitment to the

European project in the late 1980s, after the 1986 referendum in particular, as a result of the change of attitude within the Social Democratic Party. The single market plans in the 1980s constituted, in the view of the Social Democratic Party and also of the Social Liberal Party and parts of the Socialist People's Party, an important societal change that established new international conditions (Haahr 1993). It led these parties to support the introduction of majority voting in new areas of the EC. And from 1988 to 1991 there was a high level of agreement in Danish policy toward the EC; that is, an agreement that formed an important part of the background for the acceptance of the Maastricht Treaty by the majority of the political parties. Yet, the "no" at the referendum on the Maastricht Treaty in 1992 changed this more active EC/EU policy. Instead, the predominant Danish policy became codified in the so-called National Compromise, which I mentioned above. This compromise was a formal agreement on a political platform for new negotiations with the other EC states after the referendum in 1992 , and was accepted by all major parties, including also the Socialist People's Party, which had been advocating a "no" at the Maastricht referendum.[11] The compromise also included an "active part" that laid a foundation for an active Danish integration policy based on assigning a high priority to democracy, openness, subsidiarity (in its Danish interpretation, *nærhed*), environmental concerns, and employment. It included, in addition, the four Danish "reservations," four policy areas in which Denmark should avoid extensive participation: the single currency, defence cooperation, common citizenship, and supranational cooperation in justice and home affairs. While the 1992 "no" stopped the fledgling active Danish EU policy, one might claim that the National Compromise and its confirmation in the Edinburgh agreement and the subsequent referendum on "Maastricht and Edinburgh" in 1993 changed Denmark status from that of a reserved or reluctant member of the European Union to that of a "member with reservations."[12]

It is no exaggeration that since 1993 the four Danish reservations have played an important – perhaps even dominating – role in debate on Danish policies toward the European Union. Yet, in hindsight, it is clear that there have been – and still are – very different interpretations of the Danish reservations (DUPI 2000, 261). One can identify two quite different strategies in the interpretation of the reservations: one is that the reservations give Denmark a "time out" to allow for the possibility of cancelling the reservations at a later date (perhaps one by one, depending on circumstances), after watching how things develop within the problem areas in question. This interpretation has clearly been supported by the Liberals and the Conservatives, and at least in part by the social democratic and social liberal government as well. The other interpretation, supported by the Socialist People's Party and the "No-movements," has understood the reservations to be permanent conditions for Denmark's participation in the European Union; that is, not something temporary that could easily be changed, but, rather, a basis for Denmark's general policy within the Union.

I have discussed how Denmark's integration policy after 1993 as "a member with reservations" should be characterized (Branner 2000; Kelstrup 2000b). One view is that after 1993 Denmark returned to the policy of limited engagement, fragmentation, and pragmatism; and major elements of this view seem to hold. In fact, the reservations per se can be seen as a sign of limited engagement. Denmark's reservation in regard to defence (wanting defence issues treated in NATO) can be seen as a policy line of fragmentation. The construction of the "compromise" can in itself be seen as a very pragmatic approach. Another view, however, is that there were new and active elements in Danish EU policy after 1993. The Danish government in the mid-1990s accepted the four reservations, but, given their restriction, went nearly as far as it could in an active participation within the communities. Its very active part in the negotiations of the Amsterdam Treaty was an indication of this, as was its acceptance of the Schengen Agreement. More generally, since the debate about the Amsterdam Treaty, it has been the dominant understanding that Danish EU policy is primarily political, and not related Danish economic interests alone. Thus, in this respect, an aspect of Danish "fragmentation" was abandoned.

One might say that the social democratic and social liberal government in the 1990s showed considerable "pragmatism" in its interpretation of the Danish reservations. This pragmatism in some ways ran contrary to the policy line of limited engagement. Although there is some uncertainty as to which of the two "reservation-strategies" the government followed in the 1990s, most interpreters claim that the government chose – at least in its external policy – to regard the reservations as only temporary. Its policy line was that the Danish reservations should be respected and changed only after a referendum; but also that it was important to get as much active engagement in the European Union as possible within the limits of the reservations.

In the spring of 2000 there was an explicit move that challenged Denmark's position even as an active member with reservations. The Social Democratic and Social Liberal government decided to hold a referendum in regard to the reservation on Danish participation in Euro-cooperation in September 2000. The government wanted Denmark to participate fully in Euro-cooperation. But, even though this policy was supported by the major parties and most of the Danish establishment, the referendum resulted in a majority against the policy of the government and political establishment, just as in 1992. One might say that if Denmark changed after the 1993 referendum from being a reserved or reluctant member of the European Union to a "member with reservations," and after the 1998 referendum on the Amsterdam developed an even more "active" EU policy, the referendum from 2000 brought Denmark "back" to being a reserved member. Some interpreters even saw the 2000 referendum as a more general "fall of Danish foreign policy activism" (Holm 2002).[13] However, this view seems to be exaggerated.

As of June 2001, with the Social Democrat and Social Liberal government's "white book," an attempt to formulate a more active policy resurfaced – in an extensive argument for "showing that small countries can make a difference" (Udenrigs ministeriet 2001, 11). Further, the Liberal and Conservative government, which took power in 2001 and was in charge of the EU presidency in the fall of 2002, explicitly supported an active Danish EU policy and took a very active part in securing the enlargement of the European Union. In his speech of 15 January 2003 on "the Danish EU policy after the Presidency" Prime Minister Anders Fogh Rasmussen underlined again his wish for a very active Danish EU policy: "It is my ambition that Denmark will play a more proactive role in the EU ... We shall secure greater Danish influence through dynamic proposals, by daring and strategic alliances with countries whose views we share" (Rasmussen 2003, 9, my translation). During 2003 it became an even more articulated policy of the Liberal-Conservative government that it wished to pursue an active EU policy. However, it became a somewhat rhetorical position that nearly faded away after Denmark's support of the American and British war on Iraq, in opposition to countries such as Germany and France.

From this look at the history behind Denmark's EU policy we can see that its main driving force has been the Danish wish to participate in the open European economy and in a broad European, mainly intergovernmental, cooperation. When confronted with projects for supranational integration, the major political parties, at least until the late 1980s, have followed a policy of limited engagement. Since then, there has been a drive from the government and the major parties for a more active, Danish EU policy, but in the referenda of 1992 and 2000, the Danish elite learned hard lessons from a more reluctant popular majority. In these instances the immediate reaction was to reinforce a consensus-oriented policy. This was, in particular, manifest in the 1992 National Compromise, which still plays a very important role in the EU policy area. Yet, the wish for a more active Danish participation in EU integration seems to have emerged again, even after it previous defeat.

Thus, the tension between the EU policies of the major political parties and a relatively strong euro-skepticism seems to continue. Since it is clear that the European Union's new Constitutional Treaty must be subjected to a new Danish EU referendum, the present government has been very eager to be sure that the Danish reservations from 1992 are preserved in relation to the Constitutional Treaty (even though both governmental parties basically want Denmark to give up its reservations). It is understood that without such a confirmation, which has been included in a protocol to the treaty, it would simply be too difficult to get an acceptance of the Constitutional Treaty in a new Danish referendum. As a saying among the dominantly pro-EU Danish politicians goes: "Only a fool does not fear a Danish EU referendum." In its preparation for the coming EU referendum, the present government has also been eager to secure the Socialist People's Party's support for the Constitutional Treaty. Thus, all major parties (i.e., all parties in the *Folketing* except the Danish People's Party and the Unitary Movement) in November 2004 signed a new political agreement on "Denmark in the enlarged EU," which specifies the common view on the Constitutional Treaty (Regeringen, 2004). This agreement, which in the press was called the "new national compromise," is a clear sign that the government is still caught in a tension between a wish to be an active participant in at least major aspects of European integration and the need for a high degree of consensus-orientation in Danish EU policy.

SOCIAL AND POLITICAL AREAS AFFECTED BY DENMARK'S EU PARTICIPATION

Denmark's relationship to European integration is a much broader topic than Denmark's EU policy. Danish EU participation has had many *direct and indirect effects* in different social and political areas of Danish society, which the following necessarily brief and selective comments will discuss. The basic view is that Danish EU participation not only implies problems and tensions in Danish EU policy, as described in the previous section, but also requires institutional adaptation and change in important parts of the Danish political system and in the society. The question that arises is whether Danish EU integration in a broad sense really can go hand in hand with a strong Danish "corporative democracy," or whether the development runs counter to it.

EU Referenda and Normal Elections

Since 1972 Denmark has had six referenda on EU questions – in 1972, 1986, 1992, 1993, 1998, and 2000. The results are summarized in Table 1. Two of the referenda ended in "no"s, against the recommendation of the parliamentary majority, *Folketinget*. The response to the 1986 referendum was a "yes," but again contrary to the majority in the *Folketing*. Of course we could go into an elaborate discussion about the use of referenda

Table 1   Danish Referenda on EC/EU Questions

Date	Topic	Participation %	"Yes" %	"No" %
02.10.1972	Danish membership	90.1	63.3	36.7
27.02.1986	Single European Act	75.8	56.2	43.8
02.06.1992	The Maastricht Treaty	83.1	49.3	50.7
18.05.1993	The Maastricht Treaty and the Edinburgh Agreement	86.5	56.7	43.3
28.05.1998	The Amsterdam Treaty	74.8	55.1	44.9
28.09.2000	Adherence to the 3. phase of the EMU	87.6	46.8	53.2

Source: Official Danish Statistics.

Table 2   Elections in Denmark to the European Parliament

	1979	1984	1989	1994	1999	2004
Social Democrats	21.0 (3)	19.5 (3)	23.3 (4)	15.8 (3)	16.5 (3)	32.6 (5)
Social Liberals	3.3 (0)	3.1 (0)	2.8 (0)	8.5 (1)	9.1 (1)	6.4 (1)
Conservative People's Party	14.0 (2)	20.8 (4)	13.3 (2)	17.7 (3)	8.5 (1)	11.3 (1)
Centrum Democrats	6.2 (1)	6.6 (1)	8.0 (2)	0.9 (0)	3.5 (0)	–
Socialist People's Party	4.7 (1)	9.2 (2)	9.1 (1)	8.6 (1)	7.1 (1)	7.9 (1)
The June Movement			(3)	15.2 (2)	16.1 (3)	9.1 (1)
The People's Movement against the EC/EU	21.0 (4)	20.8 (4)	18.9 (4/1)	10.3 (2)	7.3 (1)	5.2 (1)
Danish People's Party					5.8 (1)	6.8 (1)
Christian People's Party	1.8 (0)	2.8 (0)	2.7 (0)	1.1 (0)	2.0 (0)	1.3 (0)
Liberals	14.4 (3)	12.4 (2)	16.6 (3)	18.9 (4)	23.4 (5)	19.4 (3)
The Progress Party	5.8 (1)	3.5 (0)	5.3 (0)	2.9 (0)	0.7 (0)	–
Participation, %	47.8	52.4	46.2	52.9	50.4	47.9

Source: Official Danish Statistics.

in Denmark, and also the appropriateness at all of having referenda on EU issues. But irrespective of the different opinions on these questions, it is quite clear *that EU participation has led to a stronger institutionalization of the use of referenda in Danish politics*. Actually, the use of referenda on EU issues goes beyond the requirements of the Danish Constitution. We might note that this is *not* part of a traditional corporatist development, rather the contrary. But it seems in some way to be *a special expression of a close relation between the leading political groups in Denmark and "the Danish people."*

Another important effect of EU integration is the very special relationship between the normal elections to the *Folketing* and the use of referenda on EU issues. The effect of the many referenda on EU matters seems to be that *EU issues disappear from normal election campaigns.* EU issues are debated nearly exclusively in relation to the referenda and the elections to the European Parliament. Many observers have criticized this, but the tendency seems to prevail. In the elections in the fall of 2001 there was hardly any debate about EU issues in spite of the immense importance these issues had had less than one year previously, in the referendum on Danish Euro-participation. The same tendency prevailed in the normal election to the *Folketing* in 2005. This might be seen as a kind of institutional adaptation to the European Union, but it is difficult not to interpret it as a *weakening of a dimension of traditional Danish democracy.*

Special Parties for the Elections to the European Parliament

The results of the Danish elections to the European Parliament are indicated in table 2. One remarkable feature of these elections is that we *two parties, the People's Movement Against the EU and the June Movement, act as parties only in elections to the European-Parliament.* Both movements have (likely for good reasons) declined the recurrent wish from other party members that they engage in normal elections like other political parties. The result is a particular adaptation of the Danish party systems to EU issues: *the Danish party system has been split in two,* the "normal" party system, which is relevant locally and in national politics, and an "EU party system" which consists of the normal parties plus the two new parties mentioned. It is difficult not to interpret this as *a weakening of another aspect of the traditional Danish democracy.*

New Cleavages in the Danish Party System

More generally, an effect of Danish EU participation is that *we experience new cleavages within the Danish party system.* The system is now structured not only in relation to the traditional *right-left dimension,* but also in relation to *a pro-EU and euro-skeptic dimension.* I have in figure 1 tried to position the different parties on the two dimensions on the basis of a somewhat similar figure by Hans Branner (Branner 2002, 73). Of course, such a figure should only be taken as a heuristic presentation and should be read with many caveats, particularly in regard to the position of the different parties. Yet, it illustrates an important change: *the Danish party system has got not only new parties, but also new cleavages through Danish EU participation.* One might add that the cleavage in regard to integration policy goes right through many of the parties, and that these cleavages have created severe problems for some (in particular for the Social Democrats and the Socialist People's Party).[14] *This picture is basically to be interpreted as a weakening of the consensus-orientation in Danish politics.*

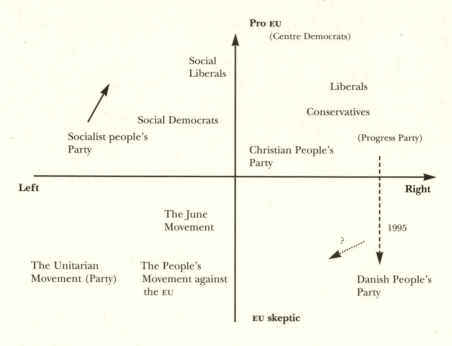

Figure 1　The Position of the Danish Political Parties vis-à-vis EU-integration
Adapted from Branner, 2002, 73.

A special feature, however, which up to now has explained the consensus-orientation among the "old" parties, is that most traditional parties are pro-EU. Further, it is interesting that until the mid-1990s Denmark did not have a euro-skeptical right wing party, but rather a euro-skeptical left wing. This was a rather unusual pattern compared to other European countries. Yet, the situation has been changing. One move took place after the formation of the Danish People's Party in 1995 (after a split in the Progress Party). A relatively strong, right wing euro-skepticism has emerged. The Danish People's Party, which in recent years is perhaps moving toward the centre on a left-right scale, has developed in the direction of being a national party with a clear national and anti-EU attitude. As such it has contributed considerably to the articulation of a new Danish nationalism, not least in relations to foreigners. Another move has recently taken place through internal debates in the Socialist People's Party. In late 2004 it adopted a more EU-positive platform and seems ready to support the acceptance of the new Constitutional Treaty. One might also add that the election to the European Parliament in 2004 resulted in a remarkable weakening of the euro-skeptical movements. Thus, there are signs that important changes are taking place in the party system. We might see this as Denmark moving toward a more "normal" pattern in party politics, although with the reservation that we do not quite know what we should consider normal in this connection. But, maybe some learning processes are taking place.

The Elite and Mass Dimensions

The referenda on EU questions has also contributed to a stronger articulation of a mass-elite division in the Danish electorate. The fact that the "no"s in 1992 and again in 2000 came in after rather elite-dominated campaigns for "yes," seems to have had an important influence on the relationship between politicians and the public in general. Yet, it is important that the elite-mass division in regard to the EU issue has been weakened over the years (Hedetoft 2000). Further, one should guard against too simplistic an interpretation of the Danish people's attitude toward the European Union as simple, parochial skepticism. There has been such skepticism, but over time there has also been a considerable change in Danish attitudes toward the Union. A recent analysis of attitudes concludes that during the 1990s the Danes became "pretty good Europeans" (Togeby et al. 317; Andersen 2002). It is pointed out that the Danes (in 1999) feared the loss of national identity, culture, and language *less* than the average among EU members. On the other hand, the Danes were, second only to the population of Luxembourg, the people that felt it had the *greatest* possibility of influencing decisions in the national political system, and – next to the Swedes – the people who felt that it had the *least* possibility of influencing decisions in the European Union (Togeby et al. 317). Maybe the interpretation of these phenomena should be that *learning processes are taking place, resulting in more positive attitudes to the European Union, but that the special relation between the Danish state and the people still is very strong.*

Denmark's EU Decision-Making System
and Parliamentary Control of EU Policy

An important aspect of Danish administrative practice is that Denmark has developed a special and very corporatist decision-making system on EU policies (Dosenrode 2000; Riis, 2002). Further, in relation to decision making on EU policies, Denmark has a special system for control of the government's EU policy (Damgaard and Nørgaard, 2000; Jensen, 2003). This system, sometimes called "the Danish model," is concentrated around the European Affairs Committee (EAC) and its possibility of "mandating" the government in regard to its participation in EU negotiations. This system has had great influence on the work of the *Folketing*. As two observers have written: "Although membership did not change the normal patterns of parliamentary coalition formation, it did introduce an elaborate and quite sophisticated system for parliamentary control of government and ministers in EU matters, with the EAC as the cornerstone. In a similar way, while the existing administrative structure was largely upheld, a new set of procedures and committees were added to handle better the EU issues that did not fit well with the traditional distinction between foreign and domestic policy" (Damgaard and Nørgaard 2000, 54). The debate about these changes of the Danish decision-making system has been concerned partly with the effectiveness of the system, and partly with the tendency that the *Folketing*, in spite of the control system, is weakened (Togeby et al. 314). Most observers interpreted the changes as *a strengthening of the corporative patterns in the Danish decision-making system.*

Has Danish EU Participation
Strengthened or Weakened Danish "Corporative Democracy"?

These brief and selective comments illustrate that Danish EU participation has had major effects on Danish political life, and that the tensions around Danish EU policy constitute only one aspect of the problems related to Danish EU participation. The descriptions could have been elaborated, and we could have added other important aspects – for instance about uncertainty in constitutional matters and, not least, in regard to mixed national/ EU policies in different sectors. The main conclusion is that Danish EU participation has had different effects in different areas. In some areas (as in the procedures for EU policy making) domestic adaptation to EU participation seems to have strengthened corporatist structures. Yet, in other areas (as in regard to the split between referenda and elections, the split of the party system, and new cleavages) we see difficulties for the traditional structures of Danish democracy. My tentative overall conclusion is that the traditional structures of "corporate democracy" have weakened, with a clearer division between corporative and traditional democratic structures.

SUCCESSFUL STATES MIGHT BE CONFRONTED WITH AN INTEGRATION DILEMMA

On the basis of the descriptions above, it is difficult to reach a simple picture of the reasons behind Denmark's great political difficulties related to its participation in European integration. The interpretation offered here, though, is that although Denmark has had relatively great success in being a coherent, corporatist, and democratic state able to take part with relative success in the open international economy, the development of a supranational political integration in Europe challenges the coherence of the Danish state and society severely. We might say that the strengthening of supranational integration provokes the integration dilemma, as we know from integration theory.[15]

The integration dilemma is the dilemma that an actor, possibly a state, experiences when it is confronted with a new important step toward further integration. The situation might be that it has to choose *either* to participate in the more intensified integration (with the possible risk of being "entrapped" and forced to accept decisions that it would otherwise reject); *or*, on the other hand, to reject the new integration step (at the risk of being "abandoned," left outside the integration process or losing influence within it). One might say that Denmark, reluctant to participate in the supranational political integration but not interested in being left out (in particular not left out of economic integration), has managed to live with this dilemma for a long time. One might also interpret the Danish reservations and the Danish policy of partial active engagement in positive integration as attempts to find partial solutions to the integration dilemma. The basic dilemma has, however, not been solved but, rather, postponed and diluted. Seemingly there are major effects of such a policy. There have been demands for domestic adaptation in many areas of Danish society and politics, also imposing new cleavages in the Danish society and politics.

A somewhat pessimistic interpretation might add that the difficulties of dealing with supranational integration might lead to other dilemmas.[16] One is that the government has to make a choice: *either* it formulates its policies in a new discourse that is relevant for the state's participation in the developing system of multi-level governance in the European Union (with the possible cost that this new discourse is not sufficiently understood by the broad public and therefore is not gathering sufficient support); *or* the government might choose to formulate its policies in old and established (often national or even nationalistic) discourses that can mobilize support (in particular to traditional ideas and identities), but has the potential cost that the policies that gain support are inadequate in regard to the actual problems and new political realities. Many will probably agree that Danish EU policy has for a long time been formulated in rather old-fashioned and somewhat national terms, with the result that much of the debate on EU policies lags heavily behind the actual problems.[17]

The government has another dilemma. *Either* it formulate its specific policy in explicit terms *or* it avoids such policy formulation, leaving policy questions in diffusion and lack of clarity. Although formulating policy would have the advantage of clarifying specific goals and objectives, the disadvantage would be that the goals might provoke disagreement, political conflict and possible lack of support. The "advantage" of avoiding policy formulation is that the government would avoid having to deal with opposition to "hidden" policies, which might be very difficult. But the cost would be that the actual policy might lose direction and be unable to generate sufficient support. Danish policies – in regard to the reservations as well as their interpretation – seem mostly in accord with such a "diffusion-strategy." One might add that a diffusion-strategy has a certain self-enforcing character; when problems have become really complex, it is extremely difficult to create a clear policy.

A more optimistic interpretation is that it *is* possible to get beyond the integration dilemma. There are two main strategies for this. The first is to increase the flexibility of the integration process. If the integration process is very inflexible and leads to a new, supranational authority that undermines the established national authority and state identity, then the integration dilemma will be very severe. On the other hand, if the new political system remains open to the preservation of substantial national identities or values, the difficulty of engaging in the political integration will be greatly reduced. In addition, the dilemma becomes much greater within an irreversible integration process than in a reversible process. Basically, flexibility in the integration process ameliorates the situation for the participants. Most observers will probably agree that Denmark has followed a policy that has resulted in a rather high degree of flexibility in the European integration process.

The second strategy is to learn from new conditions and experiences. If the integration process is slow and the learning capacity is high, it might be possible to adjust institutions, attitudes, and behaviour as the process moves forward. If the learning processes have a wide focus, it might be possible to accustom not only the political actors but also the broader population to the new levels of integration. The discussion above has pointed to the existence of learning processes and institutional adaptation in regard to Denmark's relationship to the European Union. But it is still a very open question how strong the processes of learning and adaptation are in the Danish attitudes toward European integration compared to the pressure for change.

CONCLUSIONS AND PERSPECTIVES

Denmark's EU policy is extremely complicated and contradictory, rife with paradoxes and – politically – with frustrations. Denmark is considered a rather successful state that has been able to take part in the international economy in a rather open way and has developed its own form of democracy and its welfare state in many positive ways. Why, then, does the country have such great problems in regard to the process of European integration? Denmark was at first seen in a positive light as being among the small states that were to take part in the global economy and at the same time develop as democracies and welfare states. However, this policy, although successful in the economic sphere, met with strong reservations in regard to political integration. After this, descriptions of the Danish EC/EU policy over the years emphasized the tensions involved in: i) a reserved policy based on "limited engagement," "fragmentation," and "pragmatism," ii) a policy as a "member with reservations," and iii) the re-emerging pressures for an active Danish EU policy. It seems clear that although in the present phase we once again are experiencing a move toward a more active Danish EU policy, it is not at all certain that this will be successful. Danish society and Danish politics have both been affected by Denmark's EU integration, and while some of the necessary adjustments have strengthened the dominant corporatist pattern, others have tended to undermine – at least partly – the dominant structures of "corporate democracy" and to create new cleavages in the Danish socio-political system.

Denmark closely resembles other highly developed states that participate in economic globalization and transnational and supranational political governance and which at a certain point in their participation in the integration processes, experience an integration dilemma. Perhaps for historical reasons related to the close link between the state and the people, Denmark experienced such an integration dilemma rather strongly. Yet, it has also managed to live with the dilemma and to "soften" it for quite a long time. This compromise has not been without negative effects within the socio-political system. The recent pragmatic and fragmented Danish EU policy and the country's new political cleavages can be seen in this light. One might say that in many domestic areas Denmark has had to bear the cost of its postponement of the integration dilemma.

The positive perspective for Denmark's relation to the European integration is that it might be possible to learn from experience and react in a creative way to new challenges. The negative perspective, however, might well be that these learning processes are going far too slowly. At present, in particular with the Constitutional Treaty, we have a strong impetus for moving the EU system toward a more efficient and simplified political system, perhaps also a political system with a more democratic, political structure. But it is an open question whether the Danes at the next referendum – if we have one – will dare to say "yes" to this Constitutional Treaty, or whether they prefer a "no," even at the risk of becoming marginalized in the process.

NOTES

1 For practical reasons, I shall not distinguish between EC and EU policy, but of course, we can only talk about EU policy after the formation of the European Union in 1993.

2 A majority in the Danish parliament was actually also opposed in a referendum in 1986, but at this time it was in support of the government and in an acceptance of the Single European Act.

3 Denmark can accept most of the cooperation on justice and home affairs on an intergovernmental basis through so-called parallel policies. The last reservation is no longer relevant, because the formulation – that the European citizenship does not substitute for national citizenship – has been included in the treaties.

4 In the common declaration of 14 March 2003 from the government (Liberals and Conservatives), the Social Democrats, and the Social Liberals, it is bluntly stated that: "The reservations are not today in the interests of Denmark" (my translation, Regeringen et al. 2003, 6) It is generally accepted, however, that the reservations can only be changed after a new referendum (or possibly separate referenda on each of the reservations).

5 Thus, in September 2003 a disagreement developed concerning the third reservation. Prime Minister, Anders Fogh Rasmussen, formulated it as the government's policy to try to split the reservation in regard to justice and home affairs into different parts in order to make it possible for Denmark to continue to have a reservation in regard to asylum policy but to give up the other parts of the present reservation which refer to police cooperation and the fight against terrorism. The Social Democrats reluctantly accepted this policy, while the Social Liberals were opposed.

6 Denmark's support for common EU policies has developed over the years to a stronger support for the "softer" parts of common EU policies – food safety and consumer protection, for instance. In addition, particularly on the part of the former government (i.e., the Social Democrats and the Social Liberals), there has been support for the Lisbon Process and the open method of coordination.

7 For a differentiated analysis of the European experience, see Senghaas 1982.

8 Of course, Denmark's trade relations with Great Britain also played a role in this regard.

9 Branner and Kelstrup, eds. 2000. The following text is based on the summary in Kelstrup 2000b, in particular 420–2.

10 For a discussion of how these elements can be traced back to the pattern identified as characterizing Danish policy in the 1950s, see Branner 2000, 333ff.

11 Since the referenda in 1992 and 1993 it has – rightly or wrongly – been a rather accepted view that the support of the Socialist People's Party is necessary in order to win a Danish EU referendum.

12 A thorough discussion of the National Compromise and its different elements is found in DUPI, 2000, in particular 225ff.

13 "The inability to create agreement on an EU-oriented foreign policy resulted in the "No" vote in the Euro-referendum. This was the beginning of the end

of Danish foreign policy activism. The window of opportunity was being closed – from the inside," Holm 2002, 42.

14 For a thorough analysis, see Haahr 1993 and 2000.

15 On the integration dilemma, see Kelstrup 1993, 154; Petersen, 2000; Kelstrup, 2000a. The basic idea is to draw a parallel to Glenn Snyder's analysis of the "alliance dilemma," Snyder, 1984.

16 For a more elaborate discussion, see Kelstrup, 2000b.

17 One of the criticisms of the Danish EU debate has been that it seems always to lag behind the European reality and the debates in most other EU countries (Friis 2002).

18 Three representatives from the People's Movement Against the EU changed during the election period to becoming representatives of the June Movement.

More Than Kin and Less Than Kind

The Danish Politics of Ethnic Consensus and the Pluricultural Challenge

ULF HEDETOFT

Scholarly analyses that perceive immigration as a challenge or even a threat to Danish identity and the Danish welfare state are commonly subjected either to culturalist critique or to politico-economic approbation. In the first, mostly immigrant-friendly mode, the stereotyping of ethnic minorities is castigated as unreasonable, unfounded, and based on ethnocentric prejudice, or in other words on individual or collective predispositions (see e.g., Ejrnæs 2001; Mishra and Christiansen 2002; Røgilds 1995). This is the position taken by adherents of cultural relativism and liberal cosmopolitanism. In the Danish context it is commonly referred to as *kulturradikalisme* (literally "cultural radicalism"), a tradition that has come under increasingly heavy fire, particularly since the advent of the present Liberal-Conservative government.[1] In the second and usually more immigrant-skeptical mode, immigration is viewed as an indisputable burden on state finances and welfare provisions or as a functionally undesirable intervention into a well-ordered state-citizen nexus (e.g., Mogensen and Matthiessen 2000; Nannestad 1999; Tænketanken [a think tank set up by the Ministry for Integration Affairs] 2002). The first approach is largely idealistic; the second mainly economistic, sometimes reductively so.

Unlike these two ways of approaching the problem – and without denying that questions of prejudice and economic rationality may play a role – this chapter will tackle the question differently; that is, contextually, structurally, and with regard to Denmark's track record as a small, culturally homogeneous, and economically as well as politically successful nation state trying to navigate in global waters. The question to illuminate will be: How is economic and social reality linked with cultural responses and political solutions?

SMALL STATES, HOMOGENEITY, AND IMMIGRATION

In an earlier work (Hedetoft 1995) dealing with the state of European nationalism in the context of European integration and globalization (based largely on an analysis of interview and questionnaire data collected in Germany, Denmark, and the United Kingdom , in recognizing that European nationalism will have to adapt to "new macro-political and macro-economic circumstances" in the future, I concluded that small nation states like Denmark, which combine a "non-grandiose past and large measures of national-cultural confidence," would predictably be well braced for "the tremors resulting from sitting on a faultline" (666, 668). I added that trying to deal with these challenges by attempting to recover older forms of nationalism would be misplaced and dysfunctional.

This was just before the "immigrant challenge" (combined with clash-of-civilizations panics) presented itself as the putative manifestation of globalization on the domestic scene, and before political populism began to react in precisely such a traditionalist and nostalgic mode.

A decade earlier, Peter Katzenstein (1985) had arrived at a similar conclusion but in a very different way. In *Small States in World Markets* he focused on the "democratic corporatism" of small European states, emphasizing their vulnerability to change, their dependence on world markets, their open economies, and the resultant mechanisms deployed to avoid or deflect dysfunctional internal consequences: that is, a social partnership, a centralized and concentrated system of interest groups, and the use of political bargaining and compromise to resolve conflicts. As international pressures from globalization become funnelled through different domestic structures attempting to compensate for external fluctuations, the welfare systems of small states like the Nordic countries are placed in a context of managing these pressures – or turning them to their own advantage. According to Katzenstein, global processes meet different domestic structures and capacities for absorption of change and "shock." Smallness is linked with cultural and historical homogeneity and provides the conceptual framework for explaining the robustness and relative success of many smaller nation states in a turbulent international environment.

Also, in the case of the current study, it is obviously relevant to point out that there are important differences between the state of globalization then and now. Global processes have picked up speed, the differentiation between weak and strong states has been aggravated (Bauman, 1998; Hirst and Thompson, 1996), the systems competition of the Cold War is gone, and the cultural diversity of national societies has increased as a result of migratory processes. In this context, and given that a politico-cultural compromise culture across interest and social groups has been a facilitator of national success and a cushion against external shocks, the current defence of Danish culture in the face of immigration can be seen as rooted in perceived effects of sovereignty erosion; that is, in the challenge that immigration from third countries poses to the politico-cultural framework that has historically ensured flexibility, adaptability, and consensualism. In other words, the combination of "smallness," "homogeneity," and "success," via flexible pragmatism externally and domestic socio-political consensus and trust internally (see also Katzenstein 2000), is an important parameter of Denmark's historical adaptation to changing international contexts and constraints. It has transformed itself into pride in the homogeneity of Danish culture, the consensuality of politics, and the normative value basis of political and social institutions (thus setting limits to institutional flexibility).[2]

This places on the shoulders of "national culture" a burden of political co-signification (Hedetoft 2003c), particularly since the fusion of politics and culture is always greatest in homogeneous polities and becomes foregrounded in situations of perceived crisis. This will tend to increase the pressure on political actors to "right-people the state," as Brendan O'Leary and his associates have called this process (2001).[3] In other words, there is greater pressure to ensure the cultural, linguistic, and political homogeneity that – more or less consciously, more or less rationally – is linked with welfare, well-being, and success, because "culture" and "identity" have come to be defined and substantiated in these terms.

The question is less about whether eroded sovereignty, in a new global order, *can be* compensated for through the retention of an optimum level of vertical cultural trust (for reflections on this, more to come below), and more about the specifics of the nexus between historical statehood and political and ideological responses, as well as the consequences of these responses (e.g., populism, increased mistrust of foreigners, and stereotyping of immigrants). We are here dealing with real effects of a perceived threat. Immigration may not be – indeed, is not – a material and quantitative menace because of the actual costs of integration (see note 9), but rather because it puts (or is *seen* to put) the model of "political participation among equals" and "consensual trust" in jeopardy. Globalization manifests itself domestically as a kind of culture-as-politics diversity that is difficult to reconcile with the parameters of the homogeneous model.

The process has involved a dual osmosis. The first aspect was the transformation of the previous macro-strategies applied by the Danish state for coping with smallness and vulnerability into policies and political discourses about refugees and immigrants *at the level of state and elites*. The second is the twofold transformation of these policies: first (historically), into popular attitudes, cultural resources, and sentiments about Danish identity and political culture as they rely on mainstream consensus, homogeneity, and mass-elite cultural trust in the context of welfare-state arrangements; and, second (later, now), into widespread skeptical attitudes to and discourses about refugees, immigrants, and "foreign cultures." These attitudes and discourses have cut themselves loose from their causal foundation so as to live an autonomous moral, cultural, and ideological existence with its own immanent dynamics and "logic" – the defensive ethnicism of particularist "Danishness." They will hence tend to deny their causal and historical origins, in order to be understood within the parameters of national primordialism.

To frame the question in this way is also to argue that perceptions of the "immigrant threat" contain more than sheer irrationality and prejudice. Rather, they are structurally embedded, without necessarily constituting the most appropriate political response. The question is: in what ways does diversity come to be seen and symbolically represented as a barrier to identity and well-being – not as an endorsement of anti-immigrant policies, but as an attempt to explain their "ultimate rationale" as based in a national-interest optic that takes stock of the instruments that have hitherto worked for the country while remaining within the options and scenarios that are institutionally embedded? Other possibilities or priorities cannot be excluded, however (the fact that something worked in the past does not mean that it will in future too); nor are dominant discourses that couch arguments in "existential" and "ethnic absolutism" terms for that reason more normatively acceptable. This is the point where rational-choice preferences turn irrational, and where arguments take leave of the sense-making basis from which they originally derive.

By looking at political discourse about Danish values and culture, there can be little doubt that "immigration" (as a kind of master signifier) has over the last seven or eight years come to be perceived as a significant external shock. It is interesting to ask, therefore, how the small state of Denmark tries to come to terms with new conditions for the success-culture nexus: by clinging to the old model? by tinkering with it? or by looking for an alternative trajectory involving the acceptance of diversity, a different separation between inside (domestic welfare and consensus politics) and outside (economic openness and pragmatic foreign-policy adaptation)?[4]

I will try to demonstrate that the main strategy is (still) based on the assimilationism that goes with the homogeneous welfare model, but that official discourses have become adept at framing the question in terms of "equal treatment," and then integrating elements of "diversity talk" and "diversity management" into programmatic statements: "It's not that we don't accept differences,"[5] as the recent Government White Paper from the summer of 2003 so pointedly puts it. The crucial question, of course, is what the ensuing "but" entails for the politics of integration in Denmark. Is it a prelude to the implementation of measures that would respect the differentiation between what David O'Leary calls "integration," which "stops at the public domain, permitting private cultural differences to be sustained," and "assimilation," which "through fusion or acculturation, seeks to eliminate public and private differences between people's cultures" (2001, 34)? Or are we seeing a set of policies and discourses that follow less neat lines of separation in their attempt to preserve the cultural and political specificity of Denmark's "homogeneous smallness"? Is it true for Denmark, as I have argued in a different context, that multicultural strategies are most accepted and legitimate when they are de facto little more than a mode of integrating newcomers, and are therefore both a method of inclusion and exclusion (Hedetoft 2003b, chapter 7)?

Before getting to the heart of these central questions, a brief historical outline is in order.[6]

THE DANISH CASE: ITS HISTORY AND ISSUES

Denmark, like the other Scandinavian countries, is a small, highly developed nation-state that perceives itself to possess a high degree of cultural homogeneity, social trust, and political consensualism and has traditionally cultivated a national image of tolerance, friendliness, and internationalism. Since World War II, it has developed a very specific form of universalistic welfare state, based on a high level of public provision (health care, education, unemployment benefits, old-age pensions, for example) being accessible to all citizens and residents in the countries. These welfare-state structures entail both a significant extent of state regulation and intervention in the societal domain and (unlike welfare arrangements in many continental countries, such as Germany, for example) significant levels of socio-economic redistribution across social groups and classes. These structures are costly, ideologically basing themselves not only on conceptions of social egalitarianism and universalism (rather than, for example, freedom and initiative) but also on the assumption that citizens earn their entitlements by contributing (through taxation) over a lifetime of active work to the maintenance and growth of the national wealth. Cultural belonging and political rights are thus intertwined, and "equality" is interpreted to mean two different things simultaneously: "cultural similarity" and "political sameness" (in respect of civic rights). In the Danish language, one word covers both these meanings (*lighed*).

Cultural homogeneity, on the one hand, and the universalistic structures and ideological presumptions of the Danish welfare state on the other are key to understanding the politics of immigration/integration and its conceptual foundations – and are thus also crucial for understanding major differences between Denmark and other EU Member states. Immigration has consistently been regarded as a responsibility of the state, which has set up formalized integration programs offering courses in language, civics, and history, and which has offered the same – or at least very similar – public provisions to immigrants as to its own ethno-national citizenry. It should be noted, nevertheless, that although refugees were accepted from the late 1970s onward in compliance with international conventions, their acceptance ran counter to the official and still active stop to labour immigration, dating back to 1973, which resulted from the so-called oil crisis.

Denmark has thus emphasized efforts to acculturate immigrants as speedily as possible, by means of public control and regulation, and attempts to extend egalitarian universalism to cover "old" citizens as well as newcomers. In this sense, the welfare state has been viewed as a possibility and an instrument for smooth integration. At the same time it is important to realize that the political framework for recognition has always been the successful individual inclusion and acculturation to the mores of Danish life, since the Danish political system – unlike the systems of the other Nordic countries – does not base itself on the recognition of minorities and makes no juridical or political allowance for minority rights and cultural claims based on minority status.[7] Thus, for instance, the Roma have achieved minority status and concomitant rights in Finland, Sweden, and Norway, but not in Denmark, where they are commonly regarded as a peculiar sort of people with a propensity to petty theft, but, in formal terms, as individual citizens. In this sense, the Danish political regime is a citizens' state like the French: egalitarian, secular, and assimilationist – but (so far, at least) without the component of outgoing cultural universalism that characterizes France, without a clear separation of Church and State, and without the notion of territorial citizenship (*ius soli*) which accompanies this modernized version of imperial mentality.[8]

Over time, however, the two historical staples of homogeneity and equality have increasingly come to be seen as obstacles to integration – and the immigrants to be seen as a more or less uncomfortable challenge – as cultural assimilation has revealed itself to be more difficult to bring about than originally imagined, as claims for some sort of multicultural policies have picked up speed, and as "old" citizens as well as political actors have started to focus on (and often ideologically exaggerate) the financial burden that newcomers place on the provisions of the welfare system.[9] In the ideological domain, this has exacerbated negative immigrant stereotyping: refugees are routinely branded as "welfare scroungers" or "refugees of convenience," who unfairly take advantage of a system that was never intended for their benefit.

Concurrently, the relatively high level of welfare benefits and the general conceptual approach to integration seem to work as a barrier for the integration of immigrants into the labour market, since: (i) many immigrants stand to gain nothing or very little in terms of real income by getting a job; (ii) state-regulated induction programs seem to have a "pacifying" effect and often impede geographical mobility; (iii) the close-knit nature of civic society tends to exclude culturally distinct immigrants from the social and informational networks that are frequently the gateway to participation in both the labour market and in civic and political institutions; and (iv) the readiness to accept and utilize alternative social and educational resources of immigrants is mostly rather low (especially among employers) and such resources (bilingualism, for example) are frequently stigmatized as an obstacle to rather than a possibility for better integration.

The most important lesson is that, whereas the welfare state is excellent at receiving and catering for refugee immigrants, it is vulnerable when the humanitarian consensus reaches its (cultural) limits, and fragile when it comes down to integrating immigrants into the labour market, the educational system, or civic/political institutions. Even in Sweden, which among European countries has gone furthest toward defining itself as a multicultural society, the success rate in these areas is at best only marginally higher than in Denmark, and in some areas even worse (Tænketanken 2004, 107).

There are three major kinds of barriers: political, cultural, and economic. Politically, the welfare state depends on a history of "vertical trust" between state and society, to the extent that the two "domains" are often culturally and ideologically perceived as one – a bond now widely claimed to be threatened by large-scale immigration. In practice, this image of an ethnically pure polity is translated into political reality in two ways: on the one hand, through a system of representation that allows differences of interest and opinion to organize themselves and be represented within the political system; and on the other, through practices of consensual negotiation, balancing, and mainstreaming of interests, as well as a pragmatism of conflict resolution. This means that public debates can often assume oddly antagonistic forms while simultaneously maintaining the ideal and endgoal of "finding the political middle ground." Culturally, this consensual welfare system – whereby the right to articulate dissenting, disgruntled, or disaffected views comes with the territory of belonging to what some have called the tribal community of Danishness (Mellon 1992; Gundelach 2002) – engenders a host of negative immigrant stereotypes. These stereotypes are based both on the suspicion that the newcomers may not be "real refugees" and, more fundamentally, on the premise that they have not contributed to and do not share the cultural *doxa* of this small but successful community. These negative images, in turn, provide material for the national media and the populist politicians to frame immigrants as "a problem" (Vikkelsø Slot 2001). And, economically, there is a discrepancy between the "skills structure" of the labour market and that of (most) immigrants – not surprisingly, since the majority have entered as refugees and not as economic migrants coming into a political regime allowing for the influx of non-Danes into the labour market.[10]

The three areas also interact: the level of welfare provisions is a disincentive to employment if compared with the minimum wage levels (Mogensen and Matthiessen 2000; Pedersen 2002); unwillingness among employers to hire immigrants is probably due – at least in part – to cultural considerations of social cohesion and linguistic interaction in the workplace (though solid research in the area of labour-market discrimination is still lacking – cf. Hedetoft and Hummelgaard et al. 2002); assumptions of ethno-cultural homogeneity inspire assimilationist strategies and are an obstacle to the acceptance of difference and the institutional elasticity required for successful integration (Ejrnæs 2002; Holmen 2002; Schmidt 2002); and government-controlled induction programs have sometimes developed into social incubators, insulating immigrants from society rather than preparing them for it (Järvinen and Mik-Meyer 2003). It would seem that the more extensive and universal the social benefits – and the more regulated the educational institutions and the labour market– the more difficult it is for immigrants to enter these institutions – and subsequently the labour market – on an equal footing and in the same proportions as the indigenous populations (Necef 2002). Thus, the core value of "equality" not only seems to impede more liberalist integration measures but to some extent also engenders its own inequalities and disparities, because Danish politics and society have difficulty coping adequately with cultural and social difference that falls outside the perimeters of the traditional political compact between government and citizens, which has proved itself to be a workable, multifunctional model for international adaptation, economic redistribution, social peace, and political consensus at the same time.

The conclusion so far is that there are three ways of approaching the welfare state/immigration nexus (see also Brochmann and Dölvik 2004). The most common and ideologically most acceptable one is to frame immigration as a menace to the welfare state – an argument difficult if not impossible to substantiate. Additional expenses to the tune of some DKK 10–15 billion are no doubt considerable, but in relation both to the total annual fiscal budget (some DKK 500 billion) and to total annual welfare expenditure (some DKK 170 billion) can hardly justify apocalyptic projections. Neither can the social and cultural cohesion that constitutes the foundation of solidarity for the functionality of the welfare state be said to be threatened by an "ethnic" population which – depending on the categories and variables used – makes up between 4.9 and 8 percent of the total population (Danish Immigration Service 2002, 47–8).

As already indicated, it is more fruitful to turn the tables and regard the relationship as one in which the welfare system poses a set of barriers to "successful integration" – in light of institutional inflexibilities, different forms of tacit knowledge and public attitudes, the cultural closure of the state-society compact in Denmark, and the pervasiveness of regulation, monitoring, and control that is key to the welfare state and constrains more liberalistic and pluralistic policies of integration. It must be pointed out, however, that this is an ideological rather than an objectively determined nexus; preferences have in a sense become culturally endogenized.[11] Otherwise it would be hard to explain the fact that there are significant differences between integration indicators in Denmark and Norway, countries that are structurally similar and whose immigration histories resemble each other (cf Tænketanken 2004, chapter 4). A lot depends, in other words, on specific policies, cultural framings, and public/political debates and attitudes.

This is why the third perspective, which Andrew Geddes amongst others has succinctly argued, is the most satisfying and inclusive as regards a general framework of conceptualization: "It is more useful to explore the organisational and ideological changes within European welfare states and the effects that these in turn have on understandings of migration" (Geddes 2003, 152). On this view, the perception of immigration as a threat to the welfare state is an oblique reflection of the more general problem that welfare states, not least small ones, are currently being challenged by profound upheavals in the global conditions of existence and survival of states, particularly tightly organized and homogeneous welfare states. This is starting to be realized (and theorized) by scholars (see, for example, Pedersen 2003; Smith 2003; Swank, 2002), but only sporadically comes to the fore in public debates about the "crisis" of the welfare state. This is particularly true in Denmark, where the overriding tendency has increasingly been to blame ethnic minorities, as the most visible and politically most useful element in a set of more comprehensive problems.[12] I return to the issue in the fourth and concluding section.

The next section will look in more detail at some salient themes and junctures in the recent Danish immigration debate and the strategies pursued by the former and the present governments in order to deal with the immigrant challenge to the Danish regime of ethnic consensualism – or, we might say, with the problem of "right-peopling" Denmark in a context of cultural and ethnic plurality.

THE POLITICS OF ETHNIC CONSENSUS IN DENMARK:
THE STRANGE MARRIAGE OF PLURICULTURAL DISCOURSE
AND SELF-RIGHTEOUS *KULTURKAMP*

"This is all about what makes a modern society function. And to that end, not all cultures are equally good."[13] Thus goes a central passage in a leading article (headlined "The weight of culture")[14] in one of Denmark's largest daily newspapers, *Jyllandsposten*, characterizing and acclaiming the Government White Paper on "integration," titled "The Government's Visions and Strategies for Better Integration" (June 2003).[15] The cited passage is as revealing as the White Paper itself (which will be scrutinized below). "Integration" of immigrants and their descendants is now debated, and (at least allegedly) resolved, in terms of "culture" as the pivotal benchmark,' that is, of "culture" seen not only as a relative notion but also as an absolute and axiomatic yardstick of "core values" (*fundamentale grundværdier*)[16] by which newcomers must be measured and before which their own "culture" must yield.

This is not the "thin" concept of cultural relativism or a culturally differentiating notion (see, for example, Suárez-Orozco 2002), but a thick, condensed, and politicized notion of culture as a bundle of non-contestable values, behavioural practices, and universal orientations imagined to guarantee the functionality of "a" modern society. The non-national universalism of modernity entailed in the use of "a" rather than "this" is, of course, in one sense not to be taken at face value, since we are indisputably faced with a set of rather heavy-handed national demands on ethnic newcomers (so-called New Danes). On the other hand, it is not mere window-dressing either; it reveals the imprint of recent debates and new-found convictions in the Western world about commonalities such as human rights, cultural superiority, moral and ethical foundations, democratic polities, and so forth.

Such explicit demands for cultural transformation represent a novel consensual discourse in Denmark – currently wrapped in the tinsel foil of a much-needed *kulturkamp* ("cultural struggle"), directed not only at coping with the external menace of immigration but simultaneously targeted at the enemy within, the Old Guard of "cultural radicals" and their putative defense of "soft values," their ill-concealed admiration for leftist values, and their wrong-headed Europeanism and cosmopolitanism. What is new, however, is not the assimilationist discourse itself, but, first, its near-total political hegemony (it has entirely superseded former discourses of humanitarianism, tolerance, and compassion); and second, the nexus between "culture," "cohesion," and "social functionality" that underlies both discourses and policies in the integration domain in an ever more intimate fashion (thus in a sense transcending the divide between the culturalist and the economistic approaches to integration with which this article began); and third, the way in which it has nevertheless, on its own terms and within a new kind of logic, started to assimilate, in a pragmatic-functional way, what I have here chosen to term "pluricultural discourses" ("we must leave room for diversity and learn to benefit from it," as the GWP *Resumé* has it).[17] Before delving further into this new type of ethnic policy regime in Denmark, it is relevant to diagnose a few other representative events and then to address the question of the transformative process of immigration/integration discourse and politics over the past decade: How did we get to this point, and should we conceive of it in terms of rupture or continuity?

The present Liberal-Conservative government came to office in November 2001, ousting the old Social Democratic/Radical (that is, social liberal) Party coalition after a general election fought largely on the issue of immigration. The then opposition parties, including the Danish People's Party (DPP) which now provides parliamentary backing for the government, accused the governing coalition of inconsequential, ambivalent, and far too lenient policies and practices in the domain of asylum-seekers and refugees (integration, family reunification, residence permits, citizenship, and much more), ultimately prevailing in an election fought – in a post 9/11 atmosphere dominated by widespread Islamophobia – on a rather populist agenda promising stricter controls (fewer immigrants, more severe conditions for residence, reunification, and naturalization) and tougher policies (increased demands on those who make it to – or are already in Denmark). The general tone of the debate was acrimonious, bordering on vengefulness, immigration being projected as the most imminent and most serious threat to the history, culture, identity, and homogeneity of "little Denmark." The governing coalition, somewhat to its surprise, found itself on the defensive, in spite of having pushed through an array of proposals, policies, and practices over the previous five or six years, all of which contributed toward a tighter Danish immigration and integration regime.[18] And the opposition, astutely capitalizing on a debating climate pervaded by diffuse fears, moral panics, and unspecified enemy images, created unrealistic expectations: not only could they put a virtual stop to any further inflows of undesirable aliens but they would also be able to reinstate Denmark to its imagined former status as a peaceful, stable, ethnically homogeneous, and politically sovereign welfare state – to roll back or at least counterbalance the adverse effects of globalization and Europeanization. The opposition thus successfully projected itself as the authentic and legitimate spokespersons for the people *against* their elites, who had let them down and allowed their true identity to be compromised.

In an important sense, therefore, the present government owes its life to the question of immigration and depends for its continued popular backing largely on its policies and successes in this field.[19] Consequently, one of its first initiatives was to create, the Ministry for Refugees, Immigrants and Integration, a new and separate ministry for these matters, which had previously been handled by the Ministry of the Interior. Second, the tone set in the election campaign was continued not just by a barrage of tougher policy proposals but, significantly, by a matching no-nonsense discourse of responsible behaviour, demands, values, obligations, and self-reliance – a heavily ideologized, value-ridden discourse strangely mixing particularistic demands for national acculturation and expressions of gratitude for being allowed to live in the country, with a laissez-faire, self-help message of market-oriented individualism: "Prove that you can fend for yourselves ," in the process relieving the state of financial burdens.

Accordingly, the prime minister, Anders Fogh Rasmussen, in his New Year's speech to the Danish people, aired on 1 January 2003, emphasized that "Danish society rests on certain fundamental values which must be accepted by people wanting to live here," that these values were currently being "challenged," and that Danes differ from many immigrants in having a freedom-loving and rights-respecting culture that will not allow gender discrimination, the politicization of religion, or genital mutilation. The prime minister characterized the toleration of such practices hitherto as "gullible" (*tossegode*) attitudes: "We have not dared to say out loud that certain things are better than others. But that is what we have to do now," continuing to assert – in defense of the well-behaved immigrants – that he would not permit "those who fled the darkness of the Mullahs to experience that ... medieval forces find fertile soil in Danish society" (see the text of the speech in *Politiken*, 2 January 2003).

This discourse and the policy initiatives that have continuously flowed from the new ministry under the leadership of Haarder and Hvilshoj, particularly the twenty-four-year age threshold for transnational marriages intended to curb family reunification,[20] inspired a leading article in the Danish daily *Politiken* (18 January 2002) to characterize the new government's policies as focused on "ethnic purity" and on "protecting the Danish tribe," which supposedly "cannot abide being mixed with other inhabitants of the globe." Hence, Denmark is to be "protected against immigration," a project which in the view of the columnist was as depressing as it was illusory. "Denmark for the Danes" may have been the state of affairs in the past, but was allegedly impossible in the present and future of globalization.

The counter-argument commonly heard is twofold: One is functional/economistic: effective integration cannot be had without severe limitations on immigration.[21] However, on the background of the programmatic culturalism of the prime minister's speech (and a host of similar discourses), the functional argument comes across as unconvincing pragmatism packaging a real motive of protecting the Danish *ethnie* and the benefits of its homogeneous composition. The functionality lies here – not in any necessary limitation/integration nexus and the sophisticated statistical "numbers game" that routinely accompanies it[22] – but in the political, institutional, and social realities of the Danish welfare state which are thoroughly geared to, or rooted in, what Benedict Anderson (1983) has termed the "horizontal comradeship" of this political community and the tacit cultural normativities that underpin and partly constitute it.

Such arguments can also be heard in more straightforward form. Ideological spokespersons for the preservation of historical Danishness (especially – but far from exclusively – belonging to or sympathizing with the DPP) rarely justify their attack on immigration in functional terms, but prefer to couch their objection in existential, often apocalyptic, language. In April 2002, for instance, Søren Krarup, MP, vicar in the Church of Denmark and a central representative of the DPP, put forth the following argument during the First Reading in Parliament of a proposal for the "naturalization" of specified foreign citizens: "Danes are increasingly becoming foreigners in their own country ... Parliament is permitting the slow extermination of the Danish people." He continued by predicting that "our descendants" will "curse" those politicians who are responsible for the increasing "alienation of Danes in Denmark." For the next generations, he said, will experience the "consequences of these disastrous immigration policies" involving a "senseless and irresponsible conferment of Danish citizenship to 6163 alien adults and children."

Krarup's discourse – along with many similar contributions to current political debates about immigration[23] – is based on allegations against the powers-that-be for unpatriotic activities bordering on high treason (*landsskadelig virksomhed*) against the foundational identity of Danishness, which in Krarup's terms does not need to be explained or justified (it is as natural as "the air we breathe," a basic condition of life itself), and hence cannot be acquired by foreigners. Thus, by admitting immigrants, Parliamentarians allegedly fail to "take care of Denmark" and to "safeguard the future of the Danes." The consensual compact of homogeneous Danishness is in danger of breaking down, due to politicians' betrayal of the national cause. The external menace – globalization as represented by hordes of cultural aliens – has entered into an unholy alliance with "our own" elites, people elected to defend our interests and our collective historical destiny. It is this collusion, whether intended or not, which is supposedly putting the very future of Danishness in jeopardy.[24]

It is noteworthy that these statements are made by a political actor who explicitly sees himself and his party as the authentic representatives of Danishness, who at the time of the debate were – and still are – much closer to the government and its central processes than the politicians he fulminates against. This fact reveals such nationalist indignation to be far removed from the powerless rantings of marginalized and "alienated" groups. Rather, Krarup and his associates and sympathizers are on the rampage, settling the score with old political opponents of the "cultural-radical" kind, constructing enemy imagery and moral panics for the revitalization of Danish nationalism in an ethno-religious mode blending nostalgia and fundamentalism,[25] and simultaneously making inroads on traditional social-democratic welfare territory. For despite the existentialism of Krarup's concerns for the survival of the special Danish species, the welfare state is very pragmatically at the heart of DPP policies when it comes to showing the way forward and identifying adequate political instruments. Immigration is projected as a threat both to historical Danishness and to the civic solidarity of all citizens, which the welfare state encapsulates. Hence welfare is all for the good and good for all, as long as this "all" only involves authentic Danes who truly belong here. In this way, welfare policies and the welfare state become focally linked to the migration and asylum regime in Denmark. They are doubly positioned: both as an end-goal of ethnonational policies and – via the exclusion of aliens as "welfare abusers" – as an ideological instrument for their attainment, in the process justifying the DPP's "ethnic purity" and "immigrant repatriation" platform.[26]

Catalysts for Transformation

The populist policies[27] articulated by people such as Krarup, Pia Kjærsgaard (leader of the DPP), and Ole Hasselbalch, and currently setting both the dominant tone of public debates and the tenor of government policies in the immigration and integration arena, have acted as the main catalyst for the transformation of assumptions and discourses in this sensitive policy field over the last decade or so. As indicated, the core of these developments – which can be categorized neither as smooth continuity nor as dramatic rupture[28] – can briefly be captured in terms of three crucial transformative processes, conditioned but not exclusively caused by the advent of the DPP on the political stage in 1995.[29]

From humanitarianism to nationalism: The first transformation consists in the gradual supersession of humanitarian and compassion-based approaches to the question of asylum and refugees by certain discourses and policies: (i) of national interest and utility ("What's the benefit for us? How many can we take?"); of identity scares ("Can Danishness survive the religious and civilizational challenge?"); (iii) of social cohesion ("How can we deal with criminal immigrants and ethnic ghettoes? How can we make them integrate?"); and (iv) of welfare-state policies and political participation ("Can the universalist welfare model survive? Can we afford to pay the benefits?

And is it right for 'them' to have rights without having contributed and without participating?"). In the course of the 1990s, answers to such questions, by political actors, media opinion-leaders, and ordinary citizens variously, became increasingly negative or skeptical, resulting in a barrage of legislative initiatives intended to introduce stricter controls and more tough-minded conditions for obtaining asylum and gaining access to social opportunities and welfare provisions.

This gradual abandonment of humanitarian and rights-based positions does not mean that these were ever the dominant, let alone hegemonic policy-determining, discourse, but since the 1970s they had enjoyed legitimacy and had been embraced, at least in part and sometimes for reasons of image projection only, by representatives of nearly all political parties (even by the Progress Party in the 1970s, when "immigration" had not yet developed into a key component of their nationalist policies). These positions and discourses had thus been locked in a permanent struggle with more chauvinist and utilitarian positions, sometimes blending with them, at other times representing the difference between the political left and the political right (or dividing parties such as the Social Democrats down the middle), but even more frequently standing in a relationship of "discourse/rhetoric" versus "policy" to one another – increasingly restrictive policies often being conveniently wrapped in a coating of humanitarian and immigrant-friendly rhetoric.[30]

The most significant change over the past decade in this field is that policies and discourses are no longer worlds apart, but have gradually approached each other to the extent that there is now a virtual overlap between them. What I have termed the nationalist position has gained the upper hand, not just in the area of immigration and integration policies but in the domain of discourse and rhetoric as well. The "stranger" has increasingly – without much public contestation – come to be represented as a challenge or a menace to "welfare" and "us-ness." The political domain, the media and "public opinion," and the views of the ordinary citizen have increasingly converged around a set of national "givens" and have come to express this new national consensus (and attendant demands and expectations on newcomers) in an increasingly unabashed way. Examples already given above, from the prime minister to Søren Krarup, should suffice to substantiate this claim.

From defensive to offensive "kulturkamp": The second transformation process consists of a change from a defensive stance regarding the question of identity, values, and belonging, to a new position characterized by national self-assertiveness and carried by the conviction that "our" values and culture are indisputably superior and, not least, the right ones.[31] This is a change caused and framed by the macro-political global shift from cultural relativism and interethnic harmony and tolerance to the cultural and polit-ical absolutism accompanying the victory of the free world in the Cold War, the "clash of civilizations" discourses of the '90s, and the "war on terror" following 9/11 (Hedetoft, 2003a and b). The field of migration becomes intimately linked with security concerns and the need to monitor and con-trol the flow of people – for reasons of high global politics. Nevertheless, champions of the national cause are presented with an opportunity to have the ethnonational identity circumscribed and legitimized by a novel, potent, and all-embracing discourse of universal human rights, pinpoint-ing and denigrating other cultures, religions, and traditions as inferior and (to varying degrees) dangerous.

A notable feature of this transformation is that the very universal rights and ethnic plurality which in the post–World-War-II era underpinned the dominant paradigm of cultural relativism now become harnessed to its suc-cessor paradigm of Western, U.S.-led globalism as well as the offensive and often populist *kulturkamp* targeting Third World immigrants in most Western nation-states: "Human rights are threatened – by immigration," as Mogens Camre, a prominent DPP politician (formerly a Social Democrat) headlined a contribution to *Jyllands-Posten* on 19 July 2003. In Denmark, it has thus provided welcome ammunition for already smouldering national-ist concerns and has reinstated the cause of small-nation homogeneity and suspicion of foreigners to respectability, legitimacy, and centrality – under the guise of *værdikamp* (value struggle) or *kulturkamp* (cultural struggle).[32] Alleged taboos have thus been broken in the name of "the right of free speech" – the recurrent mantra routinely invoked as justification for dis-seminating even the most vulgar anti-immigrant stereotypes – and, as already shown above (see note 24), even overt racist talk can now be flaunted as a matter of pride in the public domain. Even moderately assim-ilationist positions – commonly sold as "integration projects" – often fall on deaf ears, premised as they are on what many perceive to be the illusion (respectively the undesirability) of assimilability between incommensurable identities and forms of belonging. Should they be scrutinized in a more positive spirit nevertheless, then it is chiefly because the alternative project of (more or less openly enforced) repatriation/resettlement is realized as impracticable – and even then only on condition that the "new Danes" demonstrate their willingness to acculturate, their loyalty to Denmark, and their ability to fend for themselves. The first two of these two demands have now been formalized by the introduction of a solemn oath of allegiance to Denmark upon conferment of citizenship. The third and last condition provides the substance for the third transformation process.

From "dependence" to "self-reliance," "rights" to "duties": Unlike the second process, which belongs in the domain of assimilationist (if not exclusivist) demands on newcomers, the third transformation is of an integrationist nature, if by "integration" we mean (as O'Leary above) inclusionary processes that respect the private/public divide. Whereas the integrationist model, according to the humanitarian approach to refugees and asylum-seekers, is based on state-regulated integration by means of the social welfare system – and thus on the dependence of immigrants on state services – the new, liberalist modality demands that ethnic minorities prove their economic self-reliance through educational performance, snappy acquisition of linguistic skills, and proactive integration into the labour-market (for example, through individual entrepreneurship), thus ridding themselves of dependence on government aid. Failing that, they have to carry the penalty in the form of reduced payments (or none at all) and additional demands, incentives or pressures to return "home," diminished hopes for permanent residence (let alone citizenship), or a life lived permanently on the margins of society. Good behaviour, on the other hand, increases the prospects of obtaining residence after five years (otherwise the limit is seven), of being allowed to be geographically mobile within Denmark (otherwise mobility is restricted during the first three years of residence), and of being permitted to bring family members from countries of origin to Denmark – family re-unification depending on whether the new resident can support a family and can offer a "fitting home" – and on whether, in the case of marriages for those above twenty-four years of age, authorities deem that the family's "aggregate affiliation" (*samlede tilknytning*) to Denmark is more substantial than to any other country.

This modality also implies a shift from a rights-based to a duty-based integration regime, and from an emphasis on equality to a stress on freedom. Newcomers should no longer expect to be treated with kid gloves by welfare institutions, but must learn to manage on their own resources and contribute economically to the Danish national product. They are here to give, not to take. The official watchwords are "equal treatment" and "equal opportunities," but with a difference – the difference being that absolute equality only applies to thoroughbred Danes, whereas public payments to immigrants will tend to be lower than the common standard for up to seven years. This differential treatment is intended to work as an incentive for the newcomers to find work and relieve state and local government coffers of expenditure in this policy area. In current parlance, it is referred to as the "quid pro quo" principle – in return for permission to live and work in the country, immigrants should live and work for the country. No more spoon-feeding of refugees by local governments and municipalities; as the Minister for Integration Affairs recently (mid-October 2003) put it in no uncertain terms: what immigrants really need is to get their hands dirty by working in pigsties and slaughterhouses. And once in the workplace, dedication and "diversity management" are the proper instruments for extracting full benefit from the immigrants' resources (GWP 26ff.; but see also Lauring and Jonasson 2004). To this end, discriminatory attitudes on the part of employers are strongly discouraged in favour of a more modern approach to the advantages of a plural workforce (see further below). On the other hand, legal sanctions against discriminatory behaviour – let alone a proper anti-discrimination or anti-racist policy – are not in the cards (see Bleich 2003, for a comparative look at Britain and France).

Is this the adoption of a full-blown U.S. model of market-oriented integration? Yes and no. The American model (or what is often perceived as such) has clearly worked as inspiration, but here the shift is more clearly traceable to the adoption of discourses of market-oriented liberalism than to the domain of policy and policy implementation. After all, Denmark still maintains mandatory state-controlled induction programs for all immigrants. The 1973 ban on labour immigration is still in place – although a recent Green Card arrangement allowing for a limited influx of qualified employees who will be given temporary residence (and are not required to enroll in the induction programs) moderates this somewhat. Geographical mobility is restricted and supervised. Demands for cultural and social assimilation to the dominant national *ethnie* are pervasive – after all, this transformative process interacts and co-exists with the two other processes. Discriminatory practices are widespread, and public perceptions as well as political discourses tend to stigmatize ethnic minorities. And finally, unlike the United States, Denmark has no understanding for ethnically based claims-making, affirmative action, or descriptive political representation, and minorities hence cannot benefit from a consensual ethos of social and market-based success. This limitation makes it hard for them to compensate for their "ethnic" disadvantage through economic performance in the open and regulated labour market and refers them in large measure to the shadow economy (in the context of a civic society that still cultivates values of equality rather than freedom) (Rezaei 2004). In sum: the liberalization of integration processes by means of the labour market is narrowly circumscribed by dominant assumptions and practices of a homogeneous and consensual polity and by an institutionally embedded tradition of state-regulated governance in the immigration arena.

Principles and Strategies

Let me finally take a brief look at how these developments and assumptions are embedded in the Government White Paper (GWP) entitled "Visions and Strategies for Better Integration" (June 2003), which has been alluded to on several occasions above and is the most comprehensive statement by the Liberal-Conservative government of its thinking, discourse, and intentions in the area. Space does not permit a detailed analysis of this 84-page document (exclusive of a 16-page *Resumé*). The aim is only to illustrate and contextualize the processes and configurations that have been foregrounded above before proceeding to synthesize this section on the question of what constitutes the peculiarities of the Danish immigration regime.

The GWP contains four "principles" and three "strategies." The *principles* are:

- We must leave room for diversity and learn to benefit from it;
- We must put an end to "clientilization" [dependency] and show respect by making demands;
- We must put an end to inconsistency in all its possible forms;
- We must not excuse oppressive family forms by reference to "culture."

These principles are in turn to be implemented by three *strategies*:

- Efforts to safeguard a cohesive and open democratic society (initiatives to tackle normative integration problems);
- Efforts to ensure that persons with a different ethnic background than Danish fare better in the education system;
- Efforts to facilitate that more foreigners can acquire jobs.[33]

These program components are held together by an overarching "vision" that builds on the following premises: "The core values on which Danish society rests must be respected. Individual possibilities for self-realization must not happen at the expense of these values ... A growing part of the population have been raised with cultural traditions and norms which are different from those which are otherwise pervasive in Danish society. In addition we have the 'welfare-related problems' which arise when welfare provisions and caregivers replace the will to be self-supportive which most foreigners bring with them" (6). The vision statement in the corollary *Resumé* (which is probably the text read by most people, being briefer and textually more accessible) underlines in addition the urgent need for self-supportive initiatives through the projection (which comes across as factual truth) that "insufficient integration of foreigners in the labour market will, *grosso modo*, cost the public sector more than DKK 23 billion annually from 2005."

This emphatic foregrounding of the need for "foreigners" to acculturate to Danish norms and values (simultaneously contextualized as being based on "universal rights of freedom" [4ff.]) – and for them at the same time to relieve themselves of "clientilizing" habits vis-à-vis the public sector, is counterbalanced by a firm commitment to "equal opportunities," "responsible citizenship," and the "enrichment" of Danish society through plurality and diversity. "Diversity is a boon" since it can be used in Denmark's "intensive contact with other countries" to create "possibilities for dynamism and progress" (11). Nevertheless, the White Paper continues, we should "pay attention to the vast differences of cultures, attitudes and norms in our society. It's not that we don't accept differences ... But a number of integration problems are due to the fact that there has not been a thorough discussion of the significance and implications of the meeting of many different cultures ... A number of integration problems ... are attributable to the fact that many people of foreign descent for self-evident reasons have other ideas of right and wrong than those which are prevalent in Denmark" (11–12).

Both a close and a contextual reading of the quoted passage lead to the same conclusion: this is not, as the mention of "thorough discussion" might lead one to believe, a question of insufficient debate, possibly including a negotiation of different values and a resultant mediation between them or an acceptance of real plurality based on mutual recognition. For the "problems" originate – this is apparently beyond debate and a hard fact of life – in the lack of adaptation of the "foreigner" to values "which are prevalent in Denmark" – values that have previously been described as fundamental and which cannot be tinkered with. The immigrants, in other words, are the problem – not "us." It follows that the "thorough discussion" is not to be about homogeneity or plurality, but about the ways in which and the extent to which a moderate degree of diversity is commensurable with Danishness – identifying the line where "freedom does not transcend rationality" (13). It's not that we don't accept differences – but we prefer not to, and then only if they are innocuous or can be turned to national advantage.

As for innocuous differences, the authors are struck by the thought that, notwithstanding all the talk about "our values," "social cohesion," and "harmony," the majority population is not after all an entirely "homogeneous group" (12). This is not specified, but it apparently works as a pacifier to assure us (and possibly the authors too) that a modicum of diversity is compatible with Danish cohesiveness and consensuality. It should therefore be possible to accept other religious beliefs and cultural practices in the family, at school, and in the workplace, as long as they do not interfere with "core values" and the orderly conduct of daily routines. Often, in fact, "employees [of foreign origin] will achieve the best results if their expectations are not presented as absolute demands, but as an invitation to a dialogue" (28). As regards the family, too, there are limits to diversity and "culture is no excuse": long-distance, arranged marriages cannot be tolerated, because "the distance to Danish society is maintained" (22); cousin marriages will soon be prohibited (because they will be interpreted as "forced"); and, as for religion, it is "problematic if religious missionaries disseminate attitudes which militate against fundamental values concerning the integrity of the individual or the equality of people" (*Resumé*, 5).34 Furthermore, immigrants' feelings of solidarity must be directed toward the state and not to the "family, clan or tribe"– this might also contribute toward less tax evasion and moonlighting (29); immigrants should stop caring for their offspring at home and rather place them in childcare institutions; and they should induce their kids to participate more in sports associations in order to mingle with Danish youth (31; see Anderson, 2002). In general, there is a need for *holdningsbearbejdende initiativer*– efforts to influence and change attitudes (23). Ethnic "isolation" must be broken (*Resumé*, 7) and it is legitimate for "society" – within limits – to "interfere with the way that parents bring up their children" (ibid.). Here better integration into and use of the educational institutions (like liberal boarding schools and folk high schools, keeping pupils isolated from their family environment) are, in the view of the GWP, a "greenhouse of co-citizenship" (38), both for imparting knowledge and understanding of Danish history, culture, and democracy ("tacit norms, values and rules of the game" *Resumé*, 8), and for striking the right balance between assimilationist demands, individual initiative, and the utilization of ethnic resources for an "open and diverse labour market" (26).

This is the second point, and the crux of the tolerance displayed in the GWP toward some measure of plurality: "There is a lot of money to be gained by having employees with another ethnic background than Danish." Here the government is not thinking of its own savings on diminished welfare and induction provisions, but of the economic interests of corporate Denmark. Since immigrants are knowledgeable about "foreign languages, markets and cultures and can contribute to a better servicing of a plurally composed group of customers and clients" (27), companies might "gain access to a growing market and perhaps secure invaluable marketing" (25). In this connection, it is important for ethnic employees to temper diversity expertise with acculturation, since they often come from "a more authoritarian workplace culture, where they are used to taking orders rather than independent initiatives" (26). How this alleged authoritarianism squares with the "culture of independence" and "caring for oneself" which the GWP repeatedly claims for the newcomers (e.g., 6 and *Resumé*, 11), is a riddle that the text does not help us to solve.

What it does make clear, however, is that the way the government envisages the adaptation of the Danish welfare model to the "immigrant challenge" – the fact that "our basic perceptions are being put to the test" (11) – is by way of deploying universalist human-rights discourse in the defense of Danish particularism and assimilationist requirements, based on the consensualism and orderliness of Danish society. This allows for the incorporation of diversity, freedom, and equality into the strategic vision, but also for the transgression of the private/public divide wherever necessary. Otherness is acceptable and diversity can be tolerated – but only in depoliticized forms or in pragmatically advantageous (economically lucrative) contexts. Otherwise "consistent" state interventionism, into family values, patterns and practices, for example, is called for. Thus, where the "old" divide between humanitarianism and nationalism was superseded by a new-found consensus on consistency between discourses and policies (hence the proclamatory character of the third principle: "Putting an end to inconsistency in all its possible forms"), this new mainstream consensus has seemingly opened the door to a new area of (much more moderate) contestation, a new discourse/policy divide: integration and diversity in discourse, assimilation in political and social practice.

Briefly, the peculiarity of the modernized Danish integration policy regime can thus be described as a combination of three apparently divergent elements:

Assimilation: employs culturalist and universalist/Western human rights discourse and legitimates trangressing the public/private divide, wherever functional or morally called for – reflects the incontrovertible "claims of culture" (Benhabib 2002) in Denmark, the importance of maintaining "Danish homogeneity." Politically, this position is most vehemently championed by the DPP, but it has by now been very widely accepted across the entire spectrum, and most emphatically by the government coalition between Liberals and Conservatives.

Integration: employs "equal footing" and "equal access" discourse, both as a set of demands on ethnic minorities and in defense of calls on employers to behave in a non-discriminatory manner. This discourse respects the public/private divide, being liberal, republican, and legalist in an almost "French" mode. It also involves market-oriented self-help and self-reliance measures – but surprisingly little emphasis on equality of political participation in the civic domain (*medborgerskab*). The traditional spokespersons for this approach come from influential sections of the Social Democrats, the Social Liberal Party, and, recently, the Socialist People's Party as well.

Pluriculturality: employs diversity (management) discourse, reflecting the fact of ethnic diversity and a plural world, but within a pragmatic-instrumental modality (*let's take advantage of it!*) and probably also as lip service to pervasive claims to be allowing for multicultural policies and respecting international conventions. This stance has traditionally been championed by political actors from the left of the political middle, notably the Unity List and the Socialist People's Party (as well as a minority in the Social Democratic Party), but has now – because of the company-oriented instrumentality of diversity-management strategies – come to be broadly accepted.

The order of the three is far from random, their priority ranking within the – by now near-hegemonic – discourse of the Danish ethnic regime being that in which they are listed, as befits a program intended to modernize a consensual polity and restore social trust as well as political cohesion.[35] In this way, the model comes across as a strange marriage of interest-based pragmatism and identity-based nationalism. As a result, assimilationism poses as diversity management, and integrationist policies and discourses are positioned in the middle as seemingly neutral mediators.

THE POWER OF CULTURE
AND THE PLIGHT OF MINORITIES

This hybrid model for coping with immigration and ethnic minorities is intended as the solution to the practical puzzle of how to retain the traditional advantages – domestically and internationally – of the consensual welfare state and its compromise culture while at the same time coping with the pluricultural challenge. It is thus both a reaffirmation of the axiomatic given that not all cultures are "equally good" at making "a modern society function" (see the statement from *Jyllandsposten* with which the previous section began) and an utterance to the following effect: (i) that diversity, thus understood, may, under certain conditions, be compatible with the Danish model of ethnic consensus and "deep" cultural cohesion – or differently; (ii) that the functional benefits as well as the identity components of Danish homogeneity can be salvaged in the face of the threat posed by global migration flows; (iii) that it is possible to control borders effectively; (iv) and *that* "foreigners," given that their numbers are not excessive, can even be turned to national advantage. The price, according to this discourse, is, on the one hand, the shedding of misconceived humanitarianism toward people who for the most part are not seen to be "real refugees," and, on the other, the abandonment of ethnic minorities much more than previously to the mercy of the market and their own capacity for self-preservation. In both areas – the international and the domestic – the main recipe thus has "less pity, more consistency" writ large all over.

Critics of the recipe – and they are relatively few and quite low-key these days –fall largely into two categories. There are those who still find the toughness unpalatable and argue for more compassionate policies, a greater responsiveness to needy, poor, and persecuted people, as well as more multicultural policies of social recognition. They are frequently supported by advocates of international institutionalism and legalism, who warn political actors that their policies or intentions violate international human-rights conventions that Denmark has signed up to. Critics in this category further argue that Danish politics is bad at coping with cultural diversity, does not recognize essential Otherness and has no strategy for incorporating ethnic minorities into the Danish political system – no strategy, in other words, for what in Danish is called *medborgerskab*, the co-citizenship of the immigrant Other.

The second category of critics – the largest – argue, on the other hand, that policies of ethnic assimilationism constitute political nostalgia in a world of globalization and – as the *Politiken* columnist above – that "Denmark for the Danes" is based on an illusion of ethnic purity – in a world where borders are crumbling, sovereignties are being undermined, the North-South divide is widening, and the "demographic population bomb" in the Third World is about to explode. For such reasons, these kinds of integration policies and border control measures are supposedly doomed to fail. The watchword of this criticism boils down to a modernized version of an old Clinton attack against George Bush Sr: "It's globalization, stupid" – and it can't be hemmed in. Is this in fact the case?

Let me contextualize these criticisms and discuss them in the listed order. The problems that the Danish welfare state now faces in terms of integrating immigrants are rooted in two interconnected processes and phenomena. One is that the viability and success of this type of nation-state are seen to depend on its being a culturally homogeneous and politically autonomous entity. The second is that policies of entry and integration have been inadequately geared to distinguishing between different "categories" of immigrants (e.g., economic migrants *vs.* refugees; immigrants with varying educational, religious, and geographic backgrounds; male *vs.* female immigrants), and have also been unprepared for the increase in the number of asylum-seekers. Both problem areas are linked to the challenge that global processes as well as EU integration pose for the traditional welfare states. All EU Member States, and Denmark too, clearly need to find new avenues toward functional cohesion and to cope with diversity in ways that promote intercultural trust. In a sense, the new Danish model is cognizant of these challenges and proposes a way to deal with them – regardless of how provocative and even distasteful it may be to more cosmopolitan-minded critics.

It is no doubt true that the extensive recourse to labour-market liberalization measures is a double-headed monster and thus cannot be regarded as an automatic panacea for the problem of cultural diversity. When immigrants are increasingly thrown back on their own inventiveness and resources for integration into the labour market and have to demonstrate that they want to (and are able to) belong, this might diminish the need for the same level of socio-political consensus as hitherto and, in certain cases, may prove to have the beneficial effects for companies on which the

GWP is premised – though, as indicated, this is doubtful. On the other hand, because of the low priority it gives to political participation, this recourse to labour-market liberalization tends to jeopardize the state panoply protecting and furthering socioeconomic trust and equality (the culture of compromise) – an important parameter of the success of "smallness"; and it tends to hamper the incorporation of minorities (as collectivities as well as individuals) into the political system – something that has traditionally been pivotal for the maintenance of social peace and political consensus.

The tension between "Social Democratic" and "Danish People's Party" versions of social-welfare arrangements – one insisting that homogeneity and diversity are somehow compatible, the other that a welfare polity of the Danish kind must be predicated on ethnic purity and, if need be, assimilation – is a precise reflection of this National/Global squeeze.[36] On balance, this challenge, however real and however much it may be based on logical and practical incommensurabilities between assimilation and pluralism, must be assessed as manageable – since immigrant numbers are moderate, minorities are weak and politically disorganized, and the welfare state has, after all, a history of coping with marginalized, disaffected, or poorly integrated groups without for that reason falling apart – for example, youth protesters in the '60s, the political left in the '70s, house squatters (*bz'ere*) and anarchists (*autonomes*) in the '80s, motorcycle gangs (*Hell's Angels* and *Bandidos*) in the '90s, and so on. It cannot therefore be regarded as functionally detrimental to the reformed assimilationist model, which the current government embodies.

Another critical approach argues that the "Danish solution" is quite merciless, functionalist, and nationalist as well, cynically giving priority to "our own" interests and prosperity over those of newcomers looking for shelter, protection, and a prospect for the future. This is a moral-political criticism voiced with varying degrees of sincerity, but which in its serious and nuanced versions is quite damaging.[37] Whereas knee-jerk cultural relativism and automatic support for immigrant cultures, no matter what they may entail, make little sense (Hedetoft 2003b, chapter 7), criticizing official policies does not necessitate a normative partiality for immigrant cultures or ethnic claims-making. Nevertheless, charges of national self-sufficiency and myopic instrumentalism in dealing with immigrants or keeping the numbers of refugees at a minimum are no doubt to the point. In this context, the devil's in the details, and this exposé so far has attempted to unravel some of these critical minutiae.

The overarching objective of this chapter, however, has been to contextualize political responses to the immigrant challenge in view of their adequacy for the continued functionality of the consensual Danish compromise model of state interventionism and universal welfare. In this regard, the charge against the new assimilationist model for being idealistic, back-ward-looking, and ultimately impossible due to "globalization" is central and deserves a few final comments.

The argument is paradoxically predicated on much the same normative view of the "demographic challenge" from the outside as that which underpins policies of stricter immigration rules: ever more people are being born in the Third World and ever more people will therefore want to move to our part of the world in search of higher living standards and a more secure and stable social and political environment (Lintrup and Olesen, 2002). Faced with this situation/assessment, "restrictionists" argue that immigration flows must be controlled, limited, or stopped – whereas "globalists" argue either that this cannot be done or that immigrants and/or cultural diversity should be regarded as an asset that might help defuse the impending "age/pension bomb" in Europe.

This is not the place to deal with the two positions in any kind of detail. However, it would seem that – apart from the fact that we are here dealing with uncertain statistical projections and their even more uncertain social consequences in the future – the argument about the "impossibility" or "impracticability" of stemming and monitoring immigration flows on a national basis has very little going for it (Andreas and Snyder 2000; Joppke and Guiraudon 2001). This is not a normative, but an analytical position. Globalization does not, as I have argued elsewhere, annul or erode the nation-state (Hedetoft 1995, 1998, 2003b). It repositions and refunction-alizes it, changes the parameters of its autonomy, and does indeed, in one sense, exert a pressure on national polities for more open and porous bor-ders and for adjustments of domestic politics as well (Cohen and Clarkson 2004; Grande and Pauly 2005; Hedetoft 2003a). These imperatives apply less obviously, however, to the area of population movements, in situations where nation-states basically retain their traditional autonomous powers. In addition, national and European immigration regimes, complementing each other, are now geared toward stepped-up controls, deploying new-fangled technologies (such as biometrics) and more sophisticated forms of police collaboration. They are developing Third World aid into an instru-ment of restricting migration flows to the developed world, and can already show tangible results of their efforts in the form of stable, even moderately declining immigration figures in recent years.[38] It is true that one result of recent control measures and the budding global migration management regime (Düvell 2003) is an increase in human trafficking and probably also in other forms of irregular migration to Western coun-tries (Kyle and Koslowski 2001), but this is in large measure because gov-ernments and business (for obvious reasons of narrow national self-inter-est) are of two minds about the desirability of putting a total stop to the influx of unauthorized migrants. In any case, the main population movements in the world are not those that take place between South and North, East and West, but those within the countries and regions of the South – as voluntary or, more often, forced displacements. Nor does history support the "flooding" argument; the number of people (relative to the total world population) living outside the country of their birth has remained rather stable for more than 100 years at between two and three percent of the world population (see, e.g., Faist, 2000).

Finally, consider the commonsensical argument: why – given the political will, the economic resources and the technological apparatus – should control (not absolute, but approximate and nationally sufficient) *not* be possible? The argument only makes (imagined) sense if one conjures up literally millions and millions of barbarian hordes physically knocking down the gates of Paradise and invading the Promised Land – or more surreptitiously conspiring against us.[39] Both sets of arguments/images belong more in the domain of Science Fiction than the real world – but they are being given a certain degree of plausibility, the former argument by the wider and more diffuse "globalization" scare, the second by Islamic fundamentalism and the "war on terror."

The answer, therefore, to the question heading this section is affirmative: This model may very well work, at least in the short term. Does this imply that the government is on secure ground, that there is no real threat to the consensual model, and that Danish homogeneity is safeguarded by the current policies? In one sense, the answer is affirmative. Immigration and ethnic minorities do not constitute a serious problem – economically, politically, or culturally – though their presence no doubt brings "challenges" (of marginalization, "new poverty," and lack of political participation) that must be handled deftly.

In quite a different sense, however, there probably is a very real threat to the welfare state, the consensual model, and the well-ordered mass-elite nexus in Denmark. It does originate in the pressures of globalization, not from the migration compartment of globalization processes, however, but from the loss of traditional sovereignty which the state must face in many other policy areas: from the European integration process; from "de-industrialization," outsourcing, and the transition to a service-based and high-tech economy; from the impact of capital flows and corporate location strategies on the national taxation basis; from the loss of political authority; and from the globalization of cultures – to mention but a few (see e.g., Baylis and Smith 1997; Beck 2000; Hirst and Thompson 1996; *Jyllandsposte* 2005).

One of the significant consequences – with different implications and in different configurations on a country-by-country basis – is a growing distrust of political actors, more domestic social divisiveness, more anomie, and, at least in the formulation of much voguish political discourse, less respect for time-honoured values.[40] It is reasonable to see political populism as a response, however misguided, to this set of problems. There are a few notable indications of government awareness of this context in the GWP – for example, such statements as: "Danish society has, for a number of years, been challenged by a series of changes ... Core values of society are being challenged, both because the new citizens violate them in some areas, *and because the remaining population do the same*" (8, my emphasis). This indicates a process whereby immigrants, being the objects of a tough assimilationist regime, are taken hostage – in a process of inculcating law and order and the "right values" in a politically engineered situation of external and domestic cultural emergency – to the entire population. The ongoing "value battle," extending far afield and recently involving the question of how properly to understand twentieth-century Danish history[41] – gives credence to this reading, as do "quid-pro-quo" policies and discourses emanating from the government (e.g., Sander, Hovmand, and Frederiksen 2004). Such discourses are indications of the real problem for the "Danish model." It *is* globalization, stupid – but not like that.

I argued initially that the danger inherent in the ethnic power politics of assimilation is that the lures of populism prove too seductive and that the historical "success momentum" of Danish adaptability to changing international circumstances is drowned in a sea of national sentimentalism. The national impetus that has shown itself as a progressive force in Danish history may well revert to its opposite and become a millstone round the neck of Danish politics and political actors. The allowances made for diversity in the modernized/hybrid model indicate an awareness of this danger. On the other hand, modifications are clearly reluctant in spirit, minimal in substance, and doubtful in consequence. The pitfalls of a path-dependent and nostalgic politics of identity have not been overcome, only skirted momentarily. Evidently, minorities are still in need of more flexible institutions of political recognition and cultural accommodation, new avenues of democratic participation, alternative ways of regulating inter-ethnic communication, and firmer legal protection against social and economic discrimination. The central point in the context of this volume, however, is that in order to remain on a track of successful adaptation to more severe and inclement forms of globalization, while continuing to turn dependency and vulnerability into an advantage, the Danish welfare state and its economic beneficiaries may well need these reforms too.

NOTES

1 See, for example, Ole Hyltoft, "*Kulturradikalismens endeligt*" ("The Demise of Cultural Radicalism"), op-ed (*kronik*) in *Jyllandsposten*, 30 March 2002.

2 A problem is how the key variables interact and what role they play in the aggregate configuration – smallness, cultural/historical homogeneity, political culture of compromise – and which is the most important in the Danish context? This cannot be investigated in this paper, but the assumption is that it is the combination of the three elements which is significant rather than each factor being taken in isolation.

3 Meaning the political and ideological process of adapting territory, state, people, and culture to one another in the way that seems to be optimal at any given time.

4 And does immigration really matter – seeing that the liberalization of the social democratic welfare regime is inherent in globalization/Europeanization rather than just in one of its (visible) manifestations, that is, "immigration/migrants"?

5 *Ikke fordi der ikke må være forskelle.* For an analysis of the context and implications of this passage, see section 3, where the Government White Paper, the GWP (*Regeringens vision og strategier for bedre integration*) is scrutinized.

6 A thorough discussion of recent Danish immigration history can be found in Togeby 2003.

7 The exception is the status of the exterritorial entities within the Kingdom of Denmark, Greenland, and the Faroe Islands, each of which is represented by two members in the Danish Parliament, and the German-speaking minority in South Jutland, which – following an agreement struck between Copenhagen and Bonn in the 1950s – enjoys special cultural rights. Both cases, however, must be treated as exceptions to the rule of political and cultural homogeneity and have no precedent-setting effects.

8 Brubaker 1992; Ireland 1994. Recently, however, universalist arguments, based on human rights, have found their way into the Danish immigration debate – but also here in a uniquely Danish fashion. See the next section. For general reflections on the Danish integration regime (and its changing features) in relation to regimes in other European countries, see also Togeby 2003, 29–32.

9 In 1997 net public expenditure due to immigration was, by three ministries, estimated at DKK 10. 3 billion (after an estimated positive net effect of immigrants from the Nordic Countries, EU, North America, Switzerland, Australia and New Zealand had been deducted) (Tænketanken, 2002, 37). Other calculations and more recent figures estimate a net loss to GNP upward of DKK 23 billion as from 2005 (ibid., 10) – when an estimated loss of tax revenue (if immigrants' employment rate were the same as that of other Danes) is factored into the estimate. Methods employed by Lars Haagen Pedersen/DREAM, however, result in significantly lower net costs for the state (Haagen Pedersen 2002, 34). A balanced estimate indicates that current net costs, inclusive of expenditure toward the upkeep of asylum seekers (Danish Immigration

Service 2002, 24), are in the DKK 10–15 billion range. For further details, see also Pedersen 2002.

10 It is important to add that racist stereotyping based on welfare arguments does not imply that negative images of immigrants would disappear if these substantiations of deeply held attitudes and, sometimes, normative world-views based on ethnic stratification and images of differential belonging were not forthcoming. Here we must differentiate between reasons and justifications, grounds and manifestations, and subtexts and pretexts, as much scholarship into the structures of racial thought, discourse, and action has shown. This does not mean that the contextual justifications of negative stereotypes (here: the cultural aspects of welfare systems) are completely random or devoid of specific consequences – only that they should not be accepted at face value as the root cause of racist attitudes, which are multi-layered structures containing both contingent and more permanent features. See, for example, my discussion of these issues in Hedetoft 1995, part I, chapters 1, 2, and 3.

11 I owe this formulation to Peter Katzenstein.

12 The opposing view holds that immigration is an essential component in the solution of the "demographic age bomb." See, for example, Blomgren-Hansen 2003.

13 "Sagen drejer sig derimod om, hvad der skal til for at få et moderne samfund til at fungere. Og til det formål er alle kulturer ikke lige gode" (*Jyllandsposten*, 17 June 2003).

14 "Kulturens vægt," by Ralf Pittelkow.

15 "Regeringens vision og strategier for bedre integration."

16 White Paper, *Resumé*, 3.

17 *Resumé*, 7. I use the term "pluricultural" rather than "multicultural" in order to avoid the multiple political and ideological connotations of the latter notion.

18 Particularly the *Integration Act* of 1999.

19 The currently ongoing debate in Denmark about a possible revision of the Danish EU exemption in the area of Justice and Home Affairs (TEU, 3rd Pillar competencies) is topical evidence of this fact. The Government's current position is that the opt-out should be removed with the explicit exception of the area of asylum and refugees, where national autonomy should be retained in full.

20 The law specifies that marriages between ethnic youth settled in Denmark and foreign residents can only take place if both parties have reached 24 years of age. It has had a number of unintended consequences involving "genuine" Danes, for which reason the law is now under revision so that it may only affect naturalized Danes or people with permanent resident status from non-Western countries.

21 This is of course a commonplace argument for justifying restrictive immigration policies in most Western nation-states, and is not specific to Denmark, although its application is contextually specific.

22 Immigration and asylum policies over the last six years have to a large extent pivoted around statistical projections for the alarming proportional increase of ethnic minorities over the next three or four decades in light of the differential birthrate between Danes and immigrants and on the assumption that the inflow characterizing the '90s might constitute a continuing trend.

23 Some of the main protagonists vociferously representing immigrant-skeptical views based on the putative detrimental effects of immigration on Danish culture, history, and identity are Ole Hyltoft, Bent Jensen, Mogens Camre, Ole Hasselbalch and Jesper Langballe.

24 The translation of Krarup's views into English is mine. For the entire debate, which lasted for the entire day, 2 April 2002, see <http://www.folketinget.dk/samling/20012/salen.htm>.

25 Krarup's particular variant of essentialist Danishness is based on an almost pietistic Lutheranism combined with explicit non-democratic and in a sense highly non-populist elitism drawing its inspiration from enlightened absolutism. The ground tenor is that Danishness cannot be debated or relativized – it constitutes the absolute, natural, and incontestable conditioning of the very existence of "ethnic Danes," whether they are aware of it or not. His nationalism is thus a form of religiously inspired ethnic primordialism.

26 In its purest ideological form, this position of ethnic purity in the current Danish debate was recently articulated by Professor Ole Hasselbalch, a member and former chairman of the "Danish Society" (*Den danske Forening*), who in an op-ed article (*kronik*) in *Jyllandsposten* (16 September 2003) argued: "We have come to the point where it is no disqualification to be labelled a racist, since the accusation can be rooted in an outright honourable effort to secure the right of the Danes to be left in peace on their own soil."

27 As indicated in note 19, "populism" only partially captures the political nationalism of the DPP, which strictly speaking is an odd *mélange* of populist nostalgia, welfare-state ideologies, and non-democratic elitism.

28 The change of government in 2001 has been widely regarded as a rupture, but it is probably more correct to analyse it as a peculiar intertwining of continuities of policy and ruptures of discourse. See further below.

29 The Danish People's Party was created as a result of a split in the Progress Party, a populist anti-tax party that came into being in the early 1970s. For a brief history and analysis of the DPP, see Trads 2002.

30 This mode of discourse is still visible in the above-mentioned immigration/integration nexus: we close the door to new immigrants in order to help those who are here to integrate better and faster – ultimately we have their best interests at heart.

31 See, for example, an editorial in *Jyllandsposten* titled "The Right Values" (*"De rigtige værdier"*), 2 January 2001.

32 This is not a development distinctive to the period after the advent of the present government. The former government had already spoken about the need to impress "Danish values" on immigrants, and the government-appointed think-tank on integration, in a report published in August 2001on the integration of foreigners in Denmark, entitled chapter 9 "Fundamental Values and Norms"(Tænketanken 2001).

33 Translations from the GWP into English are mine throughout.

34 At the time of writing (March 2004), the government has tabled a proposal which, if made into law, will legalize the provision that Imams who are seen not to abide by accepted cultural norms and practices can be stripped of their Danish citizenship and expelled from the country.

35 Lise Togeby (2003) situates the Danish integration regime "more or less in the middle" between ethnic assimilation, republican monism, ethnic segregation, and pluralism, but with an inclination toward republicanism (31). On my analysis, the assimilationist tendency is dominant, as a result of declining respect for the public/private divide, the virtual absence of state/church separation, and the aggressive culturalist discourses that have characterized the Danish debate and Danish policies for the major part of the last decade.

36 It is noteworthy in this context that the "social-democratic" penchant of the DPP testifies to the strength of consensualism and welfare-state arrangements for political/electoral success in Denmark. But it is also worthy of notice that the gap between the two versions of welfare-state policies has narrowed, as the official Social Democratic program is gradually shedding much of its globalist discourse.

37 Such serious critical voices include a diverse group of scholars, journalists, politicians, and intellectuals, for example, Morten Ejrnæs (sociologist), Carsten Jensen (commentator), Kim Kjær (human-rights scholar), Hans Kornø Rasmussen (economist and journalist), and Klaus Rifbjerg (novelist, poet, and culture critic).

38 The percentage increase in the number of immigrants to "Western European States" between 1990 and 2000 was a meagre 0.7% (from 4.5% to 5.2%) of the total population (Bade 2003). Since then, indications are that the inflow is stable on aggregate, and declining in states – like Britain and Denmark – which have put very restrictive control measures in place, with the visible result that many detention camps for asylum-seekers have been closed down. As regards recent figures for Denmark, see, for example, *Jyllandsposten,* 25 February, 2004, reporting a continuing decline in the number of asylum-seekers.

39 This is the basis of currently popular Islamophobic theories – for one of these, see Helle Merete Brix et al., *In the House of War: Islam's Colonization of*

the West (Brix et al. 2003; original title: "*I krigens hus – Islams kolonisering af Vesten*"), and the interview with Brix about the book in *Politiken*, 4 October 2003.

40 The final report of the Danish Power and Democracy Project (*Magtudredningen* – Togeby et al. 2003) argues that Danish democracy is in fine shape, but nevertheless indicates the existence of several worrisome factors: growing inequality, a greater gap of power and influence between social groups, marginalization of ethnic minorities, lack of trust in EU developments, declining participation in political organizations, skepticism toward academics, and a closed administrative system. Nevertheless trust in Danish politicians is seen to be high – a conclusion which some political actors, for example, the president of the Danish Parliament, received with some disbelief (*Politiken*, 31 October 2003). See further the criticism of the project voiced in *Politiken*, 6 March 2004 ("Det er jo det rene makværk!") and for more detailed critiques, Øllgaard and Madsen 2004, and *GRUS*, no. 71, 2004.

41 Such as the prime minister's attempt in the fall of 2003 to castigate common interpretations of collaborative Danish policies vis-à-vis the Nazi occupation forces during the Second World War as rational and necessary. In light of current Danish policies giving full backing to the "war on terror" and U.S. global interventionism, the quiescent policies toward Nazi Germany strike the prime minister as misconceived and unprincipled. On this debate, see, for example, Ralf Pittelkow's contribution in *Jyllandsposten*, 30 August 2003, headlined *Værdikampen* ("The value struggle").

PART FOUR

Closing Reflections

13

Denmark and *Small States*

PETER J. KATZENSTEIN

It is in the nature of closing chapters such as these that their assignment is ambiguous. Should I celebrate, critique, or celebrate and critique? And what needs celebration and critique? Denmark, this splendid volume, or a portion of my own scholarly career that has provided a partial hook for this admirable collective enterprise? Finally, should I play the role of disinterested sage or active partisan in the pages that follow? I have a clear answer only to the last question. I will be writing as an engaged friend, of Denmark, small states, varieties of capitalism, and the editors and authors of this volume. As for my answers to the other questions, bobbing and weaving seems the most feasible response.

Let me start with an autobiographical note. I grew up in the German city of Hamburg, which, as late as the mid-nineteenth century, had been a close neighbour of Denmark. In the 1950s Denmark became a symbol of freedom for me. This was not one of the four basic freedoms that Franklin D. Roosevelt had talked about. To me, it was the fifth freedom, freedom from school, that really mattered. With my family I spent many a summer vacations in Skagen, at Denmark's northernmost tip. I adored Danish furniture, ice-cream, and girls – and not necessarily in that order. The fact that in the 1950s Danish women could smoke cigarillos in public struck this lad from a proper Hanseatic background as outlandishly cool. And in my later high-school years I learned how many ordinary Danes managed to help their Jewish compatriots to escape deportation and death during the Nazi occupation. All of which is a round-about way of saying that I am approaching my subject matter with great sympathy.

Against this background, it is not surprising that I have always disliked the assumption of those, typically living in large countries, who tend to ignore or belittle the accomplishments of Denmark and other small states. And when big countries take a fall and the small ones succeed, I take more than a normal measure of satisfaction. The cause of Europe, with its many small member states, is in my mind much advanced by every soccer match the German or French national teams lose.

The belittling of the small by the big, extends to the field of scholarship. What Michael Porter and his misguided analysis of Denmark is to the editors of this volume, Barrington Moore was for me when I wrote my two books (Katzenstein 1985, 181–6): intellectual giants who did not appreciate the deeper truth of the siren call of "small is beautiful." The story of success – economic, social, and political – that this volume illustrates is compelling. Denmark thus joins in the 1990s with the Netherlands, Ireland, Iceland, Finland, and Norway, and with a small distance also of Sweden and Austria, an illustrious group of small states, that confounds the expectations of those who assume that market efficiency can be achieved only the American way, as taught in American business schools. Few other societies in the world have matched Denmark's record in the past half century – and are likely to match it in the future. There is, then, much to celebrate about Danish accomplishments.

Yet every beauty has its warts. It is one of the great virtues of the routes that the editors mapped for this volume and the marching orders they gave to their authors, to permit ample scope for a discussion of the distributional consequences that leave some much better off than others and that mark this Social-Democratic welfare state with a surprisingly strong elitist streak.

The editors write that my work needs to be revised and updated. I could not agree more. It has been twenty years since I published two books on this subject. And while I have more recently written two papers on small states (Katzenstein 2000, 2003) they have been more extensions of and reflections on my earlier work than revisions and updating. I am thus grateful to the authors in this volume for having made one of the tasks their own. On balance, I think that the editors have treated me both too well and too harshly. They have handled with kid gloves my mis-specification of an historical argument about the foundations of democratic corporatism. And on a number of not so minor points they have glossed over or neglected altogether arguments that to my biased eyes I thought I did present clearly and which are corroborated by the impressive depth and range of evidence this volume offers.

I totally agree with the editors' insistence on taking history seriously. I did so in giving special attention to the cumulative impact of the Great Depression, the threat or the experience of Nazi occupation, and World War II in the 1930s and 1940s. These two decades witnessed a geopolitical conflict of the first order, a variable much emphasized in the editors' Introduction, combined with a deeply dislocating economic depression. The lessons elites and publics in all small European states, including Denmark, learned was simple: disagreeing with your domestic opponents was infinitely preferable to fighting with your enemies abroad or living under Nazi occupation in an impoverished and war-torn continent. Like that of the other small European states, Denmark's political economy was pretty contentious in the interwar years, notwithstanding Denmark's only recently acquired condition of national homogeneity. After 1945, however, conflict- and strike-prone societies in the small European states became much more consensual and thus laid the foundation for corporatist success in a liberal world economy.

This volume seeks to augment the historical perspective on the 1930s and 1940s by emphasizing the importance of the nineteenth century and the loss of empire as another, perhaps even more important historical experience, at least for the Danish case. On the basis of the evidence proffered in this volume, as a non-specialist I have no grounds to disagree. The loss of empire was very consequential for Denmark and laid important structural conditions for the corporatist politics that emerged after the loss of the 1864 war against Prussia.

Two interesting ideas, typically overlooked by many Danes and those who admire them as shining examples of a humane welfare state, suggest themselves as warranting further attention and reflection. Like colonies in the Third World, Iceland chose to break away from the remnant of the Danish empire during World War II while Denmark was occupied by Nazi Germany. And Denmark took another quarter of a century to accede to the demand of returning to Iceland some of the most important scrolls containing the Icelandic sagas – powerful symbols of the national identity of Iceland as Europe's oldest democracy. Furthermore, if we follow the advice Tocqueville proffered – studying the motherland through the prism of its colonies – the fate of Greenland and the Faroe Islands in the twentieth century is not one to inspire unconditional admiration in Danish rule. In the sliver of the Danish empire that remains in the twentieth century, life is often dark, and not only on account of its geographic location. Why this is so and what it tells us about Danish corporatist politics is a topic deserving further study, especially by Danish scholars.

The Danish empire left a second and more substantive legacy, rooted in what students of Asian security know as "comprehensive security," as powerfully argued by Uffe Østergård in chapter 1. Social welfare and stability become a weapon, self-consciously chosen and deployed, to defend the nation against the challenge from extremists from both left and right. This was a strategy first cultivated by Japan in the 1960s and then imitated by the newly industrializing economies in Southeast Asia in the 1970s and 1980s and by China after 1992. And like Taiwan and South Korea after 1945, Danish land-reform in the nineteenth century made for a relatively equal distribution of income and wealth that created domestic purchasing power for domestic consumption and sustained economic growth. The post-imperial Danish model of combining security with welfare thus points to intriguing parallels in other parts of the world and different historical eras. As much as it pleases admirers of the various incarnations of the Asian model to insist on the singularity of the sagacity and wisdom of the Japanese, Southeast Asian, Korean, Taiwanese, or Chinese politicians, bureaucrats, and scholars, Denmark experimented with this combination many decades earlier, and to good effect. Conversely, those celebrating Danish exceptionalism should not lose sight of the possibility, nay likelihood, of socio-political engineers in far-away lands coming up with even better ways of devising even more effective traps for catching mice.

My granting the importance of Denmark's nineteenth-century history does not mean that I wish to conceal the fact that I worked with a conception of history that was a bit different from the one advanced in this book. Rather than insisting on the difference between proximate and distant causes, as the editors do in their Introduction, I continue to view historical change like a pin-ball machine, a series of more or less important events, each of which helps shape the probability of reaching the ultimate corporatist outcome in Denmark and the other rich, small European states. This conceptualization afforded me the opportunity to devote a longish chapter to specify the historical antecedents of democratic corporatism that stretch from the twentieth century back to early European times. It is one of the many virtues of this book devoted to Denmark that its imaginative and correct insistence on the importance of Denmark's nineteenth century history enriches and strengthens further the macro-historical argument that I have advanced. And it does so without necessarily taking anything away from the importance that I attribute to the 1930s and 1940s and the historical processes I singled out, even though they preceded the nineteenth century.

That said, Østergaard's deeply illuminating chapter, which throws considerable doubt on one historical argument developed in *Small States*, needs further reflection and possible correction. I argued that Austria was the only one among the small European states which had a big state history that, in the form of the Austro-Hungarian Dual Monarchy, lasted until the twentieth century. Technically this is correct. But the loss of Denmark's empire in the nineteenth century may possibly be of comparable importance to the break-up of Habsburg at the end of World War I. I may have been ill-advised to build the entire argument around the difference between the structural foundations of the imperial legacy of Habsburg and the structural legacy of the other rich small European states, including Denmark. Since Denmark had a far-flung empire and built a remarkably strong state to administer it, the comparative argument that I etched may need correction.

I think the editors' recourse to Miroslav Hroch's (1985) application of the category of "big small state" to Denmark, however, does not solve the problem – to my satisfaction, at least. For the Czech nation, one of Hroch's examples the editors cite, as much as Austria, was part of the Habsburg Empire, by all accounts a "big big state." For comparative analysis, the editors are unnecessarily opaque on one central point and therefore risk repeating the mistake I made. The proliferation of analytical categories is less desirable than a clear-cut coding of the Danish case in comparative perspective. Either Denmark's empire was not really important, in which case my analysis in *Small States* stands; or, judging from the evidence presented in this volume, Denmark had an empire that should be compared to Austria-Hungary. Arguably, for example, shorn of its empire, like Denmark, Austria was left with a strong and over-sized state bureaucracy. Happily, my task here is to point out rather than correct the weakness of my argument – one the editors of this volume risk repeating. History is less neat than I made it look in the argument that I advanced twenty years ago. Yet it needs to be explained systematically and without taking recourse to ad hoc categories.

History is also less simple than the editors make it seem, on the basis of their reading of the uniformly excellent chapters in this book. Homogeneity, they remind the reader time and again, is a core trait of Danish corporatism and, by implication, corporatism in the other small European states. The case is a powerful one, as articulated by Ove Korsgaard in chapter 3. The consequences of the combination of the ethnic and the democratic elements of the Danish polity was the creation of two powerful shields against Denmark's overweening neighbour to the south. Denmark mobilized the ethnic shield after 1871, and the democratic shield after 1940. The argument stressing homogeneity becomes even more powerful if suitably amended, as is true also, for example, of Japan, to stress that Danish homogeneity is invoked, imagined, and politically constructed. I learned at the conference which yielded this volume that in the 1960s history teachers in secondary schools erroneously taught their students that Denmark's homogeneity was a heritage that dated back a thousand rather than a mere hundred years. Even so, Kevin O'Rourke is surely correct in pointing in chapter 4 to the settling of the national question in the nineteenth-century relations between tenant farmers and owners that favoured class compromise supported by the ideology and practice of Grundtvigianism, and a fusion of nationalism with religion (illustrated by the custom of adorning Christmas trees with small Danish paper flags), as pointing to the undeniable benefits of social homogeneity.

It is, however, easy to overstate a good point, despite Belgium's deep troubles in the 1990s. Switzerland, the Netherlands, and Austria, like Belgium members of Europe's "consociational" club of polities, have succeeded in bridging deep linguistic, ethnic, religious, and social cleavages. These consociational foundations have also yielded the conjoining of social stability with economic and political success. The politics and policy of democratic corporatism are treated in considerable detail in two excellent chapters which probe its behavioural and discursive dimensions, written by Peer Hull Kristensen and Ove Pedersen. And they are treated in the chapters by Cathie Jo Martin, Peter Abrahamson, and Per Kongshøj Madsen, which address the central issues of the role of employers and the state in labour markets, social policy, and welfare reform. And the politics and policy of corporatism require a "constitutional laxity," critiqued effectively by Hjalte Rasmussen in chapter 5, which should become a subject for investigation in other corporatist democracies. All of these contributions are adding detailed and informed assessments of the Danish case to the staple of corporatist studies. I would argue that by and large they are equally applicable to non-homogeneous polities of the consociational type. It is no accident that the 1990s witness both a Danish and a Dutch economic "miracle." An argument about the economic success of small states must look beyond homogeneity to other conditions – many of them identified in this book – that are also consequential. In a comparative perspective, homogeneity is not the only, and perhaps not even the most important, ingredient to Denmark's remarkable accomplishments. I thus take all of these chapters to update rather than revise the arguments that I developed in *Small States.*

Another main theme that the editors identify is the increasing decentralization of Denmark's corporatist arrangements. I agree that this is an important recent development and not only in Denmark (Katzenstein 1989). The liberal variant of democratic corporatism that I analysed in depth in the case of Switzerland (Katzenstein 1984) and more synthetically for the cases of the Netherlands and Belgium as well, tended toward decentralization, while the social variant that typifies Austria and the Scandinavian countries tended toward centralization (Katzenstein 1985, 125–9).

In brief, I argued that more than one road leads to Rome. Where the varieties-of-capitalism school sees only two roads – coordinated and uncoordinated market economies – I saw four. Compared to liberal market- and *étatiste* state-based forms of capitalism, democratic corporatism also provided for a viable solution. Furthermore, there was little reason to argue that centralized or decentralized corporatism enjoyed special advantages. Both followed different political logics, yet both could succeed. The move toward a more decentralized, and also more inclusive form of corporatism that marks contemporary Denmark usefully illustrates that corporatist arrangements can be more or less centralized not only across different countries but across time within the same country. This is an important empirical finding and one of undeniable consequence for Denmark.

After the end of the Cold War and the collapse of socialist political economies this point invites further reflection. The varieties of capitalism have been mightily enlarged since the Berlin Wall came down, bringing socialism with it. In line with the historical argument informing this book and my own writing, the manner by which polities extricated themselves from socialism has a lot to do with the kind of capitalism that emerged subsequently. And so did the presence and programmatic commitments of different international institutions that sought to shape that path of extrication. China, with perhaps the most dynamic of the post-socialist economies, has evolved into a form of Leninist capitalism that is beginning to have large impacts in other parts of the world. The decentralization of Danish corporatism thus points to the many ways that economic success, social stability, and political legitimacy can be brought together. This is indeed, as the editors argue, an era of capitalist hybrids that go far beyond the coordinated-uncoordinated types that have informed the writings of those adopting a varieties-of-capitalism perspective.

The importance of decentralization touches on an ancillary point that also connects to the literature on the varieties of capitalism and points to a further weakness of my own work compared to this more recent theoretical innovation. I was much less effective than were authors trying to work in this newer tradition at disaggregating my analysis to the firm and local level. I did so, in *Corporatism and Change*, in two chapters which offered a series of firm and industry studies of the textile, steel, and watch industries. The rationale for including this material was to illustrate the generative political capacity of democratic corporatism in both its centralized Austrian and decentralized Swiss versions (Katzenstein, 1984, 162–238). To be sure, my primary interest was focused on the connection between national developments in an open international economy. Yet the domestic politics of compensation that was so central to that connection required specifying the political process that started at the level of the firm and in specific localities, and tracking it as it worked itself up via regional or sectoral conduits to the national level. Prescient as my analysis of the Austrian steel industry was in concluding with a quote from Arnold Schwarzenegger's *Pumping Iron* (Katzensetin 1984, 211, note 42), its inductive method was less than fully satisfying. The initial volume articulating the varieties of capitalism perspective (Hall and Soskice 2001) promises a more deductive approach. This would be an important step forward. But on the strength of that volume and subsequent publications, this remains no more than an embryonic research program. It is no surprise that it does not yet come close to matching the robust empirical findings that have accumulated in the large literature on corporatist politics. We will be able to assess in about a decade to what extent promise has been translated into accomplishment.

The emphasis on decentralization and disaggregation appears apposite, especially in an era of globalization. Here I distinguish between globalization and internationalization, since it may be helpful in thinking about the difference between transformational changes and marginal adaptations (Katzenstein 2005, chapter 1). Globalization refers, in my way of understanding, to changes that transform the collective identities of corporate actors, for example, nation-states or corporations. Internationalization describes a continuous process of adaptation of increasingly open national economies. Sociologists and anthropologists are wont to stress the former, economists and political scientists the latter. It makes a great deal of difference whether we conceive the changes in the world with which Denmark must grapple to be global or international. The skeptics among us are likely to insist that there is little that is new under the sun and that Denmark and the other European small states are simply extending the string of accomplishments that they have spun in the last half century in an extended era of internationalization. Maybe so. It is, however, also conceivable that the world of nation-states remains unchallenged but that within the European region transformative changes are in fact occurring.

This is an idea the editors hint at without fully developing its implications. What they describe as future challenges are in fact ongoing. Denmark has exceedingly complicated relationships with the European Union, as Morten Kelstrup shows in chapter 11 and as Lisa Martin (2000, 147–89) has analysed from a rational choice perspective. And Ulf Hedetoft provides in chapter 12 a trenchant analysis of the influx of immigrants wishing to partake of the benefits of the Danish welfare state. The advantages of national control and national homogeneity are challenged profoundly by current developments in European and world politics. The split between Danish elites and Danish citizens, and the possible fissures in the Danish party system over the speed and extent of Denmark's involvement with the European Union may thus intensify. Similarly the creation of a "dual" welfare state with different rights and obligations for different classes of citizens and residents, might constitute a transformative break in the institutional foundations of the Danish polity. Here then are two processes that may transform the structural conditions that have permitted Danish success.

Nobody knows the precise mixture of global and international currents and the transformative and incremental political changes they are bringing in their wake. To answer the question of whether something is "rotten in the state of Denmark," as Michael Porter erroneously did in the early 1990s, or whether "just the opposite" is true, as the editors argue at the very end of their Introduction, thus would require a more careful analysis of the processes in world and European politics that are best captured by global or international terminology. A detailed analysis of Danish conditions simply cannot do justice to that complex issue. I share, however, the reasoned sentiment of the authors and editors of this volume: on balance, Denmark remains well placed to exploit to its advantage the conditions of a global-international world.

14

Danish Capitalism
in Comparative Perspective

PETER A. HALL

When asked about the origins of the war between Denmark and Prussia in 1864, which contributed to the Danish sense of geopolitical vulnerability prominently noted in this volume, the British prime minister, Lord Palmerston is said to have replied: "The Schleswig-Holstein question is so complicated, only three men in Europe have ever understood it. One was Prince Albert, who is dead. The second was a German professor who became mad. I am the third and I have forgotten all about it." Much the same might be said about the basis for contemporary economic success in Denmark, which has puzzled many commentators inclined toward gloomy views about the economic prospects of Europe. In that context, this book comes as a ray of light, bringing the insights of some of the most distinguished scholars of Denmark to bear on the origins of that success. Their diagnoses about how a political economy works are complicated but immensely informative.

The tension implicit in any in-depth study of a single country, however, is that, as one's view of the national case becomes more nuanced, it becomes increasingly difficult to locate that case within comparative frameworks of inquiry. For the most part, this volume avoids such problems with a resolute focus on how Danish practices measure up in cross-national terms and what they mean for theories of comparative capitalism. The purpose of this chapter is to reinforce that comparative perspective by asking: what do we learn about varieties of capitalism from this book? Where does Denmark sit among them? And what does the Danish case tell us about how political economies adjust to socioeconomic change?

On these matters, my interpretations of the evidence accord substantially with those of the editors of this volume and diverge on some crucial points. However, my goal is not to resolve such disputes definitively but to identify issues worthy of further investigation.

DENMARK AMONG VARIETIES OF CAPITALISM

Like individuals, every nation is unique in some respects but impossible to understand without a comparative frame of reference. The frame on which I have been relying in recent years distinguishes political economies according to the extent to which their firms rely on strategic interaction relative to conventional market competition for accomplishing their principal tasks, such as acquiring capital, skills, or access to new technology, setting wages or working conditions, and securing clients and suppliers (Hall and Soskice 2001). There are substantial amounts of market competition and strategic interaction in all capitalist economies. However, I would describe those economies that make the most extensive use of market competition as "liberal market economies" and those in which strategic interaction is more prominent as "coordinated market economies."[1] Of course, there is also substantial variation within both of these categories. The main point of the distinction is to draw attention to the important implications for the economy and policy that arise from the modalities through which firms coordinate their endeavours.

From this perspective, Denmark cannot be other than a coordinated market economy, albeit one with some distinctive features. The important work done by Ove K. Pedersen and others demonstrating how many issues of importance to Danish firms are negotiated, rather than regulated by fiat or market competition, confirms the point (Nielsen and Pedersen 1991). As Pedersen indicates (chapter 6), Denmark has a "negotiated economy." Although coordination in the political economy is difficult to measure and relevant indicators vary, the efforts Daniel Gingerich and I (2004) have made to assess the overall balance between market and strategic coordination across the OECD nations suggest that in Denmark the balance leans toward strategic coordination in the spheres of labour relations and corporate governance. A score of .70 on our overall coordination index locates Denmark relatively close to other coordinated market economies (CMEs) and close to the position it is assigned in the more expansive assessment of Alexander Hicks and Lane Kenworthy (1998). Figure 1 shows how Denmark is positioned vis-à-vis the other developed economies on our indices. The measures developed by Margarita Estevez-Abe, Torben Iversen, and David Soskice (2001) also indicate that, like other CMEs, Denmark tends to encourage the development of industry-specific skills, rather than the general skills on which liberal market economies (LMEs) rely more heavily (Iversen 2005). For these reasons, I would be reluctant to describe Denmark as a hybrid of the two types, as the editors of this volume do.

What tempts them to say it is a hybrid, of course, is a remarkable feature of Danish industrial relations. For at least seventy-five years, Danish gov-

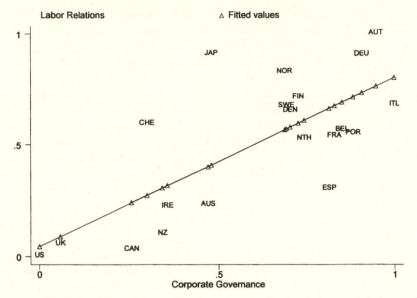

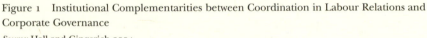

Figure 1 Institutional Complementarities between Coordination in Labour Relations and Corporate Governance

Source: Hall and Gingerich 2004.

ernments have provided relatively low levels of employment protection, firms have had little difficulty laying-off workers, and Danish workers have moved from firm to firm relatively frequently in the course of their careers. One of the distinctive features of the Danish model is its reliance on market mechanisms to allocate labour.[2] However, two key features of industrial relations distinguish Denmark from the liberal market economies that rely on market competition to allocate labour. One is a system of wage-setting that relies heavily on negotiation among trade unions and employers' associations to coordinate wage rates. The other is the most extensive system of unemployment protection in the world. As Per Kongshøj Madsen observes (chapter 9), if the average Danish worker becomes unemployed, he or she is entitled to receive 70 percent of previous wages for up to four years, and, in past years, some workers have been entitled to 90 percent of their wages for more than seven years. Coupled to these benefits is an extensive set of training programs to provide the unemployed with new skills that have been expanded in recent years. As a proportion of gross domestic product, Denmark spends more than seven times the amount that a classic liberal market economy like the United States expends on labour market policy.

This approach to managing the labour market is important for several reasons. First, it limits the extent to which firms can use labour markets to engage in wage competition. That tends to push firms toward higher value-added forms of production dependent on skilled labour. As Cathie Jo Martin indicates (chapter 7), Danish firms were much less likely than their British counterparts to use labour subsidies to extend low-cost production. Second, as Estevez-Abe and associates (2001) argue, extensive unemployment protection functions, much as employment protection does elsewhere, to encourage workers to develop high levels of industry-specific skills, thereby indirectly encouraging firms to develop production regimes that rely on such skills. In some cases, generous unemployment benefits allow firms to lay off workers temporarily in response to economic fluctuations, without losing them to other firms, thereby allowing those firms to maintain relatively long-term relationships with their skilled workers. In such respects, unemployment protection can be a substitute for the employment protection that is practised elsewhere. Finally, high levels of unemployment protection strengthen the position of the trade unions vis-à-vis employers, thereby underpinning the "negotiated economy" and limiting the adverse effects of market competition on ordinary workers.

In short, it is the intersection of several features of labour relations, rather than any single dimension of them, that has consequential impacts on the economy, as Peer Hull Kristensen (chapter 8) reports, and one effect of this system has been to give many Danish firms a production profile more like those of firms in other CMEs than those in LMEs (cf. Streeck 1992, chapter 1; Whitley 1999). One can think of this as a system well configured to encourage high-skill production regimes in an economy dominated by small and medium-sized enterprises, where the long job-tenures used to support such regimes in other coordinated market economies are not feasible, given the sensitivity of small firms to the need to control labour costs in the face of economic fluctuations, especially in a small open economy. The contributors to this volume correctly observe that Danish economic success has been built on a relatively fluid set of labour markets that allow firms to lay off labour in conditions of economic turbulence, but the fluidity of labour markets has done little to undermine the extent to which other issues of central importance to firms, as well as to the economy as a whole, are negotiated, rather than resolved through market competition.

CORPORATISM AND CULTURE

Much of the comparative literature tends to view "corporatism," or the types of strategic interaction associated with "coordination" in the political economy, as structural features of political economies. One contribution of this book is to move beyond that perspective to see these phenomena as active processes (see Regini 1984). That approach implies that such processes display enough regularity to merit description as a distinctive feature of some political economies, but it draws attention to the manifold conditions that make such processes work.

Although the literature on corporatism (or neo-corporatism) is gargantuan, curiously, it does not yield any systematic statement about the conditions required for the successful operation of a corporatist system. This is true even when corporatism is defined in relatively narrow terms as a system for securing wage moderation through regularized bargaining among trade unions and employers at the national or sectoral levels.[3] As a result, many analysts tend to associate the successful operation of corporatism with patterns of organization of trade unions and employers associations that reflect a capability to represent and discipline their membership at the national or sectoral level (see Calmfors and Driffill 1988; Alvarez et al. 1991). Because such approaches tap directly into durable features of the political economy that are subject to ready assessment, there is an argument for them. But they also tend to underspecify the conditions required for the successful operation of corporatism.

The view of the Danish political economy presented in this book provides a nice counterpoint to such approaches. Without denying the importance of the institutions structuring the political economy, it identifies a number of other factors that are also important to how well these institutions work. Taken together, the chapters in this volume suggest that four factors have influenced the successfulness of Danish corporatism and of processes of negotiation in its economy more generally. Broadly speaking, these are: i) the institutional structure of interest organization; ii) supportive government policies; iii) the character of international pressures on the economy; and iv) the climate of ideas developed in response to that pressure. In general terms, this is a realistic and useful portrait of the problem.

The most innovative aspect of this portrait is its insistence that the climate of ideas, or what Pedersen calls the "rationality context," matters to the operation of corporatism and strategic coordination more generally. Several chapters in the volume show how the thinking of governments and producer groups about the types of measures likely to advance the economy shifted during the 1980s and 1990s, generally in liberal directions that emphasized the importance of new measures to secure up-skilling and innovation. This movement was not mysterious but arose in response to experience, notably of high unemployment and more intense international competition, linked to increasing flows of goods and capital across national borders during the 1980s, and filtered through shifting economic doctrines that stressed the impact of factors on the supply side of the economy on economic growth. The incentives offered by governments, in the form of supportive social or economic policies, also made an important contribution to securing agreement from employers and trade unions to wage norms and industrial restructuring; and, as is often the case, debate among the political parties played a prominent role in the development of new approaches to such issues (see Rothstein 1991).

Macroeconomic policy was important here. While questioning some aspects of Keynesian orthodoxy and according more importance to the supply side, the governments of the 1990s mounted expansionary macroeconomic policies that, as Madsen notes (chapter 9), were a significant ingredient in the return to low levels of unemployment. Following Iversen (1999), one might add that a shift toward "harder" monetary policies helped secure wage moderation in this context. Without such moderation, a macroeconomic stimulus would not have had such beneficial effects. The upshot was that the locus of wage coordination could shift toward the sectoral level, and, in recent years, toward the firm level, allowing firms to respond more flexibly to international competition without inducing a wage spiral that would vitiate the value of macroeconomic reflation. Some views of corporatism associate its capacity to secure wage moderation with centralization of the locus of bargaining (see Golden 1993). On the basis of these essays, it would seem that Denmark secured negotiated wage moderation, even while the locus of bargaining shifted downward, partly because a hard-money regime imposed constraints on local negotiators and partly because an extensive national debate shifted interpretations about the requisites for national prosperity. The result was a more decentralized system of corporatism that was nonetheless capable of ensuring that Danish wage increases amounted to only 60 percent of those in its principal trading partners.

The editors of this volume take such points further to argue, first, that "culture" conditions strategic interaction in crucial ways, and, second, that basic features of Danish national culture with deep historical roots were crucial to the success of such negotiations. Both points are telling, but they are not the same – and the devil lies in the details. The contention that culture matters to the operation of the political economy is an important one. Soskice and I (2001) argue this point, which derives from the observation that cooperation in a context of strategic interaction will be secured only if the actors share a "common knowledge" based on shared understandings, and more than a "thin" understanding may be needed to ensure robust equilibria. Many types of cooperation require a thick set of shared understandings of the sort built up by experience over long periods of time, tantamount to a particular "culture" rooted in national history. Hence, we think culture deserves a place in analyses of the economy built on strategic interaction. Faced with the task of coordinating on one outcome out of several that would make each actor better off but would distribute the fruits of cooperation differently, actors may well reach agreement more readily if they share such elements of a common culture as a conception of social justice (see Scharpf 1997; Knight 1992).

However, our view of culture is one that sees it as a set of shared understandings deeply conditioned by experience and, hence, responsive to changes in experience. Whether modelled in Bayesian terms or otherwise, the key point is that practical experience does not simply draw on national culture but also remakes it regularly, either reinforcing or eroding the shared beliefs that underpin cooperation (see Western 2001). There is nothing especially "short-termist" about this perspective, unless that term refers to the role that immediate, as well as distant, experience plays in the determination of the relevant cooperative equilibria. But ours is a dynamic conception of culture that stresses how it is reconstituted or reconfigured by evolving experience. Many of the chapters in this volume that trace the evolution of policy and negotiation in Denmark over the past three decades describe precisely this type of process.

The pitfall to be avoided is one of seeing national culture in overly fixed terms. As these essays indicate, Denmark has a long history that impressed on its citizens a sense both of their potential vulnerability within the global economy and of the value of negotiating a strategic response to changes in that economy. As the editors suggest, this kind of historical experience may provide the basic underpinning for a negotiated economy. But the "persistence of deep-seated national identities" does not in itself guarantee successful coordination or dictate the content of the agreements.[4] The outcomes of negotiation are as likely to depend just as much on recent experience, and on the evolving conceptions of each other that actors form from it, as they are likely to depend on a long-standing sense of shared vulnerability. In this respect, however distant its roots, culture bears on the political economy only through its impact on the interpretation of contemporary experience, and such interpretations are coloured by more proximate factors, ranging from experience of the last wage round to prevailing views about the impact of developments in the European Union. For these reasons, I see the emphasis this volume puts on the contribution of culture to the management of the political economy as a salutary one, but only to the extent that it embodies a dynamic view that roots culture in contemporary as well as historical experience. Such an approach would be highly congruent with those of the varieties-of-capitalism literature.

DENMARK AS A CASE OF ECONOMIC ADJUSTMENT

Given my perspectives, I read this volume as an excellent case study of how a coordinated market economy adjusts to contemporary economic challenges. Taken together, these essays show that Denmark faced a set of challenges remarkably similar to those confronting most other European nations. Shifts in employment out of industry into the service sector generated high levels of unemployment during the 1980s, forcing governments to find new ways of creating jobs, as did rising rates of female labour force participation. More intense international competition, provoked by increasingly open international markets, forced Danish firms to seek higher levels of productivity and inspired tensions between a public sector sheltered from international competition and export industries less able to afford high wage increases (see Swenson 1991). Disillusionment with the fruits of industrial intervention stimulated a search for alternative ways to intervene on the supply side of the economy. One of the striking findings of this volume is that, despite its past success at devising formulae for survival as a small, open economy, Denmark was not immune to the economic shocks of the 1980s and 1990s. It had to find new formulae in order to handle those challenges.

That it succeeded so well is apparent. If Danish trade in goods was a startling 58 percent of GDP in 1989, by 1999, it reached 68 percent. Unemployment, after reaching 8 percent of the labour force in the early 1990s, was down to 5 percent by the end of the century. What were the ingredients of the Danish adjustment strategy?

First, like every other European government, the Danes began to look with less favour on industrial policies designed to identify national champions or subsidize industries and became more enthusiastic about letting market competition allocate resources. The focus of government intervention shifted from industrial policy toward manpower policy, where the emphasis was on skill formation, notably through programs offering the unemployed more training. By 2002 Denmark was spending more than any other OECD nation on manpower policy, and more than any but the Netherlands on active manpower policy.

Coupled to this were initiatives, reviewed by Peter Abrahamson, to reduce the level of unemployment by ensuring that the jobless took advantage of such programs. Although reforms such as those adopted in 1994 significantly shifted the emphasis of policy, they did not substantially reduce the generosity of Danish benefit programs, at least in relative international terms. Workers were still cushioned from the effects of unemployment, if now required to take on training or a subsidized job in order to receive benefits. The Danish welfare state has been remodelled but not dismantled.

In the industrial relations arena, the international challenge shifted attention to productivity issues. The demands of employers in the export sector for more flexible wage regimes were met by some decentralization in the locus of wage bargaining. As Madsen notes, in 2000, only 15 percent of collective agreements covering the private sector set central wage rates, compared with 34 percent in 1989. But widespread concerns about competitiveness kept the bulk of wage settlements, even at the firm level, well below European norms.

Finally, macroeconomic policy has also been adjusted judiciously. Beginning in 1982, Danish governments moved toward "hard money" policies that met inflationary wage increases with rising interest rates, rather than devaluation, thereby enhancing the discipline of a decentralized bargaining system. However, Denmark did not abandon Keynesianism altogether. As Madsen notes, the government adopted a fiscal stimulus in 1993 that, followed by the wealth effects of a new credit policy, set the stage for a decade of solid growth.

In many respects, the principal elements of the Danish response to economic challenge are similar to those found in many other European countries: a shift away from selective industrial policies toward manpower policies that emphasize training, modest adjustments to benefit systems to encourage the unemployed to take up reactivation programs, some decentralization in collective bargaining toward the firm level, and relatively hard monetary policies accompanied by the occasional fiscal stimulus.

What distinguishes the Danish adjustment path from some others is the extent of the resources devoted to manpower policies, both active and passive, the willingness of governments to use a fiscal stimulus on occasion, the relative freedom of firms to hire and fire employees, and the capacity of the industrial relations system to preserve wage moderation through a variety of shocks (see Auer 2000, 61). From a broader perspective, two features of the Danish adjustment path stand out; both are emphasized in this volume. One is the survival of a robust network of collective negotiations about how to respond to change. The second is the priority all actors in these negotiations accorded the problem of maintaining the nation's competitiveness.

If one takes a mechanistic approach to bargaining which associates its outcomes with how encompassing the bargaining organizations are, thereby focusing on their capacities to internalize effects that might otherwise appear as negative externalities whose costs are born by others, it is difficult to see why the type of decentralization in bargaining that Denmark experienced should not give rise to more adverse effects on economic performance (see Calmfors and Driffill 1988). By and large, however, Denmark seems to have avoided such effects. As Iversen (2000) notes, this result may be explained partly by shifts in the macro-incentives facing the actors, rooted in a hard monetary regime and higher levels of unemployment. But this volume suggests that Danish bargaining – over wages, working conditions, and public policy – has remained effective partly because it is also informed by an overarching consensus about the importance of maintaining a competitive economy.

The conditions underpinning that consensus deserve some attention. As the editors of this book note, it may have distant roots in long-standing perceptions of international vulnerability, which Peter Katzenstein (1985) and others have noted. In more proximate terms, however, it is surely conditioned by the active efforts made by Danish governments to alert social actors to the problems posed by a new international economic context and mobilize support for new approaches to them. It is probably underpinned as well by the very ubiquity of bargaining in what Pedersen terms the "negotiated economy." Rounds of bargaining that repeatedly link the specific issues at stake in them to national performance create a discursive terrain in which issues of national performance become a factor in many kinds of negotiations.

A varieties-of-capitalism perspective on this problem would suggest, however, that consensus is encouraged, not only by what Katzenstein called an "ideology of compromise," but by the structure of Danish political institutions. The latter are marked by an electoral system based on proportional representation, a legislature that is powerful vis-à-vis the executive, and a bureaucracy that provides representation to social groups. These types of institutions give producer groups substantial influence over policy making. Since they provide few avenues for one group to impose its views on others, institutions of this sort tend to press social and economic groups into a search for compromise,

Moreover, political institutions that give producer groups a strong voice in policy making also encourage Danish firms and workers to invest in the types of assets associated with coordinated market economies, such as skills that cannot readily be transferred to other sectors or production processes that require high levels of cooperation from the workforce. Firms and workers rely on policy to protect those assets, and their strong voice in policy making ensures they will be protected. If the Danish political system were more "majoritarian" economic actors might have to depend on markets to ensure the value of their assets and thereby specialize in the portable assets (such as general skills) that can readily be applied to other uses, more characteristic of liberal market economies. In short, a varieties-of-capitalism perspective stresses the contribution that political institutions make both to the achievement of compromise and to the character of the production regimes adopted in the economy.

Of course, this is not to say that bargaining is any easier in Denmark than elsewhere; nor is it a non-conflictual endeavour. Denmark lost more days to strikes during the 1980s and 1990s than most other European nations. Issues of social justice figure prominently in negotiations about the distribution of material resources. But it is difficult to escape the conclusion that, however encompassing the organizations doing the negotiating, negotiation is ubiquitous in the Danish economy, and issues of national well-being figure prominently among the considerations driving the bargains struck there.

Thus, when the problem of "comparative institutional advantage" is seen in broad perspective, the institutions of a "negotiated economy" may well be a component of Denmark's advantages, as the editors of this book note. They constitute supplements to the "invisible hand" of the market, ensuring that decisions made across the economy tend to sustain rather than erode national well-being. It may well be more practicable to operate such a system in a nation of 5.4 million people than one of 54 million. But there are enough small nations without such capacities to render the Danish achievement significant and to indicate that such practices must be nurtured if the nation is to prosper.

All coordinated market economies are distinctive in some respects, and this book outlines well the distinctive features of the Danish model. It confirms that markets are not the only institutions that can contribute to the efficiency of an economy and that strategic interaction to coordinate some endeavours may benefit firms and the economy as a whole. At the same time, the Danish experience reminds us that markets have an important role to play in coordinated economies as well, and need not undermine strategic coordination, provided that they are configured so as to be complementary to it. The mixture of markets and negotiation that Denmark has evolved deserves the attention of all who are interested in the economic future of Europe.

NOTES

I am grateful to Torben Iversen for comments on this chapter.

1 The distinction here is between economies in which firms rely heavily on competitive markets to coordinate the tasks most central to their operations and those in which relatively more of those activities are coordinated, not by markets, but by interactions among a smaller set of actors behaving strategically. This parallels the distinction between the types of equilibria familiar to neoclassical economics and the Nash equilibria on which analyses of strategic interaction focus.

2 However, it should be noted that employment protection is still much more substantial in Denmark than it is in most LMEs. Estevez-Abe et al. (2001, 165) assign it a score of .53 compared with .25 in the UK and .14 in the U.S.

3 For a more expansive definition, see Katzenstein 1985. The literature contains many studies mooting the relevance of other institutional features in the political economy, the complexion of government and its policies, and exter-

nal constraints, but it is difficult to extract from these analyses a sense of the relative importance of such factors, e.g., whether government threats or inducements matter most, and under what conditions.

4 Indeed, some elements of the negotiated economy are relatively recent. In Denmark, the 1930s were marked by extensive industrial conflict linked to high unemployment in contrast to the negotiated outcomes seen in Sweden at that time.

15

Denmark: An Ongoing Experiment

OVE K. PEDERSEN

This book is premised on the notion that history matters. But what are the implications of this insight? Can the future be projected on the basis of the conditions of the present? Will the conditions that the past has set for the present also have significance for the future? Will the long history of Denmark, as elaborated in the first part of this book, continue to have significant effects, or will the more recent short history of the last twenty or thirty years, as discussed in the rest of the volume, matter more? Does the recent short history provide the same basis for making predictions as does the long history? In other words, does the short history lead to the same sort of positive expectations for Denmark as the long history? The main question I want to discuss in concluding this volume is whether the Danish negotiated economy will still be capable of delivering the same sort of successes in the future that it did in the 1980s and 1990s. Is Denmark at the end of the past? Are we witnessing the beginning of something quite new?

In several of the contributions to this book, it is clear that describing Denmark involves a choice between understanding Denmark as a success or as a failure. For example, does Rasmussen (chapter 5) have grounds for describing Denmark as a "democratic monstrosity" or a "democratic role-model" when liberal ideals regarding constitutional rule and individual freedoms are rendered subordinate to geopolitical survival and international competitive position. Or does Abrahamson (chapter 10) provide evidence for Denmark as a "social pioneer" or a "social pathology," as aggregated data about social equality can be countered with data indicating that the Danes have a low average life expectancy, that the incidence of diagnosed depression is more widespread in Denmark than in comparable countries, and that the same is the case for the suicide rate? Or what about Denmark as a "closed" as opposed to an "open" society, as cultural and linguistic homogeneity give rise to xenophobia and a restrictive immigration policy (Hedetoft chapter 12)?

Denmark has always had two sides. The positive side is that of political stability, social equality, high growth rates, industrial modernism, and a consensus-oriented tradition for dealing with social conflict through negotiation and compromise. The negative side is that of relatively high mortality rates, low fertility rates, stress-related illnesses, and problems related to the different lifestyles of those who are socially included as opposed to those who are socially excluded.

I started to think more deeply about these issues as I read Peter Katzenstein's chapter. I was born in Skagen a few years before Katzenstein started taking his summer vacations there. And I was likely one of the many locals who curiously observed the invasion of foreigners and Danes alike who occupied Skagen every summer. I probably also stared with envy at the big boys from out of town as they ate ice cream, flirted with the girls, and holidayed while the entire town – including many of its children and youth – worked in the stores, restaurants, and hotels to earn money. Skagen is one of the beautiful places of the world. It lies between two seas – the North Sea on one side and the Kattegat on the other. The northern tip of Denmark stabs between the two seas like a curved bough, with England to the west, Norway to the north, and Sweden to the east. At Skagen's widest point, there are only a few miles between the two seas; at its tip, the two seas collide with violent force. Nothing is more beautiful than the sunrise at Skagen. Nor is anything more breath-taking than when a storm howls, and the roars from the two seas colliding can be heard throughout the entire town. Artists, authors, and royal families have been drawn to Skagen for more than a century in a romantic celebration of the sea and the sky.

SKAGEN AS EXAMPLE

Skagen is more than sea and sky, however. For centuries, Skagen was at the centre of the geopolitical conflicts of the great powers. The Skagerrak Sea has represented the gateway to the Atlantic for German and Russian fleets, and to the Baltic Sea for French, British, and American fleets. The mightiest navies in the world have sailed past and weighed anchor. Similarly, fishermen from around the world have landed their catches and come in to rest after long journeys on the Atlantic Ocean or Norwegian Sea. Long before there was any talk of globalization, Skagen was home for a plethora of languages and international trade; and as long as Denmark has been nestled in the midst of one of the world's most explosive geopolitical centres, the Skagerrak has played a central role in international conflicts. This was where fishermen could report on how Admiral Nelson's British fleet had set sail toward Copenhagen during the Napoleonic Wars; and this was where Hitler's *Wehrmacht* constructed the most fortified part of his "Festung Europa" with heavy artillery, armoured bunkers and anti-aircraft batteries. From this vantage point, the entire population could follow the British and American war planes as they came in from over the North Sea and turned south in the direction of their bombing targets in Berlin, Hamburg, or Kiel. And this was the spy-hole from which NATO could observe the Soviet fleet on its way up the Norwegian coast toward the Norwegian Sea and the Arctic Ocean. Today, one can watch Russian tankers transporting oil from St Petersburg to the global market, as well as convoys and containerships from all over the world carrying goods to the growing markets in Poland, the Baltic, and Russia.

My own memories of Skagen are mixed. In the 1950s and 1960s, Skagen was one of Europe's largest fishing towns. The city was home for roughly 500 fishing boats and trawlers from Norway, Scotland, the Soviet Union, and Sweden that were landing fish from the North Sea, the Norwegian Sea, and the Arctic Ocean. The massive fishing industry created jobs and wealth for the town. In the town there was a stink of fish, which was commonly referred to as "the smell of money." This wealth also created class divisions. A few "fishing barons" accumulated fortunes. They built ostentatious mansions and bought big American cars. My memories from that period are mostly of rotting fish and an awareness of the difference between "the others," who were rich, and the ordinary people like me, who were not. Today, Skagen is little more than a ghost town, at least in winter. Only about twenty fishing boats remain (Stensgård 2003), and the fishing industry has almost disappeared. Skagen nevertheless still remains a global meeting place. Large quantities of fish continue to be caught, but now they are processed and frozen and ready for delivery to dining tables throughout Europe before the boat has even docked. The inner harbour, instead of sheltering fishing boats, is jam-packed with luxury yachts – more than 15,000 every summer. Skagen is a good example of how Western Europe has undergone great change in the course of a short period of time. And one can hardly find a more illustrative example than Klitgården.

From 1914 to 1996, Klitgården was the summer residence for the Danish Royal Family. Until the Nazi occupation of Denmark on 9 April 1940, the Danish Royals spent every summer vacation here (Hvidt 2003). In 1996 Klitgården was put up for sale, and today the place is owned by a foundation consisting of Danish universities and professional associations. For the last seven to eight years, Klitgården – the very site where I am writing this epilogue – has served, as a retreat for researchers, journalists, authors, and other opinion makers. Throughout my childhood, I never got within 300 metres of Klitgården even though I was born a mere 500 metres from the royal room. Every time the royal family was staying at Klitgården, the King's flag was hoisted and there was no admittance to the entire area. Upon the Royal Family's return to Copenhagen, the flag was removed, but the "No Trespassing" signs remained. At the table upon which I am now writing, the Danish King sat some sixty years ago. In a moment I will be enjoying my lunch at the same dining table that the European elite and royal families sat around in years gone by. Along with the Danish Royal Family, the European upper class has disappeared from this place. Moreover, the class base of Danish society has changed, and Skagen reflects this change. Today the elite of the negotiated economy – politicians, organization leaders, industrialists, researchers, and CEOs – have turned Skagen into their summer residence, and in the summer, most of Denmark's political and financial powerbrokers gather there. Just as the royals and the European elite did in the past, this new elite is celebrating the notion of the romantic meeting between nature and culture (Stensgård 2003).

MARKET AND POLITICS

While Katzenstein is fascinated by small states and their capacity to survive and prosper, Peter Hall has long been interested in the role that knowledge plays in macroeconomic politics (Hall 1989). The Danish negotiated economy motivates him to raise the question of how negotiations and ideas play a role in the ways small states deal with strategic interaction. At the same time, it is apparent that the very concept of a negotiated economy constitutes a challenge for Hall and for the theoretical distinction he has developed with David Soskice between "liberal market economies" and "coordinated market economies" (Hall and Soskice 2001). I agree with Hall that history matters, *but experience does too*. Although one might argue that deep historical roots are crucial to the success of a negotiated economy, one cannot conclude that such roots will always cause strategic interaction to be based on negotiations, or that such negotiations will automatically lead to macroeconomic success. In the case of a negotiated economy it is important – and probably more so than in other economies – to distinguish between the short and the long history. A negotiated economy has a built-in aspect that, for lack of a better word, can be referred to as *gambling*. Every economy of course involves gambling. Households are gambling when they deposit their savings in pensions schemes; investors are gambling when they invest in bonds and shares; and CEOs are gambling when they make strategic choices. But in a negotiated economy gambling is different in three ways. First, the stakes are higher – the survival of an entire nation including the population's economic growth and welfare is at stake. Second, decision making depends on the capacity of the elite to interpret contemporary economic and other conditions for action, and to do so in a manner that will lead to successful national strategies. Third, being a small state, Denmark is forced by circumstances to adjust to geopolitical decisions taken by big states and to adapt to economic trends influenced by multinational concerns and international organizations. So, perhaps more than in liberal and coordinated economies, a negotiated economy operates in a high-risk environment – the future fate of a whole economy is based on the capacity of the elite to develop national strategies for adaptation.

I agree with Peter Hall that a negotiated economy is not identical to a "market economy" and that the Danish negotiated economy is a particular and contingent way of regulating and conducting a market economy. The question is whether this sort of contingency is also true for other economies – coordinated and uncoordinated alike? Does the liberal economy represent a particular economic regime, or do liberal and coordinated economies have the same common foundation in being coordinated? In particular, can we assume that market mechanisms are the same in liberal market economies as they are in coordinated and negotiated economies? Do market mechanisms vary according to their context? And, conversely, do liberal and coordinated market economies both contain significant elements of coordination, such that the issue is not whether one is more or less coordinated than the other, but rather whether different mechanisms of coordination operate in each? What I am wondering is whether the distinction between liberal and coordinated economies that Peter Hall adopts is too stark and extreme. That is, is it possible to determine if the Danish negotiated economy is a hybrid containing elements of both market and coordinated economies, as Katzenstein and John Campbell and John Hall emphasize in their contributions to this volume, or is it simply one variant of a coordinated economy, as Peter Hall claims?

I cannot fully answer this question here. But answering it requires that we consider the opposition between economic market mechanisms and political mechanisms, both understood as modes of coordination, and whether the two are fundamentally different. I am not sure we really know – or that anybody has given a convincing answer. Yet, determining whether Denmark is a hybrid or something else requires further thought. That said, it is important to remember that one of the most tenacious myths in political science as well as economic theory is the belief that market forces are static as well as universal (e.g., Dahl 2001) and that it is reasonable to talk about market mechanisms as if they have taken the same form and have operated in the same way everywhere even if we are constantly reminded by culture theory, anthropology, economic sociology, and comparative-historical sociology that markets emerge under varying contextual conditions, are created through varying historical processes, and change over time (Polany 1944; Edelman 1978; Reddy 1984; Biernacki 1995; and Fligstein 2001). Are market mechanisms universal or contingent? The question, of course, is open for debate. I agree with Katzenstein that contemporary comparative political economy is stretched between two theoretical ambitions that can help us resolve the issue – the one being the deductive, where the ambition is to make it possible to advance sophisticated theoretical explanations, the other being the inductive, where the aim is to conduct thick empirical descriptions. But if market mechanisms are contingent, then where does that lead us in considering the distinction between liberal and coordinated economies.? In this light, let us take another look at the development of the Danish negotiated economy.

THE GENEALOGY OF THE NEGOTIATED ECONOMY

In Denmark the most important requirements for a negotiated economy were established historically prior to the spreading of the market economy, including the creation of a labour market. This occurred more than 110 years ago when representatives for labour and capital signed the September Agreement (*Hovedaftalen for Arbejdsmarkedet*) in 1899. The September Agreement is the first of three historical compromises that created the prerequisites for a negotiated economy (Pedersen 1993). In the following, I will present a brief genealogy of the negotiated economy with the purpose of offering a double thesis. First, in the Danish case market mechanisms have been constituted through political mechanisms. Second, the nature of these political mechanisms influenced the kind of market mechanisms that were created. The main issue to be answered is this: If the development of a negotiated economy has had an impact on what Dahl (2001, 4) refers to as market systems, then perhaps market mechanisms do not have the same character in a negotiated economy that they do in a liberal economy, where "no central authorities coordinate the society" (ibid., 4).

Three types of political institutions were important in this regard: polity agreements, policy agreements, and negotiation games. All were involved in the development of market mechanisms. The three institutions have emerged from historical compromises; that is, through formal or informal agreements between class representatives about the distribution of economic and political power in a society (Korpi 1978, 350–1).[1] Historical compromises are historical in the sense that they have an impact on the distribution of economic and political power and do so by determining what are market mechanisms (and are thus left to business, labourers, and consumers to exercise) and what are political mechanisms (and are thus left to politicians and political institutions to exercise). They are also historical in the sense that, looking back from the present, they can be seen to have established a legacy or a path followed subsequently by important actors, whether involved in macro or micro economic decisions.

The September Agreement was devised in the 1890s (Pedersen 1993, 280ff.) and had three decisive consequences for the distribution of economic and political power. First, the Danish labour market became collectively organized. Central organizations were appointed to serve as legal subjects with the authority to sign and enforce collective agreements on behalf of their members. The price of labour and requirements for working conditions were subject to negotiation between the collective bodies. Second, industrial conflict became institutionally isolated. And an independent arena pertaining to labour legislation was created for determining how to enter, terminate, and maintain agreements and for how to distinguish between industrial (legal) and political (illegal) conflicts. Finally, authority was delegated from the Parliament to the labour organizations to regulate, judge, and sanction the relations between employers and employees. The September Agreement was established and enforced *prior* to the actual establishment of a liberal labour market based on individual contracts. Until 1910, wages and working conditions were set by law. Compulsory wage setting came to an end when peak organizations, through the agreement system, could regulate price setting for labour. From the beginning, then, individual contracts were embedded in collective agreements. Hence, the September Agreement was not merely an agreement about how to distribute economic and political power in society. It also involved the constitution of the market mechanisms that were to function in the labour market. Obviously, one can elaborate on which mechanisms we are talking about; but that is not the purpose here. What is more important is the claim that market mechanisms came to be of a particular type – collectively negotiated, agreed upon, and based on a norm for wage-differentiation between skilled and unskilled labour, males and females, sectors and branches, and the seniority of the individual worker. The individual wage agreement emerged from within the context of collective agreements. Not the other way around.

A second historical agreement was worked out in the 1940s during and immediately subsequent to the German occupation of Denmark. The Post-War Agreement entailed that the Danish economy would be opened to the world outside and that this opening would be followed by the establishment of a welfare state directed at facilitating the geographic and functional mobility of the labour force. Labour market policy became the most important policy in the welfare state. And the coordination of collective agreements with policies to fight unemployment was to be conducted via negotiations between the government and peak organizations. The neo-corporatist integration of politics and organizations took off. The agreement was not formalized, but the central organizations and several of the most important political parties implemented the compromise through a number of public commissions in which legislation for the labour market as well as social and education policy was agreed upon. However, the Post-War Agreement was not merely an agreement about how political power ought to be coordinated with economic power. It also involved constituting the market mechanisms that were to function in the labour market. They were negotiated collectively and agreed upon. They were also coordinated with labour market policy incentives for mobility and social policy guarantees in relation to unemployment. The individual wage agreement remained embedded in collective agreements; now, social guarantees and others were merely added to every agreement.

The third historical compromise, the Monetarist Agreement dealing with the overall monetary and fiscal stability of the Danish economy vis-à-vis other selected countries, occurred in the late 1980s. The Monetarist Agreement involved the peak organizations' de facto acceptance of the policy that the non-socialist parties had started in 1982 "by pegging the currency to the Deutschmark, liberalizing capital markets, and initiating a radical program for fiscal retrenchment" (Iversen and Swenson 2000, 15). It also involved the de facto acceptance of the notion that these policies would bring about "a gradual reduction of inflation and (real) interest rates" (ibid.) and that, being unable to effectively control inflation, interest rates, and the like, they would result in unemployment. Once again, the market mechanism was changed in the labour market.[2] It was still collectively coordinated, but was subject to monetary agreements outside the immediate control of government, peak organizations, and also (partially) the central bank. The market mechanism remained embedded in collective agreements, and continued to include social and other welfare-related guarantees, but now it was also being subjected to supranational monetary regulation.

Each of the three compromises was followed by the establishment of new types of negotiation organizations. The first compromise created conditions for polity agreements, for instance, between the Social Democratic and Social Liberal parties. Katzenstein refers to these as "the post-imperial Danish model of combining security with welfare" (see also Korsgaard, chapter 3; Korsgaard 2004, 384ff; and Højrup 2002, 332–9). In my definition, polity agreements encompass lasting interpretations of the conditions for maintaining Danish national independence and serve as the foundation for stable party alliances in the Danish parliament. As such, the post-imperial Danish model included an understanding of Denmark as being unable to defend itself militarily against any possible German aggression. Hence, it involved being forced to "form a society and construct a culture that makes it possible to survive as a people, despite territorial occupation" (Korsgaard 2004, 384, my translation). In this way the first historical compromise included an interpretation of the independence[3] of the Danish state as limited. If necessary, Denmark would have to accept its inability to defend its own sovereignty, for which reason military neutrality was to be countered by an internal consensus. Similarly, the second compromise created the conditions for polity agreements to open up the Danish economy by removing trade and other barriers for international competition. The Post-War Agreement was implemented by joining the OEEC and receiving Marshall Plan help (1948). It also involved Denmark's admission to NATO (1950) and early efforts to gain admission to the EEC (1960–61) (Lidegaard 2001, 333–64). The Post-War Agreement involved the coupling of economic policy integration and security policy integration. And although Danish independence continued to be regarded as limited, attempts were made to enlarge it by integrating the Danish state simultaneously in NATO and the EEC. The third historical compromise was implemented by linking the Danish currency to the Deutschmark (1982); through Danish participation in the Inner Market Project (1986); and by entering the first two phases of the European Monetary Union (1993). The period from the end of the 1980s to today is characterized by a change in the interpretation of Danish independence. This independence is now taken for granted in the sense that increased European integration and the crumbling of the Soviet Empire give Denmark a political and economic autonomy that the country has not enjoyed since its crushing military defeat to the Germans in 1864.

FROM ADAPTATION TO INDEPENDENCE

The paradoxical coupling of geopolitical independence and economic integration is immediately recognizable in the way the concept of competitiveness (competitive position) has been defined by governments from 1945 to the present (see Pedersen, chapter 6). From admission to the OEEC in 1948 to the beginning of the 1980s, the Danish economy has been measured in terms of its *international competitive position*. Behind this lies a conception of how Danish industry and agriculture must adapt to international economic conditions, and how labour market policy, together with other welfare policies, must be aimed at making the economy "adaptable." From the early 1980s, this concept was expanded to include the industrial sector's *technological competitive position*, which included the notions that Danish industry should adapt to technological developments, that the state should develop industrial policy programs, and that the state should facilitate reorganization of the financial market. The reactive notion that Danish industry should adapt was combined with a proactive strategy for technological adaptation (Pedersen et al. 1992). After the 1980s, the concept of technological competitiveness was expanded to encompass the *structural competitiveness* of the economy. The stage was set for a supply-oriented policy in which a large number of policies – including technology, labour market, training, and employment – were to be coordinated for the purpose of proactively promoting comparative advantages for selected regions, sectors, and businesses. National strategies for the pursuit of these goals were put on the political agenda. So were proposals for a new set of negotiation organizations.

After the Post-War Agreement of the 1940s discussed above, a number of policy agreements were negotiated in corporatist bodies, dealing with labour market issues but separately from social, educational, and other policy issues. However, after the Monetarist Agreement of the late 1980s, this sort of policy agreement was largely abandoned, traditional corporatist structures were reorganized, and a number of *social pacts* were developed and later transformed into language and negotiation games (Pedersen, chapter 6). These negotiation games and social pacts were efforts to link incomes policies, which had traditionally been the province of corporatist bargaining, to broader social bargaining by involving political parties and a broader set of interest organizations in ongoing attempts to coordinate a wide variety of policies (e.g., incomes, social welfare, education, and training) (Rhodes 2003).

All of this reveals three things. First, issues of the independence of the Danish state and the national distribution of economic and political power have always been linked. In addition, the understanding of the state's vulnerability has changed over time. Third, these developments have come to be expressed in the form of historical compromises that have laid the foundation for a variety of negotiation organizations through which the economic and political distribution of power has become institutionalized and organized. Though it is unlikely that this is a uniquely Danish phenomenon, Danish history surely has its own legacy. Nevertheless, comparable events and processes have been observed in Norway and Sweden, later in Finland and Austria, and later still in the Netherlands and other western European small states, such as Ireland. In all of these cases, small states have had to deal with two big problems: state vulnerability and class struggle. As I have shown for Denmark, the two are often linked. And the way in which they are linked – that is, the way in which states seek to protect themselves and civilize the class struggle – has important consequences for how market mechanisms and political mechanisms are constituted. Each influences the other. Indeed, through historical compromises and through the operation of negotiation organizations the distributions of economic and political power are set and reset, just as market mechanisms and political mechanisms are constituted and changed. In the Danish case, these historical compromises and linkages laid the foundation for a particular societal model – a negotiated economy.

THE NEGOTIATED ECONOMY: PROCESS

Peter Hall is right that the negotiated economy is a particular kind of coordinated economy. How particular is still an open question. He is also correct that history matters, but so does experience. How contemporary experience matters is another open question. It is one that requires us to think carefully about how societies organize the interpretation of their experience. For Denmark, the question is: how is the interpretation of experience organized in a negotiated economy?

To shed some light on this issue, let me add a new dimension to the discussion of the varieties of capitalism. Specifically, consider *knowledge regimes*. A knowledge regime consists of three parts: (i) the knowledge process – how knowledge is formed and changed; (ii) knowledge organization – how the formation of knowledge is organized; and (iii) knowledge content – the kind of knowledge being produced. The point is that there are likely to be particular knowledge regimes belonging to liberal as well as to coordinated and negotiated economies. Moreover, the type of knowledge regime in place influences which economic paradigms (knowledge content) serve as the foundation for macroeconomic and microeconomic decisions and which market and political mechanisms have the greatest influence in various production regimes. Consequently, there are several reasons why knowledge regimes are important – but especially in a negotiated economy. First, I believe that negotiated economies are more error-prone than are other economies, due to the fact that they include a particular element of gambling and risk, as I explained earlier. Second, I am convinced that this element of gambling reveals itself in the way that knowledge is organized and formed. Third, I also believe that the negotiated economy is characterized by a particular knowledge regime that makes the short history more important than ever before. Finally, this is all important because it relates back to my argument that market and political mechanisms are influenced heavily by contemporary shifts in the understanding of the vulnerability of the state.

Knowledge regimes involve three processes. First is *learning*. Learning is all about interpretation and monitoring. In Denmark it also includes how such interpretations and monitoring of things like the international competitiveness of the Danish economy have developed slowly and over many years into a socioeconomic framework of meaning to which all the important economic and political decision makers refer when making decisions (Pedersen, chapter 6). If the Danish negotiated economy is equipped with mechanisms that facilitate change and adaptability, then it is probably because learning within the Danish knowledge regime is collective and includes all of the most important actors; because the knowledge gained is cumulative and, as a result, experiences are stored in the collective memory; and because knowledge is utility-oriented and stored in macroeconomic and microeconomic databases, which are always updated and always accessible for all decision-makers. The important point is that a negotiated knowledge regime – in contrast to an ideal typical liberal knowledge regime – is not individual, but collective; not private, but public; and not contemporary, but filtered through the collective experiences of the past.

Leading is the second process. Leading is about how knowledge is utilized. In the Danish negotiated economy the collective memory is constantly used to make decisions in which collective interests are combined with special interests. This is the first reason why leadership is important in a negotiated economy – the array of special interests must be united in one common interest. A second reason why leadership is important in Denmark is that this common interest is always formulated on the basis of an interpretation of what it takes for the nation to adapt to contemporary developments in the global economy and the geopolitical environment. In the negotiated economy, this involves considerable gambling on the part of leaders, as I suggested earlier. And the stakes are very high. Not only does leadership involve an explicit effort to provide for the collective well-being as knowledge is used in negotiations between the government and other actors, but, given the orientation of Danish policy making nowadays, it is very much future-oriented insofar as leaders seek to anticipate how the very open and vulnerable Danish political economy can best adapt to changing international economic and political circumstances. Hence, leadership in Denmark is a collective art form, one based not on personal experience or intuition alone but on a collective memory that is used to develop aggregated and systematic policy prescriptions. Indeed, making decisions for an entire economy, with consequences for an entire population, via the aggregation of an array of different interests, and by coordinating a number of different policy instruments, through an all-encompassing set of structural policies, and doing so on the basis of information that is fundamentally uncertain involves considerable gambling, which may make leadership even trickier in Denmark than in other types of society.

Finally, the third process is *linking*. Linking is the ultimate purpose of learning and leading. Linking occurs when an increasing number of policies are coordinated and when several policies are linked in social pacts or through negotiation games to become strategies for national action. In the Danish negotiated economy, linking operates on many levels. National strategies combine many policies. Negotiation systems link many levels of decision-making. Indeed, policy making increasingly requires simultaneous attention to the supranational, national and local levels as well as the level of individual corporations (see Peer Hull Kristensen, chapter 8, and Cathie Jo Martin, chapter 7; also Martin and Swank 2004). And, as discussed above, knowledge is used to help link and coordinate policies in order to improve Denmark's comparative advantages by devising and taking advantage of various institutional complementarities.

Hall and Soskice define institutional complementarities in the following way: "Two institutions can be said to be complementary if the presence (or efficiency) of one increases the returns from (or efficiency of) the other" (2001, 17). The Danish negotiated economy is an example of an entire societal model that has been developed for the purpose of institutionalizing and organizing institutional complementarities. For years, Danish politicians and others have sought to establish and fine-tune such complementarities. As a result, the Danish economy is today organized around a common goal; that is, to establish comparative advantages and to discover and eliminate comparative disadvantages. In fact, one of the most important features of the negotiated economy is precisely this capacity. This capacity is a driving force behind the development of new forms of negotiation organizations. Social pacts, just like negotiation games, are developed in order to link policies as well as levels of decision making for the promotion of comparative advantages and the eradication of disadvantages. All the major social actors are involved, and the entire societal model is organized to promote institutional competitiveness throughout the economy.

INSTITUTIONAL COMPETITIVENESS

The negotiated economy may be a bit difficult to decipher, but especially so if it is regarded through liberal spectacles, or from the point of view of conventional microeconomic theory. But the fact that institutional complementarities can be promoted politically and that the Danish negotiated economy constitutes a societal model for this very purpose illustrates why all economies – coordinated and un-coordinated, negotiated and un-negotiated – must be understood as different variants of coordinated economies. As I have shown, Denmark was a coordinated economy prior to becoming a negotiated economy. It was first with the establishment of a general system of political exchange that different parts of the economy came to function in ways typically recognized in liberal theory (Pedersen, chapter 6; Pedersen 1993). The paradox is that it was through the slow creation of a negotiated economy that the individual labour contract became widespread (even if it is still embedded in collective agreements) and the walls around the domestic market were torn down and the national economy was opened up for international competition (even if there are still trade, tariff, and other barriers protecting Danish business).

The negotiated economy is hardly a perfect comprehensive societal model and it is hardly a perfect liberal economy. On the contrary, it is constantly driven by efforts to detect and advance comparative advantages, to discover and eradicate comparative disadvantages, and to seek a better mix of institutional complementarities (Hall and Soskice 2001, 17ff.). And it is not always successful. For example, Kristensen (chapter 8) points out that there are currently many problems in linking structural policy at the national level with corporate policy at the level of individual firms. Conversely, there are also problems in linking the interpretations that corporate managers have of their firm's competitive position with the interpretations of competitive position as understood by national policy-making elites. On the other hand, there have been notable successes, such as the ability to link labour security policy with labour flexibility policy (Madsen, chapter 9). In any case, every effort is bound to be temporary. This is because global circumstances are dynamic and business is confronted with new forms of global competition, particularly as the economy continues to open up. And for this reason, social pacts and negotiation games will never be all-encompassing or permanently successful. Furthermore, every intervention is bound to create unintended consequences and create new and unforeseen problems (or opportunities). As such, the negotiated economy is highly dynamic and is not easily classified as a liberal economy, a coordinated economy, or a hybrid of the two.

In my view it is only in theory that we can conceive of liberal economies. In the real world every economy is constituted and coordinated in one way or another by political and other mechanisms. If all economies are contingent upon time and place, and if market mechanisms need to be understood in historical and political context, then the juxtaposition of coordinated and liberal (i.e., un-coordinated) economies is both logically and historically wrong. The important lesson of the Danish case in this regard is that the differences between economies are not based on their being more or less liberal, but on the political, economic, organizational, and other mechanisms by which they are coordinated. So Peter Hall is right – a negotiated economy is a coordinated economy. But Katzenstein as well as Campbell and John Hall are right too – a negotiated economy is not a liberal, but a somewhat unique blend of mechanisms. In this sense, it is a variant of a coordinated economy. But then every capitalist economy is – to put a sharp point on the argument – a variety of a coordinated economy.

Then what is characteristic of a negotiated economy as one of several varieties of coordinated economies? First, it is a small state economy – interpretations of vulnerability lie behind the formulation of national strategies. Second, it is a dynamic economy – adaptation can never rest but is an ongoing process that seeks to eliminate competitive disadvantages and create competitive advantages. Third, it is an experimenting economy – knowledge is never complete and never fully trustworthy, and so every effort to create institutional and policy complementarities is based on trial-and-error logic, which makes monitoring and evaluation especially important. Fourth, it is a risky or error-prone economy – much gambling is involved and it is never clear which strategies will work.

In sum, what matters for the success or failure of a negotiated economy – and maybe for every other capitalist economy in the context of global competition – is the short history and the institutional factors that are involved. Indeed, the success or failure of all economies – including negotiated economies – is based on their institutional competitiveness and their capacity to launch competitive advantages and discover competitive disadvantages by enhancing coordination. To reiterate, the institutional competitiveness of a negotiated economy is based in large measure on its capacity to ensure growth and wealth by promoting comparative advantages for specific industrial branches and businesses through national strategies for adaptation.

SKAGEN IN THE AFTERNOON

The streets of Skagen are deserted this afternoon. It is early winter and in the middle of the week. It is cold and the days are short. In the winter Skagen is like a museum of days long gone. The hospital has been closed, as has the police station. There are not many fishing boats, but on the horizon it is possible to catch a glimpse of the container ships that serve the global economy. The tourists are gone and few people remain. Those working are few. Most of the town has been excluded and rendered dependent on social benefits. Now the welfare state is the town's single greatest employer as well as the town's most important source of income. The "included" and "excluded" live in harmony on the surface, but with considerable differences in terms of their quality of life. Transfer payments stream from the profits generated in the big cities to Skagen, Denmark's northernmost tip. The social desperation is not visible, but the mean life expectancy is lower here than it is for the average Dane. Most work here takes place only during the summer months. And the town only starts to breathe when spring arrives and the yachts sail into the harbour, the houses fill up again with tourists, and the elite from the main cities take their vacations here. In Skagen, the long history meets the short history, in ways that sometimes reflect the new class structure – and even sometimes the class conflict – of the negotiated economy. Indeed, during the summer, Skagen is hectic and occasionally violent – at least when local youth confront the rich out-of-towners. "No big problem," as they say in Skagen. Perhaps. But one wonders whether Skagen provides a glimpse of how the short history may affect the future of the negotiated economy. Will it make it or not?

In the old days, the waters around Skagen were among the most dangerous in the world. There are thousands of shipwrecks lying in the sea off of Skagen – ships that "didn't clear the point," as they say, meaning that they did not make it past the point where the two seas crash in foaming waves. Will Denmark clear the point?

There is pressure on the elite of the negotiated economy – constant and ever-present because power has been granted to them. They are obliged to interpret the global conditions for competition, analyse them in the light of past experiences, and convert this knowledge into national strategies. At the same time, they must do so while obtaining legitimacy from the population and maintaining a majority in Parliament. They decide which regions are to be excluded. They also decide how the unemployed are to be activated and how the unemployable are to be compensated through welfare benefits. In the short history, social appeasement is associated with economic engineering; and the enhancement of legitimacy is linked to the never-ending search for comparative advantages. Denmark is an experimenting economy. And its economic growth and welfare depend on the ability of the elite to make the right choices. As I have said, there is no doubt that a negotiated economy includes an important aspect of gambling. If things go wrong, they go very wrong. If things go well, they go very well. In the 1980s and 1990s, things went well thanks to good (or lucky?) producers of knowledge and decision makers. And every Dane must be grateful!

Yet the decision makers in small states must gamble under different conditions and with different consequences than must decision makers elsewhere. Maybe that is also the reason why small states have developed a different distribution of economic and political power than elsewhere; why geopolitical independence and macroeconomic decisions are two sides of the same coin for small states; and why market mechanisms are not the same in Denmark as elsewhere. The long history matters, especially in sensitizing Danes to the vulnerability of their small country. But the ways in which its vulnerability can be managed – and the nature of that vulnerability itself – have been changed dramatically by the short history. In the negotiated economy, the short history has become more important than ever before. The interpretation of independence has changed, leaving room for national strategies negotiated in social pacts and through language and negotiation games. By the same token, knowledge has come to be collectively not just privately utilized. Knowledge failures therefore also have greater significance than they do in other types of economies.

And soon dinner will be served at the dining table at Klitgården – just as in the old days but for the elite of new times.

NOTES

This essay has benefited from comments from good colleagues at the International Center for Business and Politics, Copenhagen Business School. Special thanks go to John L. Campbell, Lars Bo Kaspersen, Anker Brink Lund, and Peer Hull Kristensen.

1 Class representatives may operate either in their capacity as peak organizations at the labour market or as class-based political parties.

2 For more about monetary policy and its consequences for collective bargaining, see Franzese and Hall 2000.

3 The concept of independence is based on a crude distinction between a countries formal sovereignty (see Krasner 2001:5–7 for the set of attributes normally bound up in the understanding of sovereignty) and the *interpretation* that governments have or have had of their autonomy to act according their own reading of national interests. In this essay we are only dealing with how public authorities in Denmark have interpreted its autonomy and not how it has been able to control transborder movements or what Krasner calls its interdependence sovereignty.

References

INTRODUCTION

Albert, Michel. 1993. *Capitalism vs. Capitalism*. New York: Four Walls Eight Windows.

Alesina, Alberto and Edward Glaeser. 2004. *Fighting Poverty in the U.S. and Europe: A World of Difference*. New York: Oxford University Press.

Baldwin, Peter. 2003. "The Return of the Coercive State: Behavioral Control in Multicultural Society." 106–39 in *The Nation-State in Question*, edited by T.V. Paul, G. John Ikenberry, and John A. Hall. Princeton: Princeton University Press.

Best, Michael. 1990. *The New Competition: Institutions of Industrial Restructuring*. Cambridge: Harvard University Press.

Bille, Lars. 2002. *Fact Sheet Denmark: The Political System*. Copenhagen: Royal Danish Ministry of Foreign Affairs.

Bille, Lars and Karina Pedersen. 2004. "Ups and Downs: Electoral Fortunes and Responses of the Social Democratic Party and Liberal Party in Denmark." Unpublished manuscript, Institute of Political Science, University of Copenhagen.

Cameron, David. 1978. "The Expansion of the Public Economy: A Comparative Analysis." *American Political Science Review* 72:1243–61.

Campbell, John L. 2004. *Institutional Change and Globalization*. Princeton: Princeton University Press.

Campbell, John L. and Ove K. Pedersen. 2001. Editors, *The Rise of Neoliberalism and Institutional Analysis*. Princeton: Princeton University Press.

– 2003. "States, Politics and Globalization: Why Institutions Still Matter." 234–59 in Paul, Ikenberry and Hall.

Cox, Robert Henry. 2001. "The Social Construction of an Imperative: Why Welfare Reform Happened in Denmark and the Netherlands but not in Germany." *World Politics* 53:463–98.

Crouch, Colin and Wolfgang Streeck, editors. 1997. *Political Economy of Modern Capitalism*. Thousand Oaks, California: Sage.

Culpepper, Pepper D. 2001. "Employers, Public Policy, and the Politics of Decentralized Cooperation in Germany and France." 275–306 in Hall and Soskice.

Dahl, Robert. 1971. *Polyarchy*. New Haven: Yale University Press.

Danish Council of Social Welfare and Center for Alternative Social Analysis. 2002. *Social Trends: Social Policy in Denmark in a European Perspective*. Copenhagen: Socialpolitisk Forlag.

Esping-Andersen, Gøsta. 1985. *Politics Against Markets: The Social Democratic Road to Power*. Princeton: Princeton University Press.

Friis, Lykke. 2002. "The Battle Over Denmark: Denmark and the European Union." *Scandinavian Studies* 74:376–96.

Garrett, Geoffrey. 1998. *Partisan Politics in the Global Economy*. New York: Cambridge University Press.

Garud, Raghu and Peter Karnøe. 2001. "Bricolage vs. Breakthrough: Distributed and Embedded Agency in Technology Entrepreneurship." Working paper BCES-01-17 Berkley Center for Entrepreneurial Studies, Stern School of Business, New York University.

Gellner, Ernest. 1983. *Nations and Nationalism*. Oxford: Blackwell.

Gilpin, Kenneth N. 2003. "Layoffs Up Sharply in the U.S., Report Says." *International Herald Tribune*, September 6–7, 1.

Goldthorpe, John H., editor. 1984. *Order and Conflict in Contemporary Capitalism: Studies in the Political Economy of Western European Nations*. Oxford: Clarendon Press.

Hall, John A. 2003. "Nation-States in History." 1–28 in Paul, Ikenberry, and Hall.

Hall, Peter A., editor. 1989. *The Political Power of Economic Ideas: Keynesianism Across Nations*. Princeton: Princeton University Press.

Hall, Peter A. and David Soskice, editors. 2001a. *Varieties of Capitalism: The Institutional Foundations of Comparative Advantage*. New York: Oxford University Press.

– 2001b. "An Introduction to Varieties of Capitalism." 1–70 in Hall and Soskice.

Hattam, Victoria C. 1993. *Labor Visions and State Power: The Origins of Business Unionism in the United States*. Princeton: Princeton University Press.

Hedström, Peter and Richard Swedberg, editors. 1998. *Social Mechanisms: An Analytical Approach to Social Theory*. New York: Cambridge University Press.

Hicks, Alexander. 1999. *Social Democracy and Welfare Capitalism*. Ithaca: Cornell University Press.

Hicks, Alexander and Lane Kenworthy. 1998. "Cooperation and Political Economic Performance in Affluent Democratic Capitalism." *American Journal of Sociology* 103:1631–72.

Hollingsworth, J. Rogers and Robert Boyer, editors. 1997. *Contemporary Capitalism: The Embeddedness of Institutions*. New York: Cambridge University Press.

Hroch, Miroslav. 1985. *Social Preconditions of Patriotic Groups among the Smaller European Nations*. Cambridge: Cambridge University Press.

Ikenberry, G. John. 2003. "What States Can Do Now." 350–72 in Paul, Ikenberry, and Hall.

Jacobsson, Bengt, Per Lægreid, Ove K. Pedersen. 2003. *Europeanization and Transnational States: Comparing Central Nordic Governments.* London: Routledge.

Jensen, Lotte. 2003. "Aiming for Centrality: The Politico-Administrative Strategies of the Danish Ministry of Finance." 166–92 in *Controlling Public Expenditure,* edited by John Wanna, Lotte Jensen, and Jouke de Vries. Cheltenham, U.K.: Edward Elgar.

Karnøe, Peter. 1995. "Institutional Interpretations and Explanations of Differences in American and Danish Approaches to Innovation." 243–76 in *The Institutional Construction of Organizations,* edited by W. Richard Scott and Søren Christensen. Thousand Oaks, California: Sage Publications.

Katzenstein, Peter J. 2003. "*Small States* and Small States Revisited." *New Political Economy* 8 (1 March): 9–30.

– 2000. "Trust and International Relations." In *Disaffected Democracies: What is Troubling the Trilateral Countries,* edited by Susan Pharr and Robert Putnam. Princeton: Princeton University Press.

– 1985. *Small States in World Markets: Industrial Policy in Europe.* Ithaca: Cornell University Press.

– 1984. *Corporatism and Change: Austria, Switzerland, and the Politics of Industry.* Ithaca: Cornell University Press.

– editor. 1978. *Between Power and Plenty.* Madison: University of Wisconsin Press.

Katznelson, Ira. 1985. "Working-Class Formation and the State." 257–84 in *Bringing the State Back In,* edited by Peter Evans, Dietrich Rueschemeyer and Theda Skocpol. New York: Cambridge University Press.

Kenworthy, Lane. 1995. *In Search of National Economic Success: Balancing Competition and Cooperation.* Thousand Oaks, California: Sage Publications.

Kjær, Peter and Ove K. Pedersen. 2001. "Translating Liberalization: Neoliberalism in the Danish Negotiated Economy." 219–48 in Campbell and Pedersen.

Kristensen, Peer Hull and Jonathan Zeitlin. 2002. *Local Players in Global Games: The Strategic Constitution of a Multinational Corporation.* Unpublished manuscript, Copenhagen Business School.

Lieberson, Stanley. 1992. "Small N's and Big Conclusions: An Examination of the Reasoning in Comparative Studies Based on a Small Number of Cases." 105–18 in *What is a Case? Exploring the Foundations of Social Inquiry,* edited by Charles Ragin and Howard S. Becker. New York: Cambridge University Press.

Lieberson, Stanley and Freda B. Lynn. 2002. "Barking up the Wrong Branch: Scientific Alternatives to the Current Model of Sociological Science." *Annual Review of Sociology* 28:1–19.

Lindberg, Leon N. and Charles S. Maier, editors. 1985. *The Politics of Inflation and Economic Stagnation.* Washington D.C.: The Brookings Institution.

Locke, Richard M. and Kathleen Thelen. 1995. "Apples and Oranges Revisited: Contextualized Comparisons and the Study of Comparative Labor Politics." *Politics and Society* 23(3):337–67.

Maddison, Angus. 2001. *The World Economy: A Millennial Perspective.* Paris: OECD.

Martin, Cathie Jo. 2005. "Corporatism from the Firm Perspective." *British Journal of Political Science*. 35(1) 127–48.

Mazower, Mark. 1998. *Dark Continent*. London: Allen Lane.

McAdam, Doug, Sidney Tarrow, and Charles Tilly. 2001. *Dynamics of Contention*. New York: Cambridge University Press.

Mill, John Stuart. [1861] 1975. "Considerations on Representative Government." In *Three Essays*. Oxford: Oxford University Press.

Miller, David. 1975. *On Nationality*. Oxford: Oxford University Press.

Molina, Oscar and Martin Rhodes. 2002. "Corporatism: The Past, Present, and Future of a Concept." *Annual Review of Political Science* 5:305–31.

Monger, Joanne. 2003. "International Comparisons of Labour Disputes in 2000." *Labour Market Trends* (January). Newport, U.K.: Office for National Statistics.

Nielsen, Klaus and Stefan Kesting. 2003. "Small Is Resilient: Globalization's Impact on Denmark." Unpublished manuscript, Birkbeck College, University of London.

Nielsen, Klaus and Ove K. Pedersen. 1991. "From the Mixed Economy to the Negotiated Economy: The Scandinavian Countries." 145–67 in *Morality, Rationality, and Efficiency: New Perspectives on Socio-Economics*, edited by Richard M. Coughlin. Armonk, New York: M.E. Sharpe.

OECD. 2002. *OECD Economic Outlook, No 72*. Statistical Annex. Paris: OECD.

O'Leary, Brendan. 2001. "The Elements of Right-Sizing and Right-Peopling the State." 15–73 in *Right-Sizing the State: the Politics of Moving Borders*, edited by Brendan O'Leary, Ian S. Lustick, and Thomas Callaghy. New York: Oxford University Press.

Olsen, Mancur. 1965. *The Logic of Collective Action*. Cambridge: Harvard University Press.

Paul, T.V., G. John Ikenberry, and John A. Hall, editors. 2003. *The Nation-State in Question*. Princeton: Princeton University Press.

Pedersen, Ove K. 1993. "The Institutional History of the Danish Polity: From a Market and Mixed Economy to a Negotiated Economy." 277–300 in *Institutional Change: Theory and Empirical Findings*, edited by Sven-Erik Sjöstrand. Armonk, New York: M.E. Sharpe.

Piore, Michael and Charles Sabel. 1984. *The Second Industrial Divide*. New York: Basic Books.

Porter, Michael. 1990. *The Competitive Advantage of Nations*. New York: The Free Press.

Powell, Walter W. 2001. "The Capitalist Firm in the Twenty-First Century." 33–68 in *The 21st Century Firm*, edited by Paul DiMaggio. Princeton: Princeton University Press.

– 1987. "Hybrid Organizational Arrangements." *California Management Review* 30(1):67–87.

Putnam, Robert D. and Kristin A. Goss. 2002. "Introduction." 3–20 in *Democracies in Flux: The Evolution of Social Capital in Contemporary Society*, edited by Robert D. Putnam. New York: Oxford University Press.

Reskin, Barbara F. 2003. "Including Mechanisms in Our Models of Ascriptive Inequality." *American Sociological Review* 68:1–21.

Ricci, David M. 1993. *The Transformation of American Politics: The New Washington and the Rise of Think Tanks.* New Haven: Yale University Press.

Rodgers, Daniel T. 1998. *Atlantic Crossings: Social Politics in a Progressive Age.* Cambridge: Belknap/Harvard University Press.

Roeder, Philip G. 2001. "Ethnolinguistic Fractionalization (ELF) Indices, 1961 and 1985." February 16. <http:/weber.ucsd.edu\~proeder\elf.htm> (Web site viewed on 28 April 2003).

Royal Danish Ministry of Foreign Affairs. 1996. *Denmark.* Copenhagen: Royal Danish Ministry of Foreign Affairs.

– 1974. *Denmark: An Official Handbook.* Copenhagen: Royal Danish Ministry of Foreign Affairs.

Rubery, Jill and Damian Grimshaw. 2003. *The Organization of Employment: An International Perspective.* London: Palgrave.

Samuels, Richard J. 1987. *The Business of the Japanese State.* Ithaca: Cornell University Press.

Schmitter, Philippe C. 1979. "Still the Century of Corporatism?" 7–52 in *Trends Toward Corporatist Intermediation,* edited by Philippe Schmitter and Gerhard Lehmbruch. Beverley Hills: Sage Publications.

– and Gerhard Lehmbruch, editors. 1979. *Trends Toward Corporatist Intermediation.* Beverly Hills: Sage.

Schröter, Harm G. 1997. "Small European Nations: Cooperative Capitalism in the Twentieth Century." 176–204 in *Big Business and the Wealth of Nations,* edited by Alfred D. Chandler, Franco Amatori, and Takashi Hikino. New York: Cambridge University Press.

Schwartz, Herman. 1994. "Small States in Big Trouble: State Reorganization in Australia, Denmark, New Zealand, and Sweden in the 1980s." *World Politics* 46(July): 527–55.

Senghaas, Dieter. 1985. *The European Experience: A Historical Critique of Development Theory.* Leamington Spa, U.K.: Berg.

Shonfield, Andrew. 1965. *Modern Capitalism: The Changing Balance of Public and Private Power.* New York: Oxford University Press.

Smith, Michael R. 2004. "Corporatism and Economic Performance." Presented at the conference on the State of Denmark, Dartmouth College.

– 1992. *Power, Norms, and Inflation: A Skeptical Treatment.* New York: Aldine de Gruyter.

Sørensen, Aage B. 1998. "On Kings, Pietism, and Rent-Seeking in Scandinavian Welfare States." *Acta Sociologica* 41: 363–75.

Soysal, Yasemin. 1994. *Limits of Citizenship: Migrants and Postnational Membership in Europe.* Chicago: University of Chicago Press.

Weiss, Linda. 1998. *The Myth of the Powerless State.* Ithaca: Cornell University Press.

Western, Bruce. 2001. "Institutions, Investment and the Rise in Unemployment." 71–93 in Campbell and Pedersen.

- 1997. *Between Class and Market: Postwar Unionization in the Capitalist Democracies.* Princeton: Princeton University Press.

World Bank. 2001. *World Development Indicators.* Washington, D.C.: World Bank.

World Economic Forum. 2003. *Global Competitiveness Report, 2003–2004.* Davos, Switzerland: World Economic Forum (www.weforum.org).

Young, Brigitte. 1991. "The Dairy Industry: From Yeomanry to the Institutionalization of Multilateral Governance." 236–58 in *Governance of the American Economy*, edited by John L. Campbell, J. Rogers Hollingsworth, and Leon N. Lindberg. New York: Cambridge University Press.

Zak, Paul J. and Stephen Knack. 2001. "Trust and Growth." *The Economic Journal* 111 (April): 295–321.

Zeitlin, Jonathan. 2003. "Introduction: Governing Work and Welfare in a New Economy – European and American Experiments." 1–32 in *Governing Work and Welfare in a New Economy*, edited by Jonathan Zeitlin and David Trubek. New York: Oxford University Press.

CHAPTER ONE

Åberg, Alf. 1994. *Kampen om Skåne under försvenskningstiden.* Stockholm: Natur och Kultur.

Adriansen, Inge. 1987. "Mor Danmark, Valkyrie, Skjoldmø og fædrelandssymbol," *Folk og Kultur*, 105–63.

Ahnlund, Nils. 1956. "Dominium maris Baltici." 114–30 in *Tradition och historia*, Stockholm.

Anderson, Perry. 1974. *Lineages of the Absolutist State*, London: NLB.

Bagge, Sverre and Knut, Mykland. 1987. *Norge i dansketiden.* Politikens Forlag.

Baldwin, Peter. 1990. *The Politics of Social Solidarity: Class Bases of the European Welfare State 1875–1975.* Cambridge University Press.

Barrington Moore, Jr. 1966. *The Social Origins of Dictatorship and Democracy.* New York: Basic Books.

Beccaria, Cesare Marchese Bonesane di. 1796 (1764). *Dei delitti e delle pene.* Milano 1764, edited by Franco Venturi Torino 1965, Danish transl. Copehagen.

Bjøl, Erling. 1970. "P. Munch, sociologisk og historisk set," *Historie* ny rk. 9(1): 123–41.

Bjørn, Claus. 1979. "Den jyske Proprietærfejde." *Historie* 13: 1–70.

- 1977. "The peasantry and agrarian reform in Denmark," *Scandinavian Economic History Review* 25: 117–37.

Bohnen, K. and Jørgensen, S. Aa. 1992. *Der dänische Gesamstaat: Kiel–Kopenhagen–Altona.* Wolfenbütteler Studien zur Aufklärung 18. Tübingen.

Branner, Hans. 1992. "Danish European Policy Since 1945: The Question of Sovereignty," in Kelstrup 297–327.

- 1972. *Småstat mellem stormagter. Beslutningen om mineudlægning august 191.* Dansk Udenrigspolitisk Instituts Skriftserie 5. Copenhagen: Munksgaard.

- and Kelstrup, Morten. 2003. *Denmark's Policy towards Europe after 1945. History, Theory and Options.* Odense: University Press of Southern Denmark.

Brubaker, Rogers. 1996. *Nationalism Reframed. Nationhood and the National Question in the New Europe.* Cambridge University Press.

– 1992. *Citizenship and Nationhood in France and Germany.* Cambridge: Harvard University Press.

Childs, Marquis.1936. *Sweden: The Middle Way.* New Haven: Yale University Press.

Christiansen, Palle Ove and Østergaard, Uffe. 1993. "Folket, landet og nationen," 13–56.

Christiansen, Niels Finn. 1993. *Hartvig Frisch. Menneske og politiker.* En biografi, Copenhagen: Chr. Ejlers' Forlag.

Christmas-Møller, Vilhelm. 1970. "De små stater: Sokraterne i international politik," *Økonomi og Politik,* 4.

Clark, J.C.D. 1991. "Britain as a composite state." 55–84 in Østergård 1991b.

Colbiørnsen, Christian. 1790. *Betragtninger i Anledning af endeel jydske Jorddrotters Klage til Hs. Kgl. Høihed Kronprindsen over deres Eiendommes Krænkelse, ved Forordningen om Bondestandens frigivelse fra Stavnsbaandet til Godserne, og de flere udkomne Lovgivelser om Bøndernes Rettigheder og Pligter.* Copenhagen.

Connor, Walker. 1994. *Ethnonationalism: The Quest for Understanding.* Princeton: Princeton University Press.

Davies, Norman. 1984. *The Heart of Europe: A Short History of Poland.* London: Oxford University Press.

Degn, Christian.1974. *Die Schimmelmanns im atlantischen Dreieckshandel.* Gewinn und Gewissen, Neumünster: Karl Wachholtz Verlag.

Due-Nielsen, C. 1996. "Vindskibelighed eller vankelmod. Nogle spørgsmål til dansk neutralitetspolitik."315–24 in *Søfart – Politik – Identitet tilegnet Ole Feldbæk,* edited by H. Jeppesen. Kronborg: Handels og Søfartsmuseets søhistoriske Skrifter, XIX.

– and Petersen, N., editors. 1995. *Adaptation and Activism. The Foreign Policy of Denmark 1967–1993.* Copenhagen: DUPI.

Elliot, J.H. 1992. "A Europe of Composite Monarchies." *Past and Present,* 137: 48–71.

Engman, Max. 1991. "Historikerna och nationalstaten." *Historien og historikerne i Norden efter 1965.* Studier i historisk metode 21. Aarhus Universitetsforlag.

Esping-Andersen, Gøsta. 1990. *The Three Worlds of Welfare Capitalism.* Princeton: Princeton University Press.

– 1985. *Politics against Market: The Social Democratic Road to Power.* Princeton: Princeton University Press.

Fabricius, Knud. 1973 (1920). *Kongeloven. Dens tilblivelse og placering i samtidens natur-og arveretlige udvikling.* reprint Copenhagen: Selskabet til udgivelse af kilder til Danmarks historie.

– 1906–58. *Skaanes Overgang fra Danmark til Sverige* I–IV, Copenhagen 1906–58, reprint. Copenhagen: Selskabet til udgivelse af kilder til Danmarks historie.

Feldbæk, Ole. 1992. "Clash of Culture in a Conglomerate State: Danes and Germans in 18th century Denmark." 80–93 in *Clashes of Culture,* edited by C.V. Johansen et al. Odense University Press.

- editor. 1991–92. *Dansk identitetshistorie* I–IV. Copenhagen: C.A. Reitzels Forlag.
- and Justesen, Ole. 1980. *Kolonierne i Asien og Afrika.* Copenhagen: Politikens Forlag.

Fink, Troels. 1969 (1961). *Ustabil balance. Dansk udenrigs-og forsvarspolitik 1894–1905.* Aarhus Universitetsforlag.
- 1970 (1959). *Spillet om dansk neutralitet 1905–1909,* Aarhus: Aarhus Universitetsforlag.
- 1958. *Geschichte des schleswigschen Grenzlandes.* Copenhagen: Minksgaard.
- 1955. *Sønderjylland siden genforeningen i 1920.* Copenhagen: Schultz Forlag.

Frandsen, Steen Bo. 1996. *Opdagelsen af Jylland. Den regionale dimension i danmarkshistorien 1814–64.* Aarhus: Aarhus Universitetsforlag.
- 1995. "The Discovery of Jutland: The Existence of a Regional Dimension in Denmark." 111–26 in Sørensen 1995.
- 1993. "Jylland og Danmark – kolonisering, opdagelse eller ligeberettiget sameksistens?" 103–129 in Østergaard.

Frisch, Hartvig. 1993 (1933). *Pest over Europa. Bolschevisme – Fascisme – Nazisme .* New edition with an introduction by Uffe Østergaard. Copenhagen: Fremads forlag.
- 1933. "Nordisk Forord." 10–14 in *Pest over Europa.* Copenhagen: Henrik Koppels Forlag.

Fukuyama, Francis. 1995. *Trust: The Social Vitues and the Creation of Prosperity.* London: Hamish Hamilton.

Gad, Finn. 1984. *Grønland.* Copenhagen: Politikens Forlag.

Gregersen, H.V. 1981. *Slesvig og Holsten før 1830.* Copenhagen: Politikens Forlag.

Gow, James and Carmichael, Cathie. 2000. *Slovenia and the Slovenes. A Small State and the New Europe.* London: Hurst and Company.

Gramsci, Antonio. 1991 (1930–36). *Fængselsoptegnelser. Quaderni del Carcere.* I–II, translated and edited by Gert Sørensen. Copenhagen: Museum Tusculanum.

Green-Pedersen, Svend Erik. 1975. "The History of the Danish Negro Slave Trade 1733–1807: An Interim Survey relating in particular to its Volume, Structure, Profitability and Abolition," *Revue française d'histoire Outre Mer,* tome 60, nos. 226–7: 196–220.
- 1973. "Scope and Structure of the Danish Negro Slave Trade." *Scandinavian Economic History Review* 19, 2: 149–97.

Grundtvig, N.F.S. 1940. *Udvalgte Værker* 1–10, edited by P.A. Rosenberg. Copenhagen: Forlaget Danmark.

Gundelach, Peter. 2002. *Det er dansk.* Copenhagen: Hans Reitzels Forlag.
- 1993. "Danskernes særpræg." 133–47 in *Dansk Udenrigspolitisk Årbog.*

Gustafsson, Harald. 2000. "När blev Skåne svenskt? Ett internationallt perspektiv," Skånes renässans. Lund: *Kulturen:* 10–23.
- 1997. *Nordens historia. En europeisk region under 1200 år.* Lund: Studentlitteratur.
- 1994. *Political Interaction in the Old Regime. Central Power and a Local Society in the Eighteenth-Century Nordic States.* Lund: Studentlitteratur.

Hansen, S. Aa. 1970. *Early Industrialization in Denmark.* Copenhagen: Academic Press.

Henningsen, Bernd. 1980. *Politik eller kaos.* Copenhagen: Berlingske Forlag.

Hobsbawm, E.J. 1990. *Nations and Nationalism since 1780: Programme, Myth, Reality.* Cambridge: Cambridge University Press.

Horstbøll, Henrik. 1988. *Natural Jurisprudence, Discourses of Improvement, and the Absolutist State.* Århus: Center for Cultural Research.

– Løfting, C., Østergaard, U. 1989. "Les effets de la révolution française au Danemark," 621–41 in *L'image de la révolution française* I, edited by M. Vovelle. Oxford: Pergamon Press.

– and Østergaard, U. 1990. "Reform and Revolution. The French Revolution and the Case of Denmark," *Scandinavian Journal of History* 15: 155–79.

Hroch, Miroslav. 2000. *In the National Interest. Demands and Goals of European National Movements of the Nineteenth Century: A Comparative Perspective.* Prague: Faculty of Arts, Charles University.

– 1985. *Social Preconditions of National Revival in Europe. A Comparative Analysis of the Social Composition of Patriotic Groups among Smaller European Nations,* Cambridge: Cambridge University Press.

Hvidtfeldt, Johan. 1963. *Kampen om ophævelsen af livegenskabet i Slesvig og Holsten 1795–1805.* Åbenrå: Historisk Samfund for Sønderjylland, Skrifter nr. 29.

Japsen, Gottlieb. 1979. "Statspatriotisme og nationalfølelse i Sønderjylland før 1848," *Historie,* 107–22.

– 1973. "Betragtninger over den danske bevægelse i Nordslesvig," *Sønderjyske Årbøger,* 63–75.

Jespersen, Knud. 1994. "Rivalry without Victory. Denmark Sweden and the Struggle for the Baltic, 1500–1720." 137–76 in Rystad.

– and Feldbæk, Ole. 2002. *Revanche og neutralitet 1648–1814, Dansk Udenrigspolitiks historie* bind 2, Carsten Due-Nielsen, Ole Feldbæk, Nikolaj Petersen .red. Copenhagen: Danmarks Nationalleksikon/Gyldendal.

Kautsky, Karl. 1899. *Die Agrarfrage. Eine Uebersicht über die Tendenzen Landwirtschaft und die Agrarpolitik der Sozialdemokratie.* Stuttgart.

Kelstrup, Morten. 1991. "Danmarks deltagelse i det internationale samarbejde – fra pragmatisk funktionalisme til aktiv internationalisme."289–311 in *Fred og konflikt,* edited by Gottlieb, H., Heurlin, B., and Teglers, J. Copenhagen: SNU.

Kirk, Hans. 1953. *Skyggespil.* Copenhagen: Gyldendal.

– 1978 (1928). *Fiskerne.* Copenhagen: Gyldendal.

Kjærgaard, Thorkild. 1985. "The Farmer Interpretation of Danish History." *Scandinavian Journal of History* 10: 97–118.

Kearney, Hugh. 1991. "Nation Building – British Style." 43–54 in Østergaard 1991b.

Kelstrup, Morten, editor. 1992. *European Integration and Denmark's Participation.* Copenhagen: Political Studies Press.

Kirby, David. 1994. *The Baltic World, 1772–1993,* London: Longman.

– 1990. *Northern Europe in the Early Modern Period, 1492–1772.* London: Longman.

Kjærgaard, Th. 1989. "The Rise of Press and Public Opinion in Eighteenth-century Denmark-Norway." *Scandinavian Journal of History* 14: 215–30.

– 1979. "Gårdmandslinien i dansk historieskrivning." *Fortid og Nutid.* 28(2): 178–91. Eng. trans. "The Farmer Interpretation of Danish History." *Scandinavian Journal of History* 1985, 10: 97–118.

Knudsen, Jørgen. 2003. *Georg Brandes. Uovervindelig taber 1914–1927.* Copenhagen: Gyldendal.

– 1998. *Georg Brandes. Magt og afmagt 1896–1914.* Copenhagen: Gyldendal.

– 1994. *Georg Brandes, Symbolet og manden 1883–95.* Copenhagen: Gyldendal.

– 1988. *Georg Brandes. I modsigelsens tegn 1877–83.* Copenhagen: Gyldendal.

– 1985. *Georg Brandes. Frigørelsens vej 1842–77.* Copenhagen: Gyldendal.

Knudsen, Tim. 1995. *Dansk statsbygning.* Copenhagen: Jurist og Økonomforbundets Forlag.

– 1992. "A Portrait of Danish State-Culture: Why Denmark Needs Two National Anthems." 262–97 in Kelstrup.

Koch, Hal. 1944. *N.F.S. Grundtvig.* Ohio 1952. Danish 1944.

Kohn, Hans. 1944. *The Idea of Nationalism.* New York.

Krüger, Kersten. 1989. "Der aufgeklärte Absolutismus in Dänemark zur Zeit der Französischen Revolution" in Herzig, Stephan, Winter, (Hrsg.). *"Sie, und nicht Wir": Die Französische Revolution und ihre Wirkung auf Norddeutschland,* vol. 1 Hamburg, 289–315.

Ladewig Petersen, Erling, editor. 1984. *Magtstaten i Norden i 1600-tallet og dens sociale konsekvenser.* Odense: Odense Universitetsforlag.

Lahme, Norbert. 1982. *Sozialdemokratie und Landarbeiter,1871–1901.* Odense: Odense University Press.

Lange, Ulrich. 1996. *Geschichte Schleswig-Holsteins,* Neumünster: Wachholtz Verlag.

Lehmann, Orla. 1874 (1861). "For Grundloven. Tale ved en politisk Fest i Vejle 1861." *Efterladte Skrifter* IV. Copenhagen.

Lenin, V.I. 1964 (1907). "The Agrarian Program of the Social Democracy." In *Works* Vol. 13. Moscow.

Lind, Gunner. 1996. "Gamle patrioter. Om kærlighed til fædrelandet i 1600-tallets Danmark."

Lind, Gunner. 1994. *Hæren og magten i Danmark 1614–1662.* Odense: Odense University Press.

Lindhardt, P. G. 1978 (1953). *Vækkelse og kirkelige retninger.* Aarhus: Forlaget Aros.

– 1951. *Grundtvig. An Introduction.* Oxford: Cowley.

Lindström, Ulf. 1985. *Fascism in Scandinavia 1920–1940.* Stockholm: Almquist and Wicksell.

Lindvald, Axel. 1965. *Christian VIII før Eidsvoldgrundloven.* Copenhagen: Gad.

– 1933. "Comment le déspotisme éclairé s'est présenté dans l'histoire du Danemark." *Bulletin of the International Committee of Historical Sciences* 5(3): 714–26. VIIe Congrès International des Sciences Historiques en Varsovie.

Malling, Ove. 1992 (1777). *Store og gode Handlinger af Danske, Norske og Holstenere.* Copenhagen: Gyldendal.

Mellon, James. 1992. *Og gamle Danmark* ... Aarhus: Centrum.

Milward, Alan. 1992. *The European Rescue of the Nation State.* London: Routledge.

Molesworth, Robert. 1978 (1694). *An Account of Denmark as It Was in the Year 1692.* London. Danish translation, Århus: Wormianum.

Moore, Barrington. 1966. *The Social Origins of Dictatorship and Democracy.* Boston: Beacon Press.

Munch, Dr Peter, Ministre des Affaires étrangères du Danemark. 1931. *La politique du Danemark dans la Société des Nations.* Genève.

Møller, Erik. 1958. *Helstatens Fald.* Copenhagen.

– 1948. *Skandinavisk Stræben og svensk Politik omkring 1860.* Copenhagen: Gad.

Neumann, Iver B, editor. 1992. *Hva skjedde med Norden? Fra selvbevissthet til Rådvillhet, Europaprogrammet.* Oslo: Cappelen.

Nielsen, Johannes. 1987. *1864 – Da Europa gik af lave.* Odense: Odense Universitetsforlag.

Nørregaard, Georg. 1954. *Freden i Kiel.* Rosenkilde og Bagger. Copenhagen

Østergaard, Uffe. 2005a. "The College for the Instruction of Asiatic and Other Youth in Eastern Literature and European Science in Serampore," in *Denmark in India,* edited by Hans R. Ivesern. In press.

– 2005b. "Eidora Romani Termini Imperii," *The European Review,* Oxford. In Press.

– 2004a. "Mer, fer, terre: les clefs de l'histoire scandinave." *Geo* 302: 63–5.

– 2004b. "The Danish Path to Modernity." *Thesis eleven* 77: 25–44.

– 2004c. "La Danimarca e l'Europa. Una relazione difficile." *Nord ed Europa. Identità Scandinava e Rapporti Culturali con il Continente nel Corso dei Secoli, Atti del convegno internazional di Studi, Genova, 25–17 settembre 2003,* Quaderni del Dipartimento di Lingue e Letterature Straniere Moderne,13, a cura di Gianna Chiesa Isnardi e Paolo Morelli, Genova: Casa Editrice Tilgher-Genova, 281–312.

– 2004d. "Georg Brandes og Europa i dag." 31–46 in *Georg Brandes og Europa,* edited by Olaf Harsløf. Copenhagen: Museum Tusculanum og det Kgl. Bibliotek.

– 2003a. "Lutheranismen, danskheden og velfærdsstaten." 27–36 in *13 historier om den danske velfærdsstat,* edited by Klaus Petersen. Odense: Syddansk Universitetsforlag.

– 2003b. "For konge og fædreland. Universiteterne i den multinationale dansk-norsk-slesvigsk-holstenske Helstat." *Rubicon* 11(2): 17–41.

– 2003c. "Myter om den danske stat." *Kvan* 67: 42–61.

– 2003d. "Nationellt självbestämmande?." 23–68 in *Europeiska brytpunkt,* edited by H. Arvidson och H.-Å.Persson. Lund: Studentlitteratur.

– 2003e. "EUropa er der, hvor de rike er dødsstraf." *Kritik* 165: 51–4.

– 2002a. "The State of Denmark – Territory and Nation." *Comparative European History Review,* 200–19.

– 2000a. "Regions and Regionalism in Denmark." 4–13 in *Newsletter* 2. Århus: Jean Monnet Center.

- 2000b. "Wie klein und homogen ist Dänemark eigentlich." *Ästhetik und Kommunikation* 107: 25–32.
- 2000c. "European Identity and the Politics of Identity." 7–28 in *European Security Identities. Contested Understandings of EU and NATO*, edited by Peter Burgess and Ola Tunander. Oslo: PRIO Report 2.
- 2000d. "Danish National Identity: Between Multi-national Heritage and Small State Nationalism." 139–184 in Branner and Kelstrup.
- 1999. "Danmark i Europa," P.E. Tøjner ed. *1749*, Copenhagen: *Weekendavisen* 8 January 1999, 2.
- 1998. *Europa. Identitet og identitetspolitik.* Copenhagen: Rosinante.
- 1997a. "The Nordic Countries in the Baltic Region." 26–54 in *Neo-Nationalism or Regionality. The Restructuring of Political Space around the Baltic Rim*, edited by P. Joenniemi. Stckh.: Nord Refo.
- 1997b. "The Geopolitics of "Norden" – States, Nations and Regions." 25–71 in Stråth and Sørensen.
- 1997c. "Skandinavien und Deutschland – Vergleiche und Unterschiede." *Katalog zur Ausstellung Skandinavien und Deutschland. Eine Wahlverwandschaft.* Berlin: Deutsches Historisches Museum.
- 1997d. "Kontrafaktiske hypoteser." *Kritik* 128: 1–17.
- 1996a. "Danmark og mindretallene i teori og praksis." 44–105 in *Mindretalspolitik,* edited by J.Kühl. Copenhagen: DUPI.
- 1996b. "The Nordic Countries: Roots of Cooperation and Early Attempts." 13–50 in *Regional Cooperation and the European Integration Process. Nordic and Central European Experiences,* edited by Péter Bajtay. Budapest: Hungarian Institute of International Affairs.
- 1996c. "State, Nation and National Identity." 447–66 in *Classical and Modern Social Theory,* edited by H. Andersen and L.B. Kaspersen. Oxford: Basil Blackwell.
- 1995a. "Republican Revolution or Absolutist Reform?" 227–56 in *The French Revolution of 1789 and Its Impact*, edited by G.M. Schwab and J.R. Jeanneney. Westport Connecticut: Greenwood Press.
- 1995b. "Norden, det tyske och det moderna." 179–210 in *Vändpunkter. Europa och dess omvärld efter 1989,* edited by in Anders Björnsson och Peter Luthersson. Stckh.: Svenska Dagbladet.
- 1995c. "Der Aufbau einer färöischen Identität – Nordisch, norwegisch, dänisch – oder färöisch?" 113–40 in *Siedleridentität,* edited by Christof Dipper and Rudolf Hiestand. Frankfurt: Peter Lang Verlag.
- editor. 1993a. *Dansk identitet?* Århus Universitetsforlag.
- 1993b. "Politisk kultur og landskabsopfattelse i Danmark." 21–32 in *Syn for rum. Om byers og landskabers æstetik,* edited by L. Bek. Aarhus Universitetsforlag.
- 1992a. "Peasants and Danes." 5–31 in *Comparative Studies in Society and History.* Reprinted 179–222 in *Becoming National. A Reader,* edited by G. Eley and G. Suny, 1996. Oxford: Oxford University Press.
- 1992b. "Danmarkshistorie mellem statshistorie og nationshistorie." *Historie,* 265–89.

- 1991a. "Definitions of Nation in European Political Thought," *North Atlantic Studies* 1,2: 51–6.
- editor. 1991b. *Britain – Nation, State, Decline, Culture and History* 9/10.
- 1985. "Kafka, Praha og det østrig-ungarske dobbeltmonarki." In *Per Højholt m.fl. Kafka 100 å.*, Aarhus: Sjakalen.
- 1984. "Hvad er det danske ved danskerne?," *Den Jyske Historiker* 29–30: 85–134.
Putnam, Robert D. 1993. *Making Democracy Work. Civic Traditions in Modern Italy.* Princeton: Princeton University Press.
Rasch, Aage. 1966. *Dansk Ostindien 1777–1845.* Copenhagen: Fremad.
Rasmussen, Jens Rahbek. 1995. "The Danish Monarchy as a Composite State." 23–36 in Sørensen 1995.
Renan, Ernest. 1882. "Qu'est-ce qu'une nation?" *Oeuvres Complètes* I, Paris: Calman Lévy, 887–906.
Rerup, Lorez. 1981. *Slesvig og Holsten efter 1830.* Copenhagen: Politikens Forlag.
Roberts, Michael. 1979. *The Swedish Imperial Experience 1560–1718.* Cambridge: Cambridge University Press.
- 1973. *Gustavus Adolphus.* London: Longman.
Rothstein, Robert L. 1968. *Alliances and Small Powers.* New York: Columbia University Press.
Scavenius, Bente, editor. 1994. *Guldalderhistorier. 20 nærbilleder af perioden 1800–185.* Copenhagen: Gyldendal.
Schorske, Carl F. 1980. *Fin de siècle Vienna. Politics and Culture.* New York.
Schwartz, J. 1985. "Letter to a Danish Historian," *Den Jyske Historiker* 33: 123–4.
Seip, J.A. 1958. "Teorien om det opinionsstyrte enevelde," *Historisk Tidssktift* 38: 397–463. Reprinted in *Politisk ideologi. Tre lærestykker.* Oslo: Universitetsforlaget 1988, 13–66.
Simon, Erica. 1960. *Réveil national et culture populaire en Scandinavie. La genèse de la Højskole nordique 1844–1878.* Copenhague: Munksgaard.
Simonsen, Henrik Bredmose. 1990. *Kampen om danskheden. Tro og nationalitet i de danske kirkesamfund i Amerika.* Århus: Århus Universitetsforlag.
Sjøquist, Viggo. 1995. *Niels Svenningsen. Embedsmanden og politikeren. En biografi,* Copenhagen: Gyldendal.
- 1976. *Peter Munch. Manden. Politikeren. Historikeren.* Copenhagen: Gyldendal.
- 1973. *Erik Scavenius. Danmarks udenrigsminister under to verdenskrige.* Copenhagen: Gyldendal.
- 1966. *Danmarks udenrigspolitik 1933–1940.* Copenhagen: Gyldendal.
Sneedorf, Jens Schelderup. 1760. *Samlede skrifter.* Vol. 7
Sørensen, N.A., editor. 1995. *European Identities, Cultural Diversity and Integration in Europe since 1700.* Odense: Odense University Press.
Sørensen, Søren. 1992. *Nordens historie. en folkebog.* Copenhagen: C.A. Reitzels Forlag.
Steensgaard, Niels. 1996. "Slotsholmen og verdenshavet. Kan adelsvældens og enevældens Danmark placeres i det kapitalistiske verdenssystem." 81–9 in *Søfart*

– *Politik – Identitet tilegnet Ole Feldbæk,* edited by Jeppesen, H. Kronborg: Handels og Søfartsmuseets søhistoriske Skrifter XIX.

Stråth. Bo and Sørensen, Ø., editors. 1997. *The Cultural Construction of the Nordic Countries.* Oslo: Universitetsforlaget.

Suhm, Peter Frederik. 1776. *Historie af Danmark, Norge og Holstein udi i tvende Udtog til den studerende Ungdoms Bedste.* Copenhagen.

Swienty, Tom, editor. 1994. *Danmark i Europa.* Copenhagen: Munksgaard.

Thodberg,C. and Thyssen, A.P., editors. 1983. *N.F.S. Grundtvig. Tradition and Renewal.* Copenhagen: Det danske Samfund.

Thyssen, Anders Pontoppidan, editor. 1960. *Vækkelsernes frembrud i Danmark i første halvdel af det 19. århundrede,* I–VII. Copenhagen: Gads Forlag.

Unwin, Peter. 1996. *Baltic Approaches.* Norwich: Michael Russel.

Wilken, Lisanne. 2001. *Enhed i mangfoldighed? Eurovisioner og minoriteter.* Aarhus: Aarhus University Press.

Winge, Vibeke. 1991. "Dansk og tysk 1790–1848." 110–49 in Feldbæk.

Waahlin, Vagn. 1987. "Popular Revivalism in Denmark," *Scandinavian Journal of History* 12: 363–87.

Waahlin, Vagn and Østergaard, Uffe. 1975. Klasse, demokrati og organisation. Politiserings-og moderniseringsprocssen i Danmark 1830–48. Vols. I–VI. Aarhus University.

CHAPTER TWO

Andersen, B.R. 1983. *Two Essays on the Nordic Welfare State.* Copenhagen: AKF.

Baldwin, P. 1990. *The Politics of Social Solidarity: Class Bases of the European Welfare State, 1875–1975.* Cambridge: Cambridge University Press.

Bernild, O. 2001. "Velfærdsstaten og det livsformsorganiserede danske folk frem til 2. verdenskrig." Working chapter, Lov-project (mimeo).

Bernild, Ole. 2003. On the development of the Welfare State: the case of Denmark. Paper delivered at the *1. International Conference on Health, Humanity and Culture.* Los Angeles, October 2003.

Bjørn, C. 1990. *Fra reaktion til grundlov.* Gyldendal og Politikens Danmarkshistorie. Gyldendal/Politiken: København.

Böckenförde, E-W. 1991. *State, Society and Liberty.* Oxford: Berg Publishers.

Briggs, Asa. 1961. "The Welfare State in a Historical Perspective." *Archives européennes de sociologie* 2(2): 221–58.

Calvocoressi, P. 1991. *World Politics Since 1945.* London: Longman.

Esping-Andersen, G. 1990. *The Three Worlds of Welfare Capitalism.* Princeton: Princeton University Press.

– 1985. *Politics against Markets.* Princeton: Princeton University Press.

Flora, Peter. 1988. *Growth to Limits: The Western European Welfare States Since World War II. Sweden, Norway, Finland, Denmark.* New York: Walter de Gruyter, Inc.

– and Arnold J. Heidenheimer. 1995. *The Development of Welfare States in Europe and America.* New York: Transaction Books.

Giddens, Anthony (1985) *The Nation-State and Violence*. Cambridge: Polity Press.

Gravesen, B., N.J. Nielsen, and R. Mariager. 1999. "Arbejderbevægelsen og uden-rigspolitikken." *Arbejderhistorie* 4.

Hirst, P. and G. Thompson. 1999. *Globalization in Question*. (Second revised edition). Cambridge: Polity Press.

Hornemann-Møller, I. 1992. *Den danske velfærdsstats tilblivelse*. Copenhagen: Samfundslitteratur.

Hvidt, K. 1990. *Det folkelige gennembrud og dets mænd*. Gyldendal og Politikkens Danmarkshistorie. Gyldendal/Politiken: København.

Højrup, T. 2003. *Livsformer og velfærdsstat ved en korsvej?* København: Museum Tusculanums Forlag.

Jensen, Leon Dalgas. 1989. "Denmark and the Marshall Plan, 1947–48: The Decision to Participate." *Scandinavian Journal of History* 14.

Kaspersen, L.B. 2004. "How Denmark Became Democratic. The Impact of Warfare and Military Reforms." *Acta Sociologica* 47 (1 March): 71–89.

– 2002. "The Warfare Paradigm in Historical Sociology." *Distinktion* 5: 101–24

Knudsen, Tim, editor. 2000. *Den nordiske protestantisme og velfærdsstaten*. Aarhus: Aarhus Universitetsforlag.

Korpi, Walter. 1979. *Working Class in Welfare Capitalism: Work, Unions and Politics in Sweden*. London: Routledge.

Lidegaard, B. 2001. *Jens Otto Krag*. 2 vol. Gyldendal: Copenhagen.

– 1999. "Danmarks overlevelsesstrategi i den kolde krigs første år." *Arbejderhistorie* 4: 35–46.

– 1998a. "Vi opnaaede da, at København ikke blev bombarderet ..." In *Fra mellemkrigstid til efterkrigstid*, edited by H. Dethlefsen and H. Lundbak. Copenhagen: Museum Tusculanum.

– 1998b. "Systemet Munch – 50 år efter." *Radikal Politik* 9 (June 17).

– 1996. *I Kongens navn*. Copenhagen: Samlerens forlag.

List, F. 1999 (1837). *The National System of Political Economy*. New York: Garland Press.

Mann, M. 1993. *The Sources of Social Power: The Rise of classes and nation-states, 1760–1914*. Vol. 2. Cambridge: Cambridge University Press.

– 1986. *The Sources of Social Power: A History of Power from the Beginning to A.D. 1760*. Vol. 1. Cambridge: Cambridge University Press.

Marshall, T.H. 1975. *Social Policy*. London: Hutchinson.

Munch, P. 1905. *Det ny Aarhundrede*, 2. Aarg., 2. Bd., Copenhagen.

Nørgaard, Asbjørn Sonne. 2000. "Party Politics and the Organization of the Danish Welfare State, 1890–1920: The Bourgeois Roots of the Modern Welfare State," *Scandinavian Political Studies* 23(3): 183–215.

Pierson, C. 1998. *Beyond the Welfare State*. Cambridge: Polity Press.

Rasmussen, Erik. 1965. *Danmarks Historie. Velfærdsstaten på Vej 1913–1939*. Vol. 13. Copenhagen: Politikens Forlag.

Reifer, T. and J. Sudler. 1996. "The Interstate System." In *The Age of Transition*, edited by Hopkins, T. K., I. Wallerstein et al. London: Zed Books.

Rerup, L. 1989. *Danmarks historie*. Bd. 6, Tiden 1864–1914. Gyldendal: København.

Schmidt, Erik Ib. 1993. *Fra psykopatklubben*. Copenhagen: Gyldendal.

Schmitt, C. 1996 (1932). *The Concept of the Political*. Chicago: University of Chicago Press.

– 1988 (1934). *Political Theology*. Cambridge, Massachussets: MIT Press.

Schwartz, H. 2000. *States versus Markets*. London: Macmillan.

Senghaas, Dieter. 1985. *The European Experience*. Leamington Spa/Dover: Berg Publishers.

Skocpol, T. 1992. *Protecting Soldiers and Mothers: The Political Origin of Social Policy in the US*. Cambridge: Harvard University Press.

– 1979. *States and Social Revolutions*. Cambridge: Cambridge University Press.

Skovgaard-Petersen, V. 1985. *Danmarks historie*. Bd. 5 København: Gyldendal.

Sørensen, A.B. 1998. "On Kings, Pietism and Rent-seeking in Scandinavian Welfare States." *Acta Sociologica* 41(4): 363–75.

Sørensen, Vibeke. 2001. *Denmark's Social Democratic Government and the Marshall Plan 1947–50*. København: Museum Tusculanum.

Tamm, Ditlev. 1996. *Konseilspræsidenten*. Copenhagen: Gyldendal.

Tilly, C. 1992. *Coercion, Capital and European States*. Oxford: Blackwell.

Titmuss, R.M. 1968. *Commitment to Welfare*. London: Allen and Unwin.

Vigen, Anders. 1950. "Rigsdagen og erhversorganisationerne." In *Den Danske Rigsdag*, bd. 3 (Rigsdagen og folket). Published by Statsministeriet og Rigsdagens Præsidium. Copenhagen: J.H. Schultz.

Villaume, P. 1999. "Fra antimilitarisme til atlantisk aktivisme." *Arbejderhistorie* 4.

CHAPTER THREE

Clausen, H.N. 1870. *Det videnskabelige Livs Forhold til det borgerlige Frihedsliv*. Copenhagen: G.E.C. Gad.

Fonsmark, Henning. 1990. *Historien om den danske utopi*. Copenhagen: Gyldendal.

Fremtidens Danmark. 1945. Copenhagen: Fremad.

Gellner, Ernest. 1983. *Nations and Nationalism*. Oxford: Blackwell.

Goldschmidt, Meir. 1849. *Nord og Syd*, vols. 9 and 10.

Grundtvig, N.F.S. 1909. *Udvalgte Skrifter*, bd. 9. Copenhagen: Nordisk Forlag.

– 1965. *Taler på Marielyst Højskole 1856–71*. Copenhagen: Gyldendal.

Held, David. 1996. *Models of Democracy*. Cambridge: Polity Press.

Højskolesangbogen. 1994. Odense: Højskoleforeningens forlag.

Højrup, Thomas. 2002. *Dannelsens dialektik*. Copenhagen: Museum Tusculanum.

Katzenstein, Peter J. 2002. "Small States and Small States Revisited." Unpublished manuscript, Department of Government, Cornell University.

– 1985. *Small States in World Markets. Industrial Policy in Europe*. Ithaca: Cornell University Press.

Koch, Hal. 1970 (1945). *Hvad er demokrati?* Copenhagen: Gyldendal.

– 1942. *Dagen og Vejen*. Copenhagen: Westermann.

Korsgaard, Ove. 2004. *Kampen om folket. Et dannelsesperspektiv på dansk historie gennem 500 år.* Copenhagen: Gyldendal.

– 1999. *Kundskabskapløbet. Uddannelse i videnssamfundet.* Copenhagen: Gyldendal.

– 1997. *Kampen om lyset. Dansk voksenoplysning gennem 500 år.* Copenhagen: Gyldendal.

Krag, Jens Otto. 1956. *Kronik* in *Socialdemokraten,* 23.10.

Lidegaard, Bo. 2001. *Jens Otto Krag.* Copenhagen: Gyldendal.

Mazower, Mark 1999. *Dark Continent.* New York: Alfred A. Knopf.

Markussen, Ingrid. 1988. *Visdommens lænker.* Copenhagen: Landbohistorisk Selskab.

Nielsen, Johs. 1979. *Genrejsningshåb og undergangsangst. Dansk forsvarspolitik mellem 1864 og 1870 og folkestyrets første forsvarsordning.* Odense: Odense Universitetsforlag.

O'Leary, Brendan. 2001. "Right-Sizing and Right-Peopling." In Brendan O'Leary, Ian S. Lustick, and Thomas Callaghy, *Right-sizing the State.* Oxford: Oxford University Press.

Ørsted, A.S. 1850. *For den danske Stats Opretholdelse i dens Heelhed.* Copenhagen: Gyldendal.

Petersen, Niels 1984. *Kultusministeriet.* Copenhagen: G.E.C. Gad.

Pedersen, Ove Kaj. 1994. *Demokratiets lette tilstand.* Copenhagen: Spektrum.

Ringer, K. Fritz. 1969. *The Decline of the German Mandarins.* Cambridge: Harvard University Press.

Rousseau, J.-J. 1991(1772). "Considerations on the Government of Poland." In *Rousseau on International Relations,* edited by Stanley Hoffmann and David P. Fidler. Oxford: Clarendon Press.

Slagstad, Rune. 1987. *Rett og Politikk.* Oslo: Universitetsforlaget.

Steenstrup, M. 1865. "Skrivelse til Den danske Folkeforening." In *Udvalget for Folkeoplysningens Fremme,* 50 Aars Virksomhed 1866–1916. Copenhagen.

Weber, Eugen. 1976. *Peasants into Frenchmen.* Standford: University Press.

CHAPTER FOUR

Abramovitz, Moses. 1986. "Catching Up, Forging Ahead, and Falling Behind." *Journal of Economic History* 46: 385–406.

Anderson, R.A. 1935. *With Horace Plunkett in Ireland.* London: Macmillan.

Armstrong, David. 1989. *An Economic History of Agriculture in Northern Ireland 1850–1900.* Long Hanborough: Plunkett Foundation for Co-operative Studies.

Bairoch, Paul. 1989. "European Trade Policy, 1815–1914." 1–160 in *The Cambridge Economic History of Europe,* Vol. 8, edited by P. Mathias and S. Pollard. Cambridge: Cambridge University Press.

Barro, Robert. J. 1991. "Economic Growth in a Cross Section of Countries." *Journal of Political Economy* 106: 407–43.

Baumol, William. 1990. "Entrepreneurship: Productive, Unproductive, and Destructive." *Journal of Political Economy* 98: 893–921.

Beddy, James P. 1943. "A Comparison of the Principal Economic Features of Eire and Denmark." *Journal of the Statistical and Social Inquiry Society of Ireland* 1943: 189–220.

Bjørn, Claus, editor. 1988. *Det Danske Landbrugs Historie III: 1810–1914.* Copenhagen: Landbohistorisk Selskab.

Boyer, George R., Timothy J. Hatton, and Kevin H. O'Rourke. 1994. "Emigration and Economic Growth in Ireland, 1850–1914." 221–39 in *Migration and the International Labor Market, 1850–1939,* edited by Timothy J. Hatton and Jeffrey G. Williamson. London: Routledge.

BPP 1913. First Report of the Irish Milk Commission. Cd. 6683, British Parliamentary Papers.

– 1910. Report of the Departmental Committee on the Irish Butter Industry. Cd. 5092, British Parliamentary Papers.

Cipolla, Carlo. 1969. *Literacy and Development in the West.* London: Penguin.

Crotty, Raymond. 1966. *Irish Agricultural Production: Its Volume and Structure.* Cork: Cork University Press.

Easterlin, Richard A. 1981. "Why Isn't the Whole World Developed?" *Journal of Economic History* 41: 1–19.

Ehrlich, C. 1981. "Horace Plunkett and Agricultural Reform." In *Irish Population, Economy and Society,* edited by J.M. Goldstrom and L.A. Clarkson. Oxford: Clarendon Press.

Flora, Peter. 1983. *State, Economy and Society in Western Europe 1815–1975: A Data Handbook in Two Volumes, Vol. I, The Growth of Mass Democracies and Welfare States.* London: Macmillan.

Andrew Mellinger, John Gallup, and Jeffrey D. Sachs. 2000. "Climate, Coastal Proximity, and Development," In *Oxford Handbook of Economic Geography,* edited by Gordon L. Clark, Maryann P. Feldman, and Meric S. Gertler. Oxford: Oxford University Press.

Greif, Avner. 1994. "Cultural Beliefs and the Organization of Society: A Historical and Theoretical Reflection on Collectivist and Individualist Societies." *Journal of Political Economy* 102: 912–50.

Grousset, P. 1986. *Ireland's Disease: The English in Ireland 1887.* Belfast: Blackstaff Press.

Guinnane, Timothy G. 1994. "A Failed Institutional Transplant: Raiffeisen's Credit Cooperatives in Ireland, 1894–1914." *Explorations in Economic History* 31: 38–61.

– and Ingrid Henriksen. 1998. "Why Danish Credit Cooperatives Were So Unimportant." *Scandinavian Economic History Review* 46: 32–54.

– and Ronald I. Miller. 1997. "The Limits to Land Reform: The Land Acts in Ireland, 1870–1909." *Economic Development and Cultural Change* 45: 591–612.

Haggard, H. Rider. 1913. *Rural Denmark and Its Lessons.* London: Longman, Green and Co.

Hatton, Timothy J. and Jeffrey G. Williamson. 1998. *The Age of Mass Migration: Causes and Economic Impact.* Oxford: Oxford University Press.

Henriksen, Ingrid. 1999. "Avoiding Lock-in: Co-operative Creameries in Denmark, 1882–1903." *European Review of Economic History* 3: 57–78.

– and Kevin H. O'Rourke. 2005. "Incentives, Technology and the Shift to Year-Round Dairying in Late 19th Century Denmark." *Economic History Review* 58: 520–54.

– and Morten Hviid. 2002. "Legal Institutions and Performance: Monitoring Agreements in the Early Danish Dairy Sector." Paper presented at the ISNIE conference, Boston.

IAOS (various years). *Annual Reports of the Irish Agricultural Organisation Society, Ltd.* Dublin.

Jensen, Einar. 1937. *Danish Agriculture.* Copenhagen: J.H. Schultz Forlag.

Johansen, H.C. 1985. *Danmarks Historie, Bind 9, Danish Historical Statistics 1814–1980.* Copenhagen: Gyldendal.

Kennedy, Liam. 1976. "The Decline of the Cork Butter Market: A Comment." *Studia Hibernica* 16: 175–7.

Kindleberger, Charles P. 1951. "Group Behavior and International Trade." *Journal of Political Economy* 59: 30–46.

Landes, David. 1969. *The Unbound Prometheus: Technological Change and Industrial Development in Western Europe from 1750 to the Present.* Cambridge: Cambridge University Press.

La Porta, Rafael, Florencio Lopez-de-Silanes, Andrei Shleifer, and Robert W. Vishny. 1997. "Trust in Large Organizations." *American Economic Review Papers and Proceedings* 87: 333–8.

Lee, Joseph J. 1989. *Ireland 1912–1985: Politics and Society.* Cambridge: Cambridge University Press.

Maddison, Angus. 1995. *Monitoring the World Economy 1820–1992.* Paris: OECD Development Centre Studies.

Mitchell, Brian R. 1992. *International Historical Statistics: Europe 1750–1988.* London: Macmillan.

– 1988. *British Historical Statistics.* Cambridge: Cambridge University Press.

Mokyr, Joel. 1985. *Why Ireland Starved: A Quantitative and Analytical History of the Irish Economy, 1800–1850.* London: George Allen & Unwin.

– 1976. *Industrialization in the Low Countries.* New Haven: Yale University Press.

– and Cormac Ó Gráda. 1988. "Poor and Getting Poorer? Living Standards in Ireland Before the Famine." *Economic History Review* 41: 209–35.

Nüchel Thomsen, Birgit Thomas, and Brinley Thomas. 1966. *Dansk-Engelsk Samhandel: Et Historisk Rids 1661-1963.* Aarhus: Universitetsforlaget.

O'Donovan, James. 1940. *The Economic History of Live Stock in Ireland.* Cork: Cork University Press.

Ó Gráda, Cormac. 1975. "The Investment Behaviour of Irish Landlords 1850–75: Some Preliminary Findings." *Agricultural History Review* 23:139–55.

Ó Gráda, Cormac. 1994. *Ireland 1780–1939: A New Economic History.* Oxford: Oxford University Press.

– 1977. "The Beginnings of the Irish Creamery System, 1880–1914." *Economic History Review* 30: 284–305.

– and Kevin H. O'Rourke. 1997. "Migration as Disaster Relief: Lessons from the Great Irish Famine." *European Review of Economic History* 1: 3–25.

O'Rourke, Kevin H. 2004. "Social Cohesion, Culture and Economic Behaviour: Evidence from the Creameries." Unpublished manuscript, Trinity College Dublin.

– 1997. "The European Grain Invasion, 1870–1913." *Journal of Economic History* 57: 775–801.

– and Jeffrey G. Williamson. 1997. "Around the European Periphery 1870–1913: Globalization, Schooling and Growth." *European Review of Economic History* 1: 153–91.

– and Jeffrey G. Williamson. 1999. *Globalization and History: The Evolution of a Nineteenth Century Atlantic Economy.* Cambridge, Mass.: MIT Press.

Pedersen, J. 1926. "Irland som Danmarks Konkurrent Paa det Engelske Marked." *Nationaløkonomiske Tidsskrift,* 423–38.

Plunkett, Horace. 1982. *Ireland in the New Century.* Blackrock, Co. Dublin: Irish Academic Press.

Porter, Michael. 1990. *The Competitive Advantage of Nations.* New York: Free Press.

Prados, Leandro de la Escosura. 2000. "International Comparisons of Real Product, 1820–1990: An Alternative Data Set." *Explorations in Economic History* 37: 1–41.

Putnam, Robert D. with R. Leonardi and R.Y. Nanetti. 1993. *Making Democracy Work: Civic Traditions in Modern Italy.* Princeton, New Jersey: Princeton University Press.

Schou, R. 1910. "Landbrugsforhold i Irland og Storbritannien." *Tidsskrift for Landøkonomi,* 258–67.

Solar, Peter M. 1989–90. "The Irish Butter Trade in the Nineteenth Century: New Estimates and Their Implications." *Studia Hibernica* 25: 134–61.

Solow, Barbara. 1971. *The Land Question and the Irish Economy, 1870–1903.* Cambridge: Harvard University Press.

Smith-Gordon, Lionel and Laurence C. Staples. 1917. *Rural Reconstruction in Ireland: A Record of Co-operative Organisation.* London: P.S. King and Son.

Statistiske Meddelelser. 1915. *Mejeribruget i Danmark i 1914* 4. Rk. 49 bd. 1 h.: Copenhagen.

Taylor, Alan M. and Jeffrey G. Williamson. 1997. "Convergence in the Age of Mass Migration." *European Review of Economic History* 1: 27–63.

Temin, Peter. 1997. "Is It Kosher to Talk about Culture?" *Journal of Economic History* 57: 267–87.

Turner, Michael. 1996. *After the Famine: Irish Agriculture, 1850–1914.* Cambridge: Cambridge University Press.

Watkins, Susan C. and Jane Menken. 1985. "Famines in Historical Perspective." *Population and Development Review* 11: 647–76.

West, Trevor. 1986. *Horace Plunkett: Co-operation and Politics, An Irish Biography.* Washington D.C.: Catholic University of America Press.

Williamson, Jeffrey G. 1995. "The Evolution of Global Labor Markets Since 1830: Background Evidence and Hypotheses." *Explorations in Economic History* 32: 141–96.

Young, Alwyn. 1991. "Learning by Doing and the Dynamic Effects of International Trade." *Quarterly Journal of Economics* 106: 369–405.

CHAPTER FIVE

Andersen, Poul. 1954. *Dansk statsforfatningsret.* Copenhagen: Gyldendal.

Benson et al. 2004. *Maersk, manden og magten.* Politiken Bøger, 1. Copenhagen.

Dahl, Børge, Torben Melchior, and Ditlev Tamm, editors. 2002. *Danish Law in a European Perspective.* Second Edition. Thomson.

ECR I-2240. 1992. *EU-Court ruling in Case C-200/90.*

Fonsmark, Henning. 1990. *Historien om den danske utopi.* Copenhagen: Gyldendal.

Germer, Peter. 2001. *Dansk statsforfatningsret.* Copenhagen: DJØFs Forlag.

Kaspersen, Lars Bo. This volume, chapter 2, "The Formation and Development of the Welfare State."

Katzenstein, Peter J. 1985. *Small States in World Markets: Industrial Policy in Europe.* Ithaca: Cornell University Press.

Kelstrup, Morten et al. 1998. "Om det danske demokrati og den europæiske integration: Et demokratisk EU." *Rådet for europæisk politik* 3. Copenhagen: Systime.

Koch, Henning. 2002. "Standing to Raise Constitutional Issues." In *Parts of Danish Law in Action,* edited by Garade and Bondeson. National Report 16, Congress of International Academy of Comparative Law, Brisbane, 14–20 July.

Korsgaard, Ove. This volume, chapter 3, " The Danish Way to Establish the Nation in the Hearts of the People."

Lovbekendtgørelse. 1999. "Om dansk indfødsret," as modified by L 1999-12-29; and commentary in Karnovs Lovsamling, 1.2. Indfødsret, Note (25).

Martin, Cathie Jo. This volume, chapter 7, "Corporatism in the Post-industrial Age: Employers and Social Policy in the Little Land of Denmark."

Pedersen, Ove Kaj. 1994. *Demokratiets lette tilstand.*

Rasmussen, Hjalte. 2003. *EU-ret i Kontekst.* Copenhagen: Thomson.

– 1998. *The European Court of Justice.* Copenhagen: GadJura.

Ross, Alf. 1959. *Dansk statsforfatningsret I–II.* Copenhagen: Nyt Nordisk Forlag.

Zahle, Henrik. 1997. *Dansk forfatningset 3.* Copenhagen: Christian Ejlers' Forlag.

CHAPTER SIX

Amin, Ash and Damian Thomas. 1996. "The Negotiated Economy: State and Civic Institutions in Denmark." *Economy and Society* 25(2): 255–81.

Campbell, John L. and Ove K. Pedersen, editors. 1996. *Legacy of Change.*

Transformations of Postcommunist European Economies. New York: Aldine de Gruyter.

Cox, Robert Henry. 2001. "The Social Construction of an Imperative: Why Welfare Reform Happened in Denmark and the Netherlands but Not in Germany." *World Politics* 53(2): 463–98.

Crouch, Colin 1990. "Generalised Political Exchange in Industrial Relations in Europe during the Twentieth Century." 68–116 in *Self-Organising Policy Networks in Action*, edited by Bernd Marin. Frankfurt: Campus Verlag.

Finansministeriet. 1973. *Perspektivplanlægning* 1972–1987.

– 1971. *Perspektivplanlægning* 1970–1985. Copenhagen.

Hall, Peter. 1993. "Policy Paradigms, Social Learning, and the State: The Case of Economic Policymaking in Britain." *Comparative Politics* 25(3): 275–96.

– and David Soskice. 2002. *Varieties of Capitalism: The Institutional Foundations of Comparative Advantage.* Oxford: Oxford University Press.

Hemerijck, Anton C. and Martin Schludi. 2000. "Sequences of Policy Failures and Effective Policy Responses." 463–98 in *Welfare and Work in the Open Economy, Volume 1. From Vulnerability to Competitiveness*, edited by Fritz W. Scharpf and Vivien A. Schmidt. Oxford: Oxford University Press.

Jacobsson, Bengt, Per Lægreid, and Ove K. Pedersen, editors. 1999. *Fra opbygning til ombygning i staten*, vol. 3 in Nordic Project. Copenhagen: Jurist-og Økonomforbundets Forlag.

Jensen, Lotte. 2003. *Den store koordinator. Finansministeriet som moderne styringsaktør.* Copenhagen: Jurist-og Økonomforbundets Forlag.

Jørgensen, Henning. 2002. *Consensus, Cooperation and Conflict. The Policy Making Process in Denmark.* Cheltenham: Edward Elgar.

Katzenstein, Peter. 2002. "*Small States* and Small States Revisited." Paper presented at Cornell University, August.

– 1985. *Small States in World Markets: Industrial Policy in Europe.* Cornell University Press.

Kjær, Peter and Ove K. Pedersen. 2001. "Translating Liberalization: Neoliberalism in the Danish Negotiated Economy." 219–48 in *The Rise of Neoliberalism and Institutional Analysis*, edited by John L. Campbell and Ove K. Pedersen. Princeton: Princeton University Press.

Kastendiek, Hans. 1981. *Beiträge zur aktuellen korporativismusdiskussion.* Freien Universität Berlin.

Luhmann, Niklas. 1981. *Ausdifferenzierung des Rechts. Beiträge zur Rechtssoziologie und Rechtstheorie.* Frankfurt am Main: Suhrkamp.

Lægreid, Per and Ove K. Pedersen, editors. 1996. *Integration og Decentralisering*, vol. 2 in Nordic Project. Copenhagen: Jurist-og Økonomforbundets Forlag.

– 1994. *Forvaltningspolitik i Norden*, vol. 1 in Nordic Project. Copenhagen: Jurist-og Økonomforbundets Forlag.

Madsen, Per Kongshøj. 2003. "Flexicurity" Through Labour Market Policies and

Institutions in Denmark." 59–105 in *Employment Stability in an Age of Flexibility. Evidence from Industrialized Countries,* edited by Peter Auer and Sandrine Cazes. Geneva: International Labour Organization.

Mansbridge, Jane. 1992. "A Deliberative Perspective on Neocorporatism." *Politics and Society,* 20(4).

Marin, Bernd. 1996. "Generalisierter Politischer Austauch." 425–70 in *Organisation un Netzwerk. Institutionelle Steuerung in Wirtschaft und Politik,* edited by Patric Kenis and Volker Schneider. New York und Wien: Campus Verlag.

– 1990. "Introduction: Generalised Political Exchange." 13 in *Self-Organising Networks in Action,* edited by Bernd Marin. Frankfurt: Campus Verlag.

Nielsen, Klaus and Ove K. Pedersen. 1996. "Von der Mischwirtschaft zur Verhandlungsökonomie: Das Biespiel der Skandinavischen Länder." 357–86 in *Organisation un Netzwerk. Institutionelle Steuerung in Wirtschaft und Politik,* edited by Patric Kenis and Volker Schneider. New York und Wien: Campus Verlag.

Pedersen, Ove K. 1999. "Den Samfundsøkonomiske Forvaltning – Om Forvaltning og Interesseorganisationer." 127–50 in *Stat, Forvaltning, og Samfund efter 1950,* edited by Peter Bogason. Dansk Forvaltningshistorie, Bind 3. Copenhagen: Jurist-og Økonomforbundets Forlag.

– 1993. "The Institutional History of the Danish Polity: From a Market and Mixed Economy to a Negotiated Economy." 277–300 in *Institutional Change: Theory and Empirical Findings,* edited by Sven-Erik Sjöstrand. New York: M.E. Sharpe.

– Niels Å. Andersen, Peter Kjær, and John Elberg. 1992. *Privat Politik. Projekt Forhandlingsøkonomi.* København: Samfundslitteratur.

Schmitter, Philippe C. 1982. "Reflections on Where the Theory of Neo-corporatism has Gone and Where the Praxis of Neo-corporatism May Be Going." 259–79 in *Patterns of Corporatist Policy Making,* edited by Gerhard Lehmbruch and Philippe C. Schmitter. London: Sage.

– 1974. "Still the Century of Corporatism?" *The Review of Politics.* 36(1): 85–131.

Teague, Paul 2000. "Macroeconomic Constraints, Social Learning and Pay Bargaining in Europe." *British Journal of Industrial Relations* 38(3): 429–52.

Therborn, Gøran. 1998. "Does Corporatism Really Matter? The Economic Crisis and Issues of Political Theory." *Journal of Public Policy* 7(3): 259–84.

Traxler, Franz 1997. "The Logic of Social Pacts." 27–35 in *Social Pacts in Europe,* edited by G. Fajertag and P. Pochet. Bruxelles: European Trade Union Institut.

Traxler Franz, Sabine Blaschke, Bernard Kittel, editors. 2001. *National Labour Relations in Internationalized Markets: A Comparative Study of Institutions, Change, and Performance.* Oxford: Oxford University Press.

Treu, Tiziano. 1992. *Participation in Public Policy-Making. The Role of Trade Unions and Employers' Associations.* Berlin: Aldine de Gruyter.

Wallerstein, Michael and Bruce Western. 2000. "Unions in Decline? What Has Changed and Why." *Annual Review of Political Science* 3(1): 355–72.

494 References

CHAPTER SEVEN

Abrahamson, Peter. 1998. "Efter velfærdstaten: Ret og pligt til aktivering." *Nordisk Sosialt Arbeid* 3, 18: 133–42.

Alestalo, Matti and Stein Kuhnle. 1987. "The Scandinavian Route: Economic, Social, and Political Developments in Denmark, Finland, Norway, and Sweden." In *The Scandinavian Model*, edited by Robert Erikson et al. Armonk, New York: M.E. Sharpe.

Arbejdsmarkedsstyrelsen. 2000. "Midtvejsstatus for handlingsplan til fremme af privat jobtræning." *Arbejdsmarkedsstyrelsen* (March 16).

Arbejdsministeriet. 1999. "Danmarks Nationale Handlingsplan for Beskæftigelse 1999." København.

Bach, Hans and Anne-Birte Kylling. 1997. "New Partnership for Social Cohesion: the Danish Partnership Concept." Copenhagen: Socialforskningsinstituttet (May).

Berger, Suzanne and Ronald Dore, editors. 1996. *National Adversity and Global Capitalism.* Ithaca, New York: Cornell University Press.

Cable, Vincent. "The Diminished Nation-State: A Study in the Loss of Economic Power." *Daedalus* 124, 2: 23–53.

Campbell, John and John Hall. Introduction, this volume.

Castles, Francis. 1978. *The Social Democratic Image of Society.* London: Routledge & Kegan Paul.

Christiansen, Peter Munk. 1999. "Det fælles bedste?" 247–66 in *Den demokratiske udfordring*, edited by Jørgen Goul Andersen, Peter Munk Christiansen, Torben Beck Jørgensen, Lise Togeby, and Signild Vallgårda. København: Hans Reitzels Forlag.

– and Hilmar Rommetvedt. 1999. "From Corporatism to Lobbyism?" *Scandinavian Political Studies* 22, 3: 195–220.

Coen, David. 1997. *Journal of European Public Policy.* 4, 1: 91–108.

Crepaz, Markus. 1992. "Corporatism in Decline?" *Comparative Political Studies* 25, 2 (July): 139–68.

Crouch, Colin. 1993. *Industrial Relations and European State Traditions.* New York: Oxford University Press.

Danish National Institute of Social Research. 1997. "New Partnership for Social Cohesion." Copenhagen: Ministry of Social Affairs.

Department for Education and Employment. 1999. *United Kingdom Employment Action Plan.*

de Swaan, Abram. 1992. "Perspectives for Transnational Social Policy." *Government and Opposition* 27, 1: 33–51.

Due, Jesper, Joergen Steen Madsen, Carsten Stroeby Jensen, and Lars Kjerulf Petersen. 1994. *The Survival of the Danish Model.* Copenhagen: DJØF Publishing.

Esping-Andersen, Gøsta. 1990. *Three Worlds of Welfare Capitalism.* London: Polity Press.

Galenson, Walter. 1952. *The Danish System of Labor Relations*. Cambridge: Harvard University Press.

Geyer, Robert and Beverly Springer. 1998. "EU Social Policy After Mastricht." 207–23 in *The State of the European Union*, edited by Pierre-Henri Laurent and Marc Maresceau. Boulder Colorado: Lynne Rienner Publishers.

Gilbert, Neil. 1992 "From Entitlements to Incentives: The Changing Philosophy of Social Protection." *International Social Security Review* 45, 3: 5–17.

Goul Andersen, Jørgen. 1997. "The Scandinavian Welfare Model in Crisis? Achievements and Problems of the Danish Welfare State in an Age of Unemployment and Low Growth." *Scandinavian Political Studies* 20, 1: 1–31.

Green-Pedersen, Christoffer, Kees van Kersbergen and Anton Hemerijck. 2001."Neo-liberalism, the 'Third Way' or What? Recent Social Democratic Welfare Policies in Denmark and the Netherlands." *Journal of European Public Policy* 8, 2: 307–25.

Greenwood, Justin, Jurgen Grote, and Karsten Ronit, eds. 1992. *Organized Interests and the European Community*. Beverly Hills, California: Sage Publications.

Hall, Peter and David Soskice, eds. 2001. *Varieties of Capitalism: The Institutional-Foundations of Comparative Advantage*. New York: Oxford University Press.

Hasluck, Chris. 2000. *The New Deal for Young People, Two Years On*. Sheffield: Research Management Employment Service (February).

Henley, Andrew and Euclid Tsakalotos. 1992. "Corporatism and the European Labour Market after 1992." *British Journal of Industrial Relations* 30 (4 December): 567–86.

Hicks, Alex and Lane Kenworthy. 1998. "Cooperation and Political Economic Performance in Affluent Democratic Capitalism." *American Journal of Sociology* 6 (May): 1631–72.

Holt, Helle. 1998. *En kortlægning af dansk virksomheders social ansvar*. Copenhagen: Socialforskningsinstituttet.

Hornemann-Møller, Iver. 1992. *Den danske velfærdsstats tilblivelse*. Frederiksberg: Samfundslitteratur.

– 1994. *Velfærdsstatens udbygning*. Frederiksberg: Samfundslitteratur.

Huber, Evelyne, Charles Ragin, and John Stephens. 1993. "Social Democracy, Christian Democracy, Constitutional Structure and the Welfare State." *American Journal of Sociology* 99: 711–49.

Huber, Evelyne and John Stephens. 2001. "Welfare State and Production Regimes in the Era of Retrenchment." 107–45 in Pierson P.

Iversen, Torben. 2001. "The Dynamics of Welfare State Expansion." 45–79 in Pierson P.

– Jonas Pontusson and David Soskice, eds. 1999. *Unions, Employers, and Central Banks*. New York: Cambridge University Press.

Jacobsen, Hans Thyge. 1937. "Sociallovgivningen." 149–58 in *Konservatismens Historie I Danmark*, edited by Alfred Bindslev. Odense: Kulterhistorisk Forlag.

Katz, Harry. 1993. "The Decentralization of Collective Bargaining: A Literature

Review and Comparative Analysis." *Industrial and Labor Relations Review* 47 (1 October): 3–22.

Katzenstein, Peter. 1978. *Between Power and Plenty.* Madison: The University of Wisconsin Press.

— 1985. *Small States in World Markets.* Ithaca, New York: Cornell University Press.

Kendix, Michael and Mancur Olson. 1990. "Changing Unemployment Rates in Europe and the USA." 68–91 in *Labor Relations and Economic Performance,* edited by Renato Brunetta and Carlo Dell'Aringa. New York: NYU Press:

King, Desmond and Mark Wickham-Jones. 1998. "Training Without the State: New Labour and Labour Markets." *Policy and Politics* 26, 4: 439–55.

Kitschelt, Herbert, Peter Lange, Gary Marks, John Stephens, eds. 1999. *Continuity and Change in Contemporary Capitalism.* New York: Cambridge University Press.

Korpi, Walter 1980. "Social Policy and Distributional Conflict in the Capitalist Democracies." *West European Politics* 3: 296–315.

Lange, Peter, Michael Wallerstein, and Miriam Golden. 1995. "The End of Corporatism?"

Lash, Scott and John Urry. 1987. *The End of Organized Capitalism.* Oxford: Polity Press.

Longstreth. 1988. "From Corporatism to Dualism?" *Political Studies* 36: 413–32.

Madsen, Per Kongshøj. 2000. "The Danish Model of Flexicurity: A Paradise – with Some Snakes." 243–65 in *Labour Market and Social Protections Reforms in International Perspective,* edited by Hedva Sarfati and Giuliano Bonoli. Aldershot, Great Britain: Ashgate.

Martin, Andrew. 1979. "The Dynamics of Change in a Keynesian Political Economy."In *State and Economy in Contemporary Capitalism,* edited by Colin Crouch. London: Croon Helm.

Martin, Cathie Jo. 2005. "Corporatism from the Firm Perspective." *British Journal of Political Science* 35(1) 127–48.

Martin, Cathie Jo and Duane Swank. 2004. "Does the Organization of Capital Matter?" *American Political Science Review* 98 (November): 593–611.

Martin, Cathie Jo. 2000. *Stuck in Neutral.* Princeton: Princeton University Press.

Martin, John. 2000. "What Works Among Active Labour Market Policies: Evidence from OECD Countries' Experiences," *OECD Economic Studies* 20: 83–5.

Matzner, Egon and Wolfgang Streeck. 1991. "Introduction," *Beyond Keynesianism.* Brookfield, Vermont: Edward Elgar.

Ministry of Labour. 1996. *The Danish Labour Market Model.* Copenhagen: Ministry of Labour (June).

Ministry of Labour, Ministry of Finance, Denmark. 1996. "Labour Market Policy in Transition," (May).

Molina, Oscar and Martin Rhodes. 2002. "Corporatism: The Past, Present and Future of a Concept." *Annual Review of Political Science* 5: 305–31.

OECD. 1994. *The OECD Jobs Study.* Paris: Organization for Economic Co-operation and Development.

– 2001. *Employment Outlook.* Paris: Organization for Economic Co-operation and Development.

– 2000. *United Kingdom.* Paris: Organization for Economic Co-operation and Development (June).

– 1996. *The OECD Jobs Strategy: Enhancing the Effectiveness of Active Labour Market Policies.* Paris: Organization for Economic Co-operation and Development.

Perez, Sofia. 2001. "From De-centralization to Re-organization: Explaining the Return to National-level Bargaining in Italy and Spain." *Comparative Politics.*

Pierson, Paul, ed. 2000. *The New Politics of the Welfare State.* New York. Oxford University Press.

Pontusson, Jonas and Peter Swenson. 1996. "Labor Markets, Production Strategies, and Wage Bargaining Institutions." *Comparative Political Studies* 29, 2: 223–50.

Rhodes, Martin. 1998. "The Political Economy of Social Pacts," delivered at the New Politics of the Welfare State conference, Cambridge, Massachussets, 30 October–1 November.

Rhodes, Martin. 1997. "The Welfare State." In *Developments in West European Politics,* edited by Paul Heywood Rhodes and Vincent Wright. New York: St Martin's Press.

Rothstein, Bo. 2000. *Just Institutions Matter: The Moral and Political Logic of the Universal Welfare State.* New York: Cambridge University Press.

Sandholtz, Wayne and John Zysman. 1989. "1992: Recasting the European Bargaining." *World Politics* 42 (1 October): 95–128.

Scharpf, Fritz and Vivian Schmidt, editors. 2001. *Welfare to Work in the Open Economy.* New York: Oxford University Press.

Schmitter, Philippe. 1981. "Interest Intermediation and Regime Governability in Contemporary Western Europe and North America." In *Organizing Interests in Western Europe,* edited by Suzanne Berger. Cambridge: Cambridge University Press.

Schwartz, Herman. 2001a. The Danish "Miracle": Luck, Pluck, or Stuck? *Comparative Political Studies* 34 (2 March): 131–55.

Schwartz, Herman. 2000b. "Round Up the Usual Suspects!" 17–44 in Pierson.

Silver, Hilary. 1998. "Policies to Reinforce Social Cohesion in Europe." 38–73 in *Social exclusion: An ILO perspective,* edited by Jose Figueiredo and Arjan de Haan. Geneva: ILO Publications.

Skidelsky, Robert. 1979. "The Decline of Keynesian Politics." 55–87 in *State and Economy in Contemporary Capitalism,* edited by Colin Crouch. New York: St Martin's Press.

Social Ministry. 1999. "Det angaar os alle." Copenhagen: Social Ministry (January).

Streeck, Wolfgang. 1992. *Social Institutions and Economic Performance,* Beverly Hills, California: Sage Publications.

– and Philippe Schmitter. 1991. "From National Corporatism to Transnational Pluralism." *Politics and Society* 19: 133–64.

Swank, Duane. 2001. " Political Institutions and Welfare State Restructuring." In Pierson.

Thelen, Kathleen. 2001. In *Varieties of Capitalism*, edited by Peter Hall and Peter Lange.

Torfing, Jacob. 1999. "Workfare with Welfare: Recent Reforms of the Danish Welfare State." *Journal of European Social Policy* 9, 1: 5–28.

Treu, Tiziano. 1992. *Participation in Public Policy-Making: The Role of Trade Unions and Employer Associations*. New York: Walter de Gruyter.

Visser, Jelle and Anton Hemerijck. 1997. *"A Dutch Miracle": Job Growth, Welfare Reform, and Corporatism in the Netherlands*. Amsterdam: Amsterdam University Press.

Wallerstein, Michael, Miriam Golden, and Peter Lange. 1997. "Unions, Employers' Associations, and Wage-Setting Institutions in Northern and Central Europe, 1950–1992." In *Industrial and Labor Relations Review* 50, 3: 379–401.

Wilensky, Harold. 1976. *The "New Corporatism," Centralization, and the Welfare State*. Beverly Hills, California: Sage Publications.

Wood, Stewart. 2001. "Labour Market Regimes Under Threat? Sources of Continuity in Germany, Britain, Germany, and Sweden." In Pierson.

CHAPTER EIGHT

Ackers, Peter and Adrian Wilkinson, editors. 2003. *Understanding Work and Employment. Industrial Relations in Transition*. Oxford: Oxford University Press.

Andersen, Jørgen Goul. 2005. "Danskerne har stor indflydelse på arbejdet." (http://arkivwww.da.dk/nyhed/agenda/frontpageagenda)

– 2003. *Over-Danmark og Under-Danmark. Ulighed, velfærdsstat og medborgerskab*. Århus: Aarhus Universitetsforlag.

Andersen, Poul Houmann and Peer Hull Kristensen. 1999. "The Systemic Qualities of Danish Production." In *Mobilizing Resources and Generating Competencies. The Remarkable Success of Small and Medium Sized Enterprises in the Danish Business System*, edited by Peter Karnøe, Peer Hull Kristensen, and Poul Houmann Andersen. Copenhagen: Copenhagen Business School Press.

Arthur, Brian. 1998. *Increasing Returns and Path Dependence in the Economy*. Ann Arbor: University of Michigan Press.

Campbell, John L., John A. Hall, and Ove K. Pedersen. 2003. "The State of Denmark," mimeographed, October.

– and Ove K. Pedersen, editors. 2001. *The Rise of Neoliberalism and Institutional Analysis*. Princeton: Princeton University Press.

Casper, Steven. 2000. "Institutional Adaptiveness, Technology Policy, and the Diffusion of New Business Models: The Case of German Biotechnology," in *Organization Studies* 21(5): 887–914.

Castells, Manuel. 2000. *The Rise of the Network Society*. Oxford: Blackwell Publishers.

Chandler, Alfred D. 1977. *The Visible Hand: The Managerial Revolution in American Business*. Cambridge: Harvard University Press.

– 1962. *Strategy and Structure: Chapters in the History of the American Industrial Enterprise*. Cambridge: The MIT Press.

Cornette, Guy. 1999. "Saturn: Re-engineering the New Industrial Relations." 85–106 in *Teamwork in the Automobile Industry: Radical Change or Passing Fashion?* edited by Jean-Pierre Durand, Paul Stewart, and Juan Jose Castillo. Basingstoke: Macmillan.

Crouch, Collin. 1993. *Industrial Relations and European State Traditions.* Oxford: Clarendon Press.

Dobbin, Frank and Terry Boychuk. 1999. "National Employment System and Job Autonomy: Why Job Autonomy Is High in the Nordic Countries and Low in the United States, Canada and Australia." *Organization Studies* 20(2): 257–92.

European Commission. 2004. *Industrial Relations in Europe 2004.* Brussels: Directorate-General for Employment and Social affairs, Unit D.1.

Golding, Tony. 2001. *The City: Inside The Great Expectation Machine: Myth and Reality in Institutional Investment and Stock Market.* London: Prentice Hall.

Hall, Peter A. and David Soskice, editors. 2001. *Varieties of Capitalism: The Institutional Foundations of Comparative Advantage.* Oxford: Oxford University Press.

Hancke, Bob. 2002. *Large Firms and Institutional Change: Industrial Renewal and Economic Restructuring in France.* Oxford: Oxford University Press.

– 2000. "European Works Councils and Industrial restructuring in the European Motor Industry." *European Journal of Industrial Relations* 6(1): 35–61.

Industrirådet. 1974. *Industrivirksomhedens produktpolitik.* Copenhagen: Industrirådet.

Kjær, Peter and Ove Kaj Pedersen. 2001. "Translating Liberalization: Neoliberalism in the Danish Negotiated Economy." In Campbell and Pedersen.

Kristensen, Peer Hull. 2003. *Et Grænseløst Arbejde. En fantastisk fortælling om danske tillidsvalgtes arbejde med at sikre arbejde, indflydelse og fremtid i multinationale datterselskaber.* Copenhagen: Nyt fra Samfundsvidenskaberne.

– 1997. "National Systems of Governance and Managerial Prerogative in the Evolution of Work Systems: England, Germany and Denmark Compared." In Whitley and Kristensen.

– 1996a. "Denmark's Concealed Production Culture: Its Socio-Historical Construction and Dynamics at Work." In *Denmark, An Experimental Laboratory of Industrial Organization*, by Peer Hull Kristensen. Copenhagen: Copenhagen Business School.

– 1996b. "On the Constitution of Economic Actors in Denmark: Interacting Skill Containers and Project Containers." In Whitley and Kristensen.

– 1995. *Denmark: An Experimental Laboratory of Industrial Organization, Vols. I and II.* Doktorafhandling, Copenhagen: Copenhagen Business School.

– 1994. "Strategies in a Volatile World," in *Economy and Society*, 23(3): 305–34.

– 1986. *Teknologiske Projekter og Organisatoriske Processer,* Roskilde: Forlaget samfundsøkonomi og planlægning.

– and Claus Nygaard. 2000. *Det Industrielle Håndværk I Københavnsområdet – ved en skillevej?* Copenhagen: Copenhagen County.

– and Charles Sabel. 1997. "The Small Holder Economy in Denmark: The Exception as Variation." In Sabel and Zeitlin.

– and Jonathan Zeitlin (2005): *Local Players in Global Games: The Strategic Constitution of a Multinational Corporation*. Oxford: Oxford University Press.

– and Jonathan Zeitlin. 2001. "The Making of a Global Firm: Local Pathways to Multinational Enterprise." In Morgan et al.

Madsen, Per Kongshøj. 2003. Fyrtårn eller Slæbejolle? Dansk arbejdsmarkeds-og beskæftigelsespolitik og den Europæiske Beskæftigelsesstrategi. In Madsen and Pedersen.

– 1999. *Denmark: Flexibility, Security and Labour Market Success*. Employment and Training Papers no 53. Geneve: ILO.

– and Lisbeth Pedersen, editors. 2003. *Drivkræfter bag Arbejdsmarkedspolitikken*. Copenhagen: Socialforskningsinstituttet.

Mead, George H. 1967. *Mind, Self, and Society*, Chicago: The University of Chicago Press.

Moen, Eli and Kari Lilja. 2003. "Variety and Change in Coordinated Market Economies: The Case of Finland." Paper presented to Workshop on National Business Systems in the New Global Context, Leangkollen, Oslo, 8–11 May.

Morgan, Glenn, Peer Hull Kristensen, and Richard Whitley, editors. 2001. *The Multinational Firm: Organizing across Institutional and National Divides*. Oxford: Oxford University Press.

Mueller, Frank and John Purcell. 1992. "The Europeanization of Manufacturing and the Decentralization of Bargaining: Multinational Management Strategies in the European Automobile Industry." *International Journal of Human Resource Management* 3(1): 15–31.

Mueller, Frank. 1996. "National Stakeholders in the Global Contest for Corporate Investment." *European Journal of Industrial Relations* 2(3): 345–68.

Nygaard, Claus. 1999. *The Effect of Embeddedness on Strategic Action*. Copenhagen Business School: PhD series.

Plender, John. 2003. *Going Off the Rails. Global Capital and the Crisis of Legitimacy*. Chichester: John Wiley and Sons.

Regini, M. 1991. *Uncertain Boundaries: The Social and Political Construction of European Economics*. Cambridge: Cambridge University Press.

Rodgers, Daniel T. 1998. *Atlantic Crossings: Social Politics in a Progressive Age*. Cambridge: Harvard University Press.

Sabel, Charles F. and Jonathan Zeitlin, editors. 1997. *Worlds of Possibilities. Flexibility and Mass Production in Western Industrialization*. Cambridge: Cambridge University Press.

Tainio, Risto, Mika Huolman, and Matti Pulkkinen. 2001. "The Internationalization of Capital Markets: How International Institutional Investors are Restructuring Finnish Companies." In *The Multinational Firm. Organizing Across Institutional and National Divides*, edited by Glenn Morgan, Peer Hull Kristensen, and Richard Whitley. Oxford: Oxford University Press.

Whitley, Richard and Peer Hull Kristensen. 1996a. *The Changing European Firm: Limits to Convergence*. London: Routledge.

Whitley, Richard and Peer Hull Kristensen, editors.1996b. *Governance at Work: The Social Regulation of Economic Relations*. Oxford: Oxford University Press.

Whitley, Richard. 1999 *Divergent Capitalisms: The Social Construction and Change of Business Systems*. Oxford: Oxford University Press.

– 2000. "The Institutional Structuring of Innovation Strategies: Business Systems, Firm Types and Patterns of Technical Change in Different Market Economies." *Organization Studies* 21(5): 855–86.

Zeitlin, Jonathan and David M. Trubek. 2003. *Governing Work and Welfare in a New Economy*. Oxford: Oxford University Press.

CHAPTER NINE

Arbejdsministeriet. 1999. *Arbejdsmarkedsreformerne –en status*. København: Arbejdsministeriet.

Auer, Peter. 2000. *Employment revival in Europe. Labour market success in Austria, Denmark, Ireland and the Netherlands*. Geneva: International Labour Organization.

– and Sandra Cazes, editors. 2003. *Employment Stability in an Age of Flexibility. Evidence from Industrialized Countries*. Geneva: International Labour Organization.

Beskæftigelsesministeriet. 2002. *Flere i arbejde – analyse af den beskæftigelsespolitiske indsats*. København: Beskæftigelsesministeriet.

Bingley, Paul, Tor Eriksson, Axel Werwatz and Niels Westergård-Nielsen. 1999. *Beyond "Manucentrism": Some fresh facts about Job and Worker Flows*. Working paper 99–09. Aarhus: Centre for Labour Market and Social Research.

Boje, Thomas P. and Per Kongshøj Madsen. 2003. "Wage Formation, Institutions and Unemployment." 213–38 in *Post-industrial Labour Markets: Profiles of North America and Scandinavia*, edited by Thomas P. Boje and Bengt Furåker. London: Routledge.

Calmfors, Lars and John Driffill. 1988. "Bargaining Structure, Corporatism and Macroeconomic Performance." *Economic Policy* 6: 14–61.

Compston, Hugh and Per Kongshøj Madsen. 2001. "Conceptual Innovation and Public Policy: Unemployment and Paid Leave Schemes in Denmark." *Journal of European Social Policy* 11(2): 117–32.

Danmarks Statistik. 2003. *Statistisk Tiårsoversigt 2003*. København: Danmarks Statistik.

Dansk Arbejdsgiverforening. 2003. *ArbejdsMarkedsRapport 2003*. København: Dansk Arbejdsgiverforening.

Det Økonomiske Råds Formandskab. 2002. *Dansk Økonomi, Efteråret 2002*. København: Det Økonomiske Råd.

European Commission. 2003. *Employment in Europe 2003*. Luxembourg: European Commission.

– 2002. *Industrial Relations in Europe*. Luxembourg: European Commission.

Finansministeriet. 2001. *Finansredegørelse 2001*. København: Finansministeriet

Geerdsen, Lars Pico. 2003. *Marginalisation Processes in the Danish Labour Market*. København: Socialforskningsinstituttet.

Hall, Peter A. and David Soskice. 2001. *Varieties of Capitalism: The Institutional Foundations of Comparative Advantage.* Cambridge: Cambridge University Press

Jørgensen, Henning and Flemming Larsen. 2003. "Aktivgørelsen af aktiveringen kommer ikke af sig selv – Betydningen af institutionelt design for udviklingen af ledighedsindsatser." 164–200. In Madsen and Pedersen.

– 2002. "Labour Market Policies." 167–89 in *Consensus, Cooperation and Conflict: The Policy Making Process in Denmark,* edited by Henning Jørgensen. Cheltenham: Edward Elgar.

Katzenstein, Peter J. 1985. *Small States in World Markets: Industrial Policy in Europe,* London: Cornell.

Kristiansen, Jens. 1997. *Lønmodtagerbeskyttelsen i dansk arbejdsret.* København: GadJura.

Kærgaard, Niels and Henrik Hansen. 1994. "Den danske arbejdsløshed 1903–1990." *Samfundsøkonomen* 6: 9–13.

Larsen, Mona and Klaus Langager. 1998. *Arbejdsmarkedsreformen og arbejdsmarkedet.* København: Socialforskningsinstituttet

Madsen, Per Kongshøj. 2003. "Flexicurity" Through Labour Market Policies and Institutions in Denmark." 59–105 in *Employment Stability in an Age of Flexibility. Evidence from Industrialized Countries,* edited by Peter Auer and Sandrine Cazes. Geneva: International Labour Organization.

– 2002. "The Danish Model of *Flexicurity:* A Paradise – with Some Snakes." 243–65 in *Labour Market and Social Protections Reforms in International Perspective: Parallel or Converging Tracks?* edited by Hedva Sarfati and Giuliano Bonoli. Aldershot: Ashgate.

– Peter Munch-Madsen and Klaus Langhoff-Roos. 2001. "All Hands on Deck! – Fighting Social Exclusion in Denmark." 124–51 in *Social Exclusion and European Policy,* edited by David Mayes, Jos Berghman, and Robert Salais. Cheltenham: Edward Elgar.

– and Lisbeth Pedersen, editors. 2003. *Drivkræfter bag arbejdsmarkedspolitikken.* København: Socialforskningsinstituttet.

Mailand, Mikkel and Jesper Due. 2003. "Partsstyring i arbejdsmarkedspolitikken – perspektiver og alternativer." 202–33 in Madsen and Pedersen.

Martin, John P. 2000. "What Works among Active Labour Market Policies: Evidence from OECD Countries' Experience." *OECD Economic Studies* 30(1): 79–112.

Ministry of Labour. 2000. *Effects of Danish Employability Enhancement Programs.* København: Arbejdsministeriet.

Nielsen, Klaus and Ove K. Pedersen. 1991. "From the Mixed Economy to the Negotiated Economy: The Scandinavian Countries." 145–67 in *Morality, Rationality, and Efficiency: New Perspectives on Socio-Economics,* edited by Richard M. Coughlin. Armonk: M.E. Sharpe.

Nordic Council of Ministers. 2000. *Supply of Labour in the Nordic Countries: Experience, Developments and Political Deliberations.* København: Nordisk Ministerråd.

OECD. 2003. *Employment Outlook*. Paris: OECD.

– 2002. *Benefits and wages. OECD Indicators*. Paris: OECD.

– 1999. *Employment Outlook*, Paris: OECD.

– 1997. *Employment Outlook*, Paris: OECD.

Rosholm, Michael and Michael Svarer. 2004. "Estimating the Threat Effect of Active Labour Market Programs," *IZA Discussion Paper* no. 1300.

Smith, Michael R. 1992. *Power, Norms, and Inflation*. New York: Aldine de Gruyter.

Torfing, Jacob. 2004: *Det stille sporskifte i velfærdsstaten*. Århus: Magtudredningen, Aarhus Universitetsforlag.

Wilthagen, Ton and Frank Tros. 2004. "The Concept of 'Flexicurity': A New Approach to Regulating Employment and Labour Markets." *TRANSFER* 10(2): 166–86.

Winter, Søren. 2003. "Kanalrundfart eller Zapning? – Om kanaler og arenaer i den aktive arbejdsmarkedspolitik." 268–317 in Madsen and Pedersen.

CHAPTER TEN

Abrahamson, Peter. Forthcoming. "Futures of the European Social Model." In *The Future of the European Social Model* (working title), edited by Iona Ostner.

– 2003. "The End of the Scandinavian model? Welfare Reform in the Nordic countries." *Journal of Societal and Social Policy* 2(2): 19–36.

– 2002. "The Danish Welfare State: A Social Rights Perspective." *Journal of Societal and Social Policy* 1(1): 1–13.

– 1999. "The Welfare Modelling Business." *Social Policy and Administration* 21(4): 394–415.

– Mia Kambskard, and Cecilie Wehner. 2002. *Denmark*. Ghent: University of Ghent, Department of Social Law, Special Report, First Phase: Cross-cutting questions.

– and Cecilie Wehner. 2003. *Pension Reforms in Denmark*. London: London School of Economics and Political Science.

Andersen, Dines, Alice Appeldorn, and Hanne Weise. 1996. *Orlov: Evaluering af orlovsordningerne*. Copenhagen: National Insttute of Social Research.

Andersen, Jørgen Goul, P.A. Pettersen, Stefan Svallfors, and Hannu Uusitalo. 1999. "The Legitimacy of the Nordic Welfare States: Trends, Variations and Cleavages." In *Nordic Social Policy: Changing Welfare States*, edited by Kautto Mikko, Matti Heikkilä, Bjørn Hvinden, Staffan Marklund, and Niels Ploug. London: Routledge.

CASA and Socialpolitisk Forening. 2003. *Social Årsrapport 2003 [Social Tendencies 2003]*. Copenhagen: CASA (Centre for Alternative Social Analysis) and Socialpolitisk Forening (Danish Social Policy Association).

Castles, Francis G. and Deborah Mitchell. 1990. "Three Worlds of Welfare Capitalism or Four?" Australian National University, graduate program in public policy. Discussion paper no. 21.

Clasen, Jochen. 2000. "Motives, Means and Opportunities: Reforming Unemployment Compensation in the 1990s." *West European Politics* 23(2): 89–112.

Deacon, Bob. 1993. "Developments in East European Social Policy." 177–97 in *New Perspectives on the Welfare State in Europe*, edited by Catherine Jones. London: Routledge.

Esping-Andersen, Gøsta. 1997. "Hybrid or Unique?: The Japanese Welfare State Between Europe and America." *Journal of European Social Policy* 7(3): 179–89.

– 1996. *Welfare State in Transition: National Adaptations in Global Economies.* London: Sage.

– 1990. *The Three World of Welfare Capitalism.* Cambridge: Polity Press.

European Commission. 2002. *Joint Report on Social Inclusion.* Brussels: Directorate General V.

Eurostat. 2003. *Eurostat årbog. Statistisk guide til EU. Tiårsoversigt 1990–2000.* Luxembourg: Eurostat.

Ferrera, Maurizio, Anton Hemerijck, and Martin Rhodes. 2000. "Recasting European Welfare States for the 21st Century." *European Review* 8(3): 427–46.

Ferrera, Maurizio and Martin Rhodes. 2000. "Recasting European Welfare States: An Introduction." *West European Politics* 23(2): 1–10.

Gould, Arthur. 1993. *Capitalist Welfare Systems: A Comparison of Japan, Britain and Sweden.* London: Longman.

Hall, Peter. 1993. "Policy Paradigms, Social Learning, and the State: The Case of Economic Policymaking in Britain." *Comparative Politics* 25(3): 275–96.

– 1986. *Governing the Economy: The Policy of State Intervention in Britain and France.* New York: Oxford University Press.

Hansen, Hans. 1998. *Elements of Social Security.* Copenhagen: National Institute of Social Research.

Henriksen, Bjarne Lenau. 2003. "Villig til hvad?" *Ældresagen* (October): 14.

Holt, Helle. 1998. *En kortlægning af danske virksomheders sociale ansvar.* Copenhagen: National Institute of Social Research.

Information. 1998. "Brugerbetalingen stiger støt." The daily newspaper *Information*, 15 April: 2.

Jones, Cathrine 1993. "The pacific challenge." 198–221 in *New Perspectives on the Welfare State in Europe*, edited by Cathrine Jones. London: Routledge.

Jørgensen, Per Schultz. 2003. "Socialpolitik på børneområdet -siden regeringens start i November 2001." *Social Årsrapport 2003*: 133–8.

Kautto, Mikko and Jon Kvist. 2002. "Distinct or Extinct? Nordic Welfare States in the European Context." *SFI Working Paper 2002:7.*

Kautto, Mikko, Johan Fritzell, Bjørn Hvinden, Jon Kvist, and Hannu Uusitalo (2001). "Conclusion: the Nordic Welfare States in the European Context." 262–72 in *Nordic Welfare States in the European Context*, edited by Mikko Kautto, Johan Fritzell, Bjørn Hvinden, Jon Kvist, and Hannu Uusitalo. London: Routledge.

Knudsen, Tim and Bo Rothstein. 1994. "State Building in Scandinavia." *Comparative Politics* 26(2): 203–20.

Kuhnle, Stein and Matti Alestalo. 2000. "Introduction: Growth, Adjustments and Survival of European Welfare States." 3–18 in *Survival of the European Welfare State*, edited by Stein Kuhnle. London and New York: Routledge.

Leibfried, Stephan 1992 (1991). "Towards a European Welfare State." In *Social Policy in a Changing Europe*, edited by Zusa Ferge and Jon Eivind Kolberg. Frankfurt am Main: Campus Verlag. First published as *ZeS Arbeitspapier* Nr. 2/91. Bremen: Zentrum für Sozialpolitik, Universität Bremen.

Leibfried, Stephan and Herbert Obinger. 2000. "Welfare State Futures: An Introduction." *European Review* 8(3): 277–90.

Madsen, Per Kongshøj 2003. "Fra arbejdsmarkedspolitik til beskæftigelsespolitik: et skifte i form eller indhold?." *Social Forskning 2003: 3*.

MetroXpress. 2003a. "Udliciteringer tredoblet på få år." *MetroXpress* 3(183): 14.

– 2003b. "Roskilde amt har få ansatte" *MetroXpress* 3(183): 16.

Ministry of Social Affairs. 1999. *Sociale tendenser 1999*. Copenhagen: Ministry of Social Affairs, Den sociale Ankestyrelse.

– 1991. *Der er brug for alle II*. Copenhagen: Socialministeriet.

– 1990. *Der er brug for alle*. Copenhagen: Socialministeriet.

Ministry of State. 2003. *Kommissorium for Velfærdskommissionen*. Copenhagen: Ministry of State.

Moritz, Lone. 2003. "Langvarige kontanthjælpsmodtagere i Kgs. Enghave." *Social Årsrapport 2003*: 83–7.

NOSOSCO. (Nordic Social-Statistical Committee). 2003. *Social Protection in the Nordic Countries 2001*. Copenhagen: Nordic Social-Statistical Committee.

– 2000. *Social Protection in the Nordic Countries 1998*. Copenhagen: Nordic Social-Statistical Committee.

Olsen, Claus and Idamarie Svendsen. 2003. "Ændringer på det sociale forsørgelsesområde -med fokus på magt, ret og subjektivitet." *Social Årsrapport 2003*: 89–100.

Palme, Joakim. 1999. *The Nordic Model and the Modernisation of Social Protection in Europe*. Copenhagen: Nordic Council of Ministers.

Palme, Joakim, Åke Bergmark, Olof Bäckman, Felip Estrada, Johan Fritzell, Olle Lundberg, Ola Sjöberg, Lena Sommestad, and Martha Szebehely. 2003. "A Welfare Balance Sheet for the 1990s." *Scandinavian Journal of Public Health* 31(60): 7–143.

Pierson, Paul. 1996. "The New Politics of the Welfare State." *World Politics* 48(2): 143–79.

– 1994. *Dismantling the Welfare State? Reagan, Thatcher and the Politics of Retrenchment*. Cambridge: Cambridge University Press.

Sakslin, Maija. 2002. *Finland*. Ghent: University of Ghent, Department of Social Law, SPECIAL Report. First Phase: Cross-cutting questions.

Statistics Denmark. 2003. *Statistiske Efterretninger: Sociale forhold, sundhed og Retsvæsen 2003: 15*. Copenhagen: Statistics Denmark.

Strobel, Pierre. 2003. "Le modèle nordique de protection sociale sous le choc des réformes." *Revue française des affaires sociales* 57 (4): 7–16.

Swank, Duane. 2000. "Social Democratic Welfare States in a Global Economy."
    85–138 in *Globalization, Europeanization and the End of Scandinavian Social
    Democracy?* edited by Robert Geyer, Christine Ingebritsen, and Jonathon W.
    Moses. London: Macmillan.

Titmuss, Richard. M. 1987 (1972). "Developing Social Policy in Conditions of
    Rapid Change: The Role of Social Welfare." 254–68 in *The Philosophy of Welfare*
    edited by Brian Abel-Smith and Kay Titmuss. London: Allen and Unwin.

van Kersbergen, Kees. 2000. "The Declining Resistance of Welfare States to
    Change?" 19–36 in *Survival of the European Welfare State*, edited by Stein Kuhnle.
    London and New York: Routledge.

Van Oorschot, Wim and Peter Abrahamson. 2003. "The Dutch and Danish
    Miracles Revisited: A Critical Discussion of Activation Policies in Two Small
    Welfare States." *Social Policy and Administration* 37(3): 288–304.

Wilensky, Harold L. and Charles N. Lebaux. 1958. *Industrial Society and Social
    Welfare.* New York: Russell Sage Foundation.

CHAPTER ELEVEN

Andersen, Jørgen Goul. 2002: "Danskerne, Europa og det "demokratiske under-
    skud." Den "stille revolution" i danskernes forhold til EU," in *Europa for Folket? EU
    og det danske Demokrati,* edited by Thomas Pedersen. Magtudredningen. Århus:
    Århus Universitetsforlag.

Branner, Hans. 2002. *Det ny Europa: international politik under forandring.*
    Copenhagen: Columbus.

– 2000. "The Danish Foreign Policy Tradition and the European Context."
    185–222 in Branner and Kelstrup.

– and Morten Kelstrup, editors. 2000. *Denmark's Policy towards Europe after 1945:
    History, Theory and Options.* Odense: Odense Universitetsforlag.

– 2002. "Denmark's Policy towards Europe: A Reply." *Cooperation and Conflict,* 1
    (37, March): 90–9.

– 2000. "Denmark's Policy towards Europe in a Historical and Theoretical
    Perspective." 9–40 in Branner and Kelstrup.

Damgaard, Erik and Asbjørn Sonne Nørgaard. 2000. "The European Union and
    Danish Parliamentary Democracy." 33–58 in *Delegation and Accountability in
    European Integration,* edited by Torbjørn Bergman and Erik Damgaard. London:
    Frank Cass.

Dosenrode, Søren Z. von, 2000: "Danish EU-Policy Making." 381–402 in Branner
    and Kelstrup.

DUPI. 2000. *Udviklingen i EU siden 1992 på de områder der er omfattet af de danske forbe-
    hold.* København: DUPI.

Friis, Lykke. 2002. *Den europæiske byggeplads. Fra fælles mønt til europæisk forfatning.*
    København: Centrum.

Haahr, Jens Henrik. 2000. "Between Scylla and Charybdis: Danish Party Policies on
    European Integration." 305–33 in Branner and Kelstrup.

– 1993: *Looking to Europe*. Aarhus: Aarhus University Press.

Hansen, Lene. 2002. "Sustaining Sovereignty: The Danish approach to Europe." 50–87 in Hansen and Wæver.

– and Ole Wæver, editors. 2002. *European Integration and National Identity*. London and New York: Routledge.

Hedetoft, Ulf. 2000. "The Interplay between Mass and Elite Attitudes to European Integration in Denmark." 282–304 in Branner and Kelstrup.

Holm, Hans-Henrik. 2002. "Danish Foreign Policy Activism: The Rise and Decline."19–46 in *Danish Foreign Policy Yearbook 2002*, edited by Bertel Heurlin and Hans Mouritzen. Copenhagen: DUPI.

Ingebritsen, Christine. 1998. *The Nordic States and European Unity*. Ithaca, New York: Cornell University Press.

Jacobsson, Bengt, Per Lægreid, and Ove K. Pedersen, editors. 2001. *Europaveje. EU i de nordiske centralforvaltninger.* København: Jurist-og Økonomforbundets Forlag.

Jensen, Henrik. 2003. *Europaudvalget -et udvalg i Folketinget*. Magtudredningen. Århus: Århus Universitetetsforlag.

Katzenstein, Peter J. 1985. *Small States in World Markets. Industrial Policy in Europe*. Ithaca and London: Cornell University Press.

Kelstrup, Morten. 2001. "The European Union and Globalisation: Reflections on Strategies of Individual States." *COPRI Working Papers*, 2001/38.

– 2000a. "Integration Policy: Between Foreign Policy and Diffusion." 100–38 in Branner and Kelstrup.

– 2000b. "Danish Integration Policies: Dilemmas and Options." 414–39 in Branner and Kelstrup.

– 1994. "Dansk EU-politik: Politikfastlæggelse i et dilemma mellem diffusitet og fastlåsning." 20–56 in *Danmark og Den Europæiske Union*, edited by Bertel Heurlin. Forlaget Politiske Studier.

– 1993. "Small States and European Political Integration: Reflections on Theories and Strategies." 136–62 in *The Nordic Countries and the EC*, edited by Teija Tiilainen and Ib Damgaard Petersen. Copenhagen: Copenhagen Political Studies Press.

– editor. 1993. *European Integration and Denmark's Participation*, Copenhagen: Copenhagen Political Studies Press.

Larsen, Henrik. 2002. "Denmark and the EU Defense Dimension: Opt-out Across the Board?" 90–153 in *ESDP and the Nordic Countries: Four Variations on a Theme*, by Henrik Larsen, Nina Græger, and Hanna Ojanen. Finnish Institute of International Affairs.

Mouritzen, Hans. 1993. "The Two Musterknaben and the Naughty Boy: Sweden, Finland and Denmark in the Process of European Integration." *Cooperation and Conflict* 28: 373–402.

Mouritzen, Hans, editor. 2003. *Er vi så forbeholdne? Danmark over for globaliseringen, EU og det nære*. Århus: Århus Universitetsforlag, Magtudredningen.

Østergaard, Uffe. 2000. "Danish National Identity: Between Multinational Heritage and Small State Nationalism." 139–84 in Branner and Kelstrup.

Pedersen, Ove K., editor. 2001. *Broen fra Slotsholmen til Bruxelles. EU og den centrale forvaltning i Danmark.* København: Jurist-og Økonomforbundets Forlag.

– et al. 1994. *Demokratiets lette tilstand.* København: Spektrum

Petersen, Nikolaj. 2000. "National Strategies in the Integration Dilemma: An Adaptation Approach." 72–99 in Branner and Kelstrup.

– 1996. "Denmark and the European Union 1985–96: A Two-level Analysis," *Cooperation and Conflict* 31(2): 185–210.

– 1995. "Denmark and the European Community 1985–93." In *Adaptation and Activism: The Foreign Policy of Denmark 1967–1993*, edited by Due-Nielsen and Petersen. Copenhagen: DJØF.

Rasmussen, Anders Fogh. 2003. "Dansk europapolitik efter formandsskabet." Speech of the Prime Minister at the Danish Institute of International Studies, 15 January.

Regeringen, Socialdemokratiet og Det Radikale Venstre. 2003. "Ét Europa: mere effektivt, rummeligt og demokratisk." www.euoplysningen.dk/konvendokumenter/taler/dkeuropa

Regeringen. 2004. "Politisk aftale mellem Regeringen (Venstre og Det Konservative Folkeparti), Socialdemokraterne, Socialistisk Folkeparti og Det Radikale Venstre om Danmark i det udvidede EU." www.euoplysningen.dk

Riis, Peter. 2002. "Europaudvalget: parlamentarisk kontrol og demokratiske dilemmaer." 133–44 in *Europa for folket?* edited by Thomas Pedersen. Århus: Århus Universitetsforlag, Magtudredningen.

Senghaas, Dieter. 1992. *Von Europa lernen. Entwicklungsgeschichtliche Betrachtungen.* Frankfurt am Main: Edition Suhrkamp.

Snyder, Glenn. 1984. "The Security Dilemma in Alliance Politics." *World Politics* 86 (4).

Togeby, Lise et al. 2003. *Magt og demokrati i Danmark: hovedresultater fra Magtudredningen.* Århus: Århus Universitetsforlag.

Udenrigsministeeeriet. 2001. *Danmark og Europa: Udvidelse, Globalisering, Folkelig Forankring.* Hvidbog, June.

Wivel, Anders, editor. 1998. *Explaining European Integration.* Copenhagen: Copenhagen Political Studies Press.

Wæver, Ole. 1995. "Danish Dilemmas: Foreign Policy Choices for the 21st Century." 269–302 in *Adaptation and Activism. The Foreign Policy of Denmark 1967–1993*, edited by Due-Nielsen and Petersen. Copenhagen: DJØF.

Zilmer-Johns, Lisbeth. 2003. *Dansk sikkerhedspolitisk profil: tilbage til start?* IIS Report 2003/1. Copenhagen: Institut for Internationale Studier.

CHAPTER TWELVE

Anderson, Benedict. 1983. *Imagined Communities.* London: Verso.

Andreas, Peter and Timothy Snyder, editors. 2000. *The Wall around the West. State Borders and Immigration Control in North America and Europe.* Lanham: Rowman and Littlefield.

Anderson, Sally, 2002. "Civilizing Children: Children's Sport and Civil Sociability in Copenhagen, Denmark." Unpublished PhD thesis, Department of Anthropology, University of Copenhagen.

Bade, Klaus. 2003. *Legal and Illegal Immigration into Europe: Experiences and Challenges.* Wassenaar: Netherlands Institute for Advanced Study in the Humanities and Social Sciences.

Bauman, Zygmunt. 1998. *Globalization: The Human Consequences.* Cambridge: Polity.

Baylis, John and Steve Smith, editors. 1997. *The Globalization of World Politics.* Oxford: Oxford University Press.

Beck, Ulrich. 2000. *What Is Globalization?* Cambridge: Polity.

Benhabib, Seyla. 2002. *The Claims of Culture.* Princeton: Princeton University Press.

Bleich, Eric. 2003. *Race Politics in Britain and France.* Cambridge: Cambridge University Press.

Blomgren-Hansen, Niels. 2003. "Dynamik gennem offensiv indvandrerpolitik." *Jyllandsposten,* 12 November.

Brix, Helle Merete, et al. 2003. *I krigens hus. Islams kolonisering af Vesten.* Aarhus: Hovedland.

Brochmann, Grete and Jon Erik Dölvik. 2004. "Is Immigration an Enemy of The Welfare State? Between Human Rights and *Realpolitik* in European Immigration Policies." Forthcoming in *Managing Migration: A Policy Agenda for Economic Progress and Social Cohesion,* edited by Demetri Papademetriou. Washington, DC: Migration Policy Institute.

Brubaker, Rogers. 1992. *Citizenship and Nationhood in France and Germany.* Cambridge: Harvard University Press.

Cohen, Marjorie Griffin and Stephen Clarkson, editors. 2004. *Governing under Stress. Middle Powers and the Challenge of Globalization.* London and New York: Zed Books.

Danish Immigration Service. 2002. *Statistical Overview.* Copenhagen: The Danish Immigration Service.

Düvell, Franck. 2003. "The Globalisation of Migration Control." http://www.openDemocracy.net, 12 June. Longer version in http://www.noborder.org, 19 May.

Ejrnæs, Morten. 2001. "Integrationsloven – en case, der illustrerer etniske minoriteters usikre medborgerstatus." *AMID Working Papers,* no. 1, Aalborg University.

Ejrnæs, Morten. 2002. "Etniske minoriteters tilpasning til livet i Danmark – forholdet mellem majoritetssamfundet og etniske minoriteter." *AMID Working Papers,* no. 18, Aalborg University.

Faist, Thomas. 2000. *The Volume and Dynamics of International Migration and Transnational Social Spaces.* Oxford: Clarendon Press.

Geddes, Andrew. 2003. "Migration and the Welfare State in Europe." In *The Politics of Migration. Managing Opportunity, Conflict and Change,* edited by Sarah Spencer. Special issue, *The Political Quarterly.* Oxford and Malden, Massachussets: Blackwell.

Government White Paper (*GWP*). 2003. *Regeringens vision og strategier for bedre integration* (main report and *Resumé*). Copenhagen: The Danish Government, June.

Grande, Edgar and Louis W. Pauly, editors. 2005. *Complex Sovereignty: Reconstituting Political Authority in the 21st Century*. Toronto: University of Toronto Press.

GRUS, no. 71. 2004. Special Issue on the Final Report of the Danish Power and Democracy Project.

Gundelach, Peter. 2002. *Det er dansk*. Copenhagen: Hans Reitzel.

Haagen Pedersen, Lars. 2002. *Befolkningsudvikling, integration og økonomisk politik*. Copenhagen: DREAM (Danish Rational Economic Agents Model).

Hedetoft, Ulf. 2003a. "The Politics of Belonging and Migration in Europe." In *Identity Dynamics and the Construction of Boundaries*, edited by Bo Petersson and Eric Clark. Lund: Nordic Academic Press.

– 2003b. *The Global Turn*. Aalborg: Aalborg University Press.

– 2003c. "Culture-as-Politics: Meanings and Applications of 'Culture' in Political Studies." Opening keynote address for conference on *What's the Culture in Multiculturalism*, Danish Network of Political Theory, Department of Political Science, Aarhus University.

– editor. 1998. *Political Symbols, Symbolic Politics*. Aldershot: Ashgate.

– 1995. *Signs of Nations*. Aldershot: Dartmouth.

– and Hans Hummelgaard et al. 2002. *Integrationsforskningen i Danmark 1980–2002*. Copenhagen: The Ministry for Refugees, Immigrants and Integration.

Hirst, Paul and Grahame Thompson, 1996. *Globalization in Question*. Cambridge: Cambridge University Press.

Holmen, Anne. 2002. "Betydningen af sprog, tosprogethed og sprogligt bårne kulturformer for integrationsprocesserne." *AMID Working Papers*, no. 23. Aalborg University.

Ireland, Patrick. 1994. *The Policy Challenge of Ethnic Diversity: Immigrant Politics in France and Switzerland*. Cambridge: Harvard University Press.

Järvinen, Margaretha and Nanna Mik-Meyer, editors. 2003. *At skabe en klient. Institutionelle identiteter i socialt arbejde*. Copenhagen: Hans Reitzel.

Joppke, Christian and Virginie Guiraudon, editors. 2001. *Controlling a New Migration World*. London: Routledge.

Jyllandsposten, 3 January 2005. Leading article titled "Globalisering" ["*Globalization*"].

Katzenstein, Peter. 2000. "Confidence, Trust, International Relations, and Lessons From Smaller Democracies." In *Disaffected Democracies: What's Troubling the Trilateral Countries?*, edited by Susan J. Pharr and Robert D. Putnam. Princeton: Princeton University Press.

– 1985. *Small States in World Markets*. Ithaca and London: Cornell University Press.

Kyle, David and Rey Koslowski, editors. 2001. *Global Human Smuggling: Comparative Perspectives*. Baltimore: Johns Hopkins University Press.

Lauring, Jakob and Charlotte Jonasson. 2004. "Organisational Diversity and Knowledge Sharing." Paper presented at conference on *Ethnic Minorities, Integration and Marginalisation.* The Graduate School for Integration, Production and Welfare, Copenhagen, February 26–27.

Lintrup, Jens, and Gunnar Olesen. 2002. *Danmark i Verden.* Gylling: Narayana Press.

Matthiessen, P.C. and Gunnar Mogensen, editors. 2000. *Integration i Danmark omkring årtusindskiftet. Indvandrernes møde med arbejdsmarkedet og velfærdssamfundet.* Rockwool Research Unit. Aarhus: Aarhus University Press.

Mellon, James. 1992. *Og Gamle Danmark....* Gylling: Narayana Press.

Mishra, Mrutyuanjai and Marie Louise Schougaard Christiansen. 2002. "Glem tvangsassimilation." *Politiken,* 31 May.

Nannestad, Peter. 1999. *Solidaritetens pris. Holdningen til indvandrere og flygtninge i Danmark 1987–1993.* Aarhus: Aarhus University Press.

Necef, Mehmet, 2002. "Immigration, the National State and the Welfare State." In Peter Ludvigsen et al, WORKLAB *Newsletter* no. 5. Copenhagen: The International Association of Labour Museums.

O'Leary, David et al. 2001. *Right-Sizing the State.* Oxford: Oxford University Press.

Øllgaard, Jørgen and Mogens Ove Madsen, editors. 2004. *Magt.dk – en kritik af Magtudredningen.* Copenhagen: Frydenlund.

Pedersen, Peder J. 2003. "Velfærdsstatens styrke og svagheder." *Jyllandsposten,* 25 November.

– 2002. "Arbejdsmarkedsintegration, arbejdsmarkedspolitik og overførselsindkomster." AMID *Working Papers,* no. 7. Aalborg University.

Rezaei, Shahamak. 2004. *Det duale arbejdsmarked i et velfærdsstatsligt perspektiv.* Roskilde University: Department of Social Science and Business Economics.

Røgilds, Flemming. 1995. *Stemmer i et grænseland. En bro mellem unge indvandrere og danskere?* Copenhagen: Politisk Revy.

Sander, Helge, Svend Erik Hovmand, and Claus Hjort Frederiksen. 2004. "Noget for noget." *Jyllandsposten,* 23 February.

Schmidt, Garbi. 2002. "Betydningen af familieformer og familietraditioner for integrationsprocesserne". AMID *Working Papers,* no. 21, Aalborg University.

Smith, Nina. 2003. "Danskerne kan arbejde mere." *Politiken,* 25 November.

Suárez-Orozco, Marcelo M. 2002. "Everything You Ever Wanted to Know about Assimilation but Were Afraid to Ask." In *Engaging Cultural Differences: The Multicultural Challenge in Liberal Democracies,* edited by Richard Schweder, Martha Minow, and Hazel Rose Marcus. New York: Russell Sage Foundation.

Swank, Duane. 2002. "Withering Welfare? Globalisation, Political Economic Institutions and Contemporary Welfare States." In *States in the Global Economy: Bringing Institutions Back In,* edited by Linda Weiss. Cambridge: Cambridge University Press.

Togeby, Lise. 2003. *Fra Fremmedarbejdere til Etniske Minoriteter.* Magtudredningen: Aarhus University Press.

– et al. 2003. *Magt og Demokrati i Danmark – Hovedresultater fra Magtudredningen.* Magtudredningen: Aarhus University Press.

Trads, David. 2002. *Danskerne først. Historien om Dansk Folkeparti.* Copenhagen: Gyldendal.

Tænketanken. 2004. *Udlændinge- og integrationspolitikken i Danmark og udvalgte lande.* Copenhagen: Ministry for Refugees, Immigrants and Integration.

– 2002. *Indvandring, integration og samfundsøkonomi.* Copenhagen: Ministry for Refugees, Immigrants and Integration.

– 2001. *Udlændinges integration i det danske samfund.* Copenhagen: Ministry for Refugees, Immigrants and Integration (originally published by the Ministry for the Interior).

Vikkelsø Slot, Line. 2001. "Betragtninger over nyhedsmediernes (re)produktion af etniske minoriteter som problemdiskurs." Unpublished MA thesis, Department of Sociology, Copenhagen University.

CHAPTER THIRTEEN

Hall, Peter A. and David Soskice, editors. 2001. *Varieties of Capitalism: The Institutional Foundations of Comparative Advantage.* New York: Oxford University Press.

Hroch, Miroslav. 1985. *Social Preconditions of National Revival in Europe: A Comparative Analysis of the Social Composition of Patriotic Groups among the Smaller European Nations.* Cambridge: Cambridge University Press.

Katzenstein, Peter J. 2005. *A World of Regions: Asia and Europe in the American Imperium.* Ithaca: Cornell University Press.

– 2003. "*Small States* and Small States Revisited," *New Political Economy* 8 (1 March): 9–30.

– 2000. "Confidence, Trust, International Relations, and Lessons from Smaller Democracies," 121–48 in *Disaffected Democracies: What's Troubling the Trilateral Countries?* edited by Susan J. Pharr and Robert D. Putnam. Princeton: Princeton University Press.

– editor. 1989. *Industry and Politics in West Germany: Toward the Third Republic.* Ithaca: Cornell University Press.

– 1985. *Small States in World Markets: Industrial Policy in Europe.* Ithaca: Cornell University Press.

– 1984. *Corporatism and Change: Austria, Switzerland and the Politics of Industry.* Ithaca: Cornell University Press.

Martin, Lisa. 2000. *Democratic Commitments: Legislatures and International Cooperation.* Princeton: Princeton University Press.

CHAPTER FOURTEEN

Alvarez, Michael at al. 1991. "Government Partisanship, Labor Organization and Macroeconomic Performance." *American Political Science Review* 85 (2 June): 539–56.

Auer, Peter. 2000. *Employment Revival in Europe*. Geneva: International Labour Office.

Calmfors, Lars and John Driffill. 1988. "Centralization of Wage Bargaining." *Economic Policy* (April): 13–61.

Estevez-Abe, Margarita, Torben Iversen, and David Soskice. 2001. "Social Protection and Skill Formation: A Reinterpretation of the Welfare State." 145–83 in Hall and Soskice.

Golden, Miriam. 1993. "The Dynamics of Trade Unionism and National Economic Performance." *American Political Science Review* 87 (2, June): 439–54.

Goldthorpe, John H., editor. 1984. *Order and Conflict in Contemporary Capitalism*. New York: Oxford University Press.

Hall, Peter A. and Daniel Gingerich. 2004. "Varieties of Capitalism and Institutional Complementarities in the Macroeconomy: An Empirical Analysis." Working Paper of the Max Planck Institut für Gesellschaftsforschung, Köln.

Hall, Peter A. and David Soskice. 2001. "An Introduction to Varieties of Capitalism." 1–68 in *Varieties of Capitalism: The Institutional Foundations of Comparative Advantage*, edited by Peter A. Hall and David Soskice. Oxford: Oxford University Press.

Hicks, Alexander and Lane Kenworthy. 1998. "Cooperation and Political Economic Performance in Affluent Democratic Capitalism." *American Journal of Sociology* 103 (6, May): 631–72.

Iversen, Torben (forthcoming). *Capitalism, Democracy, and Welfare*. New York: Cambridge University Press.

– 1999. *Contested Institutions*. New York: Cambridge University Press.

Katzenstein, Peter J. 1985. *Small States in World Markets*. Ithaca: Cornell University Press.

Knight, Jack. 1992. *Institutions and Social Conflict*. New York: Cambridge University Press.

Nielsen, Klaus and Ove K. Pedersen. 1991. "From the Mixed Economy to the Negotiated Economy: The Scandinavian Countries." 145–65 in *Morality, Rationality, and Efficiency*, edited by Richard M. Coughlin. Armonk, New York: M.E. Sharpe.

Przeworski, Adam and Michael Wallerstein. 1982. "The Structure of Class Conflict in Democratic Capitalist Societies." *American Political Science Review* 76: 215–38.

Regini, Marino. 1984. "The Conditions for Political Exchange: How Concertation Emerged and Collapsed in Italy and Great Britain." 124–42 in Goldthorpe.

Rothstein, Bo. 1991. "Explaining Swedish Corporatism: The Formative Moment," *Scandinavian Political Studies* 15 (3): 173–92.

Scharpf, Fritz. 1997. *Games Real Actors Play*. Boulder, Colorado: Westview.

Streeck, Wolfgang. 1992. *Social Institutions and Economic Performance*. Beverly Hills: Sage Publications.

Swenson, Peter. 1991. "Bringing Capital Back In, or Social Democracy Reconsidered: Employer Power, Cross-Class Alliances and Centralization of Industrial Relations in Denmark and Sweden." *World Politics* 43 (4): 513–44.

Western, Bruce. 2001. "Bayesian Thinking about Macrosociology." *American Journal of Sociology* 107: 353–78.

Whitley, Richard. 1999. *Divergent Capitalisms: The Social Structuring and Change of Business Systems.* Oxford: Oxford University Press.

CHAPTER FIFTEEN

Biernacki, Richard. 1995. *The Fabrication of Labor: Germany and Britain, 1640–1914.* Berkeley: University of California Press.

Campbell, John L. 2004. *Institutional Change and Globalization.* Princeton: Princeton University Press.

Edelman, Bernard. 1978. *La legislation de la classe ouvrière.* Paris: Christian Bourgeois Editeur.

Fligstein, Neil. 2001. *The Architecture of Markets. An Economic Sociology of Twenty-First-Century Capitalist Societies.* Princeton: Princeton University Press.

Franzese, Robert J. and Peter A. Hall. 2000. "Institutional Dimensions of Coordinating Wage Bargaining and Monetary Policy." 173–204 in *Unions, Employers, and Central Banks,* by Torben Iversen, Jonas Pontusson, and David Soskice. Cambridge. Cambridge University Press.

Hall, Peter A. and David Soskice. 2001. "An Introduction to Varieties of Capitalism." 1–70 in *Varieties of Capitalism: The Institutional Foundations of Comparative Advantage,* edited by Peter A. Hall and David Soskice. Oxford: Oxford University Press.

Hvidt, Kristian. 2003. *Klitgården.* Copenhagen: Rhodos.

Højrup, Thomas. 2002. *Dannelsens dialektik: Etnologiske udfordringer til det glemte folk.* Copenhagen: Mueseum Tusculanums Forlag.

Iversen, Torben and Jonas Pontusson. 2000. "Comparative Political Economy: A Northern European Perspective." 1–37 in *Unions, Employers, and Central Banks,* by Torben Iversen, Jonas Pontusson, and David Soskice. Cambridge: Cambridge University Press.

Krasner, Steven. 2001. "Problematic Sovereignty." In *Problematic Sovereignty. Contested Rules and Political Possibilities,* edited by Steven Krasner. New York: Columbia University Press.

Korpi, Walter. 1978. *The Working Class in Welfare Capitalism.* London: Routledge and Kegan Paul.

Korsgaard, Ove. 2004. *Kampen om folket.: Et dannelsesperspektiv på dansk historie gennem 500 år.* Copenhagen: Gyldendal.

Lidegaard, Bo. 2001. *Jens Otto Krag 1914–1961.* Copenhagen: Gyldendal.

Pedersen, Ove K. 1993. "The Institutional History of the Danish Polity: From a Market and Mixed Economy to a Negotiated Economy." 277–300 in *Institutional Change. Theory and Empirical Findings,* edited by Sven-Erik Sjøstrand. Armonk, New York: M.E. Sharpe.

– Niels Å. Andersen, Peter Kjær, and John Elberg. 1992. *Privat Politik: Projekt Forhandlingsøkonomi.* Copenhagen: Samfundslitteratur.

Polanyi, Karl. 1944. *The Great Transformation. The Economic and Political Origins of Our Time.* New York: Henry Holt and Company.

Reddy, William. 1984. *The Rise of Market Culture.* Cambridge: Cambridge University Press.

Rhodes, Martin. 2003, "National 'Pacts' and EU Governance in Social Policy and the Labor Market." In *Governing Work and Welfare in a New Economy,* edited by Jonathan Zeitlin and David M. Trubek. Oxford: Oxford University Press.

Stensgård, Pernille. 2003. *Skagen.* Copenhagen: Gyldendal.

Index